(Continued on back endsheets)

Dictionary of Literary Biography® • Volume One Hundred Thirty-Nine

British Short-Fiction Writers, 1945–1980

Dictionary of Literary Biography® • Volume One Hundred Thirty-Nine

British Short-Fiction Writers, 1945–1980

Edited by
Dean Baldwin
Pennsylvania State University – Erie

A Bruccoli Clark Layman Book
Gale Research Inc.
Detroit, Washington, D.C., London

For Vicki

Contents

Plan of the Series

. . . Almost the most prodigious asset of a country, and perhaps its most precious possession, is its native literary product – when that product is fine and noble and enduring.

Mark Twain*

The advisory board, the editors, and the publisher of the *Dictionary of Literary Biography* are joined in endorsing Mark Twain's declaration. The literature of a nation provides an inexhaustible resource of permanent worth. We intend to make literature and its creators better understood and more accessible to students and the reading public, while satisfying the standards of teachers and scholars.

To meet these requirements, *literary biography* has been construed in terms of the author's achievement. The most important thing about a writer is his writing. Accordingly, the entries in *DLB* are career biographies, tracing the development of the author's canon and the evolution of his reputation.

The purpose of *DLB* is not only to provide reliable information in a convenient format but also to place the figures in the larger perspective of literary history and to offer appraisals of their accomplishments by qualified scholars.

The publication plan for *DLB* resulted from two years of preparation. The project was proposed to Bruccoli Clark by Frederick C. Ruffner, president of the Gale Research Company, in November 1975. After specimen entries were prepared and typeset, an advisory board was formed to refine the entry format and develop the series rationale. In meetings held during 1976, the publisher, series editors, and advisory board approved the scheme for a comprehensive biographical dictionary of persons who contributed to North American literature. Editorial work on the first volume began in January 1977, and it was published in 1978. In order to make *DLB* more than a reference tool and to compile volumes that individually have claim to status as literary history, it was decided to organize volumes by topic, period, or genre. Each of these free-

From an unpublished section of Mark Twain's autobiography, copyright by the Mark Twain Company

standing volumes provides a biographical-bibliographical guide and overview for a particular area of literature. We are convinced that this organization – as opposed to a single alphabet method – constitutes a valuable innovation in the presentation of reference material. The volume plan necessarily requires many decisions for the placement and treatment of authors who might properly be included in two or three volumes. In some instances a major figure will be included in separate volumes, but with different entries emphasizing the aspect of his career appropriate to each volume. Ernest Hemingway, for example, is represented in *American Writers in Paris, 1920–1939* by an entry focusing on his expatriate apprenticeship; he is also in *American Novelists, 1910–1945* with an entry surveying his entire career. Each volume includes a cumulative index of the subject authors and articles. Comprehensive indexes to the entire series are planned.

With volume ten in 1982 it was decided to enlarge the scope of *DLB*. By the end of 1986 twenty-one volumes treating British literature had been published, and volumes for Commonwealth and Modern European literature were in progress. The series has been further augmented by the *DLB Yearbooks* (since 1981) which update published entries and add new entries to keep the *DLB* current with contemporary activity. There have also been *DLB Documentary Series* volumes which provide biographical and critical source materials for figures whose work is judged to have particular interest for students. One of these companion volumes is entirely devoted to Tennessee Williams.

We define literature as the *intellectual commerce of a nation:* not merely as belles lettres but as that ample and complex process by which ideas are generated, shaped, and transmitted. *DLB* entries are not limited to "creative writers" but extend to other figures who in their time and in their way influenced the mind of a people. Thus the series encompasses historians, journalists, publishers, and screenwriters. By this means readers of *DLB* may be aided to perceive literature not as cult scripture in the keeping of intellectual high priests but firmly positioned at the center of a nation's life.

DLB includes the major writers appropriate to each volume and those standing in the ranks immediately behind them. Scholarly and critical counsel has been sought in deciding which minor figures to include and how full their entries should be. Wherever possible, useful references are made to figures who do not warrant separate entries.

Each *DLB* volume has a volume editor responsible for planning the volume, selecting the figures for inclusion, and assigning the entries. Volume editors are also responsible for preparing, where appropriate, appendices surveying the major periodicals and literary and intellectual movements for their volumes, as well as lists of further readings. Work on the series as a whole is coordinated at the Bruccoli Clark Layman editorial center in Columbia, South Carolina, where the editorial staff is responsible for accuracy of the published volumes.

One feature that distinguishes *DLB* is the illustration policy — its concern with the iconography of literature. Just as an author is influenced by his surroundings, so is the reader's understanding of the author enhanced by a knowledge of his environment. Therefore *DLB* volumes include not only drawings, paintings, and photographs of authors, often depicting them at various stages in their careers, but also illustrations of their families and places where they lived. Title pages are regularly reproduced in facsimile along with dust jackets for modern authors. The dust jackets are a special feature of *DLB* because they often document better than anything else the way in which an author's work was perceived in its own time. Specimens of the writers' manuscripts are included when feasible.

Samuel Johnson rightly decreed that "The chief glory of every people arises from its authors." The purpose of the *Dictionary of Literary Biography* is to compile literary history in the surest way available to us — by accurate and comprehensive treatment of the lives and work of those who contributed to it.

The *DLB* Advisory Board

Introduction

Great Britain in 1945 was battered and exhausted, although buoyed by relief that World War II was over and faith that peace would bring an end to war's privations and dangers. The toll of military and civilian casualties, devastation to property, lost productivity, and financing the war was staggering. The cold statistics – 357,000 Britons killed, another 600,000 disabled, a national debt of £25 billion, 700,000 homes destroyed – only begin to tell the story. Unfortunately, the privations of war were to last several more years. In spite of the Labour party's postwar reforms – from nationalizing major industries to establishing the National Health and National Insurance – life in Britain after the war was still mean and meager, marked by shortages of everything from basic foodstuffs to whiskey, by deprivations ranging from unavailable housing to unaffordable party frocks. Even wartime conscription was not abolished, as the national service, founded in 1948, required military training and service of all young men for two years. It was not abolished until 1962. Not until at least 1953 (coincidentally the coronation year of Elizabeth II) did the country genuinely recover, and it was not until 1957 that prosperity and "good times" arrived. The immediate postwar years, then, were a period of austerity and rebuilding. It had taken six years to win the war; it would take another eight to recover from it and win the peace.

The years 1957 to 1972 were a time of rapid economic expansion; for example, there were only 2.3 million automobiles in 1950 but more than 11 million in 1970, and, by the same year, 80 percent of British homes were licensed for television. In 1956 only 8 percent of Britain's homes contained refrigerators; by 1971 the figure was 69 percent. Meanwhile, the consumer revolution was accompanied in Britain as elsewhere by the "permissive society." Commentators and social historians began to worry about the breakdown in social consensus and about the rise of a purely materialistic approach to life. While some changes – such as the loosening of censorship because of the 1960 case over the publication of the unexpurgated version of D. H. Lawrence's *Lady Chatterley's Lover* (1928) – were welcomed, increases in drug addiction, premarital sex, violent crime, and divorce were seen in many quarters as distressing declines in public and private morality. Simultaneously, others worried over

Britain's loss of its African colonies, most of which had gained independence by 1965.

Between 1973 and 1980 large trade deficits and labor strife disrupted economic growth and led to the stagflation of the late 1970s. A steady decline in the country's industrial base brought intractable problems of unemployment. Book publishing was hit particularly hard by these developments. For decades a well-produced hardcover book had been an affordable commodity for most readers. In the mid 1970s the price of books rose drastically, creating one more obstacle for authors and publishers to overcome in their attempts to reach the reading public. The rapid economic expansion of the previous period had helped to blur class lines, but the return of hard economic times – and particularly the large number of labor disputes – brought about a hardening of attitudes among all classes, and a new sourness developed. Though many intellectuals remained committed to the Labour party and the Left in general, many in the middle and upper classes lost whatever sympathy they may have had toward the working class. Exacerbating these problems was the perception that many of Britain's economic and social woes were traceable to immigration, even though in 1970 only 2.5 percent of the populace was nonwhite. Immigration controls were enacted in 1962, and an antidiscrimination bill was passed in 1966; these two pieces of legislation are in many ways symbolic of Britain's ambivalence toward race. By the 1970s racial tensions, though little discussed openly, were in many respects replacing the class issues that had been a staple of social analysis in Britain for decades. As in America, the confrontations were most frequent in economically depressed areas and neighborhoods where competition for housing and jobs – along with differences in language, customs, and mores – created tensions and conflicts. Outbreaks of racial violence, as in Bristol in 1980, have not been uncommon.

Socially, the changes in Britain between 1945 and 1980 are as incalculable as the effects of the war itself. Certainly on the surface a great deal changed during those thirty-five years. Nationalizing major industries and banks, creating the "cradle to grave" welfare system, dramatically increasing taxes and death duties on the rich, opening up and reforming the educational system, changing the empire into a commonwealth, and permitting massive immigration of "people of color" are among the most obvious and dramatic of these changes. Britain in 1945 was nearly all white racially. It was still a nation of shopkeepers where, from John o' Groat's to Land's End, the typical retail outlet was the local shop; the chief mode of transport the bicycle or the bus; and the diet of the typical family mainly bread, potatoes, sprouts, and peas, with a small weekly ration of meat and a few eggs. By 1980 many local shops had been driven out of business by supermarkets or taken over by immigrants; millions of cars moved over four-lane motorways; and major cities became polyglot centers of Indian, Pakistani, West Indian, and Oriental immigration. Under these influences and pressures the British diet and palate have been transformed: the Sunday "joint," two "veg," and potatoes have given way to the Chinese nosh, Indian take-away, and back-garden barbecue. Since 1980 such changes have been intensified by the European Economic Community and the economic boom of the 1980s.

But beneath these changes, both profound and superficial, lie many important continuities. There has been little change in the basic British character. The typical Briton remains friendly and hospitable on the outside but cool, collected, and reserved on the inside. The British may enjoy spicy southern European cooking and French wine, but they remain northern Europeans in demeanor. The stiff upper lip is still much in evidence. Cities may be polyglot and the shops may be open seven days a week and late into the night, but beneath the cosmopolitanism of London, Birmingham, and Manchester resides a deep suspicion of foreigners; a latent, sometimes barely suppressed racism; and a resentment of outside influences, whether from Europe or America. Though by 1980 the British were taking their holidays in Spain, Italy, Majorca, and North America, they remained deeply provincial: a cooked breakfast, tea at 4:00 P.M., and hot-water bottles in beds were still provided by many hotels catering to British tourists.

Feminism has changed women's education, put women into jobs and professions that before the war they could not even contemplate, shaken patterns of family life, and altered sexual practices. Although there is a woman on the throne, and although Margaret Thatcher became prime minister in 1979, women as a group have made less progress than their North American sisters. From town councils to Parliament, politics has remained a male domain; corporate boardrooms are still held by the old-boy network; and university faculties have remained almost entirely male.

Most impervious of all to change has been the class system. Despite the efforts of postwar Labour governments, despite educational reforms that abolished the old eleven-plus examinations and created comprehensive high schools, despite the increase in the number of universities from seventeen in 1945 to forty-four in 1970, and despite the leveling effects of everything from income taxes to popular culture, Britain remains stratified by class. Of course there has been increased social mobility; by one measure, 30 percent of working-class youths have moved up to white-collar jobs, the same percentage as in America, but to a surprising degree the old tribal divisions and loyalties have remained. At one end are the labor unions, jealously guarding perquisites and refusing to acknowledge new realities, supposedly in the name of saving jobs and opposing privilege but also in response to long-standing suspicions. At the other end are the so-called public schools and Oxford and Cambridge Universities, theoretically open to anyone but still primarily the training grounds for the upper-middle class and still the passports to the regions of power and influence. By 1970 only 15 percent of Britain's secondary-education graduates were pursuing some form of higher education, and most of them were members of the upper-middle class.

Geographically, Britain remains two nations, north and south. Many in the north, where working-class values predominate and unemployment has been chronic, regard the south as effete and snobbish. For an ambitious young man or woman to leave Liverpool or Nottingham and seek greater opportunity in the south is still regarded in some quarters as an act of class betrayal. Many in the south regard the north almost as a foreign country, the home of beer-drinking louts, welfare cheats, and people with incomprehensible dialects. Fortunately, all of these tensions – racial, regional, economic, and gender-based – are held in dynamic tension by the British fear of radical change, by fundamental decency, and by social safety valves that permit the truly ambitious, the talented, and the determined to progress economically and socially. The postwar record of economic and social change is, of course, complex and mixed. There is no question that living standards have risen, social mobility has increased, and many of the daily amenities have improved. But progress has been uneven, and many have not benefited from the overall rise in the standard of living.

How well has the short story responded to and reflected these changes and tensions? The war caused nearly as much devastation to authors and publishers as it did to the rest of the economic and cultural life of the country. Symbolic of the damage was the bombing of London's Paternoster Row – the heart of British publishing – and the loss of millions of books. Wartime paper rationing severely limited the number of books and magazines published and reduced those that were printed to crabbed, utilitarian unattractiveness. Although the mistakes of World War I were avoided – meaning that writers were put to useful war work instead of being sent to the front to die – careers were interrupted and reputations lost; novels, poems, plays, and stories went unwritten. But while publishing as a whole recovered along with the rest of the economy, fundamental changes occurred in magazine publishing, particularly under the influence of radio and television. The flourishing short-story market that had supported many writers before the war rapidly declined. In 1940 the *Writers' and Artists' Yearbook* listed at least 165 adult magazines that published short fiction. That figure held almost constant in 1950, but by 1970 it had dropped precipitously to 74. By 1980 there were only 65 such publications, two-thirds of which were women's magazines. More important than sheer numbers was the rapid decline in quality periodicals. In 1940 there were at least twenty of these, including *Blackwood's*, *Lilliput*, and *Windsor Magazine*. Most of them survived the war, but by 1970 there were only nine left, and by 1980 only the *Anglo-Welsh Review, Blackwood's*, the *Listener, London Magazine*, the *Spectator*, and *Stand*. American outlets, particularly the *New Yorker*, partly filled the void, but there can be no doubt that the British audience for short fiction has shrunk drastically since the war. By 1980 the days when young writers could count on the short story to launch their careers or supplement their incomes were long over.

In spite of its steady decline as a popular medium, the short story reflects many of the major changes in British life, though not as clearly as the novel. The novel has a long history as a social barometer and agent of change; the short story has less often been social or political in nature. Because of its length and its tendency to focus on interior rather than exterior changes, the short story seems unsuited to the role often assigned to the novel. Nevertheless, the British short story did not retreat into preciousness nor turn its back on the issues of the day.

This trend toward seriousness of subject matter was especially evident immediately after the war and in the 1950s. Many of the stories in William Sansom's *Something Terrible, Something Lovely* (1948) are based on his experiences as a fireman during the war or deal with postwar issues of occupation and reconstruction. No less topical in many ways are the stories of Angus Wilson, whose collections *The Wrong Set and Other Stories* (1949) and *Such Darling Dodos and Other Stories* (1950) heralded a new mood

in British fiction. Political issues, the generation gap caused by the war, materialism, and class conflict are the staples of Wilson's stories. Behind the social and political issues lie Wilson's themes of cruelty, lack of understanding and communication between classes and generations, and the dangers of complacency and lack of self-knowledge. Doris Lessing's three collections published during the 1950s often deal with racial issues, though in an African context. Similarly, Francis King's *So Hurt and Humiliated and Other Stories* (1959) reveals the cultural clashes experienced by Britons abroad. King also tested the frontiers of censorship by dealing with homosexual themes at a time when homosexuality was still illegal in England. Such issues soon faced Britons directly, as did the demands of feminism, which are important concerns in the works of Lessing, Sylvia Townsend Warner, and A. L. Barker. The most explosive social commentary of the period, however, came from Alan Sillitoe, whose "Loneliness of the Long-Distance Runner" (from the 1959 collection of that title) exposed the raw nerve of working-class disaffection.

Mention of Sillitoe naturally raises the angry-young-man phenomenon. In addition to Sillitoe, this group includes John Wain, Stan Barstow, and Kingsley Amis, although the label covers more than it reveals. Perhaps the only thing that connects these disparate writers is the general tone of disillusionment expressed by many of their characters and themes. In this respect their works are accurate barometers of the social scene, and at least one social scientist has seen in their works not only signs of class conflict but also indications of the impending revolution in values, particularly sexual mores, that was the hallmark of the 1960s and 1970s. For these writers at this time, the short story was very much an instrument of social commentary. Barstow's *The Desperadoes and Other Stories* (1961) delves into the psychologies and mores of the working and middle classes. Amis's *My Enemy's Enemy* (1962) contains stories that attack do-gooders and bureaucrats, two increasingly common enemies in the welfare state. The stories in Wain's *Nuncle and Other Stories* (1960) are wide-ranging in subject and theme, but he, too, catches the country's mood and mores in such stories as "Christmas at Rillingham's" (*Nuncle and Other Stories*). The most important story of the decade – indeed one of the finest of the century – is the title piece of V. S. Pritchett's *When My Girl Comes Home* (1961). Behind Pritchett's apparent comedy of manners and emergence from narrative ambiguities is a clear sense of moral confusion directly traceable to the exigencies of war. For Pritchett, the war and its aftermath required so much compromise, expediency, and outright moral myopia that they undermined many old decencies and certainties, blurring the line between acceptable and criminal conduct. Similarly, the early stories of Frank Tuohy, including those in *The Admiral and the Nuns, with Other Stories* (1962), express pessimism about life in general. Tuohy reflects the racial tensions building in England by dealing with culture clashes abroad, and he also reveals the permissive, often perverse, sexuality of the time. Brian Glanville's stories deal not so much with a social issue as a social phenomenon – sports. Because professional sports are often seen as a clear reflection of society as a whole, such stories should not be dismissed as escapist. Ruth Prawer Jhabvala's *A Stronger Climate: 9 Stories* (1968) rounds out the decade. Almost all of her stories are set in India, and many concern the inevitable culture clashes that occur between Indians and Europeans; but the Indian caste system has its obvious parallel in England, as does India's repressive treatment of women.

Elspeth Davie, John Fowles, Giles Gordon, and Susan Hill published many of their works during the 1970s, but none of their fiction can be classed as socially conscious in the usual sense. The most biting social criticism has come from Sillitoe and Wain. Sillitoe's two collections of short fiction extend his themes of working-class frustration and disillusionment, while several of Wain's stories are direct commentaries on consumerism and the phony values of advertising and publicity. William Trevor's *Angels at the Ritz and Other Stories* (1975) contains stories that detail the sexual excesses of the decade and comment on the troubles in Ireland. Writers such as Lessing, Tuohy, and Jhabvala continued in their respective veins of racial and feminist themes in the 1970s. Overall, however, the use of short fiction as direct social commentary appears to have lessened during the decade.

Surveying literature, especially short fiction, by its supposed relevance to contemporary issues, however, can be dangerous and distorting. The short story differs from the novel in generally avoiding partisan politics and (except rarely) references to specific political issues. (Fred Urquhart's "Maggie Logie and the National Health" [*The Collected Stories, Volume One: The Dying Stallion*, 1967] is a conspicuous exception.) Front-page issues such as the cold war, nuclear politics, labor relations, economic policy, and foreign affairs are not usually the province of the short story. Most often, the short story takes place against the assumed background of such issues and problems rather than incorporating them into the plot or dialogue. Moreover, focusing too sharply on social issues detracts from one of the real strengths of the short story – its ability to deal with the internal lives of ordinary people.

In this broader sense of delving into the spiritual and psychological lives of its characters, the short story has accurately reflected the anxieties and complexities of the period, mainly through its treatment of individual consciousnesses. In this respect the postwar story resembles and closely follows its prewar predecessor. Frank O'Connor's insight that the short story often focuses on people at the fringes of society applies better than most generalizations to the twentieth-century British short story. Many of the writers in this volume might accurately be called humanists, concerned about the effects of consumerism, sexual license, lack of economic and social mobility, and racism on the psyche and soul. Others are bemused or angry over the continued absurdities of the class system; interested in the particular plight of the aging or the adolescent; fascinated by the individual quirks and eccentricities by which ordinary people cling to their dignity; and moved by the bravery and hardiness of some, the defeats of others, and the frustrations, disappointments, and small victories of the vast majority. The Beatles' "Eleanor Rigby" (1966), with its refrain, "Ah, look at all the lonely people," might be the theme song for Britain's short-story writers of this period. By examining the inner lives of Britons from every class and background, British short-story writers collectively have probed the national character and its shifting moods, values, mores, and ideas. If the specifics of politics, economics, and other public issues have been part of the assumed background rather than the clearly delineated foreground, they have not therefore been neglected – only relegated to the place they occupy in the lives of most people.

The great achievement of the postwar British story has been its exploration of the British people, usually its urban and suburban middle classes. (An interesting feature of British fiction is the lack of rural settings after the war. Trevor's stories of the rural Irish and Urquhart's of the rural Scots are rare exceptions.) In general the writers in this volume deal with the themes of isolation, lack of communication, frustration, and quiet desperation. Sometimes – as in the stories of Muriel Spark, L. P. Hartley, and Urquhart – the problem is discussed as a lack of spiritual depth or awareness. These and other writers often see postwar people as mired in the material world, unable to experience any spiritual dimension. This view in part accounts for the continued popularity of the ghost story, where characters and readers are forced to confront the unknown and nonmaterial. Spiritual fulfillment is also a frequent subject in stories of intercultural confrontation, as in those of King and Jhabvala. Most often, however, loneliness and lack of communication are seen as environmental or psychological phenomena, the result of the loss of community and the depersonalization of modern life. For instance, Pritchett's quirky characters retreat into eccentricity or reach out from it to find human contact. Similarly, the characters in stories by writers as disparate in outlook as Rhys Davies, Elizabeth Taylor, Barker, Hartley, Urquhart, Davie, Hill, and Trevor concern individuals in some sense isolated from parents or children, spouses or coworkers, neighbors or relatives. In this respect the postwar British story is predominantly pessimistic in spite of its flashes of warmth and humor, and this description generally applies to postwar novels, dramas, and poetry. Pessimism is, for better or worse, the great theme of modern and postmodern art.

Formally and technically the postwar story has kept continuity with the past. The period began with what appeared at the time to be a burst of new energy and a new tone, if not an entirely new aesthetic. The stories of Sillitoe, Amis, and Wilson, though broadly traditionalist in manner, seemed highly original and refreshingly iconoclastic. Since then there have been many experiments and new departures. In some of Sansom's stories time moves almost like a series of stop frames, and the emotions of the moment are minutely detailed; this experiment did not prove widely influential. Before the war Dylan Thomas's wild prose poems appeared to signal an age of experimentation, but even he became increasingly traditional. Iain Crichton Smith's juxtaposition of the ordinary with the fantastic, Spark's use of the religious and supernatural to defamiliarize the ordinary world, and Hartley's fantasies (which in many ways anticipate the magic realism of Latin American fiction) also represent important experimental directions. Gordon is the most relentlessly experimental writer of the period, using techniques varying from surrealism to metafiction. Trevor has been credited with (or accused of) minimalism. Barstow's most recent stories show the influence of metafiction and complex narrative perspectives.

Overall, however, the postwar British story has shown more interest in continuity with the modernist movement than in new technical departures. To some extent this tendency reflects the fact that many postwar writers started their careers, or even established their reputations, before the war — Gwyn Jones, J. B. Priestley, Davies, Hartley, Pritchett, Sansom, Thomas, Taylor, Urquhart, Warner, and Wilson were all born before 1915. Only Wilson actually began writing after the war. All of these writers are regarded as essentially modernist in sen-

sibility and traditional in technique. Perhaps, too, the traditional methods of British short-story writers reflect the restricted market for stories: there is no longer an *English Review* as there was for D. H. Lawrence, no such series as John Lehmann's *New Writing* to encourage experimental techniques. *Granta,* perhaps Britain's foremost literary magazine for the past two decades, seems more interested in politics and travel writing than fiction.

It is a mistake, however, to equate experiment with originality or literary significance, as reviewers and academic critics often do. These two groups may naturally look at the British short story and wonder why it lacks the brashness of a Donald Barthelme or a Robert Coover, the philosophical and narrative novelty of a Jorge Luis Borges or a Carlos Fuentes. But the British have rarely been innovators in this or any other form; after all, one has to extend the term "British" to include James Joyce, William Butler Yeats, and T. S. Eliot. This assessment is not meant to diminish the achievements of Ford Madox Ford, Joseph Conrad, Virginia Woolf, Malcolm Lowry, or other innovators, only to put such innovation in context. Moreover, Britain's contributions to the arts since World War II have primarily been in performance rather than creation: British film, television, theater, and music are justly famous for their actors, directors, performers, and conductors but are not well known (with some few exceptions) for their innovative writers and composers. British conservatism operates in literary as well as social and political arenas and should not be counted necessarily as a defect. Such a statement may be interpreted as an apology, but it should not be. What matters is not the newness of the style or technique but the originality and freshness of the vision.

Nowhere are these concerns better illustrated than in the stories of Pritchett. In many ways his fiction resembles that of Anton Chekhov, Guy de Maupassant, and Katherine Mansfield. But such a view tells only a small part of the story, and critics will need to exercise the full range of their ingenuity to analyze the qualities of Pritchett's style and narrative technique before they begin to crack its surface. The same may be said for many other writers represented in this volume. All have written excellent stories that deserve to be read and remembered; all have contributed to the art of fiction and to the collective growth of the short story since the war. That they are not all as well known or widely appreciated as they deserve to be is due more to the overall state of the short story and to the vagaries of literary politics than to the quality of their works.

The aim and scope of this volume, therefore, are to survey and evaluate the achievements of British short-story writers since World War II. The dividing line is not arbitrary: the war and its aftermath denote in many ways a genuinely new period in British short fiction. As with any such volume, the decision to include a writer in this time period was to some extent arbitrary. H. E. Bates and Graham Greene, for example, could as easily have been assigned to this volume as to a prewar one. Conversely, Pritchett and Warner could have been included among prewar writers, since they and many others discussed here began writing well before the war. All the writers chosen for this volume, however, published the majority of their stories or solidified their reputations after the war.

Many of the writers selected for this volume are not well known within Britain, let alone outside it. This obscurity is due in part to the perennial fate of short-story writers – to live in the shadow of novelists. British literary history can provide only two writers whose fame rests largely or entirely on short stories – Rudyard Kipling and Mansfield. Most often, fame as a novelist calls attention to a writer's short stories; the reverse is almost never the case. This problem has worsened since the war because of the decline in magazine readership and the resultant disappearance of the short story as a popular medium. Many historians and critics will not see this as a great loss, given the fact that the vast majority of magazine short fiction has always been trivial and formulaic. But what has disappeared with the popular short story is the system that supported authors in the past and made it possible for writers such as Lawrence, A. E. Coppard, Bates, and Mansfield to reach an audience at all. In those as in many other cases, success with magazines led to book publication and the chance at least to reach the reading public.

As magazines have disappeared, so have the opportunities for short-story writers to procure book contracts. There has been a significant decline in the number of volumes of short stories published in Britain since 1970. Moreover, that country has not produced, as the United States has, a bumper crop of "little" and academic journals to fill the vacuum created by the death of popular and literary magazines. American writers may not be able to earn a living by the short story any more than can their British counterparts, but at least they can count on publication, albeit in obscure journals with small circulations. British writers no longer have even this small encouragement, unless they can avail themselves of the American market. Unfortunately, as this aspect of the American market has expanded over the past twenty years, another side of it has shrunk. American textbooks and anthologies, which used to carry a considerable percentage of British short fiction, have been excluding British writers in favor of a variety of authors of many different nationalities, in their efforts to be multicultural. As a result, contemporary American students are studying the short story without reading modern or contemporary Britishwriters.

This volume, then, serves an important function in that it surveys – and in some cases investigates in considerable depth – the achievements of British short-story writers since the war. Some of the entries here – notably those on Barker, Barstow, Davie, Davies, Glanville, Hill, Jones, King, Smith, Taylor, Tuohy, Urquhart and George Mackay Brown – provide the only criticism aside from reviews available on the author. Some of the other authors have been studied as novelists or poets but not as short-story writers. Only a few of the authors have received extended critical assessment as short-story writers: Lessing, Sillitoe, Thomas, Wilson, and Pritchett. For students, teachers, and scholars this volume will serve as an indispensable introduction to many fine British writers and provide the most comprehensive, detailed discussions available on the postwar British short story.

British short-fiction writers since World War II have probed the British mind and character, illuminating the dark places of the psyche, questioning values, prying behind appearances, and revealing surprises. They have done what short-fiction writers have always done, and done it with skill. It now lies with readers and critics to assess with care what these writers have achieved. The essays in this volume are an important step in that direction and, their authors hope, incentives to further exploration.

– *Dean Baldwin*

ACKNOWLEDGMENTS

This book was produced by Bruccoli Clark Layman, Inc. Karen L. Rood is senior editor for the *Dictionary of Literary Biography* series. David Marshall James was the in-house editor.

Production coordinator is George F. Dodge. Photography editors are Edward Scott, Timothy C. Lundy, and Robert S. McConnell. Layout and graphics supervisor is Penney L. Haughton. Copyediting supervisor is Bill Adams. Typesetting supervisor is Kathleen M. Flanagan. Julie E. Frick is editorial associate. The production staff includes Phyllis Avant, Joseph Matthew Bruccoli, Ann M. Cheschi, Patricia Coate, Wilma Weant Dague, Brigitte B. de Guzman, Denise W. Edwards, Sarah A. Estes, Joyce Fowler, Laurel M. Gladden, Jolyon M. Helterman, Rebecca Mayo, Kathy Lawler Merlette, Sean Moriarty, Pamela D. Norton, Patricia F. Salisbury, and William L. Thomas, Jr.

Walter W. Ross and Deborah M. Chasteen did library research. They were assisted by the following librarians at the Thomas Cooper Library of the University of South Carolina: Linda Holderfield and the interlibrary-loan staff; reference librarians Gwen Baxter, Daniel Boice, Faye Chadwell, Cathy Eckman, Gary Geer, Qun "Gerry" Jiao, Jean Rhyne, Carol Tobin, Carolyn Tyler, Virginia Weathers, Elizabeth Whiznant, and Connie Widney; circulation-department head Thomas Marcil; and acquisitions-searching supervisor David Haggard.

British Short-Fiction Writers, 1945–1980

Dictionary of Literary Biography

Kingsley Amis
(16 April 1922 -   )

Mathew David Fisher
Ball State University

See also the Amis entries in *DLB 15: British Novelists, 1930–1959; DLB 27: Poets of Great Britain and Ireland, 1945–1960;* and *DLB 100: Modern British Essayists.*

SELECTED BOOKS: *Bright November: Poems* (London: Fortune Press, 1947);

A Frame of Mind: Eighteen Poems (Reading, U.K.: University of Reading School of Art, 1953);

Lucky Jim (London: Gollancz, 1954; Garden City, N.Y.: Doubleday, 1954);

Kingsley Amis, Fantasy Poets series no. 22 (Eynsham: Fantasy Press, 1954);

That Uncertain Feeling (London: Gollancz, 1955; New York: Harcourt, Brace, 1956);

A Case of Samples: Poems 1946–1956 (London: Gollancz, 1956; New York: Harcourt, Brace, 1957);

Socialism and the Intellectuals (London: Fabian Society, 1957);

I Like It Here (London: Gollancz, 1958; New York: Harcourt, Brace, 1958);

New Maps of Hell: A Survey of Science Fiction (New York: Harcourt, Brace & World, 1960; London: Gollancz, 1961);

Take a Girl Like You (London: Gollancz, 1960; New York: Harcourt, Brace & World, 1961);

The Evans Country (Oxford: Fantasy Press, 1962);

My Enemy's Enemy (London: Gollancz, 1962; New York: Harcourt, Brace & World, 1963);

One Fat Englishman (London: Gollancz, 1963; New York: Harcourt, Brace & World, 1964);

The James Bond Dossier (London: Cape, 1965; New York: Harcourt, Brace & World, 1965);

The Egyptologists, by Amis and Robert Conquest (London: Cape, 1965; New York: Random House, 1966);

Kingsley Amis, 1980 (photograph by Rex Coleman, Baron Studio, London)

The Book of Bond; Or Every Man His Own 007, as Lt. Col. William ("Bill") Tanner (London: Cape, 1965; New York: Viking, 1965);

The Anti-Death League (London: Gollancz, 1966; New York: Harcourt, Brace & World, 1966);

A Look Round the Estate: Poems 1957–1967 (London: Cape, 1967; New York: Harcourt, Brace & World, 1968);

Colonel Sun: A James Bond Adventure, as Robert Markham (London: Cape, 1968; New York: Harper & Row, 1968);

Lucky Jim's Politics (London: Conservative Political Centre, 1968);

I Want It Now (London: Cape, 1968; New York: Harcourt, Brace & World, 1969);

The Green Man (London: Cape, 1969; New York: Harcourt, Brace & World, 1970);

What Became of Jane Austen? and Other Questions (London: Cape, 1970; New York: Harcourt Brace Jovanovich, 1971);

Girl, 20 (London: Cape, 1971; New York: Harcourt Brace Jovanovich, 1972);

On Drink (London: Cape, 1972; New York: Harcourt Brace Jovanovich, 1973);

Dear Illusion (London: Covent Garden Press, 1972);

The Riverside Villas Murder (London: Cape, 1973; New York: Harcourt Brace Jovanovich, 1973);

Ending Up (London: Cape, 1974; New York: Harcourt Brace Jovanovich, 1974);

Rudyard Kipling and His World (London: Thames & Hudson, 1975; New York: Scribners, 1976);

The Alteration (London: Cape, 1976; New York: Viking, 1977);

Jake's Thing (London: Hutchinson, 1978; New York: Viking, 1979);

The Darkwater Hall Mystery (Edinburgh: Tragara Press, 1978);

An Arts Policy? (London: Centre for Policy Studies, 1979);

Russian Hide-and-Seek: A Melodrama (London: Hutchinson, 1980);

Every Day Drinking (London: Hutchinson, 1983);

Stanley and the Women (London: Hutchinson, 1984; New York: Summit, 1985);

How's Your Glass? (London: Weidenfeld & Nicolson, 1984);

The Old Devils (London: Hutchinson, 1986; New York: Summit, 1987);

The Crime of the Century (London: Dent, 1987);

Difficulties with Girls (London: Century Hutchinson, 1988; New York: Summit, 1988);

Memoirs (London: Hutchinson, 1991; New York: Summit, 1991);

The Russian Girl (London: Hutchinson, 1992);

The Pleasure of Poetry (London: Cassell, 1992);

Mr. Barrett's Secret and Other Stories (London: Hutchinson, 1993).

Editions and Collections: *Collected Poems, 1944-1979* (London: Hutchinson, 1979; New York: Viking, 1980);

Collected Short Stories (London: Hutchinson, 1980; enlarged, 1987);

Amis Story Anthology: A Personal Choice of Short Stories, selected by Amis (London: Hutchinson, 1992).

OTHER: *Oxford Poetry, 1949,* edited by Amis and James Michie (Oxford: Blackwell, 1949);

Oscar Wilde: Poems and Essays, second edition, edited by Amis (London: Collins Classics, 1956);

"You That Love England; or, Limey, Stay Home," in *New World Writing,* edited by Stewart Richardson and Corlies M. Smith (Philadelphia: Lippincott, 1960), pp. 135-145;

Samuel Butler, *Erewhon, or Over the Range,* edited by Amis (New York: Signet Classic, 1961);

Spectrum: A Science Fiction Anthology, volumes 1-5, edited by Amis and Robert Conquest (London: Gollancz, 1961-1966; New York: Harcourt, Brace, 1962-1967);

"Communication and the Victorian Poet," in *British Victorian Literature: Recent Revaluations,* edited by S. K. Kumar (New York: New York University Press, 1969), pp. 39-52;

"Pernicious Participation," in *The Black Papers on Education* (London: Davis & Poynter, 1971), pp. 170-173;

"A Short Educational Dictionary," in *The Black Papers on Education* (London: Davis & Poynter, 1971), pp. 215-223;

Selected Stories of G. K. Chesterton, edited by Amis (London: Faber, 1972);

Tennyson, Selected by Kingsley Amis, edited by Amis (Harmondsworth, U.K.: Penguin, 1973);

"I.L.E.A. Confidential," by Amis and Conquest, in *Black Paper 1975: The Fight for Education,* edited by C. B. Cox and Rhodes Boyson (London: Dent, 1975), pp. 60-61;

Arthur Hutchings, *Mozart: The Man, the Music,* introduction by Amis (London: Schirmer, 1976);

Harold's Years: Impressions from the "New Statesman" and the "Spectator," edited by Amis (London: Quartet, 1977);

The New Oxford Book of Light Verse, edited, with an introduction, by Amis (London: Oxford University Press, 1978); republished as *The New Oxford Book of English Light Verse* (New York: Oxford University Press, 1978);

The Faber Popular Reciter, edited by Amis (London: Faber & Faber, 1978);

"Getting It Wrong," in *The State of the Language,* edited by Leonard Michaels and Christopher Ricks (Berkeley: University of California Press, 1980), pp. 24-33;

The Golden Age of Science Fiction, edited by Amis (London: Hutchinson, 1981);

"Oxford and After," in *Larkin at Sixty,* edited by Anthony Thwaite (London: Faber, 1982), pp. 23–30.

Author of seventeen novels, three poetry collections, and more than twenty short stories, Kingsley Amis is a writer whose literary style defies categorization. In *Kingsley Amis* (1989) Richard Bradford warns the reader that "Amis is an 'experimental' writer, but his experiments are aimed at the sort of person who could be amused, annoyed and even forced to think about the relationship between literature and post-war society without necessarily having to pigeonhole his reactions under such predetermined labels as 'tradition,' 'stylistic inheritance,' 'experiment,' 'realism,' 'fantasy.' . . . A person attempting to do such things will . . . find his critical competence under severe strain." Amis's unconventional approach to literature, criticism, morality, and politics clearly informs his writing and identifies him as a significant voice in modern British fiction. Although more critical attention has been paid to Amis's novels, his short stories "allow us perhaps a clearer vision of the intent as well as the logic of the career as a whole," according to James Vickery in *Kingsley Amis in Life and Letters* (1990), edited by Dale Salwak.

In the preface to his novella *Dear Illusion* (1972), Amis states, "Some novelists find it easy and natural to express themselves in the short-story form as well; I never have, and when I do produce something too short to be called a novel, it is because I have thought of an idea which is suitable for a narrative but which cannot be stretched to the length of a novel." This difficulty aside, the fact that Amis published short fiction over the years 1955 to 1986 suggests that if such ideas came infrequently, he did not abandon the genre.

Amis was born on 16 April 1922 in a south London nursing home, the only child of William Robert and Rosa Lucas Amis. His father was a senior clerk for Colman's Mustard, a devotee of Sir William Gilbert and Sir Arthur Sullivan's operettas, and an ardent tennis and cricket player. Amis inherited his mother's interest in literature; in *Memoirs* (1991) he writes that she "continued all her life as inveterate a reader as I was in my youth: a book was as much part of her accoutrements at home as handbag and knitting."

He began his education at the local schools, including Norbury College, to which he refers as "one of the most peaceable places I have ever known." In 1934 he embarked on seven years of studies at the City of London School, which his father and two

uncles had previously attended. In *Memoirs* Amis confesses to "a minor but contemptible lie I used until recently tell, describing myself as a 'scholarship boy' all the way up the ladder. Well, actually Dad paid for my first year at the City of London School, gambling successfully that I would get a scholarship in the year that followed." He received an exhibition to read English literature at Saint John's College, Oxford, where he met Philip Larkin, who remained a friend until his death in 1985.

In the introduction to the 1964 edition of his novel *Jill,* Larkin writes that Amis was engaged in one of his characteristic displays of mimicry when the two met and that "for the first time I felt myself in the presence of a talent greater than my own." In *Memoirs* Amis recalls his friend as "an almost aggressively normal undergraduate of the non-highbrow, non-sherry-sipping sort, hard-swearing, hard-belching, etc., treating the college dons as fodder for obscene clerihews and the porter as a comic ogre, gregarious, going to the English Club, admittedly, but treating its sessions as incidents in beery nights out and/or targets for more derision, being fined by the Dean." While attending Oxford, Amis edited the publication sponsored by the University Labour Club and professed strong liberal, even pro-Soviet, political convictions. These underwent drastic alteration when, after only a year at Oxford, Amis was drafted for military service. In 1942 he was commissioned in the Royal Corps of Signals, eventually rising to the rank of lieutenant, serving in France, Belgium, and Germany.

The first three stories in Amis's first collection of short stories, *My Enemy's Enemy* (1962), were inspired by his service in the Signal Corps. The collection met with varied critical response, but R. G. G. Price (*Punch,* 3 October 1962) detected a real growth in Amis's writing, a maturing compassion: "For the first time, he seems equally aware of the forces operating on all his characters." The first story, "My Enemy's Enemy," was previously published in *Encounter* (1955). In *Kingsley Amis: An English Moralist* (1989) John McDermott suggests that this story, along with "Court of Inquiry" and "I Spy Strangers" — all set against the backdrop of the Signal Corps and including a recurring cast of characters — cannot be considered "parts of an unfinished or discarded novel; [they] are best read together as a coherent and overlapping sequence." Amis's treatment of the British army is predictably iconoclastic. He exposes the pettiness of the Byzantine bureaucracy and the tensions that form relationships among the military hierarchy and its underlying civilian caste system, all the while utilizing these foils to demonstrate deeper human truths. In opposition to the absurdity of the military background Amis sets values that become recurring themes in his fiction: loyalty, sincerity, and moral obligation.

Told from the perspective of Capt. Tom Thurston, "My Enemy's Enemy" concerns the petty hatred felt by the dictatorial Adjutant toward one "Dally" – Lieutenant Dalessio – a line-maintenance supervisor. Thurston, who loathes the Adjutant, finds himself embroiled in the conflict between the two men when the Adjutant confides in him that he has planned a surprise inspection in order to run Dalessio out of the unit. Threatened with reassignment, Thurston does not warn Dalessio of the coming inspection. Instead, one of the regular army officers gets wind of the conspiracy and warns Dalessio. Afterward, in language that highlights Amis's masterful control of colloquial usage, that officer reproaches Thurston:

> I've no doubt you have your excuses for not letting on. In spite of the fact that I've always understood you were the great one for pouring scorn on the Adj. . . . and the rest of that crowd. Yes, you could talk about them till you were black in the face, but when it came to doing something, talking where it would do some good, you kept your mouth shut. And, if I remember rightly, you were the one who used to stick up for Dally when the others were laying into him behind his back. You know what I think? I don't think you care tuppence. You don't care beyond talking, any road. I think you're really quite sold on the Adj.'s crowd, never mind what you say about them. Chew that over. And chew this over and all: I think you're a bastard, just like the rest of 'em. Tell that to your friend the Adjutant, Captain bloody Thurston.

"Court of Inquiry," the least satisfying of the three Signal Corps stories, also concerns an abuse of military authority. Here an unnamed narrator describes the proceedings of a court-martial conducted by obsessively militaristic Major Raleigh against young Lieutenant Archer. Charged with misplacing an obsolete generator, Archer melodramatically apologizes to the major and the other assembled officers, effectively embarrassing them into absolving him. When the narrator confronts Archer, the reader learns that this emotional outburst was intentional: " 'That was what Raleigh wanted,' he went on. 'If I'd stood up for my rights or anything, he'd just have decided to step up his little war of nerves in other ways. As it was I think I even made him feel he'd gone too far.' "

"I Spy Strangers," a novella, is the most polished of the three Signal Corps stories. Its characters are more developed, and the issue of authority

is dealt with more evenhandedly. While the moral position in "My Enemy's Enemy" and "Court of Inquiry" is dictated, here it is only suggested. An older Archer appears in the story, set sometime after the fall of the Third Reich but before the end of the war. Because his Signal Corps has lost much of its usefulness, Major Raleigh has organized a mock-Parliament to keep his men occupied. He harbors great misgivings about the political direction of postwar Great Britain: "Something monstrous and indefinable was growing in strength, something hostile to his accent and taste in clothes and modest directorship and ambitions for his sons and redbrick house at Purley with its back-garden tennis-court."

Although Raleigh insists on the impartiality of the visitor's gallery, his political conservatism is well represented by an orderly-room sergeant named Doll, who is convinced that the Russians and their politics represent Great Britain's postwar enemies. Raleigh's dramatic foil is present in the form of Hargreaves, a young signalman with decidedly left-wing loyalties. During the climactic debate Raleigh is so incensed by Hargreaves's description of Great Britain's future that he rises from the visitor's gallery and delivers a platitudinous diatribe, spurring Hargreaves to proclaim loudly, "I spy strangers," the parliamentary phrase calling for the gallery to be cleared. Raleigh later retaliates, assigning both Hargreaves and Archer to the continuing battle in the Far East, but Archer is spared by an early release from the army.

Although some critics characterize *My Enemy's Enemy* as at least in part Tory propaganda, the unique strength of "I Spy Strangers" is, as Philip Gardner notes in *Kingsley Amis* (1981), "its fairness to the wide range of English types involved in the end-of-war political shift." Gardner further points out that the final statements in this story – and indeed in this trilogy – are symptomatic of Amis's own swing from left- to right-wing politics. Tellingly, Amis gives the last thought to ultraconservative, but not unsympathetic, Major Raleigh:

> But the world was wide. Bad things could happen and it all went on as before. . . . Much of what he believed in must survive. And the guarantee of that was England. . . . She had weathered every storm, she had never gone under. All that was needed was faith. Despite everything that Hargreaves and Archer and the rest of them might do, England would muddle through somehow.

In 1945 Amis, like Archer, returned to Oxford, where he obtained first-class honors in 1947,

Anthony Powell, Amis, Philip Larkin, and Hilary Amis in London, 1958

at which time he commenced a two-year term as research student. Amis married Hilary Ann Bardwell the following year. In 1949 he received a position in the English department at the University College of Swansea, Wales, where he remained for the next twelve years. There he became acquainted with John Wain, author of *Hurry on Down* (1953), which – along with John Osborne's *Look Back in Anger* (1957), John Braine's *Room at the Top* (1957), and Amis's *Lucky Jim* (1954) – came to be a literary hallmark of a group of young British writers to whom critics referred as the angry young men.

These writers shared an inclination to question the validity of a social structure that seemed so different from what it was prior to 1939 and the proficiency to do so in a simple, accessible writing style. Amis bristled at the idea of their constituting a cohesive unit. After the *Daily Mail* (London) suggested that writer Colin Wilson was also an angry young man, Amis attacked Wilson's opportunism. In *What Became of Jane Austen?* (1970) Amis states that – along with Henri Barbusse, Jean-Paul Sartre, Albert Camus, Søren Kierkegaard, Friedrich Nietzsche, and others – Wilson was guilty of "a tendency to erect one's boredoms into a system with oneself sitting in the middle."

Amis vents his social concerns in "Morale Fibre" (first published in *Esquire,* 1958), the fourth story in *My Enemy's Enemy*. In the story John Lewis and his wife, Jean, reappear from *That Uncertain Feeling* (1955). The Lewises have just hired "twice-a-week domestic help," Betty Arnulfsen. Her employment has been arranged by Mair Webster, a local social worker married to a colleague of John. Throughout the story Mair attempts to reform Betty, to whom John initially refers as a woman not "really fallen, just rather inadmissibly inclined from the perpendicular." Eventually, however, Betty quits working for the Lewises, reverts to her old hangout, and turns to prostitution. When she visits John and propositions him, he notes that she is "really fallen now, right smack over full length." Later, when Betty's husband returns from Norway, he and Mair whip Betty back into shape. Mair cajoles John into visiting Betty and her husband. Betty, who at first seems beaten down, strikes out at Mair and her interference. Two weeks later she is arrested for breaking into a shop.

It is hard to miss Amis's point in "Morale Fibre"; most certainly the story is an investigation of Labour party politics and its moral agenda. Despite some contemporary reviews that found Amis's treatment of Mair unfair and exaggerated, the value of "Morale Fibre" lies precisely in the fact that he is at least evenhanded in resisting the no doubt tempting impulse to paint Mair as a relentless, meddling, do-gooder. Although John finds Mair and her constant intercession into the lives of others repugnant, he admires her "creed of take-off-your-coat-and-get-on-with-it." And, as the story ends, John points out that while Mair will probably go on intruding on Betty's life by visiting her in jail and beyond, he will not. He admits finally that the people best suited to do anything about society's ills are those least likely to do so. As Gardner puts it: "Amis looks shrewdly and realistically at the difficulty of reconciling the individuality and freedom of real if erratic people with the demands of social responsibility and order."

Another typically Amis theme, miscommunication, is treated humorously in "Interesting Things," also found in *My Enemy's Enemy*. This story, which first appeared in *Pick of Today's Short Stories* 7 (1956) but is omitted from *Collected Short Stories* (enlarged edition, 1987), concerns the first date of Gloria Davies and Mr. Huws-Evans, an overly conventional, drab income-tax inspector. As the evening is seen primarily through Gloria's perspective, the reader is subjected to a rich inventory of Mr. Huws-Evans's quirks, including an ever-present string bag full of potato chips and his violent admonishments against the producers of razor blades. During the evening Gloria laments that Mr. Huws-Evans does not make advances, but when he finally does, she makes an awkward emotional outburst in protest.

In the end, when the couple arrives at a party, the reader learns that Gloria has agreed to the date in order to meet Mr. Huws-Evans's brother: "It was because of him — she'd seen him once or twice when he called in at the office — that she'd accepted Mr. Huws-Evans's invitation." Although "Interesting Things" is the shortest and perhaps least developed story in *My Enemy's Enemy,* Amis still manages to provide each of the characters with a wide range of — in this case rather idiosyncratic — attributes. However, the story relies more heavily on character than on plot.

Whereas "Interesting Things" sacrifices plot for character development, "All the Blood Within Me," first published in *Spectator* (1962), is a fertile blend of the two, the fullest piece of fiction in *My Enemy's Enemy*. Some critics have pointed to this story as one of Amis's most impressive works. It concerns a trio of friends: Alec "Mac" McKenzie and Betty and Jim Duerden. At the outset Betty has recently died, and Mac is taking a train to the fu-

neral. During the funeral Mac's mind wanders; he comments to himself about Betty and Jim's daughter, Annette, and her husband, Frank (a half-Italian laundry owner), and Mac considers the nature of death. Amis skillfully interweaves the minister's poignant metaphysical comments with Mac's memories of Betty.

At dinner that night Mac erupts at Frank about his Catholicism and makes several barely veiled insulting remarks about foreigners. When Annette approaches Mac outside the restaurant, she reveals several unsavory things about her mother. She tells him that Betty was overtly hostile about Frank's ethnicity and that she looked on and treated Mac with disdain. Of Mac's love for Betty, Annette comments: "I know the sort. That's the best sort, the sort you don't have to do anything about or get to know the person, and it was fine for her. The way she used to put on a big tolerant act Sunday mornings when we came back from Mass when we stayed with them. Tolerant."

As in "My Enemy's Enemy" and "Morale Fibre," Amis draws the reader into sympathizing with the protagonist and his outlook and then uses an unexpected agent — here Annette — to turn the reader's perceptions topsy-turvy. One thinks this story is about a sincerely genuine, noble "love from afar" until Annette makes her revelations. One of the best features of Amis's fiction is his ability to extract spectacular emotions and truths about human nature out of common characters placed in common situations, using common language. Perhaps nowhere else in Amis's short fiction is this feature so forcibly demonstrated as in the last lines of "All the Blood Within Me." Responding to Annette's conciliatory invitation to visit her family more frequently in the future, Mac replies, "It's a pity it's such a long way." Gardner points out that this simple statement "can stand equally for that [distance] between people, between imagination and 'reality,' between the present and the past, and between the living and the dead."

After *My Enemy's Enemy* ten years passed before Amis published more short fiction. *Dear Illusion* is a humorous, oddly touching story about Great Britain's leading but nevertheless obscure poet Edward Potter and a reporter, Susan MacNamara, sent to interview him. Before their meeting MacNamara is dubious, questioning not only Potter's sincerity but whether his poetry is really any good at all. During the interview Potter understands that she has a low opinion of his work. He tells her that he produces his lyrics to assuage a general feeling of life's worthlessness and that "to be able to function as a human being" he writes poems. "Some words came into my mind," he tells her, "and straight away I felt a little better. I forget what they were, but they brought more words with them and they made me feel a little better still. By the time the words stopped coming I felt at peace." He also informs her that he has found a doctor who promises that a regimen of chemotherapy will allay the sensation of pointlessness that draws him to write.

One year later Potter is presented an award for his most recent critically acclaimed collection, *Off*. At the ceremony he reveals, however, that he wrote all the poems in this collection in one day, "in any style I could think of." Satisfied now, as he tells Susan, that he was "never any good," Potter commits suicide soon afterward.

Many critics have pointed to *Dear Illusion* as evidence of Amis questioning his literary value and whether the product really justifies the intense process, in literature and in life in general. More important, this story ponders the enigmatic nature of human relationships, what Gardner calls "the mysteriousness of life and the impulses that enable people to sustain it." In the *Collected Short Stories* "Dear Illusion" follows "All the Blood Within Me" and is a particularly good companion piece to it because "Dear Illusion" views with stark realism the kind of shocking epiphanies Amis's characters often experience in constructing their fragile worlds.

With the publication of *Lucky Jim* Amis established his reputation as an accomplished writer. He produced two other novels during the 1950s: *That Uncertain Feeling* and *I Like It Here* (1958). In 1958 Amis accepted a fellowship at Princeton University to give a series of lectures on science fiction; these were published in *New Maps of Hell: A Survey of Science Fiction* (1960). For the next five years, along with his friend Robert Conquest, Amis edited *Spectrum*, a series of science-fiction anthologies.

New Maps of Hell, often cited as the first major critical work on the then-much-maligned genre, is a lighthearted but serious attempt at legitimizing science fiction. Amis writes:

> Often, I think that part – and I mean part – of the attraction of science fiction lies in the fact that it provides a field which . . . allows us to doff that mental and moral best behaviour with which we feel we have to treat George Eliot and James and Faulkner, and frolic like badly brought up children among the mobile jellyfishes and unstable atomic piles.

In Salwak's *Kingsley Amis in Life and Letters*, both Brian Aldiss and Harry Harrison bemoan the fact that Amis is not better recognized as one of the truly great contributors to the genre. Harrison praises Amis for his groundbreaking approach to science fiction in *New Maps of Hell* but also commends Amis's original contributions to the field, particularly the novel *The Alteration* (1976), which, like Amis's most successful science fiction, is a blend of "mainstream fiction and science fiction at the same time."

Amis's contribution to short science fiction is established in the second half of the 1987 edition of the *Collected Short Stories*. McDermott suggests that while the stories in the first half (most from *My Enemy's Enemy*) are realistic, the second half is distinguished by the experimental – "parody, pastiche and genre." The first of the experimental stories, "Something Strange" (first published in the *Spectator*, 1960), is the only science-fiction piece in *My Enemy's Enemy*.

In "Something Strange" a small team of what the reader assumes must be scientists living in an isolated space station begins to encounter absurd and increasingly threatening occurrences that cannot be explained. After a cataclysm of sorts occurs, the reader discovers that the team was really trapped in a bizarre government-sponsored experiment. This revelation, however, plunges one of the team, Myri (notably the creative writer of the group), into a catatonic state. Only Bruno's declaration of love for her brings Myri out of her coma. As McDermott observes, "Love in Amis is always a strong reviver." "Something Strange" illustrates well a shortcoming in Amis's science-fiction stories: he sometimes abandons characterization in order to develop a fantasy concept.

On Drink (1972) covers a topic to which Amis frequently turns in his nonfiction writing. Essays such as "Aperitifs: As If You Needed Any Encouragement to Start Drinking, Here's What to Start With" and "Stout Work: A Day in the Life of a Bottle of Guiness, Lovingly Recorded by Kingsley Amis" reveal his enthusiasm for the subject of alcoholic beverages. In the 1987 edition of the *Collected Short Stories*, the four stories following "Something Strange" blend his interest in spirits with his equally keen interest in science fiction. "The 2003 Claret" (first published in *The Compleat Imbiber*, 1958), "The Friends of Plonk," "Too Much Trouble" (first published in *Penguin Modern Stories II*, 1972), and "Investing in Futures" (first published in *The Compleat Imbiber*, 1986) are all what McDermott refers to as "the new genre, 'SF-drink.'"

These four stories all feature the same team of researchers, who are ostensibly involved in projecting one of their number, Simpson, into the future by use of the TIOPEPE (Temporal Integrator, Ordinal Predictor, and Electronic Propulsion Equipment) in order to learn about the social and political changes to come. The team is most interested in the state of drink to come. In each story Simpson relates a depressing assessment of the drinking habits of the future.

In "The 2003 Claret" Simpson reports a widening gulf between the pretentious snobbery of wine drinkers and the equally affected antisnobbery of beer drinkers. In 1964, one year before his second marriage, to Elizabeth Jane Howard, Amis published his next "SF-drink" story, "The Friends of Plonk," in which Simpson encounters a small group of men in the year 2145. They are trying to rekindle the ability to make and enjoy alcoholic beverages, recently lost during nuclear war between Wales and Mars. In "Too Much Trouble" Simpson reports to his colleagues that in 1983 they will be serving "packets" of powder that, when mixed with water, produce stout, scotch, gin, vodka, and bitter that bears "very much the same relation to our bitter as powdered coffee to coffee."

In "Investing in Futures," the concluding piece to this series, Simpson is sent back to the Middle Ages and procures root cuttings from Burgundy vineyards. The research team grows rich off its investment in these vines because they have not been weakened by growers' attempts to ward off "phylloxera XO, the deadly subspecies of vine-aphids first seen in the Bordeaux vineyards in 1984." Although the "SF-drink" stories offer lighthearted satire, there is that underlying level of serious social criticism consistently found in much of Amis's realistic fiction. As James Gindin writes in "Changing Social and Moral Attitudes" (*Kingsley Amis in Life and Letters*), these stories "all suggest in various ways that Amis's impulse to turn to the future and the extraterrestrial was, at least in imaginative inception, a function of his assessment of the present and the terrestrial."

Of the remaining science-fiction pieces in the *Collected Short Stories*, "Hemingway in Space" (first published in *Punch*, 1960) belongs to a group of literary experiments in style and structure that includes "The Darkwater Hall Mystery" and "To See the Sun." "Hemingway in Space" is about Philip Hardacre, a caricature of the Ernest Hemingway hero. Hardacre is on a "xeeb" hunt with a young man (much beleaguered by his domineering wife) and a faithful sidekick, Ghlmu, an old Martian who eventually dies saving the hero's life. Amis manages to incorporate something of the Hemingway code of life in Hardacre's character, and the language – es-

pecially when Hardacre explains to his Martian friend why he should not take part in the hunt – positively drips Hemingway:

> "This is not your hunt, Ghlmu," he said in the archaic Martian courtly tongue.
> "I am still strong and he is big and he comes fast."
> "I know, but this is not your hunt. Old ones are hunted more than they hunt."
> "All my eyes are straight and all my hands are tight."
> "But they are slow and they must be quick. Once they were quick but now they are slow."
> "Har-dasha, it is thy comrade who asks thee."
> "My blood is yours as in all the years; it is only my thought that must seem cruel, old one. I will hunt without you."

As "Hemingway in Space" borrows substance and style from Hemingway, "The Darkwater Hall Mystery" (first published in *Playboy*, 1978) is Amis's spin on Sir Arthur Conan Doyle. Dr. Watson, the familiar narrator, recounts a mystery that in Sherlock Holmes's absence he was obliged to solve. The mystery revolves around Sir Harry Fairfax, who has been threatened by Black Ralph, an ex-convict Sir Harry had sent to jail for poaching. Through no spectacular deductions Watson solves the case, and Black Ralph is brought to justice.

Amis employs the stock Doyle formula here to get at something altogether different: the reader discovers that much more goes on at Darkwater Hall than the Black Ralph puzzle. On his second night there Watson's sleep is interrupted by the sounds of a whip and screams coming from the room above his chambers. On opening the door to this room Watson discovers Sir Harry and his wife "garbed after the fashion of a hundred years before. Emily Fairfax wore a gown of black bombazine; he who must be her husband was unrecognizable by reason of the red velvet mask that, apart from eye-holes, covered all his face above the mouth."

Although Watson accepts the couple's explanation that they are engaged in nothing more than acting out a dramatic scene, he later speculates about the merit of "the view, put forward by a Viennese colleague to whom I recently recounted the outline of this story, that Sir Harry's amateur theatricals might have been something other than what I had taken them to be, and in some abstruse way – which I could not wholly follow – connected with his failure to produce an heir." But, as Watson relates, even this is not the most enigmatic feature of his Darkwater Hall experience. On the last page of the story the reader learns that his interrogation of one of the female servants, Dolores, actually took place in his bed. Finally, the reader understands that Amis has utilized Doyle's familiar mystery-writing format to comment on a mystery whose substance is uncharacteristic of Doyle. In the last paragraph Watson muses: "Dolores, what was it in you, or in me, or in both of us that brought it about that in your arms I experienced a joy more intense and more exquisite than any before or since? . . . To me, that is the real Darkwater Hall mystery, as impenetrable and as wonderful now as it was then, forty years ago."

"To See the Sun," first published in the 1987 edition of the *Collected Short Stories,* is a Bram Stoker–like Dracula story. Here a scholar, Stephen Hillier, researching vampirism, visits a castle in Nuvakastra, Dacia, reputed to be the ancestral home of one of Europe's oldest vampire families. During the course of the story, written in an epistolary style, Hillier and young (in appearance, at any rate) Countess Valvazor fall deeply in love. The countess's love for Hillier forces her to revoke her loathsome life, and she commits suicide by exposing herself to the full morning sun. Hillier, finally comprehending the countess's true nature, flees Dacia and abandons his vampire study in favor of an investigation of early Hungarian literature.

By modeling this story after an established formula, Amis again manipulates the reader's sense of the expected. Because the majority of the letters that make up the narrative are from Hillier to his wife in England, Amis is able to juxtapose two distinct worlds: the mundane one of a married couple separated by a great distance and the fantastic one of vampires. The two chief characters are equally juxtaposed. Hillier belongs to a drab academic world; at the end of his letter to a colleague, A. C. Winterbourne, he writes: "Good luck with the James Barnes Hitchens prize." Countess Valvazor is concerned with whether she can resist the vampire's temptation to drink Hillier's blood long enough to commit suicide.

Amis's pastiche exercises point out his interest in the value of "lower forms" of literature. As McDermott suggests:

The adversion to such models is a further gesture in approval of a comparatively innocent literary culture that pre-dates any deep divide between highbrow and popular literature. Moreover, major writers of the last century would and could (he maintains) work across such a divide (as today happens only with [Graham] Greene, perhaps, Amis himself, and a handful of others).

"The House on the Headland" (first published in the London *Times,* 1979) continues the macabre theme set in "To See the Sun" and, like "The Darkwater Hall Mystery," employs a surprise ending that turns the reader's perceptions upside down. Amis utilizes this convention with better results in "All the Blood Within Me" and "Something Strange." In "The House on the Headland" the narrator, a military-intelligence agent in 1938, is given an old file concerning events shortly after Turkey pulled its troops from Crete in the late 1800s. The file, compiled by Courtenay, the British agent stationed in Crete, records the strange behavior of Count Axel, later revealed as a Swedish émigré.

The count's odd actions, such as bricking up the windows of his isolated manor, intrigue Courtenay, who, with the assistance of a junior officer, Barnes, subsequently investigates and is murdered. Barnes later witnesses the count's strange, naked menagerie of wildly deformed women: one "evidently an Asiatic half-caste with exquisite features and the look of being some months gone in pregnancy"; and another with two faces, human and tapir, whom Barnes reports he sees the count embracing. Barnes records that Courtenay's last words were "Terror . . . to fill," but the narrator clarifies: "Courtenay's last words to him [Barnes] had nothing to do with terror; he was trying to say a single word that I, with my ancient as well as Modern Greek, can identify, though I have never encountered it: teratophilia, erotic attraction to monsters."

The narrator further discloses that he was born in the Levant slightly less than one year after the date of this report and that he has Nordic coloring, Asiatic eyes, and a disturbing scar near his right hip. Fearing the worst about his origin after reading the file, he breaks off his engagement and enlists in the army. A note appended to the story informs the reader that the narrator has died in France, "showing complete disregard for his own safety, [when] he attacked an enemy tank with hand-grenades."

Perhaps the most interesting piece in the second half of the 1987 edition of the *Collected Short Stories* is "Who or What Was It?" (first published in *Playboy,* 1972). Amis begins, "I want to tell you about a very odd experience I had a few months ago," and goes on to relate in a refreshingly conversational manner a story in which a character named Kingsley Amis visits an inn called the Green Man and essentially finds himself within one of his own novels. Toying with several layers of what could be real and what must be dream, Amis – the persona – tries, as in the novel, to keep a monster called the

Amis lecturing at Vanderbilt University, fall 1967

Green Man from attacking the innkeeper's daughter. He leaves his wife in the room and sets out for where he knows the monster, "made of tree-branches, twigs, and clusters of leaves," must materialize. When Amis throws a cross at the monster, it vanishes, as does the daughter. He returns to the inn only to have his wife tell him that he never left the room and that they made love during the time that he thought and reported he was fending off the Green Man. When their doctor reports that she is not pregnant, Amis comments: "A relief, of course. But in one way, rather disappointing."

The two remaining stories in the 1987 edition of the *Collected Short Stories,* "Affairs of Death" (first published in *Shakespeare's Stories,* 1982) and "Mason's Life" (first published in the London *Sunday Times*), are probably the least developed pieces in the second half of the collection. "Affairs of Death" is an imaginative examination of a meeting between Pope Leo IX and Macbeth, wherein Macbeth wishes to establish the true story of his ascension to the crown. He tells the pope that he is afraid that people will get the story wrong after his death: "If it were not for this record, who could guess what might be believed of me in centuries to come? That I took innocent lives, that I murdered my friend,

murdered children, that I consorted with witches and saw visions, that I — how to put it? — supped full with horrors."

"Mason's Life" — at about a thousand words the briefest story in the collection — involves the title character's meeting with an apparent madman, Pettigrew, in a bar. Pettigrew repeatedly insists that Mason is not real, that he is merely dreaming his existence. In the end Mason grabs Pettigrew and is astounded to find that Pettigrew begins to fade. Mason is even more astounded when he looks at his own hand and sees "with difficulty that it likewise no longer had fingers, or front or back, or skin, or anything at all."

In his introduction to the 1987 edition of the *Collected Short Stories,* Amis writes: "Anyway, the things that only the short story can do, the impression, the untrimmed slice of life, the landscape with figures but without characters, make little appeal to me. This collection is really one of chips from a novelist's work-bench." However, his short stories — perhaps even better than his novels — display the development of Amis's career and concerns. Taken as a whole, Amis's stories demonstrate the striking skill of a writer able to illuminate great ideas using common people, situations, and language. Even his most outlandish science fiction and his most macabre pastiches center on ideas such as friendship, deteriorating morality, and the mystery of love and communication. From the Signal Corps to science fiction, from ultraliberal to conservative attitudes, from the seriousness of "All the Blood Within Me" to the lightheartedness of "Hemingway in Space," Amis's short fiction displays an impressive scope of topics and moods.

Interviews:

Pat Williams, "My Kind of Comedy," *Twentieth Century,* 1970 (July 1961): 46–50;

John Silverlight, "Profile: Kingsley Amis," *Observer,* 14 January 1962, p. 13; reprinted as "Kingsley Amis: The Writer, the Symbol," *New York Herald Tribune Book Review,* 21 January 1962, p. 6;

Harry Fieldhouse, "Penthouse Interview: Kingsley Amis," *Penthouse,* 2 (October 1970): 35–39, 42;

Peter Firchow, "Kingsley Amis," in his *The Writer's Place: Interviews on the Literary Situation in Contemporary England* (Minneapolis: University of Minnesota Press, 1974), pp. 15–38;

Clive James, "Kingsley Amis," *New Review,* 1 (July 1974): 21–28;

Melvyn Bragg, "Kingsley Amis Looks Back," *Listener,* 20 February 1975, pp. 240–241;

Michael Barber, "The Art of Fiction – LIX: Kingsley Amis," *Paris Review,* 16 (Winter 1975): 39–72;

Dale Salwak, "An Interview with Kingsley Amis," *Contemporary Literature,* 16 (Winter 1975): 1–18;

Auberon Waugh, "Amis: A Singular Man," *Sunday Telegraph Magazine,* 17 September 1978, pp. 33–36.

Bibliographies:

Rubin Rabinovitz, "Kingsley Amis Bibliography," in his *The Reaction Against Experiment in the English Novel, 1950–60* (New York & London: Columbia University Press, 1967), pp. 174–178;

Jack Benoit Gohn, *Kingsley Amis: A Checklist* (Kent, Ohio: Kent State University Press, 1976);

Dale Salwak, *Kingsley Amis: A Reference Guide* (Boston: G. K. Hall, 1978);

John McDermott, "A Kingsley Amis Checklist," in his *Kingsley Amis: An English Moralist* (New York: St. Martin's Press, 1989), pp. 243–250.

References:

Richard Bradford, *Kingsley Amis* (London: Arnold, 1989);

Philip Gardner, *Kingsley Amis* (Boston: Twayne, 1981);

James Gindin, *Postwar British Fiction: New Accents and Attitudes* (Berkeley: University of California Press, 1962);

Dale Salwak, ed., *Kingsley Amis in Life and Letters* (London: Macmillan, 1990);

Denis Vannatta, ed., *The English Short Story, 1945–1980* (Boston: Twayne, 1985).

Papers:

The Harry Ransom Humanities Research Center, University of Texas at Austin, possesses some of Amis's letters, working materials for many of his novels (notably the manuscript, typescript, and notes for *Lucky Jim*), and the typescript of *The James Bond Dossier*. Manuscripts of several of his early poems are in the Lockwood Memorial Library, State University of New York at Buffalo.

A. L. Barker

(13 April 1918 –)

Alice L. Swensen
University of Northern Iowa

See also the Barker entry in *DLB 14: British Novelists Since 1960.*

BOOKS: *Innocents: Variations on a Theme* (London: Hogarth, 1947; New York: Scribners, 1948);

Apology for a Hero (London: Hogarth, 1950; New York: Scribners, 1950);

Novelette, with Other Stories (London: Hogarth, 1951; New York: Scribners, 1951);

The Joy-Ride and After (London: Hogarth, 1963; New York: Scribners, 1964);

Lost Upon the Roundabouts (London: Hogarth, 1964);

A Case Examined (London: Hogarth, 1965);

The Middling: Chapters in the Life of Ellie Toms (London: Hogarth, 1967);

John Brown's Body (London: Hogarth, 1969);

Femina Real (London: Hogarth, 1971);

A Source of Embarrassment (London: Hogarth, 1974);

A Heavy Feather (London: Hogarth, 1978; New York: Braziller, 1979);

Life Stories (London: Hogarth, 1981);

Relative Successes (London: Hogarth, 1984; New York: Salem House, 1986);

No Word of Love (London: Chatto & Windus/Hogarth, 1985);

The Gooseboy (London: Hutchinson, 1987);

The Woman Who Talked to Herself: An Articulated Novel (London: Hutchinson, 1989; New York: Vintage, 1991);

Any Excuse for a Party: Selected Stories (London: Hutchinson, 1991);

Zeph (London: Hutchinson, 1992).

A. L. (Audrey Lillian) Barker has been acclaimed for her short stories, although she has written nine novels as well. Critics have noted, however, that her truncated, episodic style fails to lend itself to the longer form. In *Life Stories* (1981), a collection of autobiographical essays and short fiction, she writes that "in my credo the short story was one of two literary forms in which it was just possible that complete integration could be achieved: the

A. L. Barker

other form, which often blazingly achieved it, being poetry." Whether in novels or short stories, an aspect of that integration is her lifelong concern with the themes of innocence, experience, and the impossibility of understanding another person or communicating, along with the resultant absurdities of such conditions.

Barker began writing when she was nine years old. In *Life Stories* she recalls a childhood episode in which she saw a red-tiled floor through a puddle of water: "It magnified every crack, every grain. . . . It is water as I remember as my eye of childhood, a vision crystal clear and scrupulous. I like to think I saw everything like that. It is sentimentality, of course, for I had learned already to look without seeing." In this passage she closes in on what is special about her prose: it is "crystal clear and scrupulous."

Barker was born on 13 April 1918 in Saint Paul's Cray, Kent, to Henry and Elsie Dutton Barker. She writes about her parents in *Life Stories*: "I could never do my father justice. He was a stranger. . . . He thought I was a snob, and I was. . . . My mother spoke whatever came into her mind at the moment of its coming and in the manner of its coming, straight out of the rampant spirit she inherited from her mother. She was not afraid of anyone."

Barker discontinued her secondary-school education at age sixteen to become a secretary in a London office. She later found work more conducive to her interests in a literary agent's office and then as a subeditor at Amalgamated Press. When World War II began, she left this position to serve with the British Land Army and the National Fire Service. After demobilization she joined the staff of the British Broadcasting Corporation. In 1947 she won the Somerset Maugham Prize for *Innocents: Variations on a Theme,* her first collection of short stories, and she was consequently able to travel to France and Italy and launch her career as a freelance writer. Barker has summed up her affinity for and approach to writing short fiction:

> I am by choice and capacity a short story writer. . . . The possibilities for the short story have always been enough to occupy me. It is a lifetime's engagement, and as life time dwindles, tantalisingly the scope increases. Technically a form, it now seems to be blessedly formless. . . . The moment is all, is what I want to catch, with a turn of phrase, a hint, an implication, a repetition. Ideally, the moment should persist, like a flavor, so that the reader after reading, or days or years later, finds the moment complete, for better or worse, and beyond reproach or censure.

In "Submerged" (*Innocents*) a young boy, Peter Hume, reflects that "it was his parents who really irritated him by their transparent tact. They treated the subject as too extreme to fall within his knowledge or understanding. It confirmed his suspicion that there was nothing but a great deal of wilful mystery in adult affairs." Barker's theme of antagonism between the young and old is thus set in motion.

The eight stories in this collection also depict the themes of innocence and experience. Although the protagonists are often young people, they are not always innocent. In the title story young Richard Tustin "had watched one [bomb] drop like a catapulted bird, and was lucky enough to arrive just as the remains of a local tobacconist and his wife were taken from the ruins. The experience appealed to Richard. With just such an irreverent flick had he destroyed toys and the silly prized possessions of his friends. But he had never achieved such a scale of disaster, it was the method of a giant. Beside it, his efforts were puny indeed, and he was eager to study and admire."

Richard is a child of his time – World War II – which lacks innocence. Barker's stories reflect the individual's relation to reality, and because that reality is often grim the individual is often misshapen, even grotesque in his or her perspective. Richard's aunts, the Misses Goodge, live in a substantial brick house in Berkshire, away from the bombing, so Richard is sent to live with them: "Observing him, Miss Sabrina Goodge sometimes wondered why he, particularly, was being safeguarded while so many had to take their chance." She notes that "he was not lovable, he was often quite repellent."

As it turns out, Sabrina Goodge is right: Richard coldly and precisely carves up the prospects and happiness of two unsuspecting adults, his teacher and his aunts' skittish companion, Miss Sillico, a fragile woman used to depending "on the kindness of strangers." By withholding a bracelet that his aunts have asked him to find, he sets in motion events that lead to his teacher having to leave the district and Miss Sillico having to give up all hope for marriage: The story ends with Richard reaping a reward for the bracelet's return without a twinge of guilt. Throughout the collection innocence and experience are unrelated to good or to the causes and effects of fortune and misfortune. Barker views her characters, young and old, with the eye of a physician performing a delicate operation; she examines them skillfully and without sentiment.

Although *Innocents* won critical acclaim, reviewers were less enthusiastic over *Apology for a Hero* (1950), Barker's first novel. They cited weak characterization and plot, and indeed this criticism has plagued Barker's other novels. She returned to short fiction, and her next book, *Novelette, with Other Stories* (1951), includes the themes of innocence and experience and explores the nature of reality.

Barker adapted one of the stories, "Pringle," for a 1958 teleplay. The story concerns a lodger who besets a family with financial difficulties. The clever plot worked well for a television drama, but much of the story's appeal was lost through the paring of its images and lucid prose. In the story the detached author's point of view is not unlike that of a Gulliver watching little, not-too-bright people: "It was always a pity when a family splits and the small peas break loose from the pod." The point of view disengages the reader from sympathizing with the characters. Instead Barker's lean prose, honed images, and carnival humor capture the reader's attention.

In a scene involving the central characters, Mr. and Mrs. Byward, the wife is consoling but the husband is deprecating. He bemoans their plight while she looks on the bright side – they have each other, their three daughters, and a roof over their heads – until, exasperated, he cries, "Don't be sensible. . . . I can't stand you being sensible tonight." Then, in a complete turnabout, she says, "What do you want me to be – frivolous? On your pay?" The facade thus collapses, revealing the little savage behind the wifely concern and sympathy. Barker exposes both the fragile and funny sides of the structures people build through ritual and imagination. This technique is a trademark of her fiction. In *Life Stories* Barker comments, "There is mercifully no chance of knowing what reality is and the knowledge would in any case be worse than useless. The attempt is what matters."

The Joy-Ride and After (1963) is a collection of three loosely connected stories involving people in an automobile accident who reconstruct the event. The reconstructions spin out from the background of the facts but are distorted by the characters' needs to see themselves in a good light, with the result, as so often happens in Barker's work, that the characters appear out of focus – grotesque and bizarre. *Lost Upon the Roundabouts* (1964), a collection of ten short stories, won critical praise for its immaculate images and precise details. In "Agnes Araby" a recurring theme in Barker's fiction emerges: a character – usually young and lonely, often in some degree of hardship – imagines events, frequently to her detriment.

Agnes is a sixteen-year-old orphan who works for a widow with three children, one an infant. Agnes trudges about her tasks in hand-me-down shoes: "She'd been taught to watch for every need but her own and it was a needy world she was in." One day she walks with the children to a store, and on the way they are nearly run down by the local squire. Young and handsome, he is eager to make amends for nearly killing her and the children. Agnes misinterprets his intention to hire her as a kitchen helper. She thinks he is in love with her; terrified, she runs away, thereby losing a chance to alleviate her hard lot:

> If you knew Agnes Araby and she knew you, you could be pretty sure that monstrous fancy had been at work on your behalf. What you could never tell . . . was whether she'd chosen you a plush heaven or a sticky end. It had little to do with her liking or disliking, she wouldn't have spared her best friend if she'd had one. There was a bit of the artist in her.

Barker could be writing about herself in this passage. Like Agnes she will not spare anyone: her imagination is a "monstrous fancy," and she has more than "a bit of the artist in her."

Although critics continued to praise Barker's short fiction, they withheld acclaim for her second novel, *A Case Examined* (1965). The main character, Rose Antrobus, seems to be charitable, but, like so many of Barker's characters, she is self-deceptive. In *Life Stories* the author notes that Rose is sent abroad "to acquire not so much a polish as some cracks in the glaze." Similarly, Barker spent time outside of England as a stipulation of the Somerset Maugham Prize. She traveled to France and stayed at the Chateau Montaigne:

> I think it was while I was there that I realized that the net value of any experience fluctuates, depending not on its quality, or nature, or on whether it is first- or second-hand, but on who has digested it. Because after something has happened, it has to be broken down to manageable proportions. I saw that people took only what they could use, from any one sequence of events.

In Barker's third novel, *The Middling: Chapters in the Life of Ellie Toms* (1967), the title character's life disintegrates into drunkenness and disillusion. The novel is episodic, a structure Barker favors possibly because of her penchant for the short story. Critics, however, found its form fragmented and its narrative lacking cohesiveness. This was not the case, however, with *John Brown's Body* (1969), which critics praised for its narrative consistency and sharp details. This novel, a mystery, is propelled by the protagonist's self-deception, isolation, and inability to communicate. Although those characteristics are found in her previous work, they come together in this novel with renewed vigor. Marise, the main character, convinces herself that her neighbor, Ralph Schilling, is a wanted criminal because of his faint resemblance to a fugitive murderer, and she convinces others as well. Through Marise, Barker explores the ways in which people construct reality, often to the detriment of others as well as to themselves.

Women are the focus of *Femina Real* (1971), a collection of stories broaching the subjects of strength, vulnerability, and manipulation in women's roles as daughters, wives, and mothers, young and old. A ten-year-old handicapped girl outwits the man who is holding her prisoner; a sickly woman uses her frailty to dominate those around her. One of the stories, "Noon," is about an almost-thirteen-year-old girl who likes to sunbathe in the nude. Her younger friend Jane wonders, " 'Why do you do it?' Even as she asked she suspected that Davina would tell her such a small fraction of the truth as to constitute a lie. 'Don't pretend it's just to get brown all over because I know it's not.' "

Jane is correct: Davina is experiencing the power of her emerging sexuality, and she needs someone to verify it, a male witness who will affirm its power and beauty:

> She rolled on her face. Here was one: arching her quaking stomach she gently lowered it to the burning sand. With fingers and toes she scrabbled until, under the surface, she found icy cold and wetness. To experience this extra hotness and coldness at the same moment was indescribably important. How could she possibly describe it? Or the feeling that she was full of sea, that she was the quick of the sea, that pierce her and pain would run out into the Indian Ocean? Or the sounds which she did not so much hear as transmit? Which came up through the sand and sounded through her bones? At best they were a kind of music and she the one instrument it could be played on, but generally they were intimations of something else entirely going on. Life at another level. How could she tell anyone that this was her private history which poor little Jane would try to forget?

The passage reveals the complexity of the feelings and desires of the young girl becoming a woman, and it is also an example of Barker's skill in weaving the disparate parts of the girl's innocence and experience into a whole.

That the male witness happens to be Jane's father is of little importance to Davina. However, she is momentarily disappointed: " 'Go away! Shoo!' she said aloud, but of course he went on looking through his medicine-blue lenses, he probably thought she didn't speak English, probably he thought she was a big blue shrimp." In this exquisitely honed story of a young woman of the type that the painter Balthus Klossowski often portrays in seductive self-awareness, Barker enlists the theme of entrapment: the young woman trapped in her body's awakening and the older man trapped in his desire.

Maternity is at the center of the conflict in "Almost an International Incident," in which a group of American tourists makes an unexpected stop in Quattro Santo, an Italian village about to celebrate the festival of Santa Lidia. One of the tourists, Pearl, who is seven months pregnant, falls into a romantic reverie over the quaint streets, houses, and inhabitants. Pearl likes Quattro Santo "as she knew she wouldn't like any other place on the trip and as she would probably never be able to like any other place again." Enraptured, she exclaims, "I feel that the people here are my friends. They may be more than that, I'm not sure whether it's a blood tie." She is particularly drawn to Gilda, a young servant who seems to return Pearl's affection. While Pearl is dressing and Gilda is turning down the bed covers, they talk about children, and Gilda says that al-

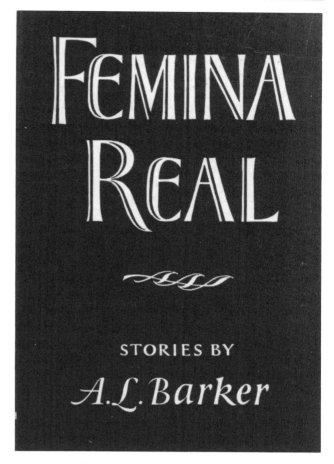

Dust jacket for Barker's 1971 collection of short fiction, which focuses on women's roles as wives, mothers, and daughters

though she has been married nearly five years she and her husband have no children: "We have never — I never have. . . . Not once." Then, noticing that Pearl is putting on her stockings, "Gilda went on her knees. . . . She gently drew on each one, smoothing Pearl's stockings over her ankles. 'Dolcemente, signora. You should be careful of yourself.' "

At this point the story is a clichéd scenario of cozy feelings between people of different cultures and classes, but in Barker's world, the common is often suspect and complex. Later, in a tableau of street revelers dancing and cavorting, signs of cruelty stain the idyllic; the cliché begins to unravel. Pearl notices a man selling wild birds, their twiggy legs bound with string, their tiny heads swaying as the seller holds them upside down; she sees a jester debasing himself as he mimics others. The scene culminates in an unprovoked attack on the American tourists: "They were laughing and aiming at the Americans with rubbish from the basin of the fountain, mostly rotten fruit and balled-up cartons, wet and unpleasant but not dangerous. Gilda, the hotel-maid, was with them. . . . She was excited, her cheeks flaming, her full lips laughing, crying out or pressed to her wrist in delight." Gilda's act awakens Pearl to the villagers' three-dimensionality, which is more complex than what Pearl has so dreamily and egotistically imagined through the pink cloud of her contentment and sense of well-being. Barker thus strips away the patterned surfaces and exposes the spaces in which people live.

Some critics have found Barker's views of women in *Femina Real* harsh, unsympathetic, and skewed. But the author's perceptions – no matter on what or on whom – have always been relentlessly her own: no sentimental coating, no off-the-rack ideas. Age, race, religion, and sex are not exempted from her penetrating gaze, from her ability to strip away the veneer of manners and the camouflage of drawing-room posturings.

Barker's unrelenting gaze is modified by distance, tapered by a detached narrator and a tongue-in-cheek tone. Critics have noted the amused tolerance of the narrator of the novel *A Source of Embarrassment* (1974). The hero, Edith, may or may not have a brain tumor. Her husband wants to discern the truth because he wants to know how to proceed with his current paramour. Although critics have praised the novel's detached humor, they have pointed out that the events and characters seem haphazard and incidental. *A Heavy Feather* (1978) has been criticized for its lack of unity. In *Life Stories* Barker writes:

> My novel, *A Heavy Feather,* was to have been about the impossibility of communicating. I was convinced, for the purposes of the book anyway – every book convinces when it is first purposed – that everyone was an island and everyone had a lot to discover. I believed that I was meant to know. I was sealed off inside my skin and so was everyone else. One could only signal waving or drowning.

A Heavy Feather is written in nine chapters, each divided into several parts. Each part is separated by asterisks, giving the effect of a montage of images and sensory impressions. This structure reinforces Barker's theme of isolation, of being "sealed off," and it also reflects the impossibility of unifying subject matter, of pummeling it into traditional plots. David Profumo (*Times Literary Supplement,* 21 July 1978) writes that Barker's best work "has drawn strength from avoiding the artificial neatness that narrative shapeliness imposes on the representation of life."

Barker's vision and style save characters from becoming pathetic or absurd. For instance, the forty-eight-year-old mother in "Belle Amie" (*No Word of Love,* 1985) teeters on the edge of the absurd as she preens herself in the light of an attractive young man's attentions. She thinks that he is smitten by her; actually all he wants is a free ride home from the beach. Barker makes the mother and the other characters neither losers nor winners; rather, they are encapsulated in absurd situations constructed by their imaginations.

The imagination often works in strange and disturbing ways in Barker's fiction. In "The Twichild" (*No Word of Love*) the narrator returns from America to England after a twenty-five-year absence. She looks up a former lover and a best friend who are married and have three children – two sons and a daughter. When the narrator meets her former lover, Harold Pritchard, for dinner, she does not recognize him:

> He had been a gaunt youth. . . . He was fully finished now: if anything he was overdone. Gone was the hungry look which I used to cherish because I was the only one, I thought I was, who could make it disappear. Gone was the mane of yellow hair which I used to comb with my fingers. He took off his hat and he had a few tabby strands disposed across his cranium.

The following day the narrator is to dine with Harold, Jean (her best friend), and their daughter, Beatrice. The sons are at boarding school. The narrator soon discovers that Jean has undergone a radical transformation – she is more like a boy than a matron of nearly fifty. She wears faded jeans and scruffy tennis shoes; she rides her son's bicycle around and around the driveway; she decorates her bedroom (separate from Harold's) with posters of rock stars, and a poster of Dracula hangs above her bed. Although the narrator has known that Jean role-plays, she is unprepared for Jean-as-young-boy. The story ends on a disturbing note:

> [Beatrice] perched on the arm of his [her father's] chair, looking down at the top of his head and disposing a strand of his hair that had become undisposed. . . . There they sat, Hal and his daughter, and as he gazed up at her, widening his eyes as he always had when he was moved, I saw, through the extra flesh he had put on over the years, the raw bones of the Hal I had known. And I saw something else I had known – his hungry look.

The reader is left to speculate whether Jean's transformation through her imagination into a boy is the cause of the covert incestuous relationship between Harold and Beatrice or whether her transformation is the result or escape from that relationship.

The *Observer* (23 April 1989) called *The Gooseboy* (1987) a "beautifully crafted little novel." It is divided into three novella-length sections and narrated by twins, Douglas Bysshe ("rhymes with fish") and Ducie Bysshe Pike. The gooseboy lives on Douglas's estate in southern France; one side of his face is handsome, the other "the color of raw meat, an old rawness in which blood had darkened and the living tissue had dried hard and rigid as wood." He cannot speak but he is not pitiful — not in Barker's world. He seems no more deformed or pitiable than the other characters, and like the others he retains a modicum of dignity and an aura of attractiveness: "The oieboy [Douglas's French for gooseboy] had come into the yard, his arms full of brown roses. He carried them carefully, his head bowed, solicitous, even tender." When someone asks what the gooseboy likes, insinuating that what he would like would be grotesque or abnormal, Douglas responds, "Living, breathing, putting flowers in his hair, dancing with the geese."

Each twin has a story to tell. Douglas's story — from the point of view of an aging romantic actor cast in the role of a doctor treating lepers in Africa — verges on the disjointed and bizarre. From an airplane Douglas perceives Africa as a "dish of cooked spinach. People down there were cooked too, half digested and still clinging to a separate existence: the whites soft-boiled, the blacks glossy with gastric juices. There was another extreme, people picked to the bone and rocks bitten into dust." Ducie's story centers on the twin facts that, unlike her brother who is exceptionally good-looking, she is homely and that her best friend's daughter has run off with her husband, Pike. On the one hand Ducie is the plain, spurned wife, but on the other she is a feisty wit triumphant. She confronts her husband's young lover: "She gazed up at me out of his arms. 'We love each other.' For her that solved everything. I don't call it innocence, or ignorance, I call it dimness, underendowment, and it's dangerous. Not to her, to everyone else." To be innocent is to be dim and dangerous in the etiology of Barker's fiction.

Barker — responding to criticism that her novels lack unified structures and plausible characterizations — anticipates the reception of *The Woman Who Talked to Herself: An Articulated Novel* (1989) by laying the groundwork for the reader. The novel is a series of stories loosely connected so as to allow flexibility of movement. The narrator, a "celebrity storyteller," is being interviewed by a journalist, and the novel is comprised of the stories and anecdotes she tells the interviewer. The storyteller, Winnie Appleton, is in her kitchen: "I didn't have a doll's house. I made houses in the furz. It takes willpower to believe you're having domestic and social encounters in thorn bushes. I had to stretch my imagination and I've never been able to get it back to normal. Whatever normal is."

The *Observer* (12 May 1991) notes: "This novel begins with a gauche journalist coming to interview a novelist; the novelist is covered in flour, she rolls out pastry and stories (she's better at fiction than pie). This is A. L. Barker on first-class form — sad and diverting by turns." Walter Nash (*London Review of Books*, 9 November 1989) states that the narrator "is almost inarticulate. The articulation of her uncertainties, transient perceptions, guesses at the truth of things, takes the form of little fables, humorous and disturbing, each of them a self-contained short story, all of them related, as myth is related to the commonplace or as daydream is related to the dull event, to the incidental facts of Winnie's experience." This is Winnie's encounter with door-to-door religion peddlers:

"You may expect hell, madame. . . . You may expect to fry along with the tares and the organs of unclean beasts."
"Don't they make those into pet food?"
"There will be no suspended sentence, exculpation or pardon. You will burn for all eternity."
"So that's settled. Thank you for calling."

Winnie admits to the journalist that storytellers manipulate people's minds: "It's what we're here for, it's become big business. But I don't mean to banish anything, least of all reality. What is reality?" The reader is pulled into the "reality" of the interview. But the reader must beware of this Barkeresque reality, for there is no interview: Winnie has all along been talking to herself.

Barker is at home with the short-story form, whether linked loosely into a novel-length structure or standing alone. The short story lends itself to Barker's particular vision — whether in isolation or as a part of a whole, as in a mosaic. *Any Excuse for a Party: Selected Stories* (1991) is a collection of sixteen stories covering more than forty years of Barker's attempt to achieve what she calls a "perfect encapsulation," a "moment complete . . . beyond reproach or censure." Adam Mars-Jones (*Times Literary Supplement*, 1 March 1991) notes that "in her later work, Barker learns to hold off from the story she is telling, and to fight the epigrammatic tendencies in her style. Her punctuation becomes casual, regularly preferring a comma to a stronger pause, and her prose acquires a syncopation of sense and grammar. . . . At the same time, her subject matter becomes more elusive." "Elusive" describes the dialogue between husband and wife from the title story in the collection. The wife, Leonie, has just learned that he is having an affair, but he does not know that she knows:

> "I think I'll have a bath before dinner."
> "We're having your favorite – grilled halibut."
> "Halibut?" He frowned. "I don't especially enjoy it."
> "You mean it's not your favorite?" Leonie clapped both hands over her mouth. "How awful! How thoroughly unsatisfactory of me not to get it right! I did so want to do something you'd like."
> "It doesn't matter."
> "Did you mean that remark to be hurtful? If I were emotionally unbalanced, as women who are left alone all day are said to be, it could prey on my mind with tragic consequences.... But I'm not unbalanced. Being alone delights me and I know you didn't mean to be hurtful. You meant to be kind – which of course can amount to the same thing and be absolutely devastating?"

The exchange is not only elusive, but it also demonstrates a recurrent theme reflecting a marriage or a relationship adrift.

Barker's wit is also elusive, as in "A Fairly Close Encounter" (*Any Excuse for a Party*). Miranda's fiancé, an obtuse and conventional man, and Miranda's lively aunt are meeting her at an airport:

> Perhaps it was the sight of the relentlessly revolving luggage on the carousel which provoked the aunt to fatalism.
> "It is asking for trouble to assume that another person is having your same thoughts and emotions as precisely the same moment as yourself."
> "I like to think that Miranda and I complement rather than duplicate each other, that we are two halves of one whole."
> "One whole of what? A lemon?" The aunt burst out laughing. "What a droll fellow you are!"
> Miranda smiled. "He can be very funny when he chooses."

Ironically, it is the last thing he chooses to be at that moment, so intent is he on his importance and profundity – on his individuality.

Another story in the collection, "Submerged," is from Barker's first published book, *Innocents*. Peter Hume, "diving into the river . . . always felt he was entering something of his own." As a reader of Barker's fiction one enters something of one's own: a unique

world in which the guide directs one's gaze to humanity's foibles, alienation, pretensions, inability to communicate, and lack of innocence. She also shares the comic aspects of the human condition in a "crystal clear and scrupulous" style. Mars-Jones concludes that "at her best she is formidable, and from a bare corner of human relations gathers a rich harvest." One can argue that the corner is "bare" or that what Barker writes about is "from a *corner* of human relations," but one cannot argue that she is formidable. Her subjects – fused with the themes of innocence and experience, alienation and the inability to communicate – cover a panorama of human events, not just a corner.

In her work Barker dwells on the boundaries of story and novel. Her fiction, whether short or long, is a collection of narratives related or unified by theme, character, or both. The illusion of the distant author pervades her work; she seems to be a puppeteer manipulating characters who struggle and twist in events manufactured by their dreams, imaginings, and desires. The overall effect is that of satire. Barker's sharp eye, intrusions of wit, and economy bring to her work images and characters unblemished by cliché and sentimentality: the gooseboy, "his reflection . . . amber-colored, and quaking with the movement of the water"; Doolally, mesmerized by a crafty storyteller in a daffodil-yellow mackintosh; Winnie Appleton, storyteller extraordinaire, interviewed by a cat in a chair; and Agnes Araby, whose very name suggests the incongruous, imagining she is Cinderella, in hand-me-down shoes, being courted by a prince.

The themes of innocence and experience, of isolation and the impossibility of free-floating communication, and of the ambiguous nature of the imagination lend themselves to Barker's sense of the real, which is neither glorious nor tragic but always alive because of her keen eye and refusal to sugarcoat with the usual store of clichéd sentiments and bleached truisms. In *Beginning Again: An Autobiography of the Years 1911 to 1918* (1963) Leonard Woolf writes that Katherine Mansfield's "gifts were those of an intense realist, with a superb sense of ironic humor and fundamental cynicism." That could be said of another short-story writer – A. L. Barker.

Papers:

Barker's manuscripts are in her personal possession at her home in Surrey, England.

Stan Barstow

(28 June 1928 –)

John L. Grigsby
Lincoln Memorial University

See also the Barstow entry in *DLB 14: British Novelists Since 1960*.

BOOKS: *A Kind of Loving* (London: Joseph, 1960; Garden City, N.Y.: Doubleday, 1961);

The Desperadoes and Other Stories (London: Joseph, 1961); revised as *The Human Element* (London: Longmans, 1969);

Ask Me Tomorrow [novel] (London: Joseph, 1962);

Joby (London: Joseph, 1964);

The Watchers on the Shore (London: Joseph, 1966; Garden City, N.Y.: Doubleday, 1967);

Ask Me Tomorrow [play], by Barstow and Alfred Bradley (London & New York: French, 1966);

A Raging Calm (London: Joseph, 1968); republished as *The Hidden Part* (New York: Coward-McCann, 1969);

A Season with Eros (London: Joseph, 1971);

Stringer's Last Stand, by Barstow and Bradley (London: French, 1972);

The Right True End (London: Joseph, 1976);

A Brother's Tale (London: Joseph, 1980);

A Kind of Loving: The Vic Brown Trilogy (London: Joseph, 1981);

The Glad Eye and Other Stories (London: Joseph, 1984);

Just You Wait and See (London: Joseph, 1986);

B-Movie (London: Joseph, 1987);

Give Us This Day (London: Joseph, 1989);

Next of Kin (London & New York: Joseph, 1991).

OTHER: *Through the Green Woods: An Anthology of Contemporary Writing About Youth and Children,* edited by Barstow (Leeds, U.K.: Arnold, 1968).

Stan Barstow's short stories have become progressively more noteworthy since the 1960s. That results both from increasingly complex and effective technical artistry and from increasingly profound and complex subjects and themes. His stories provide a realistic, compassionate depiction of the

Stan Barstow (photograph by Neil Barstow)

lives of the working-class English in the northern industrial – particularly coal-mining – districts. As Frederick Bowers states in *Contemporary Novelists* (1976): "Barstow sets his theme against the unsympathetic background of Cressley, a West Riding industrial town of terraced houses, ugly factories, garish cinemas, and grubby parts," and, by use of sophisticated ironic contrasts and juxtapositions, Barstow's works "rise above the ephemeral in their concrete presentation of human character, their solid settings, their natural dialogue and, above all, their forceful and moving expression of what it is to be human."

Stanley Barstow was born in Horbury, Yorkshire, on 28 June 1928, the only child of a coalmining father, Wilfred Barstow, and his wife,

Elsie. After success as a scholarship boy at the local grammar school in Ossett, Stanley became employed in the engineering industry, first as a draftsman and later as a sales executive. He married Constance Mary Kershaw in 1951, and they had two children: Neil (born in 1954) and Gillian (born in 1957). Increasingly dissatisfied with industrial employment, Barstow turned to writing fiction in the late 1950s and early 1960s, publishing his first and best-known work, *A Kind of Loving,* in 1960. The success of this novel was quickly followed by his first collection of short stories, *The Desperadoes and Other Stories* (1961). He has since written other novels – *Joby* (1964) and *A Raging Calm* (1968) being the most important – plays, television and radio scripts, and two more collections of short stories, *A Season with Eros* (1971) and *The Glad Eye and Other Stories* (1984).

All these works are centered in the mythical town of Cressley – much like William Faulkner's Jefferson – which is based on the northern English industrial districts in which Barstow has always lived. He resides in Ossett, the west Yorkshire town where he attended grammar school. Of his deliberate and perhaps mystifying choice to remain in and write only about his native region of England, Barstow has made this defense:

> The publication of some of my work in the U.S. and its translation into several European languages reassures me that I have not resisted the neurotic trendiness of much metropolitan culture for the sake of mere provincial narrowness; and the knowledge that some of the finest novels in the language are "regional" leads me to the belief that to hoe one's row diligently, thus seeking the universal in the particular, brings more worthwhile satisfactions than the pursuit of an often phony jet-set internationalism.

Barstow's technical artistry and thematic concerns have been elucidated by scholars and critics. In *The Technique of Modern Fiction: Essays in Practical Criticism* (1968) Jonathan Raban notes the similarity of first-person narrative technique in the works of Alan Sillitoe and Barstow, particularly in *A Kind of Loving* and Sillitoe's *The Loneliness of the Long-Distance Runner* (1959), stating that their "contemporary English 'vernacular' innocents" act as "a vehicle for an uncultivated sensibility whose very naivete makes for a kind of wisdom."

In *The Socialist Novel in Britain: Towards the Recovery of a Tradition* (1982) Ingrid von Rosenberg also notes Barstow's heavy dependence on first-person narrative, astutely explaining it as an attempt to show a "small slice of social reality, seen from the inside," since the "hero's thoughts are for the most part determined by his experiences in the outside world." She attributes his constant use of the vernacular in dialogue as part of his desire to embody his lower-class speech patterns without alteration or apology. However, in *The English Short Story, 1945–1980: A Critical History* (1985) Dean Baldwin notes the problem of repeated dependence on this "contemporary English vernacular innocent" point of view: "It is difficult to sustain the fiction that the working class is peopled by tough and articulate spokesmen who just happen to write well-crafted stories." This problem is particularly evident in *The Desperadoes and Other Stories,* but by the time of *The Glad Eye and Other Stories* Barstow has solved the problem through the use of a complex variety of narrative perspectives, even to the point of writing a metafictional story, "Work in Progress," about the act of writing a story. The latter collection is also free of the clichéd metaphors and other heavily imitative technical aspects that plague some of the pieces in his first collection, although it includes stories that hint at the artistic mastery of the later work.

Barstow shares some thematic concerns with other British regional writers of his time. In *The English Short Story, 1945–1980: A Critical History* Jean Pickering writes that "John Wain, Kingsley Amis, and Alan Sillitoe, all 'angry young men' who published collections during the sixties, are faithful observers of the point where the middle and lower classes intersect, and their purposes are generally . . . political." In an interview in *The British Working Class Novel in the Twentieth Century* (1984) Sid Chaplin, another working-class British writer, acknowledges the similarity of perspective of these working-class regionalists. He discusses his acquaintance with John Braine, Keith Waterhouse, Len Doherty, and Barstow, his "particular friend." Chaplin alludes to the anger in these authors' works: "Any working-class writer is by definition isolated." Von Rosenberg notes the satiric tendency toward anger in Barstow and the other regionalists' works, their emotions resulting from their experiences and observations of social and economic injustice in class terms:

> It would be wrong . . . to let the impression grow that these novels are basically acquiescent. The very resignation is mostly voiced with such bitterness and sometimes fury, that the criticism is obvious. . . . Some of them seem to take up a tradition of literary protest certainly much older than the socialist novel, perhaps even dating as far back as Thomas Nashe's *The Unfortunate Traveler:* they tell stories of individual rebellion, and

they tell them in a very impressive way, even if defeat may be the outcome.

This focus on rebellion against an increasingly technological, dehumanized, and unjust world "proves a desire to preserve the special character of working-class life as it had developed over the last hundred years," according to von Rosenberg. She writes that the nuclear threat and the new affluence of industrial society generate a focus on "psychological repression and escape," on "a new set of difficulties for the working class, more or less of a psychological nature." In Barstow's works such difficulties include how to deal with newly acquired wealth and independence when one is young and lacks guidance and stable values (as in "The Desperadoes"), how to survive in a work world in which the money earned is the only positive element, and how to comprehend, as von Rosenberg states, "deeper longings stirring obscurely in the hearts of the juvenile heroes" in a world whose nuclear uncertainty and crass commercialism produce "feelings of disorientation, insecurity and loneliness." Bowers articulates those thematic concerns, stating that – in Barstow's best novels (*A Kind of Loving, Joby,* and *A Raging Calm*), as well as in his short stories – the author focuses on the possibilities and permutations of awareness of others and the growth of love in a "materially and spiritually narrow" environment where self-indulgence and destruction of self and others are the overt manifestations. Von Rosenberg writes that Barstow's works have some affinity with the bourgeois novel because of his focus on love but that his works are not fundamentally bourgeois because of his frequently tragic bent, which shows the failure or limitedness of love resulting from materialistic vocational preoccupations and the impoverished values of undereducated, unaware families. Bowers notes that Barstow's distinctive thematic concerns distinguish him from other angry working-class writers: "Barstow's novels take social class and the industrial environment much more for granted. . . . The overriding preoccupation is with the development of human wisdom and love in an environment which is indifferent or hostile." Bowers explains that the author's fundamental thematic focus is on the possibility of the development of a "workaday human love."

Barstow's first collection of short fiction, *The Desperadoes and Other Stories,* is most characterized by unevenness of achievement, both in technical artistry and content originality and profundity. Several of the stories utilize the first-person narrative viewpoint but not with great success. For example, the

first story, "The Human Element," is told from the viewpoint of a young man caught in a competitive conflict between love for his motorbike and love for a woman. Although the young man's clichéd expressions – such as "Thelma's face lights up like a Christmas tree" and Thelma was flapping "her arms about like an angry old hen" – are realistic given his lack of education and worldly experience, his reticence and ambivalence about Thelma's sexual attributes are considerably less so.

The problem of the inappropriateness of characters' language detracts from other stories, such as "The Drum," in which the first-person, working-class narrator uses the word *apropos* in the first sentence. In "The Years Between" one of the brothers in the story describes himself as "the scholar" and the other as "the rough and ready lad" who makes his fortune by sheep farming, yet this "rough and ready" character writes a note that begins:

> My dear Sarah, the enclosed letter has only just come into my hands. It has explained many things to me and the fact that owing to a series of mischances my brother Thomas delivered it thirty years too late may help to ease what must have embittered you for so long.

Neither the vocabulary nor the syntax seems to suit a sheep farmer.

Several of the stories suffer from clichéd or overly imitative content. Geoff Sadler has noted in *Contemporary Novelists* (1986) that the pieces in *The Desperadoes and Other Stories* and *A Season with Eros* are "Lawrentian in tone." More problematic than general tone derivativeness, though, is the similarity of Barstow's "A Lonely View of the Gasworks" to Ernest Hemingway's "Hills Like White Elephants" (*transition,* August 1927; collected in *Men Without Women,* 1927). Both stories involve couples in conflict because of illegitimate relationships, with the man in each case in favor of the action proposed in each story (abortion in Hemingway's, renting a particular house together in Barstow's). There is the same emphasis on terse, emotionally loaded dialogue, which suggests imitation by Barstow given Hemingway's fame for such verbal exchanges. The title of each story is drawn from a comment made at a crucial moment by the female character, and each title is used as an ironic comment on the problematic action proposed and the sexual relationship presented. In fact, the reader is left with the impression that "A Lonely View of the Gasworks" is almost more Hemingway's than Barstow's. To a lesser degree his imitativeness extends to "The Actor," which focuses on the artistic, external-appearance-

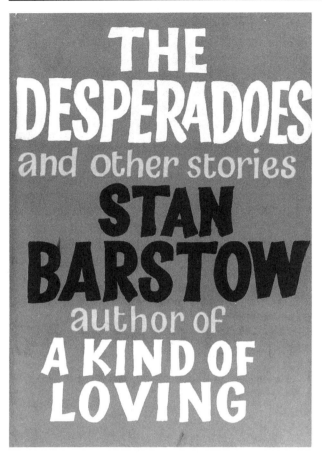

Dust jacket for Barstow's first collection of short stories, many of which deal with the tragedies of working-class characters

was once real love in the miner and his wife's relationship eventually leads her to lock him outside on what is, ironically, the night that his gambling pays off handsomely. Instead of the prosperity so near at hand, though, all the miner gains is a tragic death as he slips and kills himself while attempting to enter his home through a window on a snowy night. Skillfully symbolic and ironic, the story realistically depicts the destruction wrought by social and economic forces in the psychological and physical disintegration of the tragic couple.

"The Desperadoes" is similarly effective and central to Barstow's continuing thematic interests. In its depiction of the juvenile, eventually felonious antics of a group of male teenagers, it also derives its energy and realism to at least some extent from Barstow's experiences. Like "Gamblers Never Win" the title story is told from an omniscient viewpoint, with Vince and his gang having sufficient wealth to allow them to pursue other interests, particularly sexual ones, but in a world of disorientation, insecurity, and loneliness, a world of ongoing economic and social inequality. Vince meets a middle-class girl and pursues his interest in her, but she rejects him when a security guard at a local bar discovers them kissing. The guard represents middle-class authority and control, as well as middle-class social and civil appropriateness. Indeed, as Baldwin writes of Sillitoe's work, "The police are still the enemy; the main line of demarcation is between 'them' and 'us.' " In his anger at "them" (the girl, the guard, and the middle-class world they represent) Vince resorts to realistic tragic violence, attacking the guard as he walks home and killing him without consciously intending to do so. Thus the rage of class conflict is believably and graphically presented as Vince and his gang fail in their confrontation with a crucial psychological dilemma of modern lower-class life. Their impoverished values and the unjust society in which they live lead to their tragic rebellion, which dooms them to lives as criminals. As von Rosenberg comments, Barstow's works "illustrate the emergence of youth as a separate social and cultural group in those years [the 1950s and 1960s] wearing their particular clothes and developing their own code of behavior. But as a rule they do not find what they are craving for."

The two most noteworthy stories in Barstow's first collection are tragic. In them he realizes his special gift for ironic ambiguity and realistic (some would say pessimistic) presentation of the tragedy of the working-class world. In his later collections Barstow refines his literary technique and eschews the comic (at which he rarely succeeds) to present

versus-internal-dramatic-reality dichotomy presented by Henry James in his well-known "The Real Thing" (*Black and White,* 16 April 1892; collected in *The Real Thing and Other Tales,* 1893).

These problems aside, there is much to recommend *The Desperadoes and Other Stories.* For example, "Gamblers Never Win" is a compelling, profound story of family tragedy that illustrates several of Barstow's thematic concerns. Part of the story's power derives from its detailed focus on life in a coal miner's family, the type of life Barstow knows best, and the story perfectly illustrates von Rosenberg's point that his works achieve a "greater authenticity of representation and the conveyance of a particular atmosphere" by rendering social and economic facts instead of by long descriptions. The miner's ghastly occupation generates his excessive drinking and gambling as psychological escapes, and his poverty generates the division between him and his daughter, who marries into the relative wealth of the middle class. The diminution of what the tragic lives of his people and his region of England in ever more powerful ways.

Barstow's second volume of stories, *A Season with Eros,* reveals his greater maturity and skill as a creative writer, although it is not free of problems, particularly the matter of overimitativeness. This is most noticeable in "Twenty Pieces of Silver," about a Christian housekeeper who — through her religious faith and helpfulness to others, including the atheistic middle-class housewife for whom she works — rises to the status of Christ symbol. The housekeeper, Mrs. Fosdyke, refuses to steal the twenty pieces of silver that the housewife, Mrs. Marsden, deliberately leaves in her husband's pocket in order to test her. Her chiding response to Mrs. Marsden's comment that "I have to test the honesty of my servants" is "Twenty pieces of silver. Is that my price, d'you think? They gave Judas thirty!" At the end of the story Mrs. Fosdyke again agrees to manage the collection for the orphanage in her district.

The story closely echoes Aleksandr Solzhenitsyn's "Matryona's Home" (*Novy Mir,* January 1963), in which the title character, another older single woman, serves the teacher who comes to live with her and similarly assumes the burden of caring for the people in her community, despite temptation to do otherwise. Both stories are heavily laden with religious symbolism, and both end with specific biblical allusions, Barstow's with reference to the "poor lambs" and Solzhenitsyn's with a focus on Matryona as the "righteous one without whom . . . no village can stand." To a lesser extent the imitativeness problem is reflected in "Love and Music," whose focus on a community musical troupe resembles that in Thomas Hardy's *Under the Greenwood Tree* (1872). In neither case does Barstow acknowledge his influences. He later realized the problem, as evidenced by his postscript to "The Apples of Paradise" (*The Glad Eye and Other Stories*). In that addendum Barstow notes the debt the story owes to Hardy's "Fellow-Townsmen" (*Wessex Tales,* 1888), a tack he should have taken with at least two stories in each of his previous collections.

Despite Barstow's occasional derivativeness, clear advancements in his technical skills are evident in *A Season with Eros.* Three stories in particular demonstrate his improved use of symbolism as he goes beyond simple dialogue stories to artistic layering of meanings and ideas. In "Estuary" a young man's trip to and fascination with the ocean becomes representative of his attraction to and relationship with an older, more experienced woman he meets there. Eventually she becomes as implacably powerful as the sea itself, loving to swim in risky waters, and she initiates the young man, Parker, into the sexual world and uses him repeatedly for her pleasure:

> "Now," she said. "Be very quick."
> He was nothing. He knew it through the flare of his response. Something the sea would use and discard. He thought it in the fleeting second before she took him, unresisting, plunging down with her into the vortex of her frenzy.

Like the sea and the birds in Walt Whitman's "Out of the Cradle Endlessly Rocking" (*Leaves of Grass,* 1855), she educates Parker about the human world of love and death, but this story radically alters Whitman's symbolism to the point that imitativeness is not an issue. Rather, artistic mastery is.

The same is true of the creative symbolism in "The Assailants" and "This Day, then Tomorrow." In the first story a truck driver, Brian, is alienated from his wife Joyce and stepdaughter because of the romantic machinations of Joyce's employer. Joyce later hears a news report on the radio:

> Arriving on the same flight at London Airport was the Prime Minister of the newly independent African state of Kandaria, Mr. Walter Umbala, who is here on an unofficial visit. Our reporter asked Mr. Umbala about recent unrest and disturbances in Kandaria. He said that in a nation of mixed races and religions there were bound to be disagreements from time to time, but they only became serious when exploited by outside agencies for their own ends. "We must be ever vigilant and resist these outside elements with all our might," Mr. Umbala said. "Only then shall we go forward, united and strong, to our destiny among the free nations of the world."

Joyce fails to perceive the symbolic message and impatiently switches off the radio, just as her and Brian's impatience with each other and incomprehension of others' interference have virtually destroyed their lives together.

In "This Day, then Tomorrow" the closing symbolism involves the young main character, Ruth, who has just had a novel accepted for publication and has been struggling with the changes involved in that success, such as others' interference in her privacy as well as her concern over how much of her experiences she has revealed in the novel. She also fears how much readers will perceive as her experiences. Ruth — ambivalent and uncertain about her literary career but determined to continue it — is presented at the story's end on a train trip back home from a visit to her publisher in London. The last lines describe her as she proceeds to the dining car: "Ruth had not thought herself hungry but now she got up and made her way towards the dining-car, swaying from side to side as she balanced herself against the motion of the train." Ruth's swaying thus becomes symbolic of her psychological dilemma or ambivalence, but her hunger and progress convey her dedication and ambition to succeed in her career. Such layering of meaning represents Barstow's advance beyond graphic realism to a higher level of artistic rendering, a technical achievement continued with even more innovative and metafictional techniques in his most recent collection.

"This Day, then Tomorrow" also represents an advancement of Barstow's thematic concerns. His focus on the dilemma of the beginning writer indicates his awareness that knowledge and depiction of oneself are the ultimate source of the fiction writer's creative power and ability to render the reality and problems of society. In fact, the stories in *A Season with Eros* seem to be deliberately arranged to make this thematic point of ultimate self-responsibility for failure or success, particularly in matters of love or the lack thereof.

The first story, "A Season with Eros," depicts a marriage that has failed because of a young man's (Ruffo's) willingness to blame his mother-in-law for interfering with his marriage and controlling his wife Maureen, while Maureen blames Ruffo for what she perceives as changed behavior on his part. Neither character is willing to blame himself or herself for the failed marriage and lost love. The same is true of a different kind of love in "Principle," in which Luther Stringer, an old-style union loyalist, rejects his future son-in-law, Bob, for crossing a picket line and working during a strike. Luther's daughter, Bessie, sides with her fiancé. When Luther rejects them, his wife decides she cannot tolerate any more of his self-righteousness, and she leaves him after twenty-seven years. Instead of blaming himself at all, Luther simply "reached for his hat and coat and left the house for the pub on the corner where he was sure to find someone who spoke his language." Self-love thus wins over love of others because of generational loyalties, political affinities, class identification (Bob has middle-class ambitions), and other divisive aspects of the contemporary world.

"Waiting" depicts the excessive materialism of a son and daughter-in-law who grow impatient with the lingering, aged father in whose house they live. They begin to sell his furniture and other possessions, replacing them with more middle-class, fashionable ones. When they finally go to the extent of selling his favorite chair, he reacts in anger:

> I know what it is. You're wantin' me to die. Well, I'll tell you – I'm wantin' it an' all. There's nowt left for me sin' my Mary went. I'm waitin', just bidin' my time till the good Lord sees fit to take me to her again.... And you'll just have to bide your time an' wait anent me.

He leaves the room after neither his son nor his daughter-in-law expresses any regret, feelings of guilt, or concern for him, as clearly any love for him has long since been replaced by self-love. Nor do they admit any guilt to each other: "Neither of them spoke. In a moment they looked at each other and then they looked away." In *A Season with Eros* only the novelist Ruth in "This Day, then Tomorrow" shows sufficient self-awareness and concern for others to transcend the shallow values and limited education of those around her and to work to improve her life, and others' lives, through her writing. Thus Barstow seems to be indicating his solution to the dehumanizing vocational choices of industrialized northern England and to the unenlightened values of that world. In doing so he makes a powerful statement in "This Day, then Tomorrow" for a caring, educated, holistic humanism as the only solution to the tragedy of the lives of the less fortunate people in his world.

The Glad Eye and Other Stories is Barstow's most recent and best short-story collection. As Sadler observes, "*Glad Eye* shows a greater depth of perception . . . its effects more finished and mature than in previous collections." The greater maturity and finish are evident both in an expanded range and depth of thematic implications and in a greater variety of technical strategies. There are only ten stories in this collection as opposed to fourteen in *A Season with Eros* and fifteen in *The Desperadoes and Other Stories*. Just one story, "The Apples of Paradise," in his most recent collection is overly imitative, but Barstow acknowledges that in a postscript. His reference to a Hemingway novel in "Rue" is at least a nod to his debt to that author.

In *The Glad Eye and Other Stories* Barstow varies his first-person narration by using more female narrators than male ones (two female narrators and one male) for the first time. He adds even more variety by having one of the females use letter narration, in the style of Samuel Richardson. This technique is believable because the lady – Mrs. Raymond Hawkridge in "The Middle of the Journey" – confesses to an extramarital affair that she would much more likely divulge via a letter to a friend than via an open confession to a general audience. An even more important development in this collection is Barstow's continual progression toward more innovative narrative forms and subjects, as evident in "Work in Progress," a metafictional story in which the primary character is a writer attempting to decide how to conceive the story by Barstow in which the character appears. Although obviously influenced by such metafictional works as John Barth's "Lost in the Funhouse" (*Lost in the Funhouse,* 1968), Barstow's story is imaginatively original in its content and structure, and it raises important questions about the creative process while being intriguing and entertaining.

The greater narrative variety in *The Glad Eye and Other Stories* is indicative of an important advance in Barstow's thematic concerns. For the first time he shows real awareness of and sensitivity to the dilemmas of women within the cultural and scientific parameters that control the lives of the characters in his stories. Women are presented much more sympathetically overall in this collection, but particularly in "The Pity of It All," "Foreign Parts," "Good," and "The Middle of the Journey." In "The Pity of It All" Barstow presents Nancy Harper's psychological dilemmas as she deals with her husband's death in a mining disaster and her daughter's death in an automobile accident, implicit comments on the occupational and technological dangers of modern life.

Nancy must cope with the guilt-ridden behavior of Mr. Daymer, the driver who killed her daughter. He shadows her and almost forces her into an intimate relationship, even though she realizes their unbridgeable social and economic class differences and that he will eventually desert her and return to his wife. By presenting Nancy as irrevocably trapped in a life of low pay and dissatisfying work as a shop clerk, of car wrecks and mining disasters and human psychological wrecks such as Daymer, but as enduring despite these arbitrary and unjust controls, Barstow shows a great deal of understanding of the dilemmas working-class women face in the modern world.

Barstow shows similar sympathy for and understanding of the bored, frustrated middle-class housewife in "Good." He presents Jean Nesbit as the insufficiently educated, unambitious wife of a school principal whose only concern is that Jean deal with the children and the house and not embarrass him. Her dependence is the direct result of her impoverished childhood during the Depression and her being advised to marry well as the solution to all her problems. But being married to a frequently absent and relatively unconcerned husband is not enough, and Jean, desperate for any challenge or excitement, decides to steal an item at the local grocer's. Detected by television cameras that seem to immortalize her crime and "condemn her forever," she is faced with the likelihood of receiving the maximum legal punishment and with an outraged husband who cannot comprehend her reality and dilemmas.

Barstow thus demonstrates an astute awareness of the social and economic controls that create the desperately quiet lives of "good," economically secure women such as Jean Nesbit. He does the same in "Foreign Parts," in which a working-class woman similar to Nancy Harper has a similarly unfulfilling extramarital affair. In "The Middle of It All" another "good" housewife has lost all excitement and enjoyment while in an economically secure marriage. In those stories Barstow broadens the parameters of his thematic exposition of the monetary, educational, and technological controls that create the tragedies in the lives of his characters. He shows an understanding of how women can be trapped, which is an advance in the depth of intellectual perception in his stories.

However, the Marxist social and economic class conflict is still the foundational element in his tragic presentations; it is the causal core that generates the levels and varieties of tragedy through its permutations. That fact is perhaps most dramatically and skillfully reflected in "Rue," the long story that concludes this collection. Although Sadler overstates the case when he says that "Rue" is a "new departure" for Barstow, he is correct in his perception of the story's high quality. Here Barstow presents the economic and social class conflict most graphically, via an aging executive of a printing company, Mr. Jordan, whose wife has died. He meets a young, impoverished woman, Mrs. Nugent, in a bar, and her "direct genuineness of . . . smile" enchants him. Her simple, open friendliness represents a working-class attribute lacking in the sophisticated, subtle women of the corporate world, and he works to develop a relationship with her.

He invites her to be his live-in housekeeper and succeeds in having sexual relations with her, but she begins to smile rarely as she becomes uncomfortable in his world of polished conversation, material excess, and stringent behavioral codes. Eventually he discovers her in bed with a man of her own economic and social background. Before Mr. Jordan can overcome the shock of exposure to the relatively greater sexual freedom of the working class, she breaks into his father's collection of antique snuffboxes (symbolic of aristocratic manners and traditions), steals them, and then disappears, gone back to her own world of poverty and uneducated people, but freedom in a sense too.

In "Rue" the psychological is definitely a function of the social and ultimately the economic, for the "love" Mr. Jordan feels for Mrs. Nugent and vice versa is not stronger than the class barrier that divides the two. Although this is not a new theme for Barstow — and thus Sadler is wrong about the story as a "new departure" — it has never been presented more effectively in his other short fiction. The theme is conveyed without making either character unsympathetic. In his objective detachment he shows both characters as tragic victims of their respective environments. "Rue" and the other pieces in *The Glad Eye and Other Stories* indicate that Barstow has matured into a great writer of short fiction.

Barstow's short fiction believably and evocatively captures the tragedy in the lives of the people of his class and region of England. His works indeed dramatize the "universal in the particular," his stated goal. As von Rosenberg observes, his works are truer to life than most of the literature of his time. Sadler also attests to that enduring human concern and power in Barstow's fiction:

> Barstow views life clearly and honestly. He doesn't look away, or pretend that things are other than they are. Detesting such modern trends as TV culture and bingo-addiction, he nevertheless retains his belief in progress. Though the relationships of his characters are uncertain and fraught with danger, one senses that they will endure. More even than his honesty, Barstow shares his humanity with the reader.

Barstow's fiction should thus be understood as truly serious and profound literature designed to guide humanity to a saner means of life than those currently prevalent. Von Rosenberg notes that communicative commitment in her contrast of Barstow with escapist experimentalists such as James Joyce and in her explanation of Barstow's desire to commiserate about class conflicts, "thereby showing a social responsibility comparable to that of the bourgeois novelists of the eighteenth and nineteenth centuries." In an age of deconstructive nihilism such a humanistic sense of responsibility is crucial if, in the words of Faulkner, man is not just to endure, but prevail. Clearly, in the personal and occupational world of literary commitment, Barstow has prevailed. It is now the task of literary scholars to recognize, explain, and pay homage to his significant achievements.

References:

Dean Baldwin, "The English Short Story in the Fifties," in *The English Short Story, 1945–1980: A Critical History,* edited by Dennis Vannatta (Boston: G. K. Hall, 1985), pp. 34–74;

Frederick Bowers, "Stan(ley) Barstow," in *Contemporary Novelists,* edited by James Vinson, second edition (New York: St. Martin's Press, 1976), pp. 96–98;

Jean Pickering, "The English Short Story in the Sixties," in *The English Short Story, 1945–1980: A Critical History,* pp. 75–119;

Michael Pickering and Kevin Robins, "The Making of a Working-Class Writer: An Interview with Sid Chaplin," in *The British Working Class Novel in the Twentieth Century,* edited by Jeremy Hawthorn (London: Arnold, 1984), pp. 139–150;

Jonathan Raban, *The Technique of Modern Fiction: Essays in Practical Criticism* (London: Arnold, 1968);

Geoff Sadler, "Stan Barstow," in *Contemporary Novelists,* edited by D. L. Kirkpatrick, fourth edition (New York: St. Martin's Press, 1986), pp. 70–71;

Ingrid von Rosenberg, "Militancy, Anger, and Resignation: Alternative Moods in the Working-Class Novel of the 1950s and Early 1960s," in *The Socialist Novel in Britain: Towards the Recovery of a Tradition,* edited by H. Gustav Klaus (New York: St. Martin's Press, 1982), pp. 145–165.

George Mackay Brown

(17 October 1921 –)

David S. Robb
University of Dundee

See also the Brown entries in *DLB 14: British Novelists Since 1960* and *DLB 27: Poets of Great Britain and Ireland, 1945–1960.*

BOOKS: *The Storm and Other Poems,* illustrated by Ian MacInnes (Kirkwall, Scotland: Orkney Press, 1954);

Loaves and Fishes (London: Hogarth, 1959);

The Year of the Whale (London: Chatto & Windus/ Hogarth, 1965);

A Calendar of Love and Other Stories (London: Hogarth 1967; New York: Harcourt, Brace & World, 1968);

Twelve Poems (Belfast: Queen's University Festival Publications, 1968);

A Time to Keep and Other Stories (London: Hogarth, 1969; New York: Harcourt, Brace & World, 1970);

An Orkney Tapestry (London: Gollancz, 1969);

A Spell for Green Corn (London: Hogarth, 1970);

Lifeboat and Other Poems (Bow, Crediton, U.K.: Richard Gilbertson, 1971);

Fishermen with Ploughs: A Poem Cycle (London: Hogarth, 1971);

Poems New and Selected (London: Hogarth, 1971; enlarged edition, New York: Harcourt Brace Jovanovich, 1973); enlarged as *Selected Poems* (London: Hogarth, 1977);

Greenvoe (London: Hogarth, 1972; New York: Harcourt Brace Jovanovich, 1972);

Penguin Modern Poets 21, by Brown, Norman MacCaig, and Iain Crichton Smith (Harmondsworth, U.K.: Penguin, 1972);

Magnus (London: Hogarth, 1973);

Hawkfall and Other Stories (London: Hogarth, 1974);

The Two Fiddlers: Tales from Orkney (London: Chatto & Windus, 1974);

Letters from Hamnavoe (Edinburgh: Gordon Wright, 1975);

Edwin Muir: A Brief Memoir (West Linton, U.K.: Castlelaw Press, 1975);

The Sun's Net (London: Hogarth, 1976);

George Mackay Brown, 1992 (photograph by Gordon Wright)

Winterfold (London: Chatto & Windus/Hogarth, 1976);

Pictures in the Cave (London: Chatto & Windus, 1977);

Witch and Other Stories (London: Longman, 1977);

Under Brinkie's Brae (Edinburgh: Gordon Wright, 1979);

Six Lives of Fankle the Cat (London: Chatto & Windus, 1980);

Portrait of Orkney, text by Brown, photographs by Werner Forman (London: Hogarth, 1981); enlarged, with illustrations by Erlend Brown and photographs by Gunnie Moberg (London: John Murray, 1988);

Andrina and Other Stories (London: Hogarth, 1983);

Voyages (London: Chatto & Windus/Hogarth, 1983);

Christmas Poems, text by Brown, engravings by John Lawrence (Oxford: Perpetua Press, 1984);

Time in a Red Coat (London: Chatto & Windus/Hogarth, 1984; New York: Vanguard, 1984);

Three Plays (London: Chatto & Windus/Hogarth, 1984);

Christmas Stories, text by Brown, engravings by Lawrence (Oxford: Perpetua Press, 1985);

The Scottish Bestiary, text by Brown, illustrations by John Bellany, Steven Campbell, Peter Howson, Jack Knox, Bruce McLean, June Redfern, and Adrian Wiszniewski (Edinburgh: Paragon Press, 1986);

The Loom of Light, text by Brown, illustrations by Simon Fraser, photographs by Moberg (Nairn, Scotland: Balnain, 1986);

Keepers of the House, text by Brown, illustrations by Gillian Martin (London: Old Stile Press, 1986);

A Celebration for Magnus, text by Brown, illustrations by Fraser, photographs by Moberg and Giles Conacher, handwritten Gregorian chants by the monks of Pluscarden Abbey, handwritten musical score by Peter Maxwell Davies (Nairn, Scotland: Balnain, 1987);

The Golden Bird: Two Orkney Stories (London: John Murray, 1987);

Stone, text by Brown, photographs by Moberg (Verona: Kulgin D. Duval & Colin H. Hamilton, 1987);

Two Poems for Kenna (Dorset, U.K.: Hod House / Child Okeford, U.K.: Words Press, 1988);

Songs for St. Magnus Day, text by Brown, engravings by Lawrence (Oxford: Perpetua Press, 1988);

The Masked Fisherman and Other Stories (London: John Murray, 1989);

Tryst on Egilsay: Haakon and Magnus: Seven Poems, text by Brown, illustrations by Rosemary Roberts (Wetherby, U.K.: Celtic Cross Press, 1989);

The Wreck of the Archangel: Poems (London: John Murray, 1989);

Letters to Gypsy, text by Brown, illustrations by Fraser (Nairn, Scotland: Balnain, 1990);

Selected Poems, 1954–1983 (London: John Murray, 1991);

Vinland (London: John Murray, 1992);

Rockpools and Daffodils: An Orcadian Diary, 1979–1991, text by Brown, photographs by Gordon Wright (Edinburgh: Wright, 1992).

OTHER: "The Broken Heraldry," in *Memoirs of a Modern Scotland,* edited by Karl Miller (London: Faber & Faber, 1970), pp. 136–150;

"Two Horses, Rose and Terror," in *New Tales of Unease,* edited by John Burke (London: Pan, 1976), pp. 30–40;

Dark Angels, lyrics by Brown, music by Peter Maxwell Davies (London: Boosey & Hawkes, 1977);

"An Autobiographical Essay," in *As I Remember: Ten Scottish Authors Recall How Writing Began for Them,* edited by Maurice Lindsay (London: Robert Hale, 1979), pp. 9–21;

Fiddlers at the Wedding, lyrics by Brown, music by Davies (London: Boosey & Hawkes, 1980);

Into the Labyrinth, lyrics by Brown, music by Davies (London: Chester Music, 1986);

"Pearl," in *Scottish Short Stories 1986,* edited, with an introduction, by Deidre Chapman (London: Collins, 1986), pp. 27–31;

Edwin Muir: Selected Prose, edited, with an introduction and a memoir, by Brown (London: John Murray, 1987);

House of Winter, lyrics by Brown, music by Davies (London: Chester Music, 1987).

SELECTED PERIODICAL PUBLICATIONS – UNCOLLECTED: "Pilgrim," *Lines Review,* 26 (Summer 1968): 5–8;

"The Mercenary," *Scotia Review,* 7 (August 1974): 20–23;

"Writer's Shop," *Chapman,* 4 (Summer 1976): 23–24;

"Night Crossing," *Scottish Review,* 10 (May 1978): 9–11;

"Orpheus with his Lute," *New Edinburgh Review,* no. 44 (November 1978): 18–20;

"Jenny Barraclough," *New Edinburgh Review,* no. 50 (May 1980): 9–11;

"My Scotland: 2: Orkney and Scotland," *Scottish Review,* 36 (November 1984): 15–17.

Now past seventy, George Mackay Brown is unique among modern British writers in the scope, nature, and integrity of his achievements. A major part of his distinctiveness lies in the way he has created an entire oeuvre centered on a sparsely populated region, the Orkney Islands, which are far on the periphery of national life. Another dimension that sets him apart from all other current British writers is the vision that informs his work, a vision made up of values drawn from his religion, his sense of history, his literary allegiances, and his devotion to Orkney. Furthermore, he is one of those rare writers who combines wide accessibility and popularity with a totally uncompromised reputation as an artist of the utmost seriousness and integrity.

He has attained distinction in three literary modes: verse, the short story, and the novel. An aspect of this versatility is the tight interrelatedness that marks his work across these three genres and also in his other writing, which includes drama, essays, journalism, children's literature, and guidebooks. Indeed, so heavily integrated is his work both in subject matter and method that a brief description runs the risk of making him seem entrapped in a fatally narrow range. Direct contact with his work, however, reveals him as an author of inexhaustible invention, great humanity, and unfailing commitment to the techniques of writing. At the center of his oeuvre are his short stories, of which he has published six major collections.

Brown was born in Stromness, Scotland, on 17 October 1921, the youngest of the six children of John and Mhairi Sheena (née Mackay) Brown. There was only one daughter in the family, and one of the sons died in infancy. John Brown was a tailor who became a postman; he died of a heart attack in 1940. Even though its population is only about two thousand, Stromness is the second largest town in Orkney (after Kirkwall). It is located on the western side of Mainland, the largest of the sixty-five or so islands that make up the Orkney archipelago. The original name for Stromness was Hamnavoe, the one Brown prefers to use in his writings.

It may be difficult for outsiders to envisage the distinctiveness of the Orcadian identity. A glance at a map suggests that the Orkney Islands are merely a part of Scotland; a glance northward on a clear day from John o'Groats on the northern tip of Scotland displays the archipelago apparently just a few miles offshore. Yet those few miles of sea, combined with the sense of distance from Edinburgh – let alone from London – keep alive a sense of being different from Scotland that is the result of many centuries of separate tradition and history. During the age of the Vikings, Orkney was part of a political and cultural world that included Norway to the east, Caithness in northern Scotland to the south, the islands off the west coast of Britain (including the Isle of Man and Ireland), and territories stretching to Iceland and beyond, even to Vinland, as Brown reminds the reader in his 1992 novel of that title. To a considerable extent mainland Scotland was relevant to Orcadians solely as a source of plunder; Orkney and Shetland were formally incorporated into Scotland (as part of a dowry) in 1468–1469.

That northern world, of which Orkney was a central constituent, had its history commemorated and its separate self-awareness embodied in great sagas, including the *Orkneyinga Saga,* written by an Icelander around 1200. As Hermann Pálsson and Paul Edwards state in the introduction to their 1978 translation, the work has, for the people of Orkney, "a special significance, having become, since its first appearance in an English translation (1873), what might be called their secular scripture, inculcating in them a keener sense of their remote forebears and sharpening their awareness of a special identity." The possession of such a splendid piece of historical literature is surely one of the important reasons why, as Brown writes in *An Orkney Tapestry* (1969), "the Orkney imagination is haunted by time."

Although there were no writers in Brown's family, his sister – ten years older than he – frequently told him stories, exposing him to a tradition of oral storytelling. In the community as a whole, indeed, storytelling was a universal pastime, a form of entertainment lying at the heart of its culture. In her account of Brown's life in *The Contribution to Literature of Orcadian Writer George Mackay Brown* (1991), Hilda D. Spear quotes the author: "In Scotland, when people congregate they tend to argue and discuss and reason; in Orkney they tell stories." Evidence of Brown's skills with the written word came in his early school essays; he attended Stromness Academy until he was eighteen.

In 1941 Brown was diagnosed with tuberculosis, which has plagued him for much of his life, preventing him from strenuous labor. The enforced idleness enabled him to read extensively, however, and to move into journalism with contributions to the *Orkney Herald.* The first of these, "The Downward Trend of the Tory Party," was published on 28 November 1944. Apart from political essays his early journalism included many book reviews as well as a regular weekly diary. He has written columns for Orkney newspapers throughout his career as a writer.

In October 1951 Brown resumed his formal education, spending a year at Newbattle Abbey – an adult-education college in Dalkeith, just south of Edinburgh – under the wardenship of poet and critic Edwin Muir. One of Brown's earliest reviews was of the first version of Muir's autobiography, *The Story and the Fable* (1940). Brown has acknowledged that Muir's vision of reality, expressed in that book, has influenced him profoundly. Just how automatically that schema comes to Brown is visible in the foreword to *An Orkney Tapestry,* in which he proposes to "make a kind of profile of Orkney, which is not a likeness of today only; it has been worked on for many centuries," thereby revealing "the vision by which the people live, what Edwin Muir called their Fable." He contrasts this with "the facts of our history — what Edwin Muir called The Story" — but sees the historical record as merely a mask over something timeless: "underneath, the true face dreams on, and The Fable is repeated over and over again."

The two writers are clearly close in their outlooks, so it is not surprising that Muir accepted Brown for a place at Newbattle following an informal meeting over tea in the Stromness Hotel or that Brown found the experience that the Muirs offered at Newbattle to be "one of the happiest times I remember — perhaps the happiest." However, Brown then suffered another major bout of tuberculosis, which led to a fifteen-month stay in Kirkwall Sanatorium. The enforced idleness enabled him to develop further as a poet.

Brown had been writing verse since the 1940s, and with Muir's encouragement his first collection, the thirty-three-page *The Storm and Other Poems* (1954), was published by the Orkney Press. Muir provided an introduction, and the volume was illustrated by a local artist, the first of Brown's many collaborations with artists in other fields, of whom perhaps the most important has been the composer Sir Peter Maxwell Davies. Brown's reputation as a poet spread with his second collection, *Loaves and Fishes* (1959). He has continued to publish verse; his second collection of *Selected Poems* appeared in 1991.

Brown's first major publication of short fiction, *A Calendar of Love and Other Stories* (1967), seems at first sight to be a considerable change of literary direction, but that is far less the case than one might suppose. That volume of fourteen stories has been followed by five other major collections as well as some short-story publications of more restricted circulation. *Greenvoe* (1972) is the first of a series of novels leading up to *Vinland* (1992). Brown's copious stream of prose fiction from 1967 onward shows little obvious development or major change of emphasis.

The justification of the view that Brown's short stories are central to his lifework does not rest merely on their sheer quantity. His poems and novels have the same senses of structure and narrative that are so fully and naturally manifested in the stories. His most characteristic poetic manner is narrative; poem after poem offers Orkney characters living, loving, working, and dying. The reader of his verse must enter the essential life of Orkney, past or present. Brown is one of the least confessional of contemporary poets; almost all his poems are about a place, a way of life, and the truths and values that he believes inhere in that place and life. His gaze is directed outward to people and their environments rather than inward to his own situation. His poems are essentially and obviously fictional, and his general structural method in them is to build the verse from tiny fragments of what can only be called narrative, as in "Runes from the Island of Horses" (*Poems New and Selected,* 1971):

Winter
    Three winter brightnesses —
    Bridesheet, boy in snow,
    Kirkyard spade.

Barn Dance
    Fiddler to farm-girls, a reel,
    A rose,
    A tumult of opening circles.

Farm Girl
    Spinster, elder, moth
    Quiz till dawn
    The lamp in Merran's window.

Kirkyard
    Pennies for eyes, we seek
    Unbearable treasure
    Through a wilderness of skulls.

Mirror
    Ikey unpacked a flat stone.
    It brimmed
    With clouds, buttercups, false smiles.

Brown's novels are also marked by a confidently episodic approach to structure so that each one is built up from fragments laid side by side, like a mosaic. Many of these fragments could easily stand alone as self-contained short stories. Such an approach to the novel can appear to be limiting and a sign of limitation. His first novel, *Greenvoe*, could easily be misread as a collection of short stories that makes only a perfunctory gesture toward the kind of coherence one expects of novels. It was published soon after his first two short-story collections and is set in the same world of contemporary Orkney that one finds in them. However, its more elaborate coherence lies beneath its surface.

Brown's commitment to storytelling is irrevocably bound up with his sense of the values inherent in the traditional Orkney way of life. He has a profound sense of kinship with the generations of storytellers who have lived in Orkney for as long as the islands have been inhabited. To Brown storytelling is a profoundly natural activity, as much a part of his conception of instinctive human behavior as making love; living off the sea and the land; dwelling in a small, knowable community; and worshiping the Christian God. These values come together in his vision of the Orkney way of life as lived until recent times. In this vision the storyteller has a vital function in keeping alive the community's sense of itself, especially by renewing, through imaginative retelling, the shared knowledge of its distinctive past. Deeper still, the storyteller maintains the community's contact with its natural rhythms and the religious reality that they reflect. Through stories the community's openness to wonder, to the marvelous, is kept alive. Many of Brown's stories are clearly intended to do just that.

Brown's writing is imbued with values and attitudes of which readers of any substantial portion of his work will soon become aware. Part of Brown's complaint against the modern age is that it is inimical to the traditional habit of communal storytelling, just as it is inimical to so much else that characterized the life of Orkney before the present generations. Brown is well known for his opposition to what he calls progress. He sees both the technology of the modern age and the outlooks that produce and welcome its products as contrary to mankind's deepest needs and instincts. Several of his stories explicitly convey this attitude.

In "The White Horse Inn" (*The Masked Fisherman and Other Stories,* 1989), for example, the more sensitive characters regret the arrival of gas street lighting as diminishing the beauty of the night. Less directly "Hawkfall" (*Hawkfall and Other Stories,* 1974), in its glimpses of various phases of island life, imparts the diminution of the quality of contemporary everyday experience. Its modern Orkney is debilitating, petty in contrast to a past that was both heroic and terrible. Indeed, one of the most obvious ways in which Brown expresses his antipathy to much of the modern age is through his fundamental choice, in the whole range of his lifework, to turn his back on most of the world outside Orkney for his subject matter.

Some of Brown's stories are not set in Orkney, but most of those non-Orkney tales take place in barely defined, often vaguely oriental settings. When, as happens only occasionally, the twentieth-century world outside Orkney is portrayed, it is usually for the clear purpose of illustrating its cruelty, as in the concentration-camp sections of the novel *Magnus* (1973). When twentieth-century Orkney is treated, the mood is usually sad, satiric, or

both. This whole cluster of ideas and values comes together in the powerful little story "The Wireless Set" (*A Time to Keep and Other Stories,* 1969), in which a radio given to aged parents by their son is at first an almost comic presence in their traditional environment but then brings the awfulness of world war right into the Orkney living room. It comes to embody the twentieth-century invasion of their lives, and when the son is drowned on convoy duty, the father, rejecting what the times have done to his family, smashes the device with an ax.

In part Brown is simply reacting to the visible changes in daily Orkney life brought by the twentieth century. Until that time Orkney's isolated situation kept it largely untouched by the great industrial and social changes that swept over the lowlands of mainland Scotland in the nineteenth century. In Orkney the living patterns of an agrarian and maritime economy were able to evolve while maintaining continuity with the ways of the past. Brown is vividly — and regretfully — aware of the changes wrought by modern communications and contact with outside cultures. In addition to the general impact of the twentieth-century world, Orkney has played a prominent role, from the 1970s onward, in the North Sea oil industry. Some of the world's most advanced technology has arrived, almost literally, on Brown's doorstep.

Yet Brown is no simpleminded Luddite, and his cherishing of the community values that are being so swiftly eroded has sources deeper than mere nostalgia. In Brown's eyes the immense materialism of the current age and its craving for novelty are directly opposed to all his favored values, which are, at base, religious. Brown's values stress at least three equally important strands. He holds to the age-old religious rejection of material things as distracting, irrelevant novelties: his ideal of human life is of simplicity and, indeed, poverty. At both the personal and communal levels, furthermore, he sees human life in the present as requiring a rootedness in knowledge of the past and in the traditions deriving from the past. Yet, deeper still, he is mistrustful of any way of life that denies direct contact with the basic rhythms of nature — the rhythms of the seasonal year and their practical application in human life, the farming year. Perhaps even deeper still is his sense of the alternation of the grand opposites of fullness and dearth, of light and darkness.

Orkney is a good place to lay oneself open to such oppositions. During its summer days the light never finally departs from the skies, and during its winter days the hours of darkness almost completely overwhelm the hours of light. Brown associates storytelling with winter. Orkney shares the same latitudes as the middle of Hudson Bay and southern Alaska. The long nights cause some people a severe depression that is characteristic enough to have its own name, *morbus orcadensis*. Most of the stories in *The Masked Fisherman* are set around the winter solstice, and many of Brown's tales throughout his collections take wintry bleakness as their starting points.

Brown's belief in poverty, personal and cultural rootedness, and the rejection of the superficial seductions of success – along with his sense of how these values are essentially Christian – is made clear in "The Eve of St. Thomas" (*The Masked Fisherman*). In this story a successful author of popular fiction renews his writing, and his life as a whole, by rediscovering his roots in Orkney, drawing on the *Orkneyinga Saga,* and sloughing off his comfortable life in exchange for one of hardship and poverty. The transformation takes place at Christmas; many of Brown's stories offer a version of the Christmas miracle. Another in the same collection is "The Nativity Bell and the Falconer." Set in Viking Orkney, it depicts an isolated Christian community's fear of the Norsemen, which reaches its climax at their little Christmas Mass. The service is suddenly interrupted by the arrival of seven young warriors, but, to the amazement and relief of the congregation, the newcomers silently join the worship.

Brown's sense of religion lies at the heart of the majority of his stories. Many of them make explicit reference to the religious life, bringing the sinfulness of men and women throughout history into juxtaposition with spiritual realities. Many other stories express a religious awareness through order and shaping. Brown became a convert to Catholicism in 1961, during one of his worst periods of illness. Although brought up a Presbyterian, he never seems to have found the Presbyterian ethos congenial. Indeed, his vision of the imperfections of the modern age does not merely consist of criticism of the twentieth century. Like several other contemporary Scottish writers, Muir among them, Brown appears to regard the Scottish Reformation of the sixteenth century as a time when much more was lost than gained. In *An Orkney Tapestry* – during the course of which he gives a brief personal, poetic history of the islands – he describes how "a terrible thing happened":

> A dozen horsemen rode through the hills from Hoy. They dismounted at the chapel of Our Lady. The valley people heard the sounds of blows and smashing and dilapidation inside – it went on all morning. Presently some of the horsemen came out with bulging sacks and staggered with their loads to the edge of the crag and emptied them out into the sea below. A young man with a pale face stood at the end of the chapel and told the people that now they could worship God in a pure form; the Pope and his bishops had been cast down from their high Babylonish places; the idolatry of the Mass was abolished, abomination of desolation that it was; instead the unadulterated word would be preached to them, Sabbath after Sabbath, by him their new minister, in the kirk of Hoy five miles away.

As always in Brown's writing, the instinctive mode is of concrete, individualized narration. For him history's reality is a lived, experienced thing, best encountered in a tale.

With this new puritanism, he implies, came a new spirit of intolerance and persecution and an emphasis on religion as a thing of terror. Brown envisages the loss of Catholicism as a loss not just of truth, but of spiritual and physical beauty – a terrible impoverishment. Several of his most effective tales deal with this directly, such as "Witch" and "Master Halcrow, Priest" (both in *A Calendar of Love*). "A Treading of Grapes" (*A Time to Keep*) – a juxtaposition of three sermons imagined as being delivered in the same church in the twentieth, eighteenth, and early sixteenth centuries – highlights not just the worldliness of the two later ages in comparison with the earliest, but especially picks out the sheer poverty of thought, language, and feeling in twentieth-century religious utterance.

Brown is in no danger, however, of portraying the worlds of prehistoric, Viking, and medieval Orkney as versions of Eden. Mankind's capacity for evil and cruelty is as clear in the pages of the *Orkneyinga Saga* as it is in the chronicles of the twentieth century. In Orkney's Viking past, though, there is also miracle and transformation, as in the history of Saint Magnus, whose cathedral dominates Kirkwall. The story of Orkney's saint is central to Brown's thinking, and he has returned to it in a variety of artistic contexts. Magnus was one of two jointly ruling twelfth-century earls of Orkney whose rivalry perpetuated a terrible civil war. At a peace meeting held at Egilsay, Earl Hakon's men slew Magnus, who had envisioned his death as a solution to the problems of the earldom. Hakon proved a worthy, effective ruler whose reign greatly benefited the earldom, and Magnus's sacrifice was honored through sainthood.

This miraculous echo of Christ's earthly reality and self-sacrifice starkly contrasts with the violence and disorder of Viking Orkney. Brown is ca-

Dust jackets for Brown's 1967 and 1969 collections of short fiction, which focus on characters living in the Orkney Islands

pable of doing full justice to the horror of the times, and indeed it would be easy to see him as a predominantly somber writer. His characteristic pattern presents miracle and light suddenly, frequently briefly, entering the darkness of human experience. The violence that makes up so much of the *Orkneyinga Saga* is not, he knows, confined to its period. One of his recurring concerns – whether or not he is writing about Orkney's Viking past – is the vain, destructive pursuit of glory and ambition through war. In "King and Shepherd" (*Andrina and Other Stories,* 1983) he envisages an ancestor of Genghis Khan pushing west with his army but finding that the pull of farm rhythms is ultimately too strong for him and his men. In "Perilous Seas" (*The Sun's Net,* 1976) Brown depicts the brutality of an eighteenth-century mutiny on the high seas, while in "The Battle in the Hills" (*Andrina and Other Stories*) he tells of a battle in sixteenth-century Orkney from the point of view of the women whose men are caught up in it. In "Stone, Salt, and Rose" (*The Sun's Net*) a

young English knight is captured during the Scottish victory at Bannockburn in 1314. He gradually ascends from despair and degradation to eminence and a near fairy-tale happiness at the hands of his captor, who finally grants him his daughter's hand. Once again miracle transforms the life of one of Brown's protagonists.

Brown's faith in miracles is double-edged, not to be taken as indicating a merely naive optimism. Whether he is writing about the emptiness of twentieth-century daily life or about mankind's propensities toward cruelty and destruction, his position is not far from despair, but he can still attain to a hope derived from his Catholic faith. Brown clearly finds himself dwelling in a season of dearth, a wintry age in which the wellsprings of all that he regards as most vital to human needs are scarcely flowing.

Brown's writing about his community seems an integral part of his living there. Like Muir's poem "The Horses" (*One Foot in Eden,* 1956), which details the aftermath of a nuclear exchange,

Brown's story "The Seven Poets" (*The Sun's Net*) depicts the return to a simple community lifestyle of self-sufficient village groupings as mankind rediscovers a healthier, saner way of life:

> It can be said, with justice, that a great deal of excitement went out of the human story once this pastoral system was established. Men considered boredom to be a small price to pay for their new tranquillity. In fact there was little boredom. The simple village system had within itself endless variety.

Brown's lifework appears to demonstrate that, for writers and readers alike, the simple village system has endless variety. To an urban reader, at least, it may be a marvel how Brown can keep finding new ideas for stories among the tiny towns and villages, the isolated crofts and fishermen's huts of a sparsely populated archipelago.

One partial explanation for his remarkable success may be his love for new beginnings. Not only does each story involve a fresh start, but many of his stories are structured to be groupings of even shorter stories. The stories with such groupings are often visibly sectionalized in order to stress the separateness of their component parts. To read Brown is to experience life as an endless sequence of fresh starts. He communicates a sense of the limitless possibilities of human life. Interest, wonder, and even miracle lie around the next corner, be it ever so familiar and prosaic. Brown's sense of richness in his Orkney environment, though, would be strained were he to confine himself to portraying the Orkney of his own time.

Another dimension of Brown's stories is his diversity within a well-defined range of characteristics. He has a strong sense of structure and an instinct to make form an explicit part of the reading experience he offers. He often partitions his stories into subsections, as with the three sermons in "A Treading of Grapes" or the five sections of "Five Green Waves" (*A Calendar of Love*). His interest in stories that embody numerical patterns is the result of his enthusiasm for beginnings combined with an almost medieval inclination to ascribe beauty and additional meanings to numbers. Brown's basic realism is mated to a tendency toward clarity and stylization, as if the truth of God's universe thereby comes closer to being expressed.

Brown has produced stories of many different types by combining his extended range of Orkney material with his poet-craftsman's talent for devising new structural patterns. Those types include stories of life in twentieth-century Orkney, "web of life" stories, stories based on numerical or repeated patterns, stories set in Orkney's past, stories that juxtapose different phases of Orkney's history, ghost stories, stories that portray the entrance of miracle and mystery into modern life, and stories that express the joy of ritual.

Many of Brown's stories deal in a straightforwardly realistic way with life in contemporary Orkney. Perhaps the most powerful example of what he can do in this mode is "Celia," the opening story of *A Time to Keep*. One of his longest stories, it tells of a girl left to nurse her ailing stepfather. She has turned to drink and entertains male visitors in her room for the sake of the bottles they bring with them. Bleak as the basic situation of the story is, the effect is finally more complex than seems likely because of the love and strength she shows even in this state of weakness and degradation. Partially destroyed by her life experience, Celia nevertheless demonstrates the indestructibility of human values and almost attains the status and dignity of sacrifice as she lives her maimed life as a service both to the invalid and the emotionally needy members of the community.

Such a direct, undeviating concentration on one situation, however, is not at all frequent in Brown's tales of contemporary life. More characteristic are those that may be called his "web of life" stories. The image of life as a great God-woven tapestry is a favorite of the author's, and certain of his tales seem to be particularly direct attempts to express this idea. Such stories deal with many characters without necessarily concentrating on any one or two of them. Their structure is episodic, with each episode an apparently self-contained fragment, and the reader is challenged to find the kernel of the tale through imaginative involvement. Narrative and meaning are woven into a pattern of strands. That mosaiclike approach has the virtue of reconciling a thorough realism of texture with a powerful sense of control and stylization.

The impersonal structure of such tales might seem to militate against a strong emotional content, but in Brown's hands the result usually conveys the emotion of understatement and carries, furthermore, a powerful sense of mystery in and reverence for life. A good example is "The White Horse Inn," which is split into seven episodes, each named after a different character, such as "Fisherman," "Harvester," and "Spinster." The disparate episodes seem chaotic, but the theme of the inn's function as a focus for human life through a community as a whole, and throughout the ages, gently emerges.

"A Calendar of Love," the title story of Brown's first short-story collection, is close in method to "The White Horse Inn," although it focuses on a narrower range of characters. It has twelve main sections named after the months and tells of the triangular relationship involving Thorfinn, an irresponsible philanderer; Peter, an evangelical, even visionary, Christian; and Jean, who is trapped behind the bar of the pub she runs on behalf of her dying, demanding father. In March she gives herself to both Thorfinn and Peter. By December she has finished with both and gives birth to a son.

Brown treats each of the twelve sections as a separate tale with its own narrative principle or pattern. Some sections advance the story with simple directness, while others are more oblique. "August," for example, consists solely of the quoting of three small advertisements in the local paper; by this time they are full of meaning for the reader. With its associated cool detachment the artifice in "A Calendar of Love" allows for the rapid alternation of a wide range of tones, from comic to profoundly serious. The result is an extraordinarily vivid impression of a clearly realized set of relationships working themselves out in the context of a deftly sketched community and way of life. The underlying implication of such a panoramic story is the stress on the variety and individuality of life to be found in the communities in which these stories are set. The numerical form provided by the sequence of time in "A Calendar of Love" is closely paralleled in other stories where an even more arbitrary numbering provides a structure. Brown often selects numbers well sanctioned in oral literature: three, five, and seven.

An equally pervasive element of Brown's stories is the presentation of a moment from Orkney's long history. He either retells an episode that forms part of the historical record, such as "The Feast at Paplay" (*Andrina and Other Stories*), or invents a completely new tale set in earlier times, such as "Tartan" (*A Time to Keep*). Several stories deal with facets of what Brown considers the central event in Orkney's history, the martyrdom of Magnus, but the author also uses other episodes from the *Orkneyinga Saga* and occasionally writes about events from later centuries. A particularly memorable example from this last group is "Witch" (*A Calendar of Love*), set near the beginning of the seventeenth century. It relates the arrest and fearful punishment of a falsely accused peasant girl charged with witchcraft. In other stories he imaginatively re-creates important moments in the social or cultural develop-ment of the islands' inhabitants, as in his account of the Reformation coming to an obscure corner in "Master Halcrow, Priest" (*A Calendar of Love*) or his description of the development of writing and decorative art in an isolated Pictish community in "The Stone Rose" (*The Masked Fisherman*).

Brown's re-creations of history are inevitably conditioned by his familiarity with the style of the sagas. His stories are marked by an ability to render brutality and occasionally sickening violence forcefully but not gratuitously. He is able to suggest convincingly a primitive, largely alien perspective on the part of his ancient characters while conveying, when appropriate, continuities with the present. An excellent example of this technique is "The Story of Jorkel Hayforks" (*A Calendar of Love*), which tells of a group of seven Viking seafarers whose number is whittled down to two; several of the lost members meet sudden, violent deaths. Yet the matter-of-fact tone causes the violence to take on an almost comic edge without losing its force, and mortality itself is enfolded into a larger sense of life's flow.

Brown also creates a version of his historical short stories that involves the juxtaposition of parallel fragments from different centuries, providing a contrast between the ages. "A Treading of Grapes" is such a tale. The title piece of *Hawkfall and Other Stories* is longer and more subtle, consisting of episodes from prehistory, Viking times, the period of the Renaissance tyrant Earl Patrick, the Napoleonic period, and the present. At first glance the episodes seem to have little in common apart from a shared location, although readers are likely to discern a repeated motif of love and sex. Nevertheless, the story's deepest concern seems to be with power and authority. The episodes depict different moments in the history of the islands' governance, from the mystical process of burying one chief and the selection of another in prehistoric times to the persuasion, over an obscure shop counter, of a local businessman to join the municipal council. Yet these glimpses of the various structures of power are embedded in much fuller sketches of entire ways of life.

More mechanical – and nearer to the kind of effect Brown can achieve in some of his longer, multisectioned poems – is "The Twentieth of August" (*The Masked Fisherman*). In this story he "quotes" from fictional documents – diaries, chronicles, and letters – providing glimpses of Orkney life on 20 August of the eighty-third year of each century from 1183 onward. The inevitable change and variety brought about by time is the basic point, although a sense of equally powerful continuity is also conveyed. The story ends with a mysterious glimpse of a log from 2083.

In many stories Brown writes as an out-and-out realist, creating irreproachably convincing tales of mundane experience. Many other stories, however, deny the confines of the commonplace either by introducing the supernatural or by poetic suggestions of miraculous truths and realities. Whatever Brown may be doing, however, in the way of crossing the boundaries of the everyday, the stress is still on the reality of what is being depicted. His tales are never merely literary escapes but always invite the reader to enter a reality. If that reality is at odds with the humdrum view of reality, then there is always, at last, a religious justification.

In Brown's ghost stories the specters are usually very much part of the real world; they are often extremely physical presences. The lovers in "The Drowned Rose" (*Hawkfall*) can be seen, heard, smelled, and desired. The dead little girl in "The Tree and the Harp" (*The Masked Fisherman*) may not actually appear to her successor in the house and garden, but she still addresses her, conversationally, from her invisibility. The Orkney girl abandoned by her pirate lover in "The Pirate's Ghost" (*The Sun's Net*) ultimately has to release his spirit by traveling to London and clasping the hand of his tarred, rotting corpse in a final farewell. An Orkneyman slain in an obscure seventeenth-century battle journeys back to his homeland, only gradually coming to the realization that he is no longer alive, in "Soldier from the Wars Returning" (*The Sun's Net*).

A different approach to the rapprochement between the everyday world and the realm of the miraculous can be found in those stories in which a mysterious holy presence intrudes on the commonplace. In "Anna's Boy" (*The Masked Fisherman*), for example, the tale seems to be leading up to the revelation of whatever grotesque mystery surrounds the child who is rumored to be kept completely sequestered by his mother. The community finally gets a view of the lad when he appears at a children's school party at the moment when the newly available electrical power has failed at the height of a stormy day. He has miraculously carried a burning candle through the storm. There is no attempt to explain these circumstances; Brown leaves the little pattern of events to communicate its own meaning.

"Christmas Visitors" (*The Masked Fisherman*) is apparently the somewhat depressing stream of consciousness of an old woman who receives a small tide of visitors to break up her Christmas Day isolation: her grandchildren, the English incomer from next door, the cat from the neighboring farm, an old man who confesses to a lifelong love for her, and her eldest son. Her life seems shriveled and these brief visitations barely nourishing, but she responds to them with a growing warmth and satisfaction. Then it is revealed that she is longingly expecting one more visitor: the ghost of her husband, drowned forty-three years earlier and an invariable presence each Christmas. This year he does not come, and Brown hints that the old woman dies.

The sense of order and meaningful sequence in such stories, as well as the profound sense of religious awe found in so many of them, culminates in a group of stories that are nearer to the status of prose poems. These stories convey, more than anything else, the joy and beauty of a ritualistic patterning. A particularly pure example is "Dialogue at the Year's End" (*The Masked Fisherman*), with eleven short sections, each mainly consisting of a paragraph of reminiscence and self-congratulation from an old woman followed by a comment of ironic approval from a mysterious, Puck-like child:

> "What can anybody do in February?" said the old done woman with the grey shawl muffling her mouth. "Oh but my needles went clickety-clack, clickety-clack, and a jumper with bonny patterns brown and white fell from the knitting needles. I'll be the bonniest lass at the barn dance at the Bu come the weekend. I will."
> "No gull was ever so busy," said the flame-bright boy, and put another peat on the fire.

The descriptions of the woman and the child change each time, with increasingly poetic language, just as their musings and responses do. When the end is reached, it is (once again) as if death has overtaken the woman, but here death becomes a fairy-tale adventure and seems to take the attractive form of the complete abandonment of self. The brief story almost ceases to be a narrative and becomes instead a timeless pattern of verbal structure. Such a piece is the ultimate of that powerful tendency in Brown's writing to transform the flux of human experience into an ordered beauty.

Brown's stories, therefore, cover a wide range of subjects and modes while remaining within an apparently narrow circumscription. His various approaches to short fiction can be found in all his collections. Nevertheless, there is some progression and development in his work as a short-story writer in that with the passing of the years he has moved further and further from the sort of realistic, contemporary fiction represented by "Celia." He is increasingly drawn to the otherness of history, timelessness, and miraculous pattern. Stories set solely in contemporary Orkney become scarce in his later collections. Sometimes, as in "The Eve of St. Thomas," a substantial portion of contemporary narrative is coupled with material reflecting earlier times. The result creates implications for all time, and the sense of engagement with contemporary life as such is blunted.

Brown's enthusiasm for the historical, the timeless, and the parabolic is one of his major strengths and a prime element in his distinctiveness. It is possible to regret that he has not written even more about contemporary Orkney, but in the nevertheless considerable amount he has written on that subject the present-day life of the islands is richly assimilated into a larger context of history and the marvelous. The result thoroughly fulfills Brown's goal of making "a kind of profile of Orkney, which is not a likeness of today only; it has been worked on for many centuries." Brown has neither followed nor created a fashion in his writing; his universally accepted achievement is that of a brilliant individualist.

However, there has been surprisingly little published about Brown in academic journals or books. Alan Bold's 1978 study of the author is still the only critical book devoted to him. Brown's reputation is nevertheless high, both among the general public and professional critics. It can only be a matter of time before the unique quality of his writing stimulates a flood of academic assessment.

References:

Alan Bold, *George Mackay Brown* (Edinburgh: Oliver & Boyd, 1978);

Osamu Yamada, Hilda D. Spear, and David S. Robb, *The Contribution to Literature of Orcadian Writer George Mackay Brown: An Introduction and a Bibliography* (Lewiston, Queenston & Lampeter: Edwin Mellen, 1991).

Papers:

Collections of Brown's manuscripts are at the National Library of Scotland, Edinburgh, and the University of Edinburgh.

Roald Dahl

(13 September 1916 – 23 November 1990)

John L. Grigsby
Lincoln Memorial University

BOOKS: *The Gremlins* (New York: Random House, 1943; London: Collins, 1944);

Over to You: Ten Stories of Flyers and Flying (New York: Reynal & Hitchcock, 1946; London: Hamish Hamilton, 1946);

Some Time Never: A Fable for Supermen (New York: Scribners, 1948; London: Collins, 1949);

Someone Like You (New York: Knopf, 1953; London: Secker & Warburg, 1954);

Kiss, Kiss (New York: Knopf, 1960; London: M. Joseph, 1960);

James and the Giant Peach (New York: Knopf, 1961; London: Allen & Unwin, 1967);

Charlie and the Chocolate Factory (New York: Knopf, 1964; London: Allen & Unwin, 1967);

The Magic Finger (New York: Harper & Row, 1966; London: Allen & Unwin, 1968);

Fantastic Mr. Fox (New York: Knopf, 1970; London: Allen & Unwin, 1970);

Charlie and the Great Glass Elevator (New York: Knopf, 1972; London: Allen & Unwin, 1973);

Switch Bitch (New York: Knopf, 1974; London: M. Joseph, 1974);

Danny, the Champion of the World (New York: Knopf, 1975; London: Cape, 1975);

The Wonderful Story of Henry Sugar and Six More (New York: Knopf, 1977; London: Cape, 1977);

The Enormous Crocodile (New York: Knopf, 1978; London: Cape, 1978);

My Uncle Oswald (London: M. Joseph, 1979; New York: Knopf, 1980);

The Twits (London: Cape, 1980; New York: Knopf, 1981);

George's Marvelous Medicine (London: Cape, 1981);

The BFG (New York: Farrar, Straus & Giroux, 1982; London: Cape, 1982);

Revolting Rhymes (London: Cape, 1982; New York: Knopf, 1983);

The Witches (New York: Farrar, Straus & Giroux, 1983; London: Cape, 1983);

Dirty Beasts (New York: Farrar, Straus & Giroux, 1983; London: Cape, 1983);

Roald Dahl (courtesy of Viking Press)

Boy: Tales of Childhood (New York: Farrar, Straus & Giroux, 1984; London: Cape, 1984);

The Giraffe and the Pelly and Me (New York: Farrar, Straus & Giroux, 1985; London: Cape, 1985);

Going Solo (London: Cape, 1986; New York: Farrar, Straus & Giroux, 1986);

Matilda (New York: Viking Kestrel, 1988; London: Cape, 1988);

Rhyme Stew (London: Cape, 1989; New York: Viking, 1990);

Esio Trot (London: Cape, 1990; New York: Viking, 1990);

The Minpins (London: Cape, 1991; New York: Viking, 1991);

The Vicar of Nibbleswicke (London: Century, 1991; New York: Viking, 1992).

Roald Dahl began his career as a short-story writer after suffering through the horrors of severe canings and other punishments in oppressive British schools during the 1920s and 1930s and after enduring the horrors of military service as a Royal Air Force (RAF) pilot in World War II. In the latter context he was severely injured in an airplane crash, and extensive surgery and hospitalization were required to save his life. The importance of Dahl's school experiences is evident in his choosing to write children's stories late in his literary career, as well as in his late autobiographical work *Boy: Tales of Childhood* (1984). In *Roald Dahl* (1992) Mark West comments that Dahl's mind-set in all his works is that of "an outsider — one who distrusts not only society's authority figures but also the socializing process in general."

The centrality of Dahl's RAF service to his writing can be seen in his first collection of stories, *Over to You: Ten Stories of Flyers and Flying* (1946), which deals exclusively with the military. The war's impact on Dahl as a person and a writer is also evident in the autobiography of his war years, *Going Solo* (1986). West writes:

> According to Dahl, he had the mindset of a businessman before the crash, but afterwards he began thinking like a writer. The brush with death and the time he spent convalescing in the hospital made him more introspective and creative. He began paying attention to his dreams and fantasies and developed an interest in aesthetics.

The essential traits of Dahl's perspective and thus his fiction derive from ghastly, horrifying experiences, so it is not surprising that the fiction is bizarre, fantastic, and even grotesque to some.

Although there is considerable disagreement about the overall quality of Dahl's short fiction and the duration of his most successful literary period, there is no argument about the fact that his stories are engrossing, highly entertaining reading, since two of his collections, *Someone Like You* (1953) and *Kiss, Kiss* (1960) became best-sellers in the United States. According to Richard Brickner (*New York Times Book Review*, 21 October 1974), "an ingenious imagination, a fascination with odd and ordinary detail, and a lust for its thorough exploration, are the first strengths of Dahl's story-telling." Granville Hicks (*Saturday Review*, 20 February 1960) adds that "his great gift is for telling a macabre incident in such a way that the reader shudders and smiles at the same time." Maurice Dolbier (*New York Herald Tribune Book Review*, 7 February 1960) comments that Dahl's purpose is to entertain and that he "has little patience with short-story writers who are more

concerned to satisfy their own self-esteem than the interest of readers." Thus — despite complaints about lack of thematic profundity, about harmfully superficial and stereotypical characterization, and even about obsessively compulsive sexual fixations in his stories for adults (particularly the most recent ones) — Dahl has succeeded in being widely read and highly praised as an imaginative, original writer of carefully crafted, suspenseful, and ironically surprising stories.

Dahl was born on 13 September 1916 in Llandaff, Wales, the youngest son of Harald and Sofie Hesselberg Dahl, Norwegians who had moved to southern Wales in 1900. Harald died four years after Roald's birth. However, Dahl described his early childhood as pleasant (until his school experiences) and his family as close-knit and affectionate. He was able to attend expensive private schools, graduating from Repton School in 1932 but refusing his mother's offer to finance an Oxford education. Rather, inspired by a literature teacher's talks and by his desire to visit faraway, exotic places, Dahl accepted a job with the overseas division of Shell Oil Company and worked in eastern Africa from 1932 to 1939.

At that point he joined the RAF, as World War II had begun and British interests were severely threatened in Africa. After stints as a pilot in Greece and Syria, Dahl was injured and eventually sent back to England when persistent headaches made further combat flying unfeasible. However, Dahl remained in the military as a spy, eventually being sent to the United States as an assistant air attaché. There he met the author C. S. Forester, who asked him to write about his war experiences. Forester sent the story that Dahl wrote to the *Saturday Evening Post*, which bought it, and Dahl's literary career had begun. After the warmly praised, but moderately selling, *Over to You* and an unsuccessful novel, *Some Time Never: A Fable for Supermen* (1948), Dahl achieved success and popularity with *Someone Like You*, his second, and longest, collection of stories.

Kiss, Kiss was similarly successful with critics and readers, as were most of Dahl's children's stories, which he began to write in 1960. The most famous of those is *Charlie and the Chocolate Factory* (1964). Dahl also wrote the screenplays for the James Bond film *You Only Live Twice* (1967) and *Chitty Chitty Bang Bang* (1968). He produced one more collection of short stories for adults, *Switch Bitch* (1974), which was reviewed much less favorably than his previous collections. Dahl then published more children's stories; a novel, *My Uncle Os-*

wald (1979); several volumes of poetry, including *Revolting Rhymes* (1982); and the autobiographical works *Boy: Tales of Childhood* and *Going Solo*.

Dahl become a celebrity in America because of his residence there for part of each year after 1942, his publishing most of his stories in American periodicals, and his widely publicized marriage to actress Patricia Neal in 1953. Their union resulted in four children who at least in part prompted his career as a children's author. During the first ten years of Dahl's marriage to Neal he produced his best short stories for adults, those in *Kiss, Kiss,* which focus primarily on male/female relationships. Dahl and Neal divorced in 1979, and he spent most of the remainder of his life at his farm in Great Missenden, England. He died on 23 November 1990 in Oxford.

Despite the widespread popularity of *Someone Like You* and *Kiss, Kiss,* there has been disagreement among critics about the technical effectiveness of Dahl's stories and their thematic implications, even about whether his stories have any thematic implications at all. In "Sex Ex Machina and Other Problems" (*Kenyon Review,* 1969) James Degan states that Dahl has an "indifference to imposing a 'vision' on his stories." However, Degan goes on to qualify that assessment by noting that, although Dahl's stories are somewhat "farfetched," they are "eminently readable and despite their lack of pretension, a great deal more profound in their insight into human nature than much fiction passing as profundity today." That kind of carefully qualified praising of Dahl's work is done by Dean Baldwin in *The English Short Story, 1945–1980: A Critical History* (1985):

> The best of Dahl's stories achieve a degree of palpable horror or grim irony that is at once entertaining and revealing. Explaining the id leads Dahl into fascinating territory, from which he often derives stories of great cleverness. These can be very effective, but in large doses they appear contrived and slick.

That contrived, manipulative quality of Dahl's less effective stories is repeatedly pointed out by critics. In "The Confidence Man" (*New Society,* 27 December 1979) Michael Wood observes that, because of Dahl's imaginative fancifulness and devotion to surprising the reader, "his stories, increasingly, have become tall tales with punch lines, rather than bits of imagined life." Wood also discusses how Dahl's strength becomes his weakness:

> He has tact, timing, a clean, economic style, an abundance of ingenuity — none of them things to be sniffed at. But above all he knows how to manipulate his read-

ers; and if no decent writer is without a touch of this talent, no really good writer, I suspect, ever lets it rule him. A writer who *only* manipulates his readers becomes a confidence man, a cousin to Thomas Mann's Felix Krull.

> It is this quality in Dahl's stories which makes so many of them seem so wispy when they are done. You can't tell them to anyone, because you'll spoil the surprise; and you can't read them again yourself, because the surprise was all there was. This is not true of the better work of Maugham, or Saki, or Maupassant.

Wood then adds a qualifier: "Fortunately, it's not true of the better work of Dahl, either."

Other critics have noted the important subjects and themes of Dahl's best stories, all of which, as Baldwin observes, deal with the psychological realm of human existence. J. D. O'Hara (*New Republic,* 19 October 1974) states: "One of Dahl's subjects is the war between men and women. Another is the threat of the esoteric, the repeated suggestion that special knowledge is dangerous, or that the man with special knowledge is necessarily nutty." Another aspect of Dahl's psychological probing is discussed by Nona Balakian in a review of *Over to You* (*New York Times Book Review,* 10 February 1946): "With a feeling for essential truthfulness, he has singled out, for these stories, the inner experiences of some of the men who followed the Messerschmitts into the deserts of Egypt and Libya, into Greece and Palestine." In a review of *Kiss, Kiss* (*New York Times Book Review,* 7 February 1960) Malcolm Bradbury writes, "His characters are usually ignoble: he knows the dog beneath the skin, or works hard to find it" — further testament to Dahl's extrapolation from the powerful, self-centered needs of the human subconscious. Similarly, the *Times Literary Supplement* (28 October 1960) points out that, in his best work, "where Mr. Dahl differs from the common run of spine-chillers is in the verisimilitude of his caricature of human weakness . . . revealing a social satirist and moralist at work behind the entertaining fantast."

West agrees that characters "as caricatures of human frailty . . . lie at the core of Dahl's stories," noting that, "even though Dahl's characters may not be realistic, they are still drawn from real life." James Kelly (*New York Times Book Review,* 8 November 1953) praises the "satirical burlesque" in several stories in *Someone Like You.* West bemoans the fact that Dahl's ironic criticisms of society have received little attention: "Like the critics who reviewed *Someone Like You,* most of the reviewers who wrote about *Kiss, Kiss* praised Dahl for his ingenious plots and careful use of details, but they paid little attention to the ideas and themes that underlie his stories."

ROALD DAHL

Kiss Kiss

Michael Joseph

Eleven fine new stories by the author of SOMEONE LIKE YOU

PHOTOGRAPH BY ELI WALLACH

Roald Dahl, who was born in Wales of Norwegian parents, is forty-four years old. He is married to the actress Patricia Neal, and has two daughters. His interests include the growing of old-fashioned or species roses, collecting eighteenth-century furniture, buying and selling paintings, drinking wine and betting on horses.

Dust jacket for Dahl's 1960 collection of short stories, which depict the struggles of male/female relationships

West effectively argues that a major theme in Dahl's work is "the human response to impending death," remarking that in *Over to You* "almost all of these stories feature characters who struggle against the dehumanizing aspects of war." He also notes the theme of the danger of excessive fantasy or illusion in many of Dahl's stories as well as Dahl's sometimes-satiric presentation of class differences in England. In all of Dahl's work, West concludes, "authoritarian figures, social institutions, and societal norms are ridiculed or at least undermined."

In his best stories Dahl presents skillfully composed plots that convey powerful insights into the frequently negative depths of the human psyche. His stories often satirize the conventional norms, institutions, and hierarchies of society from the point of view of, in West's words, "an outsider." West attributes that position to Dahl's close Norwegian ties while in England and close English ties while in America as well as his profoundly negative school and war experiences. In his less effective works, however, Dahl's outsider status results in a kind of cynical condescension toward and manipulation of the reader in surprise-of-plot stories that stereotype

characters outside his self-focused realm of psychological experience. Wood states that "Dahl tends to condescend to adults," treating them "only as victims" – evident in his belief that "the reader or viewer has to be hooked, snagged in suspense, if he is not to close the book or change the channel."

Over to You is unique among Dahl's short-story collections because it focuses on a single general subject: pilots' lives during war. Although the book did not sell well, it received some positive reviews. Orville Prescott (*Yale Review,* Spring 1946) observes that "This, one never doubts, is the way British pilots talked, felt, acted. This is the way they forgot the past and the future and ignored all but the immediate present." That assessment pertains to the best stories in the collection, such as "Katina," in which the title character is a nine-year-old Greek girl whose parents have been killed in German bombing raids. She stands defiantly before the diving airplanes, tempting death, and is adopted by an RAF squadron for her bravery. The fliers devote their free time to caring for Katina, whose death upon again walking deliberately out before the strafing jets is described in emotionally affecting detail. The fliers then fight even harder because of Katina, who represents the powerful spirit of the embattled Greek people.

Balakian also praises *Over to You,* stating that Dahl "has not written the usual postmortem adventure story but tried imaginatively to bring the flier's separate world within the compass of our own." "A Piece of Cake" is the best example in the collection of such imaginative re-creation. The story, which is based on the piece that Dahl wrote at Forester's request, describes in minute, realistic detail the psychological states of a pilot who has engine trouble, crashes, is injured, and is almost burned alive in his airplane. The incidents derive from Dahl's own crash and near death. Dahl uses a slowed stream-of-consciousness technique to depict the stunned, shocked pilot trying to realize how and why he hurts (facial injuries and flames at his feet) and what he must do to escape (loosen the straps holding him in and crawl from the airplane). Dahl then presents the hallucinatory dreams of the flier, who lies unconscious in a hospital. The flier imagines he is writing jokes on his airplane to entertain the Germans, but he finally realizes they cannot appreciate the jokes because they are in English. He also imagines running uncontrollably through grassy fields, past his mother, toward a dark cliff edge that he cannot avoid even though he tries to grab his legs to stop. Such imaginative presentation of the psychological state of near death leads John Stinson, in his assessment of *Over to You* in *The English Short Story,* to say that Dahl creates "sharp, credible individuation of character and scene that manages, almost paradoxically, richly to suggest the truth of universal experience."

West praises several stories in this first collection, noting that "Katina" is the most realistic of the ten and applauding "Madame Rosette" as "a celebration of the compassionate side of human nature." Balakian also favors the latter story, in which three fliers on leave tentatively arrange through a procurer, Madame Rosette, for a sexual encounter with a shop girl but then have second thoughts and instead free fourteen young girls held in bondage by Madame Rosette. Balakian calls the story "one of the most vivid," stating that "Mr. Dahl has captured [the fliers'] spirit of mad abandon with marvelous subtle insight and genuine humor."

Not all the stories in *Over to You,* however, are so realistic, imaginative, or insightful. Michael Straight (*Saturday Review,* 9 March 1946) writes that some of them come "perilously close to exchanging content for dramatic effect." This observation applies to both "Death of an Old Old Man" and "An African Story." In the first story a German and a

British pilot touch wings and crash, and the point of view is switched problematically to relate the incident and present the consciousness of the British pilot. Also problematic is the pilot's stated death yet his continued narration of the last part of the story. Such devices generate confusion rather than creative ambiguity in Dahl's attempt to capture the emotional impact of the pilot's crash and death.

In "African Story" a pilot relates a tale told to him by an old man. That man had arranged the death of a mentally deficient acquaintance who killed the old man's dog as the result of an insane fixation on the dog's incessant paw licking. The insane character is too imitative of the obsessed, compulsive narrators of such Edgar Allan Poe stories as "The Tell-tale Heart" (1843). As in Poe's tale the old man's desire for revenge is exploited and dramatized at the expense of any serious consideration of the justifiability of the revenge taken and the philosophical and moral dimensions of the action involved. Minute attention is focused on the ghastly drama of the impaired man's death as he is duped into waiting to confront a boy who is supposedly stealing milk at night from one of the old man's cows. Instead the impaired man encounters a large mamba that fatally poisons him. Not only is the story far-fetched and imitative, but it also lacks any significant psychological insight.

Nevertheless, *Over to You* was an auspicious beginning for Dahl as a short-story writer. The fundamental strengths of Dahl's work, his creativity and originality, are present in abundance, as are insightful psychological portraits of fliers in confrontation with that universal human experience: death. The collection also contains stories with important implications, such as the impersonal treatment of fliers in hospitals in "A Piece of Cake" and the assessment in the same story of the Gladiator airplane that the British pilot flies as old, cheaply made, and "a big thing that will burn better and quicker than anything else in the world." Certainly, too, the insanity of war is implicitly criticized throughout the collection. However, Dahl does even better in his next two collections, which are the ones upon which his admirers argue he merits canonical-writer status in literary history.

Dahl's second collection of stories, *Someone Like You,* has been much more popular than *Over to You,* at least partly because of its more topical and much more varied content. Most of the fifteen stories occur in British settings ranging from working-class automobile service stations to the mansions of the fabulously wealthy, and anyone with an interest in British life and culture can learn much from the collection. Part of the reason for the greater popularity of this collection is the greater extent of the macabre in its stories. For example, in "Lamb to the Slaughter," which Baldwin calls one of Dahl's best, a wife whose husband tries to leave her strikes him with a frozen leg of lamb and kills him. When the police come to investigate the murder and search for the blunt object that killed the husband, the wife serves them the leg of lamb, thus effectively disposing of the murder weapon. As they eat the meat and ironically comment on how the murder weapon is "probably right under our very noses," the wife giggles in the next room. The story also illustrates A. H. Cheyer's assessment of Dahl's gender-warfare theme (*Wilson Library Bulletin,* February 1962): "The stories betray a Thurberesque glee as the author keeps score of skirmishes won and lost in the war between the sexes, in which the combatants employ a variety of ingenious dodges to get the better of their better halves."

As important as the stories' ingenuity in successfully embodying that theme is the fact that both female and male characters are presented believably, sometimes sympathetically and sometimes unsympathetically, which is less true in some of Dahl's later stories. For example, he is careful to point out that Mary Maloney, the wife in "Lamb to the Slaughter," is six months pregnant when her husband callously decides to leave her, making her striking him both believable and at least somewhat justified. Similarly, in "Nunc Dimittis" a wealthy British art collector is understandably offended to learn that a female companion has called him a bore, and he seeks revenge in embarrassing her by exposing a seminude painting of her. She seeks revenge by perhaps poisoning the caviar she sends to him as a gift. The story's ending is ambiguous, the art-collector narrator simply saying that he feels ill after eating a bit of the caviar, so perhaps that illness is his punishment, not death. Regardless, the cynical presentation of both characters is balanced fairly and illustrates West's observation that *Someone Like You* exposes the hidden savagery of the supposedly highly civilized.

West also indicates another important theme in this collection, explaining that in both "The Soldier" and "The Wish" the characters' behavior is governed much more by their fantasies and emotions than by reality and reason. Thus Dahl astutely integrates as his theme the weakness to which he was most prone. In "The Soldier" a former flier apparently suffering from post-traumatic stress disorder becomes so absorbed in his fantasies of life-threatening danger that he comes to believe his wife is trying to drive him crazy. He therefore confronts her, kitchen knife in hand, in a rather pathetic attempt to harm her, get attention to and help for his problem, or both. Similarly, in "The Wish" a young boy becomes so fantasy-prone that he imagines the carpet in his home is infested with snakes (the black parts of the carpet) and filled with hot coals (the red parts). He tries to cross the floor on only the yellow parts and falls in the process. His hand hits a "glittering mass of black and he gave one piercing cry of terror as it touched." Dahl adds the final ironic touch: "Outside in the sunshine, far away behind the house, the mother was looking for her son."

Dahl not only presents the theme of the danger of fantasy and illusion in "The Wish" and other stories in this collection, but he also satirizes the "sane" adults who neglect the psychological dimension of reality and desert their children to its horrors. He effectively satirizes the two "civilized" but actually barbaric and vengeful upper-class characters in "Nunc Dimittis," while the policemen as protectors of society are exposed to ridicule in "Lamb to the Slaughter." The latter satiric aspect illustrates West's remarks about Dahl's distrust of society's authority figures. In fact, *Someone Like You* is probably Dahl's most satiric collection, given the variety of British life and society reflected in it.

Especially noteworthy in showing the range of this satiric vein are the "Claud's Dog" stories that end the collection. For example, the last one, "Mr. Feasey," satirizes Claud, a dog racer, and his friend, a service-station operator, as they scheme to race a slow dog repeatedly in order to raise the odds in betting against him. They then try to substitute an identical-looking fast dog after making huge bets that he will win. They succeed in deceiving Mr. Feasey, the track operator, as to which dog is running, but the bookies simply refuse to pay when the pair's substitute dog wins, claiming that the service-station operator and Claud bet on another dog instead.

Dahl's satiric point in "Mr. Feasey" is that scheming and chicanery are so rampant in British dog racing that there is no real hope of winning, regardless of one's skill in deception, and the story is filled with graphically realistic, even ghastly, descriptions of the lengths to which gamblers (including dog owners) go in order to win (such as putting wintergreen on the dogs' skin or ginger up their anuses to make them run faster). As Kelly states, "For many readers the final scarifying story about greyhound racing and the cheating men and willing dogs who share it will live as long as any in the book." The profound satire and the detailed, informed content of the "Claud's Dog" stories illustrate Wood's point that, in Dahl's best short fiction, there is "an earned, painstaking knowledge which clearly echoes Dahl's own interests." Certainly, many of the stories in *Someone Like You* are among Dahl's best.

Kiss, Kiss, Dahl's third collection of short fiction, is less varied and contains fewer stories (eleven) than *Someone Like You,* but it was just as successful. West explains that *Kiss, Kiss* has the same kind of "tightly woven plots, macabre elements, and surprise endings," but it is different in that most of the stories "focus on tense and unhappy relationships between men and women, whereas just a few of the stories in *Someone Like You* treat this theme." Another similarity, noted by *Time* (22 February 1960), is that "as in his earlier book, *Someone Like You* . . . author Dahl specializes in the horror of normality."

The horrifying nature of male/female relationships in Dahl's fiction is perhaps best shown in "The Way up to Heaven," in which the horror is the responsibility of both sexes. A couple married for thirty years struggle for power in the relationship, focusing specifically on Mrs. Foster's wish to live near her grandchildren in Paris all the time versus her husband's wish that he and she remain in New York. In the psychological struggle Mr. Foster tortures his wife by being constantly late while knowing that fear of lateness is an obsession with her. When Mrs. Foster is ready to leave on an airplane trip to Paris to visit her beloved grandchildren, Mr. Foster hides the gift for their daughter in the car and returns to the house supposedly to search for it. Frantic minutes later Mrs. Foster goes to the door of their home, puts her key in it, and stops and listens carefully. She then removes the key, says it is too late, and tells the driver to take her to the airport. She is strangely white, with a hard expression.

After six weeks in Paris, and after hints that she will return soon, Mrs. Foster goes back to New York, seeming perhaps a bit amused that no one meets her at the airport. Arriving home she smells a strange, faint odor and purposefully goes to the rear of the house as if to "investigate a rumor or to confirm a suspicion." She returns quickly with a satisfied look and calls a repairman to report that the elevator in the house is stuck between the second and third floors. Throughout the story the horror of the husband's torture and of the wife's final revenge is graphically depicted, and the psychological reality of the subtle power struggles in marriages is superbly illustrated.

A similar situation is found in "Mrs. Bixby and the Colonel's Coat," in which, as Bradbury states, "the standard male magazine story becomes something immeasurably better because Mr. Dahl knows not only his market but his characters inside out." This is certainly true of "The Way up to Heaven" as well. Bradbury goes on to praise "The Champion of the World" and "Parson's Pleasure," two of the most surprising, and at the same time profoundly satiric, stories in *Kiss, Kiss:* "Both have great endings; both have enormous substance in the tale that is told."

The marvelously surprising ending of "Parson's Pleasure" depicts the horror of a fake parson, who is really an antique dealer, when he finds a priceless Chippendale chest of drawers in the house of Rummins, an impoverished, uneducated, and uncultured farmer who appears in one of the "Claud's Dog" stories in *Someone Like You.* In order to get the antique cheaply, the "parson" pretends that the piece is virtually worthless and that he only wants its legs to attach to another piece of furniture. Rummins, Claud, and Rummins's son, Bert, then demolish the chest of drawers in an attempt to help the parson, who has gone to get his car, since they assume that the antique will not fit in the car and they believe his story. Entertaining and ironic, the story satirizes the manipulative antics of the antique dealer, a representative of the upper class.

The same kind of surprise ending and astute satire distinguish "The Champion of the World," in which the satire is directed primarily at the scheming of Claud and his working-class cohorts. Claud and the narrator (the service-station owner) devise an apparently foolproof plan for poaching the pheasants of Mr. Hazel, a rich, arrogant landowner and pie and sausage manufacturer. They feed Mr. Hazel's pheasants raisins laced with a sleeping potion and carry off hundreds of the birds. Bessie Organ, wife of the town vicar, brings the pheasants — hidden beneath her child in its stroller — to Claud the next day. However, the pheasants awake and fly out en masse just as she arrives at the service station and just as Mr. Hazel is due to drive past. Uproariously humorous, the story ends with the birds flocking groggily around the station.

West notes the "underlying class conflict" and satiric implications of both "Parson's Pleasure" and "The Champion of the World," remarking that "in both of these stories arrogant members of the upper class discover that they do not have total control over the country folk whom they so despise." Not all the stories in *Kiss, Kiss* are of this high quality. For example, West complains that "The Landlady" – in which a woman kills, stuffs, and mounts her lodgers as exhibits – is too closely "modeled after traditional ghost stories." Hicks notes that "William and Mary" and "Edward the Conqueror" suffer from "overelaboration . . . so much preparation that the climax is a disappointment." Still, both stories center on highly original, imaginative ideas: in "William and Mary" a man's brain is surgically removed and lives on after the remainder of his body dies, and in "Edward the Conqueror" a woman finds a cat that is a reincarnation of Franz Liszt. The stories are entertaining, and both involve the male/female conflict, with a woman victorious in one instance and a man in the other. Bradbury makes a more legitimate complaint than Hicks about *Kiss, Kiss:* "His [Dahl's] poorer stories (an allegory of Hitler's natal day, a horror-tale of a landlady who practices taxidermy on her lodgers) are weaknesses in idea – not in treatment."

Switch Bitch is by far the most controversial of Dahl's collections of short fiction for adults. Comprised of only four long stories all previously published in *Playboy*, the collection is unified by the sexually explicit content and the presence of Uncle Oswald as the main character in the first and last stories. The book has its defenders, such as Peter Ackroyd (*Spectator*, 30 November 1974), who says that "the stories in this book prick the bubbles of sexual fantasy even before they have got off the ground, and they use . . . tricks of suspense and reversal, which would seem artificial within a novel, to great effect." West praises all four stories, noting the creative irony of "The Visitor" (in which the "playboy" unknowingly has sex with a leper), emphasizing the poignant qualities of "The Great Switcheroo" (in which two husbands surreptitiously manage the "perfect" wife swap) and "The Last Act" (in which a widow resorts to suicide after a disastrous sexual encounter), and applauding "Bitch" (about a perfume that makes men sexually uncontrollable) for presenting "serious implications about the relationship between sexuality and human evolution."

However, the preponderance of critical opinion about *Switch Bitch* has been negative, the fundamental complaint being that Dahl succumbs to the theme implicit in some of his earlier stories: the danger of excessive indulgence in fantasy and illusion. Imagination is replaced by unadulterated sexual fantasy despite the plot twists, which only give the impression of the puncturing of illusions. Victoria Glendinning (*New Statesman*, 22 November 1974) writes:

> Roald Dahl's stories always have a nasty sting in the tail. The four outrageous stories in *Switch Bitch* certainly do – literally – for they are all about sex. . . . It is all perhaps

a little slick; but the slickness is that of the professional entertainer. In each case Roald Dahl sets up a realistic situation, then loads it with amusing and fantastic sexual possibilities. Then, somewhere this or the other side of pornography, he produces a denouement of the banana-skin kind – black banana-skin at that. The lecher falls flat on his face, the reader is released into appalled laughter, and morality is placated.

The manipulative condescension, gimmicky plotting, and character stereotyping noted by Glendinning are evident in "Bitch." Here Uncle Oswald arranges to support an inventor in his efforts to create a perfume whose effect would be analogous to that of a "bitch dog in heat" on male dogs. After elaborate efforts to con the reader into believing that such an invention is possible and after focusing only on the arousing smell of females to males (as if the reverse type of sexual arousal were impossible), Dahl has the inventor test his product by putting a few drops on his female assistant and hiring a boxer to approach her. The boxer smells the perfume, becomes violently agitated, and rapes the assistant, although Dahl carefully avoids the word *rape*. In most troublesome stereotyping the female assistant loves the sexual assault and wants more, even going to the extent of stealing almost all the remainder of the perfume, spraying herself, and walking up to the inventor.

Such "love of rape" stereotyping continues in the plot twist at the end of the story. Oswald has saved a few drops of the perfume and decides to eliminate the American president, whom he despises, by spraying the president of the Daughters of the American Revolution (DAR) just before she meets the American president at the time of his speech to the DAR. Oswald is accidentally exposed to the perfume's odor in the woman's presence, however, and he immediately attacks her. Although she is described as disgustingly large and unattractive, the story ends with her loving the assault, saying to Oswald as he recovers and departs, "I don't know who you are, young man. . . . But you've certainly done me a power of good."

Rather than puncturing sexual illusions or fantasies, the story attempts to manipulate the reader into acceptance of one of the most damaging stereotypes of women: that they all desire to be raped and would be much happier and less frustrated if they were. Brickner comments:

> Oswald's plot misfires, unfortunately, as does the story. The giddiness of its ending left me feeling that the story was a joke with an irresistible body and a punch line which, when it opened its mouth, nullified the body's

seductiveness. Painless pain should hurt more than "Bitch" does.

Dahl's kind of slightness is difficult to keep healthy. A clumsy touch and it bruises badly.

Both Glendinning's and Brickner's comments reveal their sense of a distinctly unhealthy quality in *Switch Bitch*, an unhealthiness rooted in unnatural fantasizing and obviation of reality. O'Hara remarks on the primary plot elements in the stories, which also include an opulent desert mansion occupied by beautiful women with a bizarre secret and a switching of wives without the wives knowing: "As *Playboy* neutralizes pornography with an airbrush, so Dahl sweetens nastiness into mild amusement."

Dahl himself hinted at the fantasy tendency run amok in his late stories, as quoted by West:

For twenty-five years, I was able to write stories that were untarnished by sexual overtones of any kind. But now, in my late middle age, they're riddled with sex and copulation. What, I wonder, is the reason for this?

The fact that Dahl did not understand why his later stories are so sexually oriented is a clear indication of the extent to which such fantasy became an obsession. Wood hints at that obsessive, almost juvenile, concern, stating that "Bitch" "is just a wringing out of an old joke, and conjures up a disturbing vision of nervously chortling readers, excited elbows digging into their neighbors' ribs, all of them dim and inhibited enough to be tickled by these sad, snickering approaches to the mysteries of Eros."

Such a return to fantasies of youth helps to explain Dahl's switch to writing children's stories in 1960, and Wood argues that such regressive fantasizing is also the key to the continuing cruelty and horror in Dahl's stories. He notes the presence of revenge as a motive in many of Dahl's stories, remarking that such is "deviance's favorite mode," and he suggests that Dahl's canings at Repton are the ultimate source: "I do think it makes sense to see Dahl's writing as a kind of revenge on the world of which Repton was a picture for him. The vision is odd and tangential because the world is so deeply and finally in the wrong." It seems clear that, by the time of *Switch Bitch*, Dahl had begun to lose the creative balance between fantasy and reality that makes his best stories ingeniously inventive and profoundly insightful and satiric. Perhaps Dahl realized that, since *Switch Bitch* was his last collection of stories for adults.

Despite the substantial decline in the quality of his short fiction toward the end of his literary career, Dahl's achievements as a short-story writer are significant. They include insightful psychological presentations, creative fictional constructions, and astutely integrated and important satire of many of the illusions of twentieth-century British and American society. Dahl successfully transformed the horrors of school-age abuse and World War II into imaginative art. Joyce Carol Oates (*Southern Review,* Winter 1971) comments that Dahl's stories "are professional in form and execution – smooth and seamless and totally undisturbing. Dahl writes stories that are almost frightening and almost amusing, crafted along old-fashioned lines of 'suspense,' peopled with characters who are given proper names and one or two characteristics." In a review of *Switch Bitch* (*Books and Bookmen,* March 1975) Paul Levy indicates Dahl's limitations as a short-story writer:

Roald Dahl is a master of the short story in the tradition of O. Henry . . . but . . . will Mr. Dahl ever make the move from fiction to literature? Possibly – but not on the present showing. . . . Mr. Dahl very nearly succeeds in creating a genuine fictional character in Uncle Oswald . . . an entity whose function it is to survive for longer than the time necessary to experience one adventure. But the function of the O. Henry hero is to have only one adventure per story, and Dahl seldom has the courage to break the mold.

However, Dahl should be judged on the quality of his best short fiction, that written in the 1950s, and his late fantasy-prone and stereotype-filled work should probably be ignored. Such treatment does not mean that Dahl will be ignored, only that he will be remembered for his best, which is doubtless what he would have wanted.

References:
Dean Baldwin, "The English Short Story in the Fifties," in *The English Short Story, 1945–1980: A Critical History,* edited by Dennis Vannatta (Boston: G. K. Hall, 1985), pp. 34–74;

Joyce Carol Oates, "Realism of Distance, Realism of Immediacy," *Southern Review,* 7 (Winter 1971): 295–313;

John Stinson, "The English Short Story, 1945–1950," in *The English Short Story, 1945–1980: A Critical History,* pp. 1–33;

Mark West, *Roald Dahl* (New York: Twayne, 1992);

Michael Wood, "The Confidence Man," *New Society,* 50 (20 December 1979): 14–16.

Elspeth Davie

(20 March 1919 –   )

Marina Spunta

BOOKS: *Providings* (London: Calder, 1965);

The Spark and Other Stories (London: Calder & Boyars, 1968);

Creating a Scene (London: Calder & Boyars, 1971);

The High Tide Talker and Other Stories (London: Hamish Hamilton, 1976);

Climbers on a Stair (London: Hamish Hamilton, 1978);

The Night of the Funny Hats and Other Stories (London: Hamish Hamilton, 1980);

A Traveller's Room (London: Hamish Hamilton, 1985);

Coming to Light (London: Hamish Hamilton, 1989);

Death of a Doctor and Other Stories (London: Sinclair-Stevenson, 1992).

OTHER: "Note," in *Beyond the Words: Eleven Writers in Search of a New Fiction,* edited by Giles Gordon (London: Hutchinson, 1985), pp. 87–88;

Original Prints II: New Writing from Scottish Women, edited, with an introduction, by Davie (Edinburgh: Polygon, 1987).

With five collections published since 1965, Elspeth Davie is one of the best short-fiction writers in Scotland. Her interest in the "hidden, day-to-day experience" in "what's happening to people just below this hectic surface" is the common denominator of all her writings. Her metaphysical quest for a whole that will reunify the gaps of modern society is brilliantly conveyed through her idiosyncratic style; her blend of detailed realism with touches of impressionism; and her semisurrealistic symbolist style. Her achievement of an extremely controlled, precise form that conceals the effort of making a whole from the chaos, and of making a unity from opposite codes – along with her ability to select words pregnant with deeper meaning – gives birth to a compact world which is seemingly a universe of its own, yet one directly linked with the panorama of contemporary literature. Unfortunately, the abstract character of her narrative form has probably prevented some critics and readers from appreciating her stylistic achievements, especially in the short stories.

Elspeth Dryer was born in Kilmarnock, Ayrshire, Scotland, on 20 March 1919. Her mother, Lilian McFarland Dryer, was Canadian, and her father, Oliver, was a Scottish minister from a Norwegian family. "I was lucky to be brought up in a family which had the wider world in view," writes Davie in her "Autobiography," an unpublished manuscript held by the National Library of Scotland in Edinburgh (Account 10631/2/2). Soon after her birth the family, which included two other daughters (Joyce, who died at age three, and Lois), moved to the south of England, and Oliver worked for the International Peace Movement in London. After living for nine years in Purley, Surrey, they returned to Scotland, where Elspeth and Lois attended George Watson's Ladies College in Edinburgh. At that time the family lived in Lasswade, a country village near a large mining community, Bonnyrigg, where Oliver Davie had a parish.

After Elspeth completed the fifth form in 1936, she spent two years at Edinburgh University, studying English, philosophy, and fine arts. Her recollection of this period in her 1938–1939 diary (unpublished; National Library, Edinburgh) is an accurate though intermittent report showing her need and determination to write. The diary features some powerful descriptions of natural scenes and people rendered through quick touches, as in an impressionist painting. It also records some of her experiences at Art College, which she attended from 1938 to 1942. Despite her excellent achievements at Edinburgh University, including a prize in philosophy, Davie was unable to take a full degree, because she lacked courses in Latin and math.

After qualifying as a teacher she taught art for a while, as described in "A Portrait of George Watson's Ladies College" (Account 10631/2/2):

Teaching wasn't a voluntary decision. Sometimes I enjoyed it. I taught first in the Borders [at Hawick], then I went to Aberdeen to a big school and that was interesting. I loved being in Aberdeen [for two years]. I made friends there and there I married. Then we went to

Northern Ireland and I did a little teaching there but it was more sort of part time.

Her teaching experience constitutes the autobiographical basis of her second novel, *Creating a Scene* (1971), about an art teacher and his pupils.

From 1945 to 1969 Davie lived in Belfast, where her husband, the philosopher George Elder Davie, taught at Queen's College. Their daughter, Anne, was born in Belfast in 1946. However, the Davies took leave in Edinburgh in 1955 and from 1959 to 1960; they now reside there. Although Elspeth started to write more steadily after her time at Art College and after moving to Belfast, her passion for writing, as well as for reading, began at an early age. Despite her dream of composing a long novel about travelers — who are a frequent subject of her fiction — she first wrote short stories, which she considered the "easiest thing to start with." The nature of her imagination — directly linked to her strong visual sense, which she believes she developed with her sketching — fits the requirements of the genre as she defines it:

> It is a kind of illumination of the whole . . . perhaps you see the whole thing at the beginning and perhaps you see how to end it. A short story is perhaps more intense than a novel because you have got to make it into this short pace and keep up the tension. . . . It is just the shortness that makes it more pregnant and also easier to write, whereas a novel has this keeping things going for a long time and trying to keep it into a unity for which you have to look back and forward to see if it is consistent.

Davie considers her short narratives better than her longer ones because, in a short story, "you have to feel more excitement and feel it till the end because you have to carry it through a rather short time." Short fiction, she states, can more effectively "focus on one person or one group." Her main objective of reunifying society's gaps and her tendency for restraint correspond to her detailed writing and reflect her vision of the world. Her stories, like the reality she portrays through them, are paradoxically full of voids (silences), which are clear metaphors of contemporary society. The narration, therefore, is the result of a succession of flashes, of sparks. She discusses her technique in "Notes on the Short Story" (Account 10631/1/13):

> The short story though small has lots of room for silence. We don't get lots of talks, so we have to "put up" to make the most of gestures, looks, passing words, exclamations, all the things which are short. These are the

things the short story makes use of. It can't afford to explain things. It must show them in a flash.

She also states her aim in writing together with her vision of reality:

> Many of us live in a world of speed, noise and endless activity and there's not always much time to take a look at what's happening to people just below this hectic surface. Yet the strange, the desolating, the ludicrous is happening to us all the time between our getting up and our going to bed. This hidden, day-to-day experience — though we may talk or keep silent, laugh or cry about it — concerns everyone. Certainly it interests me and I hope, with luck to be able to express some part of it in my writing.

Davie's focus on modern society is aimed at giving a clear picture of its alienation and neuroses. She concentrates on the themes of crisis and identity, loneliness, lack of communication, and the need to adopt a mask in one's dealings with other people. She strives to overcome the individual's alienation from others, the world, and himself by sudden sparks — moments of revelation — that can lead the character to see beyond appearances. Davie's first novel, *Providings* (1965), revolves around the theme of getting rid of obsessive objects and persons in a desperate endeavor to assert one's identity.

The pieces in *The Spark and Other Stories* (1968) illuminate all her work. Davie's first collection of short fiction exemplifies in nineteen different ways the process of epiphany people may involuntarily undergo. Afterward they usually revert to their original state, the result of a society paralyzed by its neurosis. Here, "repeated again and again but without repetitional boredom, is a twofold situation where either objects dampen people right down or people spark into life," claims critic Douglas Gifford in *Books in Scotland* (Autumn 1984). Gifford, together with Alan Massie and a few others, has best discerned Davie's abilities.

The characters in *The Spark and Other Stories* are eccentrics, people out of step with reality. The result is a world of self-contained, incommunicable entities, a parody of modern society. A revelation to these characters can only come from the outside, either in the form of an accident of fate that leads to an epiphany or in the form of some other character. Such "spark characters" are mainly children who can see through the others' masks with their power of imagination. Despite these opposite, positive forces each main character passes unaltered through an antithesis that briefly negates his or her initial static situation. Each protagonist eventually goes back to his or her former state of inertia, few of them managing to undergo real change.

"Family House" illustrates Davie's use of eccentric characters and her masterly depiction of interiors. Here the accident of fate happens when Edith, one of the five siblings in the Finlay family, is hit by an old mantelpiece clock while looking for a lamp in the attic. She is forced to stay in bed, which keeps her from the family's preoccupation with household tasks. Made aware of a dangerous hollow caused by dry rot under the attic floor – a symbol of their blank identity – the family finally moves out. The situation in this story is somewhat autobiographical, as the author has revealed a love/hate feeling for her family house when she was young: "a kind of dread of being weighed down by these memories cast around" but also a "fascination" with them.

A brilliant story on the themes of loneliness, lack of communication, and the mask is "A Woman of Substance." The description of Miss Reed in her changing depressive moods is masterfully rendered from inside the character's mind. After a sudden epiphany on her real situation, the protagonist immediately retreats behind her mask in an attempt to hide her dissatisfaction with herself. She continues with her self-deception until she feels driven to throw herself against a tree in order to "show herself as a woman with weight and bulk."

Davie's ability to render the workings of the mind in its fears, delusions, and obsessions is conveyed through her impressive depiction of settings, especially internal, claustrophobic environments. "The Siege" can be taken as an example of the author's use of narrative as a metaphor for self-closure. Here a woman confines herself in her house after her husband's death, buying huge quantities of food that take up so much space that they literally immobilize her. A paradigmatic example of the author's use of children as "spark characters" is "A Private Room," in which a small girl tries in vain to reveal her aunt's true nature behind the rigid mask she has adopted after a disappointment in love. "A Visit to the Zoo" involves a similarly desperate attempt by a child to communicate with and change others that clashes with the adults' determination to remain closed.

The gift of the children and a few artists in the stories is imagination, the secret power that enables them to create their own world and penetrate the essence of reality. Davie defines imagination as "a different way of looking at reality, maybe the right one, since there is so much strangeness in the

Dust jacket for Davie's first collection of short stories, many of which involve children who spark revelations in adults

world." It is therefore their means to reach a metaphysical reality, and in this respect Davie takes after Flannery O'Connor, a writer she greatly admires. O'Connor stated that "imagination is a distortion of truth, but you may have to use a sort of distortion to get at the truth," and Davie endorses that view. An example of Davie's depiction of the power of imagination is "A Map of the World," in which Janet's ability to visualize what her uncle describes about his journeys as though "it were there before her" outdoes his verbalizations.

Davie's striving toward a whole, an order, is reflected in her effort to convey a message into a form. She believes that "the writing has to have some fairly reasonable form however much you want to write of chaotic things . . . even chaos must have some form, some smooth style to make it readable." However, she fears that her style may be "too smooth at times, patterned, or too cool," and some critics have pointed out a degree of detachment and lack of warmth in her stories. Davie has discussed her predilection for a reserved style to convey the violent feelings in her stories: "I think you have to have this detachment. I am not sure how it works but you cannot get too emotionally involved." Yet, on the other hand, she remarks that "sometimes I might sound slightly inhuman, distant. . . . Maybe I myself am not near enough. . . . It is a very difficult balance between expressing a tremendous lot of emotions and also having a certain amount of reserve."

Davie's aim is "to look realistic, if anyone can do it," and she believes that true realism is "to be found in writers who look at things others don't look at." In *The Spark and Other Stories* her striving for realism results in extended descriptions of nature, together with internal settings that are startling for their richness of detail. The insistence on color, a natural consequence of the author's powers of observation and her experience as a painter, adds to the vividness of her stories and is carried through all her work, becoming symbolic in her later collections.

The critical reception to *The Spark and Other Stories* was varied. The majority of reviewers underlined the peculiarities of Davie's lonely characters, their claustrophobic tendencies, and their obsession with possessions. A larger and more positive response, however, resulted as the author became better known to critics and the public, following reprintings of her first collection and her first two novels both in Britain and the United States. On the whole *The Spark and Other Stories* is an impressive book that illustrates Davie's world in a powerful style. Her later collections become even more surrealistic as her language gains in control and symbolism.

Creating a Scene, Davie's second novel, reflects her experience as an art teacher (in Edinburgh for six months in 1970) and focuses on the theme of art and the question of identity. *The High Tide Talker and Other Stories* (1976), her second collection of short fiction, includes some of her finest achievements in the genre. In the title story a man devises a talk show on the meaning of life every evening on the beach, but the tide always interrupts him before he reaches the "truth-bit." The other stories in the collection are also concerned with the quest for metaphysical reality. While most of them present Davie's usual obsession with objects, she more deeply ties the characters' obsessions to their identities. Modern society and its neuroses are brilliantly portrayed in fifteen pieces that differ in theme and tone from those in *The Spark and Other Stories.*

The question of identity is seen from different points of view, even by means of paranoid schizo-phrenic characters with delusions of grandeur or superiority. One of the most notable examples is Carruthers, the showman in the title story, a brilliant parody of modern questers who are but word vendors. Among the group of vacationers at the resort who gather for his daily preaching, Watson shows his disappointment at realizing that Carruthers never gets at the truth of reality in his speechifying. Another good actor and talker is Mr. Shering, the protagonist of "Waiting for the Sun." He has his picture taken in the most extraordinary places so that people may ask about his occupation, which in fact consists only of posing. The theme of the mask is clearly central in all the stories dealing with the question of identity and is directly linked with the themes of loneliness and lack of communication, which pervade Davie's fiction. "The Last Word" satirizes such disillusioned characters as Peerie, the protagonist, who decides not to waste time in reading all the books on astronomy but simply to search for the "last word," the newest discovery that could unveil the truth about the subject.

Obsessions with objects acquire a symbolic nature in her short fiction. Among her various symbols perhaps the most powerful is the egg in "Allergy," one of her best stories. It concerns the interaction between a widowed landlady and her lodger, who is allergic to eggs and of whom she takes good care until she discovers him with a young woman. Eggs are a recurrent symbol in Davie's stories, also offering an element of autobiography (her allergy to them). The egg can be taken as an emblem of her writing for its "perfect state of unified opposites." The author has commented on its meaning: "As a subject the egg had everything. It was brilliantly self-contained and clean, light but meaty, delicate yet full of complex, far-reaching associations – psychological, sexual, physiological, philosophical." She also points out the danger of a forced interpretation of symbols, a theme she develops in such stories as "The Diary" (*The Night of the Funny Hats and Other Stories,* 1980). Yet the power of symbols as double-faced units is that of healing the split universe, at least in the eyes of those gifted persons who can read it, the "spark characters." Davie believes that "symbols are something that illumines reality but in a rather difficult angle." This definition, recalling the one she gives of imagination, links the idea of symbol with the "flash," both sharing the feature of irrational illuminations. As Davie claims: "Symbols? Well, I see them after I have done them." The power of symbols to hint irrationally at a "universal significance, a metaphorical dimension," constitutes the basis of Davie's unity of realism and surrealism.

In *The High Tide Talker and Other Stories* there is an attempt to explore the unconscious in "A Lost Toy." This tendency develops toward the fantastic – or, more precisely, magical realism – in such later stories as "Geological Episode" (*The Night of the Funny Hats*) and "Green Head" (*A Traveller's Room,* 1985). "A Lost Toy" is a compact story built on a dreamlike atmosphere conveyed through the technique of the flash, a series of impressions filtered through the protagonist's mind. Logan, a widower, is followed in his quest for a toy bear that is said to be lost in a wailing neighbor's garden. In contrast to the long, detailed descriptions in *The Spark and Other Stories,* the second collection features a more concise, impressionistic, and essential style that is further developed in *The Night of the Funny Hats* and following collections. Yet *The Spark and Other Stories* demonstrates Davie's semisurrealistic style in portraying a world in which everyone is an oddity.

Climbers on a Stair (1978), a novel set in an Edinburgh tenement where the dwellers are watched in their casual encounters, was followed by *The Night of the Funny Hats,* one of Davie's best collections of short stories. Here the portrait of a split society is made more impressive by the symbolic writing and gloomier tone. Furthermore, her style grows more masterful with the use of such techniques as free direct and indirect speech, the story within a story, and modulations of oral storytelling.

The title story is one of the author's best attempts to convey her message in her idiosyncratic, semisurrealistic style. The setting – a bus trip through Western Australia – is striking for its "wonderful, strange landscapes, so totally unlike any other, with very spectacular places and so terribly lonely," as the author remembered her 1977 bus journey across the Nullarbor Plain. The power of this environment, chaotic and motionless at the same time, lies in its remoteness and alienation: "The perspective of this landscape and its light was such that every object in it appeared to exist by itself in total separateness from the rest. Each bush, tree, stone and flower lived in the naked light with its own black shadow sharply defined – a shadow which would grow longer and sharper as the sun went down." What brings all the characters together is the driver's idea of the funny hats for the last night of the journey, a variation of the theme of the mask. The silence, which is the basic feature of the landscape and also the quest of the male protagonist, reaches a climax when the death of the driver,

Dust jacket for Davie's third collection of short stories, most of which are surrealistic explorations of the effects of space and time

the only guarantor of order, is announced to the travelers waiting for the masquerade.

Besides the familiar themes of the mask and of art, the stories in *The Night of the Funny Hats* employ a new use of space and time. The settings become more evident, as in "The Time-Keeper," about an old man obsessed with time who appoints himself a guide to the city of Edinburgh. Time gains importance through the device of the story within a story. In "The Bridge" a father tells his daughter about his previous relationship; in "The Swans" a woman remembers two Russian dancers while looking outside a shop window to the ruined house where they used to live; in "Geological Episode" a geologist finds himself telling his hostess, in the middle of the night, of his encounter with a mermaid. Those stories also display a more powerful storytelling tone, as in the opening of "A Weight Problem," where a thin man, puzzled by his lack of moral weight, offers to remove himself from a flight as the plane is pronounced overweight.

Together with these refined techniques, Davie demonstrates an increased ability to simulate through a simple style the effect of a symbolic narrative. Her impressionistic technique, which leads to her semisurrealistic style, is refined in such stories as "Concerto." Here the narrator's device of perceiving the scene at the same time as readers do results in a sort of slow-motion filming of the situation, filtered through the eyes of the audience and thus made strange. The atmosphere is reinforced by the rhythm, as the narration is built on a swiftly paced description of a piece of music parallel to the disturbance of a man suddenly feeling sick.

In *The Night of the Funny Hats* Davie's language becomes deeper and more essential through a wider use of symbols. As C. Small points out in a review of the collection in the *Glasgow Herald* (10 April 1980), "Elspeth Davie has an acute ear for both nuances and banalities of common speech: still more . . . is unspoken, the dialogue of dreams, longings, intimations which people fail to utter, sometimes even to themselves." The author often parodies the ambiguity of language, especially in her story titles, which tend to mislead readers. Such titles as "A Weight Problem," "Change of Face," "The Foothold," "It Is Your Turn," "Geological Episode," and others in later collections create suspense as they imply more than their literal meanings.

Davie delights in playing with the questions of symbolism and ambiguity by pointing out the danger of a forced interpretation of symbols. The final piece, "The Diary," seems to warn readers about their understanding of the preceding stories. In this comic sketch three nieces misleadingly decode the recurrent *B* in their uncle's diary as the initial of a secret lover, whereas it stands for *bread*. Davie's greater control of the language also derives from her increased amount of free direct and indirect speech. By suppressing more and more the connective tissue of the narrative discourse — leaving only the essential, the characters' perceptions — these stories and those in the following collection achieve greater vividness and effectiveness. As A. Spence (*New Edinburgh Review*, May 1980) states, "Her writing is stylized, imaginative and creates a realism of another order."

In *A Traveller's Room,* Davie's fourth collection of short stories, the bleak tone already present in the previous collection is reinforced by the themes of old age and death, which come together with those of traveling and order. The title story features a "spark character," one of those sensitive children who people her first collection. Here a girl tells of her family's vacation in the north. Imagination enables her to feel a deep sympathy and communion with nature and other people. When given the room of a man who is traveling, she looks at his possessions and feels "a premonition of some sadness in another person, not a sharp, penetrating sadness, but the slow, enveloping kind that folds in forever to keep out air and light."

The other examples of traveling provide more chances for recollection than revelation. In "Couchettes" a woman cannot sleep because the couchettes (train berths) remind her of the prison camps during World War II. "In the Train" is a story within a story where an aunt tells her niece of what she calls an "extra-marital" relationship she had on a train. The girl cannot make the aunt aware of her mask of pretension. Another recollection of previous travel is found in the story "Kiosk Encounter," where two friends meet by chance after one returns from a journey. An out-of-order telephone booth underlines the breakdown of communication between the two friends.

This theme is reinforced by the same image in "Out of Order," where the protagonists, faced with a phone booth that is not in use, finally come to doubt the very idea of order in society: "this unknown, perfect state that makes us feel askew." In "Lines" the image of a straight line formed by ducks on a pond reminds a group of children of a crime an old woman is supposed to have committed. "Security" is a lighter sketch about a woman, a child, and a security guard in an art gallery. It conveys the woman's distrust of security as guaranteed by society.

Even more effective than those renderings of the theme of chaos versus order are the stories that deal with the fantastic — or, better stated, magical realism — as they discard social order from within. One of the best examples is "Green Head." The opening is striking for its simple, matter-of-fact style, an intrinsic characteristic of magical realism that increases the absurdity of the situation: "Not long ago the young man, Ewan, had turned eighteen years of age, he was astounded and ashamed one day to find spikes of new green grass beginning to grow in among the hair of his head." Another subversion of natural order requiring a suspension of disbelief happens in "The Return." The unnaturalness of the situation is conveyed by the oppressive silence that is maintained throughout the story until the climax, when the mother — a mermaid — returns to the sea. Here again is the intriguing, matter-of-fact style, together with the theme of silence and lack of communication.

The remaining stories in the collection, though within the conventions of realism, portray characters with peculiar obsessions. In "The Gift" a sixty-year-old retired head teacher thinks back to his fiftieth birthday and to one missing gift that turns out to be the very lamp on his table. In "A Botanist's Romance" the protagonist's search for William Shakespeare's Ophelia ironically clashes with the practical mind of one Agnes Donnelly, whom he mistakes for his heroine. In "The Stamp" people are obsessed with stamps stuck upside down, denoting lack of care. All the objects involved — the gift lamp, flowers, and stamps — are clear symbols for lack of communication. Perhaps the most vivid picture of the ego quest is "A Free Fur Coat," where the identity of a young man is threatened as he puts on the thick fur coat of his recently deceased uncle. The story ends with the protagonist's deciding to go back to his thin winter jacket, thus regaining his own identity.

In *A Traveller's Room* the stories' plots develop elaborately through flashbacks. The resulting gaps in space and time are cleverly rendered in a style that becomes even more essential through the techniques of reticence and concentration, leaving only a series of glimpses and apparently disconnected impressions. The increased use of free direct and indirect speech enables the author to concentrate the utterances and filter the narration through the mind of the speaker. Davie's obsession with ambiguous titles such as "Lines," "A Field in Space" (where the question at a conference is between a real field and field of knowledge), and "Bulbs" (flower bulbs versus lightbulbs) deliberately plays with readers' expectations, sometimes even too insistently.

The reviews of *A Traveller's Room* were mainly positive, but critics' response to *Death of a Doctor* (1992) has been less favorable on the whole. Reviewers point out Davie's insistent moralism, which seems to increase in this collection's stories, some resembling modern folk parables. Indeed, in these stories Davie trades some of her atmospheric surrealism for an increased faithfulness to everyday reality on the one hand and the fantastic on the other. In this collection, therefore, one finds unusually varied stories, even though the common theme is still the quest for meaning and identity in a fragmented universe.

Connected with the theme of identity is the leitmotiv of the gap, which here, as in previous collections, is conveyed in a variety of ways: by things missing, by people leaving, by the symbol of "white patches," by silence, and particularly by illness and death. The title story, which in Davie's manuscript dates back to 1984, sets the theme of loss and the impossibility of attaining a whole, as the doctor — the guarantor of order like the bus driver in "The Night of the Funny Hats" — suddenly dies, leaving the nurse with the task of giving the bad news to the patients. Illness is also explored in "The Stroke," an impressive picture of the void a city banker suddenly experiences on finding himself alone in a hospital, unable to phone his wife.

In those perceptive studies of characters' psychology, Davie's talent is at its best when employing metaphors of silence and color to demonstrate the concept of the communications gap. "On Christmas Afternoon" (written in the early 1950s for the *Observer* short-story competition, won by Muriel Spark) is an atmospheric story about a boy's frightened realization, in the middle of a Christmas party, of his growing up. The chaos of the party contrasts with the silence of the boy, a "haunted, unnatural child," and with his silent communication with a man who is sewing his Santa Claus costume. Silence clearly stands for the need for communication in "Write on Me," a brilliant sketch set in an art gallery where a small boy and his father are confronted with "a large square of canvas covered with a smooth, thick coating of pure white paint."

Other examples of the communication gap include realistic stories without that peculiar shift, that weird touch, that distinguishes previous collections. "Counter Movements" stages the final parting of two lovers in a bar, followed by a somewhat abstract conversation between the girl and a waiter. "The Hairdresser" portrays a boy's sadness at the news that his hairdresser is leaving. Those stories, like "Death of a Doctor" and "Waiting" — about an empty Scottish-Italian restaurant — retain only a little of the writer's idiosyncratic technique, presenting realistic, though unusual situations.

Death of a Doctor also features examples of outsiders similar to those in the earlier collections. "Absolute Delight" epitomizes the author's mixture of modes in the grotesque story of a man with "difficult feet," unable to feel the "absolute delight" the shoes he buys from a catalogue are meant to bring him. "The Man Who Wanted to Smell Books" portrays a similarly obsessed character in a sort of science-fiction story deploring the replacement of books by videos. Charlie Syson is an eccentric who likes to feel and smell books, which clearly stand as a symbol of communication against the impersonality and passivity of television screens. Behind him lies the author's complaint about a modern society where "most people don't read."

The tendency toward allegory is also the common denominator of the semisurrealistic stories. The fantastic comes to light in "Choirmaster," a sarcastic depiction of a religious choir that protests God's inequity under the direction of a mysterious and devilish aspiring leader. In "Connections" the fantastic breaks through even more clearly as the protagonist, waiting for his train, encounters a ghost struggling with a heavy suitcase. Here the moral is given by the ghost, who articulates Novalis's idea of seeing what has always been there but has never been seen before. In some stories the surrealistic touch is spoiled by an excessive moralism that shows how modern society is turned upside down. In "Through the Forest," after a brilliant opening that plays with the fairy-tale style, the author shows herself perhaps too concerned with her moral aim in criticizing "progress" versus nature. Again the falsity of modern society is demonstrated by the use of titles with double meanings. "Absolute Delight," "Counter Movements," "Waiting," "The Stroke," and "Connections" leave readers puzzled about their implications. "The Morning Mare" pictures a young girl's "nightmare" as her vacation is ruined after observing the cruelty of a milkman toward his mare.

Although she sometimes overstresses ambiguities, Davie's achievement of an extremely controlled, restrained form conceals the effort of making a whole from the chaos — a unity of opposite codes — while portraying modern society. Readers and critics may sometimes sense too much abstraction and moralizing in her stories. Nevertheless, the power of her creations and her stylistic achievements have not yet received sufficient examination or praise.

Interviews:

Alan Massie, "The Art of Elspeth Davie: Metaphysics with Reason, *Weekend Scotsman,* 31 January 1981, p. 1;

Lorn MacIntyre, "The Anatomy of a Short Story," *Weekend Scotsman,* 13 April 1985, p. 4.

References:

Douglas Gifford, "The Vital Spark: The Vision of Elspeth Davie," *Books in Scotland,* no. 16 (Autumn 1984): 9–10;

M. van Eijck, *The Novels and Stories of Elspeth Davie: An Introduction,* Ph.D. dissertation, Catholic University, Nijmegen, 1984.

Papers:

Davie's unpublished manuscripts include Accounts 10631/1/1–15, Accounts 10631/2/1–8, and two diaries (for 1938–1939 and May 1946) in the National Library of Scotland, Edinburgh.

Rhys Davies

(9 November 1901 – 21 August 1978)

D. A. Callard

BOOKS: *The Song of Songs and Other Stories* (London: Archer, 1927);

Aaron (London: Archer, 1927);

The Withered Root (London: Holden, 1927; New York: Holt, 1928);

A Bed of Feathers (London: Mandrake, 1929; New York: Black Hawk, 1935);

Tale (London: Lahr, 1930?);

Rings on Her Fingers (London: Shaylor, 1930; New York: Harcourt, Brace, 1930);

The Stars, the World, and the Women (London: Jackson, 1930);

A Pig in a Poke (London: Joiner & Steele, 1931);

A Woman (London: Capell/Bronze Snail Press, 1931);

Arfon (London: Foyle, 1931);

Daisy Matthews and Three Other Tales (Waltham Saint Lawrence, U.K.: Golden Cockerel, 1932);

Count Your Blessings (London: Putnam, 1932; New York: Covici-Friede, 1932);

The Red Hills (London: Putnam, 1932; New York: Covici-Friede, 1933);

Love Provoked (London: Putnam, 1933);

One of Norah's Early Days (London: Grayson, 1935);

Honey and Bread (London: Putnam, 1935);

The Things Men Do: Short Stories (London: Heinemann, 1936);

A Time to Laugh (London: Heinemann, 1937; New York: Stackpole, 1938);

My Wales (London: Jarrolds, 1937; New York: Funk & Wagnall's, 1938);

Jubilee Blues (London & Toronto: Heinemann, 1938);

Under the Rose (London: Heinemann, 1940);

Sea Urchin: Adventures of Jorgen Jorgensen (London: Duckworth, 1940);

Tomorrow to Fresh Woods (London: Heinemann, 1941);

A Finger in Every Pie (London: Heinemann, 1942);

The Story of Wales (London: Collins, 1943; New York: Hastings House, 1943);

The Black Venus (London: Heinemann, 1944; New York: Howell Soskin, 1946);

Selected Stories (London & Dublin: Fridberg, 1945);

Rhys Davies

The Trip to London: Stories (London: Heinemann, 1946; New York: Howell Soskin, 1946);

The Dark Daughters (London: Heinemann, 1947; Garden City, N.Y.: Doubleday, 1948);

Boy with a Trumpet (London: Heinemann, 1949; Garden City, N.Y.: Doubleday, 1951);

Marianne (London: Heinemann, 1951; Garden City, N.Y.: Doubleday, 1952);

The Painted King (London: Heinemann, 1954; Garden City, N.Y.: Doubleday, 1954);

No Escape, by Davies and Archibald Batty (London: Evans Bros., 1955);

The Perishable Quality (London: Heinemann, 1957);

The Darling of Her Heart and Other Stories (London: Heinemann, 1958);

Girl Waiting in the Shade (London: Heinemann, 1960);

The Chosen One and Other Stories (London: Heinemann, 1967; New York: Dodd, Mead, 1967);

Print of a Hare's Foot (London: Heinemann, 1969; New York: Dodd, Mead, 1969);

Nobody Answered the Bell (London: Heinemann, 1971; New York: Dodd, Mead, 1971);

Honeysuckle Girl (London: Heinemann, 1975).

Collections: *Collected Stories* (London: Heinemann, 1955);

The Best of Rhys Davies (Newton Abbot, U.K. & North Pamfret, Vt.: David & Charles, 1979);

The Selected Rhys Davies, edited, with an introduction, by D. A. Callard (Bristol, U.K.: Redcliffe, 1993).

OTHER: Anna Kavan, *Julia and the Bazooka,* edited, with an introduction, by Davies (London: Owen, 1970);

Kavan, *My Soul in China,* edited, with an introduction, by Davies (London: Owen, 1975).

In the breadth of his subject matter and the scope of his work — which includes twenty novels, in excess of a hundred short stories, two topographic books on Wales, a biography, and a play — it is not unreasonable to claim for Rhys Davies the title of Wales's greatest twentieth-century prose writer. That he is not generally recognized as such, least of all in his own land, is due in part to the "outsiderdom" that he deliberately cultivated and to his almost lifelong residence in London, divorced from the rather incestuous currents of Welsh literary life.

Davies was born on 9 November 1901 (not 1903, as he was given to claiming) in Clydach Vale, a tributary valley of the Rhondda rising steeply at right angles from the town of Tonypandy. His father, Thomas Rees Davies, was the son of an illiterate Merthyr collier. Both of Thomas's parents had died during his childhood, and he was raised in an orphanage, leaving to become a grocer's boy in Tonypandy. Rhys Davies's mother, Sarah Ann Lewis Davies, was an uncertificated schoolteacher from Ynysybwl. She was eighteen and Thomas was twenty-one when they married in 1895 and almost immediately set up the Royal Stores, a grocery shop, at 6 Clydach Road, Clydach Vale.

Since the first coal had been discovered in the 1860s, the coal-bearing valleys of south Wales, especially of the Rhondda, had acquired many of the attributes of a gold-rush area. In the years that followed, a vast influx of people poured in from rural west Wales, southwest England, and Ireland. Now

bereft of its collieries, Clydach Vale appears to be a backwater, but it was not so at the turn of the century. The Davieses' shop was equidistant from two major Rhondda pits, the Blaenclydach Colliery at the foot of the valley and, at the head, the Cambrian Colliery of D. A. Thomas, later ennobled as Viscount Rhondda. The area was the focus of a famous labor struggle, the Tonypandy Riots (1911), which were eventually suppressed by military action sanctioned by Winston Churchill.

There is a myth running through a great deal of twentieth-century Welsh writing of the rural arcadia in which the people of south Wales dwelled before being plunged into the hell of industrialism. It is found, for instance, in Dylan Thomas's "Fern Hill" (*Deaths and Entrances,* 1946) and achieved popular expression (and worldwide dissemination through director John Ford's 1941 Academy Award–winning film) in Richard Llewellyn's *How Green Was My Valley* (1939). Rhys Davies subscribed to the mythology, but in his case the grounds were rather tenuous. On his father's side both his grandparents and great-grandparents were born in the even-worse industrial hell of Merthyr Tydfil, though the family originated in the Teifi Valley in west Wales. On his mother's side his grandparents also came from the Teifi Valley, from which his maternal grandfather, John Lewis, had moved to the Rhondda to work as a timberman in the coal pits.

Both sides of Davies's family were Welsh-speaking, as were both of his parents, but they did not teach the language to their children. All schooling in Wales was conducted in English, and it was generally felt that, in the words of the great industrialist David Davies, "English was the language to make money in." It was a society in which education as a means of escape was given the highest priority, and a knowledge of the Welsh language came to be seen as an impediment. This, combined with the huge influx of English and Irish immigrants, meant that the language rapidly declined over a short period in the industrial valleys, to be replaced by a heavily Welsh-inflected English.

The Royal Stores, despite its grandiose name, was a tiny, economically precarious shop almost entirely dependent on the vagaries of the coal market and the outcome of industrial struggle. Rees Vivian Davies, as he was christened, was the fourth child of the family, which, despite its relative poverty, was still considered middle class in the eyes of the valley's inhabitants. Although it was possible in boom times for a collier to earn a good wage, there was a great gulf between a man who hewed coal for a living and a man in a white coat who cut cheese.

Besides, Thomas Davies, whom Rhys portrays as something of an impractical dreamer, had ambitions to become a man of affairs. He was a founder of the local chamber of commerce, the Liberal Club, and the local golf club; he later became a Freemason.

Because of these connections the Davies children were sometimes invited to the large white house of the Cambrian pit's colliery manager. And, since even the poorest need to eat, Rhys grew up in contact with the entire spectrum of life in Clydach Vale: in the community, but not exactly of it. During the frequent strikes and lockouts the grocer was in an invidious position. As Rhys writes in his autobiographical novel *Tomorrow to Fresh Woods* (1941):

> In a strike the tradesman was a bigger loser than either the miner or the mine owner. The miners hung idle about the place, living on credit; the owner was without profit but was not losing any of the coal in his pits. But the tradesman handed out his stock without a cash return, worked daily in his shop without a wage, and dipped into his bank balance to pay the wholesalers.

At one point the store had to be remortgaged in order for Thomas to meet debts, and in the aftermath of the 1926 General Strike bankruptcy was only narrowly avoided.

Yet there was sufficient money for the family to employ a maid, usually a country girl from west Wales, who was given a room and one pound per week. The household was virtually a matriarchy. Rhys's mother curbed what she saw as her husband's impracticality and hounded debtors who had been given credit during hard times by her more lenient husband. Rhys had an elder brother, Jack, who was killed during the closing months of World War I, and a younger brother, Lewis, born in 1913. There were also three sisters. Lewis recalls that after Jack's death the brothers grew up in a household of women. Their father was constantly busy with meetings and events: "We only really saw him on Sundays."

On Sundays the family attended services at the Welsh-speaking Goshen Nonconformist Chapel though the father was not a believer and the children had only a bare competence in the Welsh language. Lewis recalls that the parents would often irritate their children by switching to Welsh when something private was to be discussed. Few Welsh writers have much good to say about the Nonconformist tradition, which even today is pervasive in Welsh religious life, and Rhys was no exception. When he became old enough to make such decisions, he insisted on transferring his religious allegiance from stark Nonconformity to the ornate ritu-

als of High Anglicanism conducted in English at the neighboring Saint Thomas's Church. Eventually he was followed by the rest of the family, his father doubtless believing that a move to Anglicanism represented a step forward on the path of upward mobility that he was treading.

Yet the world of the chapel predominates in Davies's fiction, and chapel was the religious expression of the masses. The Great Revival of 1905 — in which Evan Roberts, a young preacher, secured the wavering faith of those battered by migration and the shock of industrialization for the Nonconformist cause — had left a deep mark on the Rhondda. Roberts, exhausted by his brief ministry, retired after six months (though he lived until 1950), but others took up the torch. Davies states in a letter: "I was also very aware of religious elements and remember as a child being impressed by the excitements of a minor religious revival — processions of singing people marching in the streets, stories of sudden conversions (short-lived in their effect, it seemed)."

With its constant political and religious turmoil the Rhondda of Davies's childhood was a thought-provoking environment, and it became the subject of nearly all his fiction from his early stories and first novel, *The Withered Root* (1927), which deals with a religious revival, up to *Tomorrow to Fresh Woods*. After 1941 he turned to writing stories and novels set in west Wales (often the Teifi Valley), to exploring the world of the London Welsh, and, finally, to working with a wholly English setting.

At the age of twelve Davies was enrolled in Porth County School, the best school in the Rhondda. However, he was not happy there, nor was he a great academic success. Classes were streamed into "A" and "B" groups, and Davies remained in the "B" stream for the duration of his stay. His independent spirit had begun to assert itself, though his encounter with Homer's *Odyssey* left him with an abiding love of Greek mythology. In later life he claimed that he had "dropped out of school before matriculation," implying that he had left at sixteen, but he actually refused to attend beyond the age of fourteen, the minimum for departure from that school.

His parents — especially his mother, who was extremely ambitious for her children — were horrified. *Tomorrow to Fresh Woods* includes a beating administered by the father to the recalcitrant hero, and this was probably based on fact. Eventually Davies's parents had to relent. He worked in his father's shop and set about a rigorous course of self-education at the library of the South Wales Miner's Federation. He was soon drawn to French writers

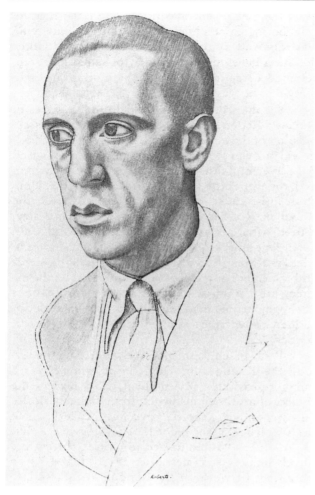

Davies in 1927 (drawing by William Roberts; courtesy of John Roberts)

and literature, notably to Gustave Flaubert's *Madame Bovary* (1857), whose title character's seductive, wanton presence colors many of the female characters Davies created. He also discovered Russian authors: Leo Tolstoy and Anton Chekhov, whom he once called "my god." He began to write derivatively, little realizing that the material that was to make his name as an author was all around him as he served in the shop and made deliveries.

"I always think of this period as a burial, with myself lying somnolent in a coffin, but visually aware of the life going on above me, and content to wait until the time came for me to rise and be myself," Davies told R. L. Megroz of his Clydach Vale adolescence. This period lasted about five years, during which he successfully evaded a parental plan to set him to work in a bank. Then, absolutely unqualified but filled with dreams of becoming a writer, he set out to encounter the world.

Davies had a brief period of employment in Cardiff in a potato and corn merchant's warehouse before he set his sights on London. He took lodgings in Manor Park, a dreary no-man's-land between the East End and what was then the dormitory town of Ilford, rooming with a young man named John Pope. He continued to write, but his initial lack of success forced him into odd jobs, including that of assistant to a gentleman's outfitter. The job provided him with his only extravagance in a fairly parsimonious life: a taste for fine, expensive clothes, almost to the point of dandyism. On his periodic returns to the Rhondda he startled the congregation at Saint Thomas's by appearing in spats and sporting a malacca cane.

His writings during these years consisted mostly of poetry with distinctly French and imagist influences, and some of these early efforts saw print when he later achieved success. He also struggled to write plays, but it was not until one wet Sunday afternoon when he wrote three naturalistic short stories of Rhondda life that he discovered his true medium.

No one had seriously treated Welsh life in English prose until Caradoc Evans's *My People* (1915). This series of stories deals with the Welsh peasantry of Cardiganshire; its idiosyncratic rendition of Welsh into English is difficult to read today. Evans's stories point out that, far from living in a rustic arcadia, the peasants were venal, narrow, and avaricious. Though the book was well received in England, his message was unappreciated in his native country, and Evans became, for a time, the most hated man in Wales.

The French influences that Davies absorbed through his reading emerge in his later writings, and the dominant voice behind his earliest stories is that of Evans. Davies, however, writes about an English-speaking, newly industrialized proletariat. This was an undiscovered subject as far as English writing went, and it fitted well with a prevailing antimetropolitan mood then current among "advanced" writers, who mostly drew their inspiration from D. H. Lawrence.

Many of these writers contributed to the *New Coterie,* a magazine that Davies initially came upon during one of his trips to the West End. His first story, "A Gift of Death," appeared in the Spring 1926 issue, the second number of that magazine. Other stories by Davies ran in numbers three, four, and six, alongside works by Lawrence, Liam O'Flaherty, T. F. Powys, Aldous Huxley, and H. E. Bates. Contributors were unpaid, and the sixth edition was the last.

The magazine brought Davies in touch with the avant-garde of contemporary London arts and letters. It was distributed by Charles Lahr, a German-born bibliophile, bookseller, and small publisher, from his Progressive Bookshop at 68 Red Lion Street. Soon Davies found his way to the tiny premises, "little larger than a sentry box," and a warm friendship grew between the two men that lasted until 1971, when Davies wrote Lahr's *London Times* obituary. Through Lahr, Davies met Bates, James Hanley, Powys, and Hugh MacDiarmid, as well as Augustus John, Nina Hamnett, and Nancy Cunard. Lahr published the first collection of Davies's stories, *The Song of Songs and Other Stories* (1927), and typed the manuscript of *The Withered Root* (1927).

As a German, Lahr published his books under the imprint of E. Archer, his wife's name before marriage, to counter anti-German prejudice prevalent after World War I. There was a fashion at that time for limited signed editions, and one thousand copies of *The Song of Songs* were printed, with a hundred signed and nine hundred numbered. *Aaron,* a single story, was published as a pamphlet later that same year.

The public was appreciative, although Davies's mother refused to read his stories after "The Sisters" ran in the third number of the *New Coterie.* On the strength of his reception Davies was approached by "three young idealistic Cambridge graduates" who had just founded what was to be a short-lived publishing house, Holden. They offered an advance for Davies to write a novel. *The Withered Root,* a somewhat melodramatic study of a religious revivalist classically torn between the spirit and the flesh, was the result. Again, public response was favorable; the book was also published in America. On the strength of that and an advance on a new novel, Davies turned completely to writing. Except for a few months of war work, he never engaged in another profession. He avoided literary journalism, writing only about a half-dozen book reviews, usually unpaid and done as favors.

The real love of Davies's literary life was the short story rather than the more economically viable novel. In the introduction to *Collected Stories* (1955) he states:

> Short stories are a luxury which only those writers who fall in love with them can afford to cultivate. To such a writer they yield the purest enjoyment; they become a privately elegant craft allowing, within very strict confines, a wealth of idiosyncrasies. Compared with the novel, that great public park so often complete with draughty spaces, noisy brass bands and unsightly litter, the enclosed and quiet short story garden is of small

> importance, and never has been much more (Tchekoff compared with Dostoevsky; Maupassant with Balzac.) The short story gives the release of a day off, when something happened which one remembers with a smile or a start of interest, with a pang or a pause of fear. These are moods when Joyce's masterly tale *The Dead* makes *Ulysses* seem an obstreperous curiosity which one doesn't return to after the age of thirty; not many winters have passed when I have not read *The Dead* with undiminished admiration.

With royalties from his first novel and an advance on the second, Davies left London in 1928 for a spell in France. He traveled from Paris to Nice where, taking a furnished room, he began work on what were to be his second and fourth novels, *Rings on Her Fingers* (1930) and *The Red Hills* (1932). Liam O'Flaherty and his wife were living in nearby La Colle, and Davies stayed with them for some time, though the period was not happy. The couple were undergoing marital problems, and Mrs. O'Flaherty tried to irritate her husband by openly flirting with Davies, who eventually left in disgust. Relations with O'Flaherty — the two men had written mutually appreciative introductions for private-press editions of each other's stories — cooled considerably. Davies thinly fictionalized the episode thirty years later in a long story, "Tears, Idle Tears" (*The Darling of Her Heart,* 1958).

However, there was a more fortunate literary encounter:

> Dear Rhys Davies,
>
> Mr Lahr sent me your address. Would you care to come here and be my guest in this small and inexpensive hotel for a few days? Bandol is about 20 minutes on the Marseilles side of Toulon: 20 minutes from Toulon. My wife and I would be pleased if you came. I'm not sure quite how long we shall stay here — but anyhow ten days.
>
> Sincerely, D. H. Lawrence

A young writer with only one novel and a few short stories to his credit might have been overawed by such an invitation, but Davies was never impressed by literary or social grandeur. (Years later he was to become, for a while, a fringe member of the salon of the formidable Ivy Compton-Burnett. He soon ceased to attend: "She's sooo boring!" was his verdict.)

Davies and Lawrence took to one another. They had a mining-village background in common, and Lawrence saw Davies as one of the literary offspring he had engendered by his solitary rebellion.

He told Davies: "All you young writers have *me* to thank for what freedom you enjoy, even as things are – for being able to say much that you couldn't even hint at before I appeared. It was *I* who set about smashing down the barriers." However, he railed against the "passivity" of younger writers who were not doing enough to continue the work he had started. Lawrence wanted Davies to launch a satiric magazine to be called the "Squib" – to which Lawrence would be a contributor – that would "singe people's bottoms." Davies politely and effectively evaded this suggestion.

This was a crucial time for Lawrence. The Orioli edition of *Lady Chatterley's Lover* (1928), which he told Davies was his magnum opus, had been published in an expensive edition of one thousand copies but was already being widely pirated. Lawrence was desperate to find a publisher brave enough to bring out a cheap edition. While Lawrence's wife, Frieda, was away visiting her mother in Germany, Lawrence and Davies traveled to Paris in March 1929 to examine possibilities. From there Davies left for England carrying a manuscript of Lawrence's *Pansies* (1929), which had been seized by customs when posted. This venture into smuggling was successful, and the booklet was eventually published by Lahr.

There was only one quarrel during Lawrence and Davies's brief but eventful friendship. One evening Davies and Frieda went out to a café in Bandol and overstayed. When they came back, Lawrence flew into a jealous rage that soon burned itself out. In fact neither Lawrence nor O'Flaherty before him had any need to be jealous: Davies was homosexual. Anecdotal evidence from his brother Lewis suggests that he had been aware of his sexuality from an early age, and this may have had something to do with rejection of educational opportunity and his precipitate flight from the Rhondda. His demeanor was entirely masculine, and he favored entirely masculine men, often guardsmen. He maintained complete discretion about his homosexuality. Women were often attracted to him, much to his discomfiture, though he enjoyed women's company a great deal. "Women have been the main problem in my life," he complained to his brother in old age.

Many of Davies's sexual contacts were fleeting. He never wrote about homosexuality, even when, as in the case of his novel *The Painted King* (1954) – clearly based on the homosexual Ivor Novello – he might have done so safely in the third person. In Davies's elegantly composed if somewhat evasive memoir, *Print of a Hare's Foot* (1969), he finds it necessary to hint throughout at a heterosexual past. Perhaps the principal effect that his sexuality had on his writing was to permit him to concentrate on his art almost to the exclusion of everything else.

Davies came to reject much of his early work as journeyman stuff. *The Withered Root, Rings on Her Fingers,* and *Count Your Blessings* (1932) were dropped from his personal bibliography of novels. When he published his *Collected Stories,* he excised more than half of his output, including nearly all of his early work. The earliest story in the volume is "Arfon" (1931), a long piece about a village half-wit gulled by a slatternly girl whom he mistakenly believes is the one person in the community who cares for him and for whom he steals to buy presents. When he eventually realizes the truth, he strangles her, thus revenging himself not only on her but also, by proxy, on the community that has rejected and mistreated him:

> This was the end. His heart knew it was the end, and if only he could forget her face lying up there he thought he would know peace. He did not want to live any more. He had had enough of all that was done under the sky. Yet he continued to weep and sob, stumbling down. The hills lay in silence all about him. They looked magnificent in their eternal tawny sleep, under the high arch of the far skies. Such strength of silence and eternity they had, Arfon should have been eased as he stumbled and crawled in disordered weeping down to the houses of the people.

The story is illustrative of Davies's somber, naturalistic mode, which derived to some degree from Caradoc Evans. Yet Davies's intention was to "give some flesh tints to Anglo-Welsh writing" and to move beyond the "savagely bleak" Evans. He succeeded in this aim in another early story, "Revelation" (*A Pig in a Poke,* 1931), which also survived self-censorship. Here an innocent, frustrated miner who has never seen his wife unclothed is sent with a message to the house of the chief engineer of the pit. When he knocks at the door, the engineer's wife answers, completely naked:

> Gomer's tongue clave in astonishment to his mouth. The gaping silence lasted several moments. A naked woman stood before him, and then slowly, slowly retreated, her fist clenched in the cleft between her breasts.
> "Mr. . . . Mr. . . . Montague asked me . . . " stammered Gomer, and could not switch his rigid gaze from the apparition.
> How lovely she was!

The encounter has the eventual effect of improving his marriage to his straitlaced wife.

Davies was soon being taken seriously as a writer with a future. In 1932, a mere five years after his first work appeared in print, Megroz's *Rhys Davies: A Critical Sketch* was published. Although Davies's output during the 1930s was little short of titanic, financial security eluded him. For most of that period, and well into the 1940s, he owned little more than a small, but expensive, wardrobe and a few crates of books and papers. This did have the advantage of permitting a highly peripatetic existence, and it is difficult to say with any certainty quite where Davies was living for much of the decade.

For some of the time he lived with Vincent Wells, an older homosexual who was the director of a city brewing firm. Wells lived in a well-appointed house in the exclusive village of Henley-on-Thames, a riverside setting that forms the backdrop for some of Davies's stories. Wells is remembered as being reclusive, unconnected with the literary world, but wealthy. He drove a Daimler and retained a manservant. This arrangement lasted intermittently from the early 1930s until 1945, when the house caught fire, destroying many of Davies's papers. Wells retired to New Zealand, and the two men thereafter had little contact. For a time in the mid 1930s Davies shared a flat in Chalk Farm with an architect named Bevan, a friend of Wells.

However, Davies frequently lacked the modest wherewithal necessary to keep himself alive in London and sometimes returned to Clydach Vale, with which he maintained a love-hate relationship, to bury himself in his work. The new stories in his second collection, *Love Provoked* (1933), mark an advance toward a more mature style. In the introduction to his *Collected Stories* he states: "That instinct to *dive,* swift and agile, into the opening of a story holds, for me, half the technical art; one must not on any account loiter or brood in the first paragraph; be deep in the story's elements in a few seconds." Davies demonstrates this technique in the opening to "Daisy Matthews" (*Love Provoked*):

She was a small woman of thirty-three or thereabouts who looked as harmless and neat as a pet white mouse. Her little round eyes, bright and alert, and her swift pattering movements, as though she were always engaged on some nervous quest were mouselike too. But she was not negligible. She had a certain amount of natural prettiness, she read poetry and played her piano intelligently, and she had a passion for wearing expensive black furs. Living alone with a housekeeper in her villa on the hill, she had been courted by some of the most respected men in the place, men of position. Yet she couldn't bring herself to marriage.

The volume is still something of a ragbag, however, bringing together new stories with ones published earlier by private presses. Much of Davies's energy during the 1930s went into a loosely connected fictional trilogy that charts life in Clydach Vale from the days of the Welsh squirearchy through industrialization, industrial strife, economic boom, and finally the Depression. These novels – *Honey and Bread* (1935), *A Time to Laugh* (1937), and *Jubilee Blues* (1938) – serve as perhaps the most artistically expressed and least ideologically distorted studies of Rhondda life. *Jubilee Blues* is by far the best of Davies's Rhondda novels.

In the late 1920s a group including Davies, Bates, and the vorticist painter William Roberts was led on a nostalgic expedition around Germany by Lahr, ending up in his home village, Steinbockenheim. Davies witnessed the rise of Nazism with his customary fascinated detachment, and Germany was of sufficient interest for him to make a second trip there two years later. From those visits came the much-anthologized story "Cherry Blossom on the Rhine" (*The Things Men Do: Short Stories,* 1936), the closest that Davies came to overt political comment. His apparent apoliticism – Welsh writers tend to be expected to adopt either a Nationalist or Socialist stance – is possibly one of the reasons for his lack of native recognition. In fact he was privately a lifelong supporter of the Labour party. In a 1929 letter to Lahr, Davies comments: "Every night in my devotions I pray for a Labour Government." In his seventies Davies expressed support for the somewhat uninspiring Labour administration of James Callaghan. And (admittedly writing for Keidrych Rhys's magazine, *Wales*) he once remarked, "I support self-government for Wales." This was, however, his only recorded statement on the subject. Like his masters, Chekhov, Flaubert, and Guy de Maupassant, he did not view fiction as a soapbox for political oratory.

The relationship between Bates and Davies was never close, but it underwent a distinct chill when Bates wrote a harsh review of *Count Your Blessings* for the magazine *Everyman*. Bates felt that Davies had real talent but did not like the book, deeming it unworthy of its author, a view shared by Megroz. Indeed, Davies later dropped the book from his bibliography. At the time, however, he was irritated. On 10 March 1932 he wrote to Lahr from Clydach Vale:

Master Bates has had his opportunity at last. It's nice to have his tribute. The only thing that's provoking is that

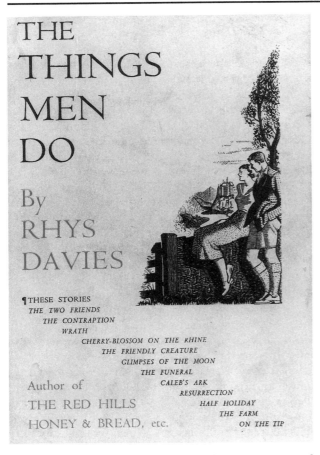

THE
THINGS
MEN
DO

By
RHYS
DAVIES

¶THESE STORIES
THE TWO FRIENDS
THE CONTRAPTION
WRATH
CHERRY-BLOSSOM ON THE RHINE
THE FRIENDLY CREATURE
GLIMPSES OF THE MOON
THE FUNERAL
CALEB'S ARK
RESURRECTION
HALF HOLIDAY
THE FARM
ON THE TIP

Author of
THE RED HILLS
HONEY & BREAD, etc.

Dust jacket for Davies's 1936 collection of short stories, most of which concern gentlewomen in straitened circumstances

grown-ups should be submitted to the printed opinion of such an adolescent, whose own books are so pallid and watery. He ought to be turned over and have his mean little bottom smacked.

Friendly, if epistolary, relations were not reestablished between Davies and Bates until the 1940s. Some of Davies's sensitivity to Bates's criticism may have sprung from the fact that *Count Your Blessings* was his first book to be published by a mainstream firm, Putnam. Lahr had published many of the early stories; others were published by small-scale or limited-edition presses. Holden, which had published *The Withered Root,* had rapidly gone bankrupt. *Rings on Her Fingers* had been published by Shaylor, ominously (or suspiciously) operating from the same address as Holden and soon suffering the same fate. *A Pig in a Poke* had been published by Joiner and Steele, which had a prestigious list but was something of a coterie publisher. For years Davies set his sights on Jonathan Cape to publish his work but never succeeded in having a manuscript

accepted there. Similar attempts at Gollancz proved fruitless. Putnam remained Davies's main publisher until 1936, when Dwye Evans persuaded him to join Heinemann's list. Heinemann thereafter published almost all of Davies's books, and Evans was Davies's editor until his retirement in the mid 1960s.

The Things Men Do is Davies's first fully realized book of short stories. The two previous volumes consist in part of old pieces, giving them a disjointed feel. All the stories in the third volume are fresh, and the flaws of the early work – the melodrama and the reliance on extreme situations for effect – are largely expunged. Extraordinary situations are sometimes used, but for comic effect, as in "Resurrection," in which a woman who has been laid out in a parlor for burial inconveniently comes to life:

> Half a day before the lid was to be screwed down on her, Meg rose in her coffin and faintly asked for a glass of water. Her two sisters were bustling about the room, tidying and dusting and admiring the flowers, and both, after a few moments of terrified shock, looked at the recently deceased with a bitter anger. Once again she was doing something improper.
> "Water!" stuttered Bertha. "Go on with you now. What do you want with water?" Gathering strength at the sound of her own voice, she went on sternly and as if speaking to a nuisance: "Lie back thee, lie back. Dead you are."

Despite the title the book is almost exclusively concerned with women locked into a dignified respectability that they try to maintain in the face of poverty; drunken, ne'er-do-well husbands; and general backbiting. As in "Resurrection" the dynamic often revolves around three sisters. Although the Rhondda of Davies's youth was a male-dominated society based on heavy industry and the masculine camaraderie of the pit, it is not surprising that he chose to portray that society principally from a woman's viewpoint. Aside from the female-dominated nature of his family circumstances, as a general assistant in his father's shop his contact with the inhabitants of the valley was primarily with women. Men worked but in general did not shop. The corner store was also a meeting place where gossip was recounted, and Davies certainly absorbed a great deal of this.

The Things Men Do is also the first volume in which Davies's wry humor comes to the fore. If he set out to add fleshy tints to the bleakness of Evans's stories, he also succeeded in adding humor, a quality often absent in Evans's work. Yet Davies was not oblivious to the ravages of the Depression, as a story such as "On the Tip" reveals. *The Things Men Do* established Davies as the foremost Welsh prose writer, and, when the publisher Jarrolds wanted to commission a book on Wales for its My Country series, it turned to Davies.

My Wales (1937) is a substantial travelogue executed with Davies's usual humanity and surprising erudition. It was a matter of great pride to him that he was "100% pure-blooded Welshman," and, though he chose not to live in the country, this did not diminish his affection for it. His feelings toward his homeland are more succinctly expressed in his answers to a 1946 editorial questionnaire in *Wales:*

1. *Do you consider yourself an Anglo-Welsh writer?*
No. I am only a writer. Does one (if I may make so bold) think of Henry James, T. S. Eliot as Anglo-American writers? Down with passports to Art!

2. *For whom do you write?*
Primarily, myself. But if persons, of either sex, wish to look over my shoulder at what I am writing, I do not discourage them; in fact, I positively welcome them.

3. *What is your opinion of the relationship between Literature and Society?*
The first attempts to lead the second into the Promised Land. A carrot held to the ass. A whip of the finest steel and of scorpions, laid to the obstinate torpid back. An enticing song to woo a weary dulled creature into brilliancy. A medicine for the sick. A vision for the blind.

4. *Should "Anglo-Welsh" Literature express a Welsh attitude to life and affairs, or should it merely be a literature "about" Welsh things?*
Neither consciously. If a writer thinks of his work along these lines it tends to become too parochial, narrow. But if he is Welsh by birth, upbringing, and selects a Welsh background and characters for his work, an essence of Wales should be in the work, giving it a national "slant" or flavour. But no flag waving. A curse on flag waving.

5. *Do you believe that a sense of Welsh nationhood is more consistent with one particular attitude to life and affairs than any other?*
But what "particular attitudes?" I find this question indefinite; these "attitudes" should be defined by the questioner. Offhand, I should say that Welsh nationhood is consistent with an attitude of minding one's business, self-sufficiency, a certain elemental instinct and appreciation of the poetry of life; vitality, humour, an attitude containing a vision of the small range but intense within this restricted orbit. (I am not sure that this small range is not advantageous and is the reason why the Welsh people, as a whole, seem so alive, their energies not dissipated into the world's spacious grandiosity and its external problems.)

Davies was the first Welsh writer to take on London as a full-blooded literary professional, but in the 1930s he was joined by a second whose notoriety and fame were to exceed his own by far. Davies's attitude toward Dylan Thomas always had a certain ambivalence. Like most writers Davies began as a poet (and some fairly creditable verses, executed in a pastiche of imagism and early Eliot, can be found in fugitive magazines), but he abandoned the form once he discovered his talent for prose. Nonetheless, he admired the genre of poetry above other literary forms, and he admired Thomas's work. Davies observes in *My Wales:* "The young poet, Dylan Thomas, another dark horse, whose furious wealth of imagery is as wild and fearsome as a Welsh preacher involved in transports of *hwyl,* promises that a considerable poet has again come out of Wales."

Davies was not a great pub socializer, but he was not a recluse either, and he sometimes relaxed in the literary pubs of Soho that Thomas frequented. While they never quarreled, it soon became obvious that the two men had little in common temperamentally, and they had little to do with one another over the years. Davies's dandified appearance gave the impression of prosperity, though he often must have been much poorer than Thomas. Davies's background had instilled in him certain petit bourgeois virtues: thrift, a horror of debt, and an insistence on paying his own way. Thomas violated all these with his spendthrift manner, which was doubly spendthrift with others' money.

In an interview with D. A. Callard, Fred Urquhart recounts an amusing anecdote of when he and Davies were drinking in a London pub. "Oh, God, here's Dylan," said Urquhart. The two men scanned the clientele, realizing that they were the only acquaintances of Thomas in the pub and that this meant they would have to spend the evening buying drinks for the allegedly impecunious poet. They then fled by the side door before Thomas could see them. Davies was nevertheless fascinated by Thomas's revival of bohemianism in the grand French manner (though preferably at a distance) and included an affectionate portrait of Thomas in his 1957 novel, *The Perishable Quality.*

The onset of World War II threw Davies into deep depression. The death of his brother Jack during the closing weeks of World War I affected Davies deeply. "He would always clam up when the subject of his brother was mentioned," Urquhart recalls, adding, somewhat in understatement, "Rhys was not the sort of man who bares his soul." Davies claimed that he wrote nothing for a year after the outbreak of World War II. This is unlikely because a well-researched biography of Danish adventurer

Jorgen Jorgensen, *Sea Urchin,* was published in 1940. Despite the fact that he was thirty-nine years old and had been categorized 4-F (the lowest medical category), he was not exempted from military service and received a call-up in 1941. His great friend Raymond Marriott and Lewis Davies had both become conscientious objectors, but Davies decided to do his bit, which proved fairly small indeed. He was sent to work at the Ministry of Information and lasted four months, somehow engineering a discharge on medical grounds. This was the only post he held after he gave up gentleman's outfitting to become a writer. In his self-penned entry for *Twentieth Century Authors* (1955 edition) the four months are expanded into the years 1939 to 1942.

Davies had an odd, diverse set of friends, one of whom, Louis Quinain, was a "literary policeman." Davies met Quinain in 1937 and was staying with him and his wife when he received his call-up. He completed his last Rhondda novel, *Tomorrow to Fresh Woods* — a roman à clef about the maturation of a young grocer's boy with literary inclinations — at their house. Davies did, however, return to Rhondda in some of his short fiction. In 1942 he took a room in the house of Mrs. Waugh-Brown, "a faded actress, purply with drink." He occupied it until 1954.

One tragicomic figure whom Davies met during these years was a namesake, Colyn Davies, an orphan who had been conscripted then discharged from the army after a breakdown and suicide attempt. He drifted into Soho and encountered Davies, who evidently found him attractive, at the Wheatsheaf pub. After living with him for a while Rhys found him a room in a half boardinghouse/half brothel on the same street as his own, and he frequently lent Colyn money to attend theatrical auditions. Colyn's tale is told in one of Davies's most celebrated stories, "Boy with a Trumpet," the title story of his 1949 collection.

When Colyn Davies was interviewed in 1991, he said that the story was substantially true, with little fictionalization. A similar basis of true life can be detected in many of Davies's stories. "Fear" (*Boy with a Trumpet*), about a young man's encounter with a strange Indian on a train, actually happened to BBC radio producer Philip Burton, best known as the adoptive father of actor Richard Burton. Philip collaborated with Davies on several radio projects. The producer recounted the incident to Davies, who turned it into the story. Among Davies's papers at the National Library of Wales, drafts of stories are frequently accompanied by the newspaper clippings that provided their genesis.

Even so apparently fanciful a story as "Resurrection" grew from a conversation that Davies overheard in which two women recounted the seemingly miraculous recovery of the victim of what appeared to be an irreversible coma. One of the women came home to find her up and cooking in the kitchen as if nothing had happened. "The Funeral" (*The Things Men Do*), in which two girls inter a doll in their garden, was based, according to Oonagh Lahr, on an actual incident involving Oonagh and her sister. Davies was, first and foremost, a naturalistic writer who seems to have strayed little from real life in order to garner his material.

The war years — despite rationing, the Blitz, and conscription — were good ones for many authors. Although paper was rationed and the quality of book production was low, there was a great public hunger for printed material, and magazines, which were exempt from paper rationing, particularly flourished. These years and their immediate aftermath saw Davies's most productive period in the field of the short story: *A Finger in Every Pie* (1942), *The Trip to London* (1946), and *Boy with a Trumpet.* During these years his style reached maturity, a fact surely not unconnected with the circumstance that the war created an enthusiastic audience for the short story.

One magazine that fell victim to the war was Keidrych Rhys's *Wales.* Rhys was an extraordinary figure, part idealistic impresario and part con man, who, in his early twenties, had decided to set up a metropolitan forum for "Anglo-Welsh" writing. Wales had no focal point for its English-language writers. Cardiff, not then a capital city, was evidently too cosmopolitan and Anglicized, and individual sparks of literary endeavor were scattered in isolation. If Wales had a literary capital, it was London, where the London Welsh still operated a relatively closed community with its own newspaper, rugby team, social institutions, and chapels. Davies characteristically avoided all of these with the exception of Will Griff's Welsh Bookshop, to which he was a frequent visitor.

Rhys mananged to co-opt both Davies and Thomas into supporting his venture. Thomas co-edited one of the last numbers of the magazine in 1939, before it temporarily folded, and Davies became an irregular contributor. The magazine did not pay its writers, and Davies, unlike many of the contributors, was a full-time professional writer. Most of his contributions during the magazine's history — a second series ran from 1943 to 1959 — tended to be labors of love probably unpublishable elsewhere rather than his more salable work. Of exceptional interest is a series of articles, *From My Notebook* (he is not known to have kept such a notebook, nor did he keep a diary), in which he ruminates on writing techniques and specifically on the creation of women characters by men. He also contributed a memoir of his great friend Nina Hamnett, the queen of London bohemia, and a well-researched article on his great hero Dr. William Price of Llantrisant, self-proclaimed Druid and public cremator of his own son, whom he had named Jesus Christ.

An odd quirk of Davies's character was that, although urbane and mild-mannered himself, he was drawn to extremes in other people. In the postwar years his closest woman friend was Anna Kavan — novelist, short-story writer, and heroin addict — of whom the description "socially difficult" would be an understatement. Davies was one of the few who managed to stay on friendly terms with Count Potocki of Montalk, self-proclaimed heir to the Polish throne, who strode Soho in a wine-colored cape and shoulder-length hair. He had been the subject of a notorious obscenity trial in the early 1930s when his booklet, felicitously titled *Here Lies John Penis,* had been prosecuted at the Old Bailey and its author sentenced to six months' imprisonment. "Rhys could handle these mad people," his brother Lewis commented with some amazement. In his postwar *Who's Who* entry Davies gave his recreation as "Collecting ruined characters."

Davies's next novel, *Under the Rose* (1940), marked a move away from the Rhondda landscapes to an unspecified locality in west Wales. In fact it is the Teifi Valley in Dyfed, the region from which both of his parents' families originated and to which he referred as "my West Wales." The theme of the vengeful woman runs through *Under the Rose* and much of Davies's other fiction. (Davies was an enthusiastic operagoer obsessed with Maria Callas; it is hardly surprising that his favorite operas were Richard Strauss's *Salome* [1905] and *Elektra* [1909].) *A Finger in Every Pie,* perhaps his most fully realized book of short stories, followed in 1942.

In these stories Davies's occasionally somber vision combines with his natural wit and irony to create an individual brand of black humor. The humor surrounding death and its attendant rituals is the subject of "Mourning for Ianto" and "The Dark World." In the latter story two bored adolescent boys pass their evenings by going around the valley paying their respects to corpses, which, according to custom, were generally laid out in the parlor prior to burial. In a twist that resembles the realization of the cynical hero in Nathanael West's

Miss Lonelyhearts (1933) — the realization that he is partaking in real human tragedy and not a macabre joke — dawns on the more sensitive of the pair:

> "Shall we look for more?" Jim said. A roused, unappeased appetite was in his voice.
>
> Thomas leaned against the wet wall of a house. Something broke in him. He put up his arm, buried his head in it, and cried. He cried in terror, in fear and in grief. There was something horrible in the dark world. A soft howling whine came out of his throat. Jim, ashamed, passed from wonder into contempt.
>
> "What's up with you!" he jeered. "You seen plenty of 'em before, haven't you? . . . Shut up," he hissed angrily. "There's someone coming." And he gave Thomas a push.

The landscape of most of the stories is recognizably that of Clydach Vale: Joyce's claim that Dublin could be reconstructed brick by brick from *Ulysses* (1922) is doubly true of Davies's rendering of his native valley in many stories. The volume ends, however, with a long story set on the Riviera, "Queen of the Côte d'Azur," which thinly fictionalizes some of the exotic friends he made there: a German masochist who liked being flogged by muscular young men and the apparently prim Englishwoman with a taste for "rough trade." In this story Davies seems to underline the fact that he was not confined by his often localized subjects.

In 1944 Davies achieved his solitary commercial success with a novel, *The Black Venus,* which revolves around the west Walian custom of courting in bed, a practice roughly similar to New Englanders' bundling. Davies's knowledge of west Walian life was sketchy, and his ties were emotional and imaginative rather than actual. He spoke no Welsh except for what he may have acquired by osmosis, and the genesis of the book seems to have been literary rather than experiential. According to Reginald Reynolds's eccentric history *Beds* (1952), *The Black Venus* was suggested by a paragraph in William Wirt Sykes's *British Goblins* (1880).

It is highly unlikely that the custom was ever used as Davies's protagonist employs it — as a means to test the suitability of prospective husbands — and this led to some feelings of umbrage from representatives of the society that he depicts. The feelings were not shared by the general public, and *The Black Venus* was Davies's only book to be republished as a mass-market paperback. Perhaps indicative of its author's psychology — Davies's relationships with women seem to have been loving but nonsexual — the book ends with a celibate marriage.

The Trip to London, Davies's 1946 volume of short fiction, marks a move away from Welsh themes to stories set in London and Henley-on-Thames. Davies's prose style, always adept at rendering dialogue, seems to acquire a fresh tautness in scene setting, as in this passage from "Orestes":

> A cone of soiled yellow lit the garage. The capped man in the office was maddeningly torpid. But, yes, perhaps a cab would be back in a few minutes. He waited at the entrance, standing under a naked electric bulb stuck out from the brick wall, his finger nails plucking at mortar until the quick burned. Two lightly drunk sailors waltzed past, arms entwined, fulfilment in their supple bodies; they were from another race, another kingdom whose language he could never speak now. The cab drew up, a scarecrow of a young man got out; and as he talked his Adam's apple leaped ludicrously and his eyes, glowing and consumptive, protruded insecurely. To be driven home by this death's head!

During much of 1946 Davies exiled himself, in the company of Urquhart, to a remote cottage in the Chiltern Hills where he worked on a dramatic adaptation of *Under the Rose.* Some of Davies's stories had been adapted for the stage musical *Jenny Jones,* which had a short run in the West End in 1944. The adaptation, with which Davies had nothing to do, was so loose as to render the stories unrecognizable. However, Davies loved the world of the theater and was determined to become a successful dramatist.

He had been an urbanite too long to adapt to rustic life. "The countryside drove Rhys mad," Urquhart recalls in an interview, adding that Davies slipped away into town for weekends, then for longer periods, and finally removed himself entirely. Thereafter he was, except for a brief period in Brighton, a committed Londoner, rarely venturing out of town.

The Dark Daughters (1947), a novel of womanly revenge set in the world of the London Welsh, was followed by *Boy with a Trumpet,* the last book of the trinity that marks Davies's great period of short-story writing. The heyday of the magazine was over. The following year even Cyril Connolly's *Horizon* ceased publication. Davies began to look elsewhere for markets, and one story, "The Dilemma of Catherine Fuschias" (*Boy with a Trumpet*), was first published in the *New Yorker.* But the commercial possibilities of the short story were withering rapidly, and Davies had no income other than that generated by his writing.

His short-story output, though never diminishing in quality, became more intermittent over the coming decades. The immutable nature of Davies's talent – that, having once discovered his genius for short-story writing, he almost simultaneously discovered a style and set of themes to which he adhered throughout his career – is demonstrated by his inclusion in *Boy with a Trumpet* of "One of Norah's Early Days," first published in 1935. Although Davies shifted preoccupations and tautened his style, there is an evenness of quality that runs through all his output.

Marianne (1951), a novel of female revenge set in what appears to be the industrial conurbation of Port Talbot, was the beginning of a new venture for Davies. The book came to the attention of Philip Burton. Burton had an impressive record at BBC Wales: he had commissioned "Return Journey" (1947) from Thomas and had even written a five-minute pastiche to extend it when it proved too short. Burton had taught in Port Talbot and was drawn to the novel, which he says was also based on a true incident. He arranged a highly successful radio adaptation, and he and Davies became great friends. However, their collaboration ended when Burton left for the United States in 1954. There were no further major collaborations for Davies, and he never developed a rapport with another producer as he had with Burton.

The Painted King – a novel loosely based on the rise of Ivor Novello, who had once dominated the West End with his light musicals – followed. This might have been a chance for Davies to explore homosexuality as a theme through the medium of his hero, but, apart from the most oblique hints, the author did not deal with it. Davies's friends recall that in the late 1940s he had a relationship of several years' duration with a Scots guardsman called Dodie. The intellectual gulf between the pair seems to have been the stumbling block to any fruitful relationship. Urquhart remembers Davies having many one-night stands, almost invariably with guardsmen, about whom the author seems to have had an erotic fixation.

With the death of Mrs. Waugh-Brown in 1954, the house in which Davies lodged passed into the hands of her lover, a man he disliked. He took a flat in Brighton; however, it was expensive, and he needed a roommate. In 1952 he had become friendly with a young Scot with show-business aspirations who was then busing tables at Lyons Corner House, where Davies breakfasted with clockwork regularity. The young man, Ron Heggie, and Davies began to share the flat.

When questioned by Callard in 1991, Heggie recalled Davies's idiosyncrasies and rigorously disciplined work routine in a letter:

He was a man of habit. After lunch . . . 1 p.m. till 5 . . . work. Always shopped at Sainsbury's . . . never missed Selfridges Sale . . . "very good for bed linen" . . . Even to his writing. First draft in pencil on lined pads. Next day correct/alter. Copy on to identical pad. . . . Continue on first pad. Five o'clock . . . Earl Grey tea and digestive biscuits. . . . He was a "bed-sit" type. Even to his studio flat in Russell Square. He seemed to prefer to live, work and sleep in one room.

Davies did not discuss his work at all, a fact commented on by other friends as well as Heggie, who also recalls that Davies would never go with him to the beach: "He hated the sun."

At this time Davies's play, *No Escape* (1955), which he had worked on in 1946 while living with Urquhart at Tring, went on a tour of the provinces. Despite his love of the theater and his self-declared theatrical ambitions, he seemed to have no real dramatic sense, and the play had been completed only with the aid of a collaborator, Archibald Batty. However, it had a full provincial tour, conventionally the prelude to a West End opening, and starred Flora Robson as a frustrated spinster and a young Miriam Karlin as a London prostitute.

Brighton was the last stop before London, and Davies went to see the play for the first time there. After the performance he went backstage and was flatly told by Robson that she refused to take the play to the West End. The character she played was somewhat unappealing, and throughout the tour Karlin, who made a spectacular stage entrance by walking down the theater aisle and onto the stage, had received all the good notices. This was the end of Davies's theatrical ambitions, an event he seems to have accepted with his customary equanimity, though all his friends were furious, as was Karlin. Many years later in an interview with Callard she described Robson as "a real bitch."

The friendship with Heggie throws a curious sidelight on Davies's sexuality. In a letter to Callard, Heggie remarks:

In all the years I knew him I never saw any indication of sexual activity whatsoever. He hinted at homosexuality in his youth and that the *Boy with the Trumpet* was someone he had known many years before. However, I now firmly believe that, by the time I met him, he was completely asexual. He never once made any overtures towards me nor to any of my friends who met him.

Yet Davies constantly gave the impression to his friends that he and Heggie were lovers. It is interesting that Davies also gave the impression to Heggie that he and the "Boy with the Trumpet" – Colyn Davies – were also lovers. Colyn admits that Da-

Davies in 1937

vies once made a pass at him, and he was certainly aware that his interest was more than charitable, but, once the advance was repulsed, Rhys accepted the situation and made no more of it. Yet again he led his friends to believe that he and Colyn were lovers. Shortly after knowing Rhys, both Colyn and Heggie married and had families, as did Dodie, so the extent of their involvement with Davies is unclear.

At about this time both of Davies's parents died within a few months of each other, and he received the bulk of their estate because, alone of the five siblings, he had spared his parents the expense of higher education. When he moved back to London in 1956, he took a studio flat at 15 Russell Court in the heart of Bloomsbury. The locale was central and the address prestigious, but the flat itself, variously described by visitors as "hideously cramped" and "a broom cupboard," was a minute living space. Nonetheless, it suited Davies's needs and was to remain his home until his death.

Publication of his *Collected Stories* in 1955 refocused public attention on Davies's mastery of the

short-fiction form. The volume was slightly mis-
titled, since it was a self-selection containing about
half of Davies's work: that which had survived his
rigorous self-censorship. He followed it in 1958
with a new collection, *The Darling of Her Heart and
Other Stories.* Even after so long an absence from the
form, Davies displays no diminution of quality in
the volume. Seven of the nine stories have a Welsh
setting, but, unlike the early stories, there is a
marked move to west Walian rusticity and petit
bourgeois characters. The Rhondda was becoming
a faded memory for Davies.

He did return to it in one of his most cleverly
plotted stories, "A Spot of Bother," in which Ormond, a young miner whose wife has left him, is
photographed in a compromising position with a
prostitute whom he has picked up on a night out in
Cardiff. When a blackmailer comes to his house
with the photographs, Ormond relies on the fact
that his wife is extremely nearsighted when showing
her the photographs, which he passes off as portrait
shots. The blackmailer flees and is captured by Ormond and his friends; the photographs are re-
trieved. When Ormond returns to the house, he discovers that his wife is not as nearsighted as he had
thought and that she had played along with his deception. After she strikes him with a stocking full of
dried beans, they quarrel and an amicable truce is
made:

> The dew was finally off the garden. They
> recognised it. Ormond crossed to her, took her shoul-
> ders, turned her round from the table. She had to be
> rediscovered. He gave her a shake. A bean fell out of his
> tight-knit curls and dropped into her bodice of flowered
> voile. Two pairs of tears also fell from behind her
> glasses.
> "Let me find my bean," he begged.
> Later, tidily with hand-brush and pan, he swept up
> all the beans from the floor. This was exceptional. In
> Bylau men are not much addicted to domestic jobs, and
> Ormond in particular, always out with the boys, was
> not partial to them. There was a vague aspect of compli-
> ant reformation about his figure as he stooped to the
> task.

Davies's fading memory of the Rhondda is
dealt with most poignantly in his 1957 novel, *The
Perishable Quality,* in which an aging but still attractive woman who has immersed herself in
Bloomsbury bohemia returns to the town of her
youth, Bylau, pursued by a younger lover. She is
amazed by the changes in the town, as Davies must
have been when he visited it for the funerals of his
parents. He never again used it as a subject for his
fiction.

His 1960 novel, *Girl Waiting in the Shade,* marks
a tautening of style and a willingness to explore
more perverse subject matter. The underlying
theme is incest, suggested rather than depicted, and,
though the book has a border Welsh backdrop, locality is secondary to character. Elements of the
protagonist, Lotte Curlow, are clearly derived from
Kavan, the novelist and short-story writer who was
perhaps Davies's closest friend during his later
years. Like Davies a solitary – and, by virtue of
years of heroin use – asexual person, Kavan formed
a curious bond with Davies that was only to end
with her death in 1968. Davies was named as her
coheir and executor. According to Lewis Davies,
Rhys did not privately admire Kavan's rather cere-
bral, experimental fiction (though he edited and introduced two posthumous volumes of her works).
Lewis believes that Kavan did not have much admiration for Davies's fiction either. The true nature of
this unusual friendship is lost, since, seeing each
other frequently and privately, they wrote only the
most perfunctory letters.

The 1960s were not productive years for Davies, but they were not unlucrative. With the collapse of most paying British magazines interested in
his kind of short story, Davies looked to America
for a market. During these years he had four stories
published in the *New Yorker,* including "The Chosen
One," which received the 1966 Edgar Award for
crime fiction. This was the title story of his 1967
collection, his last book of short stories and one of
his best. Whereas most writers experience a falling
off or diminution of intensity in their later efforts,
degenerate into whimsy and coziness as H. E. Bates
did, or lapse into repetition and self-parody, the
quality of Davies's work improved as he was released, by literary earnings and by legacy, from the
necessity of having to publish what he considered
second-rate work.

In "The Chosen One" a middle-aged spinster,
a recurring figure in Davies's fiction, deliberately
goads a young man into killing her, knowing, as an
act of revenge, that he will live to suffer the consequences while she achieves release. Odd, perverse
relationships run through nearly all the stories in
the book. In his old age Davies struck out to explore the more arcane human passions that had always fascinated him. *Print of a Hare's Foot,* a charming but uninformative memoir, followed in 1969.
Readers should bear in mind that, in addition to
Davies's evasions, the chronology of the book is extremely haphazard. For instance, his time in Maida
Vale, which did not begin until 1942, is treated as if
it occurred during the 1930s.

In 1968 Davies received the Order of the British Empire for services to literature. The year was marred, however, by the death of Kavan, though he was financially enriched by half of her estate. Welsh writer Glyn Jones remembers seeing Davies several weeks after her death and finding him still shattered by the event. Kavan, a heroin addict for more than forty years and a veteran of at least six full-blown suicide attempts, had been living one day at a time for many years: Davies had rescued and hospitalized her after two deliberate overdoses. However, the shock was not lessened. Graham Samuel, a friend of Davies, recalls in a letter to Callard: "I remember very vividly indeed the 'watershed' effect Anna's death had on his life."

Davies's 1971 novel, *Nobody Answered the Bell,* is a claustrophobic story of lesbian passion and murder set in a seaport town that is identifiably Brighton. Brief, taut, and perverse, it continues the fictional exploration, begun with *Girl Waiting in the Shade,* of unusual forms of human passion and experience. This theme is carried through his last novel, *Honeysuckle Girl* (1975).

Whatever he may have felt privately about Kavan's writing, Davies executed his duties as literary heir by editing two volumes of her short stories. He was asked by her agent, David Higham, if he could write a biography, but Davies told him that, even after many years of friendship, he did not know enough. However, the suggestion led to *Honeysuckle Girl,* which examines the life of a middle-class heroin addict and the collapse of her marriage.

The subject matter of much of his later fiction must have disturbed Davies's aging readership, though at this stage he was no longer dependent on them for an income. In addition to previous legacies, he received a large sum in the mid 1970s on the death of his friend Louise Taylor. An American by birth, she had been reared in Paris and had become the adoptive daughter and heir to Alice B. Toklas, companion to Gertrude Stein. Taylor had lived a typical expatriate literary life, had known Robert Graves in Majorca, and had come to England and married Red Taylor, a painter some twenty years her junior. They had set up a salon of sorts in Chelsea, and she had become especially close to Davies. In the mid 1950s the Taylors had left London for various country addresses, and Davies's relationship with Louise had often been epistolary rather than personal. Despite their age gap, Red Taylor had predeceased his wife, and Davies found himself, in his midseventies, with a legacy of sixty thousand pounds. He pondered a world tour; he pondered visiting Philip Burton in the United States. Yet he did nothing: his health was beginning to fail, and the stress of the long years of self-imposed discipline was starting to show.

Davies had become friendly with some younger writers, including Francis King, who recalls how, while crossing one of London's bridges one evening, Davies was struck by a panic attack and could be moved only by having both his hands held and being led across. King believes that, in his last years, Davies ventured no farther than Russell Square, where he would sit on one of the benches when the weather was fine.

A lifelong smoker and the victim of increasingly severe bronchial attacks, Davies died of lung cancer at University College Hospital on 21 August 1978. Apart from family, the only people present at the funeral were his old friend Marriott and Keidrych Rhys and his wife. After a brief secular service his ashes were scattered in the rose gardens of Golders Green crematorium.

The apparent solitude of Davies's death mirrored what had been a constant in his life. He had lived most of it alone; maintained rigorous, clockwork discipline; and pursued his vocation with an almost frightening single-mindedness, eschewing most of the comforts — a regular partner and some security of income and residence — without which life might be unbearable for many people. He did not even turn to drink, which has sustained and stymied so many Celtic talents. "It just doesn't work for me," he once said, though he always drank in moderation.

He also lacked the support of a literary group or coterie. The Lahr group was a disparate set of individuals who soon went their separate ways. After his meeting with Lawrence, Davies found himself in the drawing room of Lady Ottoline Morrell, and, had he been career-minded, he might have inveigled his way into the Bloomsbury set. All his life Davies avoided cliques, political groups, and camp followings. Generally he seems to have been unimpressed by the work of most of his contemporaries — even Lawrence receives only faint praise — turning instead for his inspiration to the nineteenth-century Russian and French masters. Though he frequented the Fitzrovian literary pubs of the 1930s and 1940s, he was an observer rather than a participant in that extraordinary effusion of bohemia. The Welsh never took him to heart; he had been in London too long for that.

His sexuality — which seems to have revolved around casual, often mercenary, contacts with guardsmen on the one hand and romantic, apparently platonic friendships with young men on the other – might almost have been designed to facilitate a huge literary output uninterrupted by emotional or domestic upset. "Was Davies ever in love?" Peter Wyndham Allen, an old friend, was asked. "Rhys Davies never loved anyone but Rhys Davies," he replied.

This may have been true, but what Davies truly loved about himself was his writing, and it was to this that he dedicated his life. The stature of his novels is open to debate, but he demonstrates development from the early novels, with their Victorian overhangs of melodrama and unlikely coincidence, to the later ones, which exhibit the tautness and economy of his best short stories. In this form he was on surer footing when dealing with his familiar Rhondda world rather than his imaginative, fanciful renderings of west Walian life.

In the field of short fiction Davies appears to have sprung up fully fledged. Even though he is often concerned with a volatile industrial milieu rather than the settled agrarian world of many of his contemporaries, his stories have a timelessness rare in what is, in effect, proletarian writing. The best of his stories will stand comparison with anything written in the English language during the twentieth century, and it is unfortunate that they are, at present, too little known.

Bibliography:

John Gawsworth, *Ten Contemporaries: Notes Toward Their Definitive Bibliography* (London: Benn, 1932).

References:

G. F. Adam, *Three Contemporary Anglo-Welsh Novelists: Jack Jones, Rhys Davies and Hilda Vaughan* (Bern: Franke, 1948?);

R. L. Megroz, *Rhys Davies: A Critical Sketch* (London: Foyle, 1932);

David Rees, *Rhys Davies* (Cardiff: University of Wales Press, 1975).

Papers:

Davies's papers are divided among the Harry Ransom Humanities Research Center, University of Texas at Austin; the National Library of Wales, Aberystwyth; and the Sterling Library, University of London.

Further source material for this entry is derived from interviews conducted by the author and correspondence with the author, who is grateful to Philip Burton, A. L. Davies, Colyn Davies, Ron Heggie, Miriam Karlin, Francis King, Oonagh Lahr, Graham Samuel, and Fred Urquhart for their cooperation.

John Fowles

(31 March 1926 –   )

David W. Endicott
Ball State University

See also the Fowles entry in *DLB 14: British Novelists Since 1960: Part 1.*

BOOKS: *The Collector* (Boston: Little, Brown, 1963; London: Cape, 1963);

The Aristos: A Self-Portrait in Ideas (Boston: Little, Brown, 1964; London: Cape, 1965; revised edition, London: Cape, 1968; Boston: Little, Brown, 1970);

The Magus (Boston: Little, Brown, 1965; London: Cape, 1966; revised edition, Boston: Little, Brown, 1977; London: Cape, 1977);

The French Lieutenant's Woman (Boston: Little, Brown, 1969; London: Cape, 1969);

Poems (New York: Ecco, 1973; Toronto: Macmillan, 1973);

The Ebony Tower (Boston: Little, Brown, 1974; London: Cape, 1974);

Shipwreck, text by Fowles and photographs by the Gibsons of Scilly (London: Cape, 1974; Boston: Little, Brown, 1975);

Daniel Martin (Boston: Little, Brown, 1977; London: Cape, 1977);

Islands, text by Fowles and photographs by Fay Godwin (Boston: Little, Brown, 1978; London: Cape, 1978);

The Tree, text by Fowles and photographs by Frank Horvat (Boston: Little, Brown, 1979; London: Aurum, 1979);

The Enigma of Stonehenge, text by Fowles and photographs by Barry Brukoff (New York: Summit, 1980; London: Cape, 1980);

Mantissa (London: Cape, 1982; Boston: Little, Brown, 1982);

A Short History of Lyme Regis (Boston: Little, Brown, 1982);

A Maggot (London: Cape, 1985; Boston: Little, Brown, 1985);

Lyme Regis Camera (Boston: Little, Brown, 1990).

OTHER: "Notes on an Unfinished Novel," in *Afterwords: Novelists on Their Novels,* edited by

photograph by Jacob Sutton

Thomas McCormack (New York: Harper & Row, 1969), pp. 160–175;

Sabine Baring-Gould, *Mehalah: A Story of the Salt Marshes,* introduction, glossary, and appendix by Fowles (London: Chatto & Windus, 1969);

Henri Alain-Fournier, *The Wanderer,* afterword by Fowles (New York: New American Library, 1971);

Sir Arthur Conan Doyle, *The Hound of the Baskervilles,* foreword and afterword by Fowles (London: John Murray & Cape, 1974);

73

Piers Brendon, *Hawker of Morwenstow: Portrait of a Victorian Eccentric,* foreword by Fowles (London: Cape, 1975);

"Hardy and the Hag," in *Thomas Hardy After Fifty Years,* edited by Lance St. John Butler (London: Macmillan, 1977), pp. 28–42;

"The Man and the Island," in *Steep Holm — A Case History in the Study of Evolution* (London: Kenneth Allsop Memorial Trust, 1978), pp. 14–22;

Marie de France, *The Lais of Marie de France,* foreword by Fowles (New York: Dutton, 1978);

Harold Pinter, *The French Lieutenant's Woman: A Screenplay,* foreword by Fowles (Boston: Little, Brown, 1981).

TRANSLATIONS: Charles Perrault, *Cinderella* (London: Cape, 1974; Boston: Little, Brown, 1976);

Claire de Durfort, *Ourika,* with introduction and epilogue by Fowles (Austin, Tex.: W. Thomas Taylor, 1977).

John Fowles has consistently distanced himself from the middle-class English society that was his familial lot and a source of much resentment toward his father. Now living in a sort of self-imposed exile in the Dorset town of Lyme Regis, Fowles has bound himself to the artistic aesthetics of innovative, naturalistic writing. Yet this image seems to conflict with that of Fowles as the author whose novels have sold millions of copies and whose collection of short fiction, *The Ebony Tower* (1974), was a best-seller in the United States. Three of his novels have been made into motion pictures, thus heightening the image of the public author in conflict with the private artist. In "The Enigma" (*The Ebony Tower*) John Marcus Fielding, a Tory member of Parliament, is described in terms that might apply to Fowles: "He feels more and more like this minor character in a bad book. . . . So he's a zombie, just a high-class cog in a phony machine. From being very privileged and very successful, he feels himself very absurd and very failed."

While much of Fowles's career has been devoted to the novel, he has also written poetry, screenplays, essays, and book reviews. Although his short fiction has largely been limited to the five stories in *The Ebony Tower* (one being a translation of a French Celtic tale), modifications of chapters from his novels have been published in this form. Fowles's short fiction displays the master storytelling abilities that have come to characterize his novels, and the existential qualities of his work are often highlighted by critics.

Fowles was born to Robert and Gladys Fowles on 31 March 1926 in the London suburb of Leigh-on-Sea, located at the mouth of the Thames River. His early life can be described as that of an only child, as his only sibling, Hazel, is more than fifteen years younger. Fowles is of simple English heritage, notably not "British," a distinction the author makes because the English have little in common with the Welsh, Scots, and Irish. In a 1989 interview with James Baker, Fowles remarked: "I was brought up in an intensely conventional suburb not far from London by, in social terms, conventional parents. I have tried to escape ever since."

Fowles is a writer whose social consciousness and awareness of nature are outweighed only by his dedication to the aesthetics of his craft. In a 1985 interview with Carol Barnum, Fowles stated: "I don't think humanity is improving. . . . My view of the world's future [is] not very optimistic." Closely related to this concern with society is Fowles's appreciation of nature, a force he sees as a possible redeemer of society, or at least a force that humanity must reevaluate. As he commented to Barnum: "The original sin of mankind is for me its age-old contempt for, or indifference to, the other species on this planet." For Fowles nature has become an escape, a means of finding in the world what cannot be found in those around him: "I would now call my relationship [with nature] one of love, certainly one of need. What most people look for in human friends and contacts, I look for in nonhuman nature."

This appreciation of nature, while not obscured by the divine aspects of Wordsworthian worship, is noticeable in the Celtic-inspired stories of *The Ebony Tower,* as is the author's interest in the integration of the aesthetics of visual art into his written work. As Lynne Vieth states in *Modern Fiction Studies* (Summer 1991), "The opposition between visual and narrative representations of reality has remained a constant theme in the fiction of John Fowles." Fowles said to Barnum: "I don't think any art or science can describe the whole reality of nature, partly because it is its experience *now.* . . . I often feel this in writing fiction — that one is trying to describe what one can't and ought not even to be trying; and is so condemned to a sort of vulgar futility, or eternal second best." This futility comes to life in the title story of *The Ebony Tower* as abstractionist artist David Williams is forced to realize the constraining comfort of his life. Other protagonists, such as the unnamed narrator of "Poor Koko," fall short of ultimate realization yet still exist in the conflict of art versus nature versus humanity of which Fowles is so acutely aware.

Through interviews Fowles has provided valuable insights into his fiction as well as his understanding of writing and an author's responsibility to the art. One of his pervading themes is the relationship of humanity to nature, which he feels is important to life as well as to art. He remarked to Baker (1989) that "the relation, between man and nature, is far more important and real to me than that between man and God, even between man and other men. . . . Men often bore, books often bore, all things human can bore; nature never." For Fowles the conflict between writing and nature that seems apparent in his conversations is merely an obstacle, not an insurmountable barrier. His appreciation of nature is foremost; his role as writer-human is a mere fact that cannot be avoided. As he stated to Baker (1989): "Nature regularly brings tears into my eyes; humans very, very seldom." His role is not to change humanity, but to get readers to reevaluate their outlooks. As he said to Barnum: "I know I have helped a little in altering people's view of life." For Fowles this is the responsibility of the artist.

The early events of Fowles's life are characteristic of the lives of English boys of his generation. He attended Bedford School as a boarder in 1939 but by 1941 had returned to his parents' home in the Devon countryside where the family had moved in 1940 to avoid the London blitz. Fowles has attributed his exit from Bedford to "a sort of nervous breakdown at the age of 15," as noted by James Aubrey in *John Fowles: A Reference Companion* (1991). A rejuvenated Fowles returned to Bedford the following term and was graduated in 1944 after achieving the distinctions of being named captain of the cricket team and head boy (in charge of the system of student discipline that he had initially viewed with shock). After leaving Bedford, Fowles received naval training in Scotland. Ironically, he completed the requirements for a commission in the Royal Marines on the same day that World War II ended in Europe. He was stationed in Okehampton, twenty-five miles from the beautiful Devon countryside, and his duties included training young marines in commando tactics.

At the age of twenty-one Fowles began to examine his life in relation to the larger society. He concluded that the military life of rules, orders, and innate violence was an extension of the middle-class conformity against which he was beginning to react. From this point on, the idea of nonconformity became an important aspect of Fowles's life and writing. This newly found system of values led Fowles to leave the Royal Marines in 1947 and enroll at Oxford, where the influence of the French existentialists, namely Jean-Paul Sartre and Albert Camus, helped develop the young man's urge to become a writer.

Fowles attended New College, enrolling in the Honours School of Language and Literature and specializing in French and German. After ultimately concentrating on French language and literature, he took an honors degree in 1950. During his years at Oxford he began to explore the rich traditions of French literature and culture that have greatly influenced his works.

After earning his degree Fowles took a series of teaching positions in France, Greece, and England. From 1951 to 1953 he lived on the Greek island of Spetsai, an experience that provided material for his novel *The Magus* (1965; revised, 1977). While the teaching seems to have been less than fulfilling for him, the environment of postwar Greece provided him with much enjoyment as well as source material. During this period Fowles wrote a set of poems later included in his one published volume of poetry, *Poems* (1973). Although Fowles returned to England in 1953, his time in Greece seems to have heightened his feelings of alienation from English society.

On 2 April 1954 Fowles married Elizabeth Whitton, whom he had met on Spetsai. When they first encountered each other, Whitton was married to another teacher at the Spetsai school. As her marriage disintegrated, Fowles developed strong feelings for her. She and her husband returned to England at the same time as Fowles. During this period Fowles began *The Magus*, a novel motivated by his feelings for Whitton as well as by his longing for the Greek countryside. After their marriage Fowles took a teaching position at Saint Godric's College in Hampstead, London. He remained there until 1963, when sales of his first published novel, *The Collector* (1963), generated enough income to allow him to pursue writing full-time.

With the publication of *The Collector* Fowles's career as a novelist developed rapidly. After moving to Lyme Regis in 1958, Fowles settled into the quiet life of a country man of letters. His publications include a philosophical work, *The Aristos: A Self-Portrait in Ideas* (1964; revised, 1968); the novels *The Magus*, *The French Lieutenant's Woman* (1969), and *Daniel Martin* (1977); *Poems*; and many nonfiction pieces. *The Collector*, *The Magus*, and *The French Lieutenant's Woman* were made into motion pictures in 1965, 1968, and 1981, respectively.

Examining *The Ebony Tower* as a collection poses a problem: should one attempt to find continuity in the stories, or should they be viewed as individual pieces bound in one book? Perhaps because of Fowles's reputation as a novelist, many critics read the collection as a loosely integrated appraisal of what Kerry McSweeney, in *Four Contemporary Novelists* (1983), sees as a central aspect of Fowles's fiction: "The relation of the individual to his cultural and historical situation and to his society." Still, the five stories function effectively when read individually, and the thematic ties are less than obvious. Yet Peter Conradi, in *John Fowles* (1982), senses a connection among the stories in that there is an "insecure tenure of the self in relation to the text." Conradi sees the connection between "The Ebony Tower" and "Poor Koko" as "the disruption of the line of artistic and cultural filiation [that speaks] of the ways in which the authority of the text itself authenticates the reading self, or fails to do so."

Fowles provides his perspective of the continuity of the collection in "A Personal Note," which precedes the translation of the medieval Celtic tale "Eliduc," the second story in the volume. Fowles states: "The working title of this collection of stories was *Variations,* by which I meant to suggest variations both on certain themes in previous books of mine and in methods of narrative presentation." He proceeds by explaining the Celtic influence on the work, which is highlighted by the landscape of Brittany as witnessed in "The Ebony Tower" and "The Cloud": "[The collection] is also a variation of a more straightforward kind, and the source of its mood, as also partly of its theme and setting, is so remote and forgotten – that I should like to resurrect a fragment of it. . . ." As Fowles explains, this is the Celtic romance.

The importance of the collection to Fowles's literary canon is often debated. While some critics view *The Ebony Tower* as a mere rehashing of themes and characters (with slight alterations) of novels such as *The Magus* and *The Collector,* others see the stories as capsules of the artistry of the novels, yet still exhibiting originality. The stories can be seen not only as variations of the novels but also of each other. Similarities between *The Ebony Tower* and the novels are apparent, but the influence of "The Eliduc" and its Celtic qualities remains pivotal. For Fowles the Celtic romance is the parent of fiction: "One may smile condescendingly at the naiveties and primitive technique of stories such as *Eliduc;* but I do not think any writer of fiction can do so with decency – and for a very simple reason. He is watching his own birth." Besides the translation the four remaining stories present variations of this inherited narrative convention, and "The Ebony Tower" and "The Cloud" are set in central France.

The title story, the first in the collection, provides an excellent example of the connection Fowles sees between novels and the medieval Celtic tradition. "The Ebony Tower" is set in Brittany, yet the theme seems to come directly out of *The Magus.* The novel, fantastic in its story, is commonly read as an awakening of self-awareness, with the narrator, Nicholas Urfe, acting as an instructor for the reader on the lessons of life. Urfe, in reaction to the grotesque manipulations of the eccentric Maurice Conchis, gains emotional and intellectual freedom. Much the same can be said of the protagonist and narrator of "The Ebony Tower," David Williams, an English art critic and minor abstractionist painter. Williams is sent to the French countryside to interview famous expatriate William Breasley, a renowned representational painter with a Hemingwayesque reputation stemming from his notorious lifestyle. Fowles's efforts to link the story to the novel are obvious; one of the two female art students living with Breasley is noticed by Williams as reading *The Magus:* "He guessed at astrology, she would be into all that nonsense."

Williams initially appears in the story as a character of strength, a fashionable contemporary artist comfortably (if not overtly happily) married to an illustrator of children's books. They are in the class of Londoners that Fowles often seems to detest. Williams has been selected to interview Breasley for a forthcoming book on the eminent artist's work. The meeting is scheduled to take place at Breasley's manor, Coetminais, in a secluded forest of Brittany. In his initial discussion of Breasley's work Williams also describes Coetminais as well as the unfolding novella of which all are participants: "'Celtic' had been a word frequently used [in interpreting Breasley's art], with the recurrence of the forest motif, the enigmatic figures and confrontations." At this early stage in "The Ebony Tower" Fowles provides the reader with a strand that unifies the entire collection, "the enigmatic figures and confrontations" of the Celtic romance. The translation of *Eliduc* – a twelfth-century French romance by Marie de France – that follows the title story provides the framework of the entire collection.

Central to the varying interpretations of "The Ebony Tower" is the role of art and the artist. In *The Romances of John Fowles* (1985) Simon Loveday points out that, "by casting both his male principals [Williams and Breasley] as artists, Fowles has thrust art into the centre of the discussion." From one perspective the conflict between Williams and Breasley (and ultimately within Williams himself) centers on the relationship between art and life. It is at this point of conflict that the crux of "the ebony tower" reaches the reader. Breasley's derogatory use of the phrase in relation to abstract art, which he openly despises, transcends its normally limited usage and applies openly to the comfortably secure life of Williams. As Diana (nicknamed "the Mouse"; she is one of the art students living with

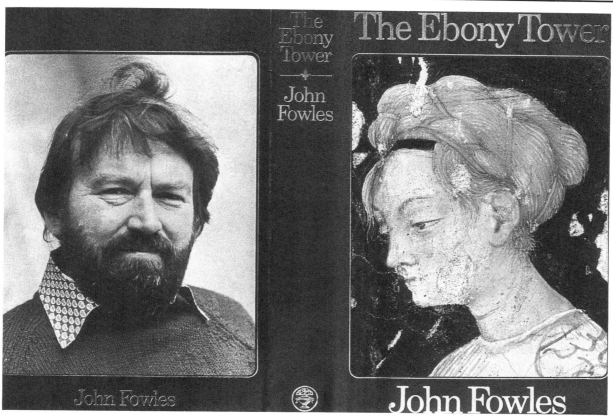

Dust jacket for Fowles's 1974 collection of stories, some of which are influenced by the traditions of the medieval Celtic romance

Breasley) explains, Breasley, in an attack on abstract art, refers to "the ebony tower" as the opposite of the ivory tower. She relates that Breasley thinks an abstractionist "is obscure because the artist is scared to be clear." Ultimately, Williams realizes this statement not only is a description of his art, but also of his life.

Remembering Fowles's detestation of upper-middle-class British society, the reader recognizes Williams not as a hero but as a pathetic character. His later unsuccessful attempt at infidelity with Diana characterizes his life as "the ebony tower," unfulfilled in spite of his comfortable marriage. Although Williams's attempt at infidelity fails, his realization of the condition of his life allows him to confront his newly perceived dilemma – that of neglecting the self in the name of comfort – what Fowles might call the dilemma of the middle class. The story ends, however, before the reader is reassured of this. Loveday sees this conflict as representative of the fundamental antithesis of Fowles's work, that of the conflict between freedom and responsibility. Loveday states: "[Fowles's] fiction, though ultimately asserting the primacy of freedom, aims at a synthesis of these apparently conflicting pairs."

Fowles follows "The Ebony Tower" with his translation of *Eliduc,* a story of quest and courtly love. The title character is a brave knight from Brittany who, in loyal service to his king, helps bring peace and prosperity to the kingdom through victorious battle. Yet rivals discredit him to the king, and Eliduc is forced to leave Brittany and seek adventure in England. Before he leaves, he promises to remain faithful to his wife, Guildeluec. The theme of faithfulness is central to "Eliduc" as well as to Fowles's novels and most of the stories in *The Ebony Tower.*

After helping the king of Devon, Eliduc falls in love and elopes with the king's daughter, Guilliadun, but he does not tell her of his wife in Brittany. When she finally hears of Guildeluec, Guilliadun falls into a deathlike trance. Ultimately Guildeluec discovers the truth of her husband's other love. She weeps for the fate of the three, but through the enchanted red flower of the weasel she is able to revive the "dead" Guilliadun. Guildeluec, recognizing her husband's love for Guilliadun, leaves him with his new wife and becomes a nun. The three are reunited by the story's end in a tribute to Christianity.

The importance of Fowles's formal training in French language and literature while at Oxford is obvious, and the story focuses the collection's varying motifs. As Mahmoud Salami points out in *John Fowles's Fiction and the Poetics of Postmodernism* (1992), the quest in "Eliduc" is similar to the one in "The Ebony Tower" in that Eliduc reaches a level of "the ideal figure to whom David [Williams] must aspire if he wishes to achieve existential freedom." "Eliduc" provides Fowles with a loose framework based on the traditions of medieval tales. Some critics believe this framework is applied to the collection as a whole. The characteristics of the medieval tale, all well represented in "Eliduc," include the predicament of the yearning male admirer, a type of punishment for the discourteous lover, a dangerous or mysterious quest, and an atmosphere of enchantment.

According to Salami the significance of "Eliduc" "is to stress the possibility of striking a balance between opposites whether they are internal as in the case of David, or whether they are between two individuals or societies as in 'The Cloud' and 'Poor Koko.' " In *John Fowles* (1978) Barry Olshen places "Eliduc" within the scope of the remainder of the collection, stating that, much like the medieval knight, "each of Fowles' protagonists can be seen to undergo a kind of ordeal at a crucial point in his or her life." That experience changes each character's self-image and alters the direction of his or her life. This thematic link places the Celtic tale squarely in the middle of *The Ebony Tower*.

Following "Eliduc" in the collection is "Poor Koko," the story of an academic writer working on a book about nineteenth-century novelist Thomas Love Peacock. In the course of a robbery the biographer suffers what seems the most brutal of attacks, the destruction of his manuscript. The aging, dwarfish university professor borrows some friends' weekend cottage to devote time to his definitive biography of the "long-dead novelist Peacock." As the protagonist states, "He is not greatly read these days." This seemingly minor observation provides the story with its initial conflict: a scholarly writer laboring over a book about a seldom-read author that will surely find a limited audience. (Fowles, however, has often expressed admiration for Peacock.) As the story progresses, the conflict leads to a larger and more obvious one: the inability and possible unwillingness of people to understand each other.

The story is presumably told some months after the robbery. The narrator-protagonist leaves London to find a quiet place in North Dorset to continue work on the slowly progressing biography. He goes to great lengths to add that he arrived mid-week, thus occupying the house when it should have been empty. He hears a burglar downstairs and decides to remain quiet, hoping that the thief will not notice him. The narrator makes much of his diminutive size: "I like to class myself – in no other but a physical sense, I hasten to add – with Pope, Kant and Voltaire." In fact, his most successful book is titled *The Dwarf in Literature*.

As if to highlight the coming linguistic confrontation, the narrator is quick to point out that the book has its shortcomings, "nor was [it] quite the model of objective and erudite analysis it pretended to be." He firmly establishes the tone of the robbery and the class conflict that leads to the larger linguistic battle as he admits that books "have been my life rather more than life itself." What follows is an ironic realization of the distancing from life to which this adoration of books has brought him: "It seems fitting that I should have been where I was that night entirely because of one [a book]."

After a short time the burglar discovers the narrator but treats him rather well. They engage in conversation as the thief continues to steal. The subjects of their exchange vary greatly: occupations, crime, literature, politics, and society. The narrator realizes that the young criminal is "someone who belonged to that baffling (to my generation) new world of the classless British young." Despite the narrator's belief that the class difference was not the reason behind the text's destruction ("No one detests class snobbery more sincerely than I do"), this conclusion seems self-justifying rather than genuine, as much of his character does. The class difference instigates the confrontation, a fact that the narrator, while acknowledging the conflict of language, continues to deny.

Although the story cannot be labeled a strong political commentary, the observations Fowles makes on the British class system are apparent. While the narrator busies himself trying to categorize the thief ("He was not even remotely like an intellectual Marxist"), he refuses to see the connection between class struggle and language's expressive (and oppressive) power within it. When the narrator states, "He attacked something quite plainly apolitical: my book," he is refusing to see the threat of the book and the power it may represent. When the narrator denies the thief's request to be the subject of the professor's writing, he passes his only chance to safeguard his manuscript. The narrator ultimately realizes this, but he fails to understand why. And the thief – the winner in the confrontation of language as he destroys the manuscript – achieves an even grander victory by becoming the subject of Fowles's story.

Similarities between "Poor Koko" and *The Collector* are obvious. While the novel deals with a woman held captive by a deranged amateur lepidopterist, the short story presents the professor as captive. Both works have been noted to deal with the "few" in conflict with the "many," a distinction Fowles also discusses in *The Aristos*. In comparing the villains from the novel and the short story, Aubrey states: "Like Clegg [the kidnapper in *The Collector*] the burglar is aware of the insurmountability of the gap between the many and the few, but he seems to understand much better than Clegg does the nature of the gap."

Of all the stories in *The Ebony Tower,* "Poor Koko" shows the least influence of the Celtic tradition. As Timothy Alderman states in *Modern Fiction Studies* (Spring 1985): "The Celtic-inspired green world [which acts for the artist Breasley as a contrast to the world he detests] also brings with it an atmosphere of magic, foreboding, and enigma." The source of the green world remains vital to "The Ebony Tower," but the professor in "Poor Koko" comes to the source, nature, for seclusion while admitting that he "missed the familiar all-night sounds from outside my London flat." As Alderman points out, "The isolation of the cottage enables the thief to act so unusually." Moreover, the narrator's stuffy academic personality makes him barely tolerable to the reader, denying him the respect that the often-abusive Breasley commands. In *Papers on Language and Literature* (Winter 1987) Ellen McDaniel states that, at this point in his life, the narrator has become "impervious to any human contact, either critical or friendly."

However, there is some Celtic influence in "Poor Koko." Loveday notes that — besides the link between the west-country setting where the cottage is located and the Cornish epigram to Brittany and the Celts that accompanies the story — "Poor Koko" possesses one of the major motifs of "Eliduc," a failure to communicate. Critical interpretation of "Poor Koko" consistently views the story as addressing not only the confrontation of classes but also of language. Loveday observes that the failure of communication hinges on the larger, more disturbing failure to listen. The thief is ultimately granted his wish of having the narrator tell his story in that the professor does recount the robbery and its intensity. In articulating the events the professor is forced to examine and represent them — in short, to comprehend.

"The Enigma" concerns the mysterious disappearance of a member of Parliament, John Marcus Fielding, a devoted family man of strict morals and habits. His patterned life makes the disappearance an unresolvable enigma. Seemingly satisfied with his successful life, Fielding had proven trustworthy in both his public and domestic affairs. To this scenario Fowles adds an unusual twist for the detective-story genre: "The Enigma" has no resolution. While speculation runs rampant throughout the story, by its conclusion the reader has no clearer idea of Fielding's fate than when it began. The story seems to move from one mystery, the disappearance of Fielding, to another, involving a beautiful woman. The reader is placated much as the protagonist, Detective Sergeant Michael Jennings, is.

Jennings has been given the task of trying to find Fielding (or clues to his disappearance) after the wheels of investigation have seemingly ground to a halt. Scotland Yard has had no success in locating the missing M.P., and some of Fielding's colleagues speculate that he has run off with an unknown mistress. In the course of his investigation Jennings interviews Isobel Dodgson, the girlfriend of the missing man's son. At this point the story begins to shift focus from Fielding toward the mystery of male-female relationships. Here Fowles breaks from the detective-story genre, creating in Isobel what Olshen labels "one more lovely variation on the intelligent, sensitive, independent female who plays so active and essential a role in the *dramatis personae* of the Fowles canon."

Isobel offers Jennings her postulate regarding the Fielding mystery. She reveals that the night before the disappearance she had told Fielding that she would be working in the British Museum the next day. The museum is the last place where Fielding had been sighted, suggesting that he had come to see Isobel, though she had not gone to work that day after all. During her interview with Jennings, Isobel, an aspiring novelist, recommends that the detective imagine himself as an author trying to write the conclusion to a book. This, she claims, could help unravel the otherwise unsolvable case. She suggests that Fielding has probably just escaped from the oppressively conservative life he had lived for so long. Jennings becomes intrigued with Isobel and her theory but receives little enthusiasm from his superiors at Scotland Yard. The story ends, disappearance unresolved, with Jennings and Isobel making love. With this final scene the story shifts emphasis from Fielding to a focus on the male-female relationship, a continuing theme in Fowles's work.

The thematic relationship of life to art, represented by Isobel, is important in "The Enigma." Robert Huffaker, in *John Fowles* (1980), states that this theme is consistent throughout *The Ebony*

Belmont House in Lyme Regis, where Fowles has resided since 1968

Tower: "Having already published a book of children's stories, Isobel is now writing a novel. Her novelist's view, while providing clues, also deepens the enigma." In fact, Isobel throws into question the realism of reality. While this does not lead to the case being solved, it does allow Fowles the freedom to make "The Enigma" much more than a detective story.

The Ebony Tower concludes with what Fowles has called the best story in the collection, "The Cloud." It follows the Celtic tradition established by "Eliduc," but in what Loveday sees as "a debased or corrupt form." Olshen goes so far as to call "The Cloud" "Fowles's most difficult work to penetrate, certainly the most opaque in *The Ebony Tower.* Everything in this delicate mood piece is understated, muted, or ambiguous."

"The Cloud" takes place in the countryside of central France, where a group of English friends is vacationing. Among the group are Paul Rogers; his wife, Annabel; their two children; Annabel's sister, Catherine; Peter, a divorced television producer; and Peter's girlfriend, Sally. From a continually changing narrative perspective Fowles creates a seemingly fluctuating reality reminiscent of Isobel's novelist's view of life. As the story unfolds, Catherine, recently widowed and suffering from depression, takes one of the children into the woods and tells her a story of a lost princess. The connection Fowles makes between life and art in much of his work is again apparent, as Catherine's story ultimately becomes her reality. By the conclusion of "The Cloud" Catherine, after a brief meeting with Peter laced with sexual overtones, disappears, left much like the princess of her story, waiting for her prince.

As the piece progresses, a theme common to the stories in the collection becomes apparent: what Huffaker describes as "the conflict between the brutalizing masculine ego and the civilizing female intelligence." Caught somewhere in between is Catherine, a character Fowles has acknowledged was written in "deliberate homage to Katherine Mansfield." A consistent theme in Fowles's work, the joining of art and literature, seems to be the story's ultimate shortcoming. While reception to "The Cloud" has been mixed, its near-surrealistic complexity appears to be its most central characteristic, whether critically praised or condemned. The story can be said to work more effectively as a rolling landscape portrait than as a self-contained piece of fiction. In discussing the story with Barnum, Fowles admitted, "Perhaps I did leave out too much" for the reader to comprehend the narrative fully. Nevertheless, for Fowles the artist, "The Cloud" completes a progression in the collection. In summarizing his perception of the story to Barnum, he stated: "It feels alright for me, if I am allowed an opinion."

The Ebony Tower has been Fowles's only venture into the short-fiction genre, and its success has been consistently acknowledged in various critical examinations. Fowles has more recently pursued nonfictional venues, such as *The Enigma of Stonehenge* (1980) and projects dealing with the rich history of the Lyme Regis area where he resides. With *The Ebony Tower* he achieves a loosely thematic balance in stories that remain rich in the traditions that have greatly influenced his growth as an author.

Interviews:

Raman Singh, "An Encounter with John Fowles," *Journal of Modern Literature,* 8 (1980–1981): 181–202;

Carol Barnum, "An Interview with John Fowles," *Modern Fiction Studies,* 31 (Spring 1985): 187–203;

Hilary DeVries, "Searching for a Moral Perspective: John Fowles Scans Past for That Which He Can't Find in the 'Amoral' Present," *Christian Science Monitor,* 8 October 1985, pp. 23–24;

James Baker, "An Interview with John Fowles," *Michigan Quarterly Review,* 25 (Winter 1986): 661–683;

Baker, "The Art of Fiction CIX: John Fowles," *Paris Review,* 31 (Summer 1989): 40–63.

References:

Timothy Alderman, "The Enigma of *The Ebony Tower,*" *Modern Fiction Studies,* 31 (Spring 1985): 135–148;

James Aubrey, *John Fowles: A Reference Companion* (Westport, Conn.: Greenwood Press, 1991);

Carol Barnum, "The Quest Motif in John Fowles's *The Ebony Tower:* Theme and Variations," *Texas Studies in Language and Literature,* 23 (Spring 1981): 138–157;

Peter Conradi, *John Fowles* (New York: Methuen, 1982);

Arnold Davidson, " 'Eliduc' and *The Ebony Tower:* John Fowles's Variation on a Medieval Lay," *International Fiction Review,* 11 (Winter 1984): 31–36;

Frederick Holmes, "Fictional Self-Consciousness in John Fowles's *The Ebony Tower,*" *Ariel,* 16 (July 1985): 21–38;

Robert Huffaker, *John Fowles* (Boston: Twayne, 1980);

John Humma, "John Fowles' *The Ebony Tower:* In the Celtic Mood," *Southern Humanities Review,* 17 (Winter 1983): 33–47;

Frank Kersnowski, "John Fowles' 'The Ebony Tower': A Discourse with Critics," *Journal of the Short Story in English,* 13 (Autumn 1989): 57–64;

Janet Lewis and Barry Olshen, "John Fowles and the Medieval Romance Tradition," *Modern Fiction Studies,* 31 (Spring 1985): 15–30;

Simon Loveday, *The Romances of John Fowles* (New York: St. Martin's Press, 1985);

Ellen McDaniel, "Fowles as Collector: The Failed Artists of *The Ebony Tower,*" *Papers on Language and Literature,* 23 (Winter 1987): 70–83;

Kerry McSweeney, *Four Contemporary Novelists* (Montreal: McGill-Queen's University Press, 1983);

Ruth Morse, "John Fowles, Marie de France, and the Man with Two Wives," *Philological Quarterly,* 63 (Winter 1984): 17–30;

Olshen, *John Fowles* (New York: Ungar, 1978);

Mahmoud Salami, *John Fowles's Fiction and the Poetics of Postmodernism* (Cranbury, N.J.: Associated University Presses, 1992);

Rimgalia Salys, "The Medieval Context of John Fowles's *The Ebony Tower,*" *Critique,* 25 (Fall 1983): 11–24;

Lynne Vieth, "The Re-Humanization of Art: Pictorial Aesthetics in John Fowles's *The Ebony Tower* and *Daniel Martin,*" *Modern Fiction Studies,* 37 (Summer 1991): 217–233.

Brian Glanville

(24 September 1931 –)

James J. Schramer
Youngstown State University

See also the Glanville entry in *DLB 15: British Novelists, 1930–1959: Part 1.*

BOOKS: *Cliff Bastin Remembers,* by Glanville and Cliff Bastin (London: Ettrick, 1950);

The Reluctant Dictator (London: Laurie, 1952);

Arsenal Football Club (London: Convoy, 1952);

Henry Sows the Wind (London: Secker & Warburg, 1954);

Soccer Nemesis (London: Secker & Warburg, 1955);

Along the Arno (London: Secker & Warburg, 1956; New York: Crowell, 1956);

Over the Bar, by Glanville and Jack Kelsey (London: Paul, 1958);

The Bankrupts (London: Secker & Warburg, 1958; Garden City, N.Y.: Doubleday, 1958);

World Cup, by Glanville and Jerry Weinstein (London: Hale, 1958);

After Rome, Africa (London: Secker & Warburg, 1959);

Soccer Round the Globe (London & New York: Abelard-Schuman, 1959);

A Bad Streak and Other Stories (London: Secker & Warburg, 1961);

Diamond (London: Secker & Warburg, 1962; New York: Farrar, Straus & Cudahy, 1962);

The Footballer's Companion (London: Eyre & Spottiswoode, 1962);

The Director's Wife and Other Stories (London: Secker & Warburg, 1963);

Know about Football (London & Glasgow: Blackie, 1963);

The Rise of Gerry Logan (London: Secker & Warburg, 1963; New York: Delacorte, 1965);

World Football Handbook (London: Hodder & Stoughton, 1964; London: Mayflower, 1966–1972; London: Queen Anne Press, 1974);

Goalkeepers Are Crazy: A Collection of Football Stories (London: Secker & Warburg, 1964);

The King of Hackney Marshes and Other Stories (London: Secker & Warburg, 1965);

Brian Glanville (photograph by Toby Glanville)

A Second Home (London: Secker & Warburg, 1965; New York: Delacorte, 1966);

A Roman Marriage (London: Joseph, 1966; New York: Coward-McCann, 1967);

People in Sport (London: Secker & Warburg, 1967);

The Artist Type (London: Cape, 1967; New York: Coward-McCann, 1968);

Soccer: A History of the Game, Its Players, and Its Strategy (New York: Crown, 1968); republished as *Soccer: A Panorama* (London: Eyre & Spottiswoode, 1969);

A Betting Man and Other Stories (New York: Coward-McCann, 1969);

The Olympian (London: Secker & Warburg, 1969; New York: Coward-McCann, 1969);

A Cry of Crickets (London: Secker & Warburg, 1970; New York: Coward-McCann, 1970);

The Puffin Book of Football (Harmondsworth, U.K.: Penguin, 1970);

Goalkeepers Are Different (London: Hamish Hamilton, 1971; New York: Crown, 1972);

Brian Glanville's Book of World Football (London: Dragon, 1972);

The Financiers (London: Secker & Warburg, 1972); republished as *Money Is Love* (Garden City, N.Y.: Doubleday, 1972);

The Thing He Loves and Other Stories (London: Secker & Warburg, 1973);

The Sunday Times History of the World Cup (London: Times Newspapers, 1973); republished as *History of the Soccer World Cup* (New York: Collier, 1974); revised as *The History of the World Cup* (London: Faber, 1980);

The Comic (London: Secker & Warburg, 1974; New York: Stein & Day, 1975);

Bass Charrington World Football Handbook (London: Queen Anne Press, 1975);

Soccer 76 (London: Queen Anne Press, 1975);

The Dying of the Light (London: Secker & Warburg, 1976);

A Bad Lot and Other Stories (London: Severn House, 1977);

The Puffin Book of Footballers (Harmondsworth, U.K.: Puffin, 1978); revised as *Brian Glanville's Book of Footballers* (Harmondsworth, U.K.: Puffin, 1982);

Target Man (London: Macdonald & Jane's, 1978);

A Book of Soccer (New York: Oxford University Press, 1979);

Never Look Back (London: Joseph, 1980);

Kevin Keegan (London: Hamish Hamilton, 1981);

The Puffin Book of Tennis (London: Puffin, 1981);

The Puffin Book of the World Cup (Harmondsworth, U.K.: Puffin, 1984);

The British Challenge (London: Muller, 1984);

Underneath the Arches: A Musical in Two Acts, by Glanville, Patrick Garland, and Roy Hudd (London: Weinberger, 1984);

Kissing America (London: Blond, 1985);

Love Is Not Love and Other Short Stories (London: Blond, 1985);

The Catacomb (London: Hodder & Stoughton, 1988);

Champions of Europe: The History, Romance and Intrigue of the European Cup (Enfield, Middlesex, U.K.: Guinness, 1991).

OTHER: *Footballers' Who's Who,* edited by Glanville (London: Ettrick, 1951);

The Joy of Football, edited by Glanville (London: Hodder & Stoughton, 1986).

Brian Glanville has had a prolific career as a sportswriter, novelist, and short-story writer. English critics who prefer writers to remain in tidy categories consider it paradoxical that he has managed to combine careers as a sportswriter and a fiction writer. Readers in the United States — where Ernest Hemingway could write a nonfiction piece on fishing, Norman Mailer can examine the first moon landing, and Joyce Carol Oates can analyze boxing — find Glanville's writing in diverse genres less surprising. Critics have called Glanville a British Damon Runyan and consider his subject matter his principal contribution to the modern short story. He has made the previously unexamined world of the professional footballer (soccer player) a subject of serious fiction. But he has done more than write the standard sports books for male adolescents (although he has also done that); he has captured the speech cadences of working-class Britons, giving voice to their aspirations and dreams. He has re-created the world from which have come both soccer's most rabid fans and its most skillful players.

Soccer is not, however, his only subject. Italy and artists also figure prominently in many of his stories. Others examine the legacy of the British Empire and what life is like for British civil servants facing the demise of British power. Less apparent to the casual observer of Glanville's work is his sometimes painful exploration of what it is like to be Jewish in British society, with its ever-so-polite exclusionary rules and socially isolating codes of conduct. Glanville is much more than a sportswriter or a writer who uses sports as his subject matter; he is a chronicler of the highs and lows of British life from the 1950s to the present.

Glanville's work has been categorized under three main headings: novels and stories of Jewish life, stories about professional soccer players, and novels and stories about Italy. Although these are far from his only topics, they are three important parts of his life. Born on 24 September 1931 in the London suburb of Golders Green, which he describes as being "made up equally of Jew and Gentile," Glanville was influenced by the romanticism of his father's family and the materialism of his mother's family. His father and mother, James Arthur and Florence Manches Glanville, were the children of eastern European Jewish immigrants. His father's family settled in Dublin, where his father was brought up, as Glanville recalls, "at once very

Jewish and very Irish." His mother's family settled in the Tower Bridge Road section of London; "as English Jews," writes Glanville, they "were far less integrated than Irish Jews."

From his mother Glanville learned about the insecurity that comes from an unfulfilled need to be loved, a theme that he develops in his fiction about Jewish family life. From his father he learned not only about an uncle who had run away from home and become the heavyweight champion of the South African Army and other characters in that family, but also about the game of soccer, his father's great love. An avid Arsenal fan, his father told him stories of the club's ascendancy to football glory. His father made him a "compulsive fan," and Glanville writes, "Keeping my Arsenal Almanacs year by year, I would turn in time into a soccer journalist, which would enable me to earn a living, buy time to write the fiction I wanted, and to travel endlessly around the world."

About his schooling, first at Newlands and then at Charterhouse, Glanville recalls:

> I lived in two quite different worlds. . . . Home was always immeasurably preferable, even with its emotional storms, its tears and rages. But school, perhaps, kept me sane, even though the coldness of it all, the repression of feeling, the occasional callowness, the perpetual undertow of anti-Semitism . . . turned it into a kind of exile.

Unable to secure a scholarship to Magdalen College, Oxford, he was placed by his father in a solicitor's office; he hated it. He wanted to write, and he had already started turning out short pieces for sports weeklies. By early 1950, after a bout with tuberculosis and a stay in a sanatorium, he had given up law and was ghostwriting an autobiography for Cliff Bastin, a former star for the Arsenal soccer club. *Cliff Bastin Remembers* (1950) was published with James Glanville's backing, and his son's literary career began. He was not yet twenty.

Although he claims that short stories have always been his real interest, Glanville first found success as a novelist. In 1952 *The Reluctant Dictator,* which he had written when he was eighteen, was published. It was, he admits, "a splendid idea, inadequately handled." During the early 1950s Glanville was busy writing about soccer, but, as he has done so often in his career, he found a way for soccer to support his other writing. In 1952 he was invited by the British Council to cover a series of international matches in Florence between England and Italy. While in Florence he was captivated not only by the city's beauty but also by the American former servicemen who figure in so much of his

later fiction. Many of them had been in the Italian campaign and were studying art or trying to write, living on the GI Bill. That the United States would pay former soldiers to study abroad, helping them to delay their return to American society, is a theme to which Glanville returns in many of his short stories set in Italy.

In Italy Glanville also observed another class of Americans, the military guardians of the postwar Pax Americana, who were often unhappy with being assigned to a country where everything seemed old and everyone had a past. In his first collection of short fiction, *A Bad Streak and Other Stories* (1961), Glanville explores the collision of cultures that occurs when times and politics change. In the title story Glanville writes about Britons living out their fading dreams of wealth, importance, and empire. Newer empires also have a place in Glanville's fictional world. The "American Empire" of the postwar years (mid to late 1950s) is examined in stories that depict young Americans studying art abroad ("Brooklyn Boy") or avoiding art and culture ("A Ride on a Tiger"). His passion for soccer also finds its way into this volume in such stories as "The Footballers," "Goalkeepers Are Crazy," "The Prodigy," and "If He's Good Enough, He's Big Enough."

"A Bad Streak" is set in the Azores. John Clark, London manager of Ajax Cable Company, and his assistant, the story's narrator, are there on business. Paul Moxon, the cable company's local representative and Clark's subordinate, is a stuffy British civil servant, among the last of a once-populous species on the islands: "When you looked at him and when you heard him speak, you thought of chota pegs and tennis sets and the lower ranks of the Colonial Service." His wife, Mary, speaks with "fictitious gaiety in a Harrod's voice."

As Paul proudly shows John and his assistant around the club, he nostalgically recalls its glory days: " 'There used to be three hundred of us here. . . . Wonderful for sport: tennis, football, cricket. Dances in the evening. Now there's only a dozen left.' " Still, they keep up standards: " 'We do insist on a collar and tie. Have to. Otherwise you get Americans coming in with those shirts.' " The club is cavernous: "the dining room was a mausoleum, dim-lit and macabre, peopled by the ghosts of minor public school men, impersonating empire builders." Mary, clapping her hands for the waiter, tells John and his assistant, " 'You'll have to forgive the service, C-R-E-T-I-N-S, you know.' " Although they have lived in the Azores for twenty-five years, the Moxons speak no more than "kitchen Portuguese";

as Paul explains, " 'When I came here, everyone you wanted to talk to spoke English.' "

The Moxons seem uneasy with the Portuguese inhabitants of the islands and are particularly wary about Carlos, a young boy John has befriended at the dock. Carlos is a fourteen-year-old con artist who hangs around the docks waiting for tourists, begging for work. His approach is a polished routine, "all a little too fluent." John, however, is taken by the boy and begins to fancy that he can help him, perhaps even adopt him. The Moxons " 'know *him*,' " and they caution John not to trust the boy because, says Paul, he has " 'a bad streak.' " John's trust in Carlos is tested when Mary accuses Carlos of stealing her gold cigarette lighter. John defends Carlos; however, it turns out that the boy has indeed taken the lighter. Using his authority over Paul in much the same way as Paul once wielded authority over his subalterns, John pressures him to get his wife to drop the charges, and Carlos is released.

Despite the boy's thievery John leaves the Azores convinced that he will write to Carlos and that Carlos is worth saving. In his own way John is only a bit better than the Moxons. They do not trust the boy; perhaps they were taken in by him themselves at one time. John excuses the boy's behavior on the grounds that, if people think you are a thief, you might as well be one. John does not realize that he is being every bit as paternalistic as the Moxons are being xenophobic. Each trait is a legacy of the conviction that empire – even dreams of former empire – gives one the right to pass judgment, pronounce sentence, or even to rehabilitate.

"A Ride on the Tiger" shows what the new imperialism is like. Janey, Mary, and Sheila – debutantes at a finishing school outside of Florence – have asked Butch, Macey, and Dave – American air force enlisted men – to the school's weekly At Home gathering. Butch, a tough from Brooklyn, fascinates Janey with his stories about street life and American violence. She treats him as if he were a strange breed of savage, which in some ways he is.

More a stereotype than a fully developed character, Butch stands for the new barbarism. He says to Janey, " 'Let's change the subject. Tell me what does anyone do with their time in Florence?' " Macey chimes in, " 'The guy's right, there just ain't notin'. Ugolino golf course. Excelsior Bar. Half-a-dozen crummy night clubs – and then what?' " When Janey replies that Florence has " 'one or two art galleries and museums,' " Butch curtly responds, " 'I'll make a deal with you, baby. You keep the art galleries, and I'll take Coney Island.' " Janey invites

all three to come back the next week for a party at the school. As the night ends, the three young women take a taxi up the hill to the school, "its square, stone mediaeval tower a beacon of light, long before it could be reached, taking on the unattainability of a fairy tale castle."

When the three airmen come to the party, held in the "fairy tale castle," the scene is predictable. Mrs. Waring, the principal, greets them with the frigid aloofness of "a duchess receiving *parvenus*, who must be tolerated, but need not be indulged." The party is also attended by some young Florentine men who object to the attention Janey is giving to the rude Americans. Paolo in particular keeps asking Janey to dance, and she keeps refusing him, preferring to dance with Macey, Dave, and, most often, Butch. Glanville compares Janey and Butch to "Calaban and Ariel; her eyes alive with the pleasure of a child at the seaside, which runs shrieking before a huge, impending wave." Janey, perhaps more a Miranda than an Ariel, is clearly fascinated by this creature from a brave new world.

The impending wave crashes at the end of the evening when the drunk Americans are jumped by some of the Italians as they walk down the hill. Butch, "hitting out with the savage calm of the experienced street fighter," smashes Paolo's nose across his face, and Janey, having seen her Caliban turn truly savage, runs in tears up the drive. Here again Glanville works with the predictable: the debutante; the fascinating savage; the jealous, hot-blooded aristocrat; the anxious, unfulfilled sexuality; the fairytale castle. "A Ride on the Tiger" is not, however, a fairy tale; beauty does not charm the beast.

"Brooklyn Boy" is another story about American vitality in the face of European passivity. Bill, the Brooklyn boy of the title, is a talented young painter who seduces and later leaves Mary, a young sculptor from Pasadena. Bill is a user, but he has the nerve to get what he wants no matter what the cost to others. This story is a study for Glanville's later novels about artists and writers, *The Artist Type* (1967) and *A Cry of Crickets* (1970). Unlike Geoff of *The Artist Type* or Kevin of *A Cry of Crickets,* who keep coming back to women they have abandoned, demanding nurturing and mothering, Bill never returns to a former lover. He might be the artist as enfant terrible, and he surely is adolescent and rude, but he has the capacity to be an artist.

Athletes as artists also figure in this collection. Among the best stories on this theme is "The Footballers." Invited by his friend Franco to see Franco's latest collection of football trainees, the narrator provides a Dantean account of his trip to the practice grounds:

> The journey began in Florence in the shadow of the Duomo; went by the fortifications, with their miniature lake, then passed speedily into no-man's land. The city's perimeter might by anywhere, functional and shallow, a compound of ugly bypasses, garrisoned by numberless, garish filling stations; of railway bridges, hurtling lorries, gray, anonymous side streets.

The narrator does not think the location incongruous: "It had always seemed right to me that the football ground should lie among this waste of factory buildings.... Industry and football belonged together, irrelevant alike to the nature of the city itself."

This statement gets at the core of Glanville's love for and, at the same time, mistrust of sport. It provides a retreat from an ugly world, and it can offer, for the talented few, the promise of fabulous rewards. Franco's protégés dream of being good enough to be signed on by one of the rich teams in the Italian league, of leaving the dirt and grime and grubby practice fields behind for the fast life of an international star. That dream can die hard; a player can hang on to the dream too long, well past the point where talent fades and desire is no longer enough.

Glanville's fictional world — from his studies of footballers to his sketches of finishing schools and their nouveau-riche students, to his perceptive explorations of snobbery and guilt at the tattered ends of empire — is one in which old ways and old values are changing. Sometimes the changes appear to be for the better, sometimes for the worse; Glanville lets his readers decide the morals of his stories. He remains a neutral observer: the artist who admires the talents of others, the sportswriter who puts a young footballer in touch with worldly agents and the glamorous world of Italian football and then watches what happens.

Italy and football again figure prominently in Glanville's next collection of short stories, *The Director's Wife and Other Stories* (1963). In "The Agents" he creates a comic world of intrigue and bombast as two agents for Italian football clubs compete for the services of a young English player. This is a seduction story, a familiar form of sports drama to American readers who marvel at the rewards thrown at the feet of young basketball or baseball players. In the end Billy Vining, the sought-after player, decides to stay in England where things are more familiar.

Football heroes are not only fickle; they are also far from perfect, as the young narrator of "Feet of Clay" discovers when he tries to get an autograph from Billy Green, a star player for Leeds. The young man passes his autograph book through a train window, but Green will not even look at it, throwing it into a puddle on the platform. This is a moral tale, and the ending is predictable. The young player works his way up from a local colliery team to the reserves for Liverpool City. He has his comeuppance with Green when he plays against him in a game and keeps him from scoring.

"The Director's Wife" is also about soccer, but the action takes place in the bedroom, not on the playing field. The vice-chairman's wife likes to have sex with all the new players, and Charlie, the story's narrator, is her latest conquest. This story shows Glanville at his best, as he turns the stuff of tabloid journalism into a classic tale of an aging cuckold, a libidinous wife, and an innocent but willing youth.

"The Men on the G.I. Bill" is among the most interesting stories in the collection. Tom and Frank have come to Italy after the war, Frank because he has served in the Italian campaign and Tom, who has served in the Far East, because he is attracted to Italy. After three years there they have made Florence their city, detesting American tourists because they are "at once a threat and a caricature." Although Tom and Frank share an avuncular concern for Anna, a young Florentine, their main concerns are for each other.

When the narrator brings a New York critic to visit them, the critic tells Tom, who is reading Henry James's *Washington Square* (1881), that James's " 'whole theme is *incest,* only of course he never makes it specific.' " Frank and Tom pass off the remark as an example of the " 'Freud kick' " that year at City College. When the same critic asks the narrator whether Tom and Frank are " 'fairies,' " he says, " 'No,' " but then pauses to think about them. He tells himself that "there was nothing between them so passionate or intense, nothing but friendship, bachelordom, a mutual hibernation."

Although Glanville undercuts the validity of the critic's remarks by caricaturing him as a New York intellectual, he uses the critic's remarks to suggest that there is something incestuous, self-absorbed, and inverted about Tom and Frank's feelings toward Anna, Florence, and themselves. Trapped in a Jamesian lassitude of inaction, they are unable to change, to do anything as their GI Bills slowly run out, "sand in a relentless hourglass." Glanville creates a new version of the Americans abroad in this story. His Americans are not wealthy young men who have come to Florence to spend time and money until they enter professions appropriate to gentlemen, nor are they the cynical, world-weary American expatriates of Ernest Hemingway's fiction. They are average people with average, even boring, dreams, trying to make their hiatus from a more sterile, pragmatic world last as long as possible by not talking about its ending.

Perhaps most symbolic of Glanville's concern with those who patiently chase after something, no matter how meaningless, is the scruffy little man in the park in "The Man Behind the Goal." He is there every day as the narrator and his friend Don practice soccer, Don standing in goal and the narrator taking shots from different angles. The little man trots behind the goal and patiently returns the shots that get past Don. He does this every time the two men come out to practice, but gradually he begins to throw in his comments about soccer and the way the game should be played. The narrator decides that the little man is a teacher in search of a disciple.

In many ways the little man turns out to be a teacher and a student of life as well as a dreamer. He tries, with no success, to turn a slow, bovine young man into a skillful player. When he tells the narrator that " 'soccer is the finest game of all: because there is nothing *evolutionary* about it,' " no sticks or mallets, and it is " 'a game Plato would have liked,' " the narrator looks more closely at the man and notices that he is ill, that he is struggling to keep himself going. When the man is finally taken to a hospital, the narrator visits but cannot bring himself to look into the man's expressionless face: "Nemesis had caught up with him, society and the weather had beaten him at last." There is nothing large or terribly important in this story; there is no sudden insight or epiphany of meaning, just the clean simplicity of a game and the cruelty of death.

Many of the topics and themes laid out in *The Director's Wife* resurface in *The King of Hackney Marshes and Other Stories* (1965). In "A Man with a Head Full of Dreams" Glanville returns to his study of Americans living on the GI Bill in Italy. This time the two former soldiers are Frank, an African-American, and Jack, his white friend. They live in Florence, and, like Glanville's characters in "The Men on the G.I. Bill," they are facing the expiration of their funds and realization that they will soon have to return home. Although Glanville does not mention it directly in this story, in the mid 1950s Frank and Jack would have to have been living abroad in order to share the affections of Helen, a young woman who has left Los Angeles and come

Glanville, circa 1967 (photograph by Peter Fisher)

to Florence looking for beauty. It is all too idyllic: the three friends – strolling arm in arm through ancient streets. It is the stuff of dreams, and when Jack asks Helen whether she has ever read Miguel de Cervantes' *Don Quixote* (1615), about " 'a man with a head full of dreams,' " the reader knows the dream is about to end. Helen tells him she thinks of him as Don Quixote. She is both Helen of Troy, who drove her rivals to war, and Dulcinea, for whom Don Quixote sets off on his hopeless quest. The dream in this story ends for Jack when he finds Helen in bed with Frank, who asks him what he expected with all of them being so close all the time.

In the title story the dreams belong to Sam, the "king" of a local field called Hackney Marshes. Because of his small size and quick moves he is perfectly suited to the narrow confines of the soccer fields that are crowded together in the area. He is good enough, in fact, to get a chance at playing with a second-division club, but his asthma, which he has kept hidden from his fellow players, makes it impossible for him to remain competitive at that level, and he returns to the occasional game at Hackney Marshes. Glanville, himself an amateur player who was never good enough to play professionally, obviously sympathizes with his character. That Sam is Jewish and has to hide his soccer playing from his concerned family members, who know about his asthma, further underscores the relationship between author and character.

Jewish family life is another topic in this collection. In "Roses in Burnt Oak" Glanville explores the relationship between a manipulative Jewish mother, Mrs. Golden, and her son, Ronnie. This story is unusual because Glanville experiments with a female narrative voice, telling the story from the point of view of Judith Levine, for whom Ronnie feels enough affection to invite home for the weekend but whom he does not love enough to protect from Mrs. Golden's withering indifference. Glanville's use of a female narrator is all that distinguishes an otherwise ordinary story about the small cruelties and indignities of upper-class life.

Perhaps the best story in the volume is "The Slogans," in which Glanville provides a closer look at British anti-Semitism and racism. Although the story was written in the early 1960s, it has an urgency that makes it relevant today in Great Britain, Europe, and America. The slogans of the title begin as thickly lettered signs on the walls of a subway tunnel: "NIGS GO HOME" and "JEWS GO HOME." The reader sees them through the eyes of Goldstein, the main character, who watches them evolve from hand-lettered slogans to stickers with "mauve little swastikas" at their corners: "Help to keep out black labour. Coloured immigrants are taking jobs from Britons."

Goldstein tries to deny what he sees. He tells himself that "it can't happen here," but his father, who saw what was going on in Germany and immigrated with his family to Britain in 1932, tells him, " 'In Germany also we said it can't happen here.' " Finally Goldstein decides he can no longer ignore the slogans, and, as the story ends, he is walking purposefully toward a group of neo-Nazis who have lowered their red flag with its black swastika until its tip is pointing at his breast like a lance. In typical fashion Glanville does not reveal how the story comes out; the point of the tale is that Goldstein is not willing to let it happen in Britain. In stories such as this Glanville writes about a Britain that is not all garden loveliness, hunt breakfasts, and watching the royals; his Britain is often ugly, intolerant, and harsh.

Throughout his career Glanville has often republished stories, especially for his American publishers; this is the case with *A Betting Man and Other Stories* (1969). Because the stories in *A Betting Man* first appeared in *A Bad Streak, The Director's Wife,* and *The King of Hackney Marshes,* this collection needs no special attention. Like many writers Glan-

ville has not only republished earlier works, he has also returned to earlier stories and themes and brought them up-to-date. Examples of his revising or reenvisioning earlier themes are found in *The Thing He Loves and Other Stories* (1973).

The title story involves a football fan who has killed a popular local footballer, Joey Black, when he walks into the path of the narrator's, John Gray's, car. For a time John feels as if his world has ended. He takes down the life-size poster of Joey in his bedroom, which is a shrine to the City club and Joey in particular. John loses interest in work, sex, and life. A year after Joey's death, however, John lays a wreath on the center spot at City's home field before the kickoff of a soccer match. He has been accepted back into the City fan club; he is back on the terraces with his friends. He has become a local celebrity of sorts, starting the Joe Black Memorial Award, which will be given each year to a young player who has shown the most promise.

The symbolism in "The Thing He Loves" is simple. John, the representative fan, kills Joey, the representative player, in an accident. The reader is invited to guess that the City club may be White City, especially if one wants to push the color symbolism evident in the characters' surnames. As he does elsewhere in his sports stories, Glanville explores the symbiotic relationship between fans and players, a theme taken up in "A Section of the Crowd" (*The King of Hackney Marshes*). In "The Thing He Loves" John replaces Joe, who lives on in the fans' memories in a way he might not have without his untimely death in the accident.

Another theme that resurfaces in the collection is the silent form of British anti-Semitism. "Join the Club" concerns an English Jew's attempt to become a member of a non-Jewish golf club. Each time Mr. Richards tries to join a club, he runs up against questions about his religion or references to the membership quota. Finally he is accepted by a gentile club, but six months later he resigns his membership and joins Mill Lodge, a Jewish club. He tells the people at Three Elms, the gentile club from which he resigns, that he would " 'just like to give someone else a chance on the quota.' "

Among the more interesting stories in *The Thing He Loves* is "Three or Four Cultures." Set in Mexico City during the 1968 Olympics – the title comes from the Plaza de las Tres Culturas (the three cultures being Aztec, Spanish, and Mexican) – this story explores the conflicts between the Olympic ideals of unpoliticized athletic competition and the realities of a world where everything has become political. The main character and narrator,

Marion, is a British competitor in the women's 200-meter run. The androgyny of Marion's name suggests her being uncommitted to any role other than that of runner. In Mexico City she is forced to confront her own sexuality and the larger, politicized world outside the Olympic village. She meets another athlete, a wrestler from Uruguay named Antonio. At the same time that the Olympics are going on, there are student protests in the streets (it is, after all, 1968). Marion has tried to keep her distance from politics: "As far as I was concerned you came to these countries, you ran and you went away, you'd got enough on your mind with your own races, you just had to shut everything else out."

In 1968 it is hard to shut everything else out. Marion, by now rather desperately in love with Antonio, agrees to go with him to a student meeting although it is the day before her race. Caught in police fire when the demonstrators are attacked, Marion and Antonio are captured by the police. Antonio, pointing to their blazers and badges, keeps repeating " '*Ateletas, ateletas*' "; Marion keeps shouting at Antonio, " 'How could you bring me here? How could you, when you know I've got to run?' " Marion finds she is unable to push aside the world outside the Olympic oval and the Olympic village. In this story Glanville examines one of the most politicized Olympics to that time; the politics of protest were in the streets and in the stadium.

In "My Son the Runner" – as in *The Olympian* (1969), in which he examines the relationship between a trainer, Sam Dee, and an Olympic-class sprinter, Ike Low – Glanville asks the reader to consider whether sport remains sport when it is not fun anymore. The narrator of the story, Graham, is a talented teenage runner coached by his father, who had also been a runner but never had the chance to develop his talent fully: " 'The thing is, Graham, I had ability, but I didn't have opportunity.' "

Graham's father dislikes the studied amateurism of British track and field; he has always admired the training regimens of the Germans, Finns, and Americans. His hero had been Paavo Nurmi, "the Flying Finn." Determined that Graham will have the opportunity to develop his ability, he takes the boy to the local track for training. When that is not enough, he sends him to California, Germany, and Sweden: any place where there is a coach from whom his son might learn more about running. In the end it is always the same: Graham's father has a falling-out with the coach, and he resumes coaching his son.

As Graham develops as a runner, he moves up from the 200-meter to the 400-meter run. He gets his big chance against top-flight competition at the European finals in Leipzig, in what was then East Germany. The toughest competitors in his qualifying heat are Davidescu of Romania and Sieloff of East Germany. Graham plans to run just fast enough to qualify, finishing third or fourth. But, as he passes Davidescu on the last lap and eases up, he hears Sieloff coming up behind and all the years of training take over "like a reflex action." Trained to run as if he were a racing thoroughbred, Graham forgets his plans and the upcoming heats and sprints for the finish, overtaking Sieloff at the tape. His pleased father asks, " 'What's next, Graham?' " Graham replies, " 'Nothing's next. I've retired.' " Although he considers the hours of lecture he will get from his father, who will never understand his decision, Graham is suddenly happy. Like Ike Low of *The Olympian* or Smith, the main character in the title story of Alan Sillitoe's *The Loneliness of the Long-Distance Runner* (1959), Graham has learned that the toughest race to run is against oneself.

"Roman Summer" is another of Glanville's experiments with assuming a female narrative voice. The narrator, Karen, is an American midwesterner who has come to Rome and, predictably, fallen in love. Her college roommate, Julie Cohn, who is from New York, tells her that " 'Mid-West girls are schizophrenic. . . . They shouldn't ever let you go East. Or once they do, they shouldn't let you back. It causes too damn much confusion.' " From works by such authors as Henry James and F. Scott Fitzgerald readers know what to expect from provincial Americans once they come to Europe. Glanville uses those expectations to create a story with a literary subtext.

Karen is engaged to Jim, a stereotypically practical American majoring in business administration at the University of Michigan. Neither Jim nor Ann Arbor can compete with Rome, where Karen meets Sergio, an Italian journalist with whom she immediately has an affair. He is described – in an apparent reference to Donatello in Nathaniel Hawthorne's *Marble Faun* (1860) – as "Pan-ish." Further allusions to Hawthorne's works surface when Sergio complains to Karen that he is "not corrupt"; he argues that she is more dangerous because she destroys people with her innocence. Karen does not respond to this, but she thinks " 'Americans, corrupting Europeans with their innocence' " is a nice twist on James.

As if the references to Hawthorne and James are not enough to inform the reader that this a story based on allusions to American literature, Karen's fiancé is named Jim Faulkner. He comes to Rome to bring her home and back to her senses. When she refuses to listen to him, he has a brief affair with Julie, but it is obvious to Julie that Jim still loves Karen. When Karen is about to leave Rome, she tells Sergio about Jim's having used Julie. He replies, with a final reference to Hawthorne, that " 'this is the Puritan character. To do what you want, and afterwards to look for justification.' " Perhaps both Jim and Karen do what they want because, at the story's close, they meet on the boat home and kiss as if nothing has ever happened.

In *A Bad Lot and Other Stories* (1977) Glanville returns to the sporting world he knows so well and about which he writes so compellingly. The title story examines the development of a young soccer player. He is a talented, if spoiled, teenager who plays the game with an easy grace that insults his teammates' work ethic, but he becomes a player who learns that pain and suffering are part of the game. As he has done before, Glanville makes this more than a story about a young player's learning about the game of life; it is also a story about the changing values in British sport and British life.

Young soccer players such as Jack Longman no longer arrive at the practice grounds hungry to play. Jack represents a new breed of player, one who comes not from the working class but from an upper-middle-class family. His father drives a Bentley; Jack wears expensive clothes that only a few star players would have been able to afford a few years before; he plays soccer with a passionless perfection that is at odds with the working-class ethic that motivates many of the older players. Yet, when he is injured and has to undergo painful rehabilitation and cortisone shots before he can play again, Jack shows that he is no longer the spoiled youngster who showed up at the Rovers' field the year before. As Arthur Redfern, the Rovers' manager, says at the close of the story, " 'He's grown up.' "

In "My Brother and Me" Glanville returns to the working-class characters so often found in his tales of sporting life. He examines the lives of two brothers, one a brawler in the stands, the other a player on the field. Tom, the brawler, has the talent to be a player, but not the discipline. Bob, who has the discipline, gives up boozing, fighting, and hanging around with his mates for the greater rewards of being a star player. It is an old story that recalls that of Cain and Abel; this time, however, Abel (Bob) survives, and Cain (Tom) murders another fan when he hits the man too hard during a brawl in the stands. Tom, for all his faults, is still Bob's brother; as Bob leaves the jail after vising Tom and learning that he will probably get a ten-to-fifteen-year term,

he thinks, " 'How long will I stay in this game, ten years, fifteen years? I reckon we could be finishing together.' " With this ironic statement Glanville underscores the relationship between the players and their fans as one in which each serves time for the other.

In "The Joker," yet another story about professional soccer, Glanville examines what happens when a talented player lets his penchant for practical jokes overcome his natural talent for the game. Bobby never turns down the chance to play a joke on his mates. To him, soccer is a game; life is a game; everything is a game. Even when a joke might cost him the chance to be selected for England's international team ever again, Bobby opts for the joke. Although Glanville never says so directly, Bobby's joking may be his way of avoiding the seriousness of professional soccer, which, with its huge salaries and concern with players' "work rates," has become less like a game and more like a business.

Despite attempts by club directors and trainers to turn the game into a business, soccer remains a sport dominated by chance. In "Where's It Gone" a young player who has previously been able to score with ease finds that his ability to put the ball in the net has left him. From scoring at a record-setting pace he goes to having the ball glance off the posts, strike the crossbar, or dribble slowly into the goalkeeper's hands. Forget the width and length of the field and the fact that a player may run three to five miles in an average game; forget the roughly eight yards of goal mouth: soccer is a game of inches. As Jimmy, the goalkeeper in "Paying the Penalty," learns, a few inches to the right or the left are what make a hero or a fallen idol.

Crouching at the goal line he nervously tries to guess which direction Pele, one of the game's greatest players, will direct a penalty kick. He waits, as the rules dictate, until Pele strikes the ball, then launches himself to his left. He guesses correctly, and the ball forcefully strikes his hands. Jimmy does not know whether it has gone in for a goal or has been deflected wide. The reader suspects he has stopped the shot because Jimmy says the crowd let out "a great, enormous sigh, the most marvelous sound I'd ever heard in my life." In soccer, as in life, the margin for error is slight, and few things are as clear as one would like them to be. In the best of his sports stories Glanville leaves the reader, as he does Jimmy, suspended in that moment of doubt.

In *Love Is Not Love and Other Short Stories* (1985) Glanville returns to the themes that have marked his best fiction: the search for the aesthetic life, the ways in which sports mirror society, the ugliness of racial and ethnic prejudice, and the bittersweet memories of old loves. Americans in Italy are the subject of "The Painters," which is set in Glanville's favorite city: "Florence that winter was full of painters: resident painters and transient painters, painters from the States and painters from Europe, painters in studios and painters in *pensioni,* painters with the G.I. Bill and painters without it."

As he has done in at least three other stories, Glanville introduces two American men, Tom and Ted, whose GI Bills are running out. They are struggling to resist the "immense, centrifugal pull of the United States with its terrible realities"; they will succeed "for a few months, perhaps longer, but at last being drawn inexorably back." Perhaps Glanville has returned to this theme once too often because he gets some things wrong. Most glaringly he describes both Tom and Ted as being from the Midwest, "where Tom was manifestly urban, from Chicago, Ted was a country man, from Idaho." English writers are not expected to be experts on American regions, but Idaho is decidedly not in the Midwest.

More current in its topic and message is "Black Magic," in which a soccer coach refuses to sign a brilliant West Indian player because he is sure that black athletes do not have the heart and stamina to stand the test of English soccer. American readers will instantly recognize the racism in this statement; after all, they have heard the same remarks made about the black players who now dominate sports such as basketball and football. Another soccer story in the volume, "All Rovers Fans," deserves mention because it looks at the hooliganism that has marred British soccer's image in recent years and puts that hooliganism within the context of Britain's resurgent anti-Semitism.

"All Rovers Fans" brings the ugliness of "The Slogans" up-to-date. The central characters are a middle-aged man, who looks as if he has seen hard times, and a rather plump sixteen-year-old boy "with a soft, dark, Jewish face." The two are riding back to London on an excursion train after watching the Rovers defeat Ashton Villa. Also on the train are skinheads who came to the match more for the fights on the terraces than the action on the field. They roam through the cars drinking beer

and crying " 'Kill the yids.' " When they come to the boy and ask why he is staring out the window, his face turned from them, the man says in a Cockney accent, " 'He's a Rovers fan, isn't 'e? 'E's Rovers.' " The man's claiming kinship with the boy through their attachment to the team saves the youth from a beating.

The title story in the collection tells of a middle-aged academic's return to what is perhaps Romania. Ten years before, on a similar cultural-exchange visit, he met Marta, a beautiful graduate student who had been assigned to show him and other visitors the country's ancient monasteries. He and Marta had a brief, passionate affair, but then he left for home. Although they wrote each other for some time, they lost touch. She has become a memory he does not expect to find on his return visit.

Marta, now an assistant professor, is there, but he scarcely recognizes her because "she had grown incongruously fat." Out of politeness he agrees to go to her aunt's house for dinner, dreading that she might try to rekindle their old love and feeling annoyed that he finds her so unappealing. She does kiss him, but it is the quick peck on the cheek one reserves for old friends. He feels relieved; he has escaped having to tell her how he feels about the way she now looks. As she walks him to the door, she smiles lovingly at him and says, " 'You used to be so handsome.' " There is a gentleness in *Love Is Not Love,* a sympathy for old loves and lost beauty that is sometimes absent in Glanville's other stories about love and its aftermath. This is the work of an older writer who is looking in the mirror at a face that he remembers as a young man's face, a face looking back at him, giving no answers.

The enigmatic, often touching, emotional quality of his fiction makes Glanville's work worth serious reading. Despite his often predictable plots and stereotypical characters he has the ability to make old themes fit new contexts. Like the soccer players he so admires, he squares away and often hits his target, whether it be the pain of prejudice, the loss of old empires and the rise of new ones, the ebbing of athletic or artistic talent and the challenge from youthful contenders, or the loss of old loves and the consolation of new ones.

Giles Gordon

(23 May 1940 –   )

Julia M. Gergits
Youngstown State University

See also the Gordon entry in *DLB 14: British Novelists Since 1960: Part 1.*

BOOKS: *Landscape Any Date* (Edinburgh: Macdonald, 1963);

Two and Two Make One (Preston, Lancashire, U.K.: Akros, 1966);

Two Elegies (London: Turret, 1968);

Book 2000: Some Likely Trends in Publishing (London: Association of Assistant Librarians, 1969);

Pictures from an Exhibition (London: Allison & Busby, 1970; New York: Dial, 1970);

Eight Poems for Gareth (Frensham, Surrey, U.K.: Sceptre, 1970);

The Umbrella Man (London: Allison & Busby, 1971);

Between Appointments (Frensham, Surrey, U.K.: Sceptre, 1971);

About a Marriage (London: Allison & Busby, 1972; New York: Stein & Day, 1972);

Twelve Poems for Callum (Preston, Lancashire, U.K.: Akros, 1972);

Walter and the Balloon, by Gordon and Margaret Gordon (London: Heinemann, 1973);

Girl with Red Hair (London: Hutchinson, 1974);

One Man, Two Women (London: Sheep, 1974);

Egyptian Room, Metropolitan Museum of Art (Rushden, Northamptonshire, U.K.: Sceptre, 1974);

Farewell, Fond Dreams (London: Hutchinson, 1975);

100 Scenes from Married Life: A Selection (London: Hutchinson, 1976);

Enemies: A Novel About Friendship (Hassocks, Sussex, U.K.: Harvester, 1977);

The Oban Poems (Knotting, Bedfordshire, U.K.: Sceptre, 1977);

The Illusionist and Other Fictions (Hassocks, Sussex, U.K.: Harvester, 1978);

Couple (Knotting, Bedfordshire, U.K.: Sceptre, 1978);

Ambrose's Vision: Sketches Towards the Creation of a Cathedral (Brighton: Harvester, 1980);

The Twentieth-Century Short Story in English (London: British Council, 1989).

Giles Gordon (photograph by Fay Godwin)

OTHER: *Factions: Eleven Original Stories,* edited by Gordon and Alex Hamilton (London: Joseph, 1974);

You Always Remember the First Time, edited by Gordon, Michael Bakewell, and B. S. Johnson (London: Quartet, 1975);

Beyond the Words: Eleven Writers in Search of a New Fiction, edited, with an introduction, by Gordon (London: Hutchinson, 1975);

"Members of the Jury – ": The Jury Experience, edited, with an introduction, by Gordon and Dulan Barber (London: Wildwood House, 1976);

Prevailing Spirits: A Book of Scottish Ghost Stories, edited, with an introduction, by Gordon (London: Hamish Hamilton, 1976);

A Book of Contemporary Nightmares, edited by Gordon (London: Joseph, 1977);

Modern Scottish Short Stories, edited by Gordon and Fred Urquhart (London: Hamish Hamilton, 1978; revised edition, London: Faber, 1982);

Shakespeare Stories, edited by Gordon (London: Hamish Hamilton, 1982);

Modern Short Stories 2: 1940–1980, edited, with an introduction, by Gordon (London: Dent, 1982);

Best Short Stories, 4 volumes, edited by Gordon and David Hughes (London: Heinemann, 1986–1991); republished as *Best English Short Stories,* 4 volumes (New York: Norton, 1989–1992);

English Short Stories: 1900 to the Present, edited by Gordon (London: Dent, 1988);

Stories, 3 volumes, edited by Gordon (New York: Norton, 1989–1991);

The Minerva Book of Short Stories, 5 volumes, edited by Gordon and Hughes (London: Minerva, 1990–1993).

Giles Gordon has written poetry, short stories, novels, and children's literature; he has edited and coedited nearly two dozen short-story collections, thereby improving the short story's status and encouraging fellow short-story writers; he has worked for several publishing houses as an advertising executive, editor, and literary agent; and he has taught creative writing at Tufts University's London branch. Businessman, teacher, and writer, he has evolved from an avant-garde poet and short-story writer into a novelist and, lately, a patron of and collaborator with fellow writers. Although the critical reception of his work has not always been warm, he has published regularly and widely throughout the thirty years of his career.

Giles Alexander Esme Gordon was born 23 May 1940 in Edinburgh, Scotland, to Alexander Esme, a noted architect, and Betsy Balmont McCurrey Gordon. Gordon apparently had a love/hate relationship with Edinburgh; after attending the Edinburgh Academy he left Scotland for London at age twenty-two. His semiautobiographical novel, *About a Marriage* (1972), provides insights into his youthful aspirations and feelings about Scotland. Gordon describes a young man alone in London, determined never to return home to Edinburgh yet haunted by his repressive, restrained upbringing.

Gordon's training for becoming a writer was eclectic. He studied bookmaking and typography at school and worked as a businessman, learning about publishing from the big-business, profit side. He was editorial director of the publisher Victor Gollancz from 1967 to 1972 and a literary agent and

director for Anthony Sheil Associates (later Sheil, Land Associates) beginning in 1972. His first books were collections of poetry: *Landscape Any Date* (1963), *Two and Two Make One* (1966), and *Two Elegies* (1968), but he began writing short fiction early in his career. His work has been published in a wide array of periodicals, including *Punch, Drama,* the *Spectator,* and *Critical Quarterly.*

Gordon's first collection of stories, *Pictures from an Exhibition* (1970), demonstrates his early abstract, antinarrative style. In a series of loosely connected stories Gordon varies narrator and perspective, putting paintings into motion and creating irrational, internally contradictory plots. His work shares many traits with such experimental writers as Alain Robbe-Grillet, the French author of *Instantanés* (1962; translated as *Snapshots,* 1966) and a participant in the New Novel movement of the 1950s. Robbe-Grillet's "The Secret Room" (*Esquire,* February 1963) is a hallucinatory description of a dead or dying woman, the victim of a sadistic murderer. The scene is supposedly a painting, but it is in motion, changing throughout the narrative. Gordon uses this technique throughout his career, but particularly in the "Pictures from an Exhibition" series.

Gordon's narrative manipulation is overt: he tricks readers into temporarily searching for meaning and plot then turns and undermines his story by pointing out his artifice. Like such existentialist writers as Franz Kafka and Jean-Paul Sartre, he makes absurdity the centerpiece of his fiction. Critics and readers do not always appreciate Gordon's self-consciously deconstructing narrative strategies. The *Times Literary Supplement* (23 April 1970) found *Pictures from an Exhibition* overdone: "For a writer who prefers to make an instantly sharp and brief impact – few of his twenty-eight stories are more than a few pages long – he is sometimes tiresomely profligate with words repeating, twisting, worrying the impression he wants, like a director going over the same shot."

Gordon's stories echo strategies shared and, in some cases, initiated by Donald Barthelme and John Barth. Barth's "Life-Story" (*Lost in the Funhouse,* 1963), for example, presents an author wrestling with ideas and artistic formats, bursting out at his readers: "The reader! You, dogged, uninsultable, print-oriented bastard, it's you I'm addressing, who else, from inside this monstrous fiction." Gordon also confronts his readers, sometimes impatiently, in order to redirect their attention or to remind them that they have foolishly believed his narrative, which is so clearly fictional.

Gordon's fiction requires readers' engagement and patience.

The stories in *Pictures from an Exhibition,* however, contain more than stylistic experimentation: they are replete with war, death, absurdity, and contradictions, suggesting that humans have little control and even less perception. The pieces in the collection work against readers' expectations to the point of mocking anyone foolish enough to try to picture scenes, follow plots, or find significance. Readers' attempts to assert order are continually frustrated. In "The Deserter" the main character steals a camel and heads to the middle of a harsh desert, not to escape but to commit suicide. To this end he inflates a ball, climbs on top, and spins himself to death while his perplexed pursuers watch.

The ball reappears in a later story, "Balls Balance/People Balance on Balls." Gordon notes that acrobats and trained animals entertain their audience by balancing on balls; it seems difficult, an activity alien to most people's experience. Although balancing on a ball is funny, it is also somehow artistic because no practical product comes of it except entertainment. Similarly writers spin their stories out for the entertainment of often-bemused readers; perhaps writers and other artists are simply involved in dancing to their deaths. In fact, spinning on balls is what humans do, literally and figuratively. The earth is a ball, spinning out of humans' control or perception, and people spin to their deaths, much like Gordon's deserter. The suicidal character simply makes the common experience of spinning to death more apparent.

Gordon establishes boundaries, raises expectations, and then destroys them with disconcerting and challenging effect. His characters kill themselves because their dolls argue ("Two Marriages"), echoing their own miserable marriages; they confuse their wives and lovers in hallucinatory weddings that end in funerals ("Two Women, Two Eyes"). He revises as he writes, speaking to the reader to say, "No, that's really not what happened. This is," and then, "No, that's not it either." Some readers may find stories that unravel in this fashion frustrating; other readers may enjoy the erratic humor.

"Habits" presents a swimmer bobbing up and down in the ocean, watching two men build a box into which nuns disappear, two at a time. The nuns are actually soldiers, entering the box to disrobe and prepare for battle. Because nuns are not ordinarily guilty of violence and treachery, the soldiers appear to have selected a clever disguise; however, their wandering down a beach in pairs and entering newly constructed boxes, definitely aberrant behavior for nuns, draws attention to them. These ersatz nuns are so wrenched out of their usual roles that they become humorous despite their supposedly destructive intentions. The "habits" of the title apply equally to the nuns' garb and the readers' tendency to predict based on perceptual data. Because the characters appear to be nuns, they must be female and pacific, not male soldiers bent on conquering a village.

As Gordon worries his readers, he creates stories that comment on race and gender; characters may be white, black, or some unknown amalgam of races. In "5" he writes, "These days of racial integration it doesn't do to be dogmatic about the colour of a man." While mocking the late 1960s and early 1970s sensitivity to race, he sprinkles his stories with people of color, surprising readers out of stereotypes they may have about characters' ethnic heritage.

His sensitivity to women's issues is less well developed, but his characterizations are by no means simplistic. In "13" the main character at first seems to be a man but turns out to be a sixty-five-year-old woman who had been gang-raped early in her life while most of her village was slaughtered. At the beginning of the story the reader expects the narrator to be a man; most of the main characters in the book seem to be men. That the narrator is a woman, and one who has been horribly violated, is at first surprising, then shocking. Again, however, Gordon plays with the plot, writing that "the narrator" married her last gang-rapist and lived a long, if not happy, life with him.

In "Two Women, Two Eyes" two women blur together in the narrator's mind, becoming separate yet identical, as two eyes are separate but somehow unitary, held in check by their service to the body. In "The Tailor's Dummy" another woman celebrates her hateful husband's death by doing her laundry, so incensing the villagers that they ostracize her as a witch. In these stories women are wives and victims; they are potentially dangerous and passive aggressive.

Gordon's personal life – particularly his 1964 marriage to Margaret Anna Eastoe and their apparently tumultuous family life – figures strongly in even his most abstract stories. He reiterates descriptions of his wife's body, their lovemaking, the tragedies of several miscarriages, betrayals, and dedication. After years of trying to conceive and bear a child to term, she succeeded in having three children, two sons and a daughter. *About a Marriage* describes a couple's shared pain caused by repeated miscarriages, along with the attendant guilt and frustration. Edward and Ann's marriage has many unattractive features: they both have affairs; their lovemaking is incredibly frequent and described in annoying detail; and they agree not to tell one another the truth about central issues for the sake of wedded harmony. In many ways theirs is a Victorian marriage in which the partners participate in an elaborate pageantry designed to protect family stability. Edward and Ann are defined and engulfed by their roles of husband and wife, mother and father. Finally Gordon affirms love and loyalty.

Through the next several years Gordon produced more books of poetry, *Twelve Poems for Callum* (1972) and *One Man, Two Women* (1974); a children's book, *Walter and the Balloon* (1973), cowritten with his wife; and a novel, *Girl with Red Hair* (1974). His raising small children, maintaining a marriage, advancing at Anthony Sheil Associates, and publishing one or two books a year indicate the level of his energy and focus at that time. His interest in short fiction did not falter. In 1974 and 1975 his edited and coedited volumes of short stories began to appear: *Factions: Eleven Original Stories* (1974), *You Always Remember the First Time* (1975), and *Beyond the Words: Eleven Writers in Search of a New Fiction* (1975). He is a strong advocate of British short stories, and he has stated that British short-story writers are overshadowed by their American counterparts.

As an editor Gordon has redressed wrongs and created an outlet for excellent writing. In his introduction to *Modern Short Stories 2: 1940–1980* (1982) he provides two definitions of short stories: "Short stories, to purloin the brilliant title of a collection by B. S. Johnson and Zulfikar Shose, are statements against corpses; an affirmation of living"; and "To me, short stories explore, crystallize and interpret singular incidents, emotions, attitudes, places, characters, relationships, concepts." Short stories, then, are life-confirming, a celebration of humanity in all its absurd, cruel, and beautiful permutations. Gordon's editorial work has enabled him to foster a genre to which he has dedicated much of his career. During the 1980s he turned more and more to editing collections of other writers' short fiction.

In the meantime Gordon produced *Farewell, Fond Dreams* (1975), a collection of stories previously published in such notable journals as *Chapman*, *Daily Telegraph*, *Paris Review*, and *Scottish International*. *Farewell, Fond Dreams* further stretches the definitions of the short story, even the definitions of narrative, plot, characterization, and language. The collection opens with "An Adult Alphabet," a suitable beginning for an ironically philosophical text. Ordinarily alphabets are teaching tools: children listen to them and begin to associate objects with letters, such as "A is for apple" and "B is for banana." Gordon's alphabet teaches adults the absurdity of their lives.

For example, "B" is for a barber who is such a perfectionist that he gradually cuts off all his hair in his search for the perfect haircut, and "J" is for a jester who refuses to wear his cap and bells, which makes the court wonder whether he is an anarchist. With no hair the barber will be suspect: how can his clients believe he will cut their hair appropriately when he is living proof of his obsession? With no bells the jester jeopardizes his livelihood: without a suitable costume, his jibes must be serious and, therefore, a threat to society. The privileged position of court jester requires careful role-playing and a uniform.

Many of the letters characterize living contradictions. "I," an inside forward on a soccer team, decides to play for his opponents because he so respects their efforts. "L," a literary critic, postulates freedom in his criticism and broadcasts his inability to do math, yet he harps on his son to do his mathematics correctly. Gordon also comments on the condition of women. "M" is a mezzo-soprano whose voice has been stolen by a jealous soprano. "Q" is a queen who kills her husband, the king, in order to assume the throne, but she forgets that the throne goes to her son, not her. In brief entries of usually a few lines or short paragraphs Gordon establishes characters defined by their occupations and betrayed by their expectations. In addition their titles include an array of stereotypical traits. The reader's recognition of the absurdity of a mezzo-soprano with no voice or a young mother who knows nothing about babies is this alphabet's "education."

In *Farewell, Fond Dreams* Gordon confronts the paradox of using prose, a dynamic medium, to recreate a static form, such as a photograph or painting, by using microscopic detail and shifting perspectives and occasionally employing direct narrative intrusion. In "Pictures from an Exhibition 9" the narrator explains, "The idea is to articulate without evoking (to evoke being an evocation of what?) the attitude of the body without reference to the conventions of nineteenth-century narrative fiction as employed by any twentieth-century novelist you care to name other than two or three."

Linear narration, clear plot movement and resolutions, and consistent or unfolding characterization are either missing or parodied. The reader learns to distrust initial observations; seldom in these stories do images remain predictable. Gordon focuses on immediate scenes, including his own ruminations about their possible significance, and then denies relevance or correctness. He manipulates readers by misusing their learned abilities to read stories and the cognitive machinery that enables them to make sense of the world. Common perceptual data are scrambled in his insistence on immediacy. In "Pictures from an Exhibition 19" he writes, "Not remembering what came before, concentrating on the present but not aware of it, trying not to anticipate what will come after, concentrating on the present but not aware of it." A painting or photograph, theoretically, works like this description; detached from its context it appears to be a fragment of time. Viewers scan for clues as to its significance, postulating solutions, gathering details, and making guesses as to its meaning. Because it does not move as viewers contemplate it, they have the luxury of examining it completely. Viewers cannot reconstruct the entire story, since the image "narrates" only one frame.

In the stories in *Farewell, Fond Dreams* Gordon concentrates on the present with all of its misunderstandings, inaccuracies, and absurdities, and he detaches it from its context. It is, after all, in context that humans perceive significance, but in Gordon's "Pictures from an Exhibition" stories unprocessed perception, plucked from ordinary context, is all-important. In "Pictures from an Exhibition 13," based on a performance of a Harold Pinter play, mirror images echo and distort the character: "Distorting mirrors caricature, catch character, enlarge, reduce, compound, confuse, con." The reader is left to wonder which mirror is the most accurate. In "Pictures from an Exhibition, 18," supposedly based on a news item in the *Evening Standard,* the narrator describes a man who has killed his whole family. The narrator plays with the murder story, having the victims find themselves dead, find the others, kill the others, and go through other situations involving the incident. Gordon poses many solutions to perceptual problems.

Violence, war, and some teasing political commentary are included in the volume. In "An Attempt to Make Entertainment out of the War in Vietnam" Richard M. Nick and Edward R. G. Health (obviously Richard M. Nixon and Edward Heath) send letters back and forth, complaining about bad publicity, requesting photographs of one another, and arguing. Nick reveals an ever-growing and apparently justified paranoia, while Health writes as a loving but duplicitous fan. Interspersed with these ridiculous letters are detailed descriptions of photographs of horrible deaths, such as a burning soldier and a naked Vietnamese girl who has suffered a napalm attack and has no flesh on her back.

The narrator notes, "It is wrong to weep at the death of millions. No one man's grief can encompass the death of millions." Only through these individual images of violent, senseless death can survivors or observers mourn properly. The leaders care little for the death and suffering of soldiers or civilians; they care only for *their* pictures and public images. Their petty arguments underscore the cruelty and ethical bankruptcy of the Vietnam War and the selfishness and egocentrism of politicians. Although the leaders are most culpable, Gordon's readers are also implicated in the critique.

Gordon eases out of *Farewell, Fond Dreams* with another play on numbered vignettes, "Fingers 5-20," this time with no reference to childhood, and the title story. In "Fingers 5-20" the vignettes are snapshots, images of Edna St. Vincent Millay and Virginia Woolf walking along, wearing hot pants and a miniskirt, respectively; a walking dead man; a voiceless woman chasing her voice; a stripping woman; and a man who decides to get rid of some unnecessary words, which retaliate. These are adult images, jokes, obscenities, and crimes.

"Farewell, Fond Dreams" assaults the reader: "Our lives are problematic enough without the unexpected intrusion of strangers. The fictional character has no right to address you, the reader, direct. Mine, not yours, is the God's eye view." Unlike the angry narrator in Barth's "Life-Story" who proclaims, "Your own author bless and damn you his life is in your hands," the narrator in "Farewell, Fond Dreams" is God. He knows the machinations and motivations (or lack thereof) of his characters. If he feels like changing his wife's name throughout the story, which he does, it is his business, literally. The narrator slips back and forth through time, remembering a coffin, a wife, a son, and a daughter. These images are broken and fevered dreams.

Gordon worked on several books that were published in 1976: *"Members of the Jury — ": The Jury Experience, Prevailing Spirits: A Book of Scottish Ghost Stories,* and *100 Scenes from Married Life: A Selection.* The first two books are edited collections that demonstrate Gordon's interest in furthering the cause of short fiction and his willingness to collaborate with fellow writers. His brief introductions make his dedication to the genre clear: he defends short stories against those who would proclaim the superiority of novels or other media, such as movies or television. He laments the shortage of outlets for publishing stories, since magazines and journals have turned away from fiction. His edited volumes are an attempt to support writers and educate readers.

100 Scenes from Married Life: A Selection, another novel about Edward and Ann, has an affinity with Gordon's short-story collections. With only the roughest structure the novel presents a complex image of a foundering marriage: Edward returns from Venice with his mistress, spends time with his children, has sex with his wife, wishes she would take better care of herself, and so on, through to a confrontation that reaffirms their marriage. Each chapter is titled, and after each one Gordon includes independent "Interludes." This device is similar to Ernest Hemingway's use of interchapters in *In Our Time* (1925). The interludes – brief vignettes involving famous lovers, such as Romeo and Juliet or Mr. and Mrs. Casanova – comment on Edward and Ann's marital problems and provide comic relief in what otherwise would be a painful story.

The simple narrative, or perhaps the illusion of a narrative, falls away as the book moves forward. The chapters go back and forth in time: sometimes Ann is pregnant and sometimes they have a newborn child. As in *About a Marriage* miscarriages and small corpses figure in the story. Time seems pegged to the ages and number of their children. Despite the pain of recurring death that stems from procreation, Edward's family members – particularly his surviving children – protect him from chaos, even though he complains and has affairs.

Edward has become more impatient with his wife's foibles and more demanding of her time and body. He returns from Venice with his mistress, a woman he "loves," and he reflects on the anomaly of not being able to visualize his wife's face. Like Ann, his mistress is undefined; her individuality, if any, is irrelevant. She is simply his mistress by definition, and other information is unnecessary. In some of his short stories Gordon presents interchangeable women who are essentially irrelevant as individuals. Edward understands women only in reference to his own needs, a solipsistic tendency that causes him immense trouble and confusion. If women do not perform as they ought to, according to his stereotypes, desires, or needs, they are mysterious and uncooperative. In the first chapter the "every wife" does not seem worried about his affair; she allows him to go his own way, certainly a male fantasy come true.

In the following interlude, "Catherine and Henry," Catherine Parr tells Henry VIII that he does not understand marriage. Edward too is con-

fused by his wife and children. He has become more prone to self-delusion, callousness, and indulgence in alcohol. In the chapter "Work" Edward complains about the inefficiency of his secretaries and switchboard operators, all women. They accidentally cut him off in the middle of a phone conversation and ignore his requests for help. Despite occupying positions of inferiority they control his ability to communicate. They can disconnect him, forget to type his letters, type them badly, or neglect to mail them – and they do.

After an afternoon of drinking and philandering with his mistress, he returns to a besotted afternoon's work, still irritated with his "help" yet unable to remember what he says or does for the next several hours. He writes letters and takes phone calls, immediately forgetting the content. Just as his "help" is a set of generic female employees about whom he occasionally fantasizes, his job is generic, not worth remembering or particularizing. This provider controls little of his life, despite the illusion that he is in charge. His secretaries are aware of his condition; his mistress refuses to pretend that they will be married; and his wife knows perfectly well that he is drinking and carousing. The female characters may be indistinguishable women, but they are not powerless.

Gordon details the couple's intimacy, including Edward's withdrawing from Ann while copulating in order to answer the doorbell, his slowly fading erection still visible under his dressing gown ("Intrusion from the Outside World"). Edward describes Ann on the toilet, "farting . . . just like a cow in a field" ("Reconstruction"). Clearly Edward has no illusions about his wife or their relationship, and his remark indicates serious distaste. At one point he ponders whether women pass gas before they are married. He cannot remember any unmarried women who did, implying that women present a false image before marriage and let themselves go afterward, a stereotypical and sexist maxim.

In a later chapter, "Ann's Story," Ann reflects on Edward's telling her that she looks "sluttish" in a photograph. Although he still avails himself of her body for sex, he is repulsed and perfectly willing to anatomize just how she falls short. Edward's unhappiness is further revealed by his proclaiming that he wants to redesign their house completely. He does not want to move, nor does he want to leave their neighborhood; he wants everything the same but completely different. This middle-aged man refuses to acknowledge that he is in crisis; he cannot accept his life, yet he does not wish to lose it. Ann snaps at him for being unreasonable and unrealistic: either

Dust jacket for Gordon's 1978 collection of short fiction, which focuses on violence, sex, and cruelty

they have to move, metaphorically destroying their relationship, or they have to stay. They cannot do both. Oddly enough – despite the crudity, messiness, and distaste – the book reaffirms marriage and love.

In 1977 Gordon produced *Enemies: A Novel About Friendship* and a book of poetry, *The Oban Poems*. Two collections of his short fiction, *The Illusionist and Other Fictions* and *Couple*, were published in 1978. The stories in *The Illusionist* are gathered from many sources, including *Brunton's Miscellany* (1977), *Labrys* (1978), and *New Worlds 9* (1975). In *The Illusionist* Gordon continues experimenting with fragmented narratives and ever-shifting realities. Circus performers and self-absorbed middle-aged men are frequent subjects, and there is a stronger emphasis on absurdity, if possible, than in earlier volumes, with brief respites offered by the birth of children and loyalty. He also persists in focusing on suicides, violence, cruelty, and sexual crudity.

In "Omega" ("Alpha" ends the collection) a hospitalized woman, apparently in great pain, is surrounded by many doctors. At first it seems as if she may be in some perverse sexual position; then it seems as if she may be dying. In fact she is giving birth under heavy sedation. She cannot remember where or who she is; for her the birth is foggy and painful.

Meanwhile, her husband is at home, drinking, wearing her underwear, and masturbating. While she is splayed out in a drugged haze, he perversely echoes her position: he is sprawled out, dead drunk, focusing on his genitals. It may be possible to glean some significance from his action beyond its repulsiveness. Perhaps he can do nothing to help her and turns to his only outlets. It is more probable, however, that the husband is disengaged from her pain and the outcome of their sex. He is only concerned with animalistic, onanistic pleasures.

Many of the other stories, such as "Nineteen Policemen Searching the Solent Shore," continue Gordon's multiple perspectives and revisions on the fly. "Visit to a Museum" presents a woman climbing stairs. One moment she is a splashed corpse on the sidewalk – her face miraculously intact but her mangled body squirming on the sidewalk – surrounded by shocked and vomiting people. Then she is on top of the building, thinking of a woman jumping into a distant pool like a circus entertainer. As she stands on the ledge, she provides the crowd with the thrill and excitement of a carnival, a place where ordinary rules do not apply. This story shares much with such earlier stories as "The Deserter": the main characters entertain a crowd by imitating circus performers or acrobats as they commit suicide.

In "Letters to a Spanish Painter" the narrator insists that he has a correspondence with Salvador Dali and that Dali writes him to express dismay that the narrator has not written often enough. Then the narrator says that the second letter is returned unopened; thus no correspondence exists. The narrator uses the short story as a vehicle to tell Dali that he does not exist because the letter was returned. Existence depends on participating in a system. If the system rejects a person, she or he does not exist. In "Seven Men Together" Gordon writes: "The individual . . . possesses no individuality as an individual, only as a member of a group. How interesting but strange, paradoxical. If taken to its illogical conclusion this means that the recluse, the saint, does not exist." The suicidal woman and the letter writer share a participation in public performances. They exist, at least as far as society is concerned, through their public activities and communication with others. Systems grant meaning, whether they be ritualistic performances, the postal service, or marriage. In *100 Scenes from Married Life* Edward clings to his marriage because the system allows him to exist. Without it he ceases to be. In effect saints do not exist because they are irrelevant to humanity; devoted to God, they do not contribute to or participate in any group. Gordon's position on systems reaffirms community and society. Even as the author negates and undercuts order, he analyzes its importance.

"The Illusionist" characterizes one of the few content men in Gordon's fiction. Zingari, a magician, thinks of himself as an artist, a misunderstood and underappreciated man capable of sublimity. With his two roommates, Sarah and Anna, watching, he combs his hair:

> He'd adjust the recalcitrant hair, and every time this happened it seemed to destroy the total effect so that he would have to start from scratch again. He worked on it for half an hour, quite oblivious to time passing, the world growing older. The time could be spent differently, but more usefully? Who was to say.

Like the title character in "B Barber" Zingari is a perfectionist, determined to accomplish miracles with his relatively ordinary hair. Like Gordon himself, Zingari works and reworks his art, inevitably ruining it before it is "done" yet determined to get it right, whatever that may mean. The women are accustomed to Zingari's hair performance, so they say nothing as he combs and recombs. When he is tired of combing his hair, he turns to his magic. He cuts Sarah in half as she reclines in a coffin-shaped box. Anna rocks patiently, staring out the window, uninterested in Zingari's magic.

It is significant that the women are passive; they create nothing except Zingari's insecurity. At the end of the story he declares that he will quit his profession because he is tired of the women's lack of interest and the importuning of fans, but he continues because his fans' requests for autographs prove that he has a specific identity as an artist and that he actually exists. This circus performer symbolizes the artist amid his work, practicing and posturing as he creates himself through his art. He manipulates himself into existence, achieving a second birth independent of a mother.

Works of art are at the center of two other stories in *The Illusionist,* "Dolores" and "Maestro." In "Dolores" two first-person speakers work through a contradictory story of the death of a woman sculptor. One speaker refuses to be rushed along as he describes a statue of a woman he finds in a deserted house. The statue is covered with a cloth, apparently soaked in blood or dyed red from clay. The speaker falls in love with the woman captured in clay; he says that she is the most beautiful woman he has ever seen. To this point the story sounds much like a rehash of the Pygmalion myth. However, when the man removes the cloak, getting its "blood" on his hands, he discovers that the sculpture is actually that of a man. He is furious that he has fallen in love with the image of a man. The woman sculptor appears in the room, grabbing the cloak from his hands; he follows and finds her dead. According to the speaker, she sculpted her image into clay as a man because she would have preferred being a man. The story shifts as the reader discovers that the speaker is charged with her murder and imprisoned.

The story raises many questions. Was the sculptor murdered or did she kill herself? Perhaps she could not face life as an unappreciated woman artist. Did the man kill her because he was infuriated at being fooled into loving a man? Being tricked into a pseudo-homosexual experience may have unsettled the speaker enough to incite him to violence. Clearly the statue means different things to the two characters. To the sculptor it signifies her longing to be a man (at least according to the male speaker, perhaps the man guilty of her murder); to the man, it is an object of love that recoils on him as he gets to know it better. Another possible reading of the statue is that the woman artist is an aberration, a monstrous and misleading anomaly; perspective makes meaning.

In "Maestro" a concert pianist appears onstage, greeted by polite applause, and a member of the audience is stricken with fear in anticipation of the torrent of notes he is about to hear. In this story the artist is actually torturing his audience, the man who wishes to relish a single note, to worship its purity and beauty. The multitude of notes the pianist pours into the air overwhelms this oversensitive listener, who tries to convince himself that he will be fine:

> I was there to listen, in advance of listening I had paid to listen, I tried to listen, I concentrated on listening, the note, notes, sound, sounds — stop full stop, full point before I, after both of them, the first two notes, finger tips touching the keyboard, stop, oh Christ, this is, was too much, relax, relax, back to the beginning, please, the fingers above the keyboard, the concentration, withdraw.

This is both torture and sexual arousal. The listener imagines himself standing up and shouting protests, groveling naked on the floor, and pleading for mercy. The purchaser of art is tortured by satiation, too much art. The listener's aesthetic is too simple; most audiences expect more than one note, unless they are hearing a John Cage piece. There is a purity in simple artwork, in delicacies: one diamond, one piece of cake, one pearl. The listener pleads for only one note to contemplate. As a gourmet would become ill from too much cake, the listener gets ill from too many notes. It maddens him that they are wasted — unappreciated and essentially unheard — and he does not have time to ingest them properly.

Couple presents more stories of disconnected mates and lovers. In "Bedrooms" a man and a woman have individual bedrooms; each feels alienated in the other's room. One lover's space is a hostile landscape for the other. In "Blade" Gordon writes and rewrites, retracting the action immediately after proposing it and changing the plot as he goes, beginning with the dramatic statement "Vernon plunged the blade into Maureen." At one point the narrator suggests that Vernon uses a sword on his wife, but the narrator scoffs at that idea: "Come on. People don't accidentally drop swords, and on their kitchen floors." Since a sword is too unbelievable, the narrator shifts to another, more credible method of destruction: a knife.

For a few minutes the wife plays with the sword metaphor, noting that "he had been born with it as part of his equipment, the sword in the stone, steel which had grown with flesh." In this obviously phallic image the wife analyzes why it is normal for her husband to have the mythic sword in the stone, the Arthurian symbol of royal lineage. Her husband's "sword," with which he was born, proves his male identity too. Gordon then shifts again, having the wife kill her husband and pretend that nothing has happened: "I understand. It's easy. Free will. That's what it's called, yes." As Gordon has done so many times, he manipulates the narrative, making it difficult to determine just what has happened, if anything. And that is precisely the point after all: since this is a short story, nothing has happened. This story is simply a collection of words that generate certain images in the reader's mind; it is the reader's fault for expecting coherence and logic.

Although the 1980s were productive for Gordon, his output did not include independent short-story collections. *Ambrose's Vision: Sketches Towards the Creation of a Cathedral* (1980) is his most recent novel, and he has continued to champion the cause of short fiction. In the introduction to *Modern Short Stories 2: 1940–1980* Gordon explains the special attractions of short fiction: "Thus both writer and reader may be daring and imaginative in the infinite pastures of the short story, and constantly be surprised and stimulated. The world may, and frequently is, being made wondrously new."

Gordon seems to have gone through a difficult time in his personal life. His wife died in 1989, leaving him with three children. In 1990 he married Margaret-Anne McKernan, and they have had one daughter. His professional life has changed, perhaps as a result of his personal upheaval or perhaps simply as a result of his maturing and shifting directions. Although his stories continue to appear in journals and edited collections, since the early 1980s the main thrust of his professional activity has been edited collections.

Gordon's influence is difficult to measure. He has been a prolific short-story writer and a dedicated advocate of the genre. Critics have not always been kind, although he has had his supporters. His stories work best in small doses because they require close attention and patience. It is tempting to read a short-story collection as a complete work, much as most people read novels. This tactic fails miserably with Gordon's work: it is too intellectual, contradictory, and intense. His stories are complex works of art, best read as his character in "Maestro" advocates: one at a time, with an ample period for pondering and savoring the story. He teaches readers not only to appreciate the short-story form and its potential, but also to read more slowly and patiently. Given time, his stories burst with significance, challenging, annoying, and teasing readers into seeing ordinary scenes, paintings, photographs, and daily married life from unusual angles.

L. P. Hartley

(30 December 1895 – 13 December 1972)

Edward T. Jones
York College of Pennsylvania

See also the Hartley entry in *DLB 15: British Novelists, 1930–1959: Part 2.*

BOOKS: *Night Fears and Other Stories* (London & New York: Putnam, 1924);

Simonetta Perkins (London & New York: Putnam, 1925);

The Killing Bottle (London & New York: Putnam, 1932);

The Shrimp and the Anemone (London: Putnam, 1944); republished as *The West Window* (Garden City, N.Y.: Doubleday, Doran, 1945);

The Sixth Heaven (London: Putnam, 1946; Garden City, N.Y.: Doubleday, 1947);

Eustace and Hilda (London: Putnam, 1947; New York: British Book Centre, 1958);

The Travelling Grave and Other Stories (Sauk City, Wis.: Arkham House, 1948; London: Barrie, 1951);

The Boat (London: Putnam, 1949; Garden City, N.Y.: Doubleday, 1950);

My Fellow Devils (London: Barrie, 1951; New York: British Book Centre, 1958);

The Go-Between (London: Hamish Hamilton, 1953; New York: Knopf, 1954);

The White Wand and Other Stories (London: Hamish Hamilton, 1954);

A Perfect Woman (London: Hamish Hamilton, 1955; New York: Knopf, 1956);

The Hireling (London: Hamish Hamilton, 1957; New York: Rinehart, 1958);

Facial Justice (London: Hamish Hamilton, 1960; Garden City, N.Y.: Doubleday, 1961);

Two for the River (London: Hamish Hamilton, 1961);

The Brickfield (London: Hamish Hamilton, 1964);

The Betrayal (London: Hamish Hamilton, 1966);

The Novelist's Responsibility: Lectures and Essays (London: Hamish Hamilton, 1967);

The Collected Short Stories of L. P. Hartley (London: Hamish Hamilton, 1968);

Poor Clare (London: Hamish Hamilton, 1968);

L. P. Hartley (photograph by Mark Gerson)

The Love-Adept: A Variation on a Theme (London: Hamish Hamilton, 1969);

My Sisters' Keeper (London: Hamish Hamilton, 1970);

The Harness Room (London: Hamish Hamilton, 1971);

Mrs. Carteret Receives and Other Stories (London: Hamish Hamilton, 1971);

The Collections (London: Hamish Hamilton, 1972);

The Will and the Way (London: Hamish Hamilton, 1973).

Collection: *The Complete Short Stories of L. P. Hartley*, introduction by David Cecil (London: Hamish Hamilton, 1973).

OTHER: "Three Wars," in *Promise of Greatness: The War of 1914–18*, edited by George A. Panichas (New York: Day, 1968), pp. 250–258.

L. P. Hartley's generally favorable critical reputation and dedicated readership in twentieth-century British short fiction have been primarily sustained through his Gothic tales, a genre he once described as the most exacting form of literary art. According to Peter Bien in *L. P. Hartley* (1963) the author began writing such stories at the request of Cynthia Asquith, who commissioned macabre tales from Hartley for her annual collections of ghost stories. Hartley's earliest successes in imaginative literature were with short stories, and his interest in this form continued throughout his life.

While the prevailing critical assessment of Hartley's oeuvre holds that he is more successful as a novelist than as a writer of short fiction and that his stories are best seen as studies, sketches, and experiments for larger works, that opinion may be undergoing revision with new appreciation for Hartley's achievement and craft in shorter forms of prose fiction. His ambition was to write the kind of story that his great predecessors – Edgar Allan Poe, Nathaniel Hawthorne, Henry James, and Charlotte and Emily Brontë – might have written had they lived in the twentieth century. As the fearsome circumstances of the late twentieth century receive fictional treatment, the darker underside of Hartley's sensibility seems increasingly relevant and persuasive. The fragmentation of the brief tale sometimes permits the extremely decorous Hartley to give voice to his more intimate and extravagant fears in an uninhibited way to a degree not observed in his novels.

Leslie Poles Hartley was born 30 December 1895 to H. B. and Mary Elizabeth Thompson Hartley at Whittlesea, a small town in the Cambridgeshire fens, but when he was a youngster, he moved with his family to an estate, Fleeton Towers, near the city of Peterborough. His father, a solicitor, practiced in Peterborough. He retired from law early in life to assume chairmanship and direction of what became a successful brickworks from which the family derived a fairly substantial fortune. In later life L. P. Hartley confessed to feelings of snobbery and shame about the family's success "in trade." He was the middle child and only son in a family of three children, none of whom ever married.

Hartley entered Harrow school in September 1910 and was named Leaf Scholar in 1915, the year of his departure. He matriculated to Balliol College, Oxford, the same year, but his education was interrupted by World War I. He enlisted in the army in April 1916 and served as a second lieutenant in the Norfolk Regiment. Although he did not participate in overseas action, he received a medical discharge from the military in September 1918. Hartley returned to Balliol, where he was named Williams Exhibitioner. He received his baccalaureate in December 1921, having passed his examination in modern history with second-class honors. Although Hartley remained at Balliol for a full academic year after his finals, he did not begin work toward a higher degree. In "Three Wars" (*Promise of Greatness: The War of 1914–18,* 1968) Hartley confirms his membership in the generation disillusioned by war and its aftermath: "The First World War shook one's belief in the essential goodness of humanity – the belief that all's for the best in the best of all possible worlds that, with many conspicuous exceptions, had dominated Victorian thought."

Something of this pessimistic attitude informs Hartley's initial collection of short fiction, *Night Fears and Other Stories* (1924). In the title story a newly hired night watchman who has been fabricating incidents of trial and stress in order to impress his wife finds himself sharing his brazier with a stranger. In conversation with this stranger the night watchman articulates the anxiety-producing circumstances of his life. The stranger, Iago-like, stimulates further submerged fears on the part of the night watchman: of his wife's fidelity, the loss of his children's affection, and the possibility of mental breakdown as a consequence of his inability to sleep during the day. In desperation the night watchman pulls a knife and in turn is murdered with it. The stranger steps over the body and disappears into a blind alley, leaving a track of dark, irregular footprints. To be sure, the night watchman may be a victim of his own dark mind; nevertheless, there is a stranger who does not feel the cold that grips and finally destroys the watchman.

From the beginning of his work in short fiction Hartley proved himself skillful in attaching fear to what Sigmund Freud calls the "uncanny": "nothing else than a hidden, familiar thing that has undergone repression and then emerged from it." Hartley's conception of the horror story seems closely allied to H. P. Lovecraft's definition of the genre in *Supernatural Horror in Literature* (1973):

The true weird tale has something more than secret murder, bloody bones, or a sheeted form clanking chains according to rule. A certain atmosphere of breathless and unexplainable dread of outer, unknown forces must be present; and there must be a hint, expressed with a seriousness and portentousness becoming its subject, of that most terrible conception of the human brain — a malign and particular suspension or defeat of those fixed laws of Nature which are our only safeguard against the assaults of chaos and the daemons of unplumbed space.

In "The Island," the longest story in *Night Fears,* a married couple, the Santanders, are shown a house that has been designed without edges and sharp angles — an architectural feature Hartley develops further in his futuristic allegorical novel *Facial Justice* (1960) — but the Santanders have grown "edges" of their own, as the wife has taken a series of lovers. Her husband finally strangles her and then drowns himself in the sea. The couple's organized life has been torn by an inner chaos, part of which is symbolized by Mr. Santander's torn fingernail, acquired while strangling his wife, with its "jagged rent revealing the quick, moist and gelatinous." Hartley's description of the island "as some crustacean, swallowed by an ill-turned starfish, but unassimilated" also anticipates the opening image in *The Shrimp and the Anemone* (1944), the first volume of the *Eustace and Hilda* trilogy.

Hartley is fond of symbolic retribution and substitution as seen in "The Killing Bottle," the title story of his 1932 collection. In this tale the would-be victim, Jimmy Rintoul, an amateur lepidopterist, survives Rollo Verdew's plot against him. Ironically, the madman in this story destroys all who, in his opinion, are unnecessarily cruel to living things. In "The Travelling Grave," the title story of Hartley's 1948 collection, the villain is trapped by the trick coffin he has planned to use on his guest. In *The Travelling Grave and Other Stories* Hartley deals with curses ("Feet Foremost"); haunted houses ("A Change of Ownership"); and vengeance and retribution ("The Travelling Grave," "A Visitor from Down Under," and "The Cotillon").

The best and most provocative of Hartley's horror stories in *Night Fears, The Killing Bottle,* and *The Travelling Grave* portray humans as sick animals, bearing within themselves an inexorable appetite for evil, revenge, and retribution. The masochism often found in Hartley's novels occasionally appears transformed into something closer to sadism in his short fiction. Hartley can be not only cold to life but even actively punishing. As a character in "Podolo" (*The Travelling Grave*) observes: "We loved her and so we had to kill her." This statement is made in a dream sequence, yet its relevance might be greater than a waking insight. Perhaps Hartley uses the horror story as a kind of little theater of

submerged passions, transforming hidden desires for punishment into freedom, play, and pleasure. He presents the ubiquity of guilt and corruption through the implication that everyone is latently a killer.

Bien quotes a passage from an essay Hartley wrote for the British periodical *Sketch,* to which he was a frequent contributor in the early 1930s. Here Hartley recommends that ghost-story writers make use of childhood fantasies, at least where macabre visitors are concerned:

> The trouble with many ghost stories is that, though the writer has quite a good idea of what constitutes an alarming ghost, he cannot make it seem a natural product of its environment. He has forgotten the sensations of his childhood; he cannot remember when a dressing-gown hung over the end of the bed looked like a witch crouching or a man with a broken neck. Consequently the spectre, when it comes, has the effect of a jack-in-the-box.

Hartley also followed the tradition of Jamesian realism in some of his short stories as well as in his longer fiction, beginning with the novella *Simonetta Perkins* (1925). Set in Venice, Hartley's favorite European city, the novella recounts what happens when a wealthy, proper Bostonian, Miss Lavinia Johnstone, becomes deeply infatuated with Emilio, her handsome gondolier. Surprised by her sudden infatuation with Emilio, Lavinia begins a kind of epistolary novel to her worldly friend Elizabeth Templeman, who is recuperating in Rome from a chill — not fatal, as with the title character in James's *Daisy Miller* (1878) — contracted after a nighttime visit to the Colosseum. Lavinia pretends she is concerned about her friend "Simonetta Perkins," who has developed a romantic attachment for a gondolier. Displacement through fictional personae is not uncommon in Hartley's later novels, nor is projection of fantasy situations that reflect on the protagonist's condition. Speaking for Simonetta, Lavinia intimates that her "friend" has talked about setting up the gondolier in some attractive occupation in the United States, possibly as chauffeur to the Perkinses. Elizabeth's advice to Simonetta, whom she perceives immediately as Lavinia, is to leave Venice at once.

Jamesian values of renunciation and of passion imagined, yet not enacted, prevail in *Simonetta Perkins.* Although people such as the honeymooning Lord and Lady de Winton see Lavinia as an unlighted candle, Hartley accords his protagonist an inward illumination of conscience and consciousness. She differs markedly from another love-struck visitor to Venice, Thomas Mann's Gustav Aschenbach in *Der Tod in Venedig* (1912; translated as *Death in Venice*, 1925). If Lavinia seems to court a destiny similar to Aschenbach's, at the end of the novella she accepts a different one, which is consistent with what she has always been. She follows her friend's advice and leaves Venice.

There is a rather poignant biographical connection between Hartley and Lavinia. A closet homosexual throughout his life, Hartley developed a passion for Venetian gondoliers that he apparently renounced less willingly than his protagonist in the novella. However, political exigencies prior to World War II kept Hartley from Venice. A homosexual subtext is more readily observed in Hartley's novels. His friend Francis King, whose candor about these matters is on public record, notes Hartley's reticence about homosexuality in a *Sunday Telegraph* (17 December 1972) piece written after Hartley's death:

> Had he been a man less scrupulous about not offending convention or shocking his friends, there is no doubt that, like E. M. Forster's, his books would have been very different. But the tensions set up between what he wanted to say and what he felt was sayable by a man of his position and age may, I suspect, have helped to generate the extraordinary electric energy that powers his finest works. Late in his career he began to be more explicit; but even over "The Harness Room" he worried aloud in my presence whether this or that friend might not be shocked and disgusted by it.

Like James, Hartley wanted to awaken his readers to the inadequacies of narrow, inflexible interpretations of reality. This may be one reason why both authors were attracted to writing ghost stories. In *The Tragic Comedians: Seven Modern British Novelists* (1963) James Hall notes the evolution of Hartley's technique from his suspense stories to his novels, in which human relations are seen "as absurdly dangerous games of hide-and-seek, though he no longer deals in mystery." What is supernaturally explicable in the tales of terror becomes more oblique in the presumed reality of the novels, where revenants are generally excluded. The writer of horror stories can reduce evil and adversaries to size by stylizing the situation to suit an abstract purpose. Supernaturalism gives the writer the means of controlling reality, if not necessarily understanding it, for magic deals in feints, ambiguities, distractions, and illusions. Likewise, many, if not most, short stories present characters overwhelmed and enthralled by something within or without them that they invest with mythic as opposed to logical significance.

Hartley's short stories demonstrate his impressive ability to turn reality into nightmare and phantasmagoria with no warning. Hartley's oeuvre seems to confirm Charles E. May's observation in "The Nature of Knowledge in Short Fiction" (*Studies in Short Fiction*, 1984): "The novel exists to reaffirm the world of 'everyday' reality; the short story exists to 'defamiliarize' the everyday."

Some of Hartley's most engaging stories explore the relationship of the literary artist to his life and work, as in two tales from *The White Wand and Other Stories* (1954), which also includes stories from *Night Fears* and *The Killing Bottle*. With almost wistful self-reference Hartley offers a comic horror story exploring the relationship of an author with his fictional creation in "W. S." Here author Walter Streeter keeps getting postcards from a "W. S." who, sounding like a critic, accuses him of moral ambiguity and spiritual lassitude in his character delineation. When "W. S." finally appears in the "flesh," he turns out to be the one completely evil character Streeter created in his youth before graduating to "ambiguity." Streeter realizes that his characters are either largely projections of himself or diametric opposites. The postcards that Streeter receives from W. S. show towers of famous cathedrals because the author, like Hartley himself, is known to admire cathedrals, a penchant that also appears in many of Hartley's novels. The character goes by the eponym William Stainsforth; he claims that Streeter made him a scapegoat, unloading all his self-hatred on a helpless character.

Streeter is given one chance to soften his portrayal of Stainsforth. All the author must do is find one virtue with which he ever credited this character, "just one kind thought – just one redeeming feature." Faced with a moral and aesthetic choice Streeter tries desperately to think of or fabricate something within the two minutes allotted him, but the author's moral rigor and the cause of goodness prevent him from asserting virtue where there is only evil. He submits to the literal iron hand of his character and is mercilessly strangled. "W. S." is a disturbing fable – given Hartley's usual component of "realistic" plausibility – of the artist capitulating to the perilous limitations of his former creations. The story effectively underscores Streeter's inability to deny his knowledge of evil in himself.

In "A Rewarding Experience" author Harry Tarrant is unable to produce a short story he has been commissioned to write. Tarrant can no longer write about objects, nor can he evoke nature in the manner of Thomas Hardy or Joseph Conrad. While in the past he has often written about the human race, nothing new on the species stirs his consciousness or imagination. Hartley's description of Tarrant and his dilemma approaches droll self-reference, even self-parody:

> Harry Tarrant was a bachelor and fiction-writing had confirmed him in the single state. The more he wrote about human beings the less he wanted to have anything to do with them. He got them where he wanted them, and that was outside. Outside, they obeyed the rules – his rules. Critics had remarked on his aloofness, but it was perfectly in order for an artist to be aloof.

Later he reminisces that he has kept "illness at bay, the war at bay, marriage at bay; he kept life itself at bay. Only art had he welcomed; and now art had gone back on him."

On a walk Tarrant encounters a dogfight. While separating the two animals and returning one to its mistress, he sustains a bloody hand. The woman is solicitous and accompanies Tarrant to his home. He enjoys the nursing attention given his hand by his new acquaintance. Her spaniel, understandably nervous after his ordeal, wets the rug, but Tarrant is inexplicably happier because his house has now been fouled and bloodstained, although he cannot articulate his feelings to the woman, who elects to leave without the sherry he has offered. But outside she and her spaniel once again discover their original attacker. Tarrant triumphantly shuts his gate, exclaiming, "Now you simply *must* come back." The implied consequence is that the writer will find his art less desiccated because of this renewed contact with life.

Another beguiling story somewhat along the same lines is "Two for the River" (*Two for the River*, 1961), which is narrated in first person by Mr. Minchin, another bachelor/writer who debates the advisability of selling his river home to a young couple. The guardian deity of his house accuses Mr. Minchin of fickleness; as the writer had once fallen in love with the house, he is now transferring his affections to the young couple. The house, Paradise Paddock, seems ill-suited to the sounds of squalling children whose din will forever drown out the voice of the house. Mr. Minchin fears that the house will be altered, broken up into flats, and that he will be left homeless.

His interior monologue is interrupted by the sounds of a swan attack on the river. The Marchmonts, the house-hunting couple, have taken their canoe on the river to give Mr. Minchin time to reach his decision about selling the house. Although he has decided to sell, his announcement is stifled by the couple's narrative of how they were attacked on the river. A male swan jumped on Mrs. Marchmont's back, and her husband killed it with a canoe paddle in order to save her from drowning. The honeymooning Marchmonts decide that Paradise Paddock is not for them. In gratitude for his hospitality they offer Mr. Minchin their canoe, and he accepts. The canoe signifies the true ownership of the river and the house.

Mr. Minchin apostrophizes the river, claiming it has let him down. In truth it has saved him through the intervention of the swan. He spies the female swan anxiously seeking her fallen mate and thinks, "She never had to call him before . . . and now he will not hear her." Mr. Minchin's identity with the house and river are once more indivisible; he is his own guardian deity:

> Stiffly I got up and climbed back to the house – my house, for it was mine after all; the swan had saved it for me. A moment's doubt remained: would the switch work? It did, and showed me what was still my own.

Hartley was devoted to rowing and for most of his life maintained a house on the Avon River in the West Country for that purpose, which figures prominently in his novel *The Boat* (1949). "Two for the River" embodies his best manner, method, and tone. The interior monologues and dream narrations succeed in penetrating beyond consciousness into the privacy of the interior self, which Hartley especially values and seeks to explore. In its evocation of the house and swans as symbolic reminders of Mr. Minchin, Hartley's writing resembles that of his friend and admirer Elizabeth Bowen. The outer world becomes a character itself as well as a symbol of the narrator's inner self.

In *Two for the River* Hartley makes wry contributions to the peculiar tradition of Christmas horror tales of which Charles Dickens's *A Christmas Carol* (1843) is the most notable example. Hartley's efforts in this vein include "Someone in the Lift" and "The Waits." The first offers the story of a grisly Oedipal accident at Christmastime. Mr. and Mrs. Maldon and their son, Peter, are spending the holiday at the Brompton Court Hotel. Peter is fascinated by the hotel's elevator, which he imagines has an occupant who disappears as soon as the lift comes to rest. Peter's mother tells him to ask his father whether someone is truly there each time, but the son hesitates risking his father's ridicule in Hartley's acknowledgment of Oedipal struggle. When his father is with him, Peter never sees the figure in the lift. Hence Peter theorizes that the someone must be his father.

Dust jacket for Hartley's 1954 collection of short stories, some of which concern writers and their relationships to their fictional characters

Two days before Christmas the lift breaks down, and Peter is forbidden to touch the button during the period of its repair. On Christmas Eve, however, as Peter awaits the appearance of Father Christmas, who he knows is really his father, he surreptitiously pushes the button and activates the lift:

> The lift was coming up from below, not down from above, and there was something wrong with its roof – a jagged hole that let the light through. But the figure was there in its accustomed corner, and this time it hadn't disappeared, it was still there, he could see it through the mazy criss-cross of the bars, a figure in a red robe with fur edges, and wearing a red cowl on its head: his father, Father Christmas, Daddy in the lift. But why didn't he look at Peter, and why was his white beard streaked with red?

The final image is of toys covered with blood at the feet of Peter's father, "red as the jag of lightning that tore through his brain." Although Peter never manifests any conscious desire to harm his father, circumstances contrive to bring the subconscious Freudian struggle to hideous reality.

In "The Waits" two ghostly carolers, a man and a boy, turn assailants with the result that Mr. Marriner, the head of the household, dies of a coronary on the grass near his garden gate. Psychological terror and visitation of evil disturb the silent night of Christmas Eve. The cozy Marriner family must say farewell to more than the ghost of another year.

Hartley examines the ultimate value of inanimate objects in some stories from *The White Wand*. In "The Price of the Absolute" Timothy Carswell is elated with his overpriced celadon vase because he feels he is the possessor of absolute beauty, having been told so by a salesman. In his introduction to *The Complete Short Stories of L. P. Hartley* (1973) David Cecil considers that the author endorses art over life in this story. In the context of "The Price of the Absolute," however, Carswell's faith in his art object is largely vitiated, even though he does not admit this fact to himself, by overhearing the salesman deliver a similar endorsement to another customer about yet another art object. To Carswell, his vase may well be unique, but Hartley dramatizes the situational absurdity of purchasing absolute beauty in the marketplace.

The ultimate reductio ad absurdum of any claim regarding the superiority of art over life is sketched in "Mr. Blandfoot's Picture" (*The White Wand*). All the fashionable ladies in Settlemarsh contrive to get a glimpse of Mr. Blandfoot's reputed masterpiece. The redoubtable Mrs. Marling succeeds in getting Mr. Blandfoot to accept an invitation to her salon to exhibit his picture, but she discovers to her shame that the picture is tattooed on her guest's chest. Social snobbery and the pretension to elegance are of little avail before such an exhibition. Mr. Blandfoot collapses during the middle of his display but is later revived. This rather Lawrentian character thrusts his physicality into the rarefied atmosphere of the drawing room in order to rebuke Settlemarsh's culture vultures. Similar situations occur in some of Hartley's longer works, especially in perhaps his two greatest novels, *The Go-Between* (1953) and *The Hireling* (1957).

Hartley's one fantasy novel, *Facial Justice,* a dystopian romance that deserves to be better known, shares many characteristics with his fantasy stories. This dimension of Hartley's works may seem more provocative now than in earlier decades, when some of these stories first appeared, before the advent of magic realism from Latin American writers and authors such as Italo Calvino. Hartley's inspiration was doubtless his beloved Hawthorne.

"Conrad and the Dragon" (*The Travelling Grave*) concerns a most unlikely dragon slayer. Conrad's older brother has died in an attempt to free Princess Hermione from the dragon, and since then Conrad's indifference to the princess has deepened into positive dislike. Yet the only way to get at the dragon is to utter words of love about the princess. Conrad's address to the dragon is a masterpiece of equivocation:

> But when I remember what you have done for me: rescued me from the dull round of woodland life; raised me from obscurity into fame; transformed me from a dreamer into a warrior, an idler into a hunter of Dragons; deigned to make yourself the limit of my hopes and the end of my endeavors – I have no words to thank you, and I cannot love you more than I do now!

Conrad's novel approach to the dragon is successful, but he slays the beast only to discover that the princess and the dragon are one and the same. The conquering hero is instantly transformed into a social pariah, somewhat paralleling the duality of the princess herself. Conrad, given the opportunity to leave the country in secret, departs with Charlotte, his deceased brother's sweetheart, to a republic where the couple marry and live happily ever after.

The import of "Conrad and the Dragon" is appropriately mysterious. At one level it provides a nightmare projection of the nascent sexual fears that Hartley's male characters frequently manifest toward women. It may be a parable of the dragons women can become because their admirers and lovers will them to be so. When Hartley turns to a wildly imaginative fable in *Facial Justice,* he wisely concentrates his moral vision on political rather than sexual issues, although recent critics have shown that the two are not easily separated. This bizarre short story compels attention as much for what it does not say as for what it does, a fact that might open it to newer theories and interpretations.

In contrast "The Crossways" (*Two for the River*) fulfills the expectations of an ideal fairy tale by suggesting the conditions necessary for a happy marriage. It serves as a harbinger of Hartley's late happy-ending novels, such as *My Sisters' Keeper* (1970). In "The Crossways" Lucindra, a stranger in a strange land, marries a strong, handsome woodsman, Michael, whose only blemish is an enormous scar left from an encounter with a bear. A peddler from her native country entices Lucindra with stories of the road to the Land of Heart's Desire, which is to be found at the Crossways deep in the forest. In time Lucindra leaves her husband and their two typically knowing Hartleian children, Olga and Peter, in search of her heart's desire. Finally, despite their father's warning, the children penetrate the forest, and they find Lucindra injured in a ditch by the Crossways. But all the road signs are blank.

When Michael finds them, he insists he has been unkind to his wife, for she must have the freedom to go where she likes. With this reaffirmation of her free will, she desires only to return home. Dependent on her husband to carry her, Lucindra expresses the renewed love she feels for all her family. The signpost suddenly becomes clear: the Land of Heart's Desire is the homeward path they must follow. This parable of wedded love is a little too clear for comfort. The supernaturally unclosed world of Hartley's fairy tale loses something in translation to the more problematic, realistic environment of his novels.

The resolution of traditional binary oppositions in "The Crossways" may give special meaning to this story, as Hartley shows how and why imagination and reality cannot live apart, nor art and society, nor the physical and spiritual aspects of the sexual relationship. On that basis Anne Mulkeen, in *Wild Thyme, Winter Lightning: The Symbolic Novels of L. P. Hartley* (1974), praises "The Crossways" as a seminal story in understanding Hartley's work: "This little fairy tale, this symbolic construct, embodying archetypal relationships in modern form, and carrying with it so many possible meanings, might serve as one of the clearest clues to what Hartley is all about and to his method of presentation." With his British reserve and urbanity, Hartley looks on men and women and finds them humorous but not absurd, fallible but not irredeemable, skeptical but not faithless. The deft social weave in some of the stories – including the fantasy ones – a feature at which British fiction excels, anticipates Hartley's novels of manners with adult protagonists.

Hartley's prolific final creative period, which extended from the late 1960s until his death in 1972, resulted in novels of a somewhat lighter tone and less symbolic structure than his earlier long fiction. A collection of short fiction published during this time, *Mrs. Carteret Receives and Other Stories* (1971), constitutes one of his best efforts in the genre and provides a summing-up of his success with short fiction. The title story approximates Anthony Trollope's tone and resembles the gentle satire Hartley presents in his novels of manners with adult protagonists. His description of just one feature of the Carterets' house in Venice demonstrates his skill:

All the rooms in the house were low by Venetian standards but the Carterets' dining-room had a ceiling by Tiepolo which one could not help looking at, so near was it to one's head. It depicted the glorification of someone – perhaps a prevision of Mrs. Carteret? – with angels, saints, and *putti* assisting at the apotheosis.

Mrs. Carteret did not like the ceiling to be remarked on, but equally she did not like it not to be remarked on. With her, it was always difficult to get things right.

The snobbish Mrs. Carteret, who is extremely careful about whom she receives, finds herself the unwilling hostess to Death. Much of the story's sophistication lies in the narrative commentary; like many nineteenth-century writers Hartley is possibly more adept at telling than at writing dialogue or showing. Mrs. Carteret has known how to allure by denying, but that game goes against her as she expires: "A cry pierced the silence too thin to be called a

scream." Comedy and horror fuse for a Hartleian fillip in short fiction.

Two stories in this last collection warn that the wages of thievery can result in death. In "Paradise Paddock" Marcus Foster hopes that his turquoise-colored beetle, possibly an Egyptian scarab, will be stolen, because a friend who has traveled extensively in the Near East has informed him that the object may be cursed. Indeed, a series of fairly trivial misfortunes has befallen members of the household at Paradise Paddock. Marcus conspicuously places the beetle on the mantel to see what will happen. Mrs. Crumble, his daily help, shortly confesses that she has accidentally knocked it off the mantel, claiming it has broken into dozens of unmendable pieces. Greatly relieved to be rid of the jinx, Marcus learns from his servant, Henry, that Mrs. Crumble slipped the beetle into her bag. The unfortunate Mrs. Crumble becomes mortally ill; upon Mrs. Crumble's death her daughter comes to return the object to its rightful owner, as requested by her dying mother. Marcus manages to palm the piece off on the daughter. Later the friend who first alerted Marcus to the danger of the beetle falls outside Paradise Paddock and suffers a broken leg. He gladly accepts this injury in lieu of the fatal one he might have received had the beetle still been in Marcus's possession. "Paradise Paddock" is a slight, almost perverse story characteristic of Hartley's dark humor.

Vivian Vosper, yet another Hartleian bachelor living alone in a small mews house in "a burglarious part of London," devises a clever retaliatory scheme against thieves in "Please Do Not Touch." He breaks out a bottle of amontillado and doctors the sherry with potassium cyanide left over from his youthful days of butterfly and moth collecting. He reflects on his lack of malice toward the poor creatures that he used to collect as opposed to the animus he feels against the burglars who have "robbed him and beaten him up and pinioned him as if he was a moth on a stretching-board." Burglars again strike at Vosper's house, but this time he discovers one of them dead in his sitting room, looking like a butterfly on a stretching-board. To Vivian's shock he recognizes the deceased burglar as an acquaintance he had met at parties.

Vosper finds his new emotion, revenge, enthralling. While revenge may stand as the historical fallout of a violent age, it gives him a renewed sense of ironic union with his fellows:

Revenge, revenge. It was an emotion as old as jealousy, from which it so often sprang. It was a classic emotion, coeval with the human race, and to profess oneself to be free of it was as dehumanizing almost as much, and perhaps more, as if one professed oneself to be free of love – of which, as of jealousy, it was an offspring.

At once humorous and frightening, "Please Do Not Touch" distills Hartley's special variety of macabre comedy and displays his mastery of emotional rhythm in short fiction. Moreover, this story confirms his understanding of Poe's principle that the short, highly unified literary work is ideal as a vehicle for producing a pronounced emotional effect. Hartley even offers a direct allusion to Poe in the story. "Please Do Not Touch" is perhaps the best-achieved tale in Hartley's final collection, proving that the elderly author had not lost his skill.

Two of Hartley's stories in *Mrs. Carteret Receives* also explore the mental and physical blockages that constitute domestic life for moneyed bachelors, characters close to Hartley's own temperament and situation. These bachelors suffer from a mixture of arrogance and insularity that unfits them to meet problems outside their restricted milieus. Hartley's portrayal of them, however, has humorous and touching moments.

In "The Prayer" Anthony Easterfield loses his expert chauffeur, Copperthwaite, whose ambition has always been to drive a Roland-Rex, which an American employer makes available to him. Easterfield's aging, temperamental automobile offers no contest against the Roland-Rex. Indeed, Anthony has previously prayed that Copperthwaite might be granted the gift of such a car; his prayer's answer, while seemingly affirmative, turns out to be profoundly disadvantageous to the original petitioner, who is left without a chauffeur.

Before long, however, Copperthwaite writes to his former employer, asking to be rehired. Easterfield fears that the returning chauffeur might become even more bossy than he had been earlier, deciding "for Anthony many small problems of food, wine, and so on, that Anthony had been too tired, or too old, or too uninterested, to decide for himself." Copperthwaite informs Easterfield of the reason for his wanting to come back: he found the Roland-Rex such a perfect car that he had nothing to do. With Easterfield's delicate old automobile, the chauffeur explains, "I *am* the car, sir." The story ends with Copperthwaite asking Easterfield to say a big prayer for the car, and Easterfield speculates that an answer to his prayer has perhaps been given to the mutual satisfaction of both men. Hartley's affection and respect for his longtime chauffeur, who died before the novelist, was often noted in observations by friends.

In "Pains and Pleasures" the well-ordered, miniaturized universe of Henry Kitson and his general factotum, Bill – who cleans up his cottage, cooks his meals, and drives his car – is disrupted by the behavior of Kitson's old tomcat, Ginger. Objecting to his ritual banishment from the house at night, Ginger claws and bites whoever performs this task. When the cat is permitted to spend the night comfortably inside, his forgotten housebreaking results in a mess each morning for Bill to clean. Kitson feels guilty about subjecting Bill to this ordeal, especially out of fear that he must choose between the cat and his employee. Bill suggests providing Ginger with a box of sawdust, but the cat prefers to use that for a bed. When Bill finally gives notice of his imminent departure, saying that he will look for a job where there are no animals, Kitson offers to clean any future messes.

Shortly thereafter Ginger dies, and Bill elects, much to Kitson's delight, to remain with his old employer. The story may be trivial, yet its tribute to Bill seems genuine and heartfelt, although, perhaps like Hartley himself, Kitson has difficulty thinking about others without serving his own psychological needs:

> With the advent of Bill, "a soundless calm," in Emily Brontë's words, descended on Henry. Domestic troubles were over: nothing to resent; nothing to fight against; no sense of Sisyphus bearing an unbearable weight uphill. No grievance at all. Had he lived by his grievances, was a question that Henry sometimes asked himself. Had his resistance to them, his instinct to fight back and assert himself and show what he was made of, somehow strengthened his hold on life and prolonged it?

In the often highly personal genre of the short story, Hartley sometimes reveals more about himself than he does in his longer fiction. Little broken bits of the author's life and habits help to substantiate some rather negligible stories, such as "Pains and Pleasures." The avuncular author, despite the outward appearance of cozy comfortableness, sometimes sought out the darker side of things imaginatively or vicariously through the experience of others. Through his ever-changing assembly of servants, for example, he appears to have extended his knowledge about human relationships. Some of his friends have suggested that Hartley may have deliberately cultivated a degree of chaos in his otherwise seemingly tranquil life by his choice of servants. On occasion their lack of references provided him with the major impetus for hiring them. If one of these employees, confused about his status as friend or servant in the Hartley household, took advantage of his employer's generosity by running up debts on the author's account, Hartley would patiently forbear for a while before dismissing him.

In his stories of domestic life Hartley, like his admired and acknowledged British antecedents, shows his countrymen to be conservative people. They dislike being jolted out of the quiet routine of a well-ordered life, and they have a horror of extremes. Hartley's often brief stories afford him little space in which to develop characters; instead, situations and attitudes occupy the foreground. Likewise the form permits no time to unwind complicated plots. The spare figures who inhabit his tales appear largely passive, more prone to reaction than action. Granted, similar characteristics abound in Hartley's novels as well, but their distillation is particularly noticeable in his short fiction.

With few exceptions Hartley's stories rarely investigate childhood perceptions and the acquisition of identity, topics that he pursues so successfully in such novels as *The Shrimp and the Anemone, The Go-Between, The Brickfield* (1964), and *The Betrayal* (1966). Perhaps his favored theme of adolescent innocence in the process of being corrupted requires the longer form for adequate development.

Hartley's literary achievements were recognized with some of England's highest literary honors and prizes, including the James Tait Black Memorial Prize for *Eustace and Hilda* as the best book published in 1947 and the Heinemann Foundation Prize of the Royal Society of Literature in 1954 for *The Go-Between*. He served as head of the English section of the International Association of Poets, Playwrights, Editors, Essayists, and Novelists (P.E.N.), and for several years he was a member of the management committee of the Society of Authors. In 1956 he was appointed Commander of the British Empire. Early in 1972 he was made a Companion of Literature by the Royal Society of Literature, an honor restricted to ten living British authors.

As Hartley aged, the realities of life in the social and political structure of the modern welfare state failed to win his approval. He especially deplored the loss of personal responsibility and individual accountability, but these conditions provided material for his writing. He doubtless drank too much, a trait sometimes ascribed to his author characters in the later short stories; his heart trouble worsened as the years passed. Like many of his characters Hartley wanted to please more than to astonish, and to charm rather than to stir passion. He was saddened at the generally poor response, critical and commercial, to his last books. In particular Hartley regretted his inability to secure an

American publisher for them. Considering his slow start in writing novels, Hartley's last prolific period seems notable as a redress of former inhibitions. He may have worried less at the end – ironically akin to the permissive spirit of the times he so often disdained – about what other people thought. Or maybe, as a slight late novel such as *The Collections* (1972) attests, Hartley steadfastly defined his life by the vast historical context in which Englishmen live, which prevented him from panicking when, in his opinion, things went wrong in modern times. Hartley died of heart failure at his London residence in Rutland Gate on 13 December 1972.

Hartley's place in twentieth-century British fiction as a minor but respected novelist seems secure. Kazuo Ishiguro's critically acclaimed novel *The Remains of the Day* (1989) demonstrates that Hartley's legacy as a novelist continues to have some influence. His reputation as a short-story writer, however, is less well defined. Since his death there has been almost no notice of his considerable achievement in short fiction, if one judges interest on the basis of such indicators as the annual bibliography published by *Studies in Short Fiction.* Renewed appreciation of his short stories may be anticipated as a corollary to the burgeoning enthusiasm for the fantastic and magical in literature.

Hartley believed that happiness cannot be a function of social organization, that it must be the responsibility of individual choice, operating with well-developed moral and emotional integrity. One of the first critics in the United States to introduce Hartley to American readers, Harvey Curtis Webster, summarizes the value of his literary work in *After the Trauma: Representative British Novelists Since 1920* (1970): "For those who believe it important to understand twentieth-century man in both his mistakes and his potentiality, for those who want to know how novels that *make* nothing happen can cause us to be more aware and less likely to make our world a mess than our predecessors did, the best of L. P. Hartley is required for survival." Despite the hyperbole the same advice has its relevance for Hartley's short stories as well, on their own terms without reference to his novels.

Many of Hartley's stories have resonance: their irony is a knife slicing through the entertainment, and it continues to cut when the stories end. His typically quiet collections of short stories are dense with details that occasionally illumine beyond the normal confines of fiction. Things seen and how they are seen constitute much of the excellence of Hartley's craft. He informs his love of things – and the people who surround or collect them – not with possessiveness but with the warmth of humor and the bittersweet knowledge that such treasures must someday disappear. Less benignly Hartley makes his readers aware of the fact that evil is an existing, everyday factor in life. This perspective may have peculiar relevance in the last decade of the twentieth century, giving Hartley an almost prophetic quality.

Hartley has his detractors, one of whom, Martin Seymour-Smith, in *Who's Who in Twentieth-Century Literature* (1976), disparages Hartley's short stories before mitigating somewhat his overall assessment of the author's work: "Hartley was a minor writer, for his gift either failed him altogether (as in the bulk of the stories) or was extremely fragile. But at his best he is highly individual, and as a relaxed comedian of manners he has hardly been surpassed."

In Hartley's stories, characters, and situations revisionist readers may find elements they can associate with the postmodern, the fragmented, and the indeterminate. Few writers delineate a combination of disintegration and persisting dignity better than Hartley. He often invests his characters with his special brand of self-knowledge: that which is carried along, sometimes acted well upon, but knowledge that in general issues no clarion call to action. Not surprising, his most convincing characters are those who most resemble their author.

Hartley's ironic view of the vagaries of human behavior, together with his deliberately domestic frame of reference, gives his stories a sometimes deceptively light tone. Nevertheless – despite being funny, clever, and even insightful – the stories frequently lack depth. Notwithstanding his abiding concern with the relations of the individual mind and conscience to the collective, Hartley does not search for unity underlying the fragmentation and pain of modern life in the stories as he does in his novels. His stories may be viewed as parables that do not preach. Less meant to be understood or explained, they may trouble the reader until, sometimes long afterward, they explode in the mind.

References:

Peter Bien, *L. P. Hartley* (University Park: Pennsylvania State University Press, 1963);

Paul Bloomfield, *L. P. Hartley* (London: Longmans, Green, 1962; revised edition, London: Longman, 1970);

James Hall, "Games of Apprehension: L. P. Hartley," in his *The Tragic Comedians: Seven Modern British Novelists* (Bloomington: Indiana University Press, 1963), pp. 112–128;

Edward T. Jones, *L. P. Hartley* (Boston: Twayne, 1978);

Francis King, "Sweet, Cosy, and Tough: On L. P. Hartley," *London Sunday Telegraph,* 17 December 1972;

Howard Phillips Lovecraft, *Supernatural Horror in Literature* (New York: Dover, 1973);

Charles E. May, "The Nature of Knowledge in Short Fiction," *Studies in Short Fiction,* 21 (Fall 1984): 327–338;

Anne Mulkeen, *Wild Thyme, Winter Lightning: The Symbolic Novels of L. P. Hartley* (Detroit: Wayne State University Press, 1974);

Martin Seymour-Smith, *Who's Who in Twentieth-Century Literature* (New York: Holt, Rinehart & Winston, 1976), pp. 151–152;

Harvey Curtis Webster, "L. P. Hartley: Diffident Christian," in his *After the Trauma: Representative British Novelists Since 1920* (Lexington: University Press of Kentucky, 1970), pp. 152–167.

Susan Hill

(5 February 1942 –   )

Ann Gibaldi Campbell
University of North Carolina at Chapel Hill

BOOKS: *The Enclosure* (London: Hutchinson, 1961);

Do Me a Favour (London: Hutchinson, 1963);

Gentlemen and Ladies (London: Hamish Hamilton, 1968; New York: Walker, 1969);

A Change for the Better (London: Hamish Hamilton, 1969);

I'm the King of the Castle (London: Hamish Hamilton, 1970; New York: Viking, 1970);

The Albatross (London: Hamish Hamilton, 1971); republished as *The Albatross and Other Stories* (New York: Saturday Review Press, 1975);

Strange Meeting (London: Hamish Hamilton, 1971; New York: Saturday Review Press, 1972);

The Custodian (London: Covent Garden Press, 1972);

The Bird of Night (London: Hamish Hamilton, 1972; New York: Saturday Review Press, 1972);

A Bit of Singing and Dancing and Other Stories (London: Hamish Hamilton, 1973);

In the Springtime of the Year (London: Hamish Hamilton, 1974; New York: Saturday Review Press, 1974);

The Cold Country and Other Plays for Radio (London: BBC Publications, 1975);

The Magic Apple-Tree: A Country Year (London: Hamish Hamilton, 1982; New York: Holt, Rinehart & Winston, 1983);

The Woman in Black (London: Hamish Hamilton, 1983; Boston: Godine, 1986);

Through the Kitchen Window (London: Penguin, 1984; Owings Mill, Md.: Stemmer House, 1984);

One Night at a Time (London: Hamish Hamilton, 1984);

Go Away, Bad Dreams! (New York: Random House, 1984);

Through the Garden Gate (London: Hamish Hamilton, 1986);

Mother's Magic (London: Hamish Hamilton, 1986);

Shakespeare Country (London: M. Joseph, 1987);

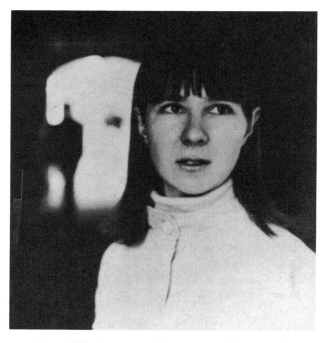

Susan Hill, circa 1970 (photograph by Jerry Bauer)

The Lighting of the Lamps (London: Hamish Hamilton, 1987);

Lanterns Across the Snow (London: M. Joseph, 1987; New York: Potter, 1988);

The Spirit of the Cotswolds (London: Viking, 1988);

Can It Be True? (London: Hamish Hamilton, 1988; New York: Viking, 1988);

Family (London: M. Joseph, 1988; New York: Viking, 1990);

Suzie's Shoes (London: Hamish Hamilton, 1989);

Glass Angels (Cambridge, Mass.: Candlewick, 1990; London: Walker, 1991);

Air and Angels (London: Sinclair-Stevenson, 1991);

Beware, Beware (Cambridge, Mass.: Candlewick, 1993);

King of Kings (Cambridge, Mass.: Candlewick, 1993);

Mrs. DeWinter (New York: Morrow, 1993).

OTHER: Thomas Hardy, *The Distracted Preacher and Other Tales by Thomas Hardy,* edited by Hill (Harmondsworth, U.K.: Penguin, 1979);

People, edited by Hill (London: Chatto & Windus, 1983);

Ghost Stories, edited by Hill (London: Hamish Hamilton, 1983);

The Parchment Moon, edited by Hill (London & New York: Penguin, 1990).

Susan Hill's career as a writer has taken some interesting and surprising turns since the publication of her first novel in 1961. *The Enclosure* was actually written when Hill was only about eighteen years old. Although she dismisses her first two novels, claiming that "neither was any good," she continued to write copiously until age thirty-two. Between 1968 and 1974 she produced six novels and two collections of short stories, all of which met with critical approbation. In 1975 she married Oxford professor Stanley Wells and did not write another novel for sixteen years. Her marriage and the birth of her first daughter, Jessica, one year later transformed Hill's career.

Between 1975 and 1991 Hill wrote books about gardening, children's books, appreciations of the English countryside, and book reviews. Her shift from critically acclaimed fiction to domestic writing mirrored the changes in her personal life. In the years during and following the pursuit of her degree in English from King's College, London, Hill perceived herself as a "solitary." She was dedicated to her art, perhaps at the expense of her personal life. In a *Sunday Times* interview (24 March 1991) she reflects on those years and expresses herself with typical directness: "I liked writing because I was good at it – you always like doing what you're good at – and I was young, energetic and very ambitious, and that's what I wanted to do. And I had nothing else to do."

During the 1980s much of Hill's and Wells's lives were consumed by efforts to conceive a second child, which culminated in the premature birth and tragic death of a daughter, Imogen, who lived only five weeks. This deeply personal event, as well as the birth of another daughter, Clemency, in late 1985, is recounted in Hill's autobiographical work *Family* (1988). After the cathartic process of expressing these experiences in writing Hill returned to writing novels with *Air and Angels* (1991).

Hill was born on 5 February 1942, the only child of R. H. and Doris Hill. They lived in Scarborough, a seaside town in Yorkshire, which had a deep influence on their daughter. In the introduction to *The Lighting of the Lamps* (1987) she refers to Scarborough as a "dramatic town, both scenically and climatically," and seaside resorts serve as the settings for several of her novels and many of her short stories. In her 1991 *Sunday Times* interview Hill remarks whimsically, "It's my party piece . . . to write about seaside towns out of season: it's such good copy."

Being an only child of older parents also helped shape Hill's career. As a young girl she grew used to solitude, becoming a voracious reader. In the introduction to *Lighting of the Lamps* she reminisces nostalgically about trips to the library with her mother and cites Lewis Carroll's *Alice's Adventures in Wonderland* (1865) and *Through the Looking-Glass, and What Alice Found There* (1872) as her favorite books from childhood. She later developed a passion for Charles Dickens, and he remains one of her favorite authors. Hill received her secondary education at a convent school and then moved on to King's College, from which she was graduated with an honors degree in English in 1963. Hill is critical of those who suggest that the study of literature is not the best training for a writer, as she states in the introduction to *The Lighting of the Lamps:* "What better way of preparing to be a writer than by spending three years immersed in the work of the greatest novelists, poets, dramatists, essayists in the English language – not in order to imitate, but to absorb and be inspired by?" While at King's College, Hill began reviewing books professionally for the publication *Time and Tide*. In 1977 she began writing her own column, "The World of Books," for the *London Daily Telegraph*.

Although most of Hill's early long fiction was well received by critics, her particular talents may be better expressed in her short fiction. The *Times Literary Supplement* (5 March 1971) observes: "The short story form offers ideal restraint to her talent." Her short fiction from the early 1970s is collected in two slim volumes: *The Albatross* (1971) and *A Bit of Singing and Dancing and Other Stories* (1973). Thematically her stories echo and complement her novels. The almost stultifying preponderance of loneliness, despair, and death in the pieces in these collections might seem odd in light of the apparent felicitousness of Hill's life. In *The Uses of Fiction* (1982) Kenneth Muir suggests a connection between the "sombre and depressing" atmosphere of Hill's fictional world and that of Dickens: "She shares his appreciation of the odd and eccentric, a compassion for the aged, the lonely and the persecuted, and his obsession with violence." Hill's protagonists are isolated and at odds with the societies around them. In some cases this isolation is self-imposed, but more often her characters long to make connections but find their attempts end in failure and rejection. As Rosemary Jackson states in *Twentieth-Century Women Novelists* (1982): "Solitary figures make pathetic attempts to release themselves from years of frustrating isolation, but they all end in ludicrous failure."

Although Hill's work in the short-fiction genre is limited to these two volumes, she makes a contribution to the late-twentieth-century development of the form. Her stories are remarkable for their intensity of both theme and style. She combines such modern techniques as epiphany and indirect narration with a powerful sense of setting and character reminiscent of the Victorian novelists she so admires. Her short fiction struggles to reconcile the powerful influence of high modernism and its stylistic experimentation with the tradition of nineteenth-century British fiction. Her stories have affinities to the short works of James Joyce and Virginia Woolf, but with greater attention to action and plot. Many of Hill's stories end with a death or some violent action.

In *The Short Story in English* (1981) Walter Allen notes: "Joyce executes his stories with, as he told his brother Stanislaus in a letter, 'a scrupulous meanness' of language. The anecdotal basis that is in most modern short stories tends to disappear almost completely." Allen goes on to cite the opening paragraph of Joyce's "Grace" (*Dubliners,* 1914), which begins, "Two gentlemen who were in the lavatory at the time tried to help him up; but he was quite helpless." This could well be the opening sentence of a story by Hill. Her stories also tend to open in medias res, often making her readers feel like voyeurs. But Hill reclaims the anecdotalism that is absent in Joyce. In addition to showing or revealing the often tragic conditions of her characters' lives, she plots stories around them that have traditional shapes, rising actions building to dramatic climaxes.

Hill's style mirrors this double purpose of showing and telling. Her syntax is remarkable for its combination of short, factual statements with longer, almost lyrical, complex sentences. A brief paragraph from the title story of *The Albatross* demonstrates this quality of her syntax:

He took nothing with him. The most important thing of all seemed that he should be by himself, the old life piled

up behind him anyhow, discarded. When he left the house, he wore only the clothes he always worked in, and his woolen jacket and Wellington boots. From the drawer in the oak dresser, he took four pound notes and some coins, all the money there was. He locked the front door.

The connotative language or imagery of "the old life piled up behind him anyhow, discarded" contrasts with the denotative factuality of the rest of the paragraph.

"The Albatross" begins in typically abrupt Hill fashion: "It was Wednesday. He had gone along the beach as usual for the fish." She confronts the reader with the main character rather than introducing him. The reader plays an important interpretative role in his or her interaction with the text. Hill refuses to pass judgments or evaluate emotions; the narrative voice is not intrusive. This absence of authorial direction can be both empowering and disturbing to the reader.

All but two of Hill's sixteen short stories are written in the third person, but it is never an omniscient or authoritative narrative voice. On the contrary, she employs the narrative technique pioneered by Henry James in such works as *The Ambassadors* (1903). The narrative voice seems always to be linked to the consciousness of one of the characters. In most cases the reader's vision associates primarily with that of one central character. But even in the most focused stories Hill occasionally abandons the mind of her protagonist in order to render an insight into the consciousness of a minor character. This narrative flexibility contributes to the stories' complexity: there are always multiple perspectives, and perception is never absolute.

It is almost impossible to trace a development or progression of either style or theme in Hill's collected stories. All sixteen were written over the period of a few years in the early 1970s. Her oeuvre is remarkable for its consistency rather than its variety. It is difficult to say whether this unity of Hill's work emerges as a strength or a weakness. A review of *A Bit of Singing and Dancing* in the *Times Literary Supplement* (30 March 1973) defends this quality: "There comes a point, which [Hill] has perhaps reached, when it is . . . important to establish an individual stamping-ground — even to the extent of being vulnerable to parody: when the reader begins to feel he recognizes 'landmarks' and signals which only this particular writer gives." Certainly Hill's two volumes of short fiction reveal a definite "individual stamping-ground": all her sixteen stories can be viewed as variations on the theme of individual loneliness. However, if there is a certain redundancy to reading these works, there is also a pervasive atmosphere that is compelling and powerful. The reader can hardly help but adapt to Hill's worldview and as a result is transformed by the despair and impotence that pervade her stories.

The opening and title story of *The Albatross* is novella length, and it serves as an excellent beginning to an examination of both collections. The first volume is the stronger of the two, and Hill probably achieves her greatest successes in its first and last stories. "The Albatross" concerns a mentally slow young man who cares for his crippled mother in a small, seedy fishing village. "Dafty" Duncan Pike, as the villagers cruelly call him, is subdued by his domineering mother, who insists on keeping herself and her son apart from the rest of society: "We live our own life, we keep ourselves to ourselves, in this town." Mrs. Pike is a rather nebulous character; her past, and thus her reasons for isolating herself, are shrouded in mystery. This nebulousness is not the result of faulty characterization on Hill's part, but rather of the focusing of the story through the consciousness of the young man: Duncan "had never understood the workings of his mother's mind." In this story Hill establishes the style of indirect narration that she employs throughout her short fiction.

Mrs. Pike had nursed her son through a dire illness in early childhood, but the reader is appalled by the capriciousness of the demands she makes on him. For example, she insists that Duncan buy their fish directly from the fishermen rather than getting it from the shop like everyone else. These trips are a source of great anxiety to Duncan, who is frightened by the roughness and teasing of these men whose lives he perceives as contrasting so sharply with his own. For, despite his fears, Duncan longs to escape, to see more of the world, to go to sea. The sea serves as an emblem of both hope and danger in "The Albatross." The story is set during the winter, a fierce season of gales and angry waves. Duncan's pervasive discontent reaches its climax on the night of a terrible storm when several of the local fishermen go out in their boats to rescue a ship that is foundering offshore. On this night Ted Flint, a fisherman of Duncan's age, is killed.

Throughout the story Flint, whose name suggests his toughness, is a central object of Duncan's thoughts. Flint takes an interest in Duncan, even coming to the Pikes' cottage one evening to invite him to the pub for a drink. Clearly Duncan idolizes Flint, yet he also remembers that Flint was one of several brutish youths who tied him up in a mackerel net and abandoned him in the bottom of a fishing boat when they were children at school to-

gether. The reader is not as quick to forgive as Duncan and is thus suspect of Flint's attentions. Depicting such ambiguity of motive is one of Hill's great strengths as a writer. Perhaps Flint repents his childish cruelty, or perhaps he merely wants to torture Duncan some more. It is impossible to arrive at any certainty in Hill's stories: she leaves the reader in a miasma of doubt and suspicion.

Whatever his motives Flint invites Duncan to go fishing with him. Throughout the story the thought of Flint fills Duncan with a sense of possibility and allows for his recurring refrain of "I could go." However, when the dream nearly becomes reality, Duncan is afraid. In the end, with his mother's assurances of his inadequacies reverberating in his mind, "he was seized with choking panic, he turned and began to run, pounding off down the beach to get away from the menace of the waves and wind."

The night of Flint's death and the terrible storm serve as a final test for Duncan. In a strange duplication of his childhood degradation he chooses to spend the night in the bottom of a boat on the edge of the churning sea. The violence of the storm and the realization of his hero's death bring the anger that has been building in Duncan to an uncontrollable point. He has cared for his invalid mother with great gentleness, even carrying her to bed every night. But after Flint's funeral he abandons her in her wheelchair at the church, and that night he goes to the pub and drinks beer for the first time.

His one day of independence culminates in violence. That night Duncan gives his mother too many of the capsules that help her to rest. While she sleeps he puts her in her wheelchair, rolls her to a cliff overhanging the beach, and pushes her over the edge. Then he goes home, burns down his cottage, and runs away. But in Hill's world no escape succeeds. Duncan is apprehended and returned to another sort of captivity. Hill is too complex a writer to allow a comfortable moral judgment to mar the pervasive anxiety she instills in her readers. Duncan's life is tragic in both his passivity and his action.

"The Albatross" is one of Hill's most acclaimed stories. A review in the *Times Literary Supplement* (5 March 1971) notes: "This is a fine story, dark and simple as Tolstoy, yet avoiding both the suggestion of brutality and the sentimental moral pleading often found in such tales of elemental relationships." A review in the *New Statesman* (12 February 1971) commends the story for its "rough edges" and remarks, "where [Hill] seems more troubled in controlling her material, paradoxically she scores her greater successes."

The *New Statesman* review is not as enthusiastic about the shorter pieces in *The Albatross,* complaining that some are "arguably too finely polished and a little contrived." The three stories that follow the title piece are all susceptible to this criticism, but they are powerful nonetheless. The second and third stories in the volume, "The Elephant Man" and "Friends of Miss Reece," work well as companion pieces. Both concern little boys from upper-middle-class families who are terrorized by the women who care for them. In "The Elephant Man," the more subtle of the two, William is consigned at age three to the care of Nanny Fawcett after the death of his previous nanny. William's mother is described "sipping a Manhattan in the oyster-grey drawing-room," and the reader realizes immediately that lonely, neglected children exist at all economic strata.

Nanny Fawcett is a good Irish Protestant whose "heart [is] filled with prejudice, most markedly against men." She complains to her young charge: "You'll be a man. . . . You'll be as bad as all the rest." William responds to her venom with genuine regret, wishing he could unsex himself, wanting to please. But Nanny Fawcett turns out to be hypocritical as well as venomous. She meets a man to whom she refers only as "My Friend" and begins using the time she is supposed to be tending to William to set up assignations with this person. William is utterly befuddled: "The fact that her friend was a man completed his sense of strangeness, everything was suddenly out of joint in his view of the world and of people."

Hill pushes this sense of freakishness to a nightmarish degree. Nanny Fawcett's friend has a mysterious profession about which William learns when he is taken to a birthday party in a hotel one afternoon. As William waits, lonely and anxious, a figure dressed in an elephant costume enters to entertain the children. William is disgusted and frightened by the figure "waving its disgusting trunk." After the entertainment William goes in search of Nanny Fawcett and finds her in a hotel bedroom with the elephant man, who removes his mask and reveals himself to be her friend.

The story ends that night when Nanny Fawcett must tend to William after he has vomited in his bed. Thinking he has gorged himself on treats at the party she warns him to shape up, promising him that in the future he will "be going to quite a number of parties, I shouldn't wonder." Working through William's consciousness, Hill conveys to the reader the nightmarishness of the boy's situa-tion without trivializing it. The reader is left with a sense of hopelessness at the climax of "The Elephant Man," as with almost all of Hill's stories.

The boy dreads the physicality of the costumed man, particularly the phallic trunk, which suggests a perverse sexuality associated with the horror of his own maleness that Nanny Fawcett has instilled in him. This veiled suggestion of sexual victimization of a child reappears in the next story, "Friends of Miss Reece." Indeed, both stories support an observation about Hill's stories made in the *Times Literary Supplement* review of *The Albatross:* "There's never been a risk that Miss Hill would be the conventional 'woman writer' – indeed, she seems happier in this excellent collection of stories, as she has in her novels, inside the skin of male characters, especially those vulnerable to dominating and selfish women."

The young boy at the center of "Friends of Miss Reece" seems a lot like William, and this virtual duplication of protagonists is a flaw in the generally excellent collection. This unnamed little boy is frequently sent by his sociable, card-playing, banquet-attending parents to stay with his aunt, who is matron at the Cedars Lawn Nursing Home. He loves old Miss Reece, who is stricken with Parkinson's disease, and in her silent isolation perceives a connection to himself. The true horror at Cedars Lawn is not the patients at all, but Nurse Wetherby. Like the Elephant Man she appears grotesque to the child. Wetherby is cruel in her talk about the patients, especially Miss Reece, and Hill implies that she has committed some sexual misconduct against the child. He can only tell his mother that Nurse Wetherby is ugly, but Hill uses ellipsis to suggest the unspeakable. "He kept his mind turned from the thought of the upstairs landings of the Cedars Lawn Nursing Home, and the attic where he must sleep, in the room next to Wetherby."

The story ends with the death of Miss Reece. The boy goes to visit her at night and finds the gas left on in her room. Earlier in the day Nurse Wetherby had been raging over the old woman's incontinence, and the reader suspects, along with the child, the nurse's murderous intent. He opens Miss Reece's window in an attempt to save her life, but the old woman dies of pneumonia the next day. That evening the child is led off to bed by Nurse Wetherby. As in "The Elephant Man" Hill expresses the helplessness of childhood in a nightmarish world of sexual exploitation.

Feminist critics, like male reviewers, have remarked on the scarcity of sympathetic women in

Hill's fiction. This is especially true in her short fiction. Jackson argues for a feminist approach to Hill: "Her victims, her peculiar cast of artists, idiots, children, lonely and dying men and women, are all romantic figures who have given up the struggle to live in an adult, 'masculine' world." Although this is true, it is hard to overlook the fact that the perpetrators of oppression – Mrs. Pike, Nanny Fawcett, and Nurse Wetherby – are often women.

The fourth story in *The Albatross,* "Cockles and Mussels," has a female protagonist. Miss Avis Parson, a sixty-nine-year-old spinster, is a resident of the genteel Delacourt Guest House. This home overlooks the sea near the Lower Bay, a seedy beach town whose Fun Fair lures day-trippers. Mrs. Hennessy, proprietress of the Delacourt, believes she provides a haven for her residents, but Miss Avis Parson, with her birdlike first name, feels trapped by her genteel surroundings, bored by the people who live at the Delacourt.

From her bedroom window Miss Parson looks out on the Lower Bay and the Fun Fair and fantasizes about this exotic realm of possibility: "As long as there had been something to watch and listen to, the attraction of the roundabout music and the lights flickering in the sky, she was never tired, her mind was filled with pictures of the scene, couples arm-in-arm together and the mothers of grown-up families, ridiculous in cardboard hats, middle-aged romances brought to a point of decision among the dodgems." Miss Parson is drawn to the romantic and procreative possibilities in the landscape that appear merely "vulgar" to Mrs. Hennessy and the other Delacourt residents. The world of mothers and middle-aged romances contrasts powerfully with Miss Parson's own, and like Duncan Pike she is attracted by everything that is different from herself.

Finally Miss Parson decides to act on her desires. Like a naughty child she must sneak out of the Guest House, not wanting to incur the disapproval of Mrs. Hennessy. In another writer's story this decision to explore might lead to delight and heightened self-awareness, but not in Hill's world. Miss Parson is initially exhilarated by the sounds, sights, and smells of the Fun Fair. She rides on the roller coaster and begins to feel a fleeting sense of involvement with the adventure-filled world, but her contentment is short-lived. As the *New Statesman* review explains, "When she manages at last to . . . get beyond the confines of middle-class gentility and into the rough-and-tumble of the day tripper's world . . . the experience is one that she cannot impose a pattern upon." Miss Parson is ultimately

overwhelmed by the strangeness of the experience and by the cockles and mussels she eats and the sherry she drinks. She returns miserable and confused to the Delacourt and dies several days later of a heart attack precipitated by food poisoning. Miss Parson's fate suggests the impossibility of living with the status quo and the futility of trying to change it, a tenet that Hill reiterates throughout her stories.

"Somerville," the fifth and final piece in *The Albatross,* is excellent, sharing the attribute of "rough edges" with the title story. "Somerville" concerns the title character, a man who has chosen a life of self-imposed isolation in a rural house on a lake. Somerville's well-being is threatened when a young, pregnant, unmarried, and dissatisfied girl from the nearby village begins paying him visits, imposing herself and her problems on his isolation.

"Somerville" is the most impressionistic story in the volume, the piece that shows the greatest influence of Virginia Woolf. Like "The Albatross," it negotiates an uneasy narrative course between the past and the present. "Somerville" has affinities with *Strange Meeting* (1971), the novel that Hill published immediately after *The Albatross.* Both involve close relationships between two men, one of whom is named Barton. In the story Somerville does not seem to be dealing well with the loss of his friend Barton. The tale opens provocatively: "Even the sight of the envelope terrified him." Somerville has received a letter, and this surprising occurrence compels him to reread a twenty-seven-year-old letter from Barton written immediately before the latter's death, presumably in World War I. It is a vivid account of the horrors of war and the slow process of freezing to death. For Somerville all letters, indeed all communications from without, are inexorably tainted with the tragedy of Barton's letter and his death.

Despite himself, Somerville becomes interested in the daughter of the village shopkeeper; he wonders about her pregnancy and her dying grandmother in a nearby hospital. Her physicality, her unhappiness, and her complaints against her family remind him of his own past, his love for Barton, and his rancor against his sister. But just as Miss Avis Parson in "Cockles and Mussels" does not profit from her explorations, so Somerville cannot gain from his exposure to the girl. His only mode of helping her proves to be negative, monstrous, and violent. When the baby is a few weeks old, the unfit mother, who "looked at it as though it were a lump of putty," suffocates her child and leaves the corpse on Somerville's property, knowing that he will find it. "He felt curiously proud, that she had trusted him," and he buries the baby at the bottom of his lake along with two unopened letters.

The irony of "Somerville" is that the man really believes he has made an affirmative connection for the first time in his life since Barton's death. At the end of the story – the end of this collection of short fiction – he is utterly content, alone except for the company of a hedgehog. Somerville's static contentment is perhaps even more disturbing than Miss Parson's death or young William's fate of continuing encounters with the Elephant Man. *The Albatross* concludes with the reiterated assurance of what the *New Statesman* terms "this inability to become involved, the incapacity for interpreting the real world." This inability and incapacity are central to Hill's fiction.

Between the publication of *The Albatross* and the appearance of *A Bit of Singing and Dancing and Other Stories* (1973), Hill produced two novels, *Strange Meeting* (inspired by the Wilfred Owen poem of the same name) and *The Bird of Night* (1972). Both novels address the love between two men, a theme that underlies "Somerville." Hill is reticent about sexuality, especially between people of the same sex. But the suggestion of male homosexuality pervades much of her work, particularly that from the early 1970s. Two of the stories in *A Bit of Singing and Dancing* fit into this pattern, and one, "How Soon Can I Leave?," considers a problematic relationship between two women.

A significant difference between Hill's two collections of short fiction is that all the stories in *A Bit of Singing and Dancing* are shorter than the two long pieces from *The Albatross* (the title story and "Somerville"). Hill seems to express a preference for the more polished, moving away from some of the "rough edges" for which she was so rightly praised in the earlier volume. Of the eleven stories in the second volume, few are as powerful and provocative as the five stories in the previous collection. However, many of them are good, as is suggested by the positive reaction of reviewers such as Miles Donald in the *New Statesman* (30 March 1973).

Hill's preoccupation with the unhappiness of children, loners, outcasts, and grotesques is abundantly apparent in her second collection. Jackson explains the numbing bleakness of Hill's outlook: "Nearly all of Susan Hill's writing presents problems in such a manner that no positive resolution seems possible: a passive acknowledgement of tragic inevitability is the dominant mood. The stories in *A Bit of Singing and Dancing* are in this vein: they are bleak pictures of ordinary people confront-

ing lost illusions, with nothing to put in the place of their romantic expectations."

Long before Hill struggled through the premature birth and death of her own daughter, she was deeply concerned with the plight of unhappy, neglected children and the relationships these children forge (or have forged for them) with the adults in their lives. This focus is evident in the opening story, "Halloran's Child," in which young Amy Halloran is afflicted with an unidentified progressive ailment complicated by rheumatic fever, leaving her emaciated, with brittle bones and transparent skin. Hill places Amy away from the center of the story, ameliorating some of the potential sentimentality. The controlling consciousness here belongs to Nate Twomey, a deaf and dumb coffin maker. Nate's disabilities, in conjunction with his less-than-felicitous profession, make him a figure of contempt and fear to the villagers.

Amy is ostracized by the healthy children in the village: "She seemed to be separated from them, almost to be less than human. . . . In the end, they were bored by her." And so the sickly child begins to visit the shop of the disabled coffin maker, and these two outsiders strike up a tenuous, subtle friendship built on silence and mutual empathy. They have an uncertain connection, but a legitimate one nonetheless: a life-affirming relationship predicated on death.

When Amy lies dying, Nate goes to see her in her parents' home. The father views this visit as a harbinger of death, and, when his daughter dies the next day, he quickly blames Nate. The inherent tragedy and injustice of this pattern are evident, but Hill presents them as inevitable and almost decorous. When the irate, grieving father punches him in the face and knocks him to the ground, Nate accepts the course of events: "His skull felt as if it would break open. But he was calm. He knew that it was what had been due him. Because he had loved the child and known of her dying, because he was a Twomey and maimed." He returns to his shop to build a tiny coffin. The story ends with a return to calmness, necessitating the interpretive dilemma that the reader must face after reading almost all Hill's stories. One wonders whether Nate is right in his stoicism, whether his resignation is the appropriate response to the death of a loved child.

In *The Albatross* Hill often tells her stories from the perspective of suffering children. Although children continue to be important to the stories in *A Bit of Singing and Dancing,* the author often aligns herself with the consciousness of an adult. This is the case in "Halloran's Child" and again in "The Custodian," which a *Times Literary Supplement* review (30 March 1973) calls "possibly the best story in the book."

"The Custodian" involves an old man whose entire life is devoted to the care of an abandoned little boy. This fine story relies more on atmosphere than plot. As the *Times Literary Supplement* review explains, the setting is Hill's favorite: "the bleak, flat, Suffolk estuary country, where the village is still a tramp away and suspicious of strangers, where gulls swoop and reeds are 'stiff and white as blades. . . .' " It is a world of scarcely restrained dangers where the allure of the beach is minimized by the terrors of an old, abandoned mill.

The simplicity of the two characters' lives explodes when the boy's father, Gilbert Blaydon, arrives unexpectedly. Blaydon's past, like that of many of Hill's characters, is mysterious and indeterminate. His intentions are also unclear, as he does not reveal his identity to the child. Over time the boy grows fond of the company of this younger man. When Blaydon offers to take the child on a brief holiday to the coast, the boy is thrilled, and the old man can think of no adequate reason to refuse. He prepares for their return by cleaning and baking, longing to establish his centrality in the boy's life. But they never come home. The once fastidious old man's reason for existing is gone, and after his abandonment he "got up later and later each day, and went to bed earlier, to sleep between the frowsty, unwashed sheets." The story concludes with a brief view of the child in a "small town flat" with his father. Youth is flexible, but the elderly custodian is irreparably broken.

In her feminist interpretation of "The Custodian" Jackson emphasizes the feminine attributes of the elderly caretaker: "the hopelessness here, despite its male protagonist, is related to the inertia and impotence which are generated by a passive female condition." Despite Jackson's argument the reader can escape neither the fact of Hill's choice to make this a male character, nor the reality of women's victimization of children in her work, abundantly evident in *The Albatross* and present again in "In the Conservatory."

"In the Conservatory" is one of Hill's most disturbing, haunting, and stylistically experimental pieces. Perhaps the ambiguity regarding the narrative center of this work contributes to its power. Here two consciousnesses alternate in their centrality, and two plot lines intertwine uneasily. An unnamed thirty-two-year-old London woman and a mentally fragile child, Leonard, clash in a conflict where the triumph of the older woman and the

death of the male child seem inevitable. The two meet at Fewings, a Victorian mansion outside London that is open to the public. The grotesque house becomes a favorite haunt of the woman and her lover. Leonard lives at Fewings with his adoptive parents, the Musrys, who are the caretakers of the mansion.

The story fluctuates between the consciousnesses of Leonard and the unnamed woman, two troubled people engaged in a bizarre battle for possession of Fewings's heart, "the conservatory that was built into the centre of the house like a great, covered courtyard, the glass roof ribbed and vaulted." The woman comes to believe that the gentle child is spying on her and her illicit companion, and Leonard's presence becomes a terrible irritant to her. One day "she caught hold of [Leonard] in one of the dark passages and held his arm tightly, pushed her face into his and told him not to come near them, to go now, right away, to stop following and spying." The boy is traumatized by her brutality, waiting months before regaining the confidence to return alone to the conservatory.

During the months of Leonard's recovery the lovers are kept from Fewings by the protracted illness of the woman's husband. When they come back after this long absence and proceed at last to the conservatory, they find Leonard floating facedown in the fish pond. The boy has presumably committed suicide in response to the return of his adversary. In true Hill fashion this tragic death makes little happen. The woman is sufficiently traumatized to terminate the affair, but then it never really seemed to matter much to her anyway. The Musrys mourn their son but continue to reside at Fewings.

The unnamed woman of "In the Conservatory" is one of Hill's most interesting female characters, exhibiting a disturbing combination of anxiety, ennui, and malevolence. In his review for the *Spectator* (19 May 1973) Douglas Dunn claims that throughout *A Bit of Singing and Dancing* "men and women (but chiefly women) wrestle with disappointment and ruminate on the lost chances which make a new life so tempting, but so difficult, to take up." The validity of Dunn's gender bias is suspect, but he is allied with Jackson in suggesting a feminist approach to Hill's second volume of short fiction. In fact, the majority of the stories in this collection continue Hill's tendency to identify with male protagonists. However, several of the pieces do focus on women, and it might be useful for future feminist critics to examine these as a set. Three of the stories follow each other: "A Bit of Singing and Dancing," "The

Peacock," and "Missy." None of these is among the strongest or most engaging pieces in the collection. Together, however, they provide insights into Hill's ideas about female victimization.

A fourth story that focuses on female characters is one of the strongest in the collection. "The two ladies who lived together were called Miss Bartlett and Miss Roscommon" begins "How Soon Can I Leave?" The spinster is a familiar figure in Hill's landscape. Miss Roscommon is the older, plumper, and more nurturing of the two. She "conceal[s] her fear of life behind frank references to babies and lavatories and the sexing of day-old chicks." Miss Bartlett is flightier, absorbed in the country crafts she makes for sale: "raffia angels," beribboned pot-pourri jars, and shell sculptures. She says almost proudly, "I'm afraid that I cannot cook . . . I live on milk and cheese and oven-baked potatoes. I would not know where to begin in the kitchen." Miss Roscommon cultivates the younger woman, luring Miss Bartlett to her larger house for home-cooked meals and companionship. When Miss Bartlett's harbor cottage is repeatedly buffeted by winter winds and wild waves, she grudgingly agrees to move in with her friend, whose more secure abode overlooks the harbor.

The arrangement should be ideal: Miss Bartlett has time to devote to her art, and Miss Roscommon has someone to nurture. But over the years the younger woman grows deeply resentful of the other's possessiveness. Although the reader is disturbed by Miss Bartlett's ingratitude, there is also something disturbing in the older woman's desperate need to be needed: "My job is to look after Mary, of course. I took that upon myself quite some time ago, when I saw that I was needed. She is such a silly girl . . . and if I were not here to worry about her meals and her comforts, she would starve, I assure you, simply starve."

After seven years of cohabitation, Miss Bartlett leaves her friend to return to the dubious comforts of the cottage she has abandoned but never sold. When a winter storm drives her to regret temporarily her burst of independence, she returns to find Miss Roscommon lying dead on the floor of the "comfortable, chintzy" living room. Two lonely women who might have brightened and ennobled each other's lives instead hurt each other. Hill is relentless in her depiction of loneliness and failure.

In "How Soon Can I Leave?" Hill makes it fairly clear that there is nothing sexual in the relationship between the two spinsters. In her treatment of the relationships of male eccentrics, Hill is more likely to suggest (though she is never explicit) ho-

mosexual ties. Two pieces that fit this pattern are "Mr. Proudham and Mr. Sleight" and "Ossie," the last story in *A Bit of Singing and Dancing*. They are the only two among sixteen that are narrated in the first person. The speaker in "Mr. Proudham and Mr. Sleight" is a woman who has engaged a room in a house in a seaside resort during the off-season in order to write.

Hill is on her favorite stamping ground here. With its carnival the seedy town is reminiscent of the Lower Bay in "Cockles and Mussels." Like Miss Avis Parson, the speaker in this story is drawn by the carnival atmosphere, which even in the wintertime exerts a sinister power: "I could not keep away from Gala Land. It had a particular smell which drew me . . . although it was lit from end to end with neon and fluorescent lights, everything looked somehow dark, furtive and gone to seed." The grotesqueness of this landscape is mirrored by the two gentlemen who live in the house where the narrator has rented a room. She first perceives Mr. Proudham and Mr. Sleight as "shadowy, improbable figures . . . Mr. Proudham, immensely tall and etiolated, with a thin head and unhealthy, yellowish skin: and Mr. Sleight, perhaps five feet one or two, with a benevolent, rather stupid moon of a face."

The relationship of these two peculiar men approximates, on a more bizarre plane, that of the Misses Roscommon and Bartlett. Mr. Proudham is the spokesman for the pair. He initiates contact with their new neighbor and takes the lead when the two men go walking with their large poodle. Mr. Sleight is virtually mute but possesses a surprising talent. When the narrator is invited to their apartment for tea, she finds one room filled with his creations: grotesque wax figurines. Mixed in with characters from the Brothers Grimm and African warriors, she recognizes replicas from the "Chamber of Horrors – Crippen and Haigh and Christie." Soon after her visit the two men begin to argue audibly, and Mr. Sleight runs away temporarily, to be returned several weeks later in an ambulance.

After the narrator departs the house, the name of the seaside town catches her eye in the newspaper one day: "Police were investigating the deaths of Mr. Albert Proudham and Mr. Victor Sleight, whose bodies were found in a gas-filled room." The newspaper report goes on to remark that "the flat was in considerable disorder, a large number of 'dolls and puppets' having been found, broken and mutilated, and strewn about the floor." The reader is left to speculate with the narrator about the roles the characters have played in their demise.

In his review of *A Bit of Singing and Dancing* for the *New Statesman,* Donald complains that "Mr. Proudham and Mr. Sleight" "suffer[s] from one of the [short-story] form's congenital problems – the need to produce a twist." Although his complaint may be legitimate, this is certainly one of Hill's most vivid and haunting stories. Donald goes on to group this story with "Ossie," calling both "stories about grotesques."

The last story in the collection concerns an inveterate eccentric and pleasure seeker, Ossie, as told by a childhood admirer who repeatedly meets Ossie throughout the latter's checkered life. At one point the speaker finds Ossie peddling mechanical toys on the Rialto Bridge in Venice. Ossie's economic fortunes oscillate dramatically, depending on the company he keeps. He has a penchant for dressing up in women's clothes, and he maintains a bizarre attitude of noblesse oblige toward the narrator, who makes repeated attempts to rescue him from squalor.

Despite his repeated efforts the loyal friend, whose deep fondness for Ossie is never explained or explored, feels guilty when Ossie dies of a stroke in a squalid London hospital, surrounded by "old, dying men." After his death Ossie's property is delivered to the friend, the only person who took any continuing interest in his life. In addition to women's clothes and wigs, the property includes a bizarre collection of mechanical toys. The narrator gives most of these to children's charities. The story concludes:

> But I kept one of the bicycling monkeys, and it is here on my desk. I wind it up and it circles round and round, as it circled on the steps of the Rialto Bridge in Venice. It has a grotesque, grinning face and bright pink feet. It is hideous. It reminds me constantly of Ossie.

Hill's second volume of short fiction ends with an assertion of the enduring appeal of the grotesque.

The mindlessly circling mechanical monkey is a fitting image to close Hill's collective works in the short-story genre because the grotesque figure engaged in futile activity reminds the reader of her characters, who never get anywhere.

One year after the publication of *A Bit of Singing and Dancing* Hill produced *In the Springtime of the Year,* the last novel she would write for sixteen years. Perhaps in those years that she devoted to her family and to other sorts of writing, Hill grew in ways that will make her an even greater writer of fiction than she was in the 1970s. Since she has returned to fiction with the novels *Air and Angels* and *Mrs. DeWinter* (1993), Hill may yet produce another excellent collection of short stories.

Interviews:

Sue Fox, "A Life in the Day of Susan Hill," *Sunday Times Magazine,* 23 November 1986, p. A114;

Nicolette Jones, "Breaking the Silence," *Sunday Times,* 24 March 1991, pp. C6, C8.

References:

Walter Allen, *The Short Story in English* (New York: Oxford University Press, 1981);

Rosemary Jackson, "Cold Enclosures: The Fiction of Susan Hill," in *Twentieth-Century Women Novelists,* edited by Thomas F. Staley (Totowa, N.J.: Barnes & Noble, 1982), pp. 81–103;

Kenneth Muir, "Susan Hill's Fiction," in *The Uses of Fiction,* edited by Douglas Jefferson and Graham Martin (Milton Keynes, U.K.: Open University Press, 1982), pp. 273–285;

Maria Schubert, "Susan Hill Focussing on Outsiders and Losers," in *English Language and Literature: Positions and Dispositions,* edited by James Hogg, Karl Hubmeyer, and Dorothea Steiner (Salzburg: University of Salzburg Press, 1990), pp. 91–101.

Ruth Prawer Jhabvala
(7 May 1927 –   )

Stevens Amidon
Goddard College

BOOKS: *To Whom She Will* (London: Allen & Unwin, 1955); republished as *Amrita* (New York: Norton, 1956);

The Nature of Passion (London: Allen & Unwin, 1956; New York: Norton, 1957);

Esmond in India (London: Allen & Unwin, 1958; New York: Norton, 1958);

The Householder (London: John Murray, 1960; New York: Norton, 1960);

Get Ready for Battle (London: John Murray, 1962; New York: Norton, 1963);

Like Birds, Like Fishes and Other Stories (London: John Murray, 1963; New York: Norton, 1964);

A Backward Place (London: John Murray, 1965; New York: Norton, 1965);

A Stronger Climate: 9 Stories (London: John Murray, 1968; New York: Norton, 1968);

An Experience of India (London: John Murray, 1971; New York: Norton, 1972);

A New Dominion (London: John Murray, 1972); republished as *Travelers* (New York: Harper & Row, 1973);

Heat and Dust (London: John Murray, 1975; New York: Harper & Row, 1976);

How I Became a Holy Mother and Other Stories (London: John Murray, 1976; New York: Harper & Row, 1976);

In Search of Love and Beauty (London: John Murray, 1983; New York: Morrow, 1983);

Out of India: Selected Stories (New York: Morrow, 1986; London: Constable, 1986);

Three Continents (London: John Murray, 1987; New York: Morrow, 1987);

Poet and Dancer (New York: Doubleday, 1993; London: John Murray, 1993).

SELECTED PERIODICAL PUBLICATIONS – UNCOLLECTED:
FICTION
"Before the Wedding," *New Yorker,* 33 (28 December 1957): 28–32;

Ruth Prawer Jhabvala (photograph © Jerry Bauer)

"Better than Dead," *New Yorker,* 34 (24 May 1958): 30–36;

"The Elected," *New Yorker,* 36 (30 April 1960): 40–45;

"Wedding Preparations," *Kenyon Review,* 23 (Summer 1961): 408–422;

"Light and Reason," *New Statesman,* 66 (19 July 1963): 73–74;

"Foreign Wives," *London Magazine,* new series 7 (January 1968): 12–22;

"A Very Special Fate," *New Yorker,* 52 (29 March 1976): 27–35;

"Parasites," *New Yorker,* 54 (13 March 1978): 34–43;

"A Summer by the Sea," *New Yorker,* 54 (7 August 1978): 26-34;

"Commensurate Happiness," *Encounter,* 54, no. 1 (1980): 3-11;

"Grandmother," *New Yorker,* 56 (17 November 1980): 54-62;

"Expiation," *New Yorker,* 58 (11 October 1982): 44-51;

"Farid and Farida," *New Yorker,* 60 (15 October 1984): 40-50.

NONFICTION

"Moonlight, Jasmine, and Rickets," *New York Times,* 22 April 1975, p. I35;

"Disinheritance," *Blackwood's,* 326 (July 1979): 4-14;

"Writers and the Cinema," *Times Literary Supplement,* 18 November 1983, pp. 1287-1288.

Ruth Prawer Jhabvala's achievement as an author of short stories rests in her ability to transmit the ambiguity and alienation of modern life. Her skillful narratives – whether set in India, London, or New York — are distinctive in their stylistic tendency to reach epiphany through the revelation of character in the moments her players come face-to-face with the limits of life. Jhabvala usually chooses to avoid the traditional narrative structures where the story is designed around the piecemeal disclosure of plot over a period of time. Instead she takes the reader deep into her characters and juxtaposes their responses to an event or displays their ironic misrepresentations of the world around them. Her stories often seem sliced out of the continuum that is life and avoid the deliberate dramatizations that seem to accompany more-conventional beginnings and denouements.

Although her narrative structures are innovative, she seems to skirt the deliberate linguistic experimentation seen in the stories of many short-fiction writers of the late modernist period. Jhabvala prefers to use conventional techniques to characterize the tensions that exist when the progressive forces of change collide with the entrenched forces of tradition. These collisions produce moments of both tragedy and comedy, yet ultimately her vision is dark. In spite of moments of triumph and joy her characters are trapped within the class and social structures around them.

Jhabvala's conservative style has been compared to those of Anton Chekhov, E. M. Forster, and Henry James. Yet her style most resembles Jane Austen's, particularly in the close attention Jhabvala pays to nuances, small frailties, and manners of social convention. Like Austen she prefers to treat

philosophical questions through her portraits of the intricacies of human relationships rather than through abstractions.

Ruth Prawer was born in Cologne, Germany, on 7 May 1927, the second of two children and only daughter of Marcus and Eleonara Cohn Prawer. Although Jhabvala experienced some happy years in Cologne, she has rarely returned to them in her fiction. The reluctance of her mother to depart resulted in the Prawers being one of the last Jewish families allowed to leave Nazi Germany. Jhabvala faced painful discrimination during her last years in Germany, a pain that was certainly amplified by the murder of her father's entire family in the Holocaust and his suicide in 1948.

The Prawers' 1939 immigration to England brought with it feelings of exile and isolation and was colored by the dangers of war, including bombings. The family initially lived in Coventry and finally settled in a Jewish suburb of London where Marcus Prawer started a clothing business. Jhabvala received a typical middle-class education in the local grammar school and in 1951 was graduated with an M.A. in English literature from the Queen Mary College of London University. In 1949 she met Cyrus S. H. Jhabvala, a Parsi architect, at a party in London. The son of a labor leader and a woman's rights activist, he returned to his family in India yet came back to London to marry her in 1951. The couple left for India shortly after the ceremony.

After she arrived in Delhi, Jhabvala considered herself a full-time writer, even while raising three daughters. By 1953 she had completed her first novel, *To Whom She Will* (1955), which was published in the United States as *Amrita* (1956). Her second novel, *The Nature of Passion,* was published in England in 1956 and in the United States in 1957. In July 1957 her story "The Interview" was published in the *New Yorker,* establishing a relationship between the author and the magazine that endured for more than twenty-five years. Six of the eleven stories in her 1963 collection *Like Birds, Like Fishes and Other Stories* originally appeared in the *New Yorker.*

"The Interview" is a first-person narrative told by an immature Indian husband who fancies himself a bit of a dandy. The story is noteworthy in its introduction of several motifs that run through Jhabvala's portraits of India. One is the tension that exists within the extended Indian families, where up to three generations may share a dwelling. The wife in this story is the first of many who dreams of her husband carrying her away from the subjugation and abuse of in-laws. Jhabvala also explores the food shortages endemic to India. As Rene Wine-garten notes in *Midstream* (March 1974): "Food plays an enormous part in a land where so many die of starvation every day. It figures as a token of love given and received. The preparation of the loved one's favorite dishes almost resembles a spiritual rite."

The narrator of "The Interview" realizes he is favored by his mother and sister-in-law, even over his working brother, by virtue of the extra tidbits he receives. Although he understands that only his brother's job lies between himself and starvation, he is unable to work with authority figures or hold a job. The sexual tension between the narrator and his brother's wife, though unconsummated, establishes a theme of illicit or dangerous love that recurs throughout Jhabvala's work.

The dark threat of starvation that hangs over the middle and lower classes of India keeps this story from becoming merely a comedy of manners. As the ominous cloud hovers, Jhabvala builds the story through the ironic thinking of the narrator, who clearly imagines himself as superior to those around him. The story reaches its denouement when he becomes more and more anxious while waiting for an important job interview. Just as his moment of opportunity arrives, he collapses into fear: "The official with the list came back and great panic seized me that he would read out my name. I got up, quickly, murmuring, 'Please excuse me – bathroom' and went out. The official with the list called after me, 'Hey mister, where are you going?' so I lowered my head and walked faster." When courage is demanded he displays only cowardice, going off to a café to nurse his wounds by fantasizing about his sister-in-law's breasts.

In "The Old Lady," the opening story in *Like Birds, Like Fishes*, the ironic technique is reversed. The central character considers herself inferior and uneducated compared to her "modern" children. Yet she is a quiet, contented woman, in stark contrast to her children. Her daughter Leila has a weak but loving husband whom she abuses and plans to divorce. Her youngest son, Bobo, lies around eating biscuits, while Satish, her oldest, is preoccupied with his career as a lawyer and is too hurried to enjoy life.

Jhabvala, particularly in these early stories, shows sympathy for the contemplative tradition in India, although many commentators note that she is quick to point out that the vast majority of Indians are more materialistic than spiritual. This juxtaposition of Babbittry with holiness recurs throughout her work; however, it does not indicate a hostility

toward spirituality itself. As Laurie Sucher observes in *The Fiction of Ruth Prawer Jhabvala* (1989): "If Ruth Jhabvala's fiction endorses a religion, it is a quietistic religion of private and contemplative withdrawal, passive 'waiting' for grace through meditation." In this vein the protagonist of "The Old Lady" is a precursor to Maji in *Heat and Dust* (1975) and Natasha in *In Search of Love and Beauty* (1983).

"A Loss of Faith" features a good-looking, but lazy, brother who will not work and a widowed mother who desires to escape the torment of in-laws. The main thrust of the story is Ram Kumar's descent into Babbittry in his attempts to escape a miserable life by immersing himself in his work. His tragedy is the discovery that, even with material success, he is trapped in a life and a social structure over which he has little control. Ultimately he loses faith in the one thing he truly values – his work.

"A Birthday in London" stands alone among Jhabvala's collected stories in that it contains no connection to Indians or India. Instead it focuses on German expatriate Jews living in England and the separation they feel. Jhabvala has always been hesitant to speak directly about her early life, particularly about the painful period immediately after World War II, which was punctuated by her father's suicide. Yet this story contains obvious parallels to Jhabvala's own life. When Sonia speaks of her late husband, she might as well be speaking of Marcus Prawer: " 'If only he had waited,' Sonia said. 'He never believed things could be well again one day. I would say to him "Otto, it is dark now but the sun will come again"; "no," he said, "it is all finished." He didn't want to live any more you see.' "

Sonia's children, Werner and Lilo, bear more than a passing resemblance to Jhabvala and her brother, Siegbert. Whereas Ruth left the Gentile life among the expatriate German Jews in England for an adventure in India, Lilo is a sturdy farmhand on an Israeli kibbutz. However, it would be wrong to carry these parallels too far, especially since the details of this period in Jhabvala's life are sketchy. She has never been a particularly autobiographical writer, and Indians – or Europeans living in India – remained her principal subject until the 1980s.

The best stories in *Like Birds, Like Fishes* deal with individuals who seek to escape the constraints imposed on them by society. Durga, the central character in "The Widow," is a singular, independent-minded woman who outlives her much-older husband. She refuses to accept the traditional role of the woman cursed by a husband's death, and she enjoys her status as an economically independent woman living alone. The theme of illicit love returns as she falls in love with the teenage son of her tenants, which leads to disaster. The boy rejects Durga's advances, and finally she sees herself as her scheming relatives see her — as a foolish old widow. Jhabvala ends the story on a typically ironic note:

> O yes, said the relatives, wise and knowing, nodding their heads, our ancestors knew what they were doing when they laid down these rigid rules for widows; and though nowadays perhaps, in these modern times, one could be a little more lenient — for instance, no one insisted that Durga should shave her head — still on the whole the closer one followed the old traditions, the safer and better it was.

Although Durga, in her resignation, starts to discover some of the contentment shown in "The Old Lady," the reader is left to wonder for whom these old traditions are better and safe.

The first-person narrator of "My First Marriage" faces different constraints. The daughter of a wealthy government official, she falls in love with an intelligent, but shiftless, storyteller from the lower classes instead of the man chosen by her parents to marry her. Rejecting her lot, she runs off and marries the man she loves. Surprisingly, she is content living within her brother-in-law's extended family. Even her discovery that her husband had another wife and family whom he abandoned does nothing to reduce her happiness in this marriage. The young storyteller becomes a guru of some renown, entrancing even her mother, but he eventually disappears, leaving his wife and disciples behind. She quickly divorces him and soon is to remarry, this time to the original choice of her parents. Although she knows her fiancé is a good man, somehow she still displays an almost-inexplicable attraction to her first love.

In "Like Birds, Like Fishes" Raj also pursues an illicit love, the spoiled wife of a materialistic young government official. He, too, attempts to violate the strictures of his social class by running off with the young woman. But they return because the young woman cannot stand the smell and squalor of the third-class compartment of the train. They are trapped: she by her materialism, and he by his all-consuming love for her.

The issue of class strictures and their effects is a theme addressed by many British writers of the postwar period, chiefly because of the disruptive forces of World War II and the popularity of Marxism among intellectuals. Jhabvala's explorations of this subject are all the more interesting because India's caste system is the most formal class struc-

ture of any society. As a non-Indian, she is the detached observer, dissecting the effects of class strictures on human relations within the laboratory of her fiction. Although India's system is particularly insidious, Jhabvala's latest fiction clearly demonstrates that class restraints are also a problem in Western society.

"Lekha" — the story of a simple young girl who marries a widower, an important government minister — is one of the finest pieces in *Like Birds, Like Fishes.* The story is told from the viewpoint of the wife of one of the minister's subordinates, a woman who befriends Lekha. Lekha ends up betraying her kind, but boring, husband by falling in love with Govind, an artist. The story centers on two epiphanies. In one the reader sees how Lekha comes alive through her love for Govind. In the second the reader discovers that the narrator, who at first glance appears to be a sympathetic modern woman, is in fact as prejudiced and closed-minded as the traditional Hindu society she rejects. This sophisticated, ironic use of indirect character development is also employed with great success in the novel *Heat and Dust. Like Birds, Like Fishes* received general acclaim and established Jhabvala's reputation as a short-story writer of the first rank. Santha Rama Rau, in the *New York Times Book Review* (11 March 1964), notes that "she grows better with the years, and her work, as it increases, improves."

In Jhabvala's 1968 collection, *A Stronger Climate: 9 Stories,* her focus shifts from the extended Indian family to Europeans in India. The subjects of these stories are closer to her own experience, and the characterizations are generally stronger and less stereotyped because of it. Jhabvala divides the collection into two groups of stories, the first six dealing with Europeans who are "seekers" and the last three focusing on those who are "sufferers."

"The Young Couple" appears to parallel Jhabvala's own experiences closely. Although placed in the "Seekers" section it might properly belong with the stories of "Sufferers." Cathy, a young wife who has followed her Indian husband from England, begins to feel oppressed by the "stronger climate" she finds in India. Everything about the country starts to feel heavy to her — the furniture, the decorations in her in-laws' house, the huge meals, and especially her husband's extended family:

> She could not complain that they did not care for her. The trouble was they cared too much, so much that she felt herself lapped around and drowning in more love than she had ever before, among her cool English family and friends, encountered. Everything that she and Naraian said or did, the way they looked, everything was

Dust jacket for Jhabvala's first collection of short fiction, which includes six stories first published in the New Yorker

the subject of scrupulous family concern, to be pointed out, discussed, wondered at and advised over.

Cathy's only joy is the time she spends alone with Naraian in their apartment. The fact that they often walk around naked when alone accentuates the freedom of their existence together, a freedom reminiscent of Eden. The tragedy of the story rests in its conclusion, where a pregnant Cathy and Naraian, newly appointed to a position in his uncle's business, are preparing to move into quarters in his parents' home.

The story seems to mirror Jhabvala's own experiences in India. In a September 1983 interview with Bernard Weinraub she speaks of her move to India: "In the beginning . . . I adored the summers; I loved the extreme heat after being so cold in wartime England. Then it became more and more difficult. India sucks the marrow from your bone, only you're not aware of it."

Among the English "seekers" are two friends in "In Love with a Beautiful Girl." Richard is a stiff young foreign-service officer who imagines himself liberal and modern, and his friend Mary is a bohemian secretary. Richard, who has always regarded himself as coolly unemotional and unlikely to marry, falls desperately in love with a wealthy Indian girl, Ruchira. She is vivacious but shallow and takes a dislike to Mary and her unconventional friends. Ruchira enjoys the boring foreign-service parties Richard abhors, and he begins to live a lie, pretending for Ruchira's sake to love the diplomatic life. Mary and Richard are slowly driven apart by this relationship. When Mary is posted back to England, Richard reacts to her complaint about Indian friends:

> "What's it matter," Richard said, "What you're loved for, as long as you are?" And intercepting a surprised look from Mary, he went on quite fiercely: "Why the hell should anyone love us for ourselves? We're not all that bloody marvelous are we?"

Jhabvala paints a wonderful portrait of how successfully India has educated the emotionally immature young Britons in different ways. The bohemian idealist has become a realist, and the practical materialist has learned the value of love. Jhabvala's gracefully ambivalent conclusion leaves unanswered and unimportant the question of whether the love affair will survive Ruchira's selfish immaturity.

In "A Spiritual Call" Daphne, a young Englishwoman, makes a traditional spiritual search: she has followed a Yogi named Swamiji to an ashram in India. In this story – the first of several portraits of Indian holy men found in Jhabvala's work – the Yogi is portrayed in rather mixed terms. Although he is idiosyncratic and a bit materialistic in his desire to build an up-to-date ashram and in his fondness for the amenities he expects to enjoy during an upcoming American tour, Jhabvala does not attack him in the way she does the religious figures in the later story "An Experience of India" or the novel *A New Dominion* (1972).

She does use satire to make fun of the Yogi as the reader realizes that Daphne's friend Helga is having sex with Swamiji, though Daphne is unaware of this development. Jhabvala also satirizes Daphne's silly 1960s antirationalism. When Daphne is asked to rewrite the guru's naive and grammatically incorrect manuscript, the Oxford-educated woman becomes ashamed of her own heritage:

> In spite of herself, Daphne's Oxford-trained mind rose at once, as she read, in judgement; and her feelings, in face of this judgement, were ones of embarrassment, even shame for Swamiji. Yet a moment later, as she raised her burning cheeks from his incriminating manuscript, she realized that it was not for him she need be ashamed but for herself. How narrow was her mind, how tight and snug it sat in the straitjacket her education had provided for it.

In spite of the implicit criticism of Daphne's naiveté and Swamiji's manipulation, by the end of the story both Helga and Daphne are shown to be happy with their existence. For all of his faults Swamiji is a successful Yogi who has taught her to become friends with Helga and to overcome the emotional straitjacket of her British upbringing. As the story concludes, the Yogi presents each of the two "seekers" with a white sari, the uniform of his true disciples.

In "Passion," perhaps the finest of the six stories concerning "seekers," Christine and Betsy are in search of love. The two roommates also share a common interest in Indian boyfriends. Yet, where Christine's affairs with Indian men are the experi-

mentation of youth, Betsy's passion for the sour Har Gopal is all-consuming.

There is great irony in the portrait of Har Gopal, for he is no prize. On his first visit he gets drunk and vomits on Betsy's white rug. He has a wife and three children whom he marginally supports with a low-level librarian's job. He dislikes Christine and her friends. But these matters mean little to Betsy, who falls desperately in love: "'Sometimes I tell you I feel *insane* – and what's more – what's terrible: I revel in it! I glory in it!' She rolled over on to her side to face Christine and her big breasts fell to that side and her eyes shone behind her flesh-coloured glasses."

Betsy's descent into passion accelerates as she prepares to sacrifice her apartment, her job, and all her security for a life near her love. But Har Gopal is appalled by her behavior, finding her mad. He points out that the chances of her finding a job in India are poor and that, even if she did, she would never be able to live on the salary she would be paid. As the story ends, Betsy is adamant about leaving behind the privileged life she feels she has led, and the reader is left to wonder whether Har Gopal will show any further interest in her.

Even though the story ends on a comic note, it succeeds on a higher level. Betsy's ecstasy is so powerful that the more limited emotions displayed by Christine, her lover, Manny, and Har Gopal pale in comparison. Although Betsy's love may be irrational, in some strange way she has discovered the "higher reality" that so many Europeans have sought in India.

The stories in "The Sufferers" concern Europeans who have come to India to be a part of its culture yet have failed in that task. Miss Tuhy, the central character in "Miss Sahib," was a wonderful teacher who stayed behind after India won independence from Great Britain. Although she no longer meets the new, stringent teacher qualifications, her love for the happy pupils and the warm climate have prompted her to remain in a poor neighborhood where she lives frugally on her savings. Miss Tuhy's students now have lives of their own and no longer show much interest in her, so her feelings are transferred to a young girl, Sharmila, whom she tutors. Sharmila becomes a symbol for Miss Tuhy's idealistic picture of India. In a brilliant piece of parallel character development, Sharmila marries, gives birth, and becomes estranged from her husband while Miss Tuhy becomes a stranger in India. As Sharmila grows fat and vulgar, Miss Tuhy increasingly suffers to observe the misery around her.

In one last attempt to redeem her faith Miss Tuhy uses her savings to take Sharmila and her children on a vacation at an English inn in the mountains. Here Miss Tuhy discovers she is happy in the clean boardinghouse atmosphere, while Sharmila and the children are miserable. Leaving early, they return to the poor neighborhood from which Miss Tuhy has become alienated. At last ready to return to an England she now misses, Miss Tuhy no longer has the funds for even a cheap fare. The gentle irony and ambivalence toward Indian society seen in the earlier stories has here grown into a vision of enormous weight and oppression.

The collection closes on a more balanced note with "The Man with the Dog." Told in the first person by an Indian widow who has escaped the usual fate of women in her situation, the "sufferer" in this story is her lover, Boekelman, an abusive Dutch businessman. At first the reader finds her love for this cruel user ironically comic, but it becomes tragic as it leads to her estrangement from her children. Yet Jhabvala gradually reveals to the reader a picture of their symbiotic love for each other. As the narrator grows stronger and more self-assured, Boekelman in his pride leaves her for the slovenly Lina. But he cannot live with the chaos that Lina represents. Although he may not return the widow's love, he loves their orderly life together. Jhabvala's evocative report of the widow's reaction to his return is powerful: "I thought of him gone away from here and living with Lina, or alone with his dog in some rented room; no contact with India or Indians . . . his only companions people like himself — as old, as lonely, as disappointed, and as far from hope."

The rootlessness of these Europeans in India certainly is a reflection of Jhabvala's own feelings of alienation. Driven from Europe by the Nazis and exiled from England, she recognized that her existence in India was tenuous. In her September 1983 interview with Weinraub she stated: "You can't live in a completely alien place . . . I got very homesick for Europe. It was a homesickness that was so terrible, so consuming. And the only place that reminded me of the Europe that I once knew was New York."

A Stronger Climate is also notable for the continued growth of Jhabvala's narrative skills. The stories in *Like Birds, Like Fishes* are spare, almost microcosmic portraits of Indians in and around Delhi, and the characters have a sameness of vision and rarely show much psychological growth. The characters in the best stories of *A Stronger Climate* are painted with much broader strokes. The reader is carried on odysseys into character where simplistic

judgments about motives are difficult to make. Stylistically stories such as "Miss Sahib" and "The Man with the Dog" demonstrate a far deeper integration of form with content. Although many of these changes in her fiction came with the increased technical proficiency one expects to see in a maturing author, there is at least one explanation for the relatively clear demarcation in style between the early and middle stages of her career — film.

In 1961 writer/director James Ivory and producer Ismail Merchant asked her to adapt a screenplay from her novel *The Householder* (1960). Her relationship with Ivory and Merchant has continued for more than thirty years, resulting in collaborations on more than a dozen movies. She received Academy Awards in 1987 and 1993 for her screenplay adaptations of the E. M. Forster novels *A Room with a View* (1908) and *Howards End* (1910).

Jhabvala has stated that her screenwriting career has allowed her to travel and meet a far greater variety of people than she would have met in her Delhi household. Yasmine Gooneratne points out that Jhabvala's "fiction written after 1960 ranges far more widely than before; geographically . . . deeper into India, and socially more freely than ever up and down India's infinitely varied and graded social scale . . . the later fiction begins to take on the aspects of a cosmic metaphor for life and universal experience."

Reviewers were quick to note the darker tone of *A Stronger Climate*. Margaret Parton, in the *Saturday Review* (1 March 1969), gave a typical reaction:

> Most of (the earlier works) are like Indian saris — pure silk shot through with silver threads of wit, irony, and indulgent laughter. Not this one. The Delhi setting is there, and also the wit and irony. But somehow the laughter is missing. Can it be that Mrs. Jhabvala, always the wry satirist, has become bitter?

Jhabvala addresses this criticism directly in "Myself in India," a controversial essay included as an introduction to her 1971 collection *An Experience of India:*

> There is a cycle that Europeans — by Europeans I mean all Westerners, including Americans — tend to pass through. It goes like this: first stage, tremendous enthusiasm — everything Indian is marvelous; second stage, everything Indian not so marvelous; third stage, everything Indian abominable. For some people it ends there, for others the cycle renews itself and goes on. I have been through it so many times that now I think of myself as strapped to a wheel that goes round and round.

The collection opens with two stories, "A Bad Woman" and "A Star and Two Girls," set in the area around Bombay. Along with "A Course in English Studies" (which takes place in the Midlands of England) this setting presents a departure for Jhabvala, whose earlier stories generally take place inside or around Delhi. "A Star and Two Girls" is also noteworthy in its characterization of Suraj, a film star who befriends two British girls, Gwen and Maggie. At a difficult filming session Suraj overhears one of his friends making a witty remark at the expense of the girls. Suraj angrily slaps and beats his friend, to the girls' horror. Their next meeting illuminates the cultural differences: "Suraj had forgotten about this incident and was surprised when they brought it up. 'It's all right,' he said, waving his hand to wave it all away. 'He has apologized to me.' '*He* apologized to *you!*'"

The contrast between the emotional Indian actor and the two reserved British girls gives this story its power. Although Gwen and Maggie genuinely like Suraj, his violent behavior and emotional swings are alien to their reserved civility. As the girls prepare to leave India, Suraj deals with the pain of separation by quoting "Urdu couplets about the tears of friends whose paths lie in separate directions." In contrast, the less emotional British girls promise to write.

Indian actresses are the focus of "Suffering Women," a story framed by its independent female characters, who are ironically attracted to the men who use them. Jhabvala portrays a more modern India, where the wealthy have broken out of the traditional roles yet still seem to seek out the psychological relationships that traditional roles presume. The story is also noteworthy for its mention of bisexuality among Indian men. Both homosexuals and bisexuals are scrutinized in Jhabvala's later works.

"Rose Petals" continues her portraits of Indians who live parasitically off their families. The story is unique, however, in that the central character, who prefers to lie around and do nothing, is the wife of a cabinet minister. Jhabvala's previous portraits of Indian housewives show them to be an industrious, though perhaps long-suffering, group. The story is built on the contrast between the hectic lives of the industrious minister and his equally active daughter, Mina, and the lazy existence of his wife and his brother, Biju.

"The Housewife" is another of Jhabvala's explorations of illicit love. It is one of her most powerful portraits of what Sucher calls her preoccupation with "the divinely powerful, all-knowing, demon lover." The housewife Shakuntala (the name is also the title of a well-known Sanskrit drama) pursues an orderly life as an upper-class Indian woman. With a grown daughter, a grandson, and a kind, indulgent husband, her existence is comfortable. But she has become restless with her life and begins taking voice lessons. These become her all-consuming passion, one that spreads to her music teacher, who becomes a symbol for the irrational passion that is missing from her life. Whereas her life is orderly, his is chaotic. The teacher forces her to come face-to-face with the conflict between her regular life and irregular passion when he announces that she is at last ready for a recital, an impossibility for a woman of her class. Frustrated by her inability to pursue her art publicly, her passions for singing and the teacher begin to come together. This transference is complete by the story's end, when Shakuntala gives herself to her teacher sexually.

The collection closes with the long title story, which concerns a sexually adventurous Englishwoman, the wife of a reporter. In its exploration of the intersection of the sexually liberated woman of the 1960s with the traditional Indian ashram, "An Experience of India" appears to be a precursor to *A New Dominion*. Jhabvala comments on this cultural phenomenon in the interview with Weinraub: "You had the Western woman, very introverted, vulnerable, sensitive, all carried to the extreme. And you had the gurus who seemed to me the epitome of a definite Indian type – charismatic, physically magnetic, deeply intuitive. The meeting of these two was just irresistible to me." In her works the two forces collide and do not mix well, despite the interest of many Westerners in Indian traditions.

In "An Experience in India" the conflict reaches its zenith in the dramatic scene where the central character is raped by her Yogi. She is at first afraid of this powerful man, but her fear evaporates as his behavior parallels that of the other Indian men with whom she has slept, men who seem to become excited at her sexual history but who call her "bitch" at the moment of climax: "'How many? Answer me!' he commanded urgent and dangerous. But I was no longer afraid: now he was not an unknown quantity nor was the situation any longer new or strange. 'Answer me, answer me!' he cried, riding on top of me, and then he cried 'Bitch!' and I laughed in relief."

By the time her 1976 collection *How I Became a Holy Mother and Other Stories* was published, Jhabvala's existence in India had become too oppressive, and she moved to Manhattan, although she continued to spend her winters in Delhi with her beloved husband, Jhab. The collection opens with two stories of British women married to Indian husbands. "Two More Under the Indian Sun" is built around the relationship between the widowed Margaret, an activist in charitable and spiritual organizations, and her friend Elizabeth, who is married to an Indian named Raju. The plot is ostensibly about a disagreement that occurs when Margaret asks Elizabeth to chaperon a group of orphans to the Taj Mahal. Because of the objections of Raju, who dislikes Margaret and her endless projects, Elizabeth refuses to go. Yet the real subject of the story is a character study of the two women and a friend, a holy man named Babaji. "Babaji and Margaret were having a discussion on the relative merits of the three ways towards realization. They spoke of the way of knowledge, the way of action, and the way of love."

While Margaret represents the way of action, Babaji follows the way of knowledge, and Elizabeth the way of unconditional love. The story delicately explores the difficulties of each path. Babaji has the detached attitude toward material things that typifies one who has an intimate knowledge of the spiritual universe. Although he professes to be interested only in spiritual things, he must rely on others for his creature comforts – a room in Margaret's home during the cold winter months and even the cup of tea he enjoys. Although Elizabeth gives love unconditionally, her love is abused by both Margaret, who tries to control her with guilt, and Raju, who bullies her and fails to communicate freely with her.

Margaret's difficulties are the most interesting. She professes to love India and is involved in charitable activities, but she is developing a secret hatred of the place. Whereas the entire household is a bustling colony of Indian culture, her room is separate and different from the rest. With solid European furniture, a fireplace, and family photographs, the room practically screams "England." She escapes here from the overwhelming neediness of India. The parallels between this scene and Jhabvala's own need for isolation in India can be seen in the essay "Myself in India": "So I am back again alone in my room with the blinds drawn and the air-conditioner on. Sometimes, when I think of my life, it seems to have contracted to this one point and to be concentrated in this one room."

"The Englishwoman" seems even more closely related to Jhabvala's life, in this case her decision to leave India. Like Jhabvala, Sadie is a middle-aged Englishwoman about to leave India and her husband. She has become overwhelmed with the heaviness and passion around her. The story paints a strange, vivid portrait of three individuals and the ways in which age has changed them. Annapurna, her husband's cousin and mistress, is like the mountain for which she is named and is the least changeable of the three. A woman of great physical energy, she is a blessing to Sadie, who long ago was gratified that her husband had turned to Annapurna rather than prostitutes. Yet Annapurna lives in the past, often talking about the dead as though they are still present.

Annapurna's husband has aged the most, especially physically. Once a slim Oxford student, he is now fat and nearly incapable of moving. He lies on the couch while Annapurna entertains him with her gossip and stories of the past. Once a hunter, a young man who loved fast cars and fast women, he is now calm and comfortable. Although his wife's decision to leave upsets him greatly, when his passion is spent he becomes resigned to her decision. There are similarities between his attitude and that of Suraj toward the departing girls in "A Star and Two Girls."

Sadie is the most complex character of the three. She certainly feels old and adrift in India, especially now that her children are grown. Her decision to leave is tied up with the great weight she feels, the pity of Indian relatives she resents, the guilt over her own lack of passion in passionate India, and a general homesickness for England. As she suffers insomnia the night before her departure, she looks out at her Indian garden, which she imagines as a wide English down where she stands under an oak tree. Sadie's decision to leave brings back the excitement of her youth, an excitement that may be a reflection of Jhabvala's feelings about leaving India for Manhattan.

"In the Mountains" contains some of the most vivid characterizations found in any of Jhabvala's works. Pritam is certainly the strangest and most independent Indian woman in any of her stories. "In the Mountains" is a bit of a mystery, as the reader wonders what brings this woman with her gruff and manly voice, her stern resistance to her mother's disapproval, to live virtually alone in the mountains. The reader begins to posit explanations such as lesbianism or a disastrous love affair. Although the reader is given a few clues, the story ends in as much mystery as it begins. Ultimately the success of the piece depends on the depth and attractiveness of Pritam's character. As S. M. Mollinger notes in *Library Journal* (1 December 1976), *How I Became a Holy Mother* contains stories "about misfits, life's square pegs, many of them women." Both Sadie and Pritam certainly fall into this category, as do the central characters in "Bombay."

"Bombay" centers on a man referred to only as "the uncle." His one period of happiness was the years spent with his widowed brother raising his niece, Nargis. It was a lively Parsi household where they read Persian poetry and Victorian prose and schooled Nargis at home. Eventually the beautiful Nargis married a wealthy Parsi businessman, and the widower died. Despite Nargis's protestations the uncle prefers to live now in a hovel among the beggars and street merchants of Bombay, visiting Nargis only when hunger forces him to do so. In spite of the squalor he seems to prefer, he believes in the prophecies of his landlady, who "traced the lines of his palms and said she still saw a lot of beautiful living left."

Although Nargis objects to her uncle's living conditions, she does not visit or pay him much attention. Nor does she pay much attention to her husband; she has become obsessed with her spoiled, sociopathic son, Rusi. Though brilliant, Rusi is unable to get along with schoolmates and teachers, and he dominates and terrorizes the household. He is the one antagonist in the uncle's life. Rusi also makes predictions, though his are usually full of calamity, and he often jeers at the uncle.

As the story develops, it becomes clear that the conflict between Rusi and the uncle is actually a contest for Nargis's affections. Although the uncle ostensibly visits because of hunger, the reader discovers that he receives a monthly stipend that he evidently does not use. Eventually the combination of a life of squalor and his age lead to illness. After he is stricken, Nargis brings him to her household. He seems genuinely sad at his loss of independence, and the story ends on a bizarre note, as Nargis is spoon-feeding the invalid:

> He just looked into Nargis's face. She always sat with her back to the window and the tree. Even when she got annoyed with him – saying, "You are doing it on purpose," when the food dropped on his chin – still he loved to have her sitting there. At such times it seemed to him that his landlady had been right and that his life was not over by any means.

Jhabvala's subversion of a stereotype can be seen in "Prostitutes," which concerns three generations of women: Maji, a former prostitute who still lives among the practicing whores; her daughter, Tara, who lives in a new home on the outskirts of town; and Tara's surly daughter, Leila, who never actually appears in the story. Jhabvala uses satire to show that Maji is less a prostitute than her successful, but selfish, daughter, for Tara's good fortune comes from exploiting Leila's father, Mukand Sa-

hib, who adores her. Tara cannot stand the presence of Mukand Sahib, a gentle, understanding man who wants only to be near Tara, to sit and hold her hand. Her affection is directed at the playful Bikki, who no longer visits much now that Leila has gone to boarding school. Her only use for Mukand Sahib is as a source of money.

When Tara visits Maji, the old woman is interested in news about her granddaughter, but Tara inquires about Bikki. As Maji becomes more and more evasive, it becomes clear to the reader that Bikki is Maji's lover, something that Tara fails to comprehend. Maji tells Tara a story about her young lover and "the old man," her late companion. At the time of Tara's birth, when life got difficult, the young lover left, but "the old man" remained and helped to support her. Clearly Maji is trying to draw a comparison between Mukand Sahib and Bikki, but Tara ignores the story.

When Bikki finally turns up, Tara confronts him about the source of his new necklace. As the truth of his relationship with Maji begins to dawn on her, Tara finally understands her mother's message. Although she leaves with Bikki for a pleasant shopping trip, by the story's end the reader knows that she will return to Mukand Sahib, as Bikki will to Maji.

The satiric element that has always been present in Jhabvala's fiction is taken to a much deeper level in "How I Became a Holy Mother." While earlier stories of the ashram paint an ironic, sometimes dark, picture of rape ("An Experience of India") and Babbittry ("A Spiritual Call"), the title story presents a much lighter portrait. Katie, a not-too-brilliant young Englishwoman, has an affair with Vishwa, a junior swami at the ashram who is being groomed for an American tour by "the Countess," a drill-sergeant type to whom the senior swami defers. This ashram is a hilarious place, full of initiates practicing "free sex" (in spite of the Countess's spying), complete with a "huge holy OM sign . . . lit up all round with coloured bulbs that flashed on and off."

Unlike Jhabvala's other gurus, the senior swami is neither a materialist nor a rapist. Vishwa has been chosen successor because the swami has tired of the Countess's American tours, which resemble the giant productions of rock-and-roll bands. The senior swami has reached the point where he cannot look up at a skyscraper without getting homesick for the mountain peaks that surround the ashram.

Jhabvala brings this tale to a stunning, hilarious conclusion. A "Great Yagna," or prayer meet-

Dust jacket for Jhabvala's 1976 collection of short stories, most of which concern women's relationships with husbands and lovers

ing, is given to celebrate Vishwa's recovery from a fever and his coming career as a guru in the West. At the end of the celebration the master swami directs Vishwa up to the "Pillar of the Golden Rule," a monument overlooking the ashram where, unbeknownst to them, Katie waits. Katie and Vishwa, whom the Countess has kept apart, begin copulating beneath the pillar:

> The drums and hymns down in the Meditation Hall reached their crescendo just then. Of course Vishwa was too taken up with what he was doing to notice anything going on around him, so it was only me that saw the Countess come uphill. She was walking quite slowly and I suppose I could have warned Vishwa in time but it seemed a pity to interrupt him, so I just let her come on up and find us.

The master swami comically settles everything to the Victorian Countess's satisfaction. The grand tour will begin with Vishwa as guru and Katie accompanying him — white robe and all — as the "Mother principle." In the end it is all a matter of packaging.

The collection closes on a serious note with the darkest story of all, "Desecration." Jhabvala shows that her interest is in character development rather than the dramatic necessities of plot when she announces the suicide of Sofia, the central character, in the first sentence. The classic triangle of characters includes Sofia, a young, educated Muslim woman of uncertain family; her elderly Hindu husband, Raja Sahib, a wealthy businessman who writes plays in blank verse; and the violent, passionate superintendent of police, Bakhtawar Singh. The allegorical nature of the story can also be seen in Sofia's name, which is synonymous with wisdom, and in the crumbling castle of Raja Sahib's family, a place that symbolizes the decay of the romantic past, as do the buildings that have been demolished since the events of the story.

Sofia's desecration in the central sex scene, where Singh mounts her from the rear as she recites Moslem prayers, is only part of the damage done. The lives of Sofia and Raja Sahib — as exemplified in their romantic evenings together on the roof of their home reading his plays — are also ruined:

> When he told her about the new drama he wanted her to read aloud, she was glad to oblige him. . . . As usual she didn't understand a good deal of what she was reading, but she did notice that there was something different about his verses. There was one line that read "Oh, if thou didst but know what it is like to live in hell the way I do!"

The truth of the matter is they both live in hell because of the affair. The gallant but proud Raja Sahib certainly suffers in his knowledge of Sofia's betrayal, and Sofia suffers with the fear that a confession will destroy the tender respect they have always shown for each other. It is a guilt she will not be able to carry forever. The desecration is complete with the destruction of the closeness that once existed between Raja Sahib and Sofia. She finds knowledge and wisdom when she realizes the pornographic path down which her provocative passion has taken her. Unfortunately, it is too late.

In "Desecration" Jhabvala makes no attempt to relieve the darkness of the tragedy through the little ironies and foibles of character on which she usually relies. The story achieves an almost fairy-tale quality, albeit one that shouts with the violence and pornography that have come to replace Victorian romanticism as an organizing principle in society. It is no accident that Singh is a uniformed superintendent of police — he represents the Fascist violence that disrupted the romanticism of Jhabvala's childhood.

How I Became a Holy Mother is Jhabvala's latest collection of new stories, and it has received consistently positive reviews. Paul Bailey, in the *Observer* (27 June 1976), states, "There are nine stories in her new collection . . . and every one of them is brilliant." Susannah Clapp, in the *New Statesman* (2 July 1976), considers the collection to be a greater achievement than *Heat and Dust*.

With its delicatessens and tastes of 1930s Germany, New York reawakened memories that allowed Jhabvala to reexplore her personal ancestry. "Commensurate Happiness" (*Encounter,* 1980) has similarities to "A Birthday in London," as well as her 1983 novel, *In Search of Love and Beauty*. As in the earlier story the characters revolve around a deceased father named Otto, though in this case he has died of natural causes. The story includes the widowed Jeanette; her late husband's mistress, Wanda; and Jeanette's grandchildren, Marie and Hughie. "Commensurate Happiness" is an ironic portrait of the diminished expectations found in women whose marriages are arranged or convenient.

Jeanette adored Otto for four years prior to a marriage that was arranged by their aunts. Before long Otto began an affair with Wanda, which Jeanette discovered. Despite terrible battles between Jeanette and Otto the affair continued up to Otto's death, and Jeanette eventually tolerated the relationship. After Otto's death Wanda became a part of Jeanette's extended family.

With this situation as background the story centers on Wanda's birthday party, at which Wanda presses Marie and Hughie into a marriage similar to that of Jeanette and Otto. Marie has always loved Hughie, but both Marie and Jeanette are aware of his homosexuality. In spite of this knowledge Jeanette clearly expects Marie to settle for this sort of diminished relationship in the same way she settled for Otto:

> It wasn't that Jeanette didn't feel for her, but she had to press on: "He does care for you. He loves you. As far as he can, he does. What more do you want?" she added — rather impatiently, for it seemed to her that Marie was being unreasonable in her expectations. She too would have to learn that one lived on earth and not in heaven.

The implicit criticism of women who settle for too little is a feminist critique that runs through much of Jhabvala's fiction. Her female characters rarely find more than a "commensurate happiness." As Sucher notes: "In terms of these novels and stories women have three *un*satisfactory options: they may love homosexual men (who ignore them) or heterosex-ual men (who despise them), or they may live without love altogether."

Marie represents the first case, and Jeanette the second. There is another option for intimacy — other women — but the women of Jhabvala's stories are usually too busy competing with each other for the favor of men to discover that path. Such possibilities are explored in the novels *Heat and Dust* and *In Search of Love and Beauty*. In *Heat and Dust* the narrator develops a bond with both the holy woman Maji and the spirit of Olivia, and Olivia evidently had a parallel relationship with her sister Marcia. Elizabeth Abel points out that "the psychic connection of women in *Heat and Dust* is deep and not readily explicable. In its most absorbing form it binds women who have never met in an exchange of influence that creates new identities."

Beyond this spiritual mentorism, and beyond friendship, there also exists the possibility of lesbian relationships, a situation explored by Jhabvala in the novel *Poet and Dancer* (1993). Judging from the sadomasochistic relationship into which the main characters, Angel and Lara, descend, Jhabvala evidently finds such relationships as likely to dissolve into codependency as heterosexual ones. Implicit in her criticism of failed human relationships is the desire for something more, something pure and romantic.

Friendship and homosexuality are also explored in "Grandmother" (*New Yorker,* 17 November 1980). Whereas the widowed Minnie is unable to achieve a close relationship with her daughter Sandra, she has developed one with Mickey and Ralph, a warm homosexual couple who become Minnie's extended family: "Ralph and Mickey had a lot of plans, and these always included Minnie. She was their family; they really didn't have anyone except her and each other." The closeness of this unlikely trio is undoubtedly a positive portrait of the possibilities of friendship. However, the reader is far from certain of that at the beginning of the story. Jhabvala has never hesitated to use irony in her characterizations, and, when the reader learns that Minnie is providing financial support to the two men, one might expect to be taken down a path where Minnie is being used by those she trusts. Some commentators have, in fact, reached such an interpretation regarding this story. However, the real irony here is that she receives more love and support from Ralph and Mickey than she does from Sandra and her son-in-law Tim, with whom she has made a similar investment.

"A Summer by the Sea" (*New Yorker,* 7 August 1978) is another journey into the complexities of human relationships. A first-person narrative told by a woman married to a homosexual man, this story maintains a delicate balance between the irony of a marriage probably entered into for the economic convenience of the husband and the gentle, genuine love and respect that the couple hold for each other. The story has similarities to both "On Bail" and the novel *Three Continents* (1987), but the relationship between Susie, the narrator, and Boy is unique.

The story also travels a line between allegory and realism, giving it a light, airy tone that dovetails nicely with the Nantucket beach setting and its sunny atmosphere. The allegorical strain can be seen in Jhabvala's naming of Boy — who represents a playful, sensitive strand of homosexuality — as well as in the carefully drawn portrait of Mother, who is almost a caricature of female sexuality gone out of control. Once again Jhabvala displays an uncanny skill at detailing the idiosyncrasies that bring characters to life. Mother is so preoccupied with her own desires that she is unaware of the disgust her manner inspires among Boy and his group: "We saw her — very bright in her upright bathing suit, with her gold-red hair and her jewels glistening in the sun, and her too-white skin that never tanned, and the operation scar showing over the top of her bikini."

Boy's lover, Hamid, is the male version of Mother. Although he does not display her sloppiness, his flamboyant homosexuality is certainly a counterpoint to Mother's urges. Susie sees in his eyes "an eroticism so deep that he had to keep it partly curtailed by lowering his black satin lashes." The swirling emotional intricacies that envelop Mother, Boy, and Hamid contrast sharply with Susie's passivity. At first glance the story seems to be a feminist indictment of women who let others rule and use them, for Susie is used economically by Boy and is dominated emotionally by Mother. At the conclusion Susie addresses this issue head on:

> But I'm getting tired of people deciding for me what I can stand and what I can't. How do they know? Maybe I like things the way they are. No one ever tells me it's wrong for me to love Mother for the way she is and not for how she is supposed to be. Then why not Boy — why can't I care for him the way he is?

Susie is speaking to all who make political judgments, in literary criticism as well as in life. Although Susie's situation may appear bleak, although she may be settling for too little, Jhabvala at least allows the possibility that Susie is at peace with her existence. The principles of freedom and personal autonomy certainly allow such a choice, even if her path to happiness is strange.

A far-less-positive characterization of homosexuals occurs in "Expiation" (*New Yorker*, 11 October 1982). Jhabvala uses a technique similar to that of "Desecration" when she reduces the dramatic impact of the story by immediately announcing the execution of the central character, Bablu. The story is told in first person by his older brother. Bablu's inevitable descent into crime and violence stems from a pampered existence, a life lived without limits. In spite of being given everything, Bablu steals from his brother. When his sister-in-law discovers the theft, Bablu stabs her. This terrible crime is covered up by the family, even by the wife herself, who understands her husband's tremendous love for his younger brother. After a two-year absence Bablu returns with his homosexual lover, Sachu, to live in his brother's home. While there they plan the violent kidnapping of a wealthy boy for ransom. Unfortunately the victim is killed, and both Sachu and Bablu are executed.

"A Very Special Fate" (*New Yorker*, 29 March 1976) is another guru story; however, Dr. Mohanty is the most modern of Jhabvala's holy men. He wears a suit, tie, and gold-rimmed glasses and has "the look of a wise Oriental, but at the same time . . . he gave the impression of a Western intellectual, someone sharp and analytical." His movement, Synthesis Unlimited, sounds like a 1990s New Age philosophy. Dr. Mohanty often attempts to establish harmony among his followers, especially women who are jealous of each other and whose motives are not necessarily pure.

However, Dr. Mohanty is not a "user guru" like so many of the other holy men in Jhabvala's works. There is no noticeable sexual activity among him and his disciples. In fact, he seems genuinely concerned about the needs of his followers. Still, Nancy, who came to India when she was twenty-two, is not the only follower to be "used up" in service to the movement. On a missionary trip the young, vibrant Mary-Ellen falls sick and is left behind in Bhopal. There she wastes away and dies among strangers, who must arrange her cremation. Mary-Ellen, who had replaced Nancy as Dr. Mohanty's closest secretary-follower, is herself replaced by another young, vibrant girl. Although Dr. Mohanty is not an overt user, he realizes that his personality attracts women, and he does not wish to lose their services. Even after he collapses during a European trip and dies, Nancy stays in India and edits his papers as one Synthesis Unlimited center after another closes in the vacuum left by the death of its leader – once a seeker, always a seeker; once a follower, always a follower. In yet another twist of irony the unseen narrator identifies herself as a seeker too.

The most recent of Jhabvala's uncollected stories deals with the theme of fame and success. In "Farid and Farida" (*New Yorker*, 15 October 1984) the title characters were childhood sweethearts from upper-class, but not wealthy, families. After growing up and falling in love they married and moved to London, where they attempted to convert their charm and physical beauty into business success. For fifteen years they tried one unsuccessful business venture after another and eventually ended up living off the charity of an old friend, Sunil. As the couple aged, they began quarreling, and Farid grew fat. Disgusted with the situation, Farida returned to India.

As the story opens, twenty years have passed, and Farid is now in his fifties, a slovenly drunk. Shocked by a report that Farida has become a holy woman, he borrows money from Sunil to return to India, where he finds that she holds court daily under a huge banyan tree, surrounded by admirers and acolytes. She radiates blessings and an aura of enlightenment. Farid moves into the ashram and visits her daily.

Farida has escaped the desperate search for material success that dominated their life together in London, along with the materialistic squabbles among her relatives in India over the belongings of her dead mother. Yet Farida's seemingly idyllic new life is disrupted by Sunil – now an extremely wealthy businessman – who has always been attracted to Farida. Totally out of his element in the ashram, devoid of the material comforts on which he depends, he nevertheless sees in Farida another way to make money. Before long he has publicity people taking pictures and is arranging a British tour for her. Farida becomes absorbed with the plans, just as she used to become absorbed with fruitless money-making projects in London.

Farid, however, does not want any part of Sunil's projects. His daily hikes up the mountain represent the romantic impulse that first drove Farida away from materialism. Farid insists that they go back up to the cave where Farida first found peace rather than tour Britain, but she refuses: "'There's nothing up there,' she said coldly. 'Can't you get that into your head? Absolutely nothing.' She looked at him with a face of stone." Over the protests of both Farida and Sunil, Farid insists on staying, and he watches them leave from his vantage point far above. Although he presents a sad fig-

ure at the end, perhaps his romantic hopes for a return are not misplaced: "He thought he would just wait until she came back for him. Of course this might take a long time – many years, even – but when she came at last he would say, 'Let's go up, Farida,' and after the inevitable argument she would agree."

Never part of any school or movement, Jhabvala has preferred the simple position of storyteller. She has been read largely because of her excellent characterizations, which are largely responsible for the generally favorable critical commentary her work has engendered. She continues to write out of her own rootlessness, that of a Polish-German Jew who grew up in England, raised her children in India, and now lives among other German-Jewish émigrés in Manhattan. Despite her involvement in filmmaking and publishing, businesses that value trendiness and spectacle over quality and depth, Jhabvala has always focused on nuances and manners, contrast and irony. The integrity of her vision has ultimately enabled her work to endure.

Interviews:

"A Novelist of India Reflects 2 Worlds," *New York Times*, 17 July 1973, p. 31;

Ramlal Agarwal, "An Interview with Ruth Prawer Jhabvala," *Quest*, no. 91 (1974): 33–36;

Alex Hamilton, "The Book of Ruth," *Guardian*, 20 November 1975, p. 12;

Bernard D. Nossiter, "Enjoying the Fruits of Detachment," *Washington Post*, 9 December 1975, p. C2;

Yolanta May, "Ruth Prawer Jhabvala in Conversation with Yolanta May," *New Review*, 2, no. 21 (1975): 53–57;

Paul Grimes, "A Passage to U.S. for Writer of India," *New York Times*, 15 May 1976, p. 14;

Anna Rutherford and Kirsten Holst Petersen, "*Heat and Dust*: Ruth Prawer Jhabvala's Experience of India," *World Literature Written in English*, 15 (1976): 373–377;

Lynne Edmunds, "Prize-winning Author, Bridging Two Cultures," *Daily Telegraph*, 14 April 1978, p. 17;

Melinda Camber Porter, "Scriptwriter for Ivory," *Times* (London), 13 July 1978, p. 12;

John Pym, "Where Could I Meet Other Screenwriters?," *Sight and Sound*, 48, no. 1 (1978–1979): 15–18;

Janet Watts, "Three's Company," *Observer Magazine*, 17 June 1979, p. 61;

Glenys Roberts, "A Taste for Adventures, and Love for the Best," *Times* (London), 13 July 1981, p. 9;

Bernard Weinraub, "The Artistry of Ruth Prawer Jhabvala," *New York Times Magazine*, 11 September 1983, pp. 64, 106–114.

Bibliography:

Ralph J. Crane, "Ruth Prawer Jhabvala: A Checklist of Primary and Secondary Sources," *Journal of Commonwealth Literature*, 20, no. 1 (1985): 171–203.

References:

Elizabeth Abel, "(E)Merging Identities: The Dynamics of Female Friendships in Contemporary Fiction by Women," *Signs: Journal of Women in Culture and Society*, 6 (Spring 1981): 413–435;

Nissim Ezekiel, "Cross-Cultural Encounters in Literature," *Indian P.E.N.*, 43, nos. 11 & 12 (1977): 4–8;

Earl W. Foell, "India: Comedy and Nostalgia," *Christian Science Monitor*, 26 January 1956, p. 7;

Yasmine Gooneratne, "Film into Fiction: The Influence upon Ruth Prawer Jhabvala's Fiction of Her Work for the Cinema, 1960–1976," *World Literature Written in English*, 18 (November 1979): 368–386;

Victor Howes, "Jhabvala Charms with Novels and Short Tales," *Christian Science Monitor*, 8 December 1976, p. 32;

Vasant A. Shahane, *Ruth Prawer Jhabvala* (New Delhi: Arnold-Heinemann, 1976);

Eunice de Souza, "The Blinds Drawn and the Air Conditioner On: The Novels of Ruth Prawer Jhabvala," *World Literature in English*, 17, no. 1 (1978): 219–224;

Laurie Sucher, *The Fiction of Ruth Prawer Jhabvala* (New York: St. Martin's Press, 1989);

Mason Wiley and Damien Bona, *Inside Oscar* (New York: Ballantine, 1993);

Haydn Moore Williams, "The Yogi and the Babbitt," *Twentieth Century Literature*, 15, no. 2 (1969): 89–90;

Rene Winegarten, "Ruth Prawer Jhabvala: A Jewish Passage to India," *Midstream* (March 1974): 72–79.

Gwyn Jones

(24 May 1907 –)

Esther P. Riley
East Tennessee State University

See also the Jones entry in *DLB 15: British Novelists, 1930–1959: Part 1.*

BOOKS: *Richard Savage* (London: Gollancz, 1935; New York: Viking, 1935);

Times Like These (London: Gollancz, 1936);

The Nine Days' Wonder (London: Gollancz, 1937);

Garland of Bays (London: Gollancz, 1938; New York: Macmillan, 1938);

The Buttercup Field and Other Stories (Cardiff: Penmark, 1945);

The Green Island (London: Golden Cockerel, 1946);

The Still Waters, and Other Stories (London: Davies, 1948);

A Prospect of Wales (London: Penguin, 1948);

The Flowers Beneath the Scythe (London & New York: Dent, 1952);

Shepherd's Hey and Other Stories (London: Staples, 1953);

Welsh Legends and Folk-Tales (London: Oxford University Press, 1955);

The First Forty Years: Some Notes on Anglo-Welsh Literature (Cardiff: University of Wales Press, 1957);

The Walk Home (London: Dent, 1962; New York: Norton, 1963);

The Norse Atlantic Saga (London & New York: Oxford University Press, 1964);

A History of the Vikings (London: Oxford University Press, 1968);

Kings, Beasts and Heroes (London & New York: Oxford University Press, 1972);

Selected Short Stories (London & New York: Oxford University Press, 1974);

Being and Belonging: Some Notes on Language, Literature, and the Welsh (Cardiff: University of Wales Press, 1977);

Profiles: A Visitor's Guide to Writing in Twentieth-Century Wales, by Jones and John Rowlands (Llandysul, Dyfed, Wales: Gomer, 1980);

Gwyn Jones (photograph by Julian Sheppard)

Y Nofela Chymdeithas – The Novel and Society (Aberystwyth: University College of Wales Press, 1981);

Three Poetical Prayer-Makers of the Island of Britain (London: Oxford University Press, 1981);

137

Background to Dylan Thomas, and Other Explorations (Oxford & New York: Oxford University Press, 1992).

OTHER: *Welsh Short Stories,* edited by Jones (Harmondsworth, U.K.: Penguin, 1940);

Welsh Short Stories, edited by Jones (London: Oxford University Press, 1956);

Scandinavian Legends and Folk-Tales: A Re-telling (London: Oxford University Press, 1956);

The Metamorphoses of Publius Ovidius Naso, edited by Jones (London: Golden Cockerel, 1958);

The Poems and Sonnets of William Shakespeare, edited by Jones (London: Golden Cockerel, 1960);

Twenty-five Welsh Short Stories, selected by Jones and Islwyn Ffowc Elis (London: Oxford University Press, 1971);

Fountains of Praise: University College, Cardiff 1883–1983, edited by Jones and Michael Quinn (Cardiff: University College, Cardiff Press, 1983).

TRANSLATIONS: *Four Icelandic Sagas* (New York: Princeton University Press for the American-Scandinavian Foundation, 1935; London: Oxford University Press, 1935);

The Vatndalers' Saga (New York: Princeton University Press for the American-Scandinavian Foundation, 1944);

The Golden Cockerel Mabinogion: A New Translation from the White Book of Rhydderch and the Red Book of Hergest, translated by Jones and Thomas Jones (London: Golden Cockerel, 1948);

Sir Gawain and the Green Knight (London: Golden Cockerel, 1952);

Egil's Saga (New York: Syracuse University Press for the American-Scandinavian Foundation, 1960);

Eirik the Red and Other Icelandic Sagas, edited and translated by Jones (London & New York: Oxford University Press, 1961).

During his long literary career Gwyn Jones has experimented with various genres at various times, first writing four novels, then producing four volumes of short stories, returning to the novel, and finally becoming a translator and editor of Norse and Welsh short stories and legends. However, his poetic prose, landscape descriptions, portrayals of human psychology, and intermingling of history with fiction emerge most vividly in the condensed form of the short story. "Every writer is by definition a born thief," writes Jones in the introduction to *Selected Short Stories* (1974); the fiction writer re-

shapes facts in order to move his audience with his "compulsive imaginings" and "noble feignings." Jones also stresses the impact of an author's experiences on his work, saying that a writer has two autobiographies – one fictional and one factual – and that everything he writes is part of those.

Much of the influence of people and events in Jones's life is evident in his work. He was born on 24 May 1907 at Blackwood, Monmouthshire, on the English/Welsh border. His paternal grandfather had come there from Kent to find work as a road man; his maternal grandfather had journeyed from Somerset to become a collier. Both married Welsh women, and although both couples endured hardships, they found the inner resources to enjoy life. Cecil Price quotes Jones's description of his grandfather Nethercott as "a deeply though not gloomily religious man of unquestioning piety and thankfulness to God for all he had sent him." His grandmother Nethercott was a storyteller who delighted in tales of the horrible. The budding writer imbibed these interests, which later emerged in his work.

Jones's father, George Henry Jones, also a collier, was well read and interested in religion, politics, and human nature. Although Jones deals with politics more in his novels than in his short stories, the religious ideas and interest in human nature in his short pieces reflect his father's influence. Price quotes Jones on his father: "He believed implicitly in the perfectibility of man, and was convinced that once want and penury were out of the way, all men would be wise, generous, and unselfish." From his mother, Lily Florence Nethercott Jones, Jones inherited an interest in painting and artistic expression. *The Green Island* (1946) indicates Jones's eye for color, mass, and perspective: "It was a country of low hills and wooded cwms, and from where he stood he could mark the writhing valleys of two rivers. In slow gradation the height of land changed from green to cyclamen and rose, and so faded into the purple masses of the watershed."

Early childhood experiences formed some of Jones's lifelong beliefs. In the introduction to *Selected Short Stories* he recalls two childhood memories, one of being lost on a mountain when he was two and another of being caught in the blast effect of a pit explosion when he was six. The former experience fortified his belief that "men and women are congenitally loseable and self-destructive, so that from time to time they lodge themselves in narrowing tunnels of doubt, fear, and aloneness, from which in life they must be rescued though in fiction they may press on to the dead end." The latter memory "in storytelling gave me fixations on darkness underground as an ultimate horror, and fire anywhere as our most fearsome destroyer. Also, both memories are rooted in my natal soil, and prefigure those pastoral-industrial or pastoral-paradisal settings in which my stories have always chosen to locate themselves." But removal from that environment was necessary before Jones could develop into a writer. His parents envisioned a higher calling than coal mining for their son, and with the help of scholarships he attended the County School, Tredegar, and University College, Cardiff.

At University College Jones took a first in the Honours School of English Language and Literature as well as two-year certificates in French and history. He proceeded to study Old Norse and German and in 1929 was awarded a master's degree with distinction; his thesis is titled "Legal Procedure and the Conduct of the Feud in the Icelandic Sagas." He married Alice Rees from Cardiff (who remained his wife until her death in 1979), and for the next six years he taught English at Wigan Grammar School and then at Manchester Central High School, both in northern England. While he taught he embarked on his writing career.

In 1935 Jones's translation *Four Icelandic Sagas* was published in the United States and Great Britain, and Gollancz published a historical novel, *Richard Savage,* which established him as a writer of fictional biography. He also wrote *Times Like These* (1936), a topical novel about the effects of economic depression on ordinary Welsh families. In addition he was appointed lecturer in English language and literature at University College, Cardiff. His return to Wales proved pivotal to his writing career, for it aligned him with Anglo-Welsh writers, a group of creative artists who chose to write in English.

Jones continued to write novels, including *The Nine Days' Wonder* (1937) and *Garland of Bays* (1938). Having written four successful novels in as many years, Jones did not produce another until 1952. A possible cause may be found in the fact that, although approximately 80 percent of the Welsh population speaks only English, writing by Welshmen in English did not begin until the accession of the Tudors, according to Jones in *Profiles: A Visitor's Guide to Writing in Twentieth-Century Wales* (1980). Lacking the centuries-long tradition of the Welsh writers, the Anglo-Welsh writers (many of whom reject that term) also lacked the journals and literary organizations that nurture and develop both fledgling and mature writers; consequently, they had to turn to London in order to find publishers for their works.

It was difficult for Jones to write in an atmosphere of indifference at best and hostility at worst. In an attempt to alleviate the lack of support for Welsh authors Jones joined forces with Creighton Griffiths to found the monthly *Welsh Review* in February 1939. This literary magazine and Keidrych Rhys's *Wales,* established in 1937, published short stories, poems, and articles by every Anglo-Welsh writer of any stature whose work had appeared by 1939. The wartime government's restrictions on paper distribution, however, caused Jones's magazine to cease publication in November 1939.

University College, no doubt impressed by Jones's success as a writer and editor as well as his skill as a lecturer, promoted him to a senior lectureship in 1939. In 1940 he became the chair of English language and literature at the University College of Wales, Aberystwyth, where he remained for twenty-four years. In 1944 Jones, continuing his interest in Viking history, produced another translation, *The Vatndalers' Saga,* but he was also interested in ancient Welsh history. His academic inclination toward languages and history as well as his skill in narrative writing helped him to work on the translation *Mabinogion* (1948), but he felt inadequate to cope with the arcane lore of ancient manuscripts or with medieval Welsh, so he enlisted the support of Thomas Jones, a Celtic scholar. The two men carefully rendered the narrative from Welsh into English, producing a translation that is truer to the original manuscript than any of its predecessors.

In March 1944 Jones revived the *Welsh Review,* which continued until 1948 with Jones as editor, but increasing costs and the onset of a recession eventually caused it to cease publication once more. Penmark Press, however, which Jones had established to print the magazine and to provide an outlet for Anglo-Welsh writers, continued until 1960 with him as director.

In *Profiles* Jones describes a "Second Flowering" of Anglo-Welsh writers who emerged in the 1950s and 1960s; these writers' works reveal a stronger commitment to their country and its problems than those of the more self-absorbed writers of the earlier decades of the century. In the short stories that he began publishing in the 1940s Jones writes of his countrymen struggling to maintain their old ways in the face of industrial expansion, the invasion of tourists, and the problems engendered by war and world events.

In *Selected Short Stories* Jones notes that "literature exists in context, not a vacuum, and that context tends to be the scene of our nurture." The regional writer, he argues, formed by the place from which he comes, "will understand its people, as no outsider will understand them, and be driven to act out that understanding in words: their character, personality and traditions, patterns of behaviour and impulses to action; what they believe in, their hopes and fears, bonds and severances, their relationships to each other, to the landscape around them, and the creatures they share it with."

The Buttercup Field and Other Stories (1945), his first volume of short fiction, illustrates that contention. (Several of the stories had been published in magazines and anthologies before World War II; seven of the thirteen are also collected in *Selected Short Stories*.) It is difficult to determine when the stories were written, and, although the collected volumes indicate that some stories were published in magazines, they do not identify the stories or the times. Even in these earliest pieces Jones's characteristic themes appear: humans lost in fear or aloneness, an ironic view of human brutality, the destructive effects of jealousy and revenge, sympathy for animals and for feeble and wronged humans, and biblical themes (always from the Old Testament). The stories also reveal in concentrated form Jones's ability, perhaps inherited from his mother, to characterize with a few deft strokes, to create pictorial views of the landscape, and to develop his narrative line in spare, uncluttered plots.

Nearly all these stories concern Welsh people and are set in the mining and industrial area of Monmouthshire where Jones grew up – what he calls the "pastoral-industrial" setting of his youth. Eleven of the thirteen stories are told in third person. Although the narrator possesses the voice of a sophisticated, well-read person – one especially familiar with the Bible – he is nevertheless able to depict the uneducated, the exploited, the oppressed, the fearful, and even the feebleminded with compassion and tenderness. Even though the stories often feature passionate people in dramatic circumstances, the narrator finds humor in character, dialogue, and situation. These early stories also illustrate Jones's references to his elemental fears: fire as a deadly destroyer and burial alive as the scene of a confrontation with the inner self.

The opening story, "The Pit," depicts a triangular relationship: a Welshman, his wife, and an Englishman who has designs on her. In addition to the sexual conflict, a nationalistic conflict between Welshman and foreigner develops. Driven by a need to prove his self-worth, the bored traveler becomes obsessed with two conquests: his host's wife and an abandoned coal pit known by the locals to be a dangerous place. The narrator never makes it clear whether the Englishman, Ackerman, is trapped in the abandoned mine shaft by the Welshman, Bendle, or by a natural occurrence. Nevertheless the underground experience becomes a crucible in which all of Ackerman's unacknowledged fears and inadequacies rise to the surface. The interloper is reduced to a state commensurate with his moral deficiencies: Ackerman emerges from the pit "something half-human flopping along the ground." The husband, in contrast, is elevated from his earlier brutish state to prove himself capable of forgiveness: Bendle gives a strange look to his wife, whose face is pinched and "rat-like," but he tenderly picks up Ackerman and carries him home.

The title story recalls Jones's other troubling memory – that fire is "our most fearsome destroyer." Although the title "The Buttercup Field" evokes a pastoral scene, the narrative is set in blazing heat, which symbolizes the fiery passions leading to the conflagration that consumes a woman and her husband of one day. Jones creates a frame story of an ordinary traveler who encounters an almost mythic figure, a black-clad old man swinging a sickle. The Father Time figure portentously intones that he is "looking for yesterday." He recites to the traveler the tale of a blacksmith's son with a golden voice who wins the heart of lovely Ann Morgan by "singing quietly the songs of the countryside." Conflict develops when a third figure, a poet from another town, is introduced; Eos y Fron's singing talent cannot compete with John Pritchard's "language of heaven," and the bard steals Ann Morgan from him. In revenge Eos y Fron bars the windows of their house and sets it afire with the bride and groom inside. Having told his horrifying story, the old man reveals that he is Eos y Fron, condemned to scythe the buttercups where the house once stood in a futile effort to find the gold ring he had given Ann.

"A Man After God's Own Heart" continues to explore the themes of jealousy and revenge. This is another story within a story; the listener is, as in the previous story, a traveler who meets a storyteller, but in this story he is a first-person narrator who judges the teller and his experience. The narrator describes Reedy as a "genteel-gone-shabby sort of fellow," a man from Cardiff who has fled the scene of his transgression. Like David in the Bible, Reedy fell in love with another man's wife. Unfortunately his "more than wholesome fear of God and the Devil" caused him a crisis of conscience; he overcame it to the extent that he was able to declare his passion to the wife, but "God came between him and Polly," and he was unable to touch her. He burned with desire until fate gave him an opportunity to send the husband to his death. The frame narrator comments on the ironic ending of Reedy's story: he marries his Polly as soon as he decently can, but God prevents the consummation of the union.

The parallel between Reedy and David is only partial: "both sent Uriah to his death in the forefront of the battle, that they might enjoy the man's wife," but even after David begot Solomon on Bathsheba he was "yet a man after God's own heart." Reedy thinks that God may also look kindly on him, for, unlike David, he has gained nothing from his sin.

"All We Like Sheep," also drawing on a biblical theme, takes its title from Isaiah's lament. The third-person narrator describes the thoughts of Cadno, a seventy-year-old sheepherder attending the funeral of his former friend Gwion. The stream-of-consciousness technique reveals a hard man who took for himself the justice the law denied him when he discovered his friend had been stealing his sheep. He has had his friends interrupt a performance of George Frideric Handel's *Messiah,* conducted by Gwion, by bleating loudly at the "All We, Like Sheep" section. Cadno's revenge was bittersweet, however. Although it had the effect of driving the humiliated Gwion out of the valley, it also alienated Cadno's neighbors, who considered his act blasphemous. He loses his flourishing farm, his neighbors shun him, and his customers dwindle. Cadno nevertheless refuses to repent; he sees God as a "grim Ironist" who laughs at human foibles, not as a God of forgiveness and pity.

His final act affirms his idea of justice. Sneering at the forgiving words of the other funeralgoers, Cadno signals his sheepdog, who races off to drive a bleating sheep into the open grave to beat a tattoo on the coffin. In the shocked silence Cadno has the last word: he trumpets "All We, Like Sheep" over the dead Gwion and trudges with his dog back to his lonely farm.

"Kittens" focuses on Morri, a naive, inexperienced young collier who falls under the spell of a married woman older and far more experienced than he. In her desperation to escape the mining valley Morri loves, Glenys has preyed on gullible men to gather enough money to flee her out-of-work husband. After Morri's brother describes Glenys as "the Scarlet Woman on the White Horse, and the Sixth Plague that plagued Egypt . . . the Fire that Burns" and explains what these metaphors mean, Morri finally awakens to the knowledge that he has been manipulated.

The narrator gradually develops the subtle parallel between the small, weak Glenys and the kitten that Morri pets: both are tiny and fragile, but both are capable of inflicting wounds. The mangled body of the kitten at the end of the story is evidence of the punishment this physical man inflicts on those who hurt him. The reader realizes that Morri has gone to catch Glenys before she boards the train out of town and that he will crush her as unthinkingly as he did the kitten that scratched him in play.

"Shacki Thomas" provides relief from the first five stories of revenge and destruction by painting the tender portrait of a fifty-two-year-old unemployed miner who comes to terms for the first time in his life with the idea of human mortality. Jones uses the stream-of-consciousness technique to record Shacki's thoughts as he walks to the hospital to visit his sick wife. His principal emotions are loneliness and fear. The conversations he has along the way do little to dispel "the worm fear" that is "at Shacki's heart like a maggot," for all his friends can talk of is cancer and death. Even the church offers no comfort; the angel poised on the cenotaph in whose shadow they gather spreads her wings over the group, but her eyes are fixed on the door of the pub opposite.

The narrator traces Shacki's fluctuating emotions: love when he buys a gift for his wife, despair when he receives no reassurances from his friends, and hope when he thinks of something amusing to lift his wife's spirits. The simple laborer is intimidated by the starchy professionalism of the hospital matron, but, when she tells him that his wife will be home soon, the emotion that he has been suppressing all day breaks through. The "murderous hate of all living things" and the sense of injustice that has grown out of his fear dissolves, and Shacki is filled with love.

The punning title of "Ora Pro Boscis" prepares the reader for the sly humor with which Jones plots the deflation of the self-important Sir Rhodri Plas Mawr's ego. An absentee landowner and magistrate who has not "sat for a dozen times in as many years, just now and then when for the look of the thing he paid a visit to Plas Mawr," Sir Rhodri is rude and supercilious to the ordinary people who live near his country estate. Sir Rhodri is so self-absorbed that he views his disproportionately large nose as a "virile organ." He fails to understand why his gamekeeper and the sergeant urge him not to attend the trial of a poacher caught on his land.

The trial is a travesty: the undercurrent of levity suggests that "this was what they'd been waiting for, the dole-drawers, the mouchers, the rabbit-snatchers — to see old Privilege up on the Plas with a stoat on the end of his nozzle." The defendant sports a proboscis just as magnificent as Sir Rhodri's noble organ. Sir Rhodri patronizingly assumes that his father must have strayed over the fence to produce this insignificant fellow, but when he asks Tomos whether his mother had worked at the Plas, Tomos's offhand answer completes the pompous man's humiliation: "No, not my mam. But my dad was always about the house. That would be before you were born, I fancy. Biggest nose in Wales, my old dad."

"The Dreamers" also has a light tone. The story pokes gentle fun at a reclusive scholar, forty-five-year-old Rhisiart Rhisiarts, whose dream of a wedding awakens him to the fact that life has passed him by while he was buried in dreams of the past. His comic quest for a wife — he accosts a prostitute; he is driven off by women who think him demented — suggests his inadequacy for the task. Discouraged, he returns home only to learn that he may have one more opportunity; his neighbor has died, leaving behind a plump, wealthy widow. She is a dreamer too: a dream has predicted her husband's death, and another has suggested she will remarry soon. Her second dream comes true; she has received a proposal from another neighbor that very day. Rhisiarts's dream fails, the narrator suggests, because, lacking any practical knowledge, he has allowed his books to dictate his behavior.

Dreams also come true in "A Night at Galon-Uchaf," which evokes the mood of Welsh legends and folktales. The combination of both a peculiar atmospheric formation, "the red wind of Shrewsbury," and a potent liquor brewed by Gurnos, a bard with second sight, tilts visitors to the farm into a dimension where they are free to act on their desires. The Widow Simon is the best example of repression: she had been so intimidated by her husband that when he died, leaving her a young, buxom widow, on his orders she slept with a wooden effigy of him rather than seek a warm, human bedfellow. Each of the other guests is similarly prevented from achieving happiness in marriage. Under the spell of the liquor and the red wind, they lose their inhibitions and "awaken well-pleased with themselves." The comic ending has Mordecai turn the red wind blue with the smoke from the burning effigy of Simon.

In another comic story, "Gwydion Mathrafel," the protagonist is also a scholarly dreamer with a quest: he seeks King Arthur's grave. Traditional enmity between the Welsh and the English provides the humor here: Gwydion encounters Martin Do-

lorous (based on the Dolorous Stroke in Arthurian legend — the sword stroke dealt by Balyn to King Pellam that presaged the fall of Arthur's kingdom), and the two engage in a bragging/storytelling contest that inevitably ends in blows. Gwydion perceives himself as Arthur's knight, fighting for the honor of his king. Before the day is over he has a vision of Arthur leading his troops out of the moat of the ruins of Castell Mor, and he imagines that he is knighted by the long-dead king. In contrast to "The Dreamers" this story suggests that dreams are more comforting than real life, which in Rhisiarts's case means living with his "bent-nosed, beetle-backed wife who nagged him" and his sister, "an untrodden, drab-feathered hen for ever cackling of the black hawk Death."

The first-person narrator of "The Passionate People" weaves an intriguing story of a two-hundred-year-old mystery. Documenting the history of his ancestress with quotations from court documents and news reports, he illustrates the thesis of the title by telling of two murders motivated by passion and revenge. A gold earring is used as evidence that a murderer cheated the gallows once, only to die by drowning. The irony of the ending underlines the point that the Welsh are a passionate people, for two hundred years later the descendants of the players in this tragedy are still feuding.

"Their Bonds Are Loosed from Above" is the only story in the collection to allude to wartime conditions; it is set in a Nazi bombing raid. The destructive war act upsets the natural order of things, and natural law is suspended for Mrs. Manod. The epigraph — recounting the death of Sisera, the Caananite general, at the hands of Jael to fulfill the prophecy that Israel should be delivered by the hands of a woman — explains why Mrs. Manod is terrified when she learns that the bombs have disinterred bodies in the cemetery. The narrator, however, suggests that she had driven a nail into her husband's head to rid herself of a drunken and abusive man, not because of nationalistic fervor. A courageous woman, Mrs. Manod struggles to outwit her husband's risen corpse, but the Nazi bombs defeat her. Her neighbor's decision not to rebury Mr. Manod until Mrs. Manod's body is ready for burial is grimly ironic; having committed murder to escape him in life, she is doomed to sleep with him through eternity.

"Take Us the Foxes, the Little Foxes" refers to the lines in Song of Solomon that speak of catching the foxes that damage the vineyards, for the vines are in bloom. The conflict is between Davies, the gamekeeper who has killed a vixen with three off-

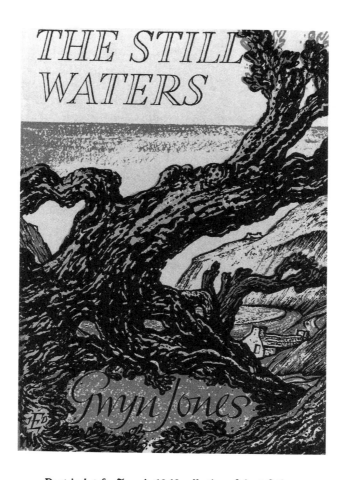

*Dust jacket for Jones's 1948 collection of short fiction,
unsentimental examinations of country people in Wales*

spring, and Dewi, the town half-wit who is without family and friends. Dewi tames one of the pups to become his only companion, inflaming his neighbors, who view the fox as predator and thief; they force him to choose between giving up his pet or killing it. Ironically only Davies, whose job is at stake, knows the secret of Dewi's midnight visits to the hills. His humanitarianism sets in sharp relief the insensitivity of a neighbor who quotes the old proverb "When there's no sense, there's no feeling."

Price quotes Jones that the move to Aberystwyth in 1940 inspired "a dozen or so short stories, comic, tragic, melodramatic, but always lyrical." His next collection, *The Still Waters and Other Stories* (1948), contains stories that are located in what Jones calls the "pastoral-paradisal setting" of his adulthood. Country people are not sentimentalized in these stories, however, nor is nature always shown as benign. Humans often prove themselves to rank lower than animals in Jones's plots; their cruelty and vindictiveness often rebound upon

them. *The Still Waters* contains ten stories, five of which had been previously published, four in magazines and one, "The Green Island," which had been printed in a limited edition in 1946. Five of these stories are included in *Selected Short Stories*.

The title story uses the same technique as "The Passionate People" to comment on Welsh history. Both narrators recite personal experiences and public records to substantiate their judgments. In "The Still Waters" the first-person narrator contends that in Llanvihangel, at least, the women rule the men. It is only partly prudence that causes men there to yield to women, he argues. The men appear to lack some essential power: "Our men are nothing, or at best but male spiders who exist to breed and be devoured." His examples demonstrate how women entrap men in their webs and then discard them when their usefulness has ended.

The first example comes from the narrator's youth – a domineering mother makes her son ready prey for a wife who will rule him with an iron hand.

The narrator muses that only the education that is denied to most rural youths could have saved Daffyd Owen from his fate. The second example, a two-hundred-year-old story, has the same plot as the first: a married woman deliberately sacrifices her amiable but ineffectual husband in order to provide for herself and her children.

The narrator's ironic tone reveals how much his education has distanced him from the matriarchal tyranny he describes. At the beginning of the story he revises the line from Ecclesiastes "Now let us praise famous men, and our fathers that begat us" by appending "and the womenfolk that bare us." He closes the story with another quotation from the same book, spoken tongue-in-cheek: "She made Daffyd happy for a month. We might perhaps count that as two, for to end, as he began, with Ecclesiastus: 'Blessed is the man that hath a virtuous wife, for the number of his days shall be double.'"

The significance of the title "Bad Blood" is evident on three levels, the most obvious being the overt application of the expression to a sheep-killing bitch and her litter. More subtly it explains why a fat farmer has allowed thistles to take over his fields, his fences to sag, and his dog not only to run loose but to breed. Finally his son gives evidence by the brutish pleasure he takes in guns and killing that he has inherited bad blood. The naturalistic theme points out the damage that results from inattention to breeding and training. The man from Glan-y-Gors can rectify the mistake of letting the dog breed, but human laws prevent him from warding off the harm the man and the boy may cause.

"Shining Morn" also emphasizes how human sensitivity can be dulled by education and training. A young boy, allowed out on his own with his new puppy, is horrified to find a rabbit caught in a trap. He agonizes over whether to forget what he has seen, to free the rabbit, or to kill it. Recalling and misinterpreting his father's words, "We must be cruel to be kind," he decides to ignore the dilemma, but his conscience forces him to return to the trap, where only a gnawed-off rabbit's foot remains. Joy over finding a lucky charm immediately erases any recollection of how he sympathized with the suffering animal; he bounds off chanting, "Poor old Bun — ain't that fun."

"Four in a Valley" draws a conscious parallel between man and nature at the same time it emphasizes the distance between the male and female points of view. Tom, a sensuous naturalist, identifies with a male hawk circling above him and his lover. He cites the hawk's freedom from human so-cial convention as an excuse for his not being willing to commit to a relationship with a woman. Dil — who, like most women, finds her behavior frequently dictated by social convention — ironically concedes that he is hawklike: he preys on women. When a farmer shoots the mate of the hawk, the male proves himself superior to Tom, who seeks only his own physical gratification, for the gallant bird makes himself a target when he remains by the ruined body of his mate. The narrator sympathetically presents Dil's misery over her loss; nevertheless, she is practical enough to recognize that she is well out of an affair with the self-absorbed man.

"The Prisoners," though set against the background of a prisoner-of-war camp, is not concerned with military imprisonment so much as it is with the entrapment of humans within irrational entanglements with each other. There are varying degrees of confinement within the story: the lobsters trapped by the islanders, who break their claws and store them in wooden cages until market time (the German prisoners ironically call these "prisoner of war cages," but they do not let their captors hear the term); the thousands of men in the prison camp "brooding in a confined space"; and the German prisoners who are released from the camp to work on the Welsh farms. The characters include Si Powell, trapped in a body dying from the damage inflicted by mustard gas; Johnny Powell, caught in a hopeless love for the woman who loves his brother; Gwen, in love with Si, who wants to break off so he can die without impediments; and Mandy, aware of the futility of her love for Johnny and driven by compassion and perhaps self-destructiveness to stay with Si. A German prisoner, able to enjoy the small pleasures of life he enjoys as a captive, is sorry to see so much misery over love: "One learned wisdom, there were chains a-plenty without those one was tempted to forge for oneself."

"Down in the Forest Something Stirred," reminiscent of a folktale, alters the tone and pace of the volume by entering the realm of fantasy to poke fun at institutional religion. The tongue-in-cheek tale of a contest between two hermits for the soul of John Lot Padog, a godless poacher, exposes the hypocrisies of the two "holy men" and suggests that honesty represents a certain natural virtue. The opening incident shows the reprobate at a moment of truth. The accidental discharge of his shotgun reveals to him that he is standing on the edge of the Pit (not a literal hole in the ground, but a figurative version just as frightening), and he determines to change his ways. Although he bargains with the two hermits in order to do the lightest penance he can, the hermits in their turn bargain with him to gain his allegiance. When he admits that liquor is too much to give up for the salvation of his soul, his mentor advises him to sacrifice water (something he never drinks). The reformed sinner is more godly than either of the self-proclaimed men of God, however, for he is truly changed, while both hermits succumb to the temptation of lust in a comic reenactment of the Garden of Eden story. Witnessing their apostasy, John Lot Padog renounces his penance and drinks water, the symbol of baptism and cleansing he had abjured at the behest of his spiritual adviser. "Damnation be damned!" he shouts.

Miss Mabli in "Guto Fewel" is another person who has stood on the edge of the Pit. Since that time she has spent her life in good works at the expense of her own happiness. Now at Guto Fewel's deathbed she seeks a sign that she has done him no harm. Although she receives no explicit answer, a flashback reveals that forty-seven years ago – when she was already a woman and Fewel was only a child – she, by inaction, sanctioned an event that ultimately sent him on the path of self-destruction.

In "Deep in the Forest Something Stirred" Jones presents a comic contrast between a roomful of suffering sinners, a self-righteous old man who panders to their taste for gossip, and an ineffectual minister, suggesting that the truly damned are those who lack the honesty to acknowledge their errors and repent them. "Gorowny's House of Gold," like "Down in the Forest Something Stirred," also has the flavor of a folktale. Gorowny is one of a series of bookish men Jones shows to be dissatisfied with the scholarly life. Gorowny has spent forty years of his life as a schoolmaster; in his retirement he becomes aware that he is unhappy because he is lonely. Taking all his money, he sets out on a quest for "some humble creature" to share his modest home. In four separate encounters with brutish humans tormenting a thrush, a dog, a cow, and a pregnant orphan girl, Gorowny's inherent kindness is frustrated because, in each case, the tormentor insists on his right to inflict pain on another being. Gorowny dissipates his meager savings in an effort to free the helpless creatures. Returning home, he is not disappointed, however. He is better off than Elijah, who had only ravens to feed him. His house, which had looked empty and dreary when he left, now appears in a golden glow as he brings his companions home. The tale drives home the point that human happiness derives from love, not power.

The closing story of the volume, "The Green Island," is thematically similar to "The Pit." The paired couples in "The Pit" are opposites. Daffyd Absalom is a craftsman, the last of his breed, and he would like to pass on his skills; his wife, the eternal Eve, wants no children. Harry Merrill, an Englishman, knows his marriage is faltering because his love for his wife has turned into pity. A cynical man, he considers most of the Welsh people he meets to be fools. Mrs. Merrill is desperate for a child; despite several miscarriages and long illnesses she threatens to leave her husband unless he gives her a child.

Harry Merrill comes to view the Green Island as symbolic of his innocent past. According to the legend of the island's origin King Bleddri had flung a clod of land after another king who was absconding with Bleddri's wife. Seeing the story of the Green Island's origin as evidence of the gullibility of cuckolds, Harry lures the not unwilling Mrs. Absalom off for a trip to the island. Unlike "The Pit," this story leaves no doubt as to why the would-be lovers become stranded: Harry's carelessness and ineptitude. Daffyd Absalom deliberately leaves them on the island with neither food nor water. The lack of necessities causes the erotic playground to become a kind of hell where the man and woman torment each other.

The experience strips Harry of his self-confidence and pride. When they are finally rescued, he can think only of food and comfort, and he feels "safety, as an animal which breaks from the trap and turns to its lair." Daffyd can afford to relent a little; his wife returns to their cottage, where she undoubtedly expects to do a little penance. Daffyd allows Mrs. Merrill to persuade him to take her husband to a doctor.

One of the themes of the story concerns self-knowledge. In a visit to the Wise Man, a local healer who seems "half-prophet, half-charlatan," Harry is struck by the man's ability to perceive unexpressed emotions. In a discussion about wisdom the Wise Man reminds him that the Bible says that wisdom is not manifest to many. Although Harry has a tendency to recognize lack of wisdom in others long before he acknowledges it in himself, it is clear at the end that his rescuers consider him a fool. The experience on the island gives Harry insight into his weaknesses; at the end his wife has hope that their marriage might be mended.

Five of the seven stories in *Shepherd's Hey and Other Stories* appeared in magazines before the collection was published in 1953. The title piece is one of Jones's longer stories. The protagonist, Craddock, is a shepherd, but, unlike the rural folk portrayed in Jones's other stories, he has seen the world and cho-

Dust jacket for Jones's 1974 collection of short fiction, which includes stories from his three previous collections

sen to return to the land. Born to mining people, he fled to the sea after his father died of black lung, but he returned five years later because "a furrow in water can't last. Nothing of your own in the whole wide waste of it. And we all want something of our own." On his farm Craddock feels "god and father among [his animals]." He struggles against weeds, snow, cold, and drought to create a flourishing farm.

His "pastoral-paradisal" world is invaded, however, by a temptress aptly named Salome, and she is followed by her husband, Harry, an opportunist who does not necessarily want his wife back. Despite Craddock's knowledge of the world he is not equipped to deal with the hardened, unscrupulous intruders. His struggles against nature have succeeded because he is single-minded and a hard worker, but these virtues are useless in a conflict with manipulative, amoral people. When Craddock refuses to submit to the weaselly Harry's blackmail, Harry uses fire to punish him. Only the necessity of

saving his sheep prevents Craddock from throwing Harry into the flames.

After the fire is under control, Craddock is momentarily depressed by the knowledge of evil — not only Harry's but his own transgression with Salome, the cause of Harry's attack. Although the pride of his flock has been destroyed by the fire, another ram has been born during the night. He will rebuild: "He was the farm's stay, and he had only one pair of hands, and there was blessedly much to do before mid-morning."

"The Brute Creation" is a starkly naturalistic story of a shepherd, a loner whose rudeness and harshness have alienated most of the people who know him. His determination to ignore the advice of other contestants not to run his year-old bitch as a novice in field trials is indicative of his obstinacy and self-destructive tendencies. As predicted, the immature dog grows confused and breaks.

Frustrated and unable to accept that he is the cause of his disappointment, the owner refuses to feed or pet his dog. He seeks comfort in alcohol and with a prostitute, but his cruelty to the dog offends the woman, who ejects him from her domicile. Casting about to blame his failure on someone else, the drunken man lures the dog closer so he can drown her, and she approaches because she is "powerless against the god she recognized in him, helpless against her craving for kindness after so horrible a day." Despite the efforts of kindhearted people to intervene on behalf of the dog during the day, she has hovered near the instrument of her death. In an ironic twist, however, she involuntarily becomes the instrument of his death.

In "Old Age" Jones uses the stream-of-consciousness technique to explain the purpose of an elderly man's visit to a house, now shabby with age, in which a blind and deaf woman lies dying. A flashback depicts his only other visit to the house, when he was a boy. His father had sent him down the mountain, telling him not to return without the pony that he had lost control of the day before. The uneducated boy, knowing just enough to be self-conscious about his clothing and speech, was too intimidated to conduct an effective search until, drawn by the life force of purebred horses in a field, he trespassed on a large estate. The owner of the property – a crude, drunken man who was alternatingly kind and violent – recognized the boy as a reincarnation of Pan, the god of flocks and herds. Learning that the boy was afraid to return home without a horse, he promised him one if he would go upstairs and get in bed with the mistress.

A shift to the woman's point of view clears up some of the ambiguity of the plot. She thought of herself as "mistress of the big house but not of herself." She would never marry this man, whom age and alcohol had rendered incapable of all but desire. Calling the older man's bluff, she invited the young man into her bed and taunted the master with his naked body. A gambler, he realized he had lost: "So it's Pan first and the rest of the field nowhere!"

When the narrative returns to the present, it is clear that they have all lost. The older man is not visible; he is probably dead. The woman is close to death, and the once-young Pan hastens to leave; he must take care of his aged body. Dreams of the past are far preferable to the ugly reality of the present.

"Copy" is an epistolary joke based on the dual meaning of the word. *Copy* refers to a manuscript to be reproduced in printing; it also means a duplicate or an imitation. One of the correspondents in this exchange is an author who feeds his ego by encouraging an aspiring female author to write to him

while at the same time he enjoys the snobbery of amusing his friend with comments about his fan's small-town notions and naiveté. On the off chance that it might be profitable he arranges a meeting with the woman, but he derisively writes to his friend that he has stood her up after seeing her. Inadvertently revealing how exploitative he is, he comments that at least he may get a story out of the episode. The final letter, from his publisher, shows that his fan has not been as naive as he thinks. She has submitted a manuscript with the same plot as his, and the publisher concludes that the earlier manuscript must be the original.

"All on a Summer's Day" is the innocuous title of a tale of bitter hatred and revenge that comes to its conclusion as inevitably and inexorably as a Greek tragedy. Murder is motivated by a mother's jealousy, a peasant's fear of losing her lands, and xenophobia. When Esther's son, Luke, joins the English army, marries a Cockney girl, Addie, and sends her to the farm so she can have their baby away from the bombs falling on London, the mother puts up with the daughter-in-law she judges to be cheap and shallow. Yet Wyndham, her grandson, wins her heart completely.

Addie, as her name suggests, is different from the stoic rural family with biblical names – Esther, Job, and Luke. Addie is bored and restless in the country and wants to go dancing instead of caring for a child. She unwittingly aids Esther in her plot to win the child away from his mother. Addie is sharp and impatient with Wyndham, but the grandmother is infinitely kind and loving. The silent battle between the women escalates when Esther finally realizes that Luke will not keep his family on the farm with her when he returns from the war.

Addie precipitates the murder plot when she has an affair with a soldier, and Wyndham innocently tells his grandmother. Esther sees a kind of poetic justice in letting the bull of Fonlas into the field through which Addie must pass on her way home. Ironically, the bull destroys the murderess's heart: Wyndham goes to meet his mother and meets his death instead. The vision of Luke in miniature on a stretcher and the living Addie coming to the house causes Esther to lock herself away from the accusing eyes of the others.

"Two Women" is another story with war hovering in the background. Costin, one of five survivors out of fourteen hundred sailors on a ship blown up at sea, has come to talk to the family of one of his friends. He is burdened by the guilt of "having robbed death and . . . his comrades" and sees this trip as a kind of penance for having survived. Wyn Maitland's family does not seem pleased to see Costin. The mother is another example of the strong women mentioned in "Still Waters," for she has sacrificed the farm and her other son so that Wyn could paint. Costin's coming is "out of the pattern she had woven so unceasingly about Manordy, about Wyn and Fred and Bronwen." Fred is "sucked-out, petulant," only a pale imitation of his vital and creative brother. Wyn's work has been enshrined in a barn; it will never be offered for sale.

Costin tries to free Bronwen, Wyn's widow, from the older woman's web. He argues that Wyn would want them to live their own lives, and he would want his work to be seen, not entombed. Bronwen loves Mrs. Maitland for her sacrifices, however, and chooses to remain. Costin leaves the two women, the brother, the paintings, and the farm all trapped in the web Mrs. Maitland has woven, but he has learned something about himself: he will not be a "sacrifice on his own altar." He will get on with his life and stop dwelling on the guilt he feels because he lived and others did not.

"A Death on Sistersland" features another island with a haunting history. Sistersland is named for two nuns who were exploited and destroyed by patriarchal authority. At the time of the story that plot is being reenacted. The island is inhabited by Yorath, an aging sheep thief; his much younger wife; and Darran, whose lust for the wife is used by Yorath to draw the weak, unscrupulous man into his schemes. The first death to occur on Sistersland is that of Yorath; whether he slips or is pushed is unclear. Mrs. Yorath quickly realizes, however, that her life is unchanged: "Childhood, girlhood, and all the baits that coax us forward — and forward to what? The graves on Sistersland, the mean grey husband, the treacherous lover." Whereas she had only the keen eye of her husband to fear before, now she has three fears: the law, Darran, and the dog.

Subsequent events reveal that Mrs. Yorath can find other protectors, but they will be as exploitative as the husband of whom she is free or the lover for whom she has no respect. Rather than continue the destructive cycle of passing from one abusive man to another, she takes her life. The singular "death" in the story's title prevents the reader from anticipating the second death, which is clearly the one to which the title refers.

Selected Short Stories includes seven of the thirteen stories in *The Buttercup Field*, five of the ten in *The Still Waters*, and five of the seven in *Shepherd's Hey*. From 1948 to 1960 Jones was associated with the Golden Cockerel Press as author and editor. He retired from the University of Wales, Cardiff (where he had been since 1964) in 1975. In 1980 he married his second wife, Mair Sivell, with whom he lives in Aberystwyth. Jones's many awards and honors include being made a commander, Order of the British Empire, for his contributions to literature.

References:

Walter Allen, *The Short Story in English* (Oxford: Clarendon, 1981);

Cecil Price, *Gwyn Jones* (Cardiff: University of Wales Press, 1976);

Dennis Vannatta, ed., *The English Short Story, 1945–1980: A Critical History* (Boston: Twayne, 1985).

Francis King
(4 March 1923 –)

Val Warner

See also the King entry in *DLB 15: British Novelists, 1930–1959: Part 1.*

BOOKS: *To the Dark Tower* (London: Home & Van Thal, 1946);

Never Again (London: Home & Van Thal, 1947);

An Air That Kills (London: Home & Van Thal, 1948);

The Dividing Stream (London: Longmans, Green, 1951; New York: Morrow, 1951);

Rod of Incantation (London & New York: Longmans, Green, 1952);

The Dark Glasses (London & New York: Longmans, Green, 1954; New York: Pantheon, 1956);

The Firewalkers: A Memoir, as Frank Cauldwell (London: John Murray, 1956);

The Widow (London & New York: Longmans, Green, 1957);

The Man on the Rock (London: Longmans, Green, 1957; New York: Pantheon, 1957);

So Hurt and Humiliated and Other Stories (London: Longmans, Green, 1959);

The Custom House (London: Longmans, Green, 1961; Garden City, N.Y.: Doubleday, 1962);

The Japanese Umbrella and Other Short Stories (London: Longmans, Green, 1964);

The Last of the Pleasure Gardens (London: Longmans, Green, 1965);

The Waves Behind the Boat (London: Longmans, Green, 1967);

The Brighton Belle and Other Stories (London: Longmans, Green, 1968);

A Domestic Animal (London: Harlow, Longmans, 1970);

Japan (London: Thames & Hudson, 1970; New York: Viking, 1970);

Flights (London: Hutchinson, 1973);

A Game of Patience (London: Hutchinson, 1974);

The Needle (London: Hutchinson, 1975; New York: Mason/Charter, 1976);

Francis King

Hard Feelings and Other Stories (London: Hutchinson, 1976);

Christopher Isherwood (London: Longman, 1976);

Danny Hill: Memoirs of a Prominent Gentleman (London: Hutchinson, 1977);

The Action (London: Hutchinson, 1978);

E. M. Forster and His World (London: Thames & Hudson, 1978; New York: Scribners, 1978);

Indirect Method and Other Stories (London: Hutchinson, 1980);

Florence (New York: Newsweek, 1982);

Act of Darkness (London: Hutchinson, 1983; Boston: Little, Brown, 1983);

Voices in an Empty Room (London: Hutchinson, 1984; Boston: Little, Brown, 1984);

One Is a Wanderer: Selected Stories (London: Hutchinson, 1985; Boston: Little, Brown, 1985);

Frozen Music (London: Hutchinson, 1987; New York: Harper, 1988);

The Woman Who Was God (London: Hutchinson, 1988; New York: Weidenfeld & Nicolson, 1988);

Punishments (London: Hamish Hamilton, 1989; New York: Viking, 1989);

Visiting Cards (London: Constable, 1990);

The Ant Colony (London: Constable, 1991);

Secret Lives: Three Novellas, by King, Tom Wakefield, and Patrick Gale (London: Constable, 1991);

Florence: A Literary Companion (London: John Murray, 1991);

Yesterday Came Suddenly (London: Constable, 1993).

OTHER: *Introducing Greece,* edited by King (London: Methuen, 1956; revised, 1968);

"The Snake Temple" and "To the Camp and Back," in *Penguin Modern Stories 12,* edited by Judith Burnley (Harmondsworth, U.K.: Penguin, 1972), pp. 39–88;

Osbert Sitwell, *Collected Stories,* edited by King (London: Duckworth, 1974);

New Stories 3, edited by King and Ronald Harwood (London: Hutchinson, 1978);

Prokofiev by Prokofiev: A Composer's Memoir, edited by King, translated by Guy Daniels (London: Macdonald & Jane's, 1979);

"The Interment," in *Winter's Tales 26,* edited by A. D. MacLean (London: Macmillan, 1980), pp. 35–55;

My Sister and Myself: The Diaries of J. R. Ackerley, edited by King (London: Hutchinson, 1982);

Lafcadio Hearn, *Writings from Japan,* edited by King (Harmondsworth, U.K.: Penguin, 1984);

Twenty Stories: A South East Arts Collection, edited by King (London: Secker & Warburg, South East Arts, 1985);

"Credit," in *Best Short Stories 1986,* edited by Giles Gordon and David Hughes (London: Heinemann, 1986), pp. 123–130;

"A Lost Opportunity," in *Winter's Tales New Series 6,* edited by Robin Baird-Smith (London: Constable, 1990), pp. 257–271;

"Vibrations," in *The Minerva Book of Short Stories 3,* edited by Gordon and Hughes (London: Minerva, 1990), pp. 145–151;

"The Pistol Shot," in *Signals,* edited by Alan Ross (London: Constable, 1991), pp. 116–124;

"A Taste of Salt," in *Fathers and Sons,* edited by John Hoyland (London: Serpent's Tail, 1992), pp. 187–205.

SELECTED PERIODICAL PUBLICATIONS – UNCOLLECTED:

NONFICTION

"The Years in the Refrigerator: Leaving School," *London Magazine,* 5 (July 1965): 28–35;

"The State of Fiction: A Symposium," by King and others, *New Review,* 5 (Summer 1978): 48–49;

"Retrospect and Reconciliation: The Farewell Address of Francis King as Outgoing International [PEN] President at Maastricht," *Pen* (Autumn 1989): 9;

"A Love Affair," *European Gay Review,* 6/7 (1991): 68–71.

TRANSLATIONS: Philippe Jullian, *Robert de Montesquiou: A Fin-de-siècle Prince,* translated by King and John Haylock (London: Secker & Warburg, 1967);

Saint Ours, *An Angel in Sodom* (London: Quartet, 1977).

The *Times Literary Supplement* (4 December 1959) called Francis King "a writer perfectly equipped for the short story." John Nicholson (London *Times,* 20 November 1980) writes: "His themes are grand, and his achievement is to blind us to the limitations of the short story, and to make us forget why it has gone out of fashion." For the past forty years King's stories have appeared in such major British periodicals as the *Listener, London Magazine, Encounter,* and *New Review* and in such major anthologies as *Winter's Tales, Best Short Stories,* and *Penguin Modern Stories.* He has explored personal relationships in a humanist, realist tradition, often focusing on the "desirous passion, not uninformed by morality" identified by Barbara Hardy as his main theme, sometimes amid social comedy and in a variety of global settings – especially Greece, Japan, and England – "a genuinely cosmopolitan writer," as Sylvia Clayton calls him (*Times Literary Supplement,* 14 November 1980). His storytelling gift functions through unadorned but witty prose, described by David Plante, in *New Review* (Summer 1978), as being "as clear as the clearest awareness, and which, like anything so clear, is depthless."

Francis Henry King was born on 4 March 1923 in Adelboden, Switzerland, the third of four children and the only son of Eustace Arthur Cecil and Faith Mina Read King. At the time of Francis's birth his parents were in Switzerland from India to visit Arthur King's mother, who had moved there after World War I to escape anti-German feeling in England. Arthur King served in the Indian Police before becoming deputy director of the Intelligence Bureau in India. His son, who draws on his early memories of India in the novel *Act of Darkness* (1983) and the novella *Frozen Music* (1987), has described his childhood in India and Switzerland as an earthly paradise, from which he was expelled at age eight.

In keeping with the convention of the day he was sent to England to attend boarding school. Totally unprepared for that life, he was unhappy at Rose Hill Preparatory School in Banstead, Surrey. However, he won a classics scholarship to the famous public school at Shrewsbury, where he was contented and began to write poetry. His novel *Never Again* (1947) fictionalizes his childhood and adolescence. When King was fourteen, his father died from tuberculosis at age forty-five. Faith King returned to England with her two youngest daughters, a situation reflected in King's novel *The Widow* (1957), based on his mother's life. For the first time he had a home in England with his immediate family, albeit not in the luxurious lifestyle his family had enjoyed as part of the British Raj in India.

King won a classics scholarship to Balliol College, Oxford, but World War II was affecting life in Britain. King had shown his pacifist convictions, shared with his aunt and a sister, when at fourteen he had refused to join the Officers' Training Corps at Shrewsbury School. After two terms at Oxford he appeared before a tribunal as a conscientious objector and was sent to work on the land in Essex and then in Surrey – a way of life recalled in his novel *A Game of Patience* (1974). Returning to Oxford four and a half years later with a large "bank account" of books read, he felt callow compared with contemporaries who had been abroad fighting. His novel *Punishments* (1989), although not autobiographical, features soldiers turned students.

King, who from age ten had wanted to be a writer, used his war years' "lucid, if glacial, calm" to get his career off to a precocious start. J. R. Ackerley, literary editor of the *Listener* (a politics and arts weekly published by the British Broadcasting Corporation), was the first editor of a national magazine to encourage him, publishing his poems and later his short stories. Ackerley became a close friend, and King acted as his literary executor and edited his diaries as *My Sister and Myself* (1982). From 1945 to 1950 King was poetry reviewer for the *Listener*. When he took his degree in English lan-

guage and literature in 1949, he was already the author of three novels: *To the Dark Tower* (1946), *Never Again,* and *An Air That Kills* (1948). In 1948 he was elected a fellow of the Royal Society of Literature.

Eager to leave England, he joined the British Council. His novel *The Ant Colony* (1991) focuses on expatriates in postwar Florence, where he worked as a lecturer from 1949 to 1951 and wrote his fourth novel, *The Dividing Stream* (1951), which is set in that city. For this novel, in which for the first time he felt he had found "a voice of my own," he won the Somerset Maugham Award (1952). C. P. Snow listed him as one of his "six bright hopes" for the English novel. *Rod of Incantation* (1952) remains King's only collection of poems, although he has written poetry all his life. King was posted to Greece by the British Council as a lecturer in Salonika (1951–1952) and Athens (1953–1957). His novels *The Dark Glasses* (1954), *The Firewalkers: A Memoir* (1956), and *The Man on the Rock* (1957) are all set in Greece, as are many stories in his first collection of short fiction, *So Hurt and Humiliated and Other Stories* (1959).

Short fiction as a form has always attracted King. In his early teens he admired Maugham's short stories for a mastery of narrative technique that Hardy and others have highlighted in King's own work. He read the short stories of Ivan Bunin, the first Russian Nobel literature laureate, admiring especially the title story of *The Gentleman from San Francisco* (1916). Although King's first collection was his tenth book, his first short story had been published fifteen years earlier. In addition to four subsequent collections of short stories, he has also produced four novellas, two in *Flights* (1973), *Frozen Music,* and the title piece in *Secret Lives* (1991), about a British establishment man dying from AIDS and his Japanese lover. *Frozen Music* – which focuses on a father's act of affirmation in "giving" his young second wife to his son after the young couple have fallen in love on a trip to India – has been his most successful book, translated into twelve languages. King has identified the deterrent to writing short fiction not as the notorious lack of magazine outlets in later-twentieth-century Britain, but as publishers' preference for novels.

In *So Hurt and Humiliated* the dominant setting is Greece, with other stories set in England, Egypt, Italy, and Germany. Mostly written in the same realist tradition as his novels, the stories generally focus on personal relationships in the postwar decade, with the exception of "Mona," in which a thirteen-year-old girl befriends a soldier shell-shocked in World War I. Foreigners often feature in the stories set in England; many of these are also concerned with family relationships, a recurrent theme in King's work. All the stories set abroad, except "The Way Out," show English expatriates involved with locals. "The Way Out," about a harassed English honorary consul who bullies his timid nine-year-old son into suicide, is set in Egypt, where King's 1956 British Council posting coincided with the Suez Crisis.

The title story concerns the relationship of an English colonel's daughter with a feckless, poor, yet attractive Greek, Costa. The story was written in 1951, and Costa seems a prototype of the con man Spiro in *The Man on the Rock*. The virgin Rosamund is seduced but is both unwilling and unable to exert influence through her father for Costa to receive a scholarship to study in England. The story's pivot is the sexual encounter, yet Rosamund presaged hurt or humiliation before she met him, "so that when she met Costa Arslanoglou she had the feeling of having come to the mouth of a dark tunnel which she had often already explored in her dreams." The same economic reality underlies "The Bitter End," though here it is America, in the person of the film director Lee, that could offer a better chance to Sotirius, a Greek peasant boy turned actor. When the few months of filming end, he teases Lee: "you have made an American of me."

From the first King has been more prepared to experiment with the short story than with the novel. "The Master," about a Greek youth's "apprenticeship" to a mysterious, sinister old man, is told as a fable. The comic story "An Informal Report" comprises an account to the headquarters of a cultural organization (like the British Council) by a writer on a lecture tour of an unnamed Scandinavian country with the organization's representative, Shephard. The monologue form allows the writer to damn himself as he details his unrealized faux pas and patronizes Shephard, a distinguished author.

The most interesting and longest piece in King's first collection is the significantly titled "A True Story," a key story in King's development. Narrated by an unnamed novelist using second- and thirdhand accounts, it shifts from 1940s England via 1930s Germany to 1950s Greece. The story centers on the wife of a German prisoner of war "suicide-case" and vividly portrays his relationship with his father-in-law, who engineered the marriage. This story distills ideas present in King's earlier works about the dependence of truth on perception, with the resultant plurality of truth, and points to later provisional resolutions of this dilemma.

In fiction the problem of perception is often the technical problem of viewpoint. In his next two novels, *The Custom House* (1961) and *The Last of the Pleasure Gardens* (1965), King writes from both first- and third-person angles. His first novel, *To the Dark Tower,* is written explicitly from the viewpoints of two characters, encompassing their pasts as well as the present, and implicitly from the viewpoint of a third, a novelist named Frank Cauldwell, who is writing a novel titled "To the Dark Tower."

The parallels between the unnamed novelist in "A True Story" and King are even closer than the text allows. The unnamed novelist is working on a novel about German prisoners of war, the subject of one of two unpublished novels King wrote before achieving publication. The story "To the Camp and Back" (*Hard Feelings and Other Stories,* 1976) is shaped from a passage in that novel. King is only a whisker away from introducing "Francis King" as a character in his fiction, as he does in his next collection, *The Japanese Umbrella and Other Stories* (1964), and as he intended to do in *The Firewalkers*. When the British Council obliged him to publish pseudonymously that affectionately ironic evocation of the dilettante Colonel Grecos's infatuation with a physically unattractive man in turn infatuated with a girl, King chose for his pseudonym – and for the first-person narrator's name – "Frank Cauldwell."

It is not surprising that the unnamed narrator in "A True Story" mentions Greece and his novels as the "things about which at that time I cared more than about anything else." In his introduction to the 1985 edition of *The Firewalkers,* King describes that book as "an album of snapshots, taken in the brilliant sunshine of Athens before its Smog Age set in and of my new-found liberation at the moment when my personal Smog Age had dissipated." As a man who realized he was homosexual, King found postwar Britain a deeply repressive society. Male homosexuality was illegal until 1967 and frequently prosecuted. King has described his years in Greece as a "period of extreme promiscuity."

In 1960 Penguin had to fight a court case in order to publish the unexpurgated version of D. H. Lawrence's *Lady Chatterley's Lover* (1928), and the constraints on publishing homosexual subject matter were far greater. Although in *The Firewalkers* the only sex involves a minor character and happens offstage, King ran afoul of his regular publisher, Longmans, Green, which refused to publish it; John Murray was bolder. From the first King had to bear in mind what was publishable. *So Hurt and Humiliated* includes his first published story, "A Visit to the General," written in 1943 and presaging *To the*

Dark Tower, not least in its homoeroticism. A pair of male lovers figures perfunctorily in "A Friend for Christmas." "Getting Ready" involves a senior man in an unnamed organization, similar to an embassy, obliging a junior to resign on account of a long-term relationship with an indigenous female lover, while the senior secretly awaits the arrival of a short-term indigenous lover, gender unstated, but whose arrival on bicycle in an Arab country suggests a man.

So Hurt and Humiliated was well received by critics, including Naomi Lewis in the *New Statesman* (12 December 1959), who highlights "a stylish consistency." The anonymous reviewer in the *Scotsman* (26 December 1959) notes "a Chekhovian strength," a comparison later made in the *Observer* by Anthony Thwaite regarding *A Game of Patience.* Although the anonymous reviewer in the *Times Literary Supplement* (4 December 1959) found that King's "moments of tragic violence are the more effective for being controlled by his faultless and professional literary style," too many of the stories culminate in death.

King has written that "foreign places have always provided me with imaginative stimulation," but Finland is an exception. Although he was content working as the British Council's assistant representative in Helsinki, during the eighteen months he spent there from 1957 to 1958 he wrote virtually nothing. By contrast, during the four years (1959–1963) he spent in Japan as regional director in Kyoto, he produced *The Custom House,* his most successful novel to that date; *The Waves Behind the Boat* (1967); and most of the stories in *The Japanese Umbrella.* All the stories in that collection, like the two novels, are set in Japan.

In his article "A Love Affair" (*European Gay Review,* 1991) King writes:

> I have never made any secret of the fact that, during the first months of my stay in Japan, I was extremely unhappy there. But then, having for a while felt myself to be so much an alien in that culture, I suddenly felt myself to be wholly at home in it. . . . I was aware of a weird affinity between my own temperament and the temperaments of many of my Japanese friends. . . . Above all, I found a similarity between the stoicism which I had absorbed both through the example of my mortally ill father during my childhood and adolescence and through my classical studies at school and at Oxford, and the code by which so many of my Japanese friends ordered their lives.

Among these friends were those to whom King dedicated *The Japanese Umbrella:* "To Norikazu Fukushima and Yoshihiro and Kunio Sogabe who

Dust jacket for King's 1964 collection of short stories, all of which are set in Japan

radically changed my view of Japan." Yoshihiro Sogabe was King's lover in Japan, Kunio Sogabe was Yoshihiro's brother, and Norikazu Fukushima was a close friend. The harsh view of Japan in *The Custom House* contrasts with the warmer tone of *The Japanese Umbrella.*

Apart from "Making It All Right," in which all the characters are expatriates, the stories in *The Japanese Umbrella* involve different relationships between expatriates and the Japanese, as in the Greek stories in *So Hurt and Humiliated.* Critical attention has focused on the stories in which "Francis King" appears as a character. There are only three such stories out of thirteen, though "The Goat," like "A True Story" and "The Vultures" in the previous collection, has as its unnamed narrator a King clone.

In "A Corner of a Foreign Field" King traces the friendship of "Francis King" with Professor Kuroda, an elderly Anglophile whose summum bonum would be to visit England. As the story ends, this dream looks like it may become a reality, but the westerner realizes Kuroda will always find a pretext for not traveling there because "England might not measure up to what you require of it." A mutual interest in Lafcadio Hearn has cemented their friendship; twenty years later King edited Hearn's *Writings from Japan*.

"Francis King" reappears in "Dog and Bird" and "L'Acte Gratuit," in which it becomes clear en passant that many acquaintances in Kyoto did not know he was a novelist as well as a British Council officer. King doubtless seemed to be merely a conscientious British Council officer, with little sense of the energy, organization, toughness, and ambition that enabled him to combine two careers. Similarly, the fictional celibate "Francis King" seems to have no private life – for publication's sake. King has acknowledged the influence of Christopher Isherwood's writing – which he surveys in the pamphlet *Christopher Isherwood* (1976) – and the device of using a narrator to whom he gives his own name clearly derives from Isherwood's *Mr. Norris Changes Trains* (1935) and *Goodbye to Berlin* (1939).

Of the stories not using the "Francis King" figure, one of the best is the opening piece, "The Crack," about the strained affair of a male Japanese student and an Englishwoman married to an invalid. While wandering on Mount Hiei, they come across a spot apparently favored by suicide-pact lovers; down the mountainside is "a crack rusty with a sediment which looked like dried blood." As the story ends, they are at the foot of the mountain, inside the crack, and he seems about to rape her, in sinister fulfillment of the pervasive female sexual imagery of the title. "The Festival of the Dead" also focuses on an affair between an Englishwoman and a Japanese man, but with a contrasting tone. Colleagues who have just finished at a summer school, they draw together for a few hours before the man's grief for his lost son is revived by the Festival of the Dead, making the woman irrelevant.

According to King, in "A Love Affair," "Above all else, Japan taught me the paradox that, in literature and art, less can mean more. . . . This lesson was particularly valuable to me in . . . my short stories. . . . By the time they reach the reader, they have undergone repeated cutting and compression." Yet the stories in *The Japanese Umbrella* do not seem more spare than those in the previous collection. However, Brigid Brophy, in a review of the later collection for the *New Statesman* (6 November 1964), points out that "his sparse incidents and dialogue lie so at ease on the page that only afterwards does one appreciate the architectural strategy which has made each element do the

work of several." King's subtle use of implication requires an attentive reader ready to infer the unsaid. His understated style allows his prose to be read fast, but the reader must not miss any detail as it is unlikely to be repeated. As King states, "I have always been preoccupied with style and form. I feel that I am most successful in achieving both if the reader is unconscious of any straining for them."

Hardy, writing about King's fidelity to traditional forms, comments: "One of the refreshing aspects of his writing is its lack of trendy imitativeness. He never plays at being a modernist or postmodernist, never tries to fake Joycean or Beckettian models." Although this is an accurate description of his work, some readers may wish King were more adventuresome, even in the later stories, some of which are less traditional in form than those in *The Japanese Umbrella*.

The Japanese Umbrella was well received. The enthusiastic anonymous reviewer in the *Times Literary Supplement* (5 November 1964) placed it "in a broadly Forsterian tradition." Brophy admired the use of the Japanese setting to provide a unified focus for the collection: "Mr. King's is not only a volume of excellent stories; it is an excellent volume of stories." The anonymous reviewer in the London *Times* (5 November 1964) especially praised "A Corner of a Foreign Field," for which Brian Glanville, Olivia Manning, and Raleigh Trevelyan awarded King the 1965 Katherine Mansfield Prize. That story first appeared in the *London Magazine* (May 1964), an arts magazine edited since 1961 by Alan Ross, who has consistently published King's work. King has acknowledged the support of the magazine's founder and previous editor, John Lehmann, during the early part of his career.

At the end of 1963 King returned to England for a year's unpaid sabbatical from the British Council. He lived in Battersea, London, the symbolic setting for his novel *The Last of the Pleasure Gardens,* in which "there was nothing of myself at all." Finding he could manage financially, he chose early retirement from the British Council despite being offered an attractive posting to France. In 1964 he became a fiction reviewer for the *Sunday Telegraph,* and in 1966 he was awarded an Arts Council bursary. By then, after eighteen months in London, he had moved to Brighton, the setting for all the stories in *The Brighton Belle and Other Stories* (1968), whose title story begins:

> She was the daughter of an earl, she had been rich, she had been beautiful. I think that it was I who first gave her the nickname "The Brighton Belle."

She reminded me of one of the old first-class Pullman coaches, once elegant but now dilapidated and ramshackle, that make up that train.

The story describes the last months of Lady Dorothy Pawson with her failed-actress friend Cynthia, whose career she attempts to promote as assiduously and unrealistically as she attempts to sell her valueless objets d'art to her friends, notably the first-person narrator, a novelist named Francis. Apart from the introduction to *Danny Hill: Memoirs of a Prominent Gentleman* (1977) – purporting to explain "the manner in which this sequel to John Cleland's *Memoirs of a Woman of Pleasure* came into my possession" – and the occasional use of an unnamed novelist, as in "Love's Old Sweet Song" (*Indirect Method and Other Stories*, 1980), "The Brighton Belle" marks King's last use of himself as a character in his fiction.

Although the novelist Francis appears in only the opening story of *The Brighton Belle,* his presence affects the form of the whole volume, the most structured of King's five collections. Like the string circling a bunch of flowers, the title piece holds together the other stories, all written in the third person. The narrator's unspecified work in progress, which is mentioned in the opening story, could be the following stories.

The once-famous train *The Brighton Belle* symbolizes not only Lady Dorothy but also the formerly fashionable resort frequented by the Prince of Wales in the late eighteenth century. The town went downhill with the influx of day-trippers – as shown in Graham Greene's *Brighton Rock* (1938) – along with the criminal element that gathered around the racecourse. King's 1960s Brighton centers on the esplanade, where "respectable" middle-class married couples and elderly people of straitened means contrast with foreign students, junkie dropouts, assorted derelicts, and even the rich and their surviving servants.

"A Beautiful Old Man" is an outstanding story about a hotel porter who asks – and receives – little from life, which does not prevent his being beaten. "Cat People" reveals a Finnish student as a probable murderer; after he flees, his landlady's returning psychic powers fuse with her desire for him. In both stories different narrative threads are interwoven in a way more common in novels than short stories. Hardy comments on King's "habit of making narrative generative. . . . King generates story as some writers generate images." She ascribes this to his sheer love of storytelling, yet storytelling for King is always the means to an end. His concern is his characters'

Dust jacket for King's 1968 collection of short stories, all of which are set in Brighton and depict the faded glory of that seaside resort

emotions, the chains of causation behind their actions, and their perception by others, the rationale of "A True Story" in his first collection.

The four-page story "The Containers" distills the decay uniting the Brighton stories. It opens as "the doctor gave Brooks three containers. Made of a waxed paper that had the appearance of parchment, they seemed far too small and fragile for their intended purpose." The author avoids using the words *excrement* or *urine* – or more-euphemistic terms – in a way that structurally reflects Brooks's embarrassment, especially about the mishaps that could befall him as he carries the filled containers back to the doctor. Ironically Brooks's embarrassment protects him temporarily from worrying about the bleak diagnosis the containers will later prompt. In his next collection, *Hard Feelings,* King includes a more complicated story, "Subject and Object," with a similar point of departure: a woman apparently confronted with inexplicable dog turds in her house. Because of its brief starkness many readers may find "The Containers" more powerful than "Subject and Object."

The Brighton Belle was generally well received, although Angus Wolfe Murray, in his show-offy London *Times* review (27 April 1968), suggests that King rubs his and the readers' noses in the dirt: "He gloats at the sweat in the palms, my dear!" Others have leveled this criticism at King – as at most worthwhile writers. King's supreme strength is his clear-sightedness. *The Brighton Belle* involves decay, which does not exclude beauty, wit, and love, such as Cynthia's for Lady Dorothy. A different writer might have developed the imagery of run-down seaside hotels into a symbol of declining Britain, as Maggie Gee does in *Grace* (1988), in which "the Empire was the name of a second-rate hotel," but King always focuses on the individual. His characters' problems, like Brooks's illness, do not have directly political causes.

After four and a half years King moved back to London, settling in the Kensington house where he still lives. He was elected to the executive committee of the English branch of the International Association of Poets, Playwrights, Editors, Essayists, and Novelists (P.E.N.), serving from 1969 to 1973, and to the executive committee of the Society of Authors in 1974, serving as chairman from 1975 to 1977. King supported the public-lending right to provide payment from public funds to authors whose books are borrowed from public libraries, a system enacted in 1979. A founding member of the Writers' Action Group, King became chairman of the Authors' Lending Rights Society in 1974. In 1968 King met actor David Atkin, who became his lover and lived with him in London. At a P.E.N. meeting in London on 14 February 1990, twenty-one months after his partner's death from AIDS at age forty-five, King said he found a love with Atkin that was totally reciprocal.

In 1969 King's novel *A Domestic Animal* (1970) was withdrawn a week before publication day when an acquaintance threatened a libel suit on the grounds that he was portrayed as a minor female character. King was forced to rewrite the passages where Penny (previously Winny) appears. He later used this experience in his novel *The Action* (1978), where Hazel's novel resembles his own novel *The Last of the Pleasure Gardens*. Arguably King's finest novel, *A Domestic Animal* suffered on first publication both from literary editors' irritation at its reappearance and from homophobia. However, this portrayal of a homosexual man's hopeless love for a heterosexual man was better received in subsequent paperback editions, in a less intolerant climate.

All the stories in *Hard Feelings* except two are set in England. The title story describes the reunion between Adrian, an antiques dealer, and his former lover/employee, whom he had banished until he had repaid previous thefts. But Adrian no longer trusts him enough to leave him alone in their bedroom with his wallet, as the other realizes. Because the two characters happen to be homosexual, this could be called a "homosexual story," although the theme of theft – a preoccupation of King – could as well be applied to a heterosexual relationship. Certainly King has always aligned himself with those authors who feel that their identity as writers transcends race, sexuality, gender, and nationality.

"The Tree" opens by apparently apostrophizing the water closet: "How I loathe the W.C. It has its uses, of course; civilization would be unthinkable without it. But it's so unreliable in performing its necessary functions. It's so unaesthetic. And, let's face it, it *stinks*." In the next paragraph the reader learns that the "old, famous, rich politician" to whom these thoughts belong is referring to the working class, not the water closet. The narrative alternates between the courteous former minister's love for his lofty lime tree and the permanently diminished horizon of an elderly working-class woman in a house at the end of "a mean, squat row" abutting on his large garden. The old woman poisons the old man's lime tree. Both are shown as the products of their different environments, respectively privileged and deprived.

"A Nice Way to Go" is among the best stories in *Hard Feelings*. After a suicidal widower has had to take his elderly Siamese cat to be euthanized, he notices a Siamese cat stuck up a tree. Despite his age and angina he climbs the tree. Heartened by the prospect of a new friendship with the cat's female owner, he destroys his hoard of sleeping pills but dies in his sleep. King writes unsentimentally and frequently about animals. All of his books contain an example of a happy relationship between a human and an animal, generally a cat or dog, reflecting his love for these pets.

Always a writer rich in ambiguities, King is well fitted to deal with the supernatural, where the only certainty may be doubt. "A Scent of Mimosa" is set at the presentation of the Katherine Mansfield Prize at Menton to an imaginary writer, Lenore, who seems possessed by Mansfield's spirit. Lenore is drawn to a young New Zealander named Leslie. Back in London she remembers that Mansfield's beloved brother, killed in World War I, was named Leslie. Given the New Zealander's insistence to her in Menton that they will meet again seems irrational, some readers may see this man – who is encountered by characters other than Lenore – as ghostly.

Hard Feelings was generally less well received than King's earlier collections. After the acclaim of King's "Japanese" books, his "English" books were underrated until *Voices in an Empty Room* (1984). Susannah Clapp, in a moderately favorable review in the *Times Literary Supplement* (24 September 1976), praises King's "ease of writing, a deft handling of small wan subjects." Like Jacky Gillot's enthusiastic review in the London *Times* (23 September 1976), Clapp's notice highlights the punning collective title, though of all King's collections the stories in *Hard Feelings* are least closely bound together.

In *Indirect Method and Other Stories,* each story is either set abroad or involves foreigners in Britain. In the apparent exception, "The Glass House," the title structure was built by the central character's architect husband, a Jewish refugee from Holland. In "Indirect Method" Liz, an accomplished doctor, returns to Japan on a professional visit and arranges to meet her former houseboy as well as her former lover, now a businessman with a family: "It is really for him and not for Professor Ito and his colleagues in the medical faculty of Kyoto University that she has come all this way." The former houseboy, Osamu, had learned English from Liz and her family by the direct method, but he uses an indirect method to seal off their past irretrievably with an expensive gift.

"Appetites," written in an impressionistic style, concerns a Greek girl dying of anorexia in London. "Love's Old Sweet Song" displays King's interest in the theater and his excellent ear for dialogue. An entire relationship is mapped through a fatuous German-American homosexual man's monologues about his lover to a silent writer friend. This story first appeared in *Gay News* (16 December 1976), the longest-running British publication for homosexuals (1972–1983).

"The Wake," which is set in Athens, involves the mourning of the son of Frosso, "one of the greatest of the *bouzouki* singers of her day." The story contains some of King's finest writing, opening with this striking image: "For so many years Frosso had been there, head held high and bosom thrust out, on the invisible escalator a few steps above me." In the final story, "Voices," Pearl discovers as a schoolgirl that she has extraordinary ESP powers, which later she and her Indian lover exploit commercially. When Pearl's telepathy wanes after she has an abortion, she attempts to recover her abilities with a "scientific" gadget placed

in her tooth. King's belief in ESP is stronger than the average reader's. In a 1974 interview with Kay Dick he declares: "I believe that if you really will a thing, if you want it strongly enough, you get it. . . . I believe in this extra-sensory perception. I think it is possible to communicate like that, impose your will on another person."

The reviews of *Indirect Method* were generally favorable, but Sylvia Clayton, in the *Times Literary Supplement* (14 November 1980), found King "less successful when his material is in itself sensational," citing "Little Old Lady Passing By," where there is indeed no need for the old woman whom Roz befriends to be revealed finally as a famous ballerina. John Nicholson, in the London *Times* (20 November 1980), identifies King's strength: "It is their [the stories'] psychological locales which give them their power."

In 1980 King's only play, *Far East,* had a modest run in Coventry. In 1978 he had started reviewing theater for the *Sunday Telegraph* while continuing to review fiction. At present he critiques fiction for the *Spectator*. From 1980 to 1981 he served on the executive committee of the National Book League. In 1977 he was elected vice-president of the English branch of P.E.N., and from 1978 to 1985 he served as its president. He was honored in 1979 by the state as an officer of the Order of the British Empire, and in 1985 he was named a commander of the Order of the British Empire.

In *One Is a Wanderer: Selected Stories* (1985) King includes stories from all five collections, arranged not chronologically but to reflect off each other. He opens with "Voices." In this context the woman's ability to know what other people are saying seems a metaphor for a writer's creating characters, their conversations, and their thoughts. The two previously uncollected stories in the volume involve Shakespearean themes. The closing story, "His Everlasting Mansion," is a monologue by Timon of Athens in his last days amid actual and metaphoric "filth of the world, a world of filth." "The Silence Is Rest?" takes the form of a love letter from Hamlet to Horatio, explaining the bloody goings-on at Elsinore, apparently all at his hand.

The pieces in *One Is a Wanderer: Selected Stories,* characterized by Jane Thynne in the *Sunday Times* (8 September 1985) as "crisis-points where emotional violence bursts through cracks in the social decorum that this author observes so acutely," were well received. However, Nicholas Shakespeare, in a half-admiring review in the London *Times* (29 August 1985), voiced a recurrent criticism: "The author shares the oriental composure, almost coldness, of many of his subjects." Yet the author is not cold but clear-sighted.

From 1986 to 1989 King served as president of International P.E.N. Aided by glasnost, he helped to establish a P.E.N. center in the Soviet Union and negotiated with the Soviets to open a center in Lithuania. A Nigerian P.E.N. center also opened during his tenure as president. The fictional setting for his novel *The Woman Who Was God* (1988) is actually Senegal, which he visited for P.E.N. But 1988 was the worst year of his life, with the death of Atkin, his partner of twenty years, followed by his own collapse from cancer. He gave up theater reviewing but has continued with all his other activities, during convalescence writing the comic novel *Visiting Cards* (1990), about the fictional WAA (World Association of Authors).

King still works for P.E.N., even visiting Slovenia for a regional conference in May 1992 during the Yugoslavian civil war. His literary friends have included Angus Wilson, whom he encouraged to start writing; L. P. Hartley, whom he helped write *Poor Clare* (1968); Olivia Manning, to whom he dedicated *The Brighton Belle;* Ivy Compton-Burnett; John Braine; and C. H. B. Kitchin. King is currently writing an autobiography. Francis King the short-fiction writer will always be overshadowed by Francis King the novelist, but, with his wit, technical skills, and understanding of people, his short stories alone ensure him a significant place in postwar British fiction.

Interviews:

Kay Dick, Interview, in her *Friends and Friendship: Conversations and Reflections* (London: Sidgwick & Jackson, 1974), pp. 109–134;

Michael Mason and Peter Burton, "A Domestic Animal?: An Interview with Francis King," *Gay News* (29 July 1976): 23–24; reprinted in *Talking to . . . : Peter Burton in Conversation with . . . ,* edited by Burton (Exeter, U.K.: Third House, 1991), pp. 68–80;

Susanne McDadd, "Francis King: An Interview," *Pen* (Autumn 1989): 24–25;

Michael Leech, "Our Gracious Kings: Francis King, the Writer, and His Mother, Faith," *Sunday Times Magazine,* 25 March 1990, pp. 12–16.

References:

Barbara Hardy, "Francis King's Obscured Passions," *European Gay Review,* 6/7 (1991): 52–67;

John Mellors, "Waves and Echoes: The Novels and Stories of Francis King," *London Magazine,* 15 (December 1975–January 1976): 74–82.

Papers:

A collection of King's manuscripts is at the Harry Ransom Humanities Research Center, University of Texas at Austin.

Doris Lessing

(22 October 1919 –)

Fiona R. Barnes
University of Wisconsin – Madison

See also the Lessing entries in *DLB 15: British Novelists, 1930–1959: Part 1* and *DLB Yearbook: 1985*.

BOOKS: *The Grass Is Singing* (London: M. Joseph, 1950; New York: Crowell, 1950);

This Was the Old Chief's Country (London: M. Joseph, 1951; New York: Crowell, 1952);

Martha Quest (London: M. Joseph, 1952);

Five: Short Novels (London: M. Joseph, 1953);

A Proper Marriage (London: M. Joseph, 1954);

A Retreat to Innocence (London: M. Joseph, 1956; New York: Prometheus, 1959);

The Habit of Loving (London: MacGibbon & Kee, 1957; New York: Crowell, 1958);

Going Home (London: M. Joseph, 1957; New York: Ballantine, 1968);

A Ripple from the Storm (London: M. Joseph, 1958; New York: Simon & Schuster, 1966);

Fourteen Poems (Northwood, Middlesex, U.K.: Scorpion, 1959);

In Pursuit of the English: A Documentary (London: MacGibbon & Kee, 1960; New York: Simon & Schuster, 1961);

Play with a Tiger: A Play in Three Acts (London: M. Joseph, 1962);

The Golden Notebook (London: M. Joseph, 1962; New York: Simon & Schuster, 1962);

A Man and Two Women (London: MacGibbon & Kee, 1963; New York: Simon & Schuster, 1963);

Martha Quest and a Proper Marriage (New York: Simon & Schuster, 1964);

African Stories (London: M. Joseph, 1964; New York: Simon & Schuster, 1965);

Landlocked (London: MacGibbon & Kee, 1965);

A Ripple from the Storm and Landlocked (New York: Simon & Schuster, 1967);

Particularly Cats (London: M. Joseph, 1967; New York: Simon & Schuster, 1967);

The Four-Gated City (London: MacGibbon & Kee, 1969; New York: Knopf, 1969);

Briefing for a Descent into Hell (London: Cape, 1971; New York: Knopf, 1971);

The Story of a Non-Marrying Man and Other Stories (London: Cape, 1972); republished as *The Temptation of Jack Orkney and Other Stories* (New York: Knopf, 1972);

The Summer Before the Dark (London: Cape, 1973; New York: Knopf, 1973);

Memoirs of a Survivor (London: Octagon, 1974; New York: Knopf, 1975);

Shikasta (London: Cape, 1979; New York: Knopf, 1979);

The Marriages Between Zones Three, Four and Five (London: Cape, 1980; New York: Knopf, 1980);

The Sirian Experiments (London: Cape, 1981; New York: Knopf, 1981);

The Making of the Representative for Planet 8 (London: Cape, 1982; New York: Knopf, 1982);

Documents Relating to the Sentimental Agents in the Volyen Empire (London: Cape, 1983; New York: Knopf, 1983);

The Diary of a Good Neighbour, as Jane Somers (New York: Knopf, 1983; London: M. Joseph, 1983); republished as part of *The Diaries of Jane Somers* (London: M. Joseph, 1984; New York: Knopf, 1984);

If the Old Could . . . , as Somers (London: M. Joseph, 1984; New York: Knopf, 1984); republished as part of *The Diaries of Jane Somers;*

The Good Terrorist (London: Cape, 1985; New York: Knopf, 1985);

The Wind Blows Away Our Words (London: Pan, 1987; New York: Vintage, 1987);

Prisons We Choose to Live Inside (London: Cape, 1987; New York: Harper & Row, 1987);

The Fifth Child (London: Cape, 1988; New York: Knopf, 1988);

The Real Thing: Stories and Sketches (New York: HarperCollins, 1992); republished as *London Observed: Stories and Sketches* (London: HarperCollins, 1992);

African Laughter: Four Visits to Zimbabwe (London & New York: HarperCollins, 1992).

Doris Lessing, circa 1949

Editions and Collections: *A Small Personal Voice: Essays, Reviews, and Interviews,* edited by Paul Schlueter (New York: Knopf, 1974);

Collected Stories, 2 volumes (London: Cape, 1978); republished as *Stories,* 1 volume (New York: Knopf, 1978);

The Doris Lessing Reader (New York: Knopf, 1988; revised edition, London: Cape, 1989).

OTHER: "The Small Personal Voice," in *Declaration,* edited by Tom Maschler (London: MacGibbon & Kee, 1957), pp. 11–27;

Each His Own Wilderness, in *New English Dramatists: Three Plays,* edited by E. Martin Browne (Harmondsworth, U.K.: Penguin, 1959);

Olive Schreiner, *The Story of an African Farm,* afterword by Lessing (Greenwich, Conn.: Fawcett, 1968);

Lawrence Vambe, *An Ill-Fated People: Zimbabwe Before and After Rhodes,* foreword by Lessing (London: Heinemann, 1972);

The Singing Door, in *Second Playbill Two,* edited by Alan Durband (London: Hutchinson, 1973).

Doris Lessing's literary career spans more than four decades; consequently her texts, both fiction and nonfiction, are valuable at the most basic level as historical records that tackle the central political, spiritual, and psychological questions of the last half of the twentieth century. In most of her works Lessing's focus is on marginal characters — people living on the fringes of society, sometimes collected in resistant subcultures — whom she tends to champion as underdogs. Despite her disavowal of feminism she is perhaps most successful (and most renowned) for her portrayals of the changing female consciousness as it reacts to problems of the age. Her works display a continuing self-conscious exploration of the limits of genre and form; most of her texts work on metafictional levels.

While known primarily for her novels Lessing has written short fiction throughout her career, and it forms an integral part of her oeuvre. Her stories are often closely linked with the novels she is working on at the time. As Claire Sprague asserts in *Re-Reading the Short Story* (1989):

> Doris Lessing is not unusual in having begun her career with short stories. She is unusual in having continued to write short stories for a long time after she established her reputation as a novelist ... her short story writing paralleled her novel writing, perhaps her very best novel writing, for a very long time. Sometimes they preceded and deeply affected her novel writing.

Doris May Tayler was born in Kermanshah, Persia, on 22 October 1919. Her father, Alfred Cook Tayler, had gone to work for the Imperial Bank of Persia after being invalided out of World War I with a wounded leg. Her mother, Emily Maude McVeagh Tayler, met her husband while nursing him after his amputation. In 1924 the Taylers moved to a large farm in Southern Rhodesia, looking for a brighter financial future and better education for their children, Doris and her younger brother, Harry. However, Alfred Tayler's attempts at farming were unsuccessful, so the family struggled with poverty for at least twenty years in an isolated area in the district of Banket, one hundred miles west of Mozambique.

Doris was educated first at a convent school and then at a government school for girls, both in the capital city of Salisbury. She returned home at about age twelve because of recurrent eye troubles and received no further formal education. At age sixteen she began working as a typist for a telephone company and was later employed by a law firm. She also worked as a Hansard secretary in the Rhodesian Parliament, then as a typist for the *Guardian,* a South African newspaper based in Cape Town.

In 1939 Doris married Frank Wisdom, a civil servant in Salisbury. They had two children, Jean and John, who remained with their father when the parents divorced in 1943. In 1945 the author married Gottfried Lessing, a half-Jewish German immigrant whom she had met at a Marxist discussion group. In 1947 their son, Peter, was born, and in 1949 she moved to England following another divorce. Although she has traveled widely, Lessing has lived in London ever since; she has never remarried.

In 1950 Lessing published her first novel, *The Grass Is Singing,* which was hailed as one of the first honest presentations of the horrors of the apartheid system and the hypocrisies of the white colonial society that maintained it. However, Lessing was not pleased with such narrow political or sociological readings of her work. She complained that *The Grass*

Is Singing and her first collection of short stories, *This Was the Old Chief's Country* (1951), "were described by reviewers as about the colour problem ... which is not how I see, or saw, them."

Throughout her career Lessing has resisted labels and external literary proscriptions. She was well aware of the material expected of her as a new colonial writer from Rhodesia, and she found such expectations limiting. Lessing sums up the advantages and disadvantages of being a writer from Africa:

> Writers brought up in Africa have many advantages – being at the centre of a modern battlefield; part of a society in rapid, dramatic change. But in a long run it can also be a handicap: to wake up every morning with one's eyes on fresh evidence of inhumanity; to be reminded twenty times a day of injustice, and always the same brand of it, can be limiting. There are other things in living besides injustice, even for the victims of it.

And yet despite Lessing's impatience with those who would hold her to a proscribed role, she has continued unrelentingly to expose injustice and inhumanity in her short fiction as well as her novels. Her short stories benefit from the creative tension caused by the unsettling contrast between the ethical, at times political, commitment of her vision and the cool, frequently humorous, detachment of her ironic tone.

The ten stories in *This Was the Old Chief's Country* present a dramatic, realistic portrait of the social history of white-settler society in southern Rhodesia, which Lessing calls "Zambesia" in her fiction. She translates the divided nature of the hierarchical society into the antagonistic narrative structure of the stories. All of them are structured on polarities or conflicts: between white and black, male and female, English settlers and Afrikaners, children and adults, and dreams and reality. She crafts her fiction so that both content and structure enact the contradictions of colonialism. The high-handedness of the white settlers' attitudes toward their adopted country is seen in their dealings with the land and its people. The male settlers, mostly farmers, view the land as a challenge, their own virgin territory to conquer and control. This militaristic attitude is underlined by the titles of the male protagonists, Majors Gale and Carruthers, in "The De Wets Come to Kloof Grange" and "The Second Hut."

In the stories that depict interactions between blacks and whites, Lessing clearly details the feudal nature of the master/servant relationships in Southern Rhodesia, exposing the injustices and inequities of what she calls "that monstrous thing, the colour bar" in *Going Home* (1957). The title character of "Leopard George" initially appears to be the one exception to the bigoted white landowners in Zambesia. Regarded as an eccentric by his community, this bachelor prefers a wild, isolated piece of land to a lush farm and does not permit hunting on his property. As a result of this — as well as his friendship with his father's servant Old Smoke — George has an unusual closeness to Africa and Africans.

However, he destroys this trust by sleeping with Old Smoke's young wife. George sends her home at night, and she is killed by a leopard. After this episode he places his fear, guilt, and anger at himself onto leopards as symbols of the Africa he cannot tame, and he becomes a ruthless hunter alienated from his African workers. He eventually marries an older white woman and assimilates into white-settler society.

Hence Lessing portrays Africa as an adventurous escape — or at least an elemental challenge — for the men who seek to conquer the land. However, for the white women who marry these men and try to make homes for their families, Africa is both a prison and a cultural desert. If the white men sometimes break through to a limited understanding of Africa, the white women seldom connect with the land or the culture. Lessing portrays white-settler women as doubly alienated from African life: they remain exiles because of their stubborn British identification and outsiders by virtue of their gender.

In "The Second Hut" Major Carruthers's wife is homesick and incapable of being assimilated into her environment. In "Winter in July" Kenneth says, "In a marriage it's necessary for one side to be strong enough to create the illusion," and Lessing portrays how this duty generally falls to the wives. This story shows the chilling results of emotional dishonesty and sterility in relationships; there is a growing moral corruption that seemingly infects most of the white population in Lessing's Zambesia.

"The Second Hut" and "The De Wets Come to Kloof Grange" not only expose gender differences and inequalities in Southern Rhodesia's farm communities, but also explore the ethnic differences between English settlers and their Afrikaans counterparts. While the English farm owners are repelled by the Afrikaners' poverty and lack of sophistication, they grudgingly recognize their ability to survive and adapt to African soil in ways impossible for the English settlers. In the uncomprehending exchanges between blacks and whites, English and Afrikaners, Lessing depicts how the stratified racist society in Rhodesia dehumanizes and separates the people who need each other's strengths and skills in

order to survive. In "The De Wets Come to Kloof Grange," for example, Mrs. Gale attempts to "save" the Afrikaans overseer's wife from what she judges to be a lonely and limited existence, but she ends up alienating the young couple by her total misunderstanding of their culture.

Lessing has a gift for realistic dialogue, especially when expressing social codes through her white characters' accents, vocabularies, and tones; the silences and gaps in their conversations are even more subtly revealing. In contrast, in most of her early stories Africans are silent background figures, although they figure prominently in three of the stories, "No Witchcraft for Sale," "The Nuisance," and "Little Tembi." However, the African characters in "No Witchcraft for Sale" and "Little Tembi" are presented rather paternalistically by Lessing as naive moral touchstones who highlight the callousness of the whites. The little black boy Tembi is "adopted" by the tenderhearted farmer's wife Jane when she is childless, but he is thrown over by her once she has her own children. He is unwilling (or unable) to understand her subsequent abandonment of him and resorts to a life of crime partly as revenge and partly in order to regain her attention. In this tragic story of mutual incomprehension Lessing attacks the inefficacy of liberal values and the misguidedness of charity work without a concomitant program of political and social reform.

In "No Witchcraft for Sale" the protagonist, Gideon, retains his dignity and independence by resisting Western conscription of his healing arts. Lessing portrays the whites' disrespectful behavior as disgracefully uncivilized; they unsuccessfully badger the supposedly uncultured Gideon for his secrets. She also reveals that the whites are the losers in their determined struggle to dominate another culture:

> The Magical drug would remain where it was, unknown and useless, except for the tiny scattering of Africans who had the knowledge, natives who might be digging a ditch for the municipality in a ragged shirt and a pair of patched shorts, but who were still born to healing, hereditary healers, being the nephews or sons of the old witch doctors whose ugly masks and bits of bone and all the uncouth properties of magic were the outward signs of real power and wisdom.

In "The Nuisance" Lessing shows how a good black worker literally gets away with murder in the corrupt society. The fate of the Long One's old wife — the nuisance of the title, she is murdered and thrown down a well — underlines the fact that a black woman's life in this country is valueless. Because the Long One is an invaluable worker, the white family shuts its eyes to his wife's murder, thereby supporting his cruelty and violence.

"The Old Chief Mshlanga" and "A Sunrise on the Veld" are the first of Lessing's many perceptive and powerful coming-of-age stories in which the child's-eye view is dramatically presented. In these two mythic stories the children confront for the first time the fear of isolation and alienation in a foreign land. "The Old Chief Mshlanga," set on a farm in the 1930s, is probably the best-known story of the collection. A sensitive fourteen-year-old white girl confronts the reality that her father's farm originally "was the Old Chief's Country" and that she also bears the collective burden of her race's guilt for dispossessing the original inhabitants. Her mental alienation from Africa, compounded by an education rooted in European myths and literature, is contrasted with the old chief's literal displacement at the end of the story when her father has the offending tribe removed from its ancestral place. She learns the painful lesson that her youth and gender do not exonerate her from culpability: "If one cannot call a country to heel like a dog, neither can one dismiss the past with a smile in an easy gush of feeling, saying: I could not help it. I am also a victim."

In "Sunrise on the Veld" a boy's initial romantic idealization of the rural world that surrounds him as he leaves home before dawn to hunt culminates in an adolescent epiphany:

> There is nothing he couldn't do, nothing! A vision came to him, as he stood there, like when a child hears the word "eternity" and tries to understand it, and time takes possession of the mind . . . and he said aloud, with the blood rising to his head: . . . there is no country in the world I cannot make part of myself, if I choose. I contain the world. I can make of it what I want. If I choose, I can change everything that is going to happen: it depends on me, and what I decide now.

This arrogant, imperialistic vision of life – so characteristic for Lessing of the white colonials' attitude to the land – is crushed by the final scene of the story. The boy's hunt is destroyed by the sight of a wounded duiker being eaten alive by thousands of ants. This countervision confronts him with the impersonal power of nature and the knowledge of his own fragility and mortality:

> It was a swelling feeling of rage and misery and protest that expressed itself in the thought: if I had not come it would have died like this: so why should I interfere? All over the bush things like this happen; they happen all the time; this is how life goes on, by living things dying in anguish. He gripped the gun between his knees and

felt in his own limbs the myriad swarming pain of the twitching animal that could no longer feel, and set his teeth, and said over and over again under his breath: I can't stop it. I can't stop it. There is nothing I can do.

In 1952 Lessing published *Martha Quest,* the first in her five-volume Children of Violence series. The novel is based on autobiographical details, but, in response to what she saw as reviewers' misreadings of the texts, Lessing emphasizes that the series is a "study of the individual conscience in its relations with the collective." The five novels – which also include *A Proper Marriage* (1954), *A Ripple from the Storm* (1958), *Landlocked* (1965), and *The Four-Gated City* (1969) – progress from a conventional bildungsroman form to an apocalyptic global vision. The first four give an extended view of the white-settler society in Rhodesia through the eyes of a disaffected young girl who can find no place for an independent woman in that community. The last novel shows her as an immigrant in London – once more in exile – who turns to various modes of consciousness in order to construct a new society able to survive the inevitable apocalypse.

In *Five: Short Novels* (1953) Lessing experiments with the form described by Dorothy Brewster, in *Doris Lessing* (1965), as "too long for a short story and too short for a novel." "Hunger" seems formulaic and didactic, yet it has proved popular with many readers. The story features the classic "country boy comes to the city" plot, in which the protagonist experiences many trials, succumbs to temptation, but finally breaks through to a vision of truth and redemption. Jabavu – an intelligent, ambitious African boy full of hubris and helpless anger against his menial life – learns from his sufferings and disappointments that he needs a vision of community to sustain him against his isolation.

In *Doris Lessing's Africa* (1978) Michael Thorpe likens "Hunger" to a morality tale, stating that "because there is so much ammunition in the story that may be used against white rule and for African solidarity it has been, as Lessing thinks, one of her 'most liked' despite, or because of, its artistic simplification." The simplistic political message at the end contrasts with the subtler messages in Lessing's other African stories; in *Doris Lessing* (1983) Lorna Sage describes it as "a version of urban pastoral, tinged with a dubious nostalgia for the collective conscience."

"A Home for the Highland Cattle," a highly ironic tale, tells of the "new" kind of settler in Rhodesia: "These days, when people emigrate . . . all they want is a roof over their heads." The story opens with dry geographical, historical, and sociological descriptions of Salisbury. The liberal-minded Gileses come looking for wealth, good company, and a house of their own; instead they find narrow-mindedness, prejudice, and a housing shortage. Marina is left behind in a subleased, semidetached box of an apartment while Philip travels in pursuit of his agricultural research. She confronts the everyday realities of racism, and her liberal values trap her into a paternalistic attitude toward her black male servant, Charlie.

The highland cattle of the title are portrayed in a mid-Victorian painting that symbolizes for Marina the hidebound, tasteless life of its owner. For Charlie, however, the African symbolism of cattle as wealth causes him to revere the awful heirloom piece. The increasing significance of the painting in the story demonstrates how skillfully Lessing infuses even the most mundane, realistic tales and objects with symbolic resonance. The inability of each character to understand the other's attitude toward the picture is symbolic of the cultural chasm that lies between them and their failure to appreciate the other's perspectives. With time Marina inevitably becomes just another white settler who accepts the racist values of the society into which she realizes she must assimilate in order to survive.

"Eldorado," Lessing's rewriting of the classic adventure story, focuses on a trio of people who love each other yet can never understand one another's dreams. Alec Barnes, the father, is a dreamer who begins farming maize but then is lost to his family in his visions of discovering gold. His practical Scottish wife, Maggie, sees his dream merely as "getting something for nothing." She desperately believes that "knowledge freed a man," but their son, Paul, cannot live up to his mother's dreams for his advancement through education because he lacks the ability. Maggie wants both men to adhere to the ways of their hardworking, pragmatic forefathers, but both have been infected by the romantic adventure tales of Africa. The mythic figure of the gold prospector entrances both father and son, and the story ends ironically on a qualified success story when Paul and his miner-mentor, James, find gold on the farm.

"The Antheap" is based on the triangular relationship between old Mr. Macintosh, a millionaire mine owner; Tommy Clarke, Macintosh's engineer's son, whom Macintosh loves as his own; and Dirk, Macintosh's real son, a half-caste rejected by his father. The friendship that develops between the two boys breaks through the barriers of race so that they form a brotherhood united against Macin-

tosh's hypocrisy and pride. Both strive for an equality in the stubborn old man's eyes and finally achieve a grudging concession on his part when he agrees to pay for their university education.

Tommy's art is the key both to his heightened sensitivity toward the emotional and political issues at stake in their lives and to his close relationship to African earth. His creative use of the African soil is in direct contrast to Macintosh's rape of the land. Ironically it is Dirk, born into an oppressed race, who will go on to study law and government in order to claim back power from his oppressors. But the future will not be so simple, and Lessing evades a sentimental conclusion by generalizing outward to the larger political issues behind the story: "The victory was entirely theirs, but now they had to begin again, in the long and difficult struggle to understand what they had won and how they would use it."

"The Other Woman" – a painful tale of love, trust, and abandonment – is the only story set in England. Rose learns to move outward from her parents' home, where she lives as a dutiful daughter, to accept responsibility for herself and to recognize her need to love others. She falls in love with Jimmy, who mistakenly loves her for what he sees as her vulnerability and helplessness. Once she assumes the role of wife and the power in the relationship shifts, he tries to leave. Enlightened by Jimmy's savvy first wife, Rose bands together with her to raise his children and the daughter of Rose's former boyfriend, who was killed during World War II.

This final, bittersweet scene dramatizes how women were assuming more central, active roles in order to support themselves and their children in the disrupted society brought on by the war. All five stories depict societies in transition. Much as Lessing experiments with new forms in the collection, her protagonists struggle to come to terms with new modes of living and social structures.

In 1956 Lessing produced *A Retreat to Innocence,* a novel that she has since disowned and blocked from republication. The text, with its uncritical pro-Communist stance, is a product of Lessing's continuing commitment to Marxism in the 1950s. After the Soviet Union invaded Hungary in 1956, Lessing left the English Communist party as did many other disillusioned members. *A Retreat to Innocence,* while propagandist in nature, is interesting as a historical marker in Lessing's career and ideological development. In 1956 Lessing visited Rhodesia after seven years in England. She was declared a prohibited immigrant on her departure because of her opposition to the racist regime, expressed in *Going Home* (1957), a factual, anecdotal account of her return to Rhodesia.

The Habit of Loving, Lessing's third collection of short stories, was also published in 1957. Only six of the seventeen stories are set in southern Africa, indicating her gradual shift from African themes and settings. Thorpe chronicles Lessing's African narratives, placing *The Habit of Loving* within what he calls her "African period": "The African stories belong almost entirely to the early and mid-'fifties, the period during which the first three books of the 'Children of Violence' sequence came out – in 1952, 1954, and 1958. This period, 1950–1958, may truly be called her 'African' period, when her work drew most intensively upon her African experience and involvement."

"Lucy Grange" and "Getting off the Altitude" sympathetically describe the deprivations and emotional stagnation of white women confined to isolated farms in Rhodesia. "Getting off the Altitude" gives the young-girl narrator a glimpse into the emotional and sexual entanglements of the Slatters' marriage. Mrs. Slatter's helplessness in the face of her husband's brutality and her continued presence despite his flagrant infidelity do not promise an independent or happy future for the narrator as she becomes a woman.

Lucy Grange is yet another cultured woman married to an unsympathetic partner. Her alienation from her surroundings leads her to give herself to the first sympathetic man who presents himself – an unattractive insurance salesman. From this opportunist she learns that "in a country like this we all learn to accept the second-rate," Lessing's succinct condemnation of the transplanted-settler society and its future.

In "Flavours of Exile" Lessing portrays a mother's perpetuation of what M. J. Daymond (*Ariel,* July 1986) calls "the cultural lie" – her blind clinging to the nostalgia of a long-dead English past idolized as "Home." While her daughter's "thoughts were on my own inheritance of veldt and sun," the mother refuses to accept the needs and realities of the present. "A Mild Attack of Locusts" is a story of survival and adjustment. The swarm of locusts that devastates a farm precipitates a crisis in which Margaret is forced to change from a city girl who does not understand or appreciate the rigors of farm life to a woman who has confronted the awful power of nature and learned to survive.

In three of the coming-of-age stories in this collection – "Flavours of Exile," "The Words He Said," and "Through the Tunnel" – Lessing explores how the male socialization process seems far less complicated than that of females. The boy in "Through the Tunnel" puts himself through a physical test in order to prove to himself that he is a man, whereas the two young-girl protagonists are initiated into womanhood by being rejected and hurt by two young men. The latent sexual danger in these stories is made manifest in the menacing, surrealistic "Plants and Girls," in which the male protagonist kills a young girl in a pantheistic sexual frenzy.

The coming-of-age stories in *The Habit of Loving* are counterbalanced by stories centered on the dilemmas and deprivations of middle and old age. The old-age stories feature various selfish old men. In "The Woman" two old men remember sexual conquests and vie for the attention of a young waitress who regards them with contempt. In "The Witness" a self-deluded voyeur and drunkard loses his last shred of dignity at work but refuses to come to terms with himself in his one brief moment of self-recognition. In "The Habit of Loving" aging George Talbot, who has made his living through the theater, is ironically taken in by the role-playing of Bobby, a thirty-five-year-old cabaret artist. Her rejection of all romantic illusions is the final blow that destroys George's protective screen, and he comes face-to-face with his own selfishness. However, this self-knowledge comes too late to save their relationship or end her suffering.

In contrast to the brutal tales of old age's disappointments, "Flight" is a sympathetic treatment of the selfishness and jealousies of old age. Lessing treats a grandfather's inability to let go of his granddaughter with compassion and honesty. In a symbolic last scene of leave-taking and love the grandfather releases his favorite racing pigeon into flight, much as he learns to let his last granddaughter go to find happiness with her future husband.

The stories of old men's weaknesses are counterbalanced by stories of middle-aged women's limitations and disappointments in love. "Wine" is told by a dispassionate narrator who simply names the protagonists as "the man/he" and "the woman/she," thereby universalizing the couple and their tired alienation from each other in Paris, traditionally the city of lovers. In "He" a downtrodden wife, after a brief mutinous period, finally decides to return to a life of drudgery with a selfish husband rather than settle for a lonely but independent existence without someone who needs her. In these stories Lessing exposes how both genders are trapped in their conflicting social roles, incapable of helping the other change or compromise and therefore doomed always to disappointment in each other.

Lessing scrutinizes tourists and tourism in at least two stories in *The Habit of Loving*. In "Pleasure" Mary Rogers confronts her self-aggrandizing motives for traveling to the south of France for her annual vacation. In "The Eyes of God in Paradise" two British doctors discover that the past lives on to menace the present while on a vacation in Bavaria in 1951. Instead of enjoying a picture-postcard holiday in the mountains, the couple are oppressed by the shadow of Nazism looming over every social contact and event. This Kafkaesque story is weighted too heavily with historical and sociological observations that darken, and at times overwhelm, the action. In both stories Lessing emphasizes the voyeuristic nature of tourism.

"The Day Stalin Died" is an anomaly in the collection. This dry, diarylike piece chronicles the narrator's day in London, full of incidental conversations, meeting, decisions, actions, and thoughts. At the end of the story the news of Joseph Stalin's death is presented as one of these daily trifles. The tone and subject matter are in marked contrast to those of *A Retreat to Innocence,* and the story is the epitome of the ironic, detached style for which Lessing is so well known.

Lessing's 1950s short stories demonstrate her commitment to social realism. As Jenny Taylor explains in *Notebooks/Memoirs/Archives: Reading and Rereading Doris Lessing* (1982): "Her colonial identity also contributed to her passionate and explicit adherence to classic realism both as a style and as an attitude – that of racial liberal humanism – in the 1950s." From 1957 to 1962, however, Lessing experimented with other genres of writing, including the nonfictional *Going Home;* a collection of poetry, *Fourteen Poems* (1959); *In Pursuit of the English: A Documentary* (1960), in which, as an immigrant, she defamiliarizes and lightly satirizes English society; and two plays, *Each His Own Wilderness* (1959) and *Play with a Tiger* (1962), both of which were produced in London.

In 1962 Lessing published *The Golden Notebook,* which is generally regarded as her greatest work. This complex novel tells of Anna Freeman Wulf's life and struggles for self-definition through interlocking "notebooks." The novel is set entirely in England, and Sprague asserts in *Re-Reading the Short Story* (1989), that "*The Golden Notebook* is Lessing's first successful novel about her 'adopted' country; in that novel her fiction, so to speak, catches up with her life." *A Man and Two Women* (1963) contains stories written during the composition of *The Golden Notebook.* As a consequence the two texts are intimately related, both in form and content. The

form of *The Golden Notebook* is episodic, what the protagonist denigrates as "pastiche" and what Sprague describes as "a loosely woven collection of short stories and novellas." Lessing incorporates short stories within the novel, in which she also examines the generic assumptions about and limitations of the short-fiction form. As a result *The Golden Notebook* is a highly self-conscious text that also introduces issues explored in Lessing's later literary projects.

A Man and Two Women contains nineteen stories that interrelate in various ways and appear to move inexorably toward the final story as a result of its teleological title, "To Room Nineteen." The collection examines relationships between men and women who are attracted or repelled by one another in various social configurations and emotional situations. Lessing appears to hold out little promise of compromise or mutual understanding between the sexes. These stories generally portray private psychological dramas and are consequently stylistically more disjointed and experimental than her earlier stories.

Three stories dramatize the explosive quality of sexual attraction and the closeness of its connection with the lust for power. In the opening story, "One Off the Short List," a self-hating former novelist thinks he can regain his lost self-esteem by sexually dominating a series of up-and-coming women on his "short list." He forces himself on a successful theater designer in order to prove himself both personally and publicly. However, the woman retains her dignity despite his raping her, and the man ultimately recognizes that he has engineered his own humiliation and defeat.

In "A Woman on a Roof" three men working on a roof during a hot summer day in London are piqued by a sunbathing woman's indifference to their attentions. They transfer all their frustrations or fantasies onto her until the insufferable tension is broken by cooling rain, which also drives away the sunbather. "Each Other" is a Wagnerian tale of sister/brother incest in a London flat. While Freda's husband is a traditional male who attempts to dominate his wife, her brother, Fred, offers her a relationship that is an equal melding of personalities. And yet the two men seem to be complementary for the woman in this triangular relationship. With one she allows only sexual bonding, and with the other she achieves spiritual and emotional union. This story presents Lessing's perspective on the limitations of both familial and social relationships.

Some of the stories present the struggles of middle-aged women trying to create new lives and roles that allow them a measure of independence. In "Our Friend Judith" the narrator is frustrated in her attempts to analyze and mold her friend Judith, who is equally determined in her efforts to maintain detachment from other people. While the reader is partially sympathetic to Judith's evasiveness as an attempt to maintain her privacy, she ultimately alienates herself from life because of her determination to repress all emotions.

"To Room Nineteen" details the tragic result of such sustained repression of emotion and instinct in favor of the total domination of the intellect. Lorna Sage terms this story "a suicidal variant on *The Summer Before the Dark*," the 1973 novel in which Lessing also presents a middle-aged woman's confrontation with her loss of identity. "To Room Nineteen" is told by a detached third-person narrator, a device that emphasizes the way in which the protagonist pitches intelligence against emotion. The first sentence explains Susan Rawlings's problem dispassionately and incorrectly: "This is a story, I suppose, about a failure in intelligence: the Rawlings' marriage was grounded in intelligence."

Lessing portrays how a middle-aged woman finds herself trapped in the socially sanctioned roles of wife and mother, without identity or privacy. Susan tries to combat her emptiness by escaping her home, husband, and children in the dingy hotel room of the title. This room becomes symbolic of the space that Susan needs in order to learn how to reconstruct her identity. However, her husband invades this space when he has her followed by a private detective, so that Susan's final refuge is violated and she is driven to commit suicide to escape fully. Lessing presents Susan's death more as a release than a negation.

"Between Men" and "How I Finally Lost My Heart" are two humorous tales with serious undertones. "Between Men" satirizes the survival attempts of two aging women who have been betrayed by the men who keep them and for whom they live. Their drunken promises to renounce men and regain their self-respect and independence together are clearly doomed to failure, for Lessing portrays how these two women are purely male-directed. "How I Finally Lost My Heart" is a playfully parodic story that poses as an instructional tale of romance but is actually antiromantic. The female protagonist, disappointed in love one too many times, determines literally to rid herself of her heart, the root of all her sorrow. The surreal events that follow are unsettling and compelling, as is the disjunction between the protagonist's jaunty tone and her tragic subject.

The collection includes four South African stories: "The New Man," another coming-of-age story; "The Story of Two Dogs," based on Lessing's childhood memories of two dogs that ran wild; "A Letter from Home," a farcical story told in a South African vernacular that does not quite ring true; and "The Sun Between Their Feet," the most successful of the four. Another story, "Outside the Ministry," details the meeting of two African politicians and their henchmen as they decide the fate of their hapless country in a corrupt neocolonial power struggle.

"The Sun Between Their Feet" dramatizes how powerless the individual creature is to change nature's course. Lessing does not romanticize the natural order here; the actions of the dung beetles appear both mindless and courageous. Beauty and horror are inextricably linked, as are courage and futility, in the repeated attempts of the dung beetles to scale the heights of a rock with their precious cargo. The dung beetles are the symbolic center of the story, but the emotional duality experienced by the narrator gives the story its depth and subtlety.

Two stories deal directly with madness and schizophrenia, topics that fascinate Lessing and inform many of her novels and short stories. "England versus England" is her reworking of the "scholarship boy" tale. She explores the tragic effects of the class system on a sensitive young man who is driven to the point of a nervous breakdown by the conflicting codes of the two worlds in which he lives. He is haunted by a self-hating inner voice that mocks him when his divided self is at odds. His intellect is unable to save him when he becomes increasingly incapable of reconciling the values and behavior of his poverty-stricken mining family and his student life at Oxford.

"Dialogue" explores the split between the outer, visible world (the shabby London street) from which the visiting woman comes and the inner, silent world (the enclosed tower flat) of her former lover, who describes himself as "the disconnected" in his mental fragmentation and fragility. By portraying the closeness of the two characters and their struggle to connect over a common abyss, Lessing makes the reader question the nature (and interchangeability) of sanity and madness. The protective yet confining rooms in this story and "To Room Nineteen" are crucial psychological symbols.

Two stories address the importance of art in women's lives. In "A Man and Two Women" the birth of a baby upsets the fragile balance not only between marriage and career, but also between the friendship of two couples. Dorothy's postnatal withdrawal from her husband, together with her loss of interest in her art, raises questions about the all-consuming potential of motherhood for women. Lessing also satirizes the artist's self-conscious posturing, which is undermined completely by the woman's instinctual behavior after birth.

"Two Potters" questions the nature of reality and the relationship of dreams and art to life. As in *The Summer Before the Dark,* the narrator/writer is caught up in interpreting a serial dream – this time about an African potter – that develops in response to outside events. The writer takes poetic license with her dream, but she is shown by her friend the potter how best to integrate her own creative whimsy into the narrative, much as the potter integrates her own artistic vision into her everyday family life. The stories about the relation of art to life and the interconnectedness of women's creativity with their emotional well-being make it clear why Virginia Tiger (*Modern Fiction Studies,* Autumn 1990) calls *A Man and Two Women* "the most self-reflexive of Lessing's collections."

African Stories (1964) is important not only for its inclusion of Lessing's thirty stories set in Africa, but also for its succinct author's preface, which details much of Lessing's philosophy about short-story writing. Lynn Suckenick, in *Doris Lessing: Critical Studies* (1974), analyzes awareness of "the bifurcation of sense and sensibility and the meaning it presents to women." Lessing's consciousness of the intellectual/emotional split between men and women is expressed in the preface to *African Stories:*

> "The Pig" and "The Trinket Box" are two of my earliest. I see them as two forks of a road. The second – intense, careful, self-conscious, mannered – could have led to a kind of writing usually described as "feminine." The style of "The Pig" is straight, broad, direct; is much less beguiling, but is the highway to the kind of writing that has the freedom to develop as it likes.

While Lessing points to these two stories as being the poles of two separate styles of writing, many of her stories incorporate both styles successfully. "The Pig" – written in the "masculine" style – appears simple and direct, but it is actually carefully crafted so that the events and consequences seem inevitable and the action linear. The story presents a double masculine-revenge plot: it pits the white farmer against his black workers and the overseer against his wife's lover.

In contrast "The Trinket Box" has a feminine cast of characters, narrator, and theme, while its style is personal, emotionally laden, and sensuous. It appears to be more complex than "The Pig" because it focuses on emotions rather than actions.

Despite Lessing's separation of the masculine and feminine styles, her best stories are usually an amalgam of both; her talent lies in her ability to integrate both emotional and narrative development in her fiction.

"The Black Madonna" opens *African Stories,* probably because Lessing feels so strongly about it: "I am addicted to 'The Black Madonna,' which is full of the bile that in fact I feel for the 'white' society in Southern Rhodesia as I knew and hated it." The story could almost be characterized as Lessing's revenge against white colonial Rhodesian society, for she brutally exposes Zambesian philistinism and bigotry in a tragicomic tale of friendship and betrayal. Michele, an Italian intern in Zambesia during World War II, paints amateur frescoes and portraits that are revered by the ignorant white colonials. He is befriended by another exile figure, a fascist soldier named Captain Stocker, who fears women and can therefore find happiness only with subordinate black women, putting his emotions in conflict with his racist beliefs. The story ends with the collapse of their friendship when Michele laughs at the white colonial society that Captain Stocker must uphold for his own survival. With Michele's departure Stocker loses his chance at confronting his loneliness and emotional sterility.

Lessing classifies *Briefing for a Descent into Hell* (1971) as "inner-space fiction." This novel is unusual for Lessing in that a man, a classics professor named Charles Watkins, is its chief protagonist. He suffers a mental breakdown and journeys through various regions of consciousness as he searches for mental unity. Charles travels from innocence to experience in a confrontation with his own evil and that of humanity, coming to the realization that disaster threatens humankind. When he is restored to his "normal" self at the end of the novel, however, he forgets this urgent message. Once more Lessing strives for the realization that much can be learned from what is classified as "madness."

The Story of a Non-Marrying Man and Other Stories (1972; published in the United States as *The Temptation of Jack Orkney and Other Stories,* 1972) is a collection of thirteen stories. While it is notable for its diversity of narrative style and subject, all the stories demonstrate Lessing's increasingly cynical vision of human weakness and self-destructiveness. "Side Benefits of an Honourable Profession" and "An Unposted Love Letter" focus on the theater as a medium for human expression and fallibility. These two sardonic pieces examine the interchanges between art and life, truth and fiction. The anecdotal gossip that fills "Side Benefits of an Honourable

Profession" exposes the human frailties evinced by the artists when offstage, in contrast to their godlike qualities when on show. In "An Unposted Love Letter" the monologue, which Lessing frames in an epistolary form, accentuates the isolated quality of the aging actress's life; she is alone because of her decision to sacrifice her personal life for her art. An integral part of her artistry and dedication to her craft has involved the creation of a theatrical persona as her lifework.

Two related stories, "Not a Very Nice Story" and "Out of the Fountain," are metafictional pieces that explore their own narrative methods, specifically how the choice of perspective or point of view dictates meaning in life as in art. "Out of the Fountain" is presented as a modern fairy-tale allegory that ends abruptly and without the traditional happy conclusion. "Not a Very Nice Story" is, in contrast, a mundane tale of two married couples and infidelity, told in a dry, ironic style by a narrator who appears more concerned with how to tell the tale effectively than with what is being told. This device forces the reader to examine and question the characters' inner motivations, as well as to analyze the mechanics of the story. "Not a Very Nice Story" and "Out of the Fountain" are good examples of how Lessing's fiction was becoming increasingly self-referential. She exposes the limitations of language and narrative forms along with the limitations of social institutions. As her narrative control grew, she began increasingly to explore the conventions and restraints of narrative as they affect life and epistemology.

There are only two African pieces in the collection. The title "Spies I Have Known" spoofs the secrecy of espionage, while the ironic, anecdotal style adopted by the narrator emphasizes the absurdity of such tales of misunderstanding and double-dealing. "The Story of a Non-Marrying Man" is told from the perspective of a ten- or twelve-year-old who meets the man of the title, Johnny Blakeworthy, "at the end of his life." Blakeworthy goes "native" after a life of moving from wife to wife and place to place but never finding the peace and simplicity for which he longs. Finally he settles in a remote African village with a black wife who makes no demands on him and knows nothing of Western "civilization." This piece is unusual among the African stories for its sympathy toward the masculine viewpoint; Lessing portrays the women in Blakeworthy's life as domestic drudges who care only for their own material well-being.

"The Temptation of Jack Orkney" continues in the mode of *Briefing for a Descent into Hell* as Jack

Orkney, thrown into self-scrutiny by his father's death and his own temporary sabbatical from work, explores the depths of his consciousness. On his psychic journey Orkney encounters the ever-present threat of madness, and, as the title suggests, he toys with religious commitment in the face of his helplessness. Ultimately, however, Orkney realizes that religion, together with politics and the responsibilities of family, merely permits people to avoid their existential aloneness. Lessing's controlled ironic tone holds Orkney's conflicting experiences and insights in a precarious balance, skillfully mirroring the fragility of his psyche. While some critics consider the collection inconsequential, most agree that "The Temptation of Jack Orkney" is an extremely powerful story.

An apocalyptic story that foreshadows Lessing's science-fiction phase, "Report on the Threatened City" features the observations of intelligent, sympathetic alien beings who come to Earth to save humans from certain disaster. These narrators frustratedly document the intransigent stupidity of earthlings until they are forced finally to give up their mission of rescue. Lessing's dark vision of global disintegration is also portrayed in a more realistic story, "An Old Woman and Her Cat." This violent, tragic tale exposes the cruelty of humanity and its social institutions in their abandonment of an old lady to a life of wandering and destitution. She finds refuge in a dead area of London ripe for "development": "There was no glass left anywhere. The flooring was mostly gone, leaving small platforms and juts of planking over basements full of water. The ceilings were crumbling. The roofs were going. The houses were like bombed buildings." Such scenes of desolation and collapse are taken up in Lessing's novel *Memoirs of a Survivor* (1974).

The cynical, apocalyptic aspects of *The Story of a Non-Marrying Man* are broken up by three deliberately interspersed, idyllic pastoral pieces that celebrate the natural beauty of London parks: "A Year in Regent's Park," "Lions, Leaves, Roses," and "The Other Garden." These descriptive, lyrical sketches contrast starkly with the revelations of human frailty and evil in the other stories. The structural division of the collection between the dark and light sides of modern society and the human psyche is almost schizophrenic. The collection marries utopian natural beauty with dystopian human works and juxtaposes Lessing's sardonic narrative style with lyrical descriptive passages. In the three park sketches humans and nature manage to achieve a harmonious existence in scattered green oases in the heart of London, giving the

Lessing, circa 1992 (photograph by Ingrid von Kruse)

reader some hope of regeneration to counter Lessing's increasingly apocalyptic visions. After *The Story of a Non-Marrying Man* Lessing concentrated on novel writing for twenty years before she returned to the short-fiction genre.

In 1978 Lessing's English stories were collected in two volumes; the collection was published in the United States in one volume, *Stories* (1978). The thirty-five stories are mostly set in England and focus on women. All but one, "The Other Woman" (*Five*), are from *The Habit of Loving, A Man and Two Women,* and *The Story of a Non-Marrying Man.*

In 1992 Lessing produced two books: a collection of eighteen new short stories, *The Real Thing: Stories and Sketches* and *African Laughter: Four Visits to Zimbabwe.* In *African Laughter,* a nonfictional sequel to *Going Home,* Lessing sympathetically continues to document the political and social upheavals in Zimbabwean society. This work, together with Lessing's latest novels, seems to signal her return to social and literary realism, a trend that she continues in her most recent short-fiction collection. Consequently, *The Real Thing* appears to be a retreat into a traditionalism of style and content for those readers and critics who have become accustomed to Lessing's fictional experiments. As Katherine Fishburn states in her review of the collection for the *Doris Lessing Newsletter* (Winter 1993): "At first glance, what seems remarkable about these eighteen

pieces is how unremarkable they are. . . . Just a lot of ordinary folks trying to muddle through life and loving in late-twentieth-century London." For the first time Lessing appears to have put her African roots behind her in her short fiction; *The Real Thing* is a completely English collection. Nonetheless, she remains true to her original role as social critic as she continues to chronicle a society in decline.

Many of the stories demonstrate the collapse of societal structures that ironically harm the very people they are supposed to support. As the title suggests, the medical profession portrayed in "Womb Ward" dehumanizes and reduces women to their physical parts and defects. In "Casualty" the waiting patients compete pettishly for the doctors' attention until confronted with a fatality, a reminder of their own mortality. "D.H.S.S." is a bitterly ironic commentary on how the social services create resentment and dependence in those they are supposed to serve. "The Mother of the Child in Question" portrays the quiet revolt of a jaded social worker who, despite her obstruction of his work, applauds a stubborn mother's refusal to accept the labeling of her daughter as "subnormal."

Many critics have attacked the somewhat sprawling narrative style and uneven prose in Lessing's novels. Her ability to write tight, spare prose is perhaps best seen in her short fiction and is shown to particular advantage in the vignette "Principles." Here Lessing returns to one of her most central concerns: the chasm of misunderstanding and miscommunication that yawns between the genders. With an understated tone Lessing transforms the confrontation of two anonymous protagonists in a traffic jam into an ironically symbolic event.

The "schizophrenia" of *The Story of a Non-Marrying Man* is also in evidence in *The Real Thing,* for Lessing appears split between her need to expose the dark side of human nature and the fallibility of social structures and her desire to celebrate the eternal, inspirational quality of her environment. Some of the stories offer sensuous sketches of London that point out the beauty and oases that still serve to rejuvenate and delight the jaded city dwellers who take the time to enjoy and notice them. "In Defence of the Underground" is a humorous apologia for London in which Lessing celebrates the very things that most malcontents deplore about the city. The English edition of *The Real Thing* is titled *London Observed,* which perhaps sums up the serene tenor and everyday content of this work most succinctly. Critics have been strongly divided about this latest collection; some applaud

Lessing's new relaxed humor and lyrical prose, while others deplore what they consider to be the slightness of her subject matter and the conservatism of her form.

Critics have found it extremely hard to categorize Lessing, for she has at various stages of her life espoused different causes and been labeled over again: feminist, Marxist, mystic, materialist, experimentalist, realist, conservative. While she displays a powerful commitment to causes she views as vital to the survival of humankind, her greatest strength lies in her flexibility. She is always prepared to change her views to accommodate new insights and contradictions.

Lessing's oeuvre encompasses an assortment of genres: science fiction, drama, essays, bildungsroman, autobiography, short stories, and poetry. She displays a tireless interest in the interplay of idea and form; consequently her texts also explore the shaping qualities of the genre in which she writes. Feminists have found her works a fruitful ground for investigating the interplay of gender and genre. Despite her experimentation with other genres Lessing's commitment to the short story is clear: "Some writers I know have stopped writing short stories because, as they say, 'there is no market for them.' Others like myself, the addicts, go on, and I suspect would go on even if there really wasn't any home for them but a private drawer."

Interviews:

Joyce Carol Oates, "A Visit with Doris Lessing," *Southern Review,* 9 (October 1973): 873–882;

C. J. Driver, "Profile 8: Doris Lessing," *New Review,* 1 (November 1974): 17–23;

Minda Bikman, "A Talk with Doris Lessing," *New York Times Book Review,* 30 March 1980, pp. 1, 24–27;

Christopher Bigsby, "Doris Lessing: An Interview," in his *The Radical Imagination and the Liberal Tradition* (London: Junction, 1981), pp. 190–208;

Lesley Hazelton, "Doris Lessing on Feminism, Communism, and 'Space Fiction,' " *New York Times Magazine,* 25 July 1982, pp. 20–21, 26–29;

Eve Bertelsen, "An Interview with Doris Lessing," *Journal of Commonwealth Literature,* 21, no. 1 (1986): 134–161;

Paul Barker, "A Golden Notebook of 70 Years of Dreams," *Independent* (London), 16 October 1989, p. 19;

E. Jane Dickson, "City of the Mind," *Sunday Times* (London), 10 May 1992, VII: 6–7.

Bibliographies:

Catherina Ipp, *Doris Lessing: A Bibliography* (Johannesburg: University of Witwatersrand Press, 1967);

Selma Burkom and Margaret Williams, *Doris Lessing: A Checklist of Primary and Secondary Sources* (Troy, N.Y.: Whitston, 1973);

Dee Seligman, *Doris Lessing: An Annotated Bibliography of Criticism* (Westport, Conn.: Greenwood Press, 1981).

References:

Elizabeth Abel, "Resisting the Exchange: Brother-Sister Incest in Fiction by Doris Lessing," in *Doris Lessing: The Alchemy of Survival,* edited by Carey Kaplan and Ellen Cronan Rose (Athens: Ohio University Press, 1988), pp. 115–126;

Orphia Jane Allen, "Interpreting 'Flavours of Exile,' " *Doris Lessing Newsletter,* 7 (Summer 1983): 8, 12;

Allen, "Interpreting 'The Sun Between Their Feet,' " *Doris Lessing Newsletter,* 5 (Winter 1981): 1–2;

Allen, "Structure and Motif in Doris Lessing's *A Man and Two Women,*" *Modern Fiction Studies,* 26 (Spring 1980): 63–74;

Margaret Atack, "Towards a Narrative Analysis of *A Man and Two Women,*" in *Notebooks/Memoirs/Archives: Reading and Rereading Doris Lessing,* edited by Jenny Taylor (London & Boston: Routledge, 1982), pp. 135–163;

Shuli Barzilai, "Unmaking the Words that Make Us: Doris Lessing's 'How I Finally Lost My Heart,' " *Style,* 22 (Winter 1988): 595–611;

Dorothy Brewster, *Doris Lessing* (New York: Twayne, 1965);

Margaret K. Butcher, " 'Two Forks of a Road': Divergence and Convergence in the Short Stories of Doris Lessing," *Modern Fiction Studies,* 26 (Spring 1980): 55–61;

M. J. Daymond, "Areas of the Mind: The Memoirs of a Survivor and Doris Lessing's *African Stories,*" *Ariel,* 17 (July 1986): 65–82;

Sharon Dean, "Marriage, Motherhood, and Lessing's 'To Room Nineteen,' " *Doris Lessing Newsletter,* 5 (Summer 1981): 1, 14;

John Hakac, "Budding Profanity in 'A Sunrise on the Veld,' " *Doris Lessing Newsletter,* 10 (Spring 1986): 13;

Linda H. Halisky, "Redeeming the Irrational: The Inextricable Heroines of 'A Sorrowful Woman' and 'To Room Nineteen,' " *Studies in Short Fiction,* 27 (Winter 1990): 45–54;

Clare Hanson, "Each Other: Images of Otherness in the Short Fiction of Doris Lessing, Jean Rhys, and Angela Carter," *Journal of the Short Story in English,* 10 (Spring 1988): 67–82;

Hanson, "Free Shorter: The Shorter Fiction of Doris Lessing," *Doris Lessing Newsletter,* 9 (Spring 1985): 7–8, 14;

Hanson, "The Woman Writer as Exile: Gender and Possession in the African Stories of Doris Lessing," in *Critical Essays on Doris Lessing,* edited by Claire Sprague and Virginia Tiger (Boston: G. K. Hall, 1986), pp. 107–114;

Tricia Hayes, "Adolescent Awakenings in the Fiction of Doris Lessing," *Doris Lessing Newsletter,* 3 (Summer 1979): 9–10;

Mona Knapp, *Doris Lessing* (New York: Ungar, 1984);

Maurine Magliocco, "Doris Lessing's 'A Man and Two Women': It Is Universal?," *Denver Quarterly,* 17 (Winter 1983): 29–39;

Eileen Manoin, "'Not About the Colour Problem': Doris Lessing's Portrayal of the Colonial Order," *World Literature Written in English,* 21 (Autumn 1982): 434–455;

Kay McCormick, "The Child's Perspective in *Five African Stories,*" *Doris Lessing Newsletter,* 9 (Fall 1985): 13, 18;

Annis Pratt and L. S. Dembo, eds., *Doris Lessing: Critical Studies* (Madison: University of Wisconsin Press, 1974);

Virginia Pruitt, "The Crucial Balance: A Theme in Lessing's Short Fiction," *Studies in Short Fiction,* 18 (Summer 1981): 281–285;

Lorna Sage, *Doris Lessing* (London & New York: Methuen, 1983);

Angela Smith, "In a Divided Mind," *Doris Lessing Newsletter,* 8 (Spring 1984): 3–4, 14;

Claire Sprague, "Genre Reversals in Doris Lessing: Stories Like Novels and Novels Like Stories," in *Re-Reading the Short Story,* edited by Hanson (New York: St. Martin's Press, 1989), pp. 110–125;

Sprague, "The Politics of Sibling Incest in Doris Lessing's 'Each Other,'" *San Jose Studies,* 11 (Spring 1985): 42–49;

Michael Thorpe, *Doris Lessing's Africa* (London: Evans, 1978);

Virginia Tiger, "Taking Hands and Dancing in (Dis)Unity: Story to Storied in Doris Lessing's 'To Room Nineteen' and 'A Room,'" *Modern Fiction Studies,* 36 (Autumn 1990): 421–433.

Papers:
The University of Tulsa Library has typescripts for *Memoirs of a Survivor* and the story "The Temptation of Jack Orkney," as well as some letters.

J. B. Priestley

(13 September 1894 - 14 August 1984)

Bes Stark Spangler
Peace College

See also the Priestley entries in *DLB 10: Modern British Dramatists, 1900–1945: Part 2; DLB 34: British Novelists, 1890–1929: Traditionalists; DLB 77: British Mystery Writers, 1920–1939; DLB 100: Modern British Essayists, Second Series;* and *DLB Yearbook: 1984.*

SELECTED BOOKS: *The Chapman of Rhymes* (London: Moring, 1918);

Brief Diversions: Being Tales, Travesties, and Epigrams (Cambridge: Bowes & Bowes, 1922);

Papers from Lilliput (Cambridge: Bowes & Bowes, 1922);

I for One (London: Lane, 1923; New York: Dodd, Mead, 1924);

Figures in Modern Literature (London: Lane, 1924; New York: Dodd, Mead, 1924);

The English Comic Characters (London: Lane, 1925; New York: Dodd, Mead, 1925);

George Meredith (London: Macmillan, 1926; New York: Macmillan, 1926);

Talking (London: Jarrolds, 1926; New York & London: Harper, 1926);

Essays of Today and Yesterday (London: Harrap, 1926);

Open House: A Book of Essays (London: Heinemann, 1927; New York & London: Harper, 1927);

Thomas Love Peacock (London: Macmillan, 1927; New York: Macmillan, 1927);

The English Novel (London: Benn, 1927; revised edition, London & New York: Nelson, 1935);

Adam in Moonshine (London: Heinemann, 1927; New York: Harper, 1927);

Benighted (London: Heinemann, 1927); republished as *The Old Dark House* (New York: Harper, 1928);

Apes and Angels: A Book of Essays (London: Methuen, 1928); republished as *Too Many People, and Other Reflections* (New York: Harper, 1928);

The Balconinny, and Other Essays (London: Methuen, 1929); republished as *The Balconinny* (New York & London: Harper, 1930);

J. B. Priestley, September 1961

English Humour (London & New York: Longmans, Green, 1929; Folcroft, Pa.: Folcroft Library Editions, 1973; revised edition, London: Heinemann, 1976);

The Good Companions (London: Heinemann, 1929; New York: Harper, 1929);

Farthing Hall, by Priestley and Hugh Walpole (London: Macmillan, 1929; Garden City, N.Y.: Doubleday, Doran, 1929);

The Town Major of Miraucourt (London: Heinemann, 1930);

Angel Pavement (London: Heinemann, 1930; New York & London: Harper, 1930);

Dangerous Corner: A Play in Three Acts (London: Heinemann, 1932; New York, Los Angeles & London: French, 1932);

Faraway (London: Heinemann, 1932; New York: Harper, 1932);

The Lost Generation: An Armistice Day Article (London: Peace Committee of the Society of Friends, 1932);

Self-selected Essays (London: Heinemann, 1932; New York & London: Harper, 1933);

Dangerous Corner: A Novel by Priestley and Ruth Holland (London: Hamilton, 1932);

I'll Tell You Everything, by Priestley and Gerald Bullett (New York: Macmillan, 1932); republished as *I'll Tell You Everything: A Frolic* (London: Heinemann, 1933);

The Roundabout: A Comedy in Three Acts (London: Heinemann, 1933; New York: French, 1933);

Albert Goes Through (London: Heinemann, 1933; New York & London: Harper, 1933);

Wonder Hero (London: Heinemann, 1933; New York & London: Harper, 1933);

Eden End: A Play in Three Acts (London: Heinemann, 1934; New York & Los Angeles: French, 1935);

English Journey: Being a Rambling but Truthful Account of What One Man Saw and Heard and Felt and Thought during a Journey through England during the Autumn of the Year 1933 (London: Heinemann/Gollancz, 1934; New York & London: Harper, 1934);

Laburnum Grove: An Immoral Comedy in Three Acts (London: Heinemann, 1934; New York & Los Angeles: French, 1935);

Four-in-Hand (London: Heinemann, 1934) – comprises *Adam in Moonshine, Laburnum Grove, The Roundabout,* short stories, and essays;

You and Me and War (London: National Peace Council, 1935);

The Good Companions; A Play in Two Acts, dramatized by Priestley and Edward Knoblock (London, New York & Los Angeles: French, 1935);

Cornelius: A Business Affair in Three Transactions (London & Toronto: Heinemann, 1935; New York & Los Angeles: French, 1936);

Three Plays and a Preface (London: Heinemann, 1935; New York & London: Harper, 1935) – comprises "Preface," *Dangerous Corner: A Play in Three Acts, Eden End: A Play in Three Acts,* and *Cornelius: A Business Affair in Three Transactions;*

Duet in Floodlight: A Comedy (London & Toronto: Heinemann, 1935);

Spring Tide, by Priestley (as Peter Goldsmith) and George Billiam (London: Heinemann, 1936);

Bees on the Boatdeck: A Farcical Tragedy in Two Acts (London: Heinemann, 1936);

They Walk in the City: The Lovers in the Stone Forest (London: Heinemann, 1936; New York & London: Harper, 1936);

Time and the Conways: A Play in Three Acts (London: Heinemann, 1937; New York & London: Harper, 1938);

People at Sea: A Play in Three Acts (London: Heinemann, 1937);

Mystery at Greenfingers: A Comedy of Detection (London: French, 1937);

Midnight on the Desert: A Chapter of Autobiography (London & Toronto: Heinemann, 1937); republished as *Midnight on the Desert: Being an Excursion into Autobiography during a Winter in America, 1935–36* (New York & London: Harper, 1937);

I Have Been Here Before: A Play in Three Acts (London: Heinemann, 1937; New York & London: Harper, 1938);

When We Are Married: A Yorkshire Farcical Comedy (London: Heinemann, 1938; London & New York: French, 1938);

The Doomsday Men: An Adventure (London: Heinemann, 1938; New York & London: Harper, 1938);

Johnson over Jordan: The Play; and All about It (an Essay) (London & Toronto: Heinemann, 1939; New York & London: Harper, 1939);

Rain upon Godshill: A Further Chapter of Autobiography (London: Heinemann, 1939; New York & London: Harper, 1939);

Let the People Sing (London & Toronto: Heinemann, 1939; New York & London: Harper, 1940);

Postscripts (London & Toronto: Heinemann, 1940); republished as *All England Listened: The Wartime Broadcasts of J. B. Priestley* (New York: Chilmark Press, 1968);

Britain Speaks (New York & London: Harper, 1940);

The Book Crisis, by Priestley, Walpole, Geoffrey Faber, and others, edited by Gilbert McAllister (London: Faber & Faber, 1940);

Out of the People (London: Collins/Heinemann, 1941; New York & London: Harper, 1941);

Britain at War (New York & London: Harper, 1942);

Black-out in Gretley: A Story of and for Wartime (London & Toronto: Heinemann, 1942; New York & London: Harper, 1942);

Daylight on Saturday: A Novel about an Aircraft Factory (London & Toronto: Heinemann, 1943; New York & London: Harper, 1943);

British Women Go to War (London: Collins, 1943);

Three Plays (London: Heinemann, 1943) – comprises *Music at Night, The Long Mirror,* and *They Came to a City;*

The New Citizen (London: Council for Education in World Citizenship, 1944);

Manpower: The Story of Britain's Mobilization for War (London: His Majesty's Stationery Office, 1944);

Desert Highway: A Play in Two Acts and One Interlude (London: Heinemann, 1944);

Here Are Your Answers (London: Common Wealth Popular Library, 1944);

Letter to a Returning Serviceman (London: Home & Van Thal, 1945);

Three Comedies (London: Heinemann, 1945) – comprises *Good Night Children, The Golden Fleece,* and *How Are They at Home?;*

Three Men in New Suits (London & Toronto: Heinemann, 1945; New York & London: Harper, 1945);

Bright Day (London & Toronto: Heinemann, 1946; New York & London: Harper, 1946);

Russian Journey (London: Society for Cultural Relations with the U.S.S.R., 1946);

The Secret Dream: An Essay on Britain, America, and Russia (London: Turnstile Press, 1946);

H. G. Wells (London: Chiswick Press, 1946);

Ever Since Paradise: An Entertainment Chiefly Referring to Love and Marriage (London: French, 1946);

The Arts Under Socialism: A Lecture Given to the Fabian Society, with a Postscript on What the Government Should Do for the Arts Here and Now (London: Turnstile Press, 1947);

Jenny Villiers: A Story of the Theatre (London & Toronto: Heinemann, 1947; New York: Harper, 1947);

Theatre Outlook (London: Nicholson & Watson, 1947);

An Inspector Calls: A Play in Three Acts (London & Toronto: Heinemann, 1947; London & New York: French, 1948); republished with *The Linden Tree* (New York: Harper, 1948);

The Rose and Crown: A Play in One Act (London: French, 1947);

The High Toby: A Play for the Toy Theatre (Harmondsworth, U.K.: Penguin, 1948);

The Linden Tree: A Play in Two Acts and Four Scenes (London: Heinemann, 1948); republished with *An Inspector Calls* (New York: Harper, 1948);

Plays, 3 volumes (London: Heinemann, 1948-1950; New York: Harper, 1950-1952);

Delight (London: Heinemann, 1949; New York: Harper, 1949);

Home Is Tomorrow: A Play in Two Acts (London: Heinemann, 1949);

The Olympians: Opera in Three Acts, music by Arthur Bliss (London: Novello, 1949);

Bright Shadow: A Play in Detection in Three Acts (London: French, 1950);

Summer Day's Dream: A Play in Two Acts (London: French, 1950);

Going Up: Stories and Sketches (London: Pan, 1950);

Festival at Farbridge (London: Heinemann, 1951); republished as *Festival* (New York: Harper, 1951);

Dragon's Mouth: A Dramatic Quartet in Two Parts, by Priestley and Jacquetta Hawkes (London: Heinemann, 1952; New York: Harper, 1952);

Private Rooms: A One Act Comedy in the Viennese Style (London: French, 1953);

Try It Again: A One Act Play (London: French, 1953);

Mother's Day: A Comedy in One Act (London: French, 1953);

Treasure on Pelican: A Play in Three Acts (London: Evans, 1953);

The Other Place, and Other Stories of the Same Sort (London: Heinemann, 1953; New York: Harper, 1953);

The Magicians (London: Heinemann, 1954; New York: Harper, 1954);

Low Notes on a High Level: A Frolic (London: Heinemann, 1954; New York: Harper, 1954);

A Glass of Bitter: A Play in One Act (London: French, 1954);

Journey down a Rainbow, by Priestley and Hawkes (London: Heinemann/Cresset, 1955; New York: Harper, 1955);

The Scandalous Affair of Mr. Kettle and Mrs. Moon: A Comedy in Three Acts (London: French, 1956);

The Writer in a Changing Society (Aldington, U.K.: Hand and Flower Press, 1956);

All about Ourselves, and Other Essays, edited by Eric Gillett (London: Heinemann, 1956);

Thoughts in the Wilderness (London: Heinemann, 1957; New York: Harper, 1957);

The Art of the Dramatist (London: Heinemann, 1957);

Topside; or, The Future of England: A Dialogue (London: Heinemann, 1958);

The Glass Cage: A Play in Two Acts (London: French, 1958);

The Story of Theatre (London: Rathbone, 1959); republished as *The Wonderful World of the Theatre* (Garden City, N.Y.: Garden City Books,

1959); revised and enlarged as *The Wonderful World of the Theatre* (London: Macdonald, 1969; Garden City, N.Y.: Doubleday, 1969);

Literature and Western Man (London: Heinemann, 1960; New York: Harper, 1960);

William Hazlitt (London: Longmans, Green, 1960);

Charles Dickens: A Pictorial Biography (London: Thames & Hudson, 1961; New York: Viking, 1962); republished as *Charles Dickens and His World* (London: Thames & Hudson, 1969; New York: Viking, 1969);

Saturn over the Water: An Account of His Adventures in London, New York, South America, and Australia, by Tim Bedford, Painter; edited, with Some Preliminary and Concluding Remarks, by Henry Sulgrave; and Here Presented to the Reading Public (London: Heinemann, 1961; Garden City, N.Y.: Doubleday, 1961);

The Thirty-First of June: A Tale of True Love, Enterprise, and Progress, in the Arthurian and Adatomic Ages (London: Heinemann, 1961; Garden City, N.Y.: Doubleday, 1962);

The Shapes of Sleep: A Topical Tale (London: Heinemann, 1962; Garden City, N.Y.: Doubleday, 1962);

Margin Released: A Writer's Reminiscences and Reflections (London: Heinemann, 1962; New York: Harper & Row, 1962);

Sir Michael and Sir George: A Tale of COSMA and DISCUS and the New Elizabethans (London: Heinemann, 1964); republished as *Sir Michael and Sir George: A Comedy of the New Elizabethans* (Boston: Little, Brown, 1965);

A Severed Head, by Priestley and Iris Murdoch (London: Chatto & Windus, 1964);

Man and Time (London: Aldus, 1964; Garden City, N.Y.: Doubleday, 1964);

Lost Empires: Being Richard Herncastle's Account of His Life on the Variety Stage from November 1913 to August 1914, Together with a Prologue and Epilogue (London: Heinemann, 1965; Boston: Little, Brown, 1965);

Salt Is Leaving (London: Pan, 1966; New York: Harper & Row, 1966);

The Moments, and Other Pieces (London: Heinemann, 1966);

It's an Old Country (London: Heinemann, 1967; Boston: Little, Brown, 1967);

Trumpets over the Sea: Being a Rambling and Egotistical Account of the London Symphony Orchestra's Engagement at Daytona Beach, Florida, in July–August 1967 (London: Heinemann, 1968);

Essays of Five Decades, edited by Susan Cooper (Boston: Little, Brown, 1968; London: Heinemann, 1969);

The Image Men, 2 volumes (London: Heinemann, 1968, 1969) – comprises volume 1, *Out of Town;* volume 2, *London End;* republished in 1 volume (Boston: Little, Brown, 1969);

The Prince of Pleasure and His Regency, 1811–20 (London; Heinemann, 1969; New York: Harper & Row, 1969);

The Edwardians (London: Heinemann, 1970; New York: Harper & Row, 1970);

Anton Chekhov (London: International Textbook, 1970);

Snoggle: A Story for Anybody Between 9 and 90 (London: Heinemann, 1971; New York: Harcourt Brace Jovanovich, 1972);

Over the Long High Wall: Some Reflections and Speculations on Life, Death, and Time (London: Heinemann, 1972);

Victoria's Heyday (London: Heinemann, 1972; New York: Harper & Row, 1972);

The English (London: Heinemann, 1973; New York: Viking, 1973);

Outcries and Asides (London: Heinemann, 1974);

A Visit to New Zealand (London: Heinemann, 1974);

Particular Pleasures: Being a Personal Record of Some Varied Arts and Many Different Artists (London: Heinemann, 1975; New York: Stein & Day, 1975);

The Carfitt Crisis, and Two Other Stories (London: Heinemann, 1975; New York: Stein & Day, 1976) – comprises "The Carfitt Crisis," "Underground," and "The Pavilion of Masks";

Found, Lost, Found; or, The English Way of Life (London: Heinemann, 1976; Boston: G. K. Hall, 1976);

The Happy Dream: An Essay (Andoversford, U.K.: Whittington, 1976);

Instead of the Trees: A Final Chapter of Autobiography (London: Heinemann, 1977; New York: Stein & Day, 1977);

Seeing Stratford (Stratford-upon-Avon: Celandine Press, 1982);

If I Ran the B.B.C. (Washington, D.C.: National Association of Broadcasters, n.d.).

OTHER: *Essayists Past and Present,* edited, with an introduction, by Priestley (London: Jenkins, 1925; New York: Dial, 1925);

Fools and Philosophers: A Gallery of Comic Figures from English Literature, edited by Priestley (London: Lane, 1925; New York: Dodd, Mead, 1925);

Thomas Moore, *Tom Moore's Diary,* edited by Priestley (Cambridge: Cambridge University Press, 1925);

The Book of Bodley Head Verse: Being a Selection of Poetry Published at the Bodley Head, edited by Priestley (London: Lane / New York: Dodd, Mead, 1926);

Henry Fielding, *The History of the Adventures of Joseph Andrews and His Friend Mr. Abraham Adams,* introduction by Priestley (London: Lane / New York: Dodd, Mead, 1926);

Fielding, *Tom Jones: The History of a Foundling,* introduction by Priestley (New York: Limited Editions Club, 1931);

Our Nation's Heritage, edited by Priestley (London: Dent, 1939);

Home from Dunkirk: A Photographic Record in Aid of the British Red Cross and St. John, introduction by Priestley (London: Murray, 1940);

Charles Dickens, *Scenes of London Life, from "Sketches by Boz,"* edited by Priestley (London: Pan, 1947);

Stephen Leacock, *The Bodley Head Leacock,* edited by Priestley (London: Bodley Head, 1957);

Four English Novels, edited by Priestley and O. B. Davis (New York: Harcourt, Brace, 1960);

4 English Biographies, edited by Priestley and Davis (New York: Harcourt, Brace & World, 1961);

Adventures in English Literature, edited by Priestley (New York: Harcourt, Brace & World, 1963).

Priestley as a soldier in World War I

J. B. Priestley, who demonstrated mastery of several literary genres, was an English man of letters who preferred to be thought of as a professional writer practicing a time-honored craft. Assessing himself as a "fertile but careless" writer, Priestley wrote plays, essays, biographies, literary criticism (from a writer's point of view; Priestley had scant regard for academic criticism), and historical and social commentaries. He refused to be knighted for his achievements, declaring in the spirit of his working-class forebears that he would leave the world as he entered it, untitled. His deep commitment to human integrity shaped his writings and his public positions on social and political issues. Although he was criticized for writing in an Edwardian style, his interest in time theories, his awareness of the dehumanizing effects of technology, and his focus on the loneliness at the core of contemporary existence show that he was in tune with the temper of the twentieth century. Priestley believed, and asserted in his writings, that the worth of a civilization is not to be measured by technological progress but by the moral values it exemplifies.

John Priestley – he added the middle name Boynton as an adult – was born on 13 September 1894 in Bradford, Yorkshire. His father, Jonathan Priestley, a schoolmaster, was descended from working-class socialists whose views he shared. Priestley described his father in his memoir *Margin Released* (1962) as the "man socialists have in mind when they write about socialism." Although his Irish mother died soon after his birth, Priestley's stepmother encouraged his musical gifts and provided a stable home life where his romantic nature flourished.

Priestley knew early on that he wanted to be a writer, and he practiced his craft by imitating English authors whose works he admired. When he completed his schooling, he chose to work as a clerk in the wool trade rather than attend a university. Susan Cooper notes that "the years between 1910 and 1914 . . . had more effect on . . . [Priestley's] personality than any period before or after them." The memory of these years would become a touchstone by which the author would measure the modern world. During a BBC broadcast in 1940 he would observe that his youth had been lived on a "sunlit plain"; the metaphor did not represent a pastoral ideal but conveyed the sense of community he had experienced in Bradford.

When he was twenty, Priestley joined the duke of Wellington's West Riding Regiment. Wounded by an exploding mortar while fighting in France in World War I, he suffered more profound wounds in the loss of friends serving with him in the trenches and in the loss of the stable world that had existed before the war. Priestley returned to the front after recovering from his injury, fought with the Devonshire Regiment, suffered from exposure to mustard gas, and was discharged in 1919.

Three years at Cambridge University on a rehabilitation grant did little to alter Priestley's skeptical Yorkshireman's view of university dons, but he easily earned a degree with honors. Having married Pat Tempest in 1921, after graduation he moved to London. To support his wife and two daughters, Barbara and Sylvia, he wrote stories, reviews, and essays for newspapers, including the *London Mercury,* the *Outlook,* and the *Daily News;* he also read manuscripts for the Bodley Head and wrote for the *Spectator,* the *Saturday Review,* and the *Bookman.*

Although as a reader for the Bodley Head Priestley had promoted the early novels of Graham Greene and E. M. Forster, the essays in his first major collection, *Brief Diversions* (1922), seemed dated. Postwar intellectuals, enthusiastic about the novels of Forster and Virginia Woolf and the poems of Ezra Pound and T. S. Eliot, criticized Priestley for following prewar traditions that, they believed, did not represent the divided modern world. This criticism highlights an essential difference between Priestley and many of his contemporaries: as distressed by economic and political conditions as any writer of his generation, Priestley retained his faith in the ability of ordinary people to overcome adversity and to preserve their values.

Priestley also disagreed with many of his contemporaries in regard to style. He wrote for an educated general audience, as he believed all great English writers had. Fearing for the fate of English literature as modern writers appealed to an ever-shrinking elite audience, he developed themes of isolation and lost purpose similar to those of his colleagues but in more accessible forms. This distrust of elitism led him to scorn the classification "man of letters," preferring to see himself as a professional writer or craftsman.

Priestley's wife died of cancer in 1925. The following year he married the former wife of the writer D. B. Wyndham Lewis, Jane Wyndham Lewis, with whom he had three children: Tom, May, and Rachel. Jane Priestley's daughter, Angela Wyndham Lewis, also became a member of the family.

Priestley's separately published short story *The Town Major of Miraucourt* (1930) is the only fiction in which he draws on his experiences in World War I. The horrors of trench warfare are not the subject of the narrative, however; rather, the author focuses on time, a subject that came to play a central role in his fiction. The narrator, a young officer, recalls an experience that offered him a kind of oasis in time: while recuperating from the effects of an exploding gas shell, he is sent to a depot in Rouen, "which swarmed with men who never seemed quite real," to process requests for workers; "entertainers were [the] favorite commodity." Sent to a subsidiary depot on a trivial errand, the narrator is returning to Rouen by train when he arrives at the hamlet of Miraucourt. He is mystified by the old-fashioned uniforms of the motley band of soldiers he finds there. The major is a corpulent fellow much more interested in wine, women, and song than in military matters. While observing the major and his companions, all of whom are named Smith, through a window during a sleepless night, the narrator realizes that he has entered a time warp and is observing William Shakespeare's Falstaff, Pistol, Bardolph, and Nym.

Déjà vu experiences and what seemed to him to be precognitive dreams had led Priestley to read J. W. Dunne's *An Experiment with Time* (1927), which confirmed his own sense that all times coexist. Later he was influenced by P. D. Ouspensky's argument in *A New Model of the Universe* (1931) that time, like space, has three dimensions. Priestley makes use of time tunnels, time fusions, and alternate time zones in much of his fiction after 1930 and in plays such as *Time and the Conways* (1937) and *I Have Been Here Before* (1937).

In the introduction to *Four-in-Hand* (1934) Priestley explains, in a typically tongue-in-cheek fashion, that he has published the book to illustrate his unacknowledged versatility as an author. The volume comprises a novel, two plays, nine short stories, and essays. Although Priestley never acknowledged any indebtedness to Forster, several of the stories in the collection indicate that Priestley shared Forster's sense of the loneliness of modern civilized men and women. "The Town Major of Miraucourt" opens the short-story section. In "Mr.

Strenberry's Tale" the narrator, a pipe-smoking writer, visits a village tavern and hears the strange account of one of the locals, Mr. Strenberry, who has had a glimpse of the distant future and has witnessed the end of the human race. Strenberry, a schoolteacher, did not expect a vision when he visited a favorite rural scene for an afternoon's relaxation. When he saw a "thin revolving column of air," he was curious but not alarmed until he discovered that the revolving column was a time capsule with a man inside who was trying to escape. Beseeching Strenberry with his eyes, the man telepathically conveyed the events leading to his attempted escape. Just as Strenberry learned that the man, a laboratory assistant, was the last human being to inhabit the earth, the column began to revolve again, returning the doomed visitor to his own time and fate. Strenberry's life has been ruined by the vision: he can find no meaning in life when he knows that the human race is doomed to extinction.

The third story, "The Demon King," blends fantasy and realism. A theatrical company is rehearsing for the "Annual Pantomime at the old Theatre Royal, Bruddersford." As the time approaches for the evening performance, everyone becomes concerned because Mr. Ireton, the actor who plays the Demon King, has not returned to the theater; known for drowning his sorrows at a local pub, Ireton is feared to have overindulged and forgotten his engagement at the theater. Suddenly the Demon King appears in a costume of "skin-tight crimson touched with a baleful green . . . far better than the one provided by the management." The Demon King, whose face has "a greenish phosphorescent glow," is more than believable in the role. At the end a messenger announces that Mr. Ireton is in the infirmary, having been struck down by a car on his way to the theater. Some of the humor in the story is derived from the elements of disparity: high drama and low comedy on the same bill; a quarrelsome, amateurish cast ill suited for their parts; and the appearance of the "devil himself" in a provincial theater. The story is also humorous because of the dialogue: Priestley's ability to represent regional speech – as in the stagehand's report that Ireton had been seen at the Cooper's Arms, where, " 'by gow, he wor lapping it up an' all' " – yields several amusing characters.

The fourth story, "Adventure," traces the events of a single night in the life of Hubert Watson, a young, romantic gentleman who yearns for an adventure to brighten the dull routine of returning each evening to his quiet flat. One night Hubert's wish comes true, but not in the picturesque way he has imagined. Naively accepting a stranger's invitation to accompany him to a "little club," Hubert finds himself among a sinister assortment of men and women who rob him of his cash and valuables. By the end of the story Hubert is grateful to escape with his life and eager to return to his flat, which his adventure has led him to regard as a haven from the harsher realities of city life. Resembling a fable with its moral undertones, the story is redeemed by Priestley's talent for creating vivid scenes and mimicking speech. He indicates his preference for sturdy, no-nonsense Englishmen by satirizing an upper-middle-class young man who chafes at the limits of his safe, privileged life, but the satire is gentle.

"Adventure" is followed by a love story, "Going Up," which is strikingly stageworthy. The plot is rather hackneyed, involving lovers who test each other through jealousy. The comic scenes, most of which occur in a department-store elevator and involve a sequence of stops, starts, entrances, and exits, would play well on the stage. The lovers' reconciliation on the final descent indicates that true love requires no artifice.

"What a Life!" illustrates the relationship between circumstance and character. A reformed burglar who works as a waiter in a hotel bar is waiting for a call from the hospital announcing the birth of his first grandchild. He resists entreaties from his former wife to reveal the name of the hospital and, thus, to threaten his daughter's peace of mind, and, "looking monstrously unlike any possible waiter, a dangerous man," he rebuffs the threats of his old partner in crime. The final scene restores the deceptive calm of the opening as the waiter quietly serves whiskeys to a couple of late-night customers who, ironically, deplore the hotel's dull routine.

The last three stories in the collection focus on one of Priestley's favorite character types: the down-to-earth yet shrewd Englishman. The "tall, bony" Yorkshireman Mr. Hebblethwaite is a workingman whose appearance and northern accent belie his deep appreciation of music and the theater. In "Handel and the Racket" Mr. Hebblethwaite and a rich American businessman, Ongar, meet in the elevator of "a very tall building not far from Cheapside" and discover that they both like the music of George Frideric Handel. Rather than offering them common ground, Handel's music becomes a topic of hot debate as each man asserts his superior interpretation of a particular oratorio. Retiring to Ongar's hotel room to resolve their differences by examining the score of the oratorio, the two men are intruded upon by American gangsters who have followed Ongar to England, hoping to compromise his anticrime efforts in the United States. Priestley asserts the superiority of the Yorkshireman by having him, rather than the American, outsmart the criminals. The two Handel buffs feel a close bond after the danger has passed, and the story ends with the resumption of the debate, which is now a friendly competition.

In "An Arabian Knight in Park Lane" Mr. Hebblethwaite is somewhat ill at ease at a formal party in London, but once again his Yorkshire shrewdness saves the day. The senile father of the hostess is in the habit of stealing jewels from party guests and taking them upstairs to his study; one of the footmen hired for the evening, taking advantage of the old man's plunderings, removes the jewels from the study. Hebblethwaite, who witnessed the old man's thefts and followed him upstairs, is accused by a police detective of being the thief, but the Yorkshireman quickly proves the footman's guilt.

In the final story in the collection, "The Taxi and the Star," a theatrical producer usurps Hebblethwaite's place in a London taxi. Hebblethwaite vows that he will somehow find and repay this arrogant swell. Barely believable coincidence brings the two men together in the home of an actress who is a hometown friend of Hebblethwaite's and member of the producer's company, but Hebblethwaite does not succeed in teaching the producer the desired lesson. The Yorkshireman reveals an admirable side of his nature when he good-humoredly accepts his failure.

While writing these stories, Priestley also produced several novels and launched his career as a playwright with such plays as *Dangerous Corner* (1932), *Eden End* (1934), and *Cornelius* (1935). In 1937 and 1938, while living in Arizona for his wife's health, he tried his hand at screen writing. At the outbreak of World War II Priestley was back in England venturing into another medium, radio broadcasting. His Sunday night talks, "Postscripts," delivered in his Yorkshire accent, were popular, but Priestley's socialism conflicted with the views of Prime Minister Winston Churchill. The program was canceled by the government just as the Germans began to bomb London. Priestley helped the war effort by finding homes for evacuees, writing and producing propaganda films, and chairing a committee on war aims. Following the war, he was instrumental in founding the Campaign for Nuclear Disarmament and served as a delegate to UNESCO.

Although Priestley remained married to his second wife for twenty-six years, he did not find contentment in marriage until 1953, when, following a divorce from Jane Priestley, he married the anthropologist Jacquetta Hawkes. They divided their time mainly between their home, Kissing Tree House, near Stratford-upon-Avon, and their London flat. Cooper observes that Priestley was "very, very English" and that although "he traveled to every civilized country in the world and a number of uncivilized ones as well . . . he never lived voluntarily for more than a few months in any country other than England, and . . . never wanted to."

Priestley's second collection of short fiction, *The Other Place, and Other Stories of the Same Sort* was published in 1953. Priestley's concern with what he considered the dehumanizing effects of a post-industrial, technological age is reflected in the nine stories. Some characters, realizing that they have no identity, long nostalgically for meaningful lives; others, trapped in smug complacency, suddenly see through bland exteriors to the emptiness of their own lives and those of their contemporaries. Although the collection represents urban existence as bleak and empty, the stories are not altogether pessimistic. Priestley uses parallel time zones, enhanced visual perception, and benign magical powers to show that alienation can be overcome if human beings practice virtues such as tolerance and generosity.

The title story uses the framing device of an after-dinner conversation between two strangers who are visiting an English village. Harvey Lindfield, a Canadian engineer, explains to his companion, a writer, that he has returned to Blakely seeking to recapture a time journey he had experienced a few months earlier while on a business trip. The people, he says, treated him with the distant courtesy reserved for outsiders. The significance of his preamble becomes clear as he recalls his trip through a time tunnel. His adventure began when an old man, Sir Alaric, whom he saved from being run over by a truck, invited him to dinner. After the meal, the host offered to rescue Lindfield from his boring, melancholy existence by giving him a chance to visit "not *some* other place – but *the* Other Place . . . round – a different kind of corner." Lindfield moved through a time tunnel that opened onto the familiar English village; everything was the same, yet different. People were open and responsive to one another; a radiant light bathed the landscape; life seemed paced to enhance community life as the villagers cheerfully performed their tasks. Lindfield instantly fell in love with a woman named Paula, recognizing that "everything with her is dead right." For the first time in his life he was happy.

Eager to be with Paula, he disobeyed her instructions to rendezvous in her room at half past ten and made "a dash for the green door" to her room at a quarter past ten. Entering the room, he found himself back in Sir Alaric's library. Lindfield realizes that he forfeited his one chance for happiness by impatiently trying to hurry events in his ideal world; accustomed to the hurried pace and self-assertive mode of modern life, he could not wait fifteen minutes for bliss. Although he recognizes his error, he cannot find his way back to his "paradise."

Lindfield's nostalgia for "*the* Other place" may lead readers to interpret Priestley as a romantic, bemoaning the loss of England's pastoral landscape. Cooper points out, however, that Priestley was a thoroughly urban man; the fourth dimension depicted in "The Other Place" is exactly like the ordinary world except that the spirit of community replaces the superficial values and fast pace of modern life.

"The Grey Ones" is written in a more sinister vein. Mr. Patson goes to the office of Dr. Smith, a psychiatrist. Questions about the nature of evil have provoked Patson's fear that he may be losing touch with reality. Does Dr. Smith, he asks, believe in an " 'Evil Principle . . . a sort of super-devil, that is working hard to ruin humanity, and has its agents, who must really be minor devils or demons, living among us as people?' " Patson has begun to entertain such a notion after hearing a well-known painter, Fribright, explain that the demons appear as " 'grey ones . . . who try to give everything a grey look . . . to make mankind go the way the social insects went, to turn us into automatic creatures . . . to destroy the soul of humanity . . . to wipe from the face of this earth all wonder, joy, deep feeling, desire to create, to praise life.' " In a grisly final scene Dr. Smith and his cohorts reveal themselves to be members of the satanic fifth column as they bear down on Patson in the form of "semi-transparent toads" with "six eyes like electric lamps . . . burning triumphantly out of Hell . . . to silence his warning forever." The satire of this story is aimed at what Priestley considers the dehumanizing trends of the twentieth century, including psychoanalysis.

With "Uncle Phil on TV" the author shifts to black comedy to depict the emptiness of contemporary life in a consumer society. Human value for the working-class Grigsons is measured by services rendered or money paid. When Uncle Phil dies because no one remembered to place his heart pills within easy reach, the family members agree that they are better off with the £150 insurance payment than they were with a sick and quarrelsome old

man who ate their food and took up room they needed. They use the money for a television set, which, they say, "gives you everything." Once the set is installed, each member of the family begins to plan his or her life around the program schedule; but to the horror of the Grigsons, Uncle Phil appears as a member of the cast of every show they watch. While the dead uncle thus gains the attention he was denied in life, he is as mean-spirited and selfish as his kin; the effect of his appearance is chilling rather than reassuring.

The main character of "Guest of Honor," Sir Bernard Clipter, is one of several middle-aged men in Priestley's fiction who suffer from the smug assurance that all is well in their comfortable worlds. As he drives his Rolls Royce to a dinner of the Imperial Industrialists' Association where he is to be the guest of honor, he nearly runs over a man with remarkable pewter-gray eyes. Chided by the industrialist for not watching where he is going, the pedestrian warns Sir Bernard that he had better watch where *he* is going. At the dinner Sir Bernard has a strange desire to question appearances he had previously taken for granted. He wonders how the waiters really feel about the dinner guests they unctuously serve; he enters the consciousness of several distinguished guests and perceives their fatigue, boredom, and fear; he sees a greenish-white crab crawl up the leg of a successful businessman and slowly devour him. His final nightmarish vision ends with the reappearance of the old man's pewter-gray eyes. At the end Sir Bernard is back in his car, pondering whether he has dreamed the events or actually experienced them. Whichever is the case, he seems more generous and humane in the final scene than he was at the beginning of the story.

"Look After the Strange Girl" demonstrates Priestley's skill in sketching a variety of characters with one or two deftly crafted sentences. When the social historian Mark Denbow travels in time from the 1950s to 1902, he is burdened by the knowledge that the gaiety and confidence of the turn of the century will be shattered by World War I. Lonely because his travel has shown him "that distance in time was apparently harder to bear than distance in space," he meets a young woman who looks as out-of-place as he feels. Thin and angular among "ripe, soft girls" of 1902, Anne at first appears pitiable; closer inspection reveals to Denbow that she is quite lovely by 1950s standards and refreshingly sensible, and he discovers that he and Anne have journeyed from the same time. The irony derives from the possibility that Anne and Denbow are attracted to one another only because they are misfits in the gay, secure world they visit; the very likeness that draws them together in this world would make them appear too familiar for romantic interest to develop between them in their own time.

In "The Statues" the reporter Walter Voley, a "fattish man in his late forties," has begun to ask: "was this really life, all that could reasonably be expected of it, or was it a bad imitation that had somehow been foisted on him?" As he moves about London on various assignments, Voley sees enormous statues whose features suggest an unknown race. The first figure appears noble and serene, the second "represented a powerful naked man agonizingly attempting to free himself from something that gripped him," and the third and most beautiful of all is "a majestic but smiling woman" holding up "a naked laughing child." Voley tries unsuccessfully to discuss his visions with his family and friends. Finally Mr. Saunders, a librarian, suggests that the reporter may be glimpsing the future. The visions completely change Voley's life, leading first to a nervous breakdown and then to his leaving the city to write for a village paper. Seeing into the future, it would seem, brings despair when one realizes that one cannot alter the present. Voley represents the plight of a modern man trapped by meaningless expectations and duties. His choice of a simpler existence is offered as an alternative to the alienating effects of urban life, but the story does not suggest ways of humanizing the metropolis.

In "The Leadington Incident" the successful, self-satisfied, middle-aged government official Cobthorn encounters a calm, remote stranger on a train. The stranger's eyes and curiously luminous stare compel Cobthorn to talk. When he reveals that he is traveling to Leadington to speak to a large crowd on urgent matters, the stranger assures him that the only urgent matter at hand is to be truly alive. Priestley intensifies the social satire through details of setting: the train approaches a "grimy station," passing "the mills and warehouses" that cut off the sunlight; the city's name implies a heavy, dead existence. The reader discovers with Cobthorn the truth of the stranger's observation that few people in the industrialized world are really alive. At the end of the story Cobthorn is standing in front of the crowd he has come to address, shouting " 'Wake Up!' "

"Mr. Strenberry's Tale" is the only story in the collection that was previously published, having appeared in *Four-in-Hand*. Priestley included it because its style and theme complement those of the other stories. When Priestley wrote the story, he may have been mainly interested in exploring the

notion of time travel, but he had it republished in the 1950s for its social commentary. The inclusion of the story in this collection shifts the focus from the surreal and futuristic elements to the satiric ones. The dark force destroying the last man on earth may simply be the final effect of trends and attitudes dominating contemporary societies.

Completing the nine stories in *The Other Place, and Other Stories of the Same Sort*, "Night Sequence" opens dramatically with a car skidding into a ditch as a young husband, arguing with his wife, angrily attempts to turn the vehicle around on a narrow road in a heavy rain. Representative of jaded, liberated moderns, Luke and Betty Gosforth work for a film company and manifest the world-weary cynicism of the "smart set." They leave the car and trudge up a lane to a dark, secluded house. In this story, as in others, Priestley uses movement in time to grant freedom to his characters: donning eighteenth-century costumes offered them by a mysterious maid to replace their rain-soaked clothes, Luke and Betty enter an earlier period, when courtly manners and elegance prevailed. Warmed by food, wine, and hospitality, they shed their brittle, defensive shells to reveal qualities they had all but lost. Betty feels worthy of love and respect when she sips sherry with their host, Sir Edward, and Luke unburdens himself to Sir Edward's niece, Julia. Their ghostly hosts hint throughout the evening that they exist because Luke and Betty need them. The young couple had become the roles they played, losing their identities. The message Priestley intends is familiar: love flourishes between people who are more committed to their human values than to their roles in society. The author consistently portrays the disappearance of such qualities as sympathy, courtesy, kindness, thoughtfulness, and generosity as the greatest evil in the modern world.

A second theme developed in the story has to do with the film industry. Luke and Betty work for a company that makes documentaries: rather than transforming events into art or serving posterity, the process has become a formulaic routine, dehumanizing those involved. Priestley had worked in films since the 1930s and knew the dangers of making profit more important than art. He warns that commercialization dehumanizes, making the work and the artist commodities in a competitive market.

Priestley wrote mainly nonfiction during the 1960s and 1970s. In 1973 he was honored by his home city of Bradford with the Freedom of the City. *The Carfitt Crisis, and Two Other Stories* appeared in 1975; two of the stories, "The Carfitt Crisis" and

"The Pavilion of Masks," had originally been written as plays, and they retain their dramatic structure. Both works, A. A. DeVitis observes, "exhibit economy of time, place, and action, and avoid all but essential description and comments on character, feeling, and motive." Priestley had written the third story, "Underground," for the *Illustrated London News* in 1974.

Reviewing the collection for the *Spectator,* Peter Ackroyd comments that the title story "has all the scars of an after-birth": the dialogue is heavy and awkward, and it "reads like a particularly elaborate set of stage directions." The crisis is foreshadowed in a dream Marion Carfitt has as she sleeps exhaustedly one afternoon after learning that her former lover has died. In the dream her husband, Sir Brian Carfitt, in one of his "terrible rages," is pointing his shotgun at someone and is about to shoot. Such a crisis does come about, but the complex plot involves the couple's marital problems, Sir Brian's mishandling of investments, and the arrival of Marion's niece from America. A mysterious man named Engram also arrives, claiming to be on his way to visit a friend at another country estate about thirty miles away; Engram is the godlike figure who eventually strips away all the masks of deception, offers Sir Brian a way to recoup his financial losses, prevents the shooting of which Marion dreamed, opens the way for the Carfitts to rekindle their love, and sends the young niece – who turns out to be an impostor – away with a couple of local young men.

Though it requires ten chapters to accomplish the twists and turns of the plot, the story's time is compressed into a single weekend. Every character except Engram shows the effects of modern life: chicanery rules in business practices, gossip entertains the idle and bored wives, insolence and indolence characterize the young people. Engram's relaxed assurance comes, he reveals in conversations, from his decision to drop out of an "upwardly mobile" career in finance and rediscover his humanity. Since his self-esteem is no longer linked with conventional notions of success, he is free to pursue any occupation, including filling in as cook and butler for the Carfitts, without losing his dignity. He anticipates each crisis and offers a redeeming solution for each character's problems. Priestley's social commentary here is faithful to that in his earlier stories: twentieth-century people can rediscover their human identities, but they need some extraordinary means of doing so.

"Underground," which follows "The Carfitt Crisis," depicts the final journey on the London subway of a thoroughly modern young man, Ray

Dust jacket for Priestley's 1975 collection of short fiction, which includes two stories originally written as plays

Aggarstone, who is absconding with the life savings of his mother and sister. A variety of repellent cotravelers and a fairy-godmother figure try to save Aggarstone by offering him the chance to change his ways, but as his journey nears its end, Aggarstone confronts a crone who "cackles and spits" when she tells him that he is on a one-way trip. As Aggarstone's heart turns to "ice-water," Priestley abandons Aggarstone's interior monologue to end the story with a coda that offers two views of the young man's death: an official one and a moral one. Two policemen examining the body record that he apparently died of a heart attack in the Northern Line train at Hampstead. The moral version is provided by the godlike figure, a mysterious "tall man with a long chin and sharp grey eyes" who knows that "this is a world where the guilty all too often go unpunished and the innocent are increasingly victimised, robbed, ruined, maimed or murdered." This melodramatic intrusion mars an otherwise successful allegory whose message is self-evident.

Subtitled "A Comedy in a Romantic Setting," "The Pavilion of Masks" is framed by a humorous prologue in which Priestley claims to have been approached by an academic with a manuscript in need of a publisher. The obtuse Dr. A. F. D. Perkisson's fragmented story involves his ancestors in a fairytale romance that supposedly occurred in the 1840s. The central story is Priestley's rewriting of the tale. Priestley closes the frame with an epilogue in which he claims that Dr. Perkisson disliked the author's version because it changes a romance into a cynical comedy. Priestley suggests that he has both succeeded and failed to accomplish his end.

Like "The Carfitt Crisis," the story reflects its origin as a drama: all the action takes place in a single day and night at the Pavilion of Masks, the extravagant dwelling built by Prince Karl, the ruler of the southern German principality of Mexe-Dorberg, for his mistress, Cleo Torres, Countess of Feldhausen. The guards who protect the countess are moonstruck students who vacillate between bombast and cowardice. Foreign emissaries and political leaders reveal themselves to be opportunists who lust after power, money, and Cleo Torres. Cleo is reputed to be a free spirit, a woman of talent and beauty; actually, she is selfish, egotistical, and frigid. Victor Vatannes, the poet who has raced across Europe to elope to France with Cleo, is a vain, pompous publicity monger who hopes that a match with Countess Feldhausen will bring him fame and fortune. Meanwhile, disgruntled citizens threaten to overrun the pavilion and oust Cleo. Dr. Novelda, Cleo's adviser and majordomo, solves Cleo's problems and saves Prince Karl from a coup d'état by arranging for everyone to be someplace else when he and Prince Karl's wife, Princess Louise, run off together to South America. This elopement, which leads to a long and happy life for the couple under assumed names, is the romantic tale Dr. Perkisson had wanted Priestley to tell. The story is more conventional than most of Priestley's short fiction, barely hinting at the supernatural by characterizing Dr. Novelda as a godlike figure with visionary powers, but it is consistent with the social satire in his other works.

In 1977 Priestley accepted the Order of Merit, conveyed by the monarch to no more than twenty-four living artists. He remained active until his death at his home in Stratford-upon-Avon on 14 August 1984. During his long career he suffered from critics' assumption that to be a versatile writer is to be a mediocre writer. His tendency to self-deprecation encouraged such assessments, but as DeVitis and Albert E. Kalson remark: "To have written *Angel Pavement*, *Bright Day*, *Eden End*, *Time and the Conways*, and *The Linden Tree* is an accomplishment of which any writer would be proud." Although Priestley devoted most of his creative energies to novels, dramas, and nonfiction, his short fiction is expertly crafted and reveals his talent for dialogue and characterization. While his interest in the exploration of alternate time dimensions dominates much of his short fiction, Priestley's faith in people's potential to reclaim their humanity and his insistence that modern civilizations need not suffer the debilitating effects of alienation underlie all his works.

Bibliography:

Alan Edwin Day, *J. B. Priestley: An Annotated Bibliography* (New York: Garland, 1980).

Biography:

Vincent Brome, *J. B. Priestley* (London: Hamilton, 1988).

References:

John Atkins, *J. B. Priestley: The Last of the Sages* (London: Calder, 1981; New York: Riverrun, 1981);

John Braine, *J. B. Priestley* (London: Weidenfeld & Nicolson, 1978);

Susan Cooper, *J. B. Priestley: Portrait of an Author* (London: Heinemann, 1970);

A. A. DeVitis and Albert E. Kalson, *J. B. Priestley* (Boston: Twayne, 1980);

David Hughes, *J. B. Priestley: An Informal Study of His Work* (London: Hart-Davis, 1958);

Colin Wilson, "A Hell of a Talent," *Books and Bookmen*, 21 (January 1975): 26ff;

Kenneth Young, *J. B. Priestley*, Writers and Their Work, no. 257 (London: Longmans Group for the British Council, 1977).

Papers:

Some of Priestley's manuscripts are at the Harry Ransom Humanities Research Center, University of Texas at Austin. His letters to Edward Davison are at the Beinecke Library, Yale University.

V. S. Pritchett

(10 December 1900 –)

John J. Stinson
SUNY College at Fredonia

See also the Pritchett entry in *DLB 15: British Novelists, 1930–1959: Part 2.*

BOOKS: *Marching Spain* (London: Benn, 1928);

Clare Drummer (London: Benn, 1929);

The Spanish Virgin and Other Stories (London: Benn, 1930);

Shirley Sanz (London: Gollancz, 1932); republished as *Elopement into Exile* (Boston: Little, Brown, 1932);

Nothing Like Leather (London: Chatto & Windus, 1935; New York: Macmillan, 1935);

Dead Man Leading (London: Chatto & Windus, 1937; New York: Macmillan, 1937);

You Make Your Own Life (London: Chatto & Windus, 1938);

In My Good Books (London: Chatto & Windus, 1942);

It May Never Happen and Other Stories (London: Chatto & Windus, 1945; New York: Reynal, 1947);

The Living Novel (London: Chatto & Windus, 1946; New York: Reynal, 1947); revised and enlarged as *The Living Novel and Other Appreciations* (New York: Random House, 1964);

Why Do I Write?, by Pritchett, Elizabeth Bowen, and Graham Greene (London: Marshall, 1948);

Mr. Beluncle (London: Chatto & Windus, 1951; New York: Harcourt, Brace, 1951);

Books in General (London: Chatto & Windus, 1953; New York: Harcourt, Brace, 1953);

The Spanish Temper (London: Chatto & Windus, 1954; New York: Knopf, 1955);

When My Girl Comes Home (London: Chatto & Windus, 1961; New York: Knopf, 1961);

London Perceived (London: Chatto & Windus, 1962; New York: Harcourt, Brace & World, 1962);

The Key to My Heart: A Comedy in Three Parts (London: Chatto & Windus, 1963; New York: Random House, 1964);

V. S. Pritchett (photograph © Jerry Bauer)

Foreign Faces (London: Chatto & Windus, 1964); republished as *The Offensive Traveller* (New York: Knopf, 1964);

New York Proclaimed (London: Chatto & Windus, 1965; New York: Harcourt, Brace & World, 1965);

Shakespeare: The Comprehensive Soul (London: British Broadcasting Corporation, 1965);

The Working Novelist (London: Chatto & Windus, 1965; New York: Random House, 1965);

The Saint, and Other Stories (Harmondsworth, U.K.: Penguin/Chatto & Windus, 1966);

Dublin: A Portrait (London: Bodley Head, 1967; New York: Harper & Row, 1967);

185

A Cab at the Door: Childhood and Youth, 1900–1920 (London: Chatto & Windus, 1968); republished as *A Cab at the Door: A Memoir* (New York: Random House, 1968);

Blind Love and Other Stories (London: Chatto & Windus, 1969; New York: Random House, 1970);

George Meredith and English Comedy (London: Chatto & Windus, 1970; New York: Random House, 1970);

Midnight Oil (London: Chatto & Windus, 1971; New York: Random House, 1972);

Balzac (London: Chatto & Windus, 1973; New York: Knopf, 1973);

The Camberwell Beauty and Other Stories (London: Chatto & Windus, 1974; New York: Random House, 1974);

The Gentle Barbarian: The Life and Work of Turgenev (London: Chatto & Windus, 1977; New York: Random House, 1977);

Selected Stories (New York: Random House, 1978);

The Myth Makers: Literary Essays (London: Chatto & Windus, 1979; New York: Random House, 1979);

On the Edge of the Cliff (London: Chatto & Windus, 1979; New York: Random House, 1979);

The Tale Bearers: Literary Essays (London: Chatto & Windus, 1980; New York: Random House, 1980);

The Turn of the Years (Wilton, U.K.: Russell, 1981);

A Man of Letters (London: Chatto & Windus, 1985; New York: Random House, 1986);

Chekhov: A Spirit Set Free (London: Hodder & Stoughton, 1988; New York: Random House, 1988);

A Careless Widow and Other Stories (London: Chatto & Windus, 1989; New York: Random House, 1989);

At Home and Abroad (Berkeley, Cal.: North Point, 1989);

Lasting Impressions: Essays, 1961–1987 (London: Chatto & Windus, 1990; New York: Random House, 1990).

Editions and Collections: *Collected Stories* (London: Chatto & Windus, 1956);

The Sailor, Sense of Humour, and Other Stories (New York: Knopf, 1956);

Collected Stories (London: Chatto & Windus, 1982; New York: Random House, 1982);

More Collected Stories (London: Chatto & Windus, 1983; New York: Random House, 1983);

The Other Side of the Frontier: A V. S. Pritchett Reader (London: Clark, 1984);

The Complete Short Stories (London: Chatto & Windus, 1990); republished as *Complete Collected Stories* (New York: Random House, 1991);

The Complete Essays (London: Chatto & Windus, 1991); republished as *Complete Collected Essays* (New York: Random House, 1992).

OTHER: *This England,* edited by Pritchett (London: New Statesman and Nation, 1937);

Robert Louis Stevenson: Novels and Stories, edited by Pritchett (London: Pilot, 1945; New York: Duell, Sloan & Pearce, 1946);

Turnstile One: A Literary Miscellany from the New Statesman and Nation, edited by Pritchett (London: Turnstile, 1948);

The Oxford Book of Short Stories, edited, with an introduction, by Pritchett (New York: Oxford University Press, 1981).

Literary journalists and reviewers of the past ten to fifteen years have been referring to V. S. Pritchett more and more frequently as "the Grand Old Man of British letters." The highly favorable, prominently placed, and usually lengthy reviews that followed the publication of *Complete Collected Stories* (1991) and, to a slightly lesser extent, *Complete Collected Essays* (1992) brought Pritchett's achievement to a new level of general awareness. Most readers who are familiar with Pritchett as an essayist, practical literary critic, biographer, autobiographer, travel writer, and, most especially, short-story writer feel he has earned the high praise he has come to be accorded. They find quality, range, and plenitude: *Complete Collected Stories* supplies 82 stories; *Complete Collected Essays,* 203 essays. Only Pritchett's merits as a novelist have been sensibly and justifiably questioned.

Pritchett's short fiction is regarded by many as at least the equal of any written in England in the past sixty years, and at least a few reviewers consistently refer to him as the best living short-story writer. In fact Frank Kermode, one of the foremost English literary critics, has labeled Pritchett simply the "finest English writer alive." Not all, of course, are as unstinting in their acclamations as Kermode or William Trevor, one of the foremost short-story writers of the late twentieth century. Trevor states in the *New Republic* (2 August 1982) that Pritchett "has done more for the short story in his lifetime than anyone since Joyce or Chekhov. He has probably done more for the English short story than anyone has ever done."

Victor Sawdon Pritchett was born on 10 December 1900 in Ipswich, Suffolk, a few miles northeast of London. His father, Walter Sawdon Pritchett, was a traveling salesman originally from Yorkshire but of Welsh descent; his mother, Beatrice Martin Pritchett, was a former Cockney shop clerk who shared tall stories and a delight in popular comic fiction with her young son. One of her favorite authors was W. W. Jacobs, whom Pritchett praises for his successful dialogue, a form that became his own forte.

Walter Pritchett – a man full of pumped-up optimism, strutting mannerisms, and laughable social pretensions (his son refers to him as a "bumptious cocksparrow" in the first volume of his memoirs) – thought constantly, unrealistically, of "success." The cloudy, confused romantic striving that Walter never ceased to exhibit was stored away deep in the consciousness of his son and was successfully mined in some poignantly comic stories. Perhaps, too, Pritchett's penchant for, and mastery of, ironic situations coolly conveyed – as opposed to emotional moments warmly presented – is ascribable to a reaction to his father's cloudy romanticism. Walter's conversion to Christian Science when Victor was a young boy was also grist for the mill of his son's fiction, most notably in "The Saint" (*It May Never Happen and Other Stories*, 1945), a story comic, satiric, and poignant all at once.

Pritchett's early life is vividly and delightfully detailed in *A Cab at the Door* (1968), the first part of a two-volume memoir often regarded as one of the best English autobiographies of the century. The title refers to a cab being present at the door to convey the Pritchetts to yet another residence: the family moved eighteen times during Victor's first twelve years. The frequent uprootings interrupted Pritchett's formal education, which ended before he was sixteen. All in all his education was about average for an English boy of his time and class, although a period at the Rosendale Junior School in Dulwich had some beneficial effects, not the least of which was Pritchett's decision, inspired largely by an innovative teacher, to become a writer. At home he read novels by Charles Dickens, whose eye for detail influenced Pritchett's fiction.

Feelings of betrayal and disappointment were at first keen for the aspiring young writer when he was withdrawn from school by his father in 1916 and set to work as an apprentice in the leather trade in London. Soon, though, his sensitive mind was alive with the excitement of the workplace and the energy and pungency of London. At age eighty he wrote in *The Turn of the Years* (1981) that "the smell of that London of my boyhood and bowler-hatted youth is still with me. I coughed my way through a city stinking, rather excitingly, of coal smoke, gas escapes, tanyards, breweries, horse manure, and urine." Pritchett banked these rich impressions and drew on them in some of his fiction of the 1930s and 1940s, including the novel *Nothing Like Leather* (1935) and the title story and "The Chestnut Tree" from *It May Never Happen and Other Stories*.

Four years later, at age twenty, Pritchett went off to live in Paris (while still working in the leather trade) to experience the romance of the city, the exhilaration of freedom from family, and an ambience conducive to writing. There he came across a piece of advice from James M. Barrie, in *When a Man's Single* (1888), "to write on the smallest things and those near to you." Pritchett wrote and rewrote three short sketches and sent them off to English reviews and the *Christian Science Monitor*. All three were accepted. While he could not give up his day job, his writing career was under way.

The 1920s proved an eventful decade for Pritchett. In Paris he lost, without regret finally, a chastity he had previously cherished. With the fervor of many autodidacts he read much of the French and English literature he felt he had missed. He was hired by the *Christian Science Monitor* (although he was a lapsed Christian Scientist) as a correspondent, and he was sent to Ireland to report on its civil war. Pritchett filed his reports, attended the Abbey theater, met William Butler Yeats and Sean O'Casey, and married an Irish actress, Evelyn Maude Vigors. Then he was off on a new *Monitor* assignment to Spain, where he learned a new language and soaked up atmosphere; then to North Africa, the United States, and back to Ireland.

In 1926 the *New Statesman,* an English weekly journal with which Pritchett was beginning a long and valuable relationship, published his first story, "Rain in the Sierra." (In *Midnight Oil* [1971] Pritchett writes that he was rather ashamed of this story "written on the Spanish gipsy, the corniest of subjects.") The *Monitor* fired him in 1927, and somewhere during those years his marriage fell apart. While briefly back in London, he got the idea of walking across Spain to provide himself with material for a travel book. *Marching Spain,* his first book, appeared according to plan in 1928 and was favorably received. In it readers can note talents that point to his success with the short story, such as the skill in arriving at epiphanic moments and the selection of vignettes that speak volumes. *Clare Drummer* (1929), a novel set in Ireland in the period 1923–1926, was not as successful, being troubled by flaws in construction and overwriting, the latter a habit of which Pritchett, by conscious attention, was soon to break himself.

Three or four of the stories in his first collection, *The Spanish Virgin and Other Stories* (1930), are worthy, if unremarkable. The merits of many, though – including the novella-length title story – are seriously compromised by flaws in construction, uncertainty about desired effects, and melodrama. Pritchett himself soon came to regard them as apprentice work, refusing to resurrect them for any later volume, including *Complete Collected Stories* (which, then, is a bit of a misnomer). The identifying Pritchett stamps are simply not present even in those pieces – "Tragedy in a Greek Theater," "The White Rabbit," and "The Cuckoo Clock" – that are good stories with balance, economy, and unified effect. The volume lacks the distinctive voice Pritchett was so soon and so authoritatively to develop, the seemingly relaxed but deft control, the acute power of suggestiveness, and the subtleties that give a sense of unusual depth.

"Sense of Humour," the first piece in *You Make Your Own Life* (1938), is given first position as well in *Complete Collected Stories*. The story represents a remarkable leap ahead; here Pritchett is near the height of his mature short-story craft just a few years after the rather unprepossessing *Spanish Virgin*. The sudden advancement cannot be wholly explained, but much of it resides in the achievement of sharp, highly selective, individuated, totally convincing dialogue. Pritchett has explained several times that "Sense of Humour," intended as a tellingly ironic story about a dull man, turned out to be – in the first version, which employed third-person narration – simply a dull story. When he revised the story – employing first-person narration that allowed his dull, insensitive traveling salesman to talk to the reader – all its subtly encapsulated ironies came alive.

Arthur, the rather vulgar salesman, begins to win the affections of Muriel, a girl with a sense of humor who is a desk clerk at a provincial hotel. The reader understands through the words of the slick, success-driven Arthur that he is largely insensitive to the agonies of Muriel's boyfriend, Colin, an inarticulate garage mechanic who anxiously trails Arthur's car whenever he rides with Muriel. As Colin follows the couple one day, he is killed when his motorcycle careens out of control into the path of an oncoming bus. That same night Muriel gives herself sexually to Arthur for the first time, even though she does, in passionate embrace, cry out, "Colin! Colin!"

A large dollop of black humor is added by Pritchett's making Arthur's father an undertaker. Colin had that day trailed his rival and his girlfriend nearly to the rival's home, a town some considerable distance away. The easiest arrangement for conveying Colin's body back home is to employ Arthur's father's hearse with, for economy, Arthur as driver: Muriel sits up front with Arthur, and Colin still follows behind, not on his motorcycle now, but in his casket. In the story's final paragraph people on the street raise their hats in respect for the dead while Arthur and Muriel, just slightly awkward, feel self-important and, in some curious way, satisfied.

To a high degree "Sense of Humour" exemplifies the salient characteristics of the Pritchettian story. First, there is the distinctive voice and unerringly accurate rendition of colloquial conversation, as any of Arthur and Muriel's dialogue reveals. Second, there is the combination of humor and satire: humor that is droll and satire that is clothed in sophisticated ironies so uninsistent that nonastute readers will miss them. It is only the black humor in this story that is relatively rare in Pritchett. Third, there is Pritchett's fascination with eccentric characters, surely his inheritance from reading Dickens. Muriel's eccentricity resides in what she calls her "sense of humour"; several times she proudly proclaims, "I'm Irish. I've got a sense of humour." Her laughing out loud as she sits in the front seat of the hearse with her dead boyfriend behind seems a sufficient indication that her "sense of humour" is bizarre. Even the insensitive Arthur says to her (either out of a sudden rising of normal feeling and decency, or else middle-class hypocrisy and respectability), "Keep your sense of humour to yourself."

Most significantly, the story has a degree of irresolution, of ambiguity, of elusiveness. Ironies bounce off each other in ways that make it hard to tell where they cross and where their paths begin and end. The reader simply cannot pin down answers to some key questions about plot and character neatly. Why did Muriel give herself to Arthur? Why did she moan Colin's name? Is her laughter a manifestation of grief (a curious but relatively common psychological phenomenon), or is it an indication of shocking shallowness? Is Arthur a soulless modern businessman, or is there a real human being somewhere beneath, struggling to break out of the mold of go-getter salesman? Pritchett's best stories contain this resonating core of ambiguity; within a brief space he manages to convey the rich, multiple levels of meaning and ambiguity that are so much a part of real life.

The phrase "typical Pritchett story" might suggest a certain narrowness of theme and technique, but this would be entirely misleading. Pritchett's range is narrower than some authors', but definitely wider than most. One might note, for example, the title piece of *You Make Your Own Life*, a story significantly different from "Sense of Humour." "You Make Your Own Life" – almost, but not quite, a monologue – blends elements of satire, humor, and compassion as it fixes an unnervingly close and steady gaze at the limitations of small-town life. In *The Teller and the Tale* (1982) William Peden notes the Hemingwayesque character of the story: "the brevity, directness, understatement, and effective use of dialogue."

The first narrator in the story, a visitor to the small town, provides a brief frame. He sits down in the barber's chair to get a haircut, and then the barber's monologue comprises nearly the whole story. Readers will be reminded of Ring Lardner's frequently anthologized story "Haircut" (first published in 1925) and might reflect too that Lardner is also expert at capturing the rhythms and diction of contemporary colloquial speech, at the skillful employment of ironic humor, and at the exposure of false values with a light but effective touch. Most commentators agree that Pritchett is largely original, that he found his own voice and his own way. But, despite his limited formal education, Pritchett has read widely, and he is a careful and highly conscious craftsman.

You Make Your Own Life, with a variety of themes and styles, shows Pritchett still in a stage of experimentation, but by this point even his experiments were conducted with assurance. By the mid 1930s things had begun to come together for Pritchett, both in his personal and professional lives. In 1934 Pritchett met Dorothy Roberts, a young woman with whom he almost instantly fell in love. He was able to marry her in 1936, when his divorce decree was granted. Pritchett has testified several times to his belief that passionate love is a spur to artistic creativity and that Dorothy has been for him a constant source of inspiration, happiness, and renewal. *Dead Man Leading* (1937), his most imaginative and technically ambitious novel to that date, proved relatively successful and received some good reviews.

Both world and personal events, however, conspired against Pritchett's progress in literary pursuits. A daughter was born in 1938 and a son in 1940, and the Pritchetts had bought a country house requiring maintenance and constant chores. And then, of course, there was World War II.

Pritchett's exact mode of involvement is slightly unclear, but the evidence strongly indicates, as Dean Baldwin notes, some kind of work for the government, probably the Ministry of Information. The early 1940s were a fallow period for Pritchett, who found little time or emotional energy for fiction writing.

By 1945, though, Pritchett was able to combine the few stories he had written during the war years with those composed in the late 1930s to form the volume *It May Never Happen*. Its favorable reception in England prompted the firm of Reynal in New York to publish it in 1947, making it Pritchett's first collection of stories to receive American publication. In *Midnight Oil* Pritchett writes that "Sense of Humour" was the first of his stories to "make a stir and give me what reputation I have as a writer of short-stories. . . . It woke me up . . . and led me on to 'The Sailor,' 'The Saint,' and 'Many Are Disappointed.' " These three stories, all from *It May Never Happen,* are, superficially at least, different from each other and from "Sense of Humour," yet all are among Pritchett's best short fiction.

Amply present in *It May Never Happen* are the traits most closely associated with Pritchett's distinctive artistry: the revelation of character through indirect, often both subtle and ironic, means; the interest in characters who are eccentrics or "puritans" or both; the auctorially mixed styles of compassion, amusement, and satiric exposure; and the employment of a sort of haze technique, which makes it impossible for readers to be sure they have taken full, final, and definitive measure of a character. "The Sailor," the most frequently anthologized and best known of the author's stories, is (although not one of his own favorites) quintessential Pritchett, employing all of the above elements.

Although "The Sailor" seems at first to be a story of the "most unforgettable character I've ever met type" – that character being the sailor – it turns out to be something different or at least something considerably more than a sharply realized and charming sketch of a character. Deeper and more central to the story is the gradual, subtle, and ironic self-exposure of the first-person narrator – an intelligent man, but an imperceptive man when it comes to a recognition of central truths about himself. The narrator takes into his home the former sailor, an unattached man with such a propensity for getting "hopelessly, blindly" lost that the reader might suspect some neurological impairment. The narrator, a writer living in the country, recognizes an identity of sorts with the sailor in that they are both "puritans," but the reader can also see that he regards the

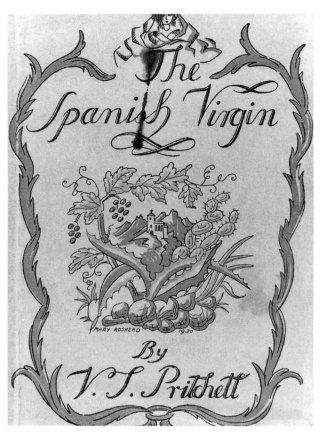

Dust jacket for Pritchett's first collection of short stories, none of which he considered worthy of inclusion in his Complete Collected Stories *(1991)*

sailor as slightly pitiable, a charity case. As the story develops, the sailor reaches out to make contact with others, and it seems probable that he has done this many times before. The narrator is more rigid and confined by his puritan nature and inheritance than is his guest. He is the one, it seems, to be pitied for emotional and spiritual sterility.

Most commentators on "The Sailor" do not seem to find much, if any, dramatic irony. In arguing against its presence they might point to its apparent inconsistency with the relaxed mood of comic whimsy and the ease of structure. Pritchett frequently withholds the two or three additional pieces of evidence explicators feel they need to provide a convincing analysis. Meaning is often equivocal in Pritchett, one of the probable reasons why three or four reviewers have mentioned Harold Pinter in comparison.

Broader, richer comedy and more obvious and pointed satire are present in "The Saint," a story so exquisitely crafted that the way it is told seems to be the easiest, the *only* way. For many,

Pritchett's artlessness makes him a writer's writer, a master of the short-story form. His selectivity and economy are all the more to be praised here since the motivating impulse for the story lies in some old wounds from Pritchett's own youth: those associated with his father's conversion to, and firm embrace of, Christian Science. In "The Saint" a sect called the Church of the Last Purification denies the existence of evil. The seventeen-year-old narrator, who is having doubts, explains: "We regarded it as 'Error' – our name for Evil – to believe the evidence of our senses, and if we had influenza or consumption, or had lost our money or were unemployed, we denied the reality of these things, saying that since God could not have made them they therefore did not exist."

The avuncular leader of the sect, Mr. Timberlake, is sent to have a heart-to-heart talk with the doubting narrator, and they go out punting on a river while they converse. The older man greatly exaggerates his skill as a punter and meets a small, but humiliating, disaster when he encounters a low overhanging branch of a willow tree. Pritchett's imagery is superbly witty as he first describes the tableaulike scene of Timberlake's being suspended from the slowly sinking branch to which he clings, then his total immersion. His black suit is gilded with buttercup pollen as he rests, thoroughly soaked, on the shore, all the while resolutely refusing to give any acknowledgment that he has met with a mishap.

Certainly one of the most successfully comic short stories of the century, "The Saint" also has depth, dimension, and even a real touch of pathos. The boy undergoes an initiation that day and comes to understand more than that the sect is a sham. While readers can laugh at Timberlake, they can also feel some sympathy and even a bit of identification with the earnestly striving figure who seems an emblem of human fallibility. These kinds of feelings are skillfully enhanced by Pritchett's use of retrospective narrative, in which the now middle-aged speaker relates that Timberlake has died young and that "the ape that merely followed me was already [the day of the immersion] inside Mr. Timberlake eating out his heart."

"It May Never Happen" provides Dickensian character sketches of eccentric individuals in a small office. The story is more than a comedy of humors, however, and it seems that the reader is expected to deduce the psychological bases for the eccentricities, especially in Mr. Phillimore, the most peculiar. Finding the "real" Phillimore is difficult, for his personality seems to demand that he engage in verbal impostures and theatrical scenes of his own devising. Despite the fact that this long story is a fairly central one in the Pritchett canon, no one has attempted any kind of analysis of this central character. By cleverly withholding some necessary evidence while suggestively providing a wealth of possibility, Pritchett causes fascinated speculation in his readers. Reviewers have complained that Pritchett sometimes carries his teasing technique too far.

In other stories Pritchett writes near the center of a modern tradition, where subtlety and indirection do lead to significant and clear meaning. "Many Are Disappointed" is Chekhovian in its delicate carefulness of structure and its establishment of meaning through the deft control of mood and atmosphere. Loneliness and longing are powerfully present in a woman who runs a tearoom far out on a country lane and in an empathizing young man among a group of cyclists who stop there and are disappointed because beer cannot be served. The story has a kind of stark, compressed lyricism reminiscent of the works of some of the best modern Welsh writers, such as Kate Roberts and Gwyn Jones.

"The Night Worker" is another successful story that shows the author's impressive range. Pritchett, whose metier is comic irony, here achieves great emotional impact, although – following his "less is more" philosophy – everything is magnificently understated. The central consciousness in the story is a seven-year-old boy who cannot comprehend that he is mostly unwanted by both his parents. The pathos results from the reader's comprehending the sadness of the boy's plight, one of which he is largely oblivious himself. Pritchett demonstrates his formidable ability to modulate and blend tones and emotions. The sadness of the boy's plight is placed against the joyful backdrop of the impending wedding of his cousin Gladys. The narrative nuances lead to interpretive richness and ambiguity. There is more than the ambiguous suggestion that the soon-to-be-married couple are going to adopt the young narrator.

"The Oedipus Complex," a self-portrait of a zany but believable dentist, is pure comedy and another testament to Pritchett's range. The whole of this frequently anthologized story consists of the words that the dentist, Mr. Pollfax, speaks to his patient in the chair. Remarkably, Pritchett has said that his own dentist supplied this monologue piecemeal; if so, the author still reveals his artistry by selecting the statements wisely.

During World War II Pritchett wrote book reviews for the *New Statesman,* which had published some of his stories. The association increased after the war; in 1946 Pritchett briefly became a director (although he soon felt burdened by the expenditure of time). He was literary editor from 1945 to 1949 and general editor from 1954 to 1956, and for years he continued to write its "Books in General" column. More important for his short-story career was the fact that the relatively high-paying *New Yorker* began to publish his stories. (The rate of payment from British periodicals, meanwhile, ranged from modest to paltry.) The *New Yorker,* almost a postwar savior of the quality short story, was also publishing works by Sylvia Townsend Warner and Muriel Spark. It was later to publish those of Penelope Gilliatt and Trevor. A few commentators have suggested that Trevor and Gilliatt (and to some extent Spark) are Pritchett's disciples or inheritors. All have the tendency to view the English as a curious species whose customs and behavior can be examined – as if from a distance – with amusement and tolerance, or as a people charmingly eccentric or delightfully quaint.

Work for the *New Statesman* heavily occupied Pritchett's time during the late 1940s and early 1950s. From 1953 to 1954 he was Christian Gauss lecturer at Princeton University. *Mr. Beluncle* (1951), his last novel, is another fiction whose obvious genesis is in his own early life. (One of the characters, Mr. Chilly, is much like the puzzling Phillimore of "It May Never Happen," except that Chilly is more fully defined.) The novel is highly flavorful, but there are problems with unity and, as Baldwin indicates, readers never get the feeling they have come to any deep, ultimate understanding of the nonetheless fascinating title character, a thinly disguised Walter Pritchett. *The Spanish Temper* (1954) is a travel book regarded by some as a modern classic. Pritchett's observations on the Spanish character, somewhat impressionistic to be sure, are sharp, illuminating, and mostly convincing.

Pritchett published little short fiction in this period, one of the reasons being that no writer could seriously think of supporting a family by the sale of short stories ("The Sailor," for example, initially brought him the sum of three pounds). *Collected Stories* (1956) contains all the pieces in *You Make Your Own Life* and *It May Never Happen* plus nine previously uncollected stories. *The Sailor, Sense of Humour, and Other Stories* (1956) contains seven pieces from *You Make Your Own Life,* thirteen from *It May Never Happen,* and five not previously collected.

Pritchett has rather consistently maintained that the title story of *When My Girl Comes Home* (1961) is the best he has ever written, and several critics – Walter Allen, Kermode, and Trevor among them — agree. Others argue the point, feeling that Pritchett has gone altogether too far with the technique of implicitness. An anonymous *Times Literary Supplement* (6 October 1961) reviewer opined that "one may perhaps feel that its obliquities and lacunae are as much the result of the temptations of a teasing technique as of artistic necessity."

Much is left to suggestion in "When My Girl Comes Home," even though it is a novella-length story. It concerns a woman's postwar return to her old London neighborhood. Family and neighbors thought she had been a prisoner of war, when actually she had been the wife of a Japanese military man. Pritchett involves the reader in some subtle, indirect play with both the illusion/reality theme and the literature/life opposition. One thematic suggestion of this complex story seems to be that people's minds were numbed during most of the war but overstimulated during its end and aftermath. The monumentality of the horror and the drama, once it had sunk in, scarcely allowed them to maintain moral or epistemological equipoise. The relatively uneducated, decent people of the woman's London neighborhood had been "common" and parochial; now they awake to the larger world, but they do so with confusion. They are no longer sure of what is true or false, right or wrong. The arrival of their "girl" back home largely coincides, then, with their enforced entry into the contemporary world. "When My Girl Comes Home" is a complex story of initiation.

The other most notable story from the volume, "The Wheelbarrow," is an excellent, albeit much more conventional, piece. Although here meaning is communicated subtly, it seems almost fully deducible. The story is a convincing, but comic, study of two characters, a man and a woman, separated by class and background as well as gender. They meet, feel some sexual chemistry, spar wittily, and part. The man, a Welsh cabdriver and lay preacher, is charming, wily, brash, and hypocritical. However, he is much more than a mere type (the religious hypocrite) or a colorful eccentric. Pritchett seldom uses two-dimensional characters and has politely objected to his characters' being labeled eccentrics. He presents his characters' lives with extreme sharpness, all the while on the lookout for the small telling oddities that, in some sense, make them more true. This is not to say that eccentrics vanish altogether from his realistic stories. As Eudora Welty writes in a review of Pritchett's *Selected Stories* (*New York Times Book Review,* 25 June 1978): "How much the eccentric has to tell us of what is central!"

"The Key to My Heart," one of the stories in *When My Girl Comes Home,* turned out to be the first of three linked stories ("Noisy Flushes the Birds" and "Noisy in the Doghouse" being the second and third), all of which were originally published in the *New Yorker.* In 1963 Pritchett brought the three stories together in a book, *The Key to My Heart: A Comedy in Three Parts.* The dust jacket for the 1964 American edition refers to the book as a novel, and the three stories are indeed tightly, integrally, and progressively linked together. *The Key to My Heart* is a successful mix of character sketch, droll comedy of manners, and farce. The psychological acuity and subtlety provide a good complement to the comic effects, enriching rather than detracting from them. The light, polished touch, the dottiness of the characters, and the overriding concern with social class can cause the book to be seen as a "very English" product, a type with which Americans were familiar through the works of Warner, Evelyn Waugh, P. G. Wodehouse, and Angus Wilson.

The 1960s proved a productive decade for Pritchett, who was already in his sixties. He had three visiting academic appointments in the United States: at the University of California, Berkeley (1962); at Smith College (1966, a time he says he particularly enjoyed); and at Brandeis University (1968). He collaborated with the photographer Evelyn Hofer on three coffee-table travel books: *London Perceived* (1962), *New York Proclaimed* (1965), and *Dublin: A Portrait* (1967). Many people know Pritchett for the London volume; his knowledgeable, beautifully styled text makes it stand far out in front of other picture books about cities. An engaging collection of his travel essays, *Foreign Faces* (republished as *The Offensive Traveller*), appeared in 1964. In 1968 he produced his justly acclaimed first volume of autobiography, *A Cab at the Door;* the second, *Midnight Oil,* was published in 1971.

Another collection of short fiction, *Blind Love and Other Stories* (1969), was also a success. All ten stories are comedies, and all are about love, whether it is unrecognized, dammed up, thwarted, or misdirected. In the stories "blind love" can mean blind because of love, blind to one's own love or that of someone else, or a blind plunge into love. Themes involving strong sexual attraction are asserted in this volume, and they resurface in Pritchett's succeeding fictional works. Some reviewers expressed mild surprise that a man then in his late sixties would seem to recognize more than ever the power of erotic love. Pritchett has suggested that it is, of course, a powerfully central force in human life, but it is also for him a means to character revelation. As erotic/romantic impulses tug at the characters, interesting fissures and divisions within their selves become apparent. In *V. S. Pritchett: A Study of the Short Fiction* (1992) Douglas A. Hughes explains that "in these late stories, which may be called comedies of Eros, the characters learn about their self-deceptions, hidden motives and fears, and what truly matters while the sympathetic reader smilingly recognizes the characters' imperfections and identifies with their profound humanity."

Three of the stories in *Blind Love* are among Pritchett's best: "The Skeleton," "The Cage Birds," and "Blind Love." The title story, a long piece of about 17,500 words, shows a side of Pritchett's craft that is not typical but that he can use to excellent advantage. The story is a relatively complex, somewhat ironic study of two characters. The structure, narrative method, and selected incident allow readers to uncover, almost layer by layer, the hidden emotions and motives of the characters. In its clearly worked out and progressive adumbration of character it resembles the similarly successful "Handsome Is as Handsome Does" (*You Make Your Own Life*).

The two characters in "Blind Love," who are nearly dual protagonists, are a well-to-do lawyer — totally blind, he was deserted by his wife some twenty years before, when he began to go blind — and his present secretary/companion — now thirty-nine, she was abandoned by her husband when he discovered, only after their marriage, that she had a birthmark extending from her neck to below one breast. At the end of the story the employer, undeterred by the physical blemish he now knows about but cannot see, comes together with his secretary to form a mutual relationship of love, sexual fulfillment, and understanding. But what occurs between beginning and end is, of course, what makes the story fascinating. The emotions of both the man and the woman are rich and fully believable, revealed within a structure of almost-symbolic incidents (including two immersions easily viewed as symbolic baptisms) reminiscent of D. H. Lawrence's "The Horse Dealer's Daughter" and "The Blind Man" (both from *England, My England and Other Stories*, 1922).

Many reviewers were impressed that Pritchett, then seventy-four, could achieve the high level of artistry he displays in *The Camberwell Beauty and Other Stories* (1974). At least four of the nine stories are excellent (the title story, "The Diver," "The Marvellous Girl," and "The Lady from Guatemala"). Several British reviewers remarked how

Pritchett's stories in general, and "The Camberwell Beauty" in particular, have an unerring eye for precisely accurate and convincing details. In the title story, which concerns the London antiques trade, Pritchett is back to dealing with eccentrics. But he has made the point that eccentricity is everywhere in real life, perhaps somewhat more so in England than elsewhere. In an interview in the *Journal of the Short Story in English* (Spring 1986) Pritchett remarks that he has been compared to Dickens "sometimes wrongly":

> People say that his [Dickens's] characters are done in caricature: I think that that is totally untrue, almost totally untrue. Especially in the English characters. A large number of English people you see walking up and down the street are acting a part. They are concealing themselves from everyone by extraordinary acts of behaviour. Strange verbiage comes out of them, certain fantasies come flying out of them, which is part of their character. They see themselves curiously, I think, on some kind of private stage.

Reviewers have noted the large assortment of liars and boasters in Pritchett's stories. The author seems to suggest that most people are liars and boasters to some extent, this perhaps being necessary for psychological self-sustainment in a modern world that constantly threatens and diminishes the individual.

The "Camberwell Beauty" is Isabel, a comely teenage girl at the beginning of the story. She is the niece of the wife of an antiques dealer, and three of the men in the trade — including the young narrator of the story — lust for possession of the beautiful and apparently naive young woman in just about the same way they lust for the possession of rare precious objects. She ends up married to the oldest of the three, an impotent man who keeps her virtually locked up and who every night commands her to undress while he looks — simply looks — at her with the same pride of possession he reserves for his most prized porcelain objects, his specialty. When he is not at home, he requires her to dress as a soldier, beat a marching drum, and blow a bugle to scare away would-be rapists and seducers.

The story can obviously be viewed as a near allegory about male possessiveness, but a few reviewers saw Pritchett going in for the improbable, the fey, and the fantastic. Pritchett seems to believe, however, that real life serves up its own metaphors for universal truths, that the artist simply has to be on a sharp lookout for these ready-made metaphors and know how to frame and present them. In *London Perceived* Pritchett notes:

The antique trade of London is tough and intimately connected; it shows a head in innumerable districts; it is a collection of tricky eccentrics, watching one another like spies, and it is the least on-coming, the most misleadingly absent-minded trade in London. And why not? A large number of its clientele – I mean the core of the business, not the casual dropper-in – are obsessed or mad.

Like the title story, "The Diver" also contains a hint of allegory. An initiation story, it subtly but memorably explores the sometimes close relationship between artistic creativity and the libido. The narrator, a young Englishman living in Paris who is proud of his virginity (much to the amazement of his French coworkers), is much like the young Pritchett self-revealed in *Midnight Oil.* Both sexually led on and mocked by an older Frenchwoman, the narrator salvages self-respect by fabricating a story about a murder (giving the mocking seducer some pause) and satisfying himself (and also her, it seems) sexually. Pritchett includes some carefully worked-out symbolic imagery involving animal skins (like Pritchett, the narrator is involved in the leather trade), and the sharp evocation of Paris in the 1920s is both thematically appropriate and colorful.

"The Marvellous Girl" concerns the severing of the last emotional ties that hold a husband and wife together and the chemically charged romantic attraction soon felt by the husband for "the marvellous girl." She is a coworker of his former wife, toward whom he still feels a confused congeries of emotions. The story provides a vivid sense of the man's feelings much more than it offers deep character study or plot. A complexity of response is produced in the reader by Pritchett's manner of presentation. From a certain point onward in the story readers can share the excitement of the young man's romantic infatuation, or they can view it ironically. They may, in fact, be able to do both at the same time, as Pritchett walks a fine line between romance and gentle mockery (or a kind of Olympian amusement) all the way through to the end. Pritchett's stories of love and erotic attraction generally provide a mixture of the comic, the ironic, and the sincerely emotional, with one treatment or mood often modulating (as in "The Marvellous Girl") into another to produce a surprised sense of depth and complexity.

Various honors and recognitions had already begun to accumulate for Pritchett, but they were capped in 1975, when he was knighted for "services to literature." The favorable reviews given *The Camberwell Beauty* probably had something to do with this

award, but additional attention had also come to the genial, hardworking Pritchett when he was elected president of the English branch of P.E.N. in 1971 and its international president in 1974. In 1971 he had also been named an honorary member of the American Academy of Arts and Letters.

Sir Victor, now a recognized master of the short-story form, had little difficulty placing his stories in those periodicals publishing quality short fiction. *On the Edge of the Cliff,* his 1979 collection, brings together nine stories, most of which had received dual publication in Britain and America. (The *New Yorker* had published three, and one had appeared in the high-paying *Playboy,* one in *Atlantic Monthly,* and two in *Encounter.*) The dominant themes in the collection are love and loneliness. Several stories seem to ask key questions about romantic love: does it necessarily involve delusion, or is it a useful force that awakens people to their true and best selves by stripping away various encrustations that lie between the surface and the real core of a person's being?

Three of the stories – "The Accompanist," "The Fig Tree," and "A Family Man" – are sharply observed tales of adultery or betrayal in love. The title story, probably the best of the collection, effectively provides a subtle modulation of tones, in this case taking readers from hard-edged realism to pathos, to poetic celebration, to comic deflation, and back again. The basic situation begins to explain how this might be done: Harry, a seventyish man, has a lovely twenty-five-year-old mistress who loves him. At one point in the story the old man strips naked, stands on the edge of a cliff overlooking some rocks and hard-breaking surf, stands there suspended in a memorable tableau, and then dives – proving, it seems, something both to himself and his young love.

Some readers will see Harry as a slightly ridiculous and repulsive old man. More will probably view him as a normal human being whose attempts to defeat the advance of time are quixotic and ungraceful. Many will see him as a representative of the constancy of human aspiration and indomitability of spirit. The author, by his shaping of form and handling of tones, will cause most readers to consider all three viewpoints. Certainly the story is no psychological parable, but it can be seen as a poetic meditation on Eros and Thanatos.

Some of the other stories in the collection – especially "The Accompanist," "The Fig Tree," and "The Wedding" – implicitly ask questions about the ways people "invent" themselves (a phrase used in several stories), "invent" people close to them, and "invent" relationships. Emotional health involves, at least in part, a balance of the elements of constancy and change. The need for constancy, though, sometimes leads people to discover self-deception or deception in those they love; the need for change sometimes causes people to make a mistake, to jump toward a false illusion. In "The Fig Tree" Sally, the wife, finds her emotional and sexual life barren and begins a sexual relationship with Teddy, a nurseryman. In the ironic, twist-in-the-tail ending uncharacteristic of Pritchett, her husband concocts both sweet revenge and an effective means of dealing with his problem. He finds a way to bring wife and lover together in enforced close contact every day in their work; soon the adulterous couple are thoroughly bored with each other.

"The Accompanist" also concerns wifely deception and adultery, in this case that of the title character, Joyce, a musical accompanist. One might suppose that her adultery is an earmark of her independence, but it is not. She is a natural accompanist in her life in general, not just in music. She is under the delusion that she is inventing herself when in actuality people are inventing her – using her to their own ends. But the other two main characters suffer delusions and neurotic torments as well. The impotent husband, Bertie, right on the edge of being a psychological basket case, is not above extorting sympathy from those around him, and sympathy of a sort seems the reason Joyce married him. He appears consistently able to use his weakness as an effective means of control. The lover, William, is the narrator, and at the end of the story he comes to envy the cozy, domestic intimacy of Bertie and Joyce; William realizes that he too might be merely an accompanist in life.

Although not at all tendentiously – like Lawrence – Pritchett often suggests that spiritual death results from a failure or unwillingness to open oneself to change, to become stratified in some environment or else to conceive of oneself as a heavily defined essence incapable of change. Like Lawrence as well, Pritchett often permits his characters, especially when they are responding to some strong emotional stimulus, to act a bit "out of character," to change. Pritchett's willingness to allow his characters a fair degree of freedom (in somewhat the same way that Lawrence talks about moving away from the "old stable ego of character") might give some readers the sense that Pritchett is guilty of flawed or inadequate plotting and implausible characterization. One needs to understand that Pritchett's art is subtle and that he has a respect for his characters, life's mysteries, and the intelligence (including emotional intelligence) of his readers.

"The Wedding," even more than "The Blind Man," is a heavily Lawrencian story. Mrs. Jackson, a divorced woman in her early thirties, teaches French in a small town in an agricultural area of England. She has humble origins as a girl in this same general area but, through education and pretense (for example, passing herself off as a member of a French émigré family), has raised herself to a different social level and married a man from a socially prominent family. But, when her marriage ends in divorce and scandal, she comes, rather prim and intellectual, to teach at the small college. She tells a male teacher that she sees nothing wrong in girls wanting to be duchesses: "Why shouldn't they think they are duchesses? I always wanted to be one. Girls are practical. A girl is a new thing: they have to invent themselves."

The transformation in her present life begins when she encounters Tom Fletcher – the father of one of her students – an earthy, indeed somewhat crude man who has been in the habit of referring to her as "the little bitch from the college." Although Fletcher is intelligent and hardworking, he really seems to believe the folklorish male "wisdom" he espouses to his friends: that Mrs. Jackson's astringent manner will melt when a man lights her sexual fire. Mrs. Jackson attends a wedding at which sexual undercurrents are strong, it being a local custom for the men to lasso the women. When she is lassoed by Fletcher, she is understandably indignant. But the ritual enactment of basic life forces and urges is a dramatically powerful moment. In an understated and carefully selective manner Pritchett allows his readers to feel the social and sexual antagonisms that exist between the farmer and the teacher, the currents that shoot across, and then reverse, within powerful fields of emotional and sexual energy. The story ends with the farmer winning her heart, but, because of Pritchett's deft management, this outcome does not seem either sentimental or hackneyed.

When *A Careless Widow and Other Stories* was published in 1989, almost every reviewer registered astonishment that a man approaching age ninety could produce stories of a quality high enough to provoke envy in almost any writer of any age. Loneliness, delusion, and the need for love – especially among the middle-aged and the elderly – are the themes of most of the six stories, although the single story that does not fit this description, "Cocky Olly," is arguably the best. It is told by Sarah, a fifty-four-year-old woman who is able to recapture, objectively, in a poetically sensitive mode of controlled nostalgia, what life was like for her when she was fourteen.

Sarah recalls the sense of wonder, joy, vitality, and confusion of her younger self, a girl raised by parents whose lives were suffused with a middle-class English dullness, suspicion, and timidity. The politically and socially reactionary fulminations of her father, while comic to the reader, produced deep, complex impressions and reactions within her. She begins to emerge from her tight, sheltered world of strict parental control when a liberal family of "advanced" ideas buys the adjoining property and she becomes acquainted with the son, a mischievous, maladjusted boy. At his house the two of them, accompanied by other children, play Cocky Olly, a game much like prisoner's base. They race about the house, shouting and flinging open doors, but his parents are perfectly and easily tolerant.

The opening of doors is a metaphor for what Sarah's new friendship is doing for her life: "At home we lived to ourselves, as my father said. Doors were always shut in our house. Here [in the new neighbors' house] all the doors were open and names were flying about." Pritchett complicates things by the introduction of some honest complexity. The new neighbors, beneath their seemingly easy liberality of spirit, are neurotically scarred by some bad experiences of the past and certain extravagances that continue in their lives. The young Sarah comes to intuit that she must somehow integrate the order and predictability represented by her father with the exuberance and spontaneity represented by the neighbors. After all, even the game of Cocky Olly ("all of us racing around") has its rules.

"A Careless Widow" is in many ways like James Joyce's "A Painful Case," but with less compression, not as much scrupulous meanness, and not as dramatic an epiphany. Depending on the reader's viewpoint, this relatively long story can both gain and lose in comparison with Joyce's. In "A Careless Widow" a successful London hairdresser and confirmed bachelor, Lionel Frazier, is the analogue of Joyce's James Duffy. Like the girl's father in "Cocky Olly," Frazier is afraid of involvement because to him it connotes "mess," a loss of personal order and control. Frazier is affable, but the "careless widow," the woman who lives in the flat beneath him, causes him deep trepidation: "She was ordinary life and ordinary life always went too far." Some readers may find that Pritchett, characteristically compassionate toward his characters, here allows some of that compassion to be eroded as

he yields to the temptation of engaging in some sly, arch humor at the expense of the timid homosexual who has ruinously repressed his emotional life along with his sexuality. Yet even here Pritchett's attitudes, encased in complex artistry, are muted, subtle, and understated.

Reviews of both the English (1990) and American (1991) editions of the complete collected short fiction were so highly favorable and so prominently placed (usually as the lead review) that readers may have assumed that Pritchett's place within the canon of major short-story writers was all but secured. It is difficult to say, however, if this is indeed the case. Pritchett's stories have never been favorites for American anthologists aiming at the college-textbook market, and in the past few years Pritchett's representation seems to have declined even more. Probably the main reason for this is that the great majority of his stories do not yield quick, neat, and wholly convincing results when subjected to New Critical, structuralist, deconstructionist, psychoanalytic, feminist, or other systematic approaches.

Another reason might be that Pritchett is not easily classifiable: he is not thought to represent any school, be the exemplar of a definable style or technique, or be the author of sharply pointed comments on the short-story form that could be valuably printed alongside a story or two as a stimulus or clue to a certain kind of analysis. He falls between stools: he is modern, certainly, but makes relatively little use of symbol or sensibility; he has escaped the tyranny of plot, but he is not an exemplar of plotlessness or nonlinear narrative.

And then, too, British short-story writers since Lawrence have not, despite some success in the *New Yorker,* been well represented in America. Pritchett's reputation, not totally justified, of being a "very English" writer does not bode well for his fiction's longevity. Many anthologists lay emphasis on the richness and diversity of all the literatures of the world, hoping to expand the horizons of American and British readers. If such anthologists deem Pritchett's stories to be of a type already too familiar – delicate, or maybe even feeble, fictions about the peculiarities of the supposedly insular English, a minute part of the world's total population – they are not at all likely to include them. Moreover, Pritchett's stories have no social urgency and might seem to be devoid of social point or moral impetus.

Pritchett is a well-read, sophisticated artist, but he is highly suspicious of both literary theories and "big" generalizations. In *The Turn of the Years* the usually tolerant author expresses some scorn for the "new and portentous verbiage" of academic theorists, finding that "their commentaries are full of self-important and comic irrelevancies." Like his contemporary Elizabeth Bowen, he seems to feel that a story, a kind of living organism, should be kept safe from critical dissection of any sort. Several reviewers have correctly remarked that Pritchett's stories often give a sense of the "vagaries of human nature." He has a strong belief in the undefined, the unpredictable, as at least a small part of life – that part of life that is most fascinating and that cries out to be artistically rendered. Overly determined meanings, then, are inimical to Pritchett's own theory and practice.

In his introduction to *The Oxford Book of Short Stories* (1981) Pritchett writes about what the short-story form can best accomplish, and he actually distills the essence of his own art: "Because the short story has to be succinct and has to suggest things that have been 'left out,' are, in fact, there all the time, the art calls for a mingling of the skills of the rapid reporter or traveller with an eye for incident and an ear for real speech, the instincts of the poet and ballad-maker, and the sonnet writer's concealed discipline of form." In his most characteristic stories Pritchett has "left out" more than readers would expect in a nonexperimental writer; the reader is virtually required to become a cocreator of meaning. In general, current taste strongly favors practices such as these. Many readers have grown weary of stories that lock them on a tight track and speed them straight down the rails to the terminal of illumination. Recent theorists have used terms such as *mimetic resistance, recalcitrance,* and *conspicuous silence* to describe structural or technical features of certain stories they admire, and the New Critics always sensibly approved of "tension." Academic critics may yet locate Pritchett and find significant riches; narratologists and reader-response critics might find that he provides fertile fields for study.

Whether exaggerated or not, Pritchett's characters are always sharply observed and faithfully represented, most especially in their speech, where the author is supremely sensitive to tone, cadence, and nuance. Whether in dialogue or in the narrative voice, Pritchett's prose is always, as Allen puts it in *The Short Story in English* (1981), "uncannily close to the speaking voice." In virtually all his interviews Pritchett has conveyed the idea that the majority of his stories had their genesis in his personal life – if not in the sense of direct emotional involvement and participation, then in the sense of his acute observation of an actual person or event.

In the *Journal of the Short Story in English* interview Pritchett remarks, "I have a trained memory for any kind of phrase, anything heard in a shop or in a train. A phrase was often more important to me than a sentence." He has explained that an overheard phrase (such as "I keep myself to myself ") can provide the imaginative spark that allows him to capture a voice (here that of the narrator in "The Sailor") and then the personality behind that voice. In the same interview he observes that, with short-story composition, "you don't want an awful lot of facts, you don't want particularly an idea, but what you really want is to hear the tune of the first sentence and the note you wish to prolong."

Pritchett is like Pinter in his expert framing of the odd bit of language or the cliché that rapidly seems to reveal the essence of character. Pritchett's characters frequently reveal themselves, as do people in real life, by their self-important and face-saving expressions, hyperboles, non sequiturs, quirky verbosities, and digressions. Pritchett's ear has long been tuned for the odd phrase; in *A Cab at the Door* he reports his delight when, sent to the store for bananas, he heard the grocer say, "Bananas out of the question!"

Several commentators have approvingly quoted Irving Howe's judgment of Pritchett: "No one alive writes a better English sentence." While that is debatable, most readers will readily concede the wit, pungency, and general felicity of phrasing that characterize so many of Pritchett's stories. Most important, whether in dialogue or narration, Pritchett's style hardly ever becomes mannered or too clever; it is always consistent with the "tune" and the "distinctive voice" that Pritchett feels crucial for a successful story. His meticulous composition process involves the pruning of phrases or sentences he considers overwritten. His arsenal of language and style is formidable, but he uses it in wise moderation.

It is only slightly stretching a point to maintain, as does English reviewer and academic Valentine Cunningham, that Pritchett's stories provide a decade-by-decade map of social change in England over the past six decades. His stories are about individuals and enduring human emotions much more than they are about the state of society, but readers attuned to nuance will see subtle, indirect reflections of changes in English society in the lives of some average English citizens. In only a few stories does Pritchett lay heavy emphasis on the favorite English theme of class distinction, but when he does – most notably in the three stories of *The Key to My Heart* – he achieves successful, delightfully light social comedy. In less overt ways the state of society makes its presence felt in most of the stories because the characteristic themes of loneliness, puritanism, initiation, the business ethic, self-delusion, and the problems of marriage attain full meaning and resonance only when placed against the backdrop of the real social world.

That Pritchett has, in recent years, represented almost exclusively the lives and dialogue of the elderly and the middle-aged is a limitation, but a minor one. The dialogue and narration in "The Rescue" (where the narrator is a sixteen-year-old girl excited about owning "the shortest mini-skirt in town") is not nearly so startlingly "right" as is usually the case with Pritchett, but it is sufficiently believable and quite far from embarrassing. Mostly, though, Pritchett prudently avoids operating out of his large circuit of excellence. He can almost magically suggest the general in the particular, and if he knows that particular well and can represent it truly, it does not matter overly much what it happens to be. What is important is that he knows a situation or environment so well that he can appear to represent it seemingly casually, in a way that is immensely suggestive.

Much more goes on in a Pritchett story than a casual reader might think, and much is there to give both reward and pleasure. In a review of *Selected Stories* (*New York Times Book Review*, 25 June 1978) Welty, herself one of the most acclaimed writers of the artistic short story, puts it this way: "Any Pritchett story is all of it alight and busy at once, like a well-going fire. Wasteless and at the same time well fed, it shoots up in flame from its own spark like a poem or a magic trick, self-consuming, with nothing left over. He is one of the great pleasure givers in our language."

Interviews:
Lewis Nichols, "Talk with V. S. Pritchett," *New York Times Book Review*, 25 April 1954, p. 16;
Douglas A. Hughes, "V. S. Pritchett: An Interview," *Studies in Short Fiction*, 13 (Fall 1976): 423–432;
"V. S. Pritchett," *Vogue* (March 1981): 326–328;
John Haffenden, "V. S. Pritchett," in his *Novelists in Interview* (London: Methuen, 1985), pp. 210–230;

Ben Forkner and Philippe Séjourné, "An Interview with V. S. Pritchett," *Journal of the Short Story in English*, 6 (Spring 1986): 11–38;
Suzanne Cassidy, "A Noticing Kind of Person," *New York Times Book Review*, 22 October 1989, p. 3;
Shusha Guppy and Anthony Weller, "The Art of Fiction CXXII: V. S. Pritchett," *Paris Review*, 117 (Winter 1990): 182–207;
Esther Harriott, "Of Aging and the Muse: Author V. S. Pritchett Reflects on Literary Longevity," *Buffalo Magazine*, 24 (January 1993): 8–11.

References:
Walter Allen, "V. S. Pritchett," in his *The Short Story in English* (New York: Oxford University Press, 1981), pp. 268–275;
Dean Baldwin, *V. S. Pritchett* (Boston: Twayne, 1987);
Ben Forkner, ed., *Journal of the Short Story in English*, special issue on Pritchett, 6 (Spring 1986);
Susan Lohafer, " 'The Wheelbarrow' by V. S. Pritchett," in her *Coming to Terms with the Short Story* (Baton Rouge: Louisiana State University Press, 1983), pp. 148–153;
William Peden, "Realism and Anti-realism," in *The Teller and the Tale: Aspects of the Short Story*, edited by Wendell M. Aycock (Lubbock: Texas Tech Press, 1982), pp. 47–62;
Peden, "V. S. Pritchett," in *The English Short Story, 1880–1945*, edited by Joseph M. Flora (Boston: Twayne, 1985), pp. 143–151;
John J. Stinson, *V. S. Pritchett: A Study of the Short Fiction* (New York: Twayne/Macmillan, 1992).

Papers:
An extensive collection of Pritchett's manuscripts and correspondence is located at the Harry Ransom Humanities Research Center, University of Texas at Austin. The Berg Collection, New York Public Library, includes many manuscripts of Pritchett's stories and reviews, plus some of his correspondence. Additional Pritchett manuscripts are held by the University of Reading (England) Library, the BBC Written Archives Centre, and the British Library.

William Sansom

(18 January 1912 – 20 April 1976)

Michael Kleeberg
Ball State University

BOOKS: *Fireman Flower* (New York: Vanguard, 1945; London: New Phoenix Library, 1952);

Something Terrible, Something Lovely (London: Hogarth, 1948; New York: Harcourt, Brace, 1954);

South (London: Hodder & Stoughton, 1948; New York: Harcourt, Brace, 1950);

The Body (London: Hogarth, 1949; New York: Harcourt, Brace, 1949);

The Passionate North (London: Hogarth, 1950; New York: Harcourt, Brace, 1953);

The Face of Innocence (London: Hogarth, 1951; New York: Harcourt, Brace, 1951);

A Touch of the Sun (London: Hogarth, 1952; New York: Reynal, 1958);

Pleasures Strange and Simple (London: Hogarth, 1953);

A Bed of Roses (London: Hogarth, 1954; New York: Harcourt, Brace, 1954);

Lord Love Us (London: Hogarth, 1954);

A Contest of Ladies (London: Hogarth, 1956; New York: Reynal, 1956);

The Loving Eye (London: Hogarth, 1956; New York: Reynal, 1956);

Among the Dahlias (London: Hogarth, 1957);

The Cautious Heart (London: Hogarth, 1958; New York: Reynal, 1958);

The Icicle and the Sun (London: Hogarth, 1958; New York: Reynal, 1959);

The Last Hours of Sandra Lee (London: Hogarth, 1961; Boston: Little, Brown, 1961);

Blue Skies, Brown Studies (Boston: Little, Brown, 1961; London: Hogarth, 1961);

Away to It All (London: Hogarth, 1964; New York: New American Library, 1966);

The Ulcerated Milkman (London: Hogarth, 1966);

Goodbye (London: Hogarth, 1966; New York: New American Library, 1967);

Grand Tour Today (London: Hogarth, 1968);

Hans Feet in Love (London: Hogarth, 1971);

The Marmalade Bird (London: Hogarth, 1973);

A Young Wife's Tale (London: Hogarth, 1974).

William Sansom (photograph by Alan Clifton)

Collection: *The Stories of William Sansom,* introduction by Elizabeth Bowen (London: Hogarth, 1963; Freeport, N.Y.: Books for Libraries Press, 1971).

When William Sansom's fiction first appeared in the 1940s, it was hailed by critics and the public alike. His trademark at the time was meticulous detail; borrowing heavily from the styles of Franz Kafka and Edgar Allan Poe, he created haunting visions out of everyday people and events. While critics at first noted his direct appeal to the eye, his later stories began to appeal to the ear, to the reader's sense of rhythm and movement. The playful, colorful language in the later stories includes puns and coinages that uniquely suit his characters and situations. Some critics, however, consider his meticulousness with sensual detail to be his main flaw. But author Elizabeth Bowen, in the introduction to *The Stories of William Sansom* (1963), describes him as "a writer whose faculties not only suit the short story but are suited by it – suited and, one may feel, enhanced."

Sansom was born in London on 18 January 1912, the third son of Ernest and Mabel Sansom. Between trips to Europe with his father, a naval architect, William received formal schooling at Uppingham from 1920 to 1928. His father steered him toward a career in banking and commercial finance. Accordingly, William traveled in Europe at length between 1928 and 1930 to learn languages. He studied German extensively and went to work for the British branch of a German bank in 1930. He spent five years in the banking business and then became a copywriter for an advertising agency. He shared an office with the poet Norman Cameron, whom Lila Chalpin, in *William Sansom* (1980), describes as "the catalyst in a moment of epiphany for Sansom." Cameron took him to an exhibition of surrealist paintings, which Sansom viewed as the purest interpretations of reality that he had ever seen. The surrealist art inspired him to suffuse his fiction with integral moments of stark reality. Sansom also possessed musical talents; he worked as a dance pianist and even wrote a waltz that was performed at Les Folies Bergère in Paris. His musical abilities doubtless influenced the appeal of rhythm and movement in his later stories.

The outbreak of World War II produced dramatic changes in Sansom's life. Too old to enlist in the military, he joined the National Fire Service in 1939. He captures the dreadful anticipation of fires caused by enemy bombers in his first published short story, "The Wall" (*Horizon,* July 1941; collected in *Fireman Flower,* 1945). An unnamed fireman serves as the narrator. He muses that nothing remarkable has happened that night besides a few "enquiring bombs" and some enormous fires, which have become so routine to him that they no longer register as remarkable. At 3:00 A.M., on the third call of the night answered by his company, he and three of his compatriots – Len, Verno, and Lofty – rush to the address and find themselves confronted by an enormous wall, behind which a warehouse furiously burns. Numb to the noise and surrounding activity, the narrator and his friends aim their jets of water at the fire. With an ear-splitting crack the wall separates from the warehouse and collapses on them.

The narrator numbly ponders the symmetrical rows of fire-brightened windows that plummet toward him. Looking to his left and right he dreamily notes potential avenues for escape but uses none of them.

He considers the angle at which the wall is descending and recounts the ways that he has seen a wall collapse. When the wall finally cracks and plunges, he kneels like a man awaiting knighthood. The wall crashes and Lofty dies; but the narrator, Len, and Verno are spared. They happen to kneel in perfect alignment with one of the windows and escape with only minor injuries. Sansom's details evoke a slow, horrible eternity of thought in the few seconds between the initial separation of the wall from the warehouse and its crash.

Other early stories by Sansom end with fate whimsically touching the characters for better or worse. In "The Vertical Ladder" (*English Story,* fifth series 1944; collected in *Something Terrible, Something Lovely,* 1948) some youthful friends dare a young man named Flegg to scale the side of an abandoned gasometer. He accepts their challenge, dismissing the uneasy second thoughts that they voice. Midway through the climb Flegg looks down and discovers that one in the group has removed the rickety wooden ladder that he has used to reach the metal ladder affixed to the side of the gasometer. Shaken, Flegg grimly resumes his climb. As he nears the top, he sees that the end of the ladder has rusted away. He can neither safely turn back nor complete the dare. The story ends with the exhausted Flegg clinging to the ladder, a few frustrating feet from realizing his goal.

"The Long Sheet" (*Horizon,* October 1941; collected in *Fireman Flower*) tells of prisoners grouped within blank-walled cubicles; a long, water-soaked sheet stretches overhead. Each group must wring the sheet dry in order to gain its freedom. One group is so daunted by the task that it never approaches the work with any real hope of accomplishing it. The next group systematically plans its approach, but the routine of wringing the sheet becomes its aim instead of gaining freedom. Another group dooms itself because each member considers only the reality of his own methodology instead of the goal of release. The last group actually dries the sheet; however, the prison keepers confess that they cannot grant the group its freedom because the group has had it all along. In *William Sansom: A Critical Assessment* (1971) Paulette Michel-Michot writes that "The Long Sheet" achieves a unique theme in which "cruelty and imprisonment become means of enlightenment, means to teach the lessons of life, and so transcend the apparent absurdity."

Many of Sansom's early stories are collected in *Fireman Flower.* Most of the characters in these pieces are alone, contemplating the astonishing twists of fate that have been dealt them. They become acute recording organisms, explaining their responses to epochal moments in their lives. Ironically, Sansom's painstaking construction of a character's response to an excruciating reality evokes a sense of nonparticipation or unreality in the reader. His minimal use of dialogue heightens this effect, as he frequently describes actions or his characters' words instead of allowing them to speak. When a voice does intervene, the narrator usually sounds detached or somehow apart from the events that he or she describes. Sansom seems to care less about characters than actions or events. His early stories strive to depict the jarring nightmare of confronting the somewhat known but not entirely understood. Rarely do his characters linger in the memory to the same extent as his events or details.

When World War II ended, Sansom entered a different phase of his writing career and encountered different influences. At first he briefly wrote screenplays for a film company. However, as his stories gained in popularity, he turned his attention toward writing short fiction full-time. He began to receive lucrative offers from magazines to produce travel essays; these are collected in five volumes: *Pleasures Strange and Simple* (1953), *The Icicle and the Sun* (1958), *Blue Skies, Brown Studies* (1961), *Away to It All* (1964), and *Grand Tour Today* (1968). He also wrote travel-related short stories, which Chalpin considers as among his best works.

In "Three Dogs of Siena" (*South,* 1948), perhaps the most endearing of his travel stories, three brothers have journeyed to Siena for the wedding of their younger sister. The brothers remain unnamed, and rightly so, for they are not the focus of the story. Each has brought along his dog. The three dogs – Enrico, Osvaldo, and Fa – become like brothers themselves, setting out to explore and enjoy the exotic new setting.

Sansom pays his customary homage to minute details in this story. In the third paragraph he concisely outlines the physical and spiritual characteristics of each dog. He also describes Siena down to the stonework in the houses that line the streets and provides insights into the town's inhabitants. Yet "Three Dogs of Siena" introduces the first extended glimpse into Sansom's sense of humor. For instance, he remarks that Enrico's tail end is stumpy and barren of hair but then concludes that the dog likely does not care much because he has never seen it.

In "Three Dogs of Siena" the reader may notice the beginnings of overdetailing in Sansom's writing. For example, a statue of Romulus and Remus being suckled by a wolf in the wilderness greatly puzzles Osvaldo, who cannot understand how the dog is able to feed the humans. Sansom

Illustration by Lynton Lamb for the story "Life, Death," in Sansom's Lord Love Us *(1954)*

cannily describes the curious lilt of Osvaldo's head as he tries to connect what he sees with what he knows. But then Sansom commits what Michel-Michot calls "philosophical intrusion," launching into a lengthy comparison of Osvaldo to a man feeling similarly confused. Sansom belabors his ideas by presenting them in many of their elementary forms; he seems reluctant to allow the reader to make connections unaided.

Sansom remained single until age forty-two. In 1954 he married Ruth Grundy, an actress and literary agent with two children from an earlier marriage. New influences came to bear on Sansom's writing. In the late 1950s the short-fiction market began tightening. Sansom therefore focused his energies on the novel and on further travel assignments, which continued to pay well. In the short stories that he did produce he started to explore relationships between people in general and men and women in particular. He also unleashed his formidable talent in appealing to the ear through the rhythm of language.

"Life, Death" (*Contact,* July–August 1950; collected in *Lord Love Us,* 1954) opens with Charley, a fishmonger, describing his work. He artfully arranges his fish on a wooden slab at his stall, giving thoughtful consideration to color and image. He arranges his lobsters in the form of a flower, finishing off the decoration with fish heads and a slice of lemon. As he works, he banters and sings with his neighbor, Jim-at-the-back. Charley obviously delights in his profession, approaching the task of selling fish with energy and imagination.

Sansom chooses his language likewise. "Life, Death" features such lines as "Out of my wits awhile I was," "So though with others smokes and girls might sound a stronger vice," and "No, I'm not broke, I'll crack a joke." The rhythm of the language makes the characters much more vivid, and Sansom also offers insights about people and relationships.

Charley begins to notice a woman who has become a regular customer at his stall and slips her extra portions of fish whenever she makes a purchase. They eventually share a smile, and he asks her to a movie. They fall deeply in love and announce their betrothal. Although Charley begins to feel an obligation to move up in his work, he rues the notion of leaving his beloved slab. He has reveled in his work at the stall and frankly admits that he will miss it. Sansom subtly depicts Charley's rite of passage from happy-go-lucky youth to responsibility-bound fiancé in artfully chosen language that makes the story all the more memorable.

An equally discomfiting transition is addressed in "Time Gents, Please" (*Time and Tide*, April 1951; collected in *Lord Love Us*). Sansom slightly alters the rhythm of his language in order to convey a more satiric tone. The similar-sounding names of the two main characters, Farquhar and Urquhart, hint that the story will address a certain sameness. Farquhar and Urquhart, two aging British gentlemen, meet every Saturday under the clock at Victoria Station, whence they journey to play cricket.

Time emerges as an important symbol in the story. Before they depart for their cricket matches, Farquhar and Urquhart set their watches to the clock in Victoria Station. This action symbolizes their rigidly measured outlooks. One Saturday a women's cricket club engages them in a match and soundly beats them. Farquhar and Urquhart, who consider cricket a man's game, are dumbfounded by their humbling. Their precious time has passed them by. On their return trip through Victoria Station their revered clock comes crashing down onto their heads. In "Time Gents, Please" Sansom creates such lyrical lines as "Thus they whiled their life away as Farquhar went his radio way while Urquhart drily cleaned." The singsong quality of the language renders the characters as nursery-rhyme caricatures, enabling Sansom to poke gentle fun at those who will not yield to an uncomfortable but inevitable mode of passage.

Sansom died in London on 20 April 1976. His last short-story collection, *The Marmalade Bird*, was published in 1973. His stories continued to feature characters who experience intense moments of definition and resolution. He also continued to explore relationships between men and women, occasionally bewildering his characters with a dose of fate. He never really left behind his fondness for exacting details, which, although occasionally distracting, add to the memorable qualities of his best short fiction.

Interview:

Walter Allen, "How They Write and Why They Do It – An Interview with William Sansom and Angus Wilson," *Queen* (15 March 1960): 143-144.

References:

A. L. Bader, "The Structure of the Modern Short Story," *College English*, 7 (November 1945): 86-92;

Dean Baldwin, "The English Short Story in the Fifties," in *The English Short Story, 1945-1980*, edited by Dennis Vannatta (Boston: Twayne, 1985), pp. 34-74;

Lila Chalpin, *William Sansom* (Boston: Twayne, 1980);

Hugo Manning, "William Sansom and Company," *Adam* (January 1947): 22;

Ronald Mason, "The Promise of William Sansom," *Wind and the Rain* (Autumn 1946): 140-146;

Paulette Michel-Michot, *William Sansom: A Critical Assessment* (Paris: Société d'Edition "Les Belles Lettres," 1971);

Howard Nemerov, "Sansom's Fictions," *Kenyon Review*, 17 (Winter 1955): 130-135;

Peter F. Neumeyer, "Franz Kafka and William Sansom," *Wisconsin Studies in Contemporary Literature*, 7 (Winter/Spring 1966): 76-84;

Jean Pickering, "The English Short Story in the Sixties," in *The English Short Story, 1945-1980*, pp. 75-119;

V. S. Pritchett, "The Short Story," *London Magazine* (September 1966): 6-9;

Isaac Rosenfeld, "Mr. William Sansom: The Body," *Partisan Review*, 16 (September 1949): 950-951;

Harvey Swados, "The Long and Short of It," *Hudson Review*, 10 (Spring 1957): 155-159;

John B. Vickery, "Sansom and Logical Empiricism," *Thought*, 36 (Summer 1961): 231-245;

James Dean Young, "William Sansom: Unwroughter," *Critique*, 7 (Spring 1964): 122-125.

Alan Sillitoe

(4 March 1928 –)

Jennifer Semple Siegel
York College of Pennsylvania

See also the Sillitoe entry in *DLB 14: British Novelists Since 1960: Part 2.*

BOOKS: *Without Beer or Bread* (Dulwich Village, U.K.: Outposts, 1957);

Saturday Night and Sunday Morning (London: Allen, 1958; New York: Knopf, 1959);

The Loneliness of the Long-Distance Runner (London: Allen, 1959; New York: Knopf, 1960);

The General (London: Allen, 1960; New York: Knopf, 1962);

The Rats and Other Poems (London: Allen, 1960);

Key to the Door (London: Allen, 1961; New York: Knopf, 1962);

The Ragman's Daughter and Other Stories (London: Allen, 1963; New York: Knopf, 1964);

A Falling out of Love and Other Poems (London: Allen, 1964; Toronto: Doubleday, 1964);

The Road to Volgograd (London: Allen, 1964; New York: Knopf, 1964);

The Death of William Posters (London: Allen, 1965; New York: Knopf, 1965);

The City Adventures of Marmalade Jim (London: Macmillan, 1967; Toronto: Macmillan, 1967; revised edition, Sheffield, U.K. & London: Robson, 1977);

A Tree on Fire (London: Macmillan, 1967; New York: Doubleday, 1968);

Guzman, Go Home, and Other Stories (London: Macmillan, 1968; New York: Doubleday, 1969);

Love in the Environs of Voronezh and Other Poems (London: Macmillan, 1968; New York: Doubleday, 1969);

Shaman and Other Poems (London: Turret, 1968);

A Start in Life (London: Allen, 1970; New York: Scribners, 1971);

Poems, by Sillitoe, Ruth Fainlight, and Ted Hughes (London: Rainbow, 1971);

Travels in Nihilon (London: Allen, 1971; New York: Scribners, 1972);

Raw Material (London: Allen, 1972; New York: Scribners, 1973; revised edition, London: Pan,

Alan Sillitoe, 1978 (photograph by Graham Miller)

1974; revised edition, London: Star, 1978; revised edition, London: Allen, 1979);

Men, Women and Children (London: Allen, 1973; New York: Scribners, 1974);

Barbarians and Other Poems (London: Turret, 1973);

Canto Two of the Rats (London: Ithaca, 1973);

The Flame of Life (London: Allen, 1974);

Somme: Steam Press Portfolio 2, by Sillitoe, Lyman Andrews, Asa Beneviste, Lawrence Durrell, Fainlight, Sylvia Plath, and Ralph Steadman (London: Steam Press, 1974);

Storm: New Poems (London: Allen, 1974);

Mountains and Caverns: Selected Essays (London: Allen, 1975);

Words Broadsheet Nineteen, by Sillitoe and Fainlight (Bramley, Surrey, U.K.: Words Press, 1975);

The Widower's Son (London: Allen, 1976; New York: Harper & Row, 1976);

Big John and the Stars (London: Robson, 1977);

Day-Dream Communiqué (Knotting, Bedfordshire, U.K.: Sceptre, 1977);

The Incredible Fencing Fleas (London: Robson, 1978);

Three Plays: The Slot-Machine, The Interview, Pit Strike (London: Allen, 1978);

From Snow on the North Side of Lucifer (Knotting, Bedfordshire, U.K.: Sceptre, 1979);

Snow on the North Side of Lucifer: Poems (London: Allen, 1979);

The Storyteller (London: Allen, 1979; New York: Simon & Schuster, 1979);

Marmalade Jim at the Farm (London: Robson, 1980);

More Lucifer (Knotting, Bedfordshire, U.K.: Booth, 1980);

The Second Chance and Other Stories (London: Cape, 1981; New York: Simon & Schuster, 1981);

Israel: Poems on a Hebrew Theme (London: Steam Press, 1981);

Her Victory (London: Granada, 1982; New York: Watts, 1982);

The Lost Flying Boat (London: Granada, 1983; Boston: Little, Brown, 1983);

The Saxon Shore Way: From Gravesend to Rye, by Sillitoe and Fay Godwin (London: Hutchinson, 1983);

Down from the Hill (London & New York: Granada, 1984);

Marmalade Jim and the Fox (London: Robson, 1984);

Sun Before Departure: Poems (London: Granada, 1984);

Life Goes On (London: Granada, 1985);

Tides and Stone Walls: Poems (London: Grafton, 1986);

Alan Sillitoe's Nottinghamshire (London: Grafton, 1987);

Out of the Whirlpool (London: Hutchinson, 1987);

The Far Side of the Street (London: Allen, 1988);

The Open Door (London: Collins, 1989);

Last Loves (London: Grafton, 1990; Boston: Chivers, 1991);

Leonard's War: A Love Story (London: HarperCollins, 1991);

Snowstop (London: HarperCollins, 1993).

Editions and Collections: *A Sillitoe Selection: Eight Short Stories,* edited by Michael Marland (London: Longmans, Green, 1968);

Down to the Bone, edited by Kenyon Calthrop, introduction by Sillitoe (Exeter, U.K.: Wheaton, 1976);

Every Day of the Week: An Alan Sillitoe Reader, edited by John Sawkins (London: Allen, 1987).

OTHER: "D. H. Lawrence and His District," in *D. H. Lawrence: Poet, Prophet,* edited by Stephen Spender (London: Weidenfeld & Nicolson, 1973), pp. 42–70;

Emrys Bryson, *Portrait of Nottingham,* introduction by Sillitoe (London: Hale, 1974), pp. 5–14;

G. H. Bowden, *The Story of the Raleigh Bicycle,* introduction by Sillitoe (London: Allen, 1975), pp. 9–10;

"Introduction to Israeli Poetry," in *The Burning Bush,* edited by Moshe Dor and Natan Zach (London: Allen, 1977), pp. 7–9;

Meir Gottesman, *Out of the Fire,* introduction by Sillitoe (Children & Youth Aliyah Committee, 1979), pp. 7–9;

"Against Ideology," in *The Writer and Human Rights,* edited by Lester and Orpen Dennys (Toronto: Arts Group for Human Rights, 1983), pp. 233–240.

TRANSLATIONS: Luis Ripoll, *Chopin's Winter in Majorca 1838–1839,* translated by Sillitoe (Palma de Majorca, Spain: Mossen Alcover, 1955);

Ripoll, *Chopin's Pianos: The Pleyel in Majorca,* translated by Sillitoe (Palma de Majorca, Spain: Mossen Alcover, 1958);

Lope de Vega, *All Citizens Are Soldiers, Fuente Ovejuna,* translated by Sillitoe and Ruth Fainlight (London: Macmillan, 1969);

Poems for Shakespeare, edited and translated by Sillitoe and Fainlight (London: Bear Gardens Museum & Arts Centre, 1979).

SELECTED PERIODICAL PUBLICATIONS – UNCOLLECTED:

FICTION

"No Shot in the Dark," *Weekly Guardian* (Nottinghamshire), 26 August 1950, p. 9;

"Late Starter," *Times* (London), 18 May 1961, p. 19;

"Harrison's Row," *Triquarterly,* 33 (Spring 1975): 179–184;

"Company," *New Yorker,* 54 (29 May 1978): 29–36;

"A Matter of Teeth," *Daily Mail Saturday Magazine,* 18 February 1989.

NONFICTION

"Portrait of Robert Graves," *Books and Bookmen* (May 1960): 7–8;

"Both Sides of the Street," *Times Literary Supplement,* 8 July 1960, p. 435;

"Arthur Seaton Is Not Just a 'Symbol,' " *Daily Worker,* 28 July 1961, p. 2;

"Shorts and Long Shorts," *Books and Bookmen* (May 1962): 16–17;

Sillitoe's birthplace in Nottingham, the city in which he grew to adulthood

"I Reminded Him of Muggleton," *Shenandoah*, 13 (Summer 1962): 4;

"Drilling and Burring," *Spectator*, 212 (3 January 1964): 11;

"Why We Signed," *Sanity: The Voice of CND*, September 1965, p. 7;

" 'Bad Form, Old Boy,' and So It Was," *Times* (London), 8 May 1972, p. 7;

"When Will the Russians Learn that Humanity is Good for Them?," *Times* (London), 10 June 1974, p. 14;

"First Day in Israel," *Transatlantic Review*, no. 50 (Autumn/Winter 1974): 91–99;

"My Israel," *New Statesman*, 88 (20 December 1974): 890–892;

"Carry on Praying," *Die Zeit*, 27 August 1975, p. 8;

"The Book I Never Wrote," *Die Welt*, 22 March 1976, p. 2;

"The State of Fiction," *New Review*, 5 (Summer 1978): 64;

"Unhappy Families," *Centre: Magazine of the North Western Reform Synagogue* (January 1979): 1–2;

"An Older Israel," *Geographical Magazine*, 52 (August 1979): 787;

"Patterson the Zionist," *Jewish Quarterly* (Winter 1980–1981): 16–18;

"My First Book," *Author*, 94 (Autumn 1983): 73–74;

"Galilee Diary, 1977," *Forthcoming: Jewish Imaginative Writing* (Spring 1984): 30–34;

"The Dread Which Artistry Cannot Conceal," *Jewish Chronicle*, 1 March 1985, p. 27;

"On Trial at the Top," *Sunday Times* (London), 2 November 1986, p. 52.

When Alan Sillitoe's *Saturday Night and Sunday Morning* was published in 1958, critics grouped the author with John Wain, Kingsley Amis, and John Braine as angry young men. The label is not entirely appropriate, even for the young author of this riveting, and often raw, first novel and the subsequent short-story collection *The Loneliness of the Long-Distance Runner* (1959): while the other "angry" writers depicted poor people trying to emulate the upper classes, Sillitoe's characters reveled in defying the elite. Furthermore, Sillitoe has often shown authority figures as inherently ignorant and ready to be manipulated by the lower classes. Although Sillitoe is known primarily for his novels, his short-story collections, especially *The Loneliness of the Long-Distance Runner,* reveal an author concerned with the tight discipline of the short-story form. Early in his career Sillitoe preferred short stories to the novel. He revealed why in a 1969 interview with Bolivar Le Franc: "a short story is more tribal, more natural. It's something that existed back in Neanderthal times when people sat around a camp-fire and started spinning out short stories while the light was still living at the end of the day. A short story is the most human form of man assessing his relationship to the natural world around him and to his fellow-men."

Scholars have particularly admired Sillitoe's increasing ability to transcend class consciousness in his five story collections: from *The Loneliness of the Long-Distance Runner* to *The Second Chance and Other Stories* (1981), Sillitoe has appealed to an increasingly broad audience while retaining the edge that has made him an important force in twentieth-century British fiction. In his review of *The Loneliness of the Long-Distance Runner* in the 29 April 1960 issue of *Commonweal,* Max Cosman predicted that Sillitoe's career would "be a notable one, especially if he gets past his savages in teddy-boy outfits to those humane and thought-conscious members of his chosen working-class." Sillitoe's short-story characters have traded their teddy-boy outfits for more conservative clothes, but they have not forgotten their roots.

Robert Haller believes that Sillitoe's first two books continue to be best-sellers because they offer "a mirror for working-class readers and a window for others into a culture with its own richness of circumstance and its own integrity." Certainly this characterization holds true for his short fiction. Some of Sillitoe's more than forty short stories are admired as minor masterpieces.

The second of five children, Sillitoe was born on 4 March 1928 in Nottingham to Sylvina Burton and Christopher Archibald Sillitoe. As a child Sillitoe witnessed much domestic violence that stemmed from his family's chronic poverty. Until late 1939 the Sillitoes depended mainly on government assistance. To dodge rent collectors the family moved to various locations in Nottingham.

In 1933 Sillitoe began school and became fascinated with the Old Testament; he later claimed that "the Christian Testament, which we were also obliged to listen to, never carried the same weight as those Old Testament chapters." His early exposure to the Bible formed the basis of his later strong pro-Israel views and contributed to his "wish to be rootless, that fixed desire to wander the face of the earth. . . ."

Sillitoe read avidly, especially adventure and detective stories by such authors as Sir Walter Scott and Sir Arthur Conan Doyle. A schoolmaster gave him the first book he ever owned, *History Day by Day,* a tantalizing volume that offered only brief synopses of historical events; Sillitoe says that "it was a book exactly suited to my avid though shallow brain." Despite his love of reading, he did not pass his eleven-plus exams, the series of tests that would have allowed him to stay in school until age seventeen. Just before leaving school in 1942 and beginning work at the Raleigh bicycle factory, Sillitoe won an award for "Proficiency in Biblical Knowledge." The prize was a limp, black, leather-bound Bible that he still possesses.

World War II brought better financial times to the Sillitoe family, although the job at the bicycle factory ended after three months because of a labor dispute. Sillitoe took jobs at various manufacturing firms until 16 April 1945, when he enlisted in the Royal Navy with plans to become a pilot; but with the war winding down, he was told to wait to be called up to a training station. He worked as an air-traffic-control assistant at Langar Airfield; then, when the navy informed him that he would have to sign on for seven years, he resigned in March 1946. He joined the Royal Air Force (RAF) six weeks later and was sent to radio school. On 8 May 1947 he shipped out for Malaya.

Returning to England in August 1948, Sillitoe was diagnosed with tuberculosis. During his sixteen-month hospitalization he read the Greek and Latin classics in translation and began writing poems, short stories, and a novel in imitation of his favorite writers: Aldous Huxley, Fyodor Dostoyevski, D. H. Lawrence, Henry Fielding, and Joseph Conrad. Many of the short stories appear, reworked, in his novel *The General* (1960). On 22 December 1949 he was discharged from the RAF and returned to Nottingham. In 1950 he wrote a poem, "Arthur Seaton," in which the title character expresses his thoughts while fishing. On 26 August 1950 his first published short story, "No Shot in the Dark" – which became a part of chapter 21 in his novel *Key to the Door* (1961) – appeared in the Nottinghamshire *Weekly Guardian;* Sillitoe received thirty shillings for it.

In the autumn of 1950 he met Ruth Fainlight, an American-born poet, in a Nottingham bookstore.

In 1952 they left together for France. After a year there they went to Spain. During this time he continued writing, supported by his RAF pension, a National Health Service allowance, and freelance translating jobs.

In 1954 the poet Robert Graves, to whom he had sent some of his poetry, invited Sillitoe to visit him. Graves advised Sillitoe to write about what he knew: Nottingham. Taking Graves's advice, Sillitoe reworked "Arthur Seaton" into a short story about a young man who gets drunk, falls down the stairs in a pub, and lies unconscious as people walk around him. The story was never published, but the hard-living protagonist Arthur Seaton, a character based on an old drinking buddy of Sillitoe's, would appear in a similar scene in his first novel.

In 1956, in Sóller, Majorca, Sillitoe began reworking several short stories set in Nottingham into a picaresque novel; within six months he had completed a four-hundred-page draft titled "The Adventures of Arthur Seaton." In the spring of 1957, while revising his novel, Sillitoe saw a performance of John Osborne's play *Look Back in Anger* and was impressed by the playwright's ability to break through establishment barriers. By August 1957 Sillitoe had completed his novel, by then one hundred pages shorter and bearing a new title: *Saturday Night and Sunday Morning*. One year and five rejection slips later, *Saturday Night and Sunday Morning* was accepted by the W. H. Allen publishing firm, and with his one-hundred-pound advance Sillitoe and Fainlight returned to England. Sillitoe insists that the novel is really "about twenty or thirty short stories stuck together with one central character. It's not a true novel in the sense of being beautifully constructed . . . and marvellously built." Chronicling the experiences of Arthur Seaton, a twenty-two-year-old factory worker who lives for the moment, spending all his money on ale, women, and flashy clothes, the book won the Authors' Club Silver Quill Award as the most promising first novel of 1958.

Early in 1959 Sillitoe and Fainlight moved to London, where he revised *The Loneliness of the Long-Distance Runner*. Later that year, with advances from publishers, Sillitoe leased a cottage in Whitwell, Hertfordshire. In November he and Fainlight were married, and *The Loneliness of the Long-Distance Runner* was published by W. H. Allen. A commercial and critical success, this short-story collection about working-class people alienated from the establishment represents some of the best fiction ever written by Sillitoe. In the title story Smith, a hardened and antisocial seventeen-year-old, must decide be-

tween winning a long-distance race for his Borstal (reform school) or remaining an outsider by losing purposefully. He revels in the routine of running around the Borstal grounds early each morning, even during the winter when "Everything's dead, but good, because it's dead before coming alive. . . ." When he realizes that those in charge are "dead" after having been barely alive, Smith has to decide whether he wants to remain "alive" by losing the race or become "dead" by winning the race for "them." Smith is probably the most idealistic character in Sillitoe's work, for the young renegade does not deviate from his personal moral code. By losing the race, he becomes a hero of the disenfranchised.

Eight more short stories complete *The Loneliness of the Long-Distance Runner*. In "Uncle Ernest" the protagonist befriends two girls who are obviously poor, buys them food, and gives them presents. He grows to think of the girls as surrogate nieces; the authorities, however, view his generosity differently and order him to leave the youngsters alone. Sillitoe captures Ernest's outrage at "them," who have so misinterpreted his motives. "Mr. Raynor the School Teacher" is told from the viewpoint of one of "them," a married, middle-aged schoolteacher who dislikes his working-class students. In "Noah's Ark" Colin, a ten-year-old version of Arthur Seaton, and Bert, his errant eleven-year-old cousin, are typical Nottingham working-class children who grab what little pleasure they can find. Although "On Saturday Afternoon" continues the alienation motif, one begins to see a hint of maturation themes. A sixteen-year-old boy who has inherited the family "bleddy blackness" – depression and angst – remembers witnessing at age ten a man trying to hang himself from a light fixture. The youth recalls the ensuing confrontation between the man and a policeman:

> "Well, what did you do it for?"
> "Because I wanted to," the bloke croaked.
> "You'll get five years for this," the copper told him. I'd crept back into the house and was sucking my thumb in the same corner.
> "That's what yo' think," the bloke said, a normal frightened look in his eyes now. "I only wanted to hang myself."
> "Well," the copper said, taking out his book, "it's against the law, you know."
> "Nay," the bloke said, "it can't be. It's my life, ain't it?"
> "You might think so," the copper said, "but it ain't."

The boy realizes the implications of such a law in the context of his own life and his relationship with the authorities.

Dust jacket for Sillitoe's second collection of short stories, in which working-class characters lash out at authority figures

"The Disgrace of Jim Scarfedale" is a tragicomedy in which a boy-narrator presents an obvious "moral": that people need to develop spirit and stubbornness so as to assert their independence and avoid the "do-gooders" of the world, who will soon tire of their work. The boy tells the story of Jim Scarfedale, who married an upper-class woman who set out to "reform" him; however, the marriage failed, for Scarfedale's wife grew weary of his simple ways. He moved back with his mother and eventually tried to prove his manhood by poaching and by frightening little girls after dark. The narrator uses Jim's story to illustrate the consequences of failing to assert one's independence early in life.

Allen Richard Penner suggests that "The Decline and Fall of Frankie Buller" is a "nostalgic sociological document" in which Sillitoe is recalling his childhood in fictional form. The narrator reminisces about his friendship with Frankie Buller, a childhood mentor. Then in his twenties, Frankie, who possessed limited intellectual abilities and identified with the neighborhood children rather than with other adults, befriended twelve-year-old boys

and taught them war games. The boys respected this man-child, attributing to him special powers that they had not yet discovered in themselves. When the narrator returns to his neighborhood ten years later he finds a changed Frankie; something vital is missing in his old mentor. More important, the narrator recognizes his own altered class consciousness. His nostalgia turns to anger when he discovers that Frankie had been hospitalized for a year and given shock treatments: "I wanted power in me to tear down those white-smocked mad interferers with Frankie's coal-forest world, wanted to wipe out their hate and presumption."

Though such "us versus them" themes prevail in the collection, Sillitoe had begun developing the more sophisticated psychological and marital motifs that would emerge more fully in his later fiction. In "The Fishing-Boat Picture" Harry, a fifty-two-year-old postman, has to deal with his former wife's attempt to establish a platonic relationship with him. As she walks up the yard for the first time in years, Harry says, "It gave me a funny feeling . . . : ten years ain't enough to change anyone so's you don't recognize them, but it's long enough to make you have to look twice before you're sure." Out of kindness Harry accepts her weekly visits and even begins to look forward to them until she asks for the return of a wedding gift: a picture of a fishing boat that depicts calmness and placidity, the opposite of their stormy marriage. This story is the first in which Sillitoe pulls away from the theme of class conflict. "The Match" continues the marital theme: Lennox and Fred attend soccer matches together but live very different lives: Lennox abuses his wife and children, while Fred adores his bride. Fred, however, is simply a younger version of Lennox, for in Sillitoe's view violence is inevitable in the Nottingham working-class family.

Anthony West praised the collection in the 11 June 1960 issue of the *New Yorker:* "These stories are, indeed, so firmly rooted in experience, and so ably handled, that they do not seem to have been written at all; they seem to be occurrences of a most engrossing and absorbing kind." On the other hand, John Updike, writing in the *New Republic* (9 May 1960), felt that Sillitoe had stereotyped all "Haves" as "pop-eyed potbellies." Still, Updike conceded that "I liked best those endings in which the boy-narrator stood right up in his shabby shoes and explained what lesson he had learned, as if he were assembling a personal Bible out of scraps of sadness and folly blowing in the gutters."

In 1960, after selling the film rights to *Saturday Night and Sunday Morning* for £4,500 ($12,600), Sillitoe wrote the screenplay, for which he was paid an additional £750 ($2,100). Also that year, *The Loneliness of the Long-Distance Runner* won the prestigious Hawthornden Prize, awarded annually to an author under forty for the best imaginative writing.

When the film version of *Saturday Night and Sunday Morning* opened in London during 1961 to good reviews, Sillitoe and Fainlight fled to Morocco for four months to get away from the limelight. On returning, he collaborated with the director Tony Richardson on the screenplay for the film version of "The Loneliness of the Long-Distance Runner." Some critics felt that Sillitoe and Richardson had excessively "sanitized" the protagonist for the screen: the hardened, antisocial criminal of the story had become a romantic hero who had been dealt a losing hand by an uncaring society. Other critics and the public, however, responded enthusiastically to the film.

Shortly after his son David's birth in 1962, Sillitoe and his family traveled to Tangier and elsewhere in Morocco. There Sillitoe revised the stories for his second collection, *The Ragman's Daughter and*

Other Stories (1963). In the title story the narrator, Tony, is stopped after work by the police, who open his suitcase for inspection: "I was lucky my suitcase had nothing but air in it. Sometimes I walk out with a box of butter and cheese from the warehouse I work at, but for once that no-good God was on my side – trying to make up for the times he's stabbed me in the back maybe." Then Tony recalls his youth, when he fell in love with Doris, the daughter of a wealthy ragman, and led her into a life of stealing. Tony was not really interested in the things he stole, for he routinely dumped his booty off the Trent bridge just to hear it splash into the water. Tony eventually got caught and spent three years in a Borstal. Now a semirespectable young working-class man with a wife and two children, Tony mourns the loss of his high spirits. At the end he says about the night he and Doris got caught: "when I switched off the light because I sensed danger, we both went into the dark, and never came out." Tony went "into the dark" by taking a comfortable job in a factory, thereby joining the system that has kept his people poor.

"The Good Women" was originally serialized in the Communist-party newspaper, the *Daily Worker.* This story is particularly significant because it demonstrated for the first time that Sillitoe could create a female character who was something more than an empty-headed working-class girl: Liza Atkin is a true revolutionary. While supporting an ailing husband and a large family she consistently bucks the system, evading the means-test man (an official who decides how much assistance families should receive) and others who would threaten her way of life: "They wain't stop me doing what I like. If the getts want to tek my few bob off me I'll throw it in their effing phizzogs."

In "The Other John Peel" Sillitoe transforms the aristocratic hunter of John Woodcock Graves's nineteenth-century ballad into a twentieth-century working-class man named Bob who moonlights as a poacher. Bob's friend Ernie is convinced that a revolution is coming and that the Russians will "liberate" them from the class system. In "The Bike" Colin is a young man just starting work in a bicycle factory. Bernard, a coworker, betrays him by selling him a stolen bike, but Colin still feels obligated to protect Bernard from the clutches of "them." Colin believes that justice will prevail when the revolution comes, for Bernard, with his "lily-white hands," will be one of the first people shot. In "To Be Collected" the brothers Donnie, Bert, and Dave eke out a precarious living by soliciting junk door-to-door. Donnie discovers a cache of Sten machine guns, a potential source of wealth and a way out of their grim life, but Dave and Bert do not want to risk getting caught selling them. After much discussion the brothers toss the guns into a reservoir, throwing away their last chance at freedom from poverty.

The narrator of "The Firebug" recalls when, as a boy, he became fascinated with the sound of fire trucks passing by his house and decided to set his own fires; he began by lighting small fires in his own yard and progressed to more serious fires. Finally he set a major blaze in the woods so that he could watch it leap out of control; the fire

> was a sheet of red flame and grey smoke, a choking wall and curtain that scared me a bit, because I was back to life, as if big hands would reach out and grab me in for good and all. Like my uncle had said hell was – though I never believed him till now.
>
> It was time to run.

His deed went unpunished, but setting fires lost its thrill for him. Although his fear of apprehension has persisted for years, the narrator remains unrepentant.

"The Magic Box" represents an important departure from the themes of Sillitoe's first story collection, foreshadowing an "us versus us" motif in which characters experience their conflicts internally rather than waging battles with the authoritarian "them." After Fred wins £250 in a football pool, he and his wife, Nan, begin to experience marital difficulties. Instead of being happy about his windfall, he is disappointed that he did not win the grand prize of £100,000. He buys a shortwave radio and sets it up in his dead son's room, where he listens to Morse-code messages from sailors to their lovers. This pastime hints at Sillitoe's increasing disenchantment with modern culture and technology: Fred retreats increasingly into a world where relationships are formed and broken through dots and dashes rather than real human contact. The old "blackness," a common malady in Sillitoe stories, falls over him; he recalls his son, a once-lively boy who had also fallen prey to the blackness before drowning in a river. Fred suffers a nervous breakdown and smashes everything in the boy's room, and Nan has him committed to a mental hospital. While he is away Nan spends her share of the football pool on drinking and "fancy-men." When she becomes pregnant, she believes that Fred will accept the child as his own. A major scene ensues, Nan dares him to leave, and he strikes her for the first time. Nan rationalizes, "He hadn't hit me before then, and he wain't hit me again, either. Maybe I deserved it though."

In the *New York Review of Books* for 5 March 1964 Stanley Kaufmann called "The Magic Box" the best story in the collection, citing Sillitoe's restraint in using a child's death not as a source of pathos but "as a cold fact of their lives." The collection itself received mixed reviews, some critics believing that Sillitoe was just rehashing his "us versus them" theme. Although most critics admired the author's technical skill, some felt that his oppression themes were oversimplified and that character development and psychological analysis suffered.

In an essay in the 25 September 1963 issue of the *Queen* titled "Poor People," which was collected in his *Mountains and Caverns: Selected Essays* (1975), Sillitoe describes the frustrations of the working class that provided the themes for his early fiction: "The poor know of only two classes in society. Their sociology is much simplified. There are *them* and *us*. Them are those who tell you what to do, who drive a car, use a different accent, are buying a house in another district, deal in cheques and not money, pay your wages, collect rent and telly dues, stop for you now and again at pedestrian crossings, can't look you in the eye, read the news on wireless or television, hand you the dole or national assistance money; the shopkeeper, copper, schoolteacher, doctor, health visitor, the man wearing the white dog-collar. Them are those who robbed you of your innocence, live on your backs, buy the house from over your head, eat you up or tread you down."

In 1963, after returning to England from Morocco, Sillitoe received an invitation from the Soviet Writers' Union to visit the Union of Soviet Socialist Republics. He remained there for a month, and later that year he spent four weeks traveling through Czechoslovakia. His travel journal *The Road to Volgograd* (1964) reveals Sillitoe's increasing dissatisfaction with British life and growing affinity for the Soviet Union.

In 1967 Sillitoe and his family went to Majorca, where they stayed in a house lent to them by Graves. There Sillitoe finished some short stories, the poetry volume *Love in the Environs of Voronezh and Other Poems* (1968), and the play *This Foreign Field,* performed in London in 1970. In September Sillitoe, who had become increasingly disenchanted with the Soviet Union's treatment of minorities and writers, returned to that country and gave a lecture at the Gorki Literary Institute titled "The Freedom for the Writer."

In the 1968 interview with Le Franc, Sillitoe, the former angry young man, commented: "I never

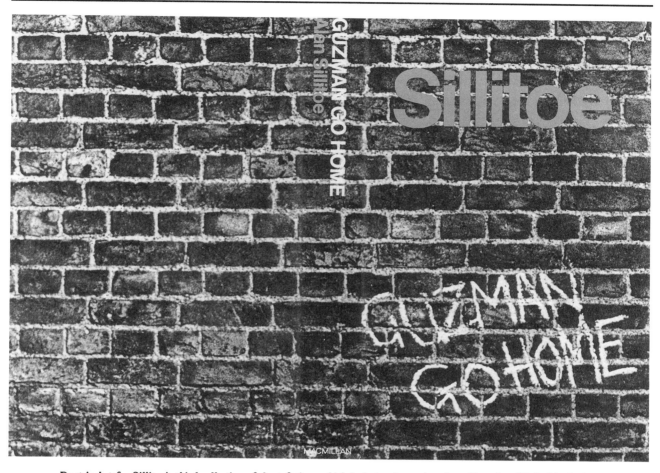

Dust jacket for Sillitoe's third collection of short fiction, which includes six stories of working-class life in Nottingham

did, in any case, trust the word anger – never had any truck with it at all. I mean, what's the point in being angry if you can't destroy what you're angry about?" At the end of the year his third book of short stories, *Guzman, Go Home, and Other Stories,* was published. In the title story the narrator, Chris, and his wife, Jane, are an English couple vacationing in Spain. When their car breaks down a man named Guzman takes them to a garage he owns. While waiting for his car to be repaired, Chris listens as Guzman reveals his past as a Nazi. Sillitoe told Le Franc that "the whole point of the story of Guzman's life is how one can be drawn, almost without knowing it, almost against one's instincts, into this terrible situation. So if there is a moral to this story it is: you can't escape politics. There's no way of living apart from politics. And also: watch your step. Every step you take, every word you say, you have to measure with great care because it's so easy, before you know it you're in some precarious situation in which you're a threat to other people."

After hearing Guzman's story, Chris decides that he cannot abandon politics.

The six remaining stories are set in Nottingham. The characters are less desperate and poor than those in Sillitoe's earlier collections, but, as Alan Hislop pointed out in the *New York Times Book Review* for 14 December 1969, "failing marriages and dying hopes" still prevail. The narrator of "Revenge," Richard, is a forty-year-old schizophrenic who fears human relationships and only understands things that are mechanical and, thus, predictable. He marries Caroline, but the marriage breaks up when he accuses her of trying to poison him. In "Chicken" Sillitoe exhibits a flair for black comedy: a foundry worker steals a neighbor's chicken for Sunday dinner and chops off its head, but the decapitated bird leads him on a merry chase right onto the neighbor's dinner table. In "Canals" Dick, a married London schoolteacher, comes home to Nottingham for his father's funeral. On a whim he visits an old girlfriend to apologize for his betrayal of her and, perhaps, to reestablish a relationship with her. Like Harry in "The Fishing-Boat Picture," however, he soon discovers that he has changed, while his former girlfriend and Nottingham have remained in the past. In "The Road" five-year-old Ivan watches his parents argue about trivial matters throughout a day trip to the beach. In "The Rope Trick" Jack steals money from a church collection box to give to a stranger whose husband has abandoned her but discovers that she, in turn, has abandoned him, leaving him holding the stolen money. Class conflict returns in "Isaac Starbuck." Isaac deserts his wife and children and finds a girlfriend. He buys a car but refuses to show his registration papers to the police, preferring to buck the system by "stealing" his own car. Unlike Smith in "The Loneliness of the Long-Distance Runner," Isaac rebels with a sense of humor and without political overtones. *Guzman, Go Home, and Other Stories* was well received by most critics; in the *Saturday Review* for 20 November 1969 Richard Clark Sterne called Sillitoe "a Chekhovian Robin Hood" who tells "wry, virile stories" about "the aborted or frustrated passions, compassions and rebellions of laborers and marginal bourgeois." Hislop in the *New York Times Book Review* said, "If the stories lack the force of those in his earlier volumes, that is because Sillitoe mapped out his territory so well. He isn't repeating himself; we are simply seeing some new parts of his world."

Sillitoe spent most of 1969 writing short stories and working on his novel *A Start in Life* (1970). When the Soviet writer Anatoli Kuznetsov, who was visiting London, ran into the *Daily Telegraph* offices and asked for political asylum in 1970, the KGB accused Sillitoe of assisting in the defection by luring Kuznetsov's guard away. Sillitoe says, "I admit that any self-respecting police force would have had reason for suspicion," but he denies that he acted as a decoy so that the Russian writer could escape.

Sillitoe spent most of 1970 writing the screenplay for *The Ragman's Daughter* (1972). He practiced his own brand of rebellion in 1971, when he paid a fine for refusing to fill out a census form. Sillitoe's fourth collection of short stories appeared in 1973. Unlike the three previous collections, *Men, Women and Children* has no title story; the title refers to the protagonists, whom the *Sewanee Review* for July 1975 described as "husbands who leave their wives, wives who leave their husbands, parents who abandon their children, lovers of all kinds who prove untrue." In "Mimic" the narrator, a mime who has forgotten how to be himself, slips into insanity and begins mimicking nature. In "Pit Strike" Joshua, a fifty-year-old coal miner, agrees to go on strike for better working conditions for his co-workers, even though his own life is already comfortable, and becomes a reluctant hero. Sillitoe combines the best and worst attributes of Smith and Guzman into Joshua, creating a more complex and interesting protagonist who agonizes over his decisions. (In 1977 a television version of "Pit Strike" was produced and directed by Roger Bamford for the BBC.) In "Before Snow Comes" Mark falls in love with a woman who later returns to her abusive husband. "Enoch's Two Letters" is the unhappy tale of an eight-year-old boy's abandonment by both parents simultaneously, each without the knowledge of the other: two "goodbye" letters arrive, one from the mother to the father and the other from the father to the mother. A sequel, "The End of Enoch?," reveals the boy's eventual fate. "The View" is a chilling story about a man who is obsessed with watching from his window as people are buried in the cemetery adjacent to his yard; when he dies, the story is continued from his wife's viewpoint. In "A Trip to Southwell" two teenagers fall in love; during their unconsummated romance, the boy and his family move away from Nottingham. When he returns to visit the girl, she is pregnant. In "The Chiker" Ken, a married, middle-aged man, is obsessed with secretly watching others make love, including his own daughter and her boyfriend. Finally, "Scenes from the Life of Margaret" tells of a woman who has been abandoned by her husband, leaving her with their three children. She falls in love with another man, who also leaves her after impregnating her. For the most part, the critics praised Sillitoe's attainment of technical sophistication in his short-story writing.

In 1973 Sillitoe traveled to the United States for the first time, spending some time in New York City before going on to Lincoln, Nebraska. In a London pub he had run into some students from the University of Nebraska and, after "a pleasant drinking bout," had promised to teach at the university for a week when he visited America. In 1974 the Israeli Foreign Office invited him to spend ten days in Israel. Sillitoe felt that visiting Israel was like "going home for the first time after two thousand years of bitter exile." Comparing writers everywhere to Jews, he sees in both groups a separateness from mainstream culture and believes that "Old Testamentism, or Judaism, is a deeply motivating force in the English non-conformist spirit." Late in 1975 he was elected a fellow of the Royal Geographical Society. Early in 1976 he attended a conference in Brussels, where he criticized the Soviet Union for its treatment of Jews. Also in 1976 Sillitoe wrote the introduction to *Down to the Bone,* a collection of his reprinted short stories.

The Second Chance and Other Stories appeared in 1981. These stories lack the rawness of those in *The Loneliness of the Long-Distance Runner:* most of the characters are sophisticated and complacent; their eyes have lost the hard glint of starving youth and are dulled from years of staring at the telly and collecting material goods. Still, Anne-Marie Brumm applauds Sillitoe's increasing exploration of "the subtleties of interpersonal relationships" between women and men.

Sillitoe's growth is especially evident in "The Second Chance." Major George Baxter, a retired RAF officer, meets Peter, a young confidence man who resembles Baxter's son, who was killed in World War II. Baxter lures Peter into acting the role of the son for Helen, Baxter's wife, who, after twenty years, is still grieving for her son; she and Baxter have never discussed the boy's death, and now they have stopped communicating altogether. When Peter begins playing his role, the fallout from twenty years of suppressed emotion becomes violent. The characters – even Helen, who has deep psychological problems – know that the scenes they are acting out are not real but that they are necessary all the same. Peter feels that the Baxters offer him a chance to make crime pay one last time before he settles down to a respectable occupation; Mrs. Baxter wants to recapture the essence of their son's life; and George Baxter sees a chance to reestablish communication in his marriage. All three have their needs met, but at a price: one of the characters is shot fatally. A new order ensues that has implications that are even more shocking than the original family order. In "The Second Chance" one finds neither working-class Nottingham people struggling for a precarious existence nor revolutionaries fighting for a cause: the setting is a country house, the Baxters are well-off, and Peter comes from an upper-class background.

"The Meeting" continues the role-playing theme. A couple meet in a bar, and the narrator, through omission, implies that they are strangers; eventually the dialogue reveals that they are former spouses who have arranged for a yearly meeting "to see if we can't get back together again and make a go of it." They discover, however, that sex is their only common denominator. In "Confrontation" a man at a cocktail party tells a woman named Mavis that he has only three months to live. When the two meet at another party a year later, Mavis is furious that he lied to her. He callously responds, "Did I?

I'm sorry about that. Parties are so deadly boring." The lie destroys his marriage, and he ends up in a doomed relationship with Mavis.

"The Sniper" is one of Sillitoe's best pieces of fiction. Nevill, an eighty-year-old man, has been hiding a sordid secret for more than fifty years: his murder of his wife's lover. Before he dies he wants to confess his guilt publicly. He jumps onto a table in a pub and begins to dance while reciting the grim details. But no one seems to care, and when the old man finally collapses the others react to his desperate dance:

> "Funny bloody story he was trying to spin us," one of them said, "about killing somebody in Robins Wood."
>
> "Couldn't make head nor tail of it. I've known him for years, and he wouldn't hurt a fly. A bit senile, I suppose."

"No Name in the Street" returns to the Nottingham poor. Albert, a middle-aged man who makes his living picking up and selling lost golf balls, communes with his dog by abusing it. "It's a good dog," he reflects, "but it gets on my nerves a bit too much at times." The dog is a metaphor for Albert himself: both are down and out, abused by those in charge. When Albert agrees to move in with a woman, the dog refuses to leave their old place: "It didn't want to leave. Well, nobody did, did they? *He* didn't want to leave, and that was a fact, but a time came when you had to. You had to leave or you had to sink into the ground and die. And he didn't want to die. He wanted to live. He knew that, now." Albert eventually tosses a golf ball to the animal, an incentive for the dog to give up his home just as the woman is an incentive for Albert to relinquish his independence. Although the setting is Nottingham and the main character lives in poverty, Sillitoe does not bring class conflict into the story; Albert is philosophical rather than angry about his lot and has learned to live with forces beyond his control.

In "A Scream of Toys" Edie remembers a childhood scene in which she and a neighborhood bully thought that they had found a large box of toys on the street. Edie soon discovered that the fancy box was empty – a foreshadowing of her bleak future. When Edie told her mother about the incident, the woman reacted in typical Nottingham fashion: she scolded Edie, telling her that "she should have had more bleddy sense because nobody leaves a box of toys at the end of the street." Thus a vestige of the old "us versus them" conflict emerges; yet the narrator blames no specific "them" but life in general: "All through life you were robbed. At the beginning the greatest act of robbery was when you were taken from the safety of your mother's womb and fobbed off with air that barely allowed you to breathe. Nobody had any choice about that, but the various robberies of life multiplied thereafter, each occasion leaving you more at the world's mercy."

In "Ear to the Ground," also set in Nottingham, the main character, middle-aged and on the dole, spends his time lamenting the state of the world and of his family; he is no longer angry at "them" for his fate. In "The Fiddle" a middle-aged Nottingham native tells the story of Harrison's Row, a block of redbrick townhouses, long since demolished, in which the people were so poor that "a rent man walked down cobblestoned Leen Place every week to collect what money he could. This wasn't much, even in the best of times. . . ." "The Gate of a Great Mansion" consists mostly of long descriptions of the terrible living conditions in Malaya; the protagonist is a thirty-five-year-old clerk who is dying of consumption. The mood is one not of anger but of sadness and despair.

"The Devil's Almanack," a macabre tale, takes place in 1866 in Kent. Twice a day Mr. Stevens, the postmaster, records the weather conditions in his almanac as a hobby. This day is anything but ordinary: his daughter, Emily, lies dead in the parlor, killed by her father to keep her from running off with a "disreputable" young soldier and leaving Stevens alone.

In "A Time to Keep" young Martin accompanies his cousin Raymond to work one day; on the job site Raymond's truck accidentally rolls over and kills a man. Raymond tells the boy, "I'm glad you came to work with me today. . . . I wouldn't have liked to drive home on my own after that little lot." The boy follows Raymond's blasé lead, assuming his normal routine when he arrives home.

In 1987 Sillitoe returned to short fiction with the novella *Out of the Whirlpool*, set in Radford Woodhouse, a tough colliery town. Peter Granby, an eighteen-year-old orphan who lives with his grandmother and works at a furniture factory, becomes a handyman for a wealthy widow who teaches him about love, sex, and the ways of the world outside of his working-class neighborhood. Unlike Sillitoe's early work, *Out of the Whirlpool* includes graphic sex scenes and profanity.

In 1989 Sillitoe's "A Matter of Teeth" was published in the *Daily Mail Saturday Magazine*. This first short story since "The Second Chance" continues the theme of noncommunication between husbands and wives. Denis, the middle-aged protagonist, endures several painful dental appointments to carry on an affair. In 1990 Sillitoe was granted an honorary doctorate by Nottingham Polytechnic and was made an honorary fellow of Manchester Polytechnic.

Sillitoe's writing reflects his affinity with the disenfranchised and the helpless. His later work retains much of the disenchantment with the establishment that earned him, at the beginning of his career, the label "angry young man," although many of his characters have aged and mellowed, becoming more philosophical and introspective and less aggressive and impulsive. Still, as the author admits, he is the writer he is today because of his humble beginnings. While Sillitoe was one of those who established the working-class-fiction genre in British literature, he has developed into a writer who is comfortable with a wide range of themes and is able to depict complex emotions.

Interviews:

"Silver Quill for New Novelist: Mr. Alan Sillitoe Looks Forward to Wider Travels," *Times* (London), 23 April 1959, p. 9;

Bob Leeson, "Return from Siberia," *Daily Worker*, 7 May 1963, p. 2;

"Alan Sillitoe," *Times* (London), 6 February 1964, p. 15;

Igor Hajek, "Morning Coffee with Sillitoe," *Nation*, 208 (27 January 1969): 122–124;

Bolivar Le Franc, "Sillitoe at Forty," *Books and Bookmen*, 14 (June 1969): 21–22, 24;

P. H. S., "Very Alive," *Times* (London), 21 July 1969, p. 4;

Brendan Hennessy, "Alan Sillitoe," *Transatlantic Review*, no. 41 (Winter–Spring 1972): 108–113;

Barry Norman, "Alan Sillitoe Avoids the Complacency Trap," *Times* (London), 26 October 1972, p. 12;

M. Lefranc, "Alan Sillitoe: An Interview," *Etudes Anglaises*, 26 (January–March 1973): 35–48;

John Halperin, "Interview with Alan Sillitoe," *Modern Fiction Studies*, 25 (Summer 1979): 175–189;

Leonie Rushforth, "Interview: Alan Sillitoe," *Bananas*, 17 (Autumn 1979): 34–36;

"In Conversation with Alan Sillitoe," *Fiction Magazine*, 1 (Spring 1982): 27;

Melanie Silgardo, "Class Is Irrelevant," *Keynote*, 1, no. 2 (April 1982): 3;

Joyce Rothschild, "The Growth of a Writer – An Interview with Alan Sillitoe," *Southern Humanities Review*, 20 (Spring 1986): 127–140.

Bibliography:

David Gerard, *Alan Sillitoe: A Bibliography* (Westport, Conn.: Meckler, 1988).

References:

Stanley S. Atherton, *Alan Sillitoe: A Critical Assessment* (London: Allen, 1979);

Anne-Marie Brumm, "Alan Sillitoe – From Angry Young Man to Universal Writer," *Neohelicon,* 14, no. 1 (1987): 89–113;

J. A. Byars, "Initiation of Alan Sillitoe's Long-Distance Runner," *Modern Fiction Studies,* 22 (Winter 1976–1977): 584–591;

David Craig, "The Roots of Sillitoe's Fiction," in *The British Working-Class Novel in the Twentieth Century,* edited by Jeremy Hawthorn (London: Arnold, 1984), pp. 94–110;

James Gindin, "Alan Sillitoe's Jungle," *Texas Studies in Literature and Language,* 4 (Spring 1962): 35–48;

Robert Haller, "Crux of Merging Deltas: A Note on Alan Sillitoe," *Prairie Schooner,* 48 (Winter 1974–1975): 151–158;

Peter Hitchcock, *Working-Class Fiction in Theory and Practice: A Reading of Alan Sillitoe* (Ann Arbor, Mich.: UMI Research Press, 1989);

N. D. Isaacs, "No Man in His Humour; A Note on Alan Sillitoe," *Studies in Short Fiction,* 4, no. 4 (1966–1967): 350–351;

Marie Peel, "The Loneliness of Alan Sillitoe," *Books and Bookmen,* 19 (December 1973): 42–46;

Allen Richard Penner, *Alan Sillitoe* (New York: Twayne, 1972);

Norma Phillips, "Sillitoe's 'The Match' and Its Joycean Counterparts," *Studies in Short Fiction,* 12 (Winter 1975): 9–14;

Eugene F. Quirk, "Social Class as Audience: Sillitoe's Story and Screenplay," *Literature-Film Quarterly,* 9, no. 3 (1981): 161–171;

Janet Buck Rollins, "Novel into Film: *The Loneliness of the Long-Distance Runner,*" *Literature-Film Quarterly,* 9, no. 3 (1981): 172–188;

D. M. Roskies, "Alan Sillitoe's Anti-Pastoral," *Journal of Narrative Technique,* 10, no. 3 (1980): 170–185;

Roskies, " 'I'd Rather Be Like I Am': Character, Style, and the Language of Class in Sillitoe's Narratives," *Neophilologus,* 65, no. 2 (1981): 308–319;

Michael K. Simmons, "The 'In-Laws' and 'Out-Laws' of Alan Sillitoe," *Ball State University Forum,* 14 (Winter 1973): 76–79;

W. J. Weatherby, "The Middle Age of the Angry Young Men," *Sunday Times Magazine,* 1 March 1981, pp. 36, 38;

Ramsey Wood, "Alan Sillitoe: The Image Shedding the Author," *Four Quarters,* 21 (November 1971): 3–10.

Iain Crichton Smith
(Iain Mac A'Ghobhainn)

(1 January 1928 –   )

Joanne Mathias Emig
York College of Pennsylvania

See also the Smith entry in *DLB 40: Poets of Great Britain and Ireland Since 1960.*

BOOKS: *The Long River* (Edinburgh: Macdonald, 1955);

Burn Is Aran, as Iain Mac A'Ghobhainn (Glasgow: Gairm, 1960; revised edition, London: Gairm, 1974);

Thistles and Roses (London: Eyre & Spottiswoode, 1961);

Deer on the High Hills: A Poem (Edinburgh: Giles Gordon, 1962);

An Dubh Is an Gorm, as Mac A'Ghobhainn (Aberdeen: Aberdeen University, 1963);

Biobuill Is Sanasan Reice (Glasgow: Gairm, 1965);

The Law and the Grace (London: Eyre & Spottiswoode, 1965);

An Coileach, as Mac A'Ghobhainn (Glasgow: An Comunn Gaidhealach, 1966);

A'Chuirt, as Mac A'Ghobhainn (Glasgow: An Comunn Gaidhealach, 1966);

The Golden Lyric: An Essay on the Poetry of Hugh MacDiarmid (Preston, U.K.: Akros, 1967);

At Helensburgh (Belfast: Festival Publications, Queen's University, 1968);

Consider the Lilies (London: Gollancz, 1968); republished as *The Alien Light* (Boston: Houghton Mifflin, 1969);

Three Regional Voices, by Smith, Michael Longley, and Barry Tebb (London: Poet & Printer, 1968);

From Bourgeois Land (London: Gollancz, 1969);

The Last Summer (London: Gollancz, 1969);

Iain Am Measg nan Reultan, as Mac A'Ghobhainn (Glasgow: Gairm, 1970);

Maighstirean Is Ministearan, as Mac A'Ghobhainn (Inverness: Club Leabhar, 1970);

Selected Poems (London: Gollancz, 1970; Chester Springs, Pa.: Dufour, 1970);

Survival Without Error and Other Stories (London: Gollancz, 1970);

Iain Crichton Smith (photograph by Christopher Barker)

My Last Duchess (London: Gollancz, 1971);

Hamlet in Autumn (Loanhead, U.K.: Macdonald, 1972);

Love Poems and Elegies (London: Gollancz, 1972);

Penguin Modern Poets 21, by Smith, George Mackay Brown, and Norman MacCaig (Harmondsworth, U.K.: Penguin, 1972);

An t-Adhar Ameireaganach Is SGeulachdan File, as Mac A'Ghobhainn (Inverness: Club Leabhar, 1973);

The Black and the Red and Other Stories (London: Gollancz, 1973);

Rabhdan is Rudan, as Mac A'Ghobhainn (Glasgow: Gairm, 1973);

Eadar Fealla-dha Is Glaschu, as Mac A'Ghobhainn
(Glasgow: University of Glasgow Celtic Department, 1974);

Goodbye, Mr. Dixon (London: Gollancz, 1974);

Orpheus and Other Poems (Preston, U.K.: Akros,
1974);

Poems for Donalda (Belfast: Ulsterman, 1974);

The Notebooks of Robinson Crusoe and Other Poems (London: Gollancz, 1975);

The Permanent Island (Loanhead, U.K.: Macdonald,
1975);

An t-Aonaran, as Mac A'Ghobhainn (Glasgow:
University of Glasgow Celtic Department,
1976);

The Village (Inverness: Club Leabhar, 1976);

The Hermit and Other Stories (London: Gollancz,
1977);

In the Middle (London: Gollancz, 1977);

An End to Autumn (London: Gollancz, 1978);

River, River: Poems for Children (Loanhead, U.K.:
Macdonald, 1978);

Na h-Ainmhidhean, as Mac A'Ghobhainn (Aberfeldy:
Clo Chailleann, 1979);

On the Island (London: Gollancz, 1979);

Am Bruadaraiche, as Mac A'Ghobhainn (Stornoway,
U.K.: Acair, 1980);

Murdo and Other Stories (London: Gollancz, 1981);

A Field Full of Folk (London: Gollancz, 1982);

The Search (London: Gollancz, 1983);

The Exiles (Manchester: Carcanet, 1984; Dublin:
Raven Arts Press, 1984);

Mr. Trill in Hades (London: Gollancz, 1984);

Selected Poems (Manchester: Carcanet, 1985);

The Tenement (London: Gollancz, 1985);

A Life (Manchester & New York: Carcanet, 1986);

Towards the Human: Selected Essays (Edinburgh: Macdonald, 1986);

An t-Eilean agus An Canan (Glasgow: University of
Glasgow Celtic Department, 1987);

In the Middle of the Wood (London: Gollancz, 1987);

Selected Stories (Manchester: Carcanet, 1990);

The Dream (London: Macmillan, 1990);

An Honourable Death (London: Macmillan, 1992).

Editions and Collections: *New Poets 1959,* by
Smith, Karen Gershon, and Christopher
Levenson, edited by Edwin Muir (London:
Eyre & Spottiswoode, 1959);

Selected Poems, 1955–1980, edited by Robin Fulton
(Loanhead, U.K.: Macdonald, 1981);

Collected Poems (Manchester: Carcanet, 1992);

Thoughts of Murdo (Edinburgh: Balnain, 1993);

Endings and Beginnings (Manchester: Carcanet,
1994).

OTHER: "Between Sea and Moor," in *As I Remember: Ten Scottish Authors Recall How Writing Began
for Them,* edited by Maurice Lindsay (London:
Hale, 1979).

SELECTED PERIODICAL PUBLICATION –
UNCOLLECTED: "Writers and Education: Iain
Crichton Smith," *Scottish Educational Journal*
(31 October 1975).

Iain Crichton Smith is a prolific writer in two
languages and several genres whose novels and
short stories are not as well known as his poetry. He
ranks with Derick Thomson and George Mackay
Brown at the forefront of the Gaelic Renaissance
and is heir apparent to Sorley Maclean's title of
elder statesman of Scottish poetry. He is also recognized as a pioneer of the short-story form in Gaelic.

Smith was born on 1 January 1928 on the Isle
of Lewis in Scotland's Outer Hebrides, in a village
where Gaelic was still the native language. In "Writers and Education: Iain Crichton Smith" (1975), an
essay about his boyhood in the village of Bayble
and his early education in the nearby town of
Stornoway, Smith describes how he "squirmed between two worlds, at home in neither," speaking English in school and Gaelic elsewhere. Attempts to
bridge the two worlds ultimately propelled Smith
into a writing career that has earned him many ac-
colades but has also caused some in Scottish and
Gaelic literary circles to regard his contributions
with reserve.

In an August 1993 interview with Joanne Mathias Emig, Smith stated: "I haven't any plans for an
autobiography. My problem is that much of my autobiography is in my books and poems, sometimes
in a disguised form." His personal essay "Between
Sea and Moor" (1979) and his children's book *On
the Island* (1979) are openly autobiographical, and
most of his stories contain recurrent images that,
taken together, reveal much of the author's nature
and background. Indeed, anyone reading the entire
canon of Smith's short fiction comes away with a
sense of having visited his village with Smith as a
guide.

Smith has also said that much of his fiction
concerns "an essentially unromantic view of human
nature" in response to the "Celtic twilight myth," an
allusion to the Irish revival in literature of the late
nineteenth and early twentieth centuries, whose
writings relied heavily on retellings of Irish (and
Gaelic) legends and folklore. The term was taken
from an 1893 collection of tales by William Butler
Yeats that emphasizes Irish mysticism and a belief

in fairies, ghosts, and spirits. Smith's break from the romantic tradition of Gaelic storytelling led to charges that he was writing under "buaidh na Beurla" (the influence of English). Early critics even implied that Smith conceived his stories in English and translated them into Gaelic.

In "Writers and Education: Iain Crichton Smith" Smith states, "Gaelic . . . is my native language," but adds that, in school, "I took Gaelic as a subject. It seems to me that there ought to have been some way in which . . . the dichotomy between Gaelic and English did not have to be so sharp and merciless." The dual-language environment at first hampered his coming to terms with his writing talent. His earliest poems are in English, modeled on the English poets he read in the classroom, but he asks, "I wonder what I would have done if Gaelic had been encouraged in a creative way in my early days?"

Reflecting further on his education, Smith notes that, as his schooling progressed, his ties to the Gaelic society of his birth were steadily weakened. At twelve he attended Nicolson Institute in Stornoway, which was on Lewis but seemed "a different place, a different world . . . a town where English is spoken practically universally." The pressure of balancing both life at home and the demands of school played on Smith to the point that he says he was glad to leave Lewis for Aberdeen University, because there he "didn't carry daily on my shoulders the weight of a village tradition and the style of the *Aeneid.*" He recalls a villager who would interrogate him as if he were a stranger, asking if he knew the number of herring in a cran, or a particular Gaelic term. Smith notes, "The awkwardness arose from the fact that though I didn't know the answers to his questions, I could have told him the relationship of the hypotenuse of a right-angled triangle to its other two sides."

But Smith's break from his family was not without pain; in his 1975 essay he writes of the day he left Lewis for the university and looked back from the boat at his younger brother, whose schooling had ended at age fourteen:

> I turned to wave to him as he stood on the quay and in a moment of vision . . . I saw that a gap was opening up between us . . . and that that gap had been steadily opening ever since he had made his choice not to leave his friends in the village.
>
> Strangely enough, he has seen more of the world than I have since that time.

Smith's older brother, Alex John (now deceased), was in charge of education in Southern Rhodesia

(now Zimbabwe) for many years: Smith's younger brother, Kenneth, lives in Australia. A recurrent theme in Smith's fiction is the relationship between brothers, often between one who has emigrated and one who has stayed in Scotland. In his novel *The Search* (1983), a scholar on a visit to Australia is drawn into a search for his long-lost brother. Several of Smith's stories bring the brother in Africa home to Scotland for a visit. Smith also used his brothers' names for some of his characters.

Smith reaches beyond his family for inspiration as well. His service as a sergeant in the British Army Education Corps (1950–1952) and his long teaching career, first at Clydebank (1952–1955) and later at Oban (1955–1977), figure prominently in many of his stories. In 1977, when he was nearly fifty, Smith retired from teaching and married a former student. Several of his stories contain images of teacher/student infatuation, with outcomes ranging from happy to tragic.

As Iain Mac A'Ghobhainn, Smith was well established as a Gaelic writer before his first works appeared in English; he produced three volumes of short stories in Gaelic before his first English novel, *Consider the Lilies* (retitled *The Alien Light* in America), was published in 1968. *Saturday Review* (8 March 1969) described Smith as "a Gaelic poet, playwright, and short-story writer [who] has written poems in English," and it was as a poet that Smith was best known to English-speaking readers. *Consider the Lilies,* set in the early nineteenth century, tells of an elderly Highland woman forced off her land by the Clearances, which allowed landlords to confiscate property for sheep grazing. Smith tackles themes of displacement and alienation as his protagonist tries to adjust to her new environment and the loss of her old community. *Saturday Review* called it "not a very good novel . . . the pattern of the simple declarative sentence, repeated at book length, gets awfully tedious," concluding that "it is too bad that for his first novel in English he has chosen material that would have been more effective as a short story."

That the short story may be Smith's forte is implied in a review of another novel, *The Tenement* (1985). The *Times Literary Supplement* (9 August 1985) described it as having "no plot – its chapters are barely connected," yet with "a cumulative power that by the end leaves one with the feeling of having been in the company of an unusually fine sensitivity." Such is the feeling evoked by many of Smith's short-fiction collections.

Smith's second book in English is his first collection of short stories in English. *Survival Without*

Error and Other Stories (1970) continues the alienation and exile themes found in *Consider the Lilies.* Smith's reputation as a poet is noted in a review of the collection by Donald John MacLeod (*Scottish International Review,* September 1970): "Some of the themes could be handled as well (if not better) in poems." MacLeod laments the lack of Gaelic background in Smith's debut in short fiction in English, pointing to the rise in ethnically generated literature in the late 1960s. He feels Smith erred in presenting mainstream fiction little colored by his Gaelic heritage. But MacLeod is writing from a Scottish background; to an American reader Smith's tales, while not notably "foreign," are clearly from a different cultural milieu.

The characters in *Survival Without Error* experience varying degrees of alienation, from the literal exile of the biblical Joseph in Egypt to the emotional gap between a dying father and the daughter who chose marriage over the chance for a university education. Smith acknowledges that "ethical" and "existentialist" are important terms in describing his fiction and cites Søren Kierkegaard as one of his greatest influences. Smith's characters live by, or purposely defy, the existentialist mandate to live life to the fullest.

In "The Ships" an elderly man and wife learn to stop living for the "someday" when their emigrant children will visit and instead "learn to be alone, for that was the way it was going to be." In "Close of Play" Neil spends the entire story in his room, listening to a broadcast of a cricket match between England and Australia. The intricacies of the play-by-play analysis may be lost on the American reader, but the tension is palpable. In trying to decide between applying for admission to a university and taking a job in London, Neil comes to regard the cricket match as a surrogate Delphic oracle. Relinquishing his Kierkegaardian free choice, he allows the arbitrary outcome of the sporting event to determine his future.

Smith cautions that, although he considers Kierkegaard a major influence, his work is not religious – that it is "at times anti-religious." Smith grew up in what he calls "a tyrannically dogmatic religious area," which "stained" his perceptions of religion. Speaking of women in his village who would go to communion and then stand gossiping on street corners afterward, Smith told Lorn Macintyre in a 1971 interview:

> I could never reconcile their talk of scandal and things like that with being religious. I never really found any evidence of joy.... I always had the feeling that reli-

gious people, if they are truly religious, ought to have more joy than they had.

Smith concluded that "it is probably true that I am Calvinistic, without theological allegiance."

In "Joseph" Smith combines his religious cynicism with themes of exile and alienation in a reworking of the biblical tale of the young man who is sold into slavery by his brothers. Smith keeps the biblical setting but paints Joseph as ambitious and cunning. In prison after refusing Potiphar's wife, Joseph decides that "since power seems to be the only important thing in life I shall gain it." Smith's Joseph is not an innocent touched by the hand of God but a politician who tells the pharaoh what he wants to hear (and what will result in Joseph's elevation in the administration). Joseph regrets selling his gifts for power but not enough to forfeit the gains he has achieved.

The analogy between Joseph in Egypt and Smith in the English-speaking world is almost too obvious to mention. Smith writes of Joseph: "Some nights he felt he did not belong to that country. Its language was not his. . . . He couldn't speak as he wished." MacLeod points out that Smith wrote a Gaelic version of the Joseph story that was printed in the Scottish publication *Gairm* in 1963 (predating his first prose publication in English) and argues that the English version suffers by comparison, offering his own translation of lines that appear to parallel Smith's English lines given above:

> I have learnt a new language and have saved my people with it. I have made myself a gall for them. I should like to write at length about Egypt but it is about my brothers and my own home that I write though they have not been kind to me. That is strange, isn't it? And I do not know how to write profoundly in the language of Egypt. That is also strange.

Smith supplies an insight in a later story, "The Brothers" (*The Hermit and Other Stories,* 1977), an eloquent tale of a writer trying to retell the Joseph story in English but who finds his typed English replaced by "Gaelic sentences, rougher and more passionate than my English ones." At first blaming ghosts from the Celtic twilight world he has forcefully rejected, the writer, after much metaphysical soul-searching, surrenders to the spirit of the moors that comes to permeate his room and to the Gaelic heritage he shares with his "brothers":

> I sat down . . . and began to type. The words were Gaelic and flowed easily and familiarly, as if I were speaking to my brothers. . . . I seemed to hear their language and

> it was their language that I wrote. It was rough and yet
> it was my own. It was their voices speaking through me.

Here Smith has accepted his place as a bridge between the two worlds.

In "The Exiles" Smith brings another exile, a Pakistani student selling clothing and linens door-to-door, into contact with an elderly Highland woman living in a council flat (akin to public housing) in the Lowlands. MacLeod criticizes Smith's syntax in this story, arguing that the standard English voice of the elderly woman detracts from the sense of her exile as parallel to that of the Pakistani student, who speaks broken English. But the woman *feels* as out of place in the Lowlands as the Pakistani, which is precisely the point – Smith knows that one need not be in a foreign country to feel displaced.

Two stories in *Survival Without Error* are harbingers of a more ambitious undertaking. "Murder Without Pain" introduces Mr. Andrew Trill, M.A., principal classics master at Eastborough Grammar School, and "Goodbye John Summers" questions the value of scholarship for scholarship's sake. In "Mr. Trill in Hades" (*Mr. Trill in Hades,* 1984) Smith sends Mr. Trill on a Dantean trek through the underworld in search of answers.

Smith's second collection of short fiction in English, *The Black and the Red and Other Stories,* was published in 1973. These stories are more Gaelic and display more literary daring than those in the previous collection. The first story, "The Dying," puts the reader at the bedside of a dying woman, clinically yet poetically describing her final moments from the viewpoint of the man attending her. Near the end of the brief story the reader realizes that the man is not her husband but her son, lost and confused by a process beyond his control. He abandons his copy of Dante and surrenders to his grief and fear: "He thought, weeping, this is the irretrievable centre where there is . . . no metaphor. At this time poetry is powerless."

In the interview with Smith, focusing primarily on his poetry, Macintyre observed that Smith's then-most-recently published poems, including several dealing with death, show a looser, less intellectual style. Macintyre asks whether they represent a departure and whether Smith thinks the coming years will be difficult for him. He responds: "I think they will be difficult ones because . . . everything I have ever done is really eventually coming to this question. What is death? What is a dead person, and in the end what is the value of writing when one is confronted by a dead person?"

Smith also admits to feelings of guilt because he had the opportunity to go out and develop his talents, while others of perhaps equal or superior intelligence were denied the chance. In the 1975 essay on his early education Smith points out that there is something wrong when so many potential leaders of a community leave it and come to perceive it as inferior: "For instance, if someone comes back to the islands after leaving them, there is a sense in which that person is thought to have failed in some manner."

Smith hints at these attitudes in "An American Sky" (*The Black and the Red*), in which John Macleod returns from America to visit his brother, who stayed behind to run the family farm. A village woman, telling John about the time his brother got the better of her in a deal, says, " 'Your brother was the cunning one. He knew a thing or two.' " She later remarks, " 'That brother of yours is a businessman. He is the one who should have gone to America.' " John walks home from the woman's cottage:

> He expected at any moment to see the ghosts of the dead stopping him by the roadway, interrogating him and asking him, "When did you come home? When are you going away?" The whole visit, he realized now, was an implicit interrogation. What it was really about was: What had he done with his life? That was the question that people, without realising it, were putting to him, simply because he had chosen to return.

The story closely parallels chapter 12 of *On the Island,* his autobiographical children's book, in which the self-named character "Iain" visits a village woman whose emigrant son has returned from America for good owing to an incurable illness. The two pieces contain many parallel images. In "An American Sky" John Macleod sees "a man who was probably her son trapped like a fly inside a net which he was repairing with a bone needle." In *On the Island* the man is "hidden behind a green net which he seemed to be endlessly repairing, so that Iain thought of him as a pleasant spider who was weaving the net out of himself in some strange way." In "Between Sea and Moor" Smith remembers watching "men seated, apparently sewing, among green netting." This could be a case of a writer refining a favorite metaphor, but, given Smith's admission that his stories are autobiographical, the repetition of images gives the reader insight into those events that have impressed Smith most vividly.

Such is the case with the title story, "The Black and the Red." The *Times Literary Supplement* (19 October 1973) called this story "the key to the recurring theme of the collection" – how to reconcile the simplicity of rural life with the corrupting effects of a liberal urban society. The story takes the form of letters from Kenneth, a naive young man newly arrived at a large university, to his family in a Highland village much like Smith's. The autobiographical echoes begin almost immediately. When Kenneth and his new schoolmate, George, arrive at the city's train station, they see a beggar "sitting on the stone pavement with his back against the wall . . . his cap – containing a few pennies – beside him." Kenneth's first letter ends, "Last night, as I was lying in bed . . . I thought I heard someone whistling a Gaelic tune. But it wasn't a Gaelic tune at all."

"Between Sea and Moor" recounts Smith's arrival at Aberdeen University with nearly identical imagery:

> When I arrived at Aberdeen Railway Station the first thing I saw was a beggar sitting on the pavement wearing black glasses, with a cap for pennies at his side.
> That night when I was lying in bed I thought I heard someone whistling a Gaelic tune past my window, but it was not a Gaelic tune at all.

The impact of the beggar on young Smith is explained in part in a 1981 interview in *Seven Poets:* "On the island of Lewis you could never have beggars . . . if there was someone who was poor, he or she would be looked after." Beyond Smith's horror at the beggar's willingness to expose his need in public (a shock to Smith's independent Calvinist heritage), the scene affected Smith because he and his brothers were raised on a one-pound-a-week widow's pension. In a different kind of society this could have been his own fate. In "Between Sea and Moor" and also in the Macintyre interview Smith admits to guilt at having "condemned" his mother to a life of hard work to support his education.

His mother's sacrifice also surfaces in "The Telegram." A nameless "fat woman" and "thin woman" drink tea and watch with apprehension as a messenger progresses through the village with a telegram. It is wartime, and the telegram can mean only that someone's son has been killed. Smith writes, "The thin woman was ambitious: she had sent her son to university though she only had a widow's pension of ten shillings a week." To ward off anxiety, the women talk of their sons in the service, and the thin woman begins a litany of the deprivations she endured to send her son "Iain" to university, ending with, " 'And for all I know he may marry an English girl and where will I be? . . . He might not give me anything after all I've done for him.' " In

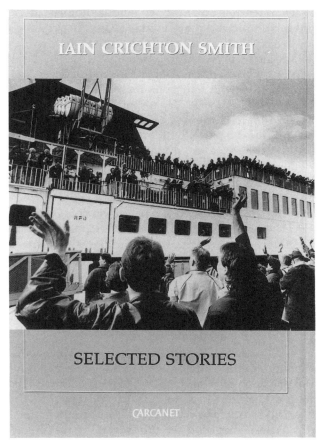

Dust jacket for Smith's 1990 collection of short fiction, which includes stories published during the 1970s and 1980s

"The Black and the Red" Kenneth's letters home repeatedly assures his family that he is working hard and knows "what has been done" for him.

But, beyond the immediate parallels to Smith's life, "The Black and the Red" presents a protagonist who acts according to Smith's own precepts: "I am much concerned with the individual's attempt to be himself as against forces that are impinging on him. His role is to question. His role is to be a 'free person' if he can be so." By the end of the story Kenneth – buffeted by the liberalizing forces of the university, the injustices of the legal system, and his ambivalent feelings for George's freethinking girlfriend, Fiona – breaks from the mores of his Highland upbringing. His final letter concludes, "I have never been so calm. Now I write out of this calmness, Fiona and I. George has gone and we are alone. We send you this letter, Fiona and I." As all the others, this letter is signed, "Your loving son, Kenneth."

Other stories in *The Black and the Red* are more abstractly philosophical. In "A Day in the Life of . . ."

a schoolteacher on her lonely annual holiday in Edinburgh reflects on her course in life throughout a day that takes her from a John Wayne movie to an avant-garde production based on the rise of Adolf Hitler. "Through the Desert" accomplishes a similar life review in four compressed paragraphs with Kafkaesque echoes. "The Crater" and "In Church" feature soldiers trapped by the horrors of war both on and off the battlefield. Smith also displays a talent for the macabre, giving many of the stories a chilling ending twist.

Smith can write a wickedly funny tale as well. In "The Professor and the Comics" a college professor espouses the literary merit of the comic character Dangerous Dan to expose the pomposities of the academic elite, in what the *Times Literary Supplement* (19 October 1973) called "a splendidly Amis-like set-piece of outrage." Professors who are caught up in, or rebel against, the strictures of academia are recurrent characters in Smith's fiction, born of his own thirty years in teaching. *Mr. Trill in Hades* is set entirely in the academic world.

"The Little People" is a cynically clever, disturbing tale that illustrates Smith's concern about the rise in tourism and the loss of local culture in his native Highlands, a concern he addressed in the Macintyre interview and that also arose in a panel discussion recorded in Aberdeen in 1970 and printed in *Scottish International Review* (September 1970). In the discussion Sorley Maclean – a premier Gaelic poet who published his first volume in 1943, when Smith was fifteen – attributes the decline of the Gaelic language in part to what he terms "the real Highland Clearance," the sale of local properties to "incomers" who use them as vacation or retirement homes. The problem, Maclean says, is that the new people "are all English speakers." Smith discusses the influx of tourists with Macintyre, calling the situation "the kind of thing where Christ might have said: In my Father's house how many mansions are all being used for bed and breakfast!"

"The Little People" concerns Matches, an information clerk and tour guide at a Stone Age archaeological site in the Highlands, "the oracle which would at regular intervals emit information to the shallow and the rich and the voyaging." The Stone Age people mystically appear one night, and Matches is seized by a desire to make contact with them. When a symbolic shower of postcards from the present to the past fails to capture their attention, he maneuvers his cat into the center of their circle. The latent wildness of the animal touches a chord in the villagers:

The cat had gone to sleep and someone was banging two stones together endlessly while others were removing the antlers from [a] deer from which eventually they would make bone needles which would lead them to the large coaches where they would come and visit themselves in pink slacks, chattering excitedly with their guidebooks and postcards.

Matches has connected; he has sent them on "their long march through history . . . as they ascend from their shell necklaces towards Woolworths."

The Hermit and Other Stories continues Smith's preoccupation with the darker side of human nature as he presents a variety of what would today be called dysfunctional relationships. *Saturday Review* (1 December 1977) noted that Smith "is particularly successful in [the] identification of the macabre element in ordinary life." The long title story examines what happens when a hermit, the personification of individualism and freedom, settles in an abandoned hut near a village. The hermit's innocuous presence disrupts the village, releasing malice, wanderlust, and repressed sexual desire among the inhabitants. The narrator, a retired headmaster, is obsessed by the hermit, perceiving – or fearing – a parallel between the hermit's life and his own as a widower. He coldly engineers what he sees as the necessary eviction of the hermit but then wonders, "What else could I think about now, now that that hut had no inhabitant, now that questions of metaphysics had been removed from me?"

The question of individual freedom, or the lack thereof, in the family setting propels "The Impulse," as a husband who has stifled his wife's intelligence, vivacity, and aspirations is baffled by his impulse to turn himself in to the police when he sees a "wanted for murder" poster. A similar relationship existing between a lame brother and his caretaker sister is carried to tragic consequences in "Timoshenko," the concise opening sentences of which could serve as a lesson for anyone aspiring to write murder mysteries:

When I went into the thatched house as I always did at nine o'clock at night, he was lying on the floor stabbed with a bread knife, his usually brick-red face pale and his ginger moustache a dark wedge under his nose. His eyes were wide open like blue marbles. I wondered where she was.

The story has a wartime setting, and the title refers to the brother's habit of calling his sister by the name of a Russian general, sardonically implying that she is even too stupid to follow the news on the radio.

"The Exorcism" is baldly philosophical, as a professor battles for the soul of a student possessed by the teachings of Kierkegaard. In "Listen to the Voice" a professor gives a maliciously honest evaluation of his dying colleague's manuscript for a book on existentialism. The story examines the darker side of the relationship between colleagues that Smith explores in "Goodbye John Summers" (*Survival Without Error*). Smith also paints unsettling portraits of a psychiatrist who is murderously jealous of his younger wife, an actor who gives a true-life performance as Macbeth, and an elderly woman who knows she must leave her home with its beloved cherry orchard and chooses to do so in a most unexpected way.

Smith continues his probing of the misfit and the maladjusted in *Murdo and Other Stories* (1981). The *Times Literary Supplement* (26 June 1981) called Smith "a fascinating story-teller" whose "sympathetic, baffled square pegs . . . cannot fit into the dark, round hole of their circumstances." In "The Visit" Smith presents a housewife who rebels against her constricted life in a whimsically nonviolent way. She imagines herself the queen of Daffodil Land, a field of flowers where she hides from "the adults" with her niece and nephew. With "The Missionary" Smith takes the reader to Africa with Reverend Black, who becomes embroiled in a harrowing cultural clash that tests his own moral convictions, yet another product of Smith's tainted view of religion.

Smith's personas of poet and teacher collide in "Mr. Heine," as the title character obliquely confronts Mr. Bingham, his former teacher, who is on the eve of retirement. Heine professes gratitude to Bingham for having guided him to his career as a writer of advertising jingles, saying that in Bingham's class he had "A revelation straight from God / That I should rhyme as I was taught." But this is not a vapid tale of scholarly gratitude; Smith is too complex for that. Bingham's nudge to Heine's career occurred when he ridiculed the latter's adolescent attempt at free verse before the entire class, comparing it unfavorably to a rhymed Tennyson poem. Bingham's blatant cruelty speaks to every teacher's fear of unwittingly stifling a budding talent, a fear that Smith addresses in "The Exorcism." After wresting an obsessed student from the grip of Kierkegaard, a professor asks, "How could I be sure that this was not indeed a second Kierkegaard, how could I be sure that I had not destroyed a genius?" There is a touch of Smith in young Heine as well, the child playing with words and discovering a talent for poetry.

With *Mr. Trill in Hades* Smith returns to the world he occupied for so many years on both sides of the desk. Here the round holes into which his square pegs must fit are those of the educational system. An essay by Ann E. Boutelle, a former student of Smith at Oban High School, in *Iain Crichton Smith: Critical Essays* (1992), draws specific parallels between the characters and incidents in some of the stories and Smith's twenty-two years at the school.

In "The Ring" a student witnesses an embarrassingly personal moment in his middle-aged mathematics teacher's life: the breakup of the teacher's courtship, which "had been a source of gossip and merriment in the school for many years." The incident strikes at the foundation of the student's need for constancy, expressed in his love for geometry: "I adored the inflexible order of the proofs, the fact that parallel lines never met, that triangles were always composed of 180 degrees. One knew where one was with geometry, it was a world of security and happiness, which sprang no surprises." Years later, at the old professor's funeral, the student learns that the man spent the years after the breakup in a slow decline. In a conclusion that could have been maudlin in lesser hands, the student reveals, "The best thing about geometry was it never lied to you, which is why I myself am a mathematics teacher as well. It has nothing to do with pain or loss."

Smith writes in "Between Sea and Moor" that he was "very poor at arithmetic and mathematics" until he began working puzzles in a book:

> I woke up and found that I could do mathematics, and that above all I had fallen in love with geometry. From then on I would do geometry problems for pleasure and when the solution clicked so elegantly it was as good as being able to write a poem. Geometry appealed to some part of my nature which has to do with a love of order and elegance.

Latin was another important subject in Smith's youth, mentioned frequently in interviews and essays. "In the School" focuses on delinquent boys who break into a school building on a summer's evening with the intent of setting it afire. The leader is "Terry, the mad one," simmering with hate and a need to destroy. Terry's rage is concentrated against Grotty, the Latin teacher, even though he "never took Latin, they said he was too stupid." Once, when Terry had made a disturbance in the room next to Grotty's, the Latin teacher had "come in and taken [Terry] out and given him six" with a belt, making "sarcastic remarks about him first in front of the class, using long words that he didn't understand." In a denouement that falls between Celtic myth and psychosis, Terry's arson plans are thwarted by a faceless band of phantom teachers in chalk-stained gowns.

On the blackboard in Grotty's classroom is the word *insula,* which the uncomprehending Terry dismisses profanely. But the Latin word held much significance for Smith in school, for he mentions "learning 'insula, insulam' etc." among the images he recalls from his secondary-school education. *On the Island* contains a brief scene of young Iain's first day in Latin class, as the "fierce-looking" teacher intones, " ' "Insula" means "island," and remember that we are living on an island. This school . . . is situated on an "insula." ' " The Latin teacher's name is Mr. Trill, and a version of him appears in "Murder Without Pain" (*Survival Without Error*). Smith mines that ground for two stories in *Mr. Trill in Hades.*

In "Murder Without Pain" Mr. Trill remembers "a young teacher of twenty-three or so, fresh from . . . the triumphs of training college and brimful of innovations and enthusiasm" who allowed his students to write plays using working-class language as well as "borrow[ing] from television some of the worst language that they heard there." This nameless young teacher becomes Mark Mason in "The Play," whose plot hinges on Mason's attempts to reach a class made up of girls marking time in school until they reach "leaving age." The girls have "a fixed antipathy to the written word"; when asked the last book she has read, one replies blankly, "Please, sir, I never read any books." Mason clings to his sense that the girls are not innately stupid; he needs only to connect with their interests.

Realizing he cannot bring the girls into his world of William Shakespeare and Sophocles, he enters theirs, proposing that they write and enact a play called "The Rise of a Pop Star." From the first impromptu scene, showing parental mockery of the singer's aspirations, Mason learns more than his students do, as the limited expectations of their lives are revealed.

Smith acknowledges D. H. Lawrence as an influence on his poetry; a Lawrencian preoccupation with class consciousness infiltrates Smith's prose as well. The unacknowledged class distinction between those destined for higher education and those presumed incapable of advanced study, illustrated by "In the School" and "The Play," is a theme Smith explores elsewhere. His poem "A Young Highland Girl Studying Poetry" (*Thistles and Roses,* 1961) uses agricultural metaphors to describe a farm girl's attempts to cultivate the "foreign rose" of literature: "Poetry drives its lines into her forehead / like an angled plough across a bare field."

The themes that have occupied Smith over the course of his long career coalesce in his existential masterpiece "Mr. Trill in Hades." The *New Yorker* (30 April 1984) inexplicably called this story "a predictable fable about a dusty teacher of Latin and Greek"; superficially, it could appear to be just that. But in these eighty-four pages, as Trill traverses the underworld, meeting famous figures of classical literature and shades from his own past, he (and the reader) must reexamine accepted truths in light of discoveries made along the way.

Smith has written often of classics teachers who are so immersed in the ancient world that they are incapable of living fully in the modern one; Mr. Trill epitomizes the type. He has lived for thirty years in the same rooming house, rarely goes out except to school, relates to children only as "beings who must be instructed in Latin," and is respected but not truly liked by students and colleagues.

The Trill stories can stand independently, but, read together, each lends depth to the other. "Murder Without Pain" works as a psychological mystery, as Trill presents a brilliant justification of a horribly inexcusable act. On its most simplistic level "Mr. Trill in Hades" can be read as a clever parody of Dante's *Inferno.* But, beyond that, the story showcases Smith's talent for characterization, as Trill's illusions are stripped away one by one, leaving him to question the naked value of his sacrifices on the altar of academia. Boutelle points out that the story was written in the period after Smith's marriage and retirement from teaching, as he sought a way to "adapt to this entirely new way of defining himself, as husband, stepfather, full-time writer, retired teacher."

"Murder Without Pain" describes Trill as "a small man with trenched cheeks rather like those of Dante," which may signal the genesis of the later story. Trill's adventures in Hades juxtapose a reinterpretation of the myths he has taught for thirty years with parallel events from his personal life. His first encounter in Hades is with the common Greek soldiers of the Trojan War. They sketch Agamemnon as a leader who "didn't know his arse from his elbow" and Ulysses as a sly cheat who stole all the credit for the victory. Trill leaves them in a daze, trying to square what he has just heard with "what [he] had read in the big Latin and Greek translations when he was still young and his parents were as usual quarrelling." Trill's father was headmaster, but his mother worked in the school canteen and saw no purpose in learning about "all that rubbish that happened long ago." If the soldiers' shades speak the truth, Trill's mother was right, and he and his father before him had indeed wasted their lives.

As Trill continues on his wanderings, he learns that Orpheus's sacrifice for Eurydice was not quite as presented in the myths; that Dido perished not from revenge but from hopelessness; that Sisyphus does not want to be released from his endless task; that the great Achilles and Agamemnon argue on; that, according to Andromache, Hector also lusted after Helen; and that the Cyclops still seeks "Noman" as well as an understanding of the treachery that robbed him of his sight. Interspliced with these meetings are insights into Trill's private and professional lives, his lost love, and his struggle for education under his mother's disapproving eye (" 'What are you doing reading those books all the time? . . . Idleness, if you ask me' ").

The last shade Trill meets is Virgil, and his last illusion is shattered. Virgil denounces his own verse, calls writing " 'the greatest labour that one can conceive of,' " and adds, " 'How tired I was of Aeneas.' " But, in explaining himself, Virgil exposes the major flaw in Trill's life: " 'I should not have stayed so long in my study . . . I should have lived off the justice of the moment.' "

Here is the crux of Trill's existential dilemma, and Smith devises a unique solution. At the center of Smith's Hades stands a castle, off-limits to all but a chosen few. Trill is taken inside and offered the chance to spend eternity reading and debating with other eternal scholars. But Trill's eyes have been opened, and he sees the sequestered academic life in all its trivialities:

> An excited voice shouted, "I have found it. I have correctly dated the Georgics."
> Heads turned towards the speaker simultaneously. One man said, "The fool. Who does he think he is?

That has already been done by Malonivitz." Another said, "I shall have to rebut whatever he says."
The headmaster gazed smilingly at Mr. Trill and said, "See? Nothing but excitement."

Trill makes the only choice he can, one that has never been picked before. He opts to return to the world, but not as a teacher. He ends his journey on a street corner, hawking newspapers full of crime, heroics, and pathos – full of life. Kierkegaard would have been proud.

Over the course of his career Smith seems to have followed the architectural dictum that "less is more." Many of his stories are told in the first person by narrators who do not give their names. The reader is plunged into the middle of the character's life and dilemma with little introduction or fanfare. But the very sense of immediacy is Smith's greatest strength. The reader is instantly thrust into the persona of someone who could be anyone at all – even the reader himself.

Interviews:

Lorn Macintyre, "Poet in Bourgeois Land: Interview with Iain Crichton Smith," *Scottish International Review* (September 1971);

"Poetry, Passion, and Political Consciousness," discussion by Smith, John McInnes, Hamish Henderson, Donald MacAuley, and Sorley Maclean, *Scottish International Review* (October 1971).

Bibliography:

Grant F. Wilson, *A Bibliography of Iain Crichton Smith* (Aberdeen: Aberdeen University Press, 1990).

Reference:

Iain Crichton Smith: Critical Essays (Edinburgh: Edinburgh University Press, 1992).

Muriel Spark

(1 February 1918 –)

Vern Lindquist
Sullivan Community College

See also the Spark entry in *DLB 15: British Novelists, 1930–1959: Part 2.*

BOOKS: *Child of Light: A Reassessment of Mary Wollstonecraft Shelley* (Hadleigh, Essex, U.K.: Tower Bridge, 1951; New York: Avon, 1974);

The Fanfarlo and Other Verse (Adlington, Kent, U.K.: Hand & Flower Press, 1952);

John Masefield (London: Nevill, 1953; Philadelphia: West, 1973; revised edition, London: Hutchinson, 1992);

The Comforters (London: Macmillan, 1957; Philadelphia: Lippincott, 1957);

The Go-Away Bird with Other Stories (London: Macmillan, 1958); republished as *The Go-Away Bird and Other Stories* (Philadelphia: Lippincott, 1960);

Robinson, A Novel (London: Macmillan, 1958; Philadelphia: Lippincott, 1958);

Memento Mori (London: Macmillan, 1959; Philadelphia: Lippincott, 1959);

The Ballad of Peckham Rye (London: Macmillan, 1960; Philadelphia: Lippincott, 1960);

The Bachelors (London: Macmillan, 1960; Philadelphia: Lippincott, 1961);

Voices at Play: Stories and Ear-pieces (London: Macmillan, 1961); republished as *Voices at Play* (Philadelphia: Lippincott, 1962);

The Prime of Miss Jean Brodie (London: Macmillan, 1961; Philadelphia: Lippincott, 1962);

Doctors of Philosophy (London: Macmillan, 1963; New York: Knopf, 1966);

The Girls of Slender Means (London: Macmillan, 1963; New York: Knopf, 1963);

The Mandelbaum Gate (London: Macmillan, 1965; New York: Knopf, 1965);

Collected Poems I (London: Macmillan, 1967; New York: Knopf, 1968); republished as *Going Up to Sotheby's and Other Poems* (London & New York: Granada, 1982);

Collected Stories I (London: Macmillan, 1967; New York: Knopf, 1968);

Muriel Spark (photograph by Jerry Bauer)

The Public Image (London: Macmillan, 1968; New York: Knopf, 1968);

The Very Fine Clock (New York: Knopf, 1968; London: Macmillan, 1968);

The Driver's Seat (London: Macmillan, 1970; New York: Knopf, 1970);

The French Window (London: Macmillan, 1970);

Not to Disturb (London: Macmillan, 1971; New York: Viking, 1972);

The Hothouse by the East River (London: Macmillan, 1973; New York: Viking, 1973);

The Abbess of Crewe (London: Macmillan, 1974; New York: Viking, 1974);

The Takeover (London: Macmillan, 1976; New York: Viking, 1976);

Territorial Rights (London: Macmillan, 1979; New York: Coward, McCann & Geoghegan, 1979);

Loitering with Intent (London: Bodley Head, 1981; New York: Coward, McCann & Geoghegan, 1981);

Bang-bang – You're Dead and Other Stories (London & New York: Granada, 1982);

The Only Problem (London: Bodley Head, 1984; New York: Putnam, 1984);

The Stories of Muriel Spark (New York: Dutton, 1985; London: Bodley Head, 1987);

Mary Shelley (New York: Dutton, 1987; revised edition, London: Constable, 1988);

A Far Cry from Kensington (London: Constable, 1988; New York: Houghton Mifflin, 1988);

Symposium (London: Constable, 1990; New York: Houghton Mifflin, 1990);

Curriculum Vitae: Autobiography (London: Constable, 1992; Boston: Houghton Mifflin, 1992).

OTHER: *Tribute to Wordsworth: A Miscellany of Opinion for the Centenary of the Poet's Death*, edited by Spark and Derek Stanford (London: Wingate, 1950);

A Selection of Poems by Emily Brontë, edited, with an introduction, by Spark (London: Grey Walls, 1952);

Emily Brontë: Her Life and Work, edited by Spark and Stanford (London: Owen, 1953; New York: British Book Center, 1953);

My Best Mary: The Selected Letters of Mary Wollstonecraft Shelley, edited by Spark and Stanford (London: Wingate, 1953; New York: Roy, 1954);

The Brontë Letters, edited, with an introduction, by Spark (London: Nevill, 1954); republished as *The Letters of the Brontës* (Norman: University of Oklahoma Press, 1954);

Letters of John Henry Newman: A Selection, edited by Spark and Stanford (London: Owen, 1957; Westminster, Md.: Newman, 1957).

SELECTED PERIODICAL PUBLICATIONS –
UNCOLLECTED: "Harper and Wilton," *Pick of Today's Short Stories*, no. 4 (1953): 191–194;

"Ladies and Gentlemen," *Chance*, 3 (April–June 1953): 40–46;

"The Pearly Shadow," *Norseman*, 13 (November 1955): 421–422;

"The Girl I Left Behind Me," *Norseman*, 16 (January 1958): 63–65;

"The End of Summer Time," *London Mystery Magazine*, 37 (June 1958): 65–69.

Although she is known primarily as a prolific novelist, Muriel Spark began her writing career with a short story. Her first published work of fiction, "The Seraph and the Zambesi" (*Observer*, December 1951; collected in *The Go-Away Bird with Other Stories*, 1958), appeared six years before her first novel, *The Comforters* (1957). According to Karl Malkoff in *Muriel Spark* (1968), Spark seems to have considered novels "an inferior way of writing" when the publisher Macmillan suggested in 1954 that she write a novel for them. Her first book of creative writing, *The Fanfarlo and Other Verse* (1952), was a volume of poetry. Even after Spark turned her attention mainly to novels, she continued to write short stories. In a 1989 interview with Jeanne Devoize and Pamela Valette she stated:

> *I* feel the short story is superior [to the novel], it's more difficult. . . . I really do think the short story is something by itself and it's superior to the novel in many ways. It's nearer to poetry and likely to have a longer life sometimes.

Spark's status as one of the most widely read contemporary British writers stems in part from the power, wit, and elegance of her short-story collections: *The Go-Away Bird with Other Stories* (1958), *Voices at Play: Stories and Ear-pieces* (1961), *Collected Stories I* (1967), *Bang-bang You're Dead and Other Stories* (1982), and *The Short Stories of Muriel Spark* (1985). Both the range of dates of these collections and the fact that Spark continues to write stories for magazines attest to her interest and success in writing short fiction. Bizarre, often supernatural plots and a detached, ironic point of view mark Spark's short fiction.

Muriel Sarah Camberg was born in Edinburgh, Scotland, on 1 February 1918 to Bernard and Sarah Elizabeth Maude Uezzell Camberg. Her father, an engineer, was Jewish; her mother was an English Presbyterian. Spark was raised a Presbyterian, and she attended James Gillespie's (Presbyterian) Girl's School as a child, an experience she writes about in "The School on the Links" (*New Yorker*, 25 March 1991). In "My Conversion" (*Twentieth Century*, Autumn 1961), however, she acknowledges that her childhood had "a kind of Jewish tinge but without any formal instruction." Still, neither Judaism nor Presbyterianism became Spark's religion; she converted to Roman Catholicism in 1954 after a year's stint as an Anglican. From early on in her life

Spark conceived of herself as a writer. Beginning at age nine she wrote poetry, and as a young girl she invented love letters to herself, leaving them where her mother could find them.

Spark lived in Edinburgh until she graduated from school in 1937; she went to Rhodesia and married S. O. Spark, whom she later came to regard as "a disastrous choice." They had a son, Robin, but divorced in 1938, and she remained in Rhodesia until she managed to return to England six years later. During World War II Spark worked for the political intelligence department of the British Foreign Office, writing anti-Nazi propaganda. She comments on this experience in the novel *The Hothouse by the East River* (1973), saying the work was "black propaganda and psychological warfare . . . a tangled mixture of damaging lies, flattering and plausible truths." Financial and health problems followed, the latter caused in part by the former. Spark supported herself and her son by working for a jewelry trade magazine, as editor of the *Poetry Review,* and as a publicity agent. Despite her difficulties she continued to write. According to Ruth Whittaker, in a letter to Derek Stanford written during this period Spark attributes the breakup of a relationship to her "selfishness" in being unwilling to dedicate her life to the man because she had to earn a living for her son, and because she wanted to write when she was not doing that.

In 1951 "The Seraph and the Zambesi" won the Christmas short-story contest sponsored by the *Observer.* This occurred just before the time that she began to be interested in Catholicism. During the summer of 1950 Spark had read "La Fanfarlo," a short story by Charles Baudelaire. The main character of that story, Samuel Cramer, reappears one hundred years later at the beginning of "The Seraph and the Zambesi." Cramer admits, in fact, to being the man about whom Baudelaire writes. This suggestion of the supernatural in Cramer's longevity contributes to a religious overtone as the story continues, the anonymous narrator claiming that she has to stay at Cramer's gasoline station "because it was Christmas week and there was no room in the hotel."

Cramer has written a "Nativity Masque" in which he will play the part of First Seraph, but at the performance an authentic seraph appears, insisting that he ought to appear in the masque because "it's been mine from the Beginning . . . and the Beginning began first." An attempt to douse the Seraph with gasoline only succeeds in burning the building, and the reader is left with a vision of the Seraph flying down the course of the river: "We watched him ride the

Zambesi away from us, among the rocks that look like crocodiles and the crocodiles that look like rocks."

One of the interesting stylistic elements of this story is the way in which even the most fantastic elements are described in a matter-of-fact, realistic tone. No explanation is attempted to account for Cramer's unnaturally long life or, as he was only a literary character to begin with, for his having a life in this story. Neither is the appearance of the fiery Seraph — who "seemed not to conform to the law of perspective, but remained the same size" when approached or regressed — explained or justified. They just exist, and the reader must accept them as possibilities in the world Spark describes. Another noteworthy stylistic component of "The Seraph and the Zambesi" is the sarcasm and wit of dialogue, as in this exchange between Cramer and the Seraph:

> "Who in hell are you?" said Cramer, gasping through the heat.
> "The same as in Heaven," came the reply, "a Seraph, that's to say."
> "Tell that to someone else," Cramer panted. "Do I look like a fool?"
> "I will. No, nor a Seraph either," said the Seraph.

In "My Conversion" Spark attributes her model for this narrative tone to Max Beerbohm, who inspired her to write "subtle English prose with the shorter words the better and a nice witty turn to it all." However, she no longer acknowledges this stylistic influence. In a 1987 interview with Sara Frankel, Spark says, "I influence myself." Indeed, the satiric and detached tone in her stories and novels distinguishes Spark's works from much of the fiction of her time.

This gift for creating such repartee may also stem from Spark's experience in London at the outset of her writing career. As she recalls in "Visiting the Laureate" (*New Yorker,* 26 August 1991), "I was a poet and living the life of a poet. It was a life of hardship, but in those years (1950–53) I felt the tremendous pull of the bohemian life in London." As editor of the *Poetry Review* Spark was much involved in the London artistic scene; but during this period she was also converting to Catholicism, which drew her somewhat away from her literary acquaintances. In *The Faith and Fiction of Muriel Spark* (1982) Ruth Whittaker observes that Spark's conversion "led to a satiric view of the fallen world and her first novel . . . sharply delineates her former literary associates and her new Catholic acquaintances." Her short story "Daisy Overend" (*The Go-Away Bird with Other Stories*) sardonically describes just such a fallen world: "the period 1920–9" and "the world of Daisy Overend, Bruton Street, W.1."

Daisy is the consummate self-absorbed, superficial Londoner. She has taken two lovers, one a political expert and one a poet, presumably to service the two sides of her public self, which the narrator remarks are "literature and politics." Still, dancing the Charleston with a prince seems to be the only important event of her life. When Daisy gives a party to advance herself in some cause, the narrator devotes herself to its destruction. She finds her chance when, in the room where the buffet has been laid, she discovers a pair of Daisy's garters lying on the table. She does not remove them as Daisy requests but instead introduces them merrily to the guests. Daisy discovers what has happened when the guests are already having much fun at her expense:

> I remember Daisy as she stood there, not altogether without charm, beside herself. While laughter rebounded like plunging breakers from her mouth, she guided her eyes towards myself and trained on me the missiles of her fury. For a full three minutes Daisy's mouth continued to laugh.

The story ends with the narrator claiming that she has "forgotten the real name of Daisy Overend," emphasizing her role as exemplar of the "charming, vicious" West End intellectual scene.

During this period Spark was also beginning a book on the poet John Masefield, and she visited him in his house on 6 December 1950. She gives a full account of the experience in "Visiting the Laureate." Yet the house of Louis MacNeice is the subject of the semi-autobiographical "The House of the Famous Poet" (*Collected Stories I*), which is set during World War II. On a journey to London the female narrator meets another young woman, who invites her to stay at the house where she works. The house turns out to be that of a famous poet, which both fascinates and troubles the narrator. She leaves the house after purchasing an "abstract funeral" (the exact nature of which is unexplained) from a soldier. She later finds that the house had been bombed that night, killing her acquaintance.

When asked about "The House of the Famous Poet" in a 1989 interview with Devoize and Valette, Spark replied:

> I did go to Louis MacNeice's house and I think I had the sensation of a dying culture or a dying event. You see, there were some very near hits. The bombs were falling and there was this Morrison shelter. . . . There was the

feeling that there could have been a direct hit at any moment.

The real house was not bombed, and Spark was not there until the 1950s. Nevertheless Spark says the house made "a very deep impression" on her.

Three of Spark's short stories were published in 1953: "Harper and Wilton," (*Pick of Today's Short Stories*, no. 4), "Ladies and Gentlemen" (*Chance*, April–June), and "The Pawnbroker's Wife" (collected in *The Go-Away Bird*). Like "Daisy Overend," "The Pawnbroker's Wife" describes a strong-willed, self-important woman, Mrs. Jan Cloote, who lives "in quite a world of [her] own." The narrator is an outsider, a woman living in Mrs. Cloote's rooms while waiting for a passage from Cape Town to England. As Spark reveals in "Venture into Africa" (*New Yorker*, 2 March 1992), "The Pawnbroker's Wife" draws heavily on her experiences while waiting for passage back to England in 1944:

> The community was divided in three: colored, black, and white. . . . I thought this quite amusing when I didn't think it tragic. . . . My story "The Pawnbroker's Wife" is set in Cape Town, and I think it expresses what to my mind was a refusal of the white people of South Africa to face the human facts around them. They were in "a world of their own."

The haughty Clootes' refusal to face facts is ironically demonstrated when they display to the narrator their most prized possession, an antique compass that they supposed has crossed the Himalayas with a famous explorer. It turns out to have been the possession of the narrator, who explains that its nicks and scratches resulted not from its use, but from its being knocked about in a drawer until it was pawned. The Clootes, who boast that they "keep ourselves to ourselves," show that in so doing they only magnify their own ignorance.

"The Twins" (*The Go-Away Bird*) satirizes in a different manner the deceptive quality of appearances. The narrator, again an outsider, visits the home of a childhood friend who has what appears to be the perfect family. The twins, however, are not the sweet children they seem to be at first. Through a series of events they show themselves to be cruel and manipulative, orchestrating the actions of their parents for their own amusement. The twins succeed in driving the narrator away, and at the conclusion they delude their parents into thinking that she has been inconsiderate, though in reality she has been the innocent victim of their machinations. The situation is reversed, in a sense, in "Miss Pinkerton's Apocalypse" (*The Go-Away Bird*).

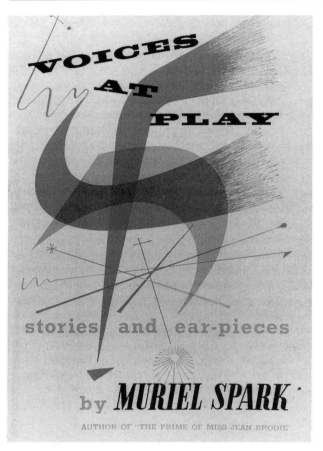

Dust jacket for Spark's 1961 collection of short fiction, which also includes four "ear-pieces," or plays

Here outrageous lies do not obscure the simple truth; instead a simple lie cloaks an outrageous truth. Miss Pinkerton and George Lake witness a flying saucer – a china saucer, possibly antique. When George declares, contrary to Miss Pinkerton's assertion, that the saucer "can't be an antique, that's absolutely certain," Miss Pinkerton repays his lack of tact by declaring to the reporter covering their incident that they had been imbibing, and that the saucer was just a figment of their drunken imaginations.

Spark's next three stories all concern ghosts. "The Pearly Shadow" (*Norseman,* November 1955) is only two pages long, which may account for its being uncollected. It concerns Mr. Nevis, who is being plagued by a pearly shadow. Dr. Felicity Grayland, "resident psychiatrist at the mental home," is attempting to rid him of this supposed delusion. But the doctor also sees the pearly shadow; in fact she takes "P. Shadow," who fears Nevis is trying to kill him, as a patient as well. Grayland diagnoses her patients thus: "Nevis illusions of being

haunted; perfectly simple. Shadow straightforward illusions of persecution." When her quivering nurse says that the last patient walked right through her, the doctor insists that the nurse is overworked and begins treatment on her as well. The self-assured psychiatrist is the deluded one, of course, and in her refusal to see the facts harks back to the Clootes in "The Pawnbroker's Wife."

Just before she wrote "The Pearly Shadow" Spark underwent Jungian therapy for nervous exhaustion. Although her therapist was a priest, not a psychiatrist, the situation may have suggested "The Pearly Shadow." "The Leaf-Sweeper" (*Collected Stories I*) shows more explicitly the influence of Jungian theory. Johnnie Geddes, founder of the Society for the Abolition of Christmas, meets his own ghost while sweeping leaves at a mental asylum. The ghost is his antiself, who likes Christmas. As they argue about Christmas, they seem to meld into one. The narrator observes: "Really, I can't say whether, when I looked a second time, there were two men or one man sweeping the leaves." Shortly after this Johnnie stops ranting about the evils of Christmas; in fact he never mentions it again and is discharged from the hospital.

"The Portobello Road" (*The Go-Away Bird*) is, in Spark's estimation, her best short story. Ghosts again play a major role in the story, and this one is even narrated by a ghost. At the outset George sees the narrator and is shocked nearly senseless; his wife, Kathleen, reminds him that the person he has seen is long dead. The reader learns that the narrator is a ghost nicknamed Needle because in life she had once found one in a haystack. She has never entirely departed this world, as "there were those odd things still to be done which one's executors can never do properly."

The narrator has much in common with Spark: she journeys to Africa because of a short-lived affair with a man (though Needle breaks off the engagement before the trip); she returns to a series of odd jobs in London; and she is confirmed a Catholic. George too has been to Africa, and while there he married and abandoned a black woman. He murdered Needle by stuffing her mouth full of hay and burying her in the haystack when she threatened to tell Kathleen (whom George then intended to wed) of his previous marriage.

The story is most remarkable for the account of the murder as told by the victim. Already dead, she is able to render a completely detached report: "He looked as if he would murder me and he did. He stuffed hay into my mouth until it could hold no more, kneeling on my body to keep it still, holding both my wrists tight in his huge left hand." The focus is on what George did, not on what Needle felt or experienced, as if she were merely a spectator to the event. The repeated sightings of Needle's ghost on the Portobello Road drive George mad not out of guilt, but because he mistakenly believes she has come back to tell Kathleen about his bigamy. He finally confesses to the murder, though nobody believes him. The ghost is singularly without malice, however, and seems genuinely concerned for both George and Kathleen, if a bit sad that they are not really as lovely as they seemed to be in their youth.

Spark did not publish any stories in 1957, but in the following year she published seven, along with her first collection, *The Go-Away Bird with Other Stories.* "The Girl I Left Behind Me" (*Norseman*, January 1958) is a three-page tale similar to "The Portobello Road" in that it is also told by the ghost of a murdered woman. Spark has not included it in any of her collections. Of the other six stories published in 1958, " 'A Sad Tale's Best for Winter,' " "Come Along, Marjorie," and "You Should Have Seen the Mess" (all in *The Go-Away Bird*) are all of a piece: character sketches about odd, marginal personages, the last two first-person narrations by rather neurotic women. (In a 1989 interview with Devoize and Valette, Spark calls "You Should Have Seen the Mess" "just really a sketch of a horrible puritanical little girl. You know, they go on like this in England."

"The Black Madonna" (*The Go-Away Bird*) is a scathing account of moral and religious hypocrisy. A new Madonna, carved out of black bog oak for the Catholic church in the new town of Whitney Clay, seems to have the mystical power of granting fertility to women who pray to it. Raymond and Lou Parker pray to her, and Lou gives birth to a beautiful black baby much to her surprise, as she and her husband are white. The reader cannot be sure whether Lou has had an affair with one of the black men the Parkers have been careful to include in their social circle or whether the black Madonna is seeking to expose the Parkers' bigotry. In any case they decide to give up their child for adoption. Their actions – and the treatment of Miss Marjorie Pettigrew by the Catholic monks in "Come Along, Marjorie" – reflect Spark's dislike of certain Catholics: "Good God, I used to think," said Spark in 1961, "if I become a Catholic, will I grow like them?"

"The Go-Away Bird," like many of Spark's stories, draws on her experiences in Africa. Nearly a novella, "The Go-Away Bird" is divided into three numbered chapters. The first shows young Daphne du Toit in Africa with her uncle Chakata and introduces the gray-crested lourie whose cry, "Go 'way, go 'way," forms the refrain of the story. Daphne is advised to leave Africa for England to keep her out of reach of Old Tuys, one of her uncle's servants, who has his mind set on taking revenge on her for Chakata's long-ago affair with Tuys's wife.

Daphne's extended trip to England, portrayed in the second section, proves a failure: money and family connections are soon exhausted, and her lover, Ralph (like the lourie), tells her, "Go away. . . . Go away and leave me in peace." In the third section she is brutally murdered by Old Tuys shortly after her return to Africa, though he thought he was only killing a deer. The story ends with Ralph visiting her grave. A lourie behind it tells him to "go 'way," which he does.

As in most of Spark's stories the male-female relationship is disastrous. In a 1987 interview with Frankel, Spark states: "I don't *deal* with men and women and love. I don't see that the relationship between men and women is very good these days." Indeed, Spark's concentration on violence and evil – and what some critics see as her relative lack of interest in good – has been cited as a fault of her fiction, but Spark repudiates this. She admits to being fascinated by violence but points out that love-story novelists portray more violence in their works than she does in hers. Another critic, Anthony Quinton, in *London Magazine* (June 1959), faults Spark as "an extremely uneven writer" who takes "too extreme" liberties in her fiction. However, a review of *The Go-Away Bird with Other Stories* in *Booklist* notes Spark's "feeling for the unusual in character, for the whims of fate, and for the supernatural" and recommends the volume to "the discriminating reader."

Voices at Play: Stories and Ear-pieces, Spark's second collection of short fiction, includes the stories she wrote after the publication of *The Go-Away Bird* as well as four plays, the "ear-pieces." Like "The Go-Away Bird," "The Curtain Blown by the Breeze" and "Bang-bang You're Dead" are both set in Africa and chronicle murders incited by sexual relationships gone bad. In a 1989 interview with Devoize and Valette, Spark discusses the genesis of "Bang-bang You're Dead":

A school-friend of mine she wasn't a close friend was murdered. She looked very like me and that was the basis of my story. . . . In the hotel where I was staying, this girl was killed. I heard it. I heard the bangs. That was a terrible experience.... We looked very much alike. Altogether this was the basis later on for a story.

The unhappiness and personal difficulties caused by her African experiences are also detailed in the reminiscence "Venture into Africa" (*New Yorker*, 2 March 1992).

Although generally somber, Spark's Africa-based stories also feature witty touches. In "The Curtain Blown by the Breeze" a husband tests the house for dust and checks the water taps before he goes out to kill his adulterous wife and her lover. "Bang-bang You're Dead" is framed as the memories that go through a woman's mind while she shows her home movies of Africa. The viewers find them entrancing as far as the tropical plants are concerned but are not at all interested in the murder.

"The Dark Glasses" also concerns a murder, but the real focus of the story is the narrator's fascination with hiding her identity as witness behind her glasses until the last line: "I think it was then she recognised me." Such dramatic irony comes into play with "A Member of the Family" and "The Fathers' Daughters" as well. Bizarre twists of plot find the woman in "A Member of the Family" getting her wish to be invited to dinner at her boyfriend's mother's house. She discovers all of his previous lovers there as well, since he never thinks romantically about any woman who has become like family. At the conclusion of "The Fathers' Daughters" Ben cancels his engagement to Carmelita (the daughter of a famous novelist) for the spinster Miss Castlemaine (the daughter of a formerly famous novelist) with no apparent reason or explanation. However, the reader can infer from a comment on the last page that Mr. Castlemaine has agreed to help Ben in his work, while Carmelita's father has not. *Voices at Play* was reviewed favorably, with the *British Book News* (September 1961) calling Spark "a remarkably original artist ... with an unerring instinct for the touch of the fantastic or the macabre which transforms the story into an inimitable creation."

The year 1967 marks a particularly high point in Spark's career. She had published eight novels in ten years, including the highly praised and extremely popular *The Prime of Miss Jean Brodie* (1961). Her *Collected Poems I* and *Collected Stories I* both appeared in 1967. The latter includes all of Spark's previously collected stories and adds four others: "The House of the Famous Poet" and "The Leaf-Sweeper," both published in the 1950s but previously uncollected; "Alice Long's Dachshunds," first published earlier that year; and "The Play-house Called Remarkable," which was written for the collection.

"The Playhouse Called Remarkable" is in one sense a witty commentary on Spark's success as a "littery figure." She had left London for New York in 1962 partly, as Alan Bold points out in *Muriel Spark* (1986), "because she felt that her literary fame and fortune had separated her from her former friends." She used an office provided by the *New Yorker* for five years, moving in 1966 to Rome, where she still lives. Another reason for the series of moves, according to Whittaker, was that Spark was spending so much time on business and publicity-related activities that her work was "becoming merely the administrative side of the set-up." These facts, and the decidedly cool critical reception of her novel *The Mandelbaum Gate* (1965), mirror the "uprise of my downfall" with which the characters in "The Playhouse Called Remarkable" are involved.

The story reads like a parable or fable, describing the genesis of art as descended from the Moon people, who brought it to humans. The earthlings were more interested in chanting "tum tum" and indulging in their "pure and primitive passions" for murder than in art (the character who incites the murder is the forefather of the founder of the London School of Economics). "And so if you ever produce a decent poem or a story," concludes Moon Biglow, "it won't be on account of anything you've got in this world but of something remarkable which you haven't got." In his review of *Collected Stories I* for *Punch*, R. G. G. Price laments that "what her fiction is really all about remains obscure ... it seems all surface." But an anonymous reviewer for *British Book News* (March 1968), while noting that Spark's stories "are sometimes slight in substance," nevertheless agrees with the more general opinion of Barbara A. Banon in *Publishers' Weekly* (15 April 1968) that "the crisp, precise, and graceful Spark style is a joy in itself."

Bang-bang — You're Dead and Other Stories adds to ten others two previously uncollected stories, "The Gentile Jewesses" and "The First Year of My Life," both first published in the *New Yorker*. Spark's heredity as the Gentile daughter of a Jewish engineer is also true of the grandmother in "The Gentile Jewesses." This character — who is married to an engineer — was a suffragette (as was Spark's maternal grandmother) and is a powerful enough storyteller to make the narrator wonder momentarily, "Was I present at the Red Sea crossing?" It is difficult, in fact, not to read the entire story as an autobiographical sketch. Spark has described her mother's habit of bowing thrice to the new moon, an action also performed by the narrator's mother. Moreover, the narrator converts to Catholicism.

Autobiography also plays a part, if only humorously, in "The First Year of My Life." Its narrator, like Spark, was born "on the first day of the second month of the last year of the First World War, a Friday." The infant narrator informs the reader that "the young of the human species are born omniscient." She illustrates this by her first smile, which is not (as her parents assume) directed at the candle on her birthday cake but at Herbert Henry Asquith, first Earl of Oxford, and Asquith's comment after the armistice: "He said that the war had cleansed and purged the world, by God!"

The Stories of Muriel Spark includes all of the author's previously collected stories (in the same order as in *Collected Stories I*), along with four new ones – "The Executor," "The Fortune-Teller," "Another Pair of Hands," and "The Dragon" – first published in the *New Yorker*. All four are told in first person, one of Spark's methods to create sympathy for a character. They all involve the supernatural: ghosts, clairvoyance, and fire-breathing dragons. The return to the fantastic, which largely had been absent from her stories since 1958, may be the result, as Whittaker maintains, of her moving to Italy, where "her social range has narrowed somewhat" and she "has fewer opportunities to exploit her ear for dialogue, and thus her facility for revealing social and class differences through conversational nuances."

Spark's stories are not meant to be taken as the truth. They are fabulous artifacts that, by their emphasis on the impossible and the bizarre, are set apart unmistakably from real life. Spark told Frankel that she sees the relationship of the writer to society as requiring "some opposition and some innovation. . . . Otherwise, he's not an artist, he might just as well be a copyist. There's no point unless you *have* something – unless you can improve on society the best thing you can do is to keep quiet." Spark does not keep quiet. Her stories' use of the fantastic, concern with social relations, bold wit, and self-consciousness as created things set them apart from the "real" world and secure them a unique and distinctive place in contemporary short fiction.

Interviews:

"Edinburgh's Muriel Spark Hides in South," *Scotsman*, 20 (August 1962): 4;

Frank Kermode, "The House of Fiction: Interviews with Seven English Novelists," *Partisan Review*, 30 (Spring 1963): 61–82;

Mary Holland, "The Prime of Muriel Spark," *Observer* (color supplement), 17 October 1965, pp. 8–10;

Ian Gillhan, "Keeping It Short – Muriel Spark Talks About Her Books to Ian Gillhan," *Listener*, 84 (1970): 411–413;

Philip Toynbee, "A Conversation with Philip Toynbee," *Observer* (color supplement), 17 October 1971, pp. 73–74;

Sara Frankel, "An Interview with Muriel Spark," *Partisan Review*, 54 (Summer 1987): 443–457;

Jeanne Devoize and Pamela Valette, "An Interview with Muriel Spark," *Journal of the Short Story in English*, 13 (Autumn 1989): 11–22.

Bibliography:

Thomas T. Tominaga and Wilma Schneidermeyer, *Iris Murdoch and Muriel Spark: A Bibliography* (Metuchen, N.J.: Scarecrow Press, 1976).

References:

Alan Bold, *Muriel Spark* (London & New York: Methuen, 1986);

Karl Malkoff, *Muriel Spark* (New York & London: Columbia University Press, 1968);

Jennifer Lynn Randisi, *On Her Way Rejoicing: The Fiction of Muriel Spark* (Washington, D.C.: Catholic University of America Press, 1991);

Velma Bourgeois Richmond, *Muriel Spark* (New York: Ungar, 1984);

Dorothea Walker, *Muriel Spark* (Boston: Twayne, 1988);

Ruth Whittaker, *The Faith and Fiction of Muriel Spark* (New York: St. Martin's Press, 1982).

Elizabeth Taylor

(3 July 1912 – 19 November 1975)

K. M. Stemmler

Clarion University of Pennsylvania

BOOKS: *At Mrs. Lippincote's* (London: Davies, 1945; New York: Knopf, 1946);

Palladian (London: Davies, 1946; New York: Knopf, 1947);

A View of the Harbour (London: Davies, 1947; New York: Knopf, 1947);

A Wreath of Roses (London: Davies, 1949; New York: Knopf, 1949);

A Game of Hide-and-Seek (London: Davies, 1951; New York: Knopf, 1951);

The Sleeping Beauty (London: Davies, 1953; New York: Viking, 1953);

Hester Lilly and Twelve Short Stories (London: Davies, 1954; New York: Viking, 1954);

Angel (London: Davies, 1957; New York: Viking, 1957);

The Blush and Other Stories (London: Davies, 1958; New York: Viking, 1959);

In a Summer Season (London: Davies, 1961; New York: Viking, 1961);

The Soul of Kindness (London: Chatto & Windus, 1964; New York: Viking, 1964);

A Dedicated Man and Other Stories (London: Chatto & Windus, 1965; New York: Viking, 1965);

Mossy Trotter (London: Chatto & Windus, 1967; New York: Harcourt Brace & World, 1967);

The Wedding Group (London: Chatto & Windus, 1968; New York: Viking, 1968);

Mrs. Palfrey at the Claremont (London: Chatto & Windus, 1971; New York: Viking, 1971);

The Devastating Boys (London: Chatto & Windus, 1972; New York: Viking, 1972);

Blaming (London: Chatto & Windus, 1976; New York: Knopf, 1976).

SELECTED PERIODICAL PUBLICATIONS –
UNCOLLECTED: "Elizabeth Taylor," *New York Herald Tribune Book Review,* 11 October 1953, pp. 23–25;

"Setting a Scene," *Writer,* 78 (July 1965): 10;

"England," *Kenyon Review,* 31, no. 4 (1969): 469–473;

Elizabeth Taylor

"Choosing Details That Count," *Writer,* 83 (January 1970): 15;

"Some Notes on Writing Stories," *London Magazine,* 9 (March 1970): 8–10.

The lack of attention given to Elizabeth Taylor's work seems especially remarkable when one examines the number of novels and short stories she wrote. In twenty-seven years Taylor published eleven novels and four collections of short stories (her final novel, *Blaming,* was published post-humously in 1976). Any mention of Taylor's work usually comments on the fact that she has not earned the critical attention that she deserves, despite rather consistent, favorable reviews of her works. Robert Liddell's comment in *Contemporary Novelists* (1976) that "her work is quiet" may be a way of explaining how she could be widely read, well received, and yet rather obscure.

The quietness of Taylor's fiction crosses over into the facts of her life. The daughter of Oliver and Elsie Coles, she was born 3 July 1912 in Reading, Berkshire, England. Taylor was educated at the Abbey School, Reading, which she left in 1930. Afterward she worked as a governess and later in a library. Taylor found these experiences valuable, commenting "I learnt so much from these jobs and I have never regretted the time I spent at them." In 1936 she married John William Kendal Taylor, who worked in the confectionary business. In 1937 she gave birth to a son, Renny, and in 1941 to a daughter, Joanna. Elizabeth Taylor died of cancer on 19 November 1975. Her friend Liddell points out in *Elizabeth and Ivy* (1986) that she died on her name day, the feast of Saint Elizabeth of Hungary.

Taylor chose to keep the facts of her personal life private, commenting in the *New York Herald Tribune Book Review* (11 October 1953): "I am always disconcerted when I am asked for my life story, for nothing sensational, thank heavens, has ever happened. I dislike much travel or change of environment, and prefer the days . . . to come round almost the same, week after week." Such routine afforded Taylor the time to spend on her writing. Despite reticence about her personal life she was quite comfortable discussing the craft and process of her fiction. Her belief that "a writer cannot rest from continually observing and being assailed by impressions" is supported in her work, which pays careful attention to the routine details of daily life.

When given the opportunity to describe her life in the *New York Herald Tribune Book Review,* Taylor avoided revealing personal information, including a claim that she had no hobbies. Instead, she directed her attention to a discussion of her writing process, which involved a great deal of time recopying drafts and revising individual sentences. Two articles by Taylor in the *Writer,* "Setting a Scene" (1965) and "Choosing Details That Count" (1970), deal with her work as a novelist, but her discussions of setting and use of details apply to her short stories as well.

Taylor's literary reputation is typically mentioned in regard to her novels, yet Florence Le-clercq comments in *Elizabeth Taylor* (1985) on Taylor's "solid reputation as a writer of short stories," an evaluation that may be based on the fact that Taylor's stories were widely published in the *New Yorker, Harpers,* and *Harper's Bazaar.* In "Some Notes on Writing Stories" (*London Magazine,* March 1970) Taylor discusses the history of the short-story genre and the neglect it has suffered: "It is not the publisher's favourite child, which means that it is not the reading public's favourite child." Despite the frequency with which Taylor's short stories were published and the reputation of the magazines in which they appeared – all the stories in *A Dedicated Man and Other Stories* (1965) originally appeared in the *New Yorker* – the reputation she struggled to earn relied mostly on her novels, even though she preferred the short-story form and its ability to intensify experience. The short-story genre also allowed Taylor to focus intensively on the presentation of character.

In "England" (*Kenyon Review,* 1969) Taylor credits the *New Yorker* for its "enormous service to the development and encouragement of the short story." She notes the personal tragedy she would feel if the short-fiction form "were not further explored for possibilities." While Taylor did not routinely experiment with the short-fiction form, she did experiment with the treatment of character and theme in the genre.

Taylor's first collection of short stories, *Hester Lilly and Twelve Short Stories,* was published in 1954. In general, the collection did not command the kind of favorable attention given to her six previously published novels. Even her obituary in the (London) *Times* (21 November 1975) resurrects the critical disagreements that spanned her career:

> In the novel form this most restful of writers never perhaps gave full enough play to her undoubted perception of human character, always stronger on her astutely observed women than in creating men. Her wit and penetration were seldom in doubt but the true asperities of modern life seemed to elude her. The short stories encouraged claims of a different kind. The short form was her metier.

Taylor was well aware of her treatment by reviewers and mentions in the *New York Herald Tribune Book Review* her astonishment that some writers manage to ignore them. She apparently was not discouraged, however, by the mixed messages of her reviews: "Good reviews seem to be extraordinary kindnesses, and although one is encouraged and uplifted by them they never seem to ring true as do the bad ones."

It seems appropriate that "Hester Lilly" should precede the twelve other stories in her first collection. A novella, it bridges the gap between Taylor's experiences with the novel and the short story. The lack of critical attention given to this collection may owe to the fact that Taylor was struggling with making transitions between forms. Some of the stories read like plot summaries of novels rather than short stories.

"Hester Lilly" introduces a common theme in Taylor's short stories, which often examine the role of jealousy and envy in characters' relationships. Muriel's jealousy of Hester Lilly, her husband's young cousin who comes to live with them, creates tension in her marriage. "Hester Lilly" resembles a short story in that events are concentrated, yet the attempt to treat the subject in a short form seems abrupt, as though Taylor is forcing the story to meet a particular required length. Like her novels, "Hester Lilly" examines the relationships between social classes, subject matter that some critics, such as Kingsley Amis, believe kept Taylor from earning the attention she deserved. Amis's review of *Angel* (1957) in the *Spectator* (14 June 1957) questions Taylor's omission from surveys of the modern novel: "The answer can start, I think, from the fact that Mrs. Taylor's work bears a superficial resemblance to the 'library novel' or 'women's novel' frequently vilified . . . in literary circles. Her favored subjects are indeed domestic and true to life as it is lived by large numbers of people."

Taylor's fondness for examining domestic relationships has caused her to be compared frequently to Jane Austen. While Taylor may have been influenced by Austen's depiction of characters' relationships or even Austen's style, Taylor's work deals more directly with the ironies of relationships. Muriel's jealousy of Hester Lilly not only addresses the issue of marital infidelity but also describes how jealousy can lead to foolish behavior and result in lack of judgment. Even if the reader's sympathies are not with Muriel at the story's end, it is difficult not to get caught up in her rapture as she dreams of making Hester's wedding cake. Even if the reader does not agree with Muriel's view, the force with which that view is presented makes it difficult for the reader to resist her response. Instead of presenting characters to the reader, Taylor has a way of bringing the reader to the characters. Thus, an examination of the characters' experiences becomes an examination of the reader's life.

The first short story of the collection, "I Live in a World of Make-Believe," deals with Mrs. Miller's desire to compete with her neighbor, Lady Luna, who represents a higher social class than the Millers. However, Mrs. Miller believes the difference can be bridged by acquiring certain symbols of class. When she has Lady Luna and her daughter, Constance, in for a visit, they are interrupted by the unexpected arrival of Mrs. Miller's sister-in-law, Auntie Flo, who has brought along a dozen eggs, a jar of pickled cabbage, and a daughter infected with ringworm. Taylor impresses upon the reader the notion that people often blindly attempt to reach beyond the limitations of their lives or social class.

In "Spry Old Character" Harry, literally blind, wants to be separated from the others in his nursing home. Taylor portrays the residents of the home as a microcosm of social classes: "In the Home there was an aristocracy – never, from decency, mentioned – of those who had once, and even perhaps recently, seen, over those blind from birth." By the end of the story the reader learns, perhaps better than Harry, that he cannot be part of the world he "sees" differently, no matter how hard he tries. A similar theme is treated in "Taking Mother Out," in which an elderly woman puts her son in his place. Roy, attempting to impress his guests with stories of his personal experiences, is exposed by his mother when she reveals that the incidents he describes have never happened to him.

Although Taylor seems preoccupied with presenting lessons to her readers, not all her stories are meant to teach readers something about themselves. While some stories serve as reminders of common human traits, others offer epiphanies that make their characters human. In *Contemporary Novelists* Taylor remarks, "I think that loneliness is a theme running through many of my novels and short stories, the different ways in which individuals can be isolated from others – by poverty, old age, eccentricity, living in a foreign country."

"A Sad Garden" shows the isolation of a woman who has lost both her son and her husband. She finally confronts her feelings of anger and grief through the unintentionally cruel treatment of her niece. "Oasis of Gaiety" treats the theme of loneliness differently. Here Taylor offers alternating views of family relationships through the eyes of various family members. Auntie recalls that nothing can really be done for young people "but to try to preserve for them some of the old days, keep up our standards, and give them an inkling of what things used to be, make a little oasis of gaiety for them." While Auntie's intentions may be good, the reader understands that it is unrealistic to think that amusing distractions can solve a person's problems.

Part of the lack of reaction in the characters and the difficulty they have in relating to each other, particularly the inability of the children to respond to their mother, is the result of "the late war." Taylor makes the post–World War II setting a subtle part of the background, suggesting an inability to return to a state of gaiety that existed before the war. The "oasis of gaiety" that Auntie can provide her daughter, Dosie, is artificial, too brief, "obviously too small." The lack of attention to the cause of reactions heightens the effect of Dosie's inability to recognize an "oasis of gaiety" or escape her loneliness: "She always felt herself leaving other people behind; they lagged after her recklessness. Even in making love she felt the same isolation – that she was speeding into a country where no one would pursue her."

Taylor does not present an entirely grim picture of the effects of the war on relationships; not every character is a Dosie, trying to dodge love's enemy. "The Beginning of a Story," however, sets romance in the presence of death. Marion, a boarder at a house where the family's grandmother has just died, is finally recognized by the son, Ronny, as a possible romantic interest. Their kiss is interrupted by a neighbor who reminds them, "It's a sad time." Taylor seems to privilege young people with a strange sense of ironic optimism by allowing them to see that there is a different way of perceiving the event of death.

Three of the stories can be grouped together to be read as an examination of the stages of life, particularly in how they relate to relationships between children and parents. "The Light of Day" deals with the birth of a child. Oddly, the woman is bored by childbirth, is not content until her husband enters the room and informs her, "You did well." The husband's approving comment seems to be the only thing that allows the woman to drift peacefully to sleep. The next story, "A Red-Letter Day," focuses on Tory, a divorced woman who has no man "to exert authority for her," who is visiting her son at school. Tory's strained relationship with her son is matched against the relationship of another mother with her boys. Tory resents the woman because she looks matronly and appears authoritative.

The third story, "The First Death of Her Life," concerns a young woman waiting for her mother to die. In the last moments of her mother's life the daughter focuses on the effect it has on her and imagines herself telling her employer of the news. The attention is shifted from the object of the event, the dying mother, to the results of the event.

The woman becomes wrapped up in the drama of her mother's death so much that, after her mother dies, the daughter leaves the hospital "like it was the end of a film." The major problem with these stories is that Taylor withholds a great deal of information, which makes it difficult to follow the events. The withholding of names or explanations for relationships does not serve the short-story form as it does in her novels.

Hester Lilly and Twelve Short Stories concludes with a powerful, ironic piece. "Swan-Moving" opens with a description of the "broken" English countryside, a village in a state of decay that "lacked even the knowledge of its own ugliness." In a heavy fog a swan happens to settle into a polluted pond. The sight of the swan eventually stirs the community to recognize how ugly the village has become, so the inhabitants begin to take pride in the appearance of their homes. Taylor allows the swan to become a symbol for the people: "The swan, preening himself daily into greater beauty, was in himself a lesson, an example in seemliness, and the village began to preen and trim itself too."

As the village becomes more beautiful, the pond's water begins to recede, so the community finds a new location for the swan. Shortly after the crowd leaves the swan in his new environment, it flies off, "away from that countryside forever." Taylor's theme lies in the fact that, as the people try to imitate the swan, they also try to impose their standards on him, assuming he wants clean water even though he was originally attracted to the polluted pond.

In many ways the lesson of the swan informs many of the stories in the collection. Taylor seems intrigued by characters' desires to create or control their own environment and the subsequent failure that accompanies such desires. This is true of Mrs. Miller's attempt to imitate another social class in "I Live in a World of Make-Believe" and Harry's attempt to behave as a person with sight in "Spry Old Character." Both characters are forced to face the fact that they cannot change their circumstances no matter how hard they try to reject their rightful place.

In Taylor's second collection of short fiction, *The Blush and Other Stories* (1958), there is noticeable development in the stories. Taylor's treatment of themes seems more controlled and subtle. The collection opens with "The Ambush," a rather long piece about Catherine, who has recently lost her fiancé, Noel. The story develops around Catherine's visit to the dead man's home to see Noel's brother, Esme, and his mother, Mrs. Ingram. Before the arrival of Freddie, an artist friend of Esme, Mrs. Ingram discusses his work: "It allows one to see how clever he has been, and that should never be. I don't want to see the wheels go round or to feel called upon to shout, 'Bravo.'"

Taylor seems to have applied Mrs. Ingram's advice to her own work in this story, as well as in the remainder of the collection. The loss of Catherine's lover is not something the reader must supply in the story; instead, Taylor constantly makes his absence known. Specifically, Catherine recalls how she once sketched Noel's ankle in the corner of one of her drawings then erased it and replaced it with filler. This memory of Noel having been removed from the picture creates a stronger sense of loss than Catherine's visit to his graveside. Such subtlety continues through the story's end, where the reader is uncertain whether Catherine's heart has recovered from a final ambush and whether she will leave the Ingrams or stay.

Taylor's observations in "England" concerning the beginning and ending of stories speak well for her technique: "As the beginning is important, so also is the drawing of the curtains, and the way that it is done is a very personal thing, a signature. The story may be wrapped up and laid away, or left trembling and exposed." The title story of the collection reveals a Taylor signature for leaving stories trembling and exposed. "The Blush" addresses the contrasts between two main characters, Mrs. Allen and her maid, Mrs. Lacey. Despite obvious differences in social class Mrs. Allen is drawn into the conversations of Mrs. Lacey's world. Mrs. Allen envies Mrs. Lacey for having a family while she has remained childless. Mr. Allen has never seen Mrs. Lacey, a thought that pleases Mrs. Allen because she knows he would not approve of their intimate conversations, and she is certain that her husband would find Mrs. Lacey appalling.

Mrs. Lacey must leave work early because she is pregnant again. In the evening Mr. Lacey comes to explain that the Allens have been overworking his wife, that she needs time off. His information of how Mr. Allen drops her off late every evening reveals to Mrs. Allen that her husband has been having an affair with the maid. Taylor's emphasis, though, is not so much on the event of the affair but on the fact that the two social classes have crossed in this infidelity. Mrs. Allen's blush at the story's close is the result of having had the illusion of her class – and life – exposed.

In *Elizabeth and Ivy* Liddell – a novelist, critic, and friend of many writers, including Ivy Compton-Burnett, Barbara Pym, and Taylor – discusses

Taylor's short stories: "They did not express or reveal but played with her own experience, or she wove fancies from tiny fragments of fact – at least this I sometimes thought I recognized." In discussing *The Blush* Liddell writes: "The story that most nearly touched me was 'The Letter-Writers.' It was not, as Elizabeth said, about herself and me – and yet there was something in it of our predicament, that of two correspondents who have never met." Where the meeting of Emily and Edmund in "The Letter-Writers" proves to be disastrous, the eventual meeting of Liddell and Taylor was successful.

Liddell's memories of his relationship with Taylor also supply two undeveloped points of Taylor's making use of autobiography in her stories: "The story 'You'll Enjoy It When You Get There' is an amusing expansion of a gaffe of her own at a 'trade banquet,' " and " 'Poor Girl' has a little of her life as a governess: her brilliant pupil is there, but not his parents. This was written for Lady Cynthia Asquith's ghost book." More important than knowing that Taylor applied her experiences as a governess to a story is an understanding of the complexities of "Poor Girl."

While the story addresses the unfortunate position in which the governess has been placed – with a rude child, a jealous and suspicious wife, and a lecherous husband – it also draws on issues of social class. Taylor's description, "The schoolroom indeed became a focal point of the house – the stronghold of Mr. Wilson's desire and his wife's jealousy," summarizes both the story's setting and conflict. But Mr. Wilson's question, "And are you happy in your position?" seems to draw on the governess's general circumstances. Beyond being a teacher she becomes the object of sexual jealousy and pursuit. Miss Chasty, the governess, is entirely isolated in the house, "cut off from the kitchen by her education," and receives no special privileges, "since maids do not wait on governesses." Taylor uses Miss Chasty as a vehicle for marking the loneliness of women in such positions.

The theme of women who devote their lives to their careers instead of marrying recurs in Taylor's short stories. "Summer Schools" not only draws on the situations of two sisters who seem destined to remain unmarried schoolteachers, but it also relies on Taylor's theme of jealousy and its effect on people. Melanie, the oldest, is jealous of an invitation that Ursula receives to spend her holiday with an old school friend whom Melanie also knew. Ursula's acceptance leads Melanie to commit one petty crime after another, all to make Ursula suffer. Al-

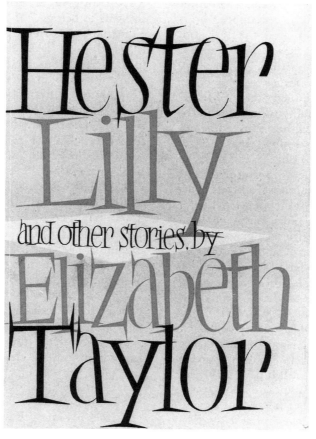

Dust jacket for Taylor's first collection of short stories, many of which depict jealousy and envy in family relationships

though both women have miserable vacations, Ursula is more honest with her feelings.

Ironically Melanie fabricates a story about an affair with a married man, while Ursula, who has had an affair, remains silent. The irony evolves from the reader's knowledge that Ursula already understands that a person often becomes "two people, the story teller and the listener," while Melanie, wrapped up in the telling and not the listening, begins to believe her own deception. Taylor is obviously alert to the dual roles that a person assumes when reading or writing a story and seems keenly aware of her roles as narrator and audience for her own work.

"Summer Schools" seems especially interesting when one considers how "The Rose, The Mauve, The White" offers a story from the opposite side of the classroom. Here the focus is on the relationship of three schoolgirls. The emphasis on adolescence allows a view of the adult world that causes Charles, the son, to shy away from "the ideal of sex-

ual love between the middle-aged." Charles's attitude contrasts with the early stages of sexual curiosity represented by the young girls in the story. While these schoolmates once valued books, their interests are becoming those of developing young women. Chances are that the girls in "The Rose, The Mauve, The White" will not end up in Melanie's or Ursula's position; the schoolmates' focus is on their physical maturation and their preoccupation with how they fit in to each other's social life.

"The True Primitive" also addresses the issue of education and how characters perceive its importance. Mr. Ransome represents book culture at the expense of experiencing romance firsthand: "He read so much about great passions, of men and women crossing continents because of love." Lily, his son's lover, represents the passion that Mr. Ransome tries to find in books. She does not understand why Harry must spend time with his father every Saturday, and Harry seems uncomfortable with her questions. When Lily spies through the shutter and finds Harry and his brother sketching the naked body of Mr. Ransome, who is surprised to see he is being watched, the impact of the story lies in its humor rather than in a moral about the value, or lack, of education.

If anything, Lily's lesson seems to draw on an observation found in "A Troubled State of Mind," which centers on Sophy's coming to terms with the fact that her best friend, Lalla, has married her father. During their discussions Sophy remarks, "It is a good thing . . . that you and I have read so many novels. The hackneyed dangers we should be safe from." Perhaps if Lily had read more, a better sense of social manners would have dictated her behavior, preventing her exposure to the hackneyed dangers of trespassing on her boyfriend's privacy.

With each new collection of short fiction Taylor's critical reputation increased. *A Dedicated Man* perhaps received more recognition because of the success of the two novels that preceded it, *In a Summer Season* (1961) and *The Soul of Kindness* (1964). *A Dedicated Man* was widely and favorably reviewed. In *Don't Never Forget* (1966) Brigid Brophy states: "Mrs. Taylor has always been an excellently unpretentious writer: if she had a fault it used to be that she was (artistically) under-ambitious. These stories seem to me to rise wholly to her talent."

A review of *A Dedicated Man* in the *Times Literary Supplement* (1 July 1965) begins, "There is a peculiar and soothing Englishness about everything Mrs. Taylor writes, which is, no doubt, part of her appeal for readers of *The New Yorker,* in which these twelve stories were first published." Although the review praises the content of the stories as well as Taylor's talent, it concludes: "Maybe these stories . . . do not add up to a very exciting or urgent contribution to current fiction. But the smoothness of Mrs. Taylor's style and her patience in recreating tiny, valuable moments of truth show once again that she is among the most craftsmanlike of any English novelists now writing." Nora Sayre, in the *New York Times Book Review* (31 March 1968), discusses the theme of violence in Taylor's work: "Violence is a neat, leisurely, rural world of red geraniums and punctual meals, good grooming and clipped lawns." Sayre notes that many of the stories in *The Blush* and *A Dedicated Man* are among Taylor's "very best work."

The first story in *A Dedicated Man* seems at first reminiscent of "The Rose, The Mauve, The White." "Girl Reading" focuses on two school friends, Sarah and Etta. Sarah comes from an upper-class family (the Lippmanns), while Etta and her widowed mother live in a poor neighborhood.

Taylor introduces "Girl Reading" with "Etta's desire was to belong," and the story combines several elements from Taylor's earlier collections. Aside from obvious issues of class difference, Etta's mother is jealous of the influence the Lippmann family – and their social class – have on Etta: "The Lippmanns' generosity depressed her. She knew that it was despicable to feel jealous, left out, kept in the dark, but she tried to rationalise her feelings before Etta." Taylor raises class issues in peculiar ways. For instance, Sarah's father continually mentions Etta's father: "He always forgot that her father was dead. It was quite fixed in his mind that he was simply a fellow who had obviously not made the grade; not everybody could."

Taylor's technique improves in this collection, extending beyond simple observations of characters' actions to include characters who reflect on observations and respond to them. Etta becomes entirely consumed with watching the relationship between Sarah's older brother and his girlfriend. Not only do they represent adult love – at least sexually – but they also symbolize a continuance of the Lippmanns' social class. Etta is not impressed by her mother's attempt at social grace – accepting sherry in the afternoon – but she is impressed by the gesture made by Sarah's brother, Roger, who confesses his love for Etta in a letter. Roger's declaration of love allows Etta finally to accept the social class that her mother and her house represent, for his statement allows her to see it all as "a place of transit, her temporary residence."

The story of the invited guest is paired with the collection's second story, "The Prerogative of Love," which evolves out of an unexpected visit from the main character's attractive niece on an evening when guests have been invited to dinner. Arabella's bad manners and behavior distract the guests, John and Helen, from seeing the strained relationship between the hosts, Lillah and Richard. The irony of the story is found in John's comment as he and his wife drive away. They compare their hosts' lives to their own, believing that their lives pale in comparison to Richard and Lillah's, but John concludes, "Well, we mustn't compare ourselves with *them.*"

Such comparisons among characters become Taylor's technique for creating conflict in stories, as in "In a Different Light," one of her few stories set primarily in a foreign locale. In *Twentieth Century Authors* Taylor comments on her love for England: "It would be painful for me to consider living in any other place. I find so beautiful, harmonious and evocative, its landscape, style, tradition, even its climate." "In a Different Light" not only challenges Taylor's words – in the character of Jane, who refuses to leave Greece – but also defends them, through Barbara's revelation that her life in England is much finer than her sister Jane's.

Barbara begins to question her ties to England with the arrival of Roland, who is visiting Greece. Roland causes Barbara to see the foreign landscape from a different perspective, though the reader understands that Barbara's new interest in Greece is in reality a fascination with Roland. Once home in England, Barbara puts any regrets about leaving Greece behind her when she sees Roland in his true domestic element with his wife, Iris. When Barbara compares her marriage to Roland's, which is clearly unpleasant, she feels fortunate.

Not all of Taylor's stories end with revelations of the characters' good fortunes, though characters' situations – often created out of lack of fortune – frequently move them to act. "The Thames Spread Out" is a peculiar story dealing with the effects of a changing landscape on character. Although Rose appears content with being the mistress to a married man, the flooding of the Thames River into her house, an event that occurs "every ten years or so," seems to suggest symbolically that she can extend her own boundaries. Rose's decision to leave Gilbert and her lifestyle behind comes as suddenly as the water's receding. Taylor has the two events occur simultaneously, so that Rose's revelation that she is free, that "nothing could stop her," sets up a comparison of Rose's life with the flood. Taylor's comment, "Such a dreadful mess she had left behind her," reads on a literal and metaphoric level.

"Mice and Birds and Boy" also focuses on a woman alone, although Mrs. May's situation is not comparable to Rose's. Here the theme of loneliness returns in the shape of an old woman who is seen by children as a witch and by members of the community as odd and untidy. When she is approached by a young boy, William, she tells him of her childhood, when she was beautiful: "It was a different world. We had two grooms and seven indoor servants and four gardeners. Yet we were just ordinary people. Everybody had such things in those days." William's family lives in what used to be Mrs. May's stables, a point of irony because William's mother sees herself as socially elevated in comparison to Mrs. May. William's father defends Mrs. May, explaining that "children sometimes see what we can't."

William's fascination with Mrs. May ends as he ages, prompting his father's comment, "The truth is, I suppose, that children grow up and begin to lose their simple vision." William's lack of interest in the woman, despite her fondness for him, is the normal result of a child's becoming aware of his peers' reactions rather than trusting his own feelings. Despite William's rejection, Mrs. May remains optimistic that "someone will come," a line she delivers to a stuffed parrot, which contrasts with the inability of the characters to hold on to what is beautiful.

"The Voices" treats the theme of isolation in a unique manner. Drawing on the setting of "In a Different Light," the story features a young woman, Laura, who listens as two elderly women, Amy and Edith, recall their daily adventures in Greece. The majority of Laura's vacation is spent passively, overhearing their conversations. Laura never meets the two women, who leave the day after her sneeze leads them to discover how easy it is to hear through the walls. The figurative walls that separate Laura from an active world are often found in Taylor's fiction, particularly in discussions of social class, as in "A Dedicated Man."

Of all the stories in the collection, "A Dedicated Man" received the most critical attention. In *Elizabeth and Ivy* Liddell comments:

> Taylor was more often at her best in each successive collection of stories, though I do not know that she ever surpassed the brilliant study of deception in the title story of *A Dedicated Man*. The "germ" of this story, I think, is the idea (I do not know who first expressed it) that couples of servants who apply for situations as man and wife have often met for the first time in the registry office. It could not have been better developed.

Silcox and Edith pose as husband and wife in order to secure employment. Silcox introduces a fictional son into their fabricated life story in order to make their relationship less suspect, but his decision backfires. Not only does the photograph of the son arouse suspicion, but it also makes Edith become obsessed with the "truth" of their son. Like Melanie in "Summer Schools," Edith begins to believe her deceptions are real. When Edith reads Silcox's mail, discovering the boy really is his son, she deserts him, forcing him out of his position at the hotel.

Silcox's lack of morality in having abandoned his real wife and son is matched by his discovery that Edith has stolen silverware from the dining room. Edith's crime – and her earlier excuse that their son has been caught stealing – prepares for the collection's final story, "Vron and Willie," which, although humorous, shows that arrogance can lead to one's downfall. Clearly Taylor is fond of examining how easily people become consumed by jealousy, pride, vanity, and greed.

Vron and Willie, bored with earning an honest living, become obsessed with shoplifting. Their success at stealing leads them to become arrogant, and they celebrate their accomplishments with loud music and dancing in their flat, surrounded by piles of stolen goods. They ignore the landlady's request to keep quiet, and their crimes are discovered by a constable whose entrance was only meant to frighten them into silence. Their aunt, attempting to cover for them, explains to her friends: "They are continuing their education."

Despite their increasingly favorable reviews of her fiction, Taylor's critics seemed reluctant to offer praise without undermining her accomplishments. Such mixed messages may have provided the foundation for Miss Smythe's observations in the story "Praises" from Taylor's fourth and final collection, *The Devastating Boys* (1972). Miss Smythe, retiring from her employment, weighs the praise she has been given and concludes: "Perhaps ... she had had too much praise all her life, and nothing else. Or might have been praised so much, *because* she had nothing else."

It is possible to view "Praises" as Taylor's response to the critical reception of her work. Critics who tended to admire Taylor's novels were often critical of her short stories, while those critical of her novels often praised her mastery of the short story. Even though she devotes a book-length study to Taylor's work, Leclercq concludes her chapter on Taylor's short stories with the comment: "In her four collections of short stories, Taylor breaks no new ground. She nevertheless broadens her scope and displays her perfected technique in a clearer, less ambiguous manner than in her twelve novels." However, a *Times Literary Supplement* review (9 June 1972) remarks: "Elizabeth Taylor must surely now be among the four or five most distinguished living practitioners of the art of the short story in the English-speaking world. Some have reservations – this reviewer among them – about her range as a novelist."

William Beauchamp's review of *The Devastating Boys* in the *Saturday Review of Science* (10 June 1972) observes: "Elizabeth Taylor's fifteenth book contains eleven elegant stories that decisively demonstrate her mastery of the techniques of traditional fiction. And yet, the reader wonders, so what?" Despite seeing the book as "flawless," Beauchamp concludes that it is likewise "unmemorable."

Perhaps the most critical review of Taylor's final collection comes from another fiction writer,

Joyce Carol Oates. Her review of *The Devastating Boys* in the *Washington Post Book World* (30 April 1972) comments on the similarity of all Taylor's stories, concluding that the collection is "quite representative of her writing." This remark suggests that Oates may not have read the fourteen works that precede *The Devastating Boys*. Her main criticism is that Taylor's characters do not seem real enough, and she finally asks, "And what about all the 'real' people, all the passionate, sometimes brutal, and always unpredictable people who refuse to be contained within the delicate confines of the old-fashioned *New Yorker* story?"

Other reviews of *The Devastating Boys* present more favorable readings of the stories. Jean Spang's review in *Library Journal* (1 April 1972) discusses the general themes of the collection, particularly the characters' search for love. Spang concludes, "An unhappy theme, but well-handled in the best Taylor tradition: her mannered technique and eye for oblique detail are perfect for this refined but frightening presentation of love at its most grotesque."

The title story, which opens the collection, revolves around the visit of two underprivileged city boys to Laura and Harold's country home. Harold does not care about the gender of the children; his only stipulation is that they be "coloured." Although Taylor does not develop the reason for Harold's request, the issue of race becomes subtly important to the story, particularly as it is recognized and expressed through the eyes of the six-year-old boys. While issues of class and race seem central to the story, reviewers tended not to comment on them. Taylor, too, does not draw attention to the issues directly; instead, she focuses on the effect the children have on the reluctant Laura.

The title comes from a remark made by Laura's untrustworthy acquaintance, the writer Helena, who represents the upper class, especially upper-class attitudes. Her comment, "Aren't they simply *devastating* boys," is mocked by Laura, and other aspects of Helena's language are mimicked by the two boys. One of the boys is named Septimus Smith, a major character in *Mrs. Dalloway* (1925) by Virginia Woolf, one of the writers Taylor most admired.

The third story, "Tall Boy," continues to feature the issues of class and race by focusing on a West Indian man named Jasper Jones who resides in a part of London where "nationalities clung together." Oates's criticism of Jasper Jones is that "he is a genteel white writer's notion of a black man, docile and childlike, and apparently without the slightest desire for, even awareness of, women."

Where such a reading suggests a Jasper Jones wrestling with sexuality, the Jasper Jones that Taylor features is concerned more with his survival and obligations: "He remained, so far, solitary, worked hard, and grieved hard over his mistakes. He saved, and sent money back home to Mam. Poverty from the earliest days – which makes some spry and crafty – had left him diffident and child-like." Not only does Taylor address what Oates misses, but she also highlights racial issues and their importance in Jasper's life: "No one here, in England, called him 'Nigger,' or put up their fists to him."

"Flesh" deals with literal issues of the flesh, even if planned marital infidelities do not turn out as hoped. It moves from a focus on Phyl's sunburn to a focus on the final outcome: in a hotel, Stanley plans to consummate his relationship with Phyl, but his gout makes it impossible for anything, including a bed sheet, to make contact with his flesh. Taylor bluntly reveals that Phyl's reason for being on vacation without her husband is because of her recent hysterectomy. In discussing their initial judgments of each other – a recurring theme in both Taylor's novels and short stories – Phyl reveals: "At the start, I thought you were . . . you know . . . one of *those*. Going about with that young boy all the time."

Although Phyl and Stanley appear to be traditional characters in the story, their frank discussions – and Taylor's frank treatment of them – make them unique. In the *New Statesman* (10 August 1973) Paul Bailey concludes his discussion of Taylor's art by observing, "She can breathe life into the oldest stock character: those unfamiliar with her writing should start by reading the story entitled 'Flesh' from *The Devastating Boys* in which she does just that."

Despite the polite descriptions reviewers gave of Taylor's work, she was, however subtly, constantly addressing issues of sexuality and sexual tensions between characters. *In a Summer Season,* for instance, centers on the main character's sexuality. The fact that her second marriage, to a younger man, is prompted by her interest in their sexual chemistry leaves her open to criticism from all the other characters in the novel. *The Soul of Kindness,* on the other hand, prominently features a homosexual character whose treatment continues the theme of loneliness found so often in Taylor's work.

"Miss A. and Miss M." is one of Taylor's rare stories narrated in the first person. It recalls the lives of Miss Alliot and Miss Martin, London schoolmistresses, through an adult's memory of childhood. Taylor touches on the androgynous ambivalence of adolescence through the memory:

"That was a time when one fell in love with who ever was *there*. In my adolescence the only males available to me for adoration were such as Shelley or Rupert Brooke or Owen Nares. A rather more real passion could be lavished on prefects at school or the younger mistresses." The narrator eavesdropped on adult conversations about hysterectomies and gynecologists, observed impromptu Shakespeare recitals, and lived generally in an "enchanted world." In addition to the mature treatment of adolescent love – of the flesh and of the world – "Miss A. and Miss M." is one of the most solid stories ever written. The control of emotion, particularly at the end, and the full sense of closure are common Taylor signatures.

Contemporary author Anne Tyler questions why Taylor is not more widely known and recognized. Tyler suggests that the reason for such oversight may be because "most of her books were published back when people still spoke of 'women's novels' without so much as a set of quotation marks to excuse the phrase. She did write exceptionally quiet tales – at least on the surface. She had a quiet, if excellent reputation." Tyler continues:

> Like Jane Austen, like Barbara Pym, like Elizabeth Bowen – soul-sisters all – Elizabeth Taylor made it her business to explore the quirky underside of so-called civilization. She cut straight to the heart of things; she could demonstrate in a phrase, in a gesture . . . that the human soul is a remarkably dark and funny object. In her delicate way, she could be absolutely savage.

Tyler does not qualify her praise with the negative comments that earlier reviewers seemed obligated to include.

Rosemary Dinnage's "The Tick of Blood in the Wrist," in the *Times Literary Supplement* (10 September 1976), is a review of *Blaming,* Taylor's final novel. Dinnage agrees that Taylor's work is "very English, nostalgic," but she adds that "such a formidably self-denying talent is not, never could be ladylike or governessy." Dinnage views *Blaming* as "a quiet conclusion" to "a most honourable literary career."

Frances J. Wallace lists Taylor's favorite writers, including Gustave Flaubert, Ivan Turgenev, Laurence Sterne, Austen, Compton-Burnett, and Woolf. There is always a temptation for critics to draw comparisons between writers. In *Elizabeth and Ivy* Liddell recalls a review he wrote of a Taylor novel in which he stated, "Mrs. Taylor does not seem to me to be very like Mrs. Woolf or Miss Compton-Burnett or Miss Bowen," because they were the writers to whom most reviewers saw Taylor indebted. Liddell's remark pleased Taylor, who responded: "I am grateful for what you wrote. It is puzzling when people say I write like this one and that one and all such different *kinds* of writers and so many of them, and it makes me feel I am nothing in myself."

In *A Very Private Eye* (1984) Pym records Taylor's death and Liddell's reaction to the news:

> Jock [Liddell] seems to have got over his eye operation very well but is still very upset about Elizabeth's death. Very little notice seems to have been taken of her but I am hoping that when her novel comes out there may be an appreciation in some of the TV book programmes. After all she was a friend of Kingsley Amis and Elizabeth Jane Howard who are well in with the 'media'. Still, what does it matter, really, such writers are caviar to the general, are they not, and fame is dust and ashes anyhow.

Although Tyler's review places Taylor in a tradition of women writers, she does not measure Taylor's worth in relation to those writers. Tyler's reading suggests that, with time, Taylor will receive the individual attention she has so long deserved.

Biography:

Robert Liddell, *Elizabeth and Ivy* (London: Owen, 1986).

References:

Kingsley Amis, "At Mrs. Taylor's," *Spectator*, 198 (14 June 1957): 784, 786;

Paul Bailey, "Artist in Miniature," *New Statesman*, 86 (10 August 1973): 192–193;

Brigid Brophy, "Elizabeth Taylor," in her *Don't Never Forget* (New York: Holt, Rinehart & Winston, 1966), pp. 162–164;

Florence Leclercq, *Elizabeth Taylor* (Boston: Twayne, 1985);

Arthur Mizener, "In the Austen Vein," *New Republic*, 129 (2 November 1953): 25;

Barbara Pym, *A Very Private Eye* (New York: Random House, 1984);

Anne Tyler, "The Other Elizabeth Taylor," *Washington Post Book World*, 21 August 1983, pp. 1–2;

Frances J. Wallace, "Elizabeth Taylor," *Wilson Library Bulletin*, 22 (April 1948): 580.

Dylan Thomas

(27 October 1914 – 9 November 1953)

John S. Bak
Ball State University

See also the Thomas entries in *DLB 13: British Dramatists Since World War II: Part 2* and *DLB 20: British Poets, 1914–1945.*

BOOKS: *18 Poems* (London: *Sunday Referee*/Parton Bookshop, 1934);

Twenty-five Poems (London: Dent, 1936);

The Map of Love (London: Dent, 1939);

The World I Breathe (Norfolk, Conn.: New Directions, 1939);

Portrait of the Artist as a Young Dog (London: Dent, 1940; Norfolk, Conn.: New Directions, 1940);

New Poems (Norfolk, Conn.: New Directions, 1943);

Death and Entrances (London: Dent, 1946);

Selected Writing (New York: New Directions, 1946);

Twenty-six Poems (London: Dent, 1950; Norfolk, Conn.: New Directions, 1950);

In Country Sleep and Other Poems (New York: New Directions, 1952);

Collected Poems, 1934–1952 (London: Dent, 1952); republished as *The Collected Poems of Dylan Thomas* (New York: New Directions, 1953);

The Doctor and the Devils (London: Dent, 1953; New York: New Directions, 1953);

Under Milk Wood (London: Dent, 1954; New York: New Directions, 1954);

Quite Early One Morning (London: Dent, 1954; enlarged edition, New York: New Directions, 1954);

Conversation about Christmas (Norfolk, Conn.: New Directions, 1954);

A Child's Christmas in Wales (Norfolk, Conn.: New Directions, 1955; London: Dent, 1978);

Me and My Bike (New York: McGraw-Hill, 1965; London: Triton, 1965);

Rebecca's Daughter (London: Triton, 1965; Boston: Little, Brown, 1965);

The Doctor and the Devils and Other Scripts (New York: New Directions, 1966);

The Death of the King's Canary, by Thomas and John Davenport (London: Hutchinson, 1976; New York: Viking, 1976).

Dylan Thomas, circa 1946

Editions and Collections: *Adventures in the Skin Trade and Other Stories* (New York: New Directions, 1955); republished as *Adventures in the Skin Trade* (London: Putnam, 1955);

A Prospect of the Sea and Other Stories and Prose Writings, edited by Daniel Jones (London: Dent, 1955);

Miscellany: Poems Stories Broadcasts (London: Dent, 1963);

Miscellany Two (London: Dent, 1966);

The Notebooks of Dylan Thomas, edited by Ralph Maud (New York: New Directions, 1967); republished as *Poet in the Making* (London: Dent, 1968);

Dylan Thomas: Early Prose Writings, edited by Walford Davies (London: Dent, 1971; New York: New Directions, 1971);

Dylan Thomas: The Poems, edited by David Jones (London: Dent, 1971; New York: New Directions, 1971);

Dylan Thomas: The Collected Stories, foreword by Leslie Norris (London: Dent, 1983; New York: New Directions, 1984);

Collected Poems, 1934–1953, edited by Davies and Maud (London: Dent, 1988);

The Notebook Poems, 1930–1934, edited by Maud (London: Dent, 1989).

OTHER: Robert Louis Stevenson, *The Beach of Falesá,* adapted by Thomas (New York: Stein & Day, 1963; London: Cape, 1964);

Maurice O'Sullivan, *Twenty Years A-Growing,* adapted by Thomas (London: Dent, 1964).

Dylan Thomas is recognized as a poet first, a scoundrel second, and a writer of fiction third. Thomas is, however, worthy of critical examination as a writer of fiction, especially short stories (though he also wrote radio scripts, two novels, and five published screenplays). While his stature as a poet has not diminished, his reputation as a fiction writer has gained considerably.

Thomas often told friends that he believed his fiction to be inferior to his poetry. He wrote to Stephen Spender on 13 May 1940 that "I do not want to write another straight prosebook yet; it would eventually get me some money, I suppose, but it would mean ten or more poems less, which, I think, would be sad and silly for me." Regardless of what Thomas said about the importance of his fiction, that he devoted as much time and effort to his fiction as he did to his poetry is evident in the notebooks he left behind containing drafts and sketches of stories. As Leslie Norris says in his foreword to *Dylan Thomas: The Collected Stories* (1983): "There is plenty of evidence that he considered poems and stories equal products of his gift, drawing no clear distinction between them, knowing they came from the same source." Thomas's stories are generally divided into what Jacob Korg calls "vigorous fantasies in poetic style, a genre he discontinued after 1939, and straightforward, objective narratives."

Dylan (pronounced "Dullan" by Welsh purists, though Thomas himself preferred "Dillan") Marlais Thomas was born on 27 October 1914 in the house at 5 Cwmdonkin Drive, Uplands, Swansea, where he spent his next twenty-three years. His father, David John Thomas, was senior English master at the Swansea Grammar School, where Dylan Thomas learned to abhor formal education. His mother, Florence Williams Thomas, was a fussy matriarch, always concerned about her children's health. He had a sister, Nancy Marles, who was nine years older than he. Although family would be an important element in Thomas's autobiographical stories, his sister and mother would, curiously, be omitted.

English was Thomas's best and favorite subject; he habitually neglected his other studies. He was editor of the school's literary magazine, in which he published a poem when he was eleven. A year later he sold a poem for the first time: "His Requiem," published on 14 January 1927 in the *Western Mail* in Cardiff and signed "D. M. Thomas," was plagiarized. After failing his examinations he left school in the summer of 1931 and thereby relinquished any prospect of a university degree, much to his father's consternation. Thomas took a job with the *South Wales Daily Post,* a Swansea evening newspaper, leaving in December 1932 after honing the reporting skills that would color the character sketches in his fiction. In 1934 he moved to London, where, living in squalor with other artists, he had a poem published nearly every month in respectable London periodicals such as the *Adelphi, New English Weekly,* and *Listener.* Most of his early stories of the fantastic and the macabre were published in journals, ranging from the *Swansea Grammar School Magazine* to *Janus* (a short-lived magazine whose editor, Royston Morley, "paid" Thomas for "The Horse's Ha" in 1936 with a cheap meal); the *Criterion,* edited by T. S. Eliot; and the *Adelphi,* edited by Sir Richard Rees. The setting of most of the stories is a Welsh seaside town called Llareggub – a pun meant to be read backward (when publishers caught the pun after Thomas's death, they changed the name to Llaregyb) – with the neighboring countryside, including a valley named Jarvis and a mountain called Cader Peak. Its inhabitants are lovesick young men, lecherous clergymen, necromancers, and mysterious girls who rise from the soil.

The stories were not all collected in any one volume in England in Thomas's lifetime, though through no lack of effort on Thomas's part. After the success of his *18 Poems* in December 1934 Thomas began trying in the spring of 1935 to solidify his reputation by having his stories published in book form. In 1936 he met Caitlin Macnamara in a London pub; they were married on 11 July 1937. In early 1938 Thomas was still sending his manuscript under the title "The Burning Baby: 16 Stories." British publishers, however, found the stories lewd and offensive. (A reader's report dated as late as January 1954 would find "The Burning Baby" "a horrible fantasy," "Prologue to an Adventure" a "welter of pornographic filth," and "The Horse's Ha" "disgustingly obscene.") Working with his literary agent, David Higham, Thomas tried to appease everyone, asking which words or phrases were found vulgar, and even suggested substituting "a story about my grandfather who was a very clean old man" for a story that had offended. In a 13 July 1938 letter to his friend Wyn Henderson, Thomas wrote, "thank you for working for them [the stories]; I do hope you succeed in making the meanies realise I'm not a smuthound."

George Reavey of Europa Press, who planned to publish the stories in Paris to avoid British censorship, told Thomas that publication of the stories "as they stand would lead to imprisonment"; but Reavey never told Thomas the "particular words, phrases, passages to which objection is taken," and the project was dropped. By November 1938 Thomas was hoping that the Hogarth Press would publish the stories under the title "In the Direction of the Beginning," but, as with Reavey and Europa Press, the publication never transpired. Richard Church of J. M. Dent finally accepted the manuscript, publishing seven short stories in August 1939 as *The Map of Love* – "The Visitor," "The Enemies," "The Tree," "The Map of Love," "The Mouse and the Woman," "The Dress," and "The Orchards" – but rejected "A Prospect of the Sea," one of Thomas's favorite stories. James Laughlin, editor of New Directions in Norfolk, Connecticut, assured Thomas that when his stories were published in America, they would not meet with similar censorship problems, and four months later New Directions released *The World I Breathe,* collecting all that was in *The Map of Love* plus five additional stories: "The Holy Six," "A Prospect of the Sea," "The Burning Baby," "Prologue to an Adventure," and "The School for Witches."

Four additional stories – "Gaspar, Melchior, and Balthasar," "Brember," "In the Garden," and "Jarley's" – were not collected until Walford Davies published them in *Dylan Thomas: Early Prose Writings* (1971). These four stories provide a study of the developing mind of a genius. They depict reality through the irrational mind of the madman, the simpleton, the fanatic, and the lecher – for the young Thomas, all synonymous with the poet. Of the four, only "Gaspar, Melchior, and Balthasar" was unpub-

lished before 1971; it comes from Thomas's private journal, which he called the "Red Notebook," and is dated 8 August 1934 – a few months before Thomas left for London and began his bohemian life as an impoverished artist. It is a caustic commentary on Christianity in which the three kings witness the birth of the Messiah during the death and destruction of a modern war that kills them and Mary just as the baby is born. "Brember," "In the Garden," and "Jarley's" were published in the *Swansea Grammar School Magazine.* "Brember," published in 1931, is reminiscent of the work of Edgar Allan Poe: George Henry Brember, the final male in a lineage, reads his family's chronicle and finds his own name already entered on the last page. Brember relives a boyhood experience before resigning himself to the fact that his family line has ended. In "In the Garden," published in 1934, a boy absorbs himself in a mysterious trunk that, although empty, he imagines to be filled with "precious stones as bright as the sun." Linden Peach holds that "In the Garden" is "an allegorical portrayal of these fears. . . . that there is something beyond death" and that the trunk symbolizes the life/death duality with its womb/coffin associations. "Jarley's," published in 1933, a story about the coming to life of wax figures in a museum, is a commentary about the struggle to give life meaning. The museum attendant, Eleazar, decides to give up blood for paraffin. The wax figures do not feel the pleasure of life, nor do they feel its pain.

The Map of Love received generally favorable reviews, although Cyril Connolly in the *New Statesman* found Thomas's writing "inflated and faked." *The Map of Love* earned Thomas seventy pounds in advances but not even that much in royalties by the time it went out of print in 1950.

"The Tree," dated 28 December 1933 in the "Red Notebook," was first published in the *Adelphi* a year later. A boy learns of the miracle of the "first tree" – suggesting both the Tree of Life and the Tree of Death, the Cross – from an old man on Christmas Eve. On Christmas Day an idiot descends from the hills near Llareggub; when the boy meets the idiot, who says that he is "from the east" – where the old man told the boy Bethlehem lies – the boy believes the idiot to be Christ and crucifies him on a tree.

"The Enemies," dated 11 February in the "Red Notebook" and first published in *New Stories* in 1934, pits the life force of a pagan couple, the Owens, against the effete Reverend Davies, who stumbles on the couple's cottage after losing his way home and refuses to leave. Thomas rebukes Christi-

A Prospect of the Sea

A Prospect of the Sea · Dylan Thomas

A Prospect of the Sea

Stories and Essays

Dylan Thomas

Dylan Thomas

DENT

Dust jacket for the 1955 collection that includes the stories from The Map of Love *and* The World I Breathe *(both 1939), plus five previously uncollected stories*

anity by having Mrs. Amabel Owen, a witchlike clairvoyant who consults a crystal ball, and Mr. Owen, who imagines the weeds in his garden screaming like babies as he tears them up, represent the vital and the fecund while the clergyman stands for death. (In a 2 May 1934 letter to his girlfriend Pamela Hansford Johnson, Thomas noted that another paper accepted the story but would not print the word *copulation;* Thomas refused to alter it, and *New Stories* printed it, "copulation & all.")

"The Dress," written in March 1934 and published in *Comment* on 4 January 1936, deals with Jack, an escaped madman imprisoned for cutting off his wife's lips "because she smiled at men." Jack has a dream in which sleep appears as a girl in a flowered dress. The dream comes true when a young woman, who has sewn a dress with flowers on it, lets the fugitive sleep with his head in her lap when he breaks into her house.

Accompanying the madmen in Thomas's world are the poets, and the next three stories in *The Map of Love* delve into the hyperimaginative, often psychotic, mind of the poet who confronts reality through fantasy and illusion. In "The Visitor,"

written in April 1934 and first published in the *Criterion* in 1935, a dying poet, Peter, is visited in his delirium by Callaghan, the spirit of death. Callaghan takes Peter from his bed and flies with him through the darkness of Jarvis Valley, where the poet sees the cyclic process of destruction and regeneration at work. When dawn is about to break, Callaghan returns the poet to his bed. His wife finds him dead, though Peter, whose soul has transcended its bodily existence, feels alive for the first time.

Written in October 1934 and first published in *The Map of Love,* "The Orchards" describes the dreams of the poet Marlais who creates an imaginary woman to fulfill his need for love. The woman comes to Marlais in the form of a scarecrow among burning orchards. When he awakes, the memory of the dream lingers, distracting him from his writing. After the dream is repeated, he journeys in search of the woman, finding her in the orchards he had before only imagined. The orchards burst into flames, and the girl becomes a scarecrow; when "the real world's wind" extinguishes the fire, Marlais is left alone, kissing a scarecrow.

"The Mouse and the Woman," first published in 1936, opens with a poet in an asylum, then examines what drove him insane. He had created a woman "upon the block of paper," and he had destroyed her after she left him: "The woman died. . . . There was dignity in such a murder." The mouse in the poet's house, though, was real, as is all evil, and the poet could not keep it out no matter how many times he boarded up its hole.

The title story, first published in the collection, explores the initiation of a boy and girl into the mysteries of sex, represented by a bewitched land and a curiously animated map. Beth and Reuben explore their sexuality guided by Sam Rib and the lecherous Great-Uncle Jarvis, a ghost of the hills who has as many lovers as he does fingers. They are Adam and Eve, able to copulate but unable to swim upstream to the first island of love, where sexuality is raw and unabashed. The story uses an impressionistic narrative style and relies heavily on the meshing of illusion and reality, religion and sexuality.

Of the five stories published in *The World I Breathe* that Dent would not include in *The Map of Love*, "A Prospect of the Sea" addresses sexual initiation that begins as a dream but turns into reality. It is difficult to imagine why Dent found this story objectionable; it is far less obscene than "The Map of Love." It is not surprising, however, that "The Burning Baby" did not find inclusion in an English volume until 1955. Written in September 1934 and first published in *Contemporary Poetry and Prose* in May 1936, the story deals with the preacher Rhys Rhys's incest with his daughter. He burns their child on a fagot of gorse and heather to rid the earth of this fruit of a "foul womb." The spectacle of a child consumed by fire is for Thomas the ultimate question for religion: how could such suffering be inflicted upon such innocence? Paul Ferris notes that the source of "The Burning Baby" was a story Glyn Jones told Thomas about Dr. Williams Price, "the Welsh eccentric who called his illegitimate son Jesus Christ and burned his body on a hill when the child died." Korg finds this story, along with "The Holy Six" and "The Enemies," examples of Thomas's condemnation of "religious hypocrisy and repression."

"The Holy Six," which first appeared in *Contemporary Poetry and Prose* for spring 1937, is a sequel to "The Enemies." Six "holy" men — stock allegorical characters with anagrams for names — head to the Owen cottage to retrieve the Reverend Davies in response to a letter from Amabel Owen telling them that Davies will not leave her home. The men's actions and thoughts are indicative of their natures: for instance, while reading Mrs. Owen's letter, Mr. Stul (Lust) imagines her feeling the "weight of her breasts on her ink-black arm" as she is writing, and Mr. Edger (Greed) "clasped everything within reach." Describing the holy men's religious affectations, Thomas gives each a sexual flavor: "The holy life was a constant erection to these six gentlemen."

First published in *Contemporary Poetry and Prose* in 1936, "The School for Witches" depicts a witch, the sister of Amabel Owen, teaching seven country girls the methods of raising the devil. When a baby is born to a mad black woman on the first night of the new year, the girls sacrifice it to Satan. The three tinkers whose paths are crossed by a black cat and who join the seven girls to form a coven are ironic portraits of the three wise men.

"Prologue to an Adventure," an unfinished story, has no real action; in the city of sin, the narrator visits two bars before the scene becomes immersed in a cleansing deluge. According to Korg, "There are no alternate realms of reality in this story. It is all an inescapable mental reality, consisting entirely of representations of the desires, fears, suspicions, and other emotions of the narrator."

A Prospect of the Sea and Other Stories and Prose Writings (1955) added three more pre-1939 stories to those of *The Map of Love* and *The World I Breathe*, plus two later stories, "The Followers" and "A Story." The three pre-1939 stories are similar in their treatments of the mad, the occult, and the surreal. "In the Direction of the Beginning," written in 1938, is a mythlike account of creation written in a surrealistic style; "The Lemon," which first appeared in *Life and Letters Today* for spring 1936, is another dream story; and in "After the Fair," written in 1934, Annie, whom Annis Pratt calls "a more orthodox version of Amabel Owen," takes her fatherless child for an endless ride on a merry-go-round.

Adventures in the Skin Trade and Other Stories (1955) added four more pre-1939 stories to those in *A Prospect of the Sea and Other Stories and Prose Writings*, including the unfinished title novel. "The Vest," dated 20 July 1934 in the "Red Notebook," deals with a man driven to madness and the mutilation of his wife by his fear of death. "The True Story," written under the title "Martha" in the "Red Notebook" and dated 22 January 1934, recounts the murder of an old woman by her young charge, who commits suicide when her lover will not help her dispose of the body. "The Horse's Ha," first published in *Janus* in May 1936, portends the coming of the white horse — the plague — to the town of

Cathmarw (Welsh for "death"). "An Adventure from a Work in Progress," first published in *Seven* for spring 1939, concerns a man's pursuit of a shadow woman through what Korg describes as "a strangely active archipelago where awesome cataclysms endanger him."

In *Portrait of the Artist as a Young Dog* (1940) Thomas has found his voice, developed his style, and matured as a writer of fiction. A collection of stories about Swansea people with a principal character based on Thomas himself, *Portrait of the Artist as a Young Dog* emerged as Thomas's self-declared "adolescent autobiography." In a 29 September 1939 letter to Bert Trick, Thomas called the stories "mostly pot-boilers" and said that "the writing of them means the writing of a number of poems less."

The ten stories in *Portrait of the Artist as a Young Dog* were written in 1938 and 1939. Critically well received but financially a disaster, the book remains the focal point of Thomas's fiction for literary scholars. Several have posited that Thomas's literary influence here was James Joyce, though Thomas fervently denied it. His title, he claimed, is less a variant on Joyce's *A Portrait of the Artist as a Young Man* (1916) than on the titles painters often give to their self-portraits. The protagonists in the stories are all variations of Thomas, from the young boy–poet at Gorsehill (the Fernhill of Thomas's youth) in "The Peaches" to the experienced poet in "One Warm Saturday."

Thomas's progression from juvenile fantasy to mature bildungsroman is a sharp one; the change in style and narrative voice parallels the change taking place in his poetic voice at the time. For whatever reason – his marriage; the birth of his first child, Llewellen, in January 1939; the impending war – Thomas matured, and his stories reflect this growth.

The ten stories, connected through the protagonist, deal with ordinary experiences from visits with relatives in the country to camping excursions with friends on the Gower to pub crawls on the docks with an older coworker. In the earlier stories, the protagonist witnesses the trials of adulthood but remains indifferent to them; in the later stories, he experiences those sufferings himself.

In "The Peaches" Thomas is too young to understand his cousin Gwilym's masturbation but old enough to learn about the tensions between social classes. Thomas's aunt and uncle, Annie and Jim Jones, are not as wealthy as Mrs. Williams, who owns "three bloody houses" and whose refusal to accept Annie's celebrated peaches creates a social schism. She tells Annie that she simply abhors peaches, but she is either missing the significance the peaches have for the Joneses, who have saved the tin since Christmas, or she is showing pity for them by not accepting their meager offering. The incident teaches Thomas that members of different social classes do not mingle.

"A Visit to Grandpa's" traces young Thomas's experiences of loneliness and old age. Of the final image of Grandpa on the bridge in "A Visit to Grandpa's," Kenneth Seib says, "Standing midway between one world and the next, but still firmly clutching the material things of this world, grandpa stares at the Heraclitean flow of time below and the imponderable seat of heaven above, with certain knowledge that he is, like all of us, heading deathward. Grandpa becomes Everyman, and the story becomes more than autobiography and pot-boiler."

In "Patricia, Edith, and Arnold" the maidservants Patricia and Edith realize that Arnold has been courting both of them. Thomas, seeing Arnold reading Edith's letters after having just told Patricia that she was his one and only, spares Patricia this painful news. While "A Visit to Grandpa's" initiates the boy into the world of loneliness and old age as he watches his grandfather on the verge of again attempting suicide, "Patricia, Edith, and Arnold" introduces him to love.

"The Fight" is based on Thomas's first meeting and subsequent friendship with Daniel Jenkyn Jones, a composer who collaborated in writing poetry with Thomas under the name Walter Bram (*bram* is Welsh for "fart"). A published poet at fifteen, the narrator pastes a copy of his poem from a local paper on his mirror "to make me blush." He lies to his new friend's father about his age because "It was exciting to have to keep wary all the time in case I contradicted myself." When the Reverend Bevan asks him to recite his last poem at the dinner table, Thomas says, "I don't think you'll like the very latest one." He is right, as all Bevan can say about the poem is that the influence was obviously Tennyson. But the artist in him has emerged.

"Extraordinary Little Cough" recalls a camping trip Thomas took to the Gower peninsula. The narrator and his friends meet up with two bullies who pick on one of them, George Hooping, nicknamed Little Cough. When the bullies challenge Little Cough to run the five-mile beach he does it, proving his masculinity in his own eyes. Thomas, meanwhile, tries to express his masculinity through love but fails. While Hooping is running, Thomas picks a girl out of a group camping nearby: "Jean, shy and curly, with butter-coloured hair, was mine." But Jean falls for one of the bullies, and Thomas's pain in failed love translates directly to his poetry. With Jean, he has finally experienced an adult emotion.

In "Just Like Little Dogs" the narrator, now a "soft-faced young man," meets two brothers, Tom and Walter, who are refraining from returning home. The narrator soon learns of the plight that keeps them away from their wives: Tom and Walter met Norma and Doris one day, paired off, and made love in the park; then, "just like little dogs," they changed partners. The girls became pregnant, and neither knew who the father was. When the judge ordered the two brothers to marry the girls, they married the wrong ones: Tom married Doris but loves Norma, though Walter "doesn't love Norma or Doris." Having experienced love firsthand in the previous story, the narrator now learns of the loneliness that can exist even in marriage.

"Where Tawe Flows" is a framed narrative that depicts Thomas and his friends discussing their contributions to a collectively written novel about life in a fictional provincial city: "Young Mr. Thomas was at the moment without employment, but it was understood that he would be leaving for London to make a career in Chelsea as a free-lance journalist"; he was also "penniless, and hoped, in a vague way, to live on women." The inner tale deals with class prejudice: the eminent Williams Hughes family will not let their son marry Mary Morgan after her wealthy uncle is found dead in the arms of a disreputable woman. The protagonist has finally experienced enough of the adult world to start writing about it.

In "Who Do You Wish Was With Us?" Thomas is on a walking tour from Uplands to Worm's Head with Raymond Price, a friend ten years his senior. He does not want to hear Ray describe yet again the lingering death of Ray's brother Harry; Thomas already knows "every cough and cry, every clawing at the air," so he avoids mentioning the word *death* and wets his feet in the incoming sea, the source of life; but death is not easily forgotten.

In "Old Garbo" Mr. Farr – Thomas's real-life mentor Freddie Farr, senior reporter at the *South Wales Evening Post* (here the *Tawe News*) – takes the budding reporter on a crawl through the seedier pubs by the docks. In "The Fishguard" pub Thomas and Farr encounter a mourning party for Mrs. Prothero's daughter. The story of the daughter's death is a lie, however, and Mrs. Prothero (known as "Old Garbo," ironically, because she is nothing like the actress), having spent the money collected for the funeral on drinks, commits suicide because she is ashamed to face the mourning women. After his drunken night Thomas awakens on Sunday to the bells of Saint Mary's ringing in his ears long after they had ceased, and he vows never to drink again.

In the last story in the collection, "One Warm Saturday," the narrator makes eye contact with a girl in the Victoria Gardens, leaves because he is shy, then meets her again in a pub. The girl, Lou, promises the narrator a night of love; but when he leaves her apartment to find a bathroom, he forgets which room is hers. He wanders among the maze of tenement rooms, stumbling into several that he thinks might be Lou's, but finds them filled with people who are, he realizes, as lonely as he.

Seib points out that, in *Portrait of the Artist as a Young Dog*, "Along with the movement from childhood to adulthood, the principal direction of the stories is from Edenic innocence to Adamic fall." Seib says that other progressions also exist: "from the private to the public, from the 'safe centre of his own identity' to the exterior world in which identity is either confused or lost; from the narrator's objective witness of life around him to subjective participation in the mean and fallen Welsh world."

The Thomases had a daughter, Aeron, in March 1943. In 1947 Thomas was awarded a £150 travel scholarship by the Society of Authors; Edith Sitwell, because she did not want him to go to America for fear that he would squander the money on drink, persuaded the society to give him the grant with the stipulation that he travel in Europe. The Thomases spent April to August 1947 in Italy. A third child, a son named Colm, was born in July 1949.

Thomas never knew a life outside of penury: on a draft of "Poem on His Birthday" a list of debtors appears among his scribblings of verse; and he was constantly writing to fellow artists, patrons, publishers, friends, and family for money, much of which he spent on drink (he claimed in 1937 to have drunk forty pints of beer in one night in Cornwall). He devoted many hours to hack-writing jobs for BBC radio and for film companies. Serious writing was hard for Thomas when he was young, and nearly impossible when he was mature; during the last six years of his life he wrote only one poem a year. He often spent months on a single poem or story, days on a single line, and hours on a single word. He had written to Johnson on 9 May 1934, describing this exhaustive process: "I write in the only way I can write, & my warped, crabbed & cabinned stuff is not the result of theorising but of

Dust jacket for the 1955 collection that includes the stories from A Prospect of the
Sea, *along with three previously uncollected stories and the unfinished title novel*

pure incapability to express my needless tortuities in any other way."

Thomas's later years were devoted primarily to writing essays and reminiscences for the BBC about growing up in Wales, for money to hold creditors at bay. He wrote the script "Memories of Christmas" for the BBC Wales Children's Hour in the fall of 1945; it was broadcast on 16 December and published in the *Listener* on 20 December and in *Wales* for winter 1946. He wrote a similar piece, "Conversations about Christmas," for the *Picture Post* of 27 December 1947. During his first American tour he combined the two for publication in *Harper's Bazaar* of December 1950 as "A Child's Memories of Christmas in Wales," for which he was paid three hundred dollars. It was published in book form as *A Child's Christmas in Wales* in 1955.

Thomas wrote three more story-essays, all broadcast between October 1946 and May 1947: "Holiday Memory," "The Crumbs of One Man's Year," and "Return Journey" were collected in *Quite Early One Morning* (1954). These late works, like his two last stories, reflect an amalgam of his two former styles. "The Followers," written in 1952, and "A Story," written in 1953, combine fantasy and autobiography.

In "The Followers," Leslie and the narrator follow a woman home, peep into the home she shares with her mother, and listen to their conversation. But they soon hear a mysterious third voice rising out of the pages of a photograph album that the two women are leafing through. "A Story" echoes both the narrative style and content of the stories in *A Portrait of the Artist as a Young Dog*. The young narrator accompanies a group of raucous

Welsh codgers on their annual pilgrimage to nearly all the pubs in western Wales.

The style of these later works, fraught with hyphenated words ("the swill-and-gaslamp smell of Saturday night"), became a Thomas trademark. The experiments with language in his poetry had finally found their way into his prose.

Thomas was aware of this development in his fiction and recognized the importance of each stage. In "Where Tawe Flows" Thomas pays homage to his fantasy period: the young Mr. Thomas announces to the literary group that he has been working on a story of "a cat who jumped over a woman the moment she died and turned her into a vampire." Receiving strange looks from the others in the group, who have written realistic narratives, he responds: "There's no need, is there . . . for us to avoid the fantastic altogether?"

In October 1951 Thomas wrote the American poet Oscar Williams, his unofficial literary agent in the United States, "I've spent months writing this poem, and hope you can squeeze out a real huge cheque from some moneyed illerate — it's me that illerate, I meant illiterate — bastard for it." With a wife and three children and no steady work, Thomas saw America as his only hope for financial security.

He went to the United States on lecture tours four times beginning in February 1951, leaving the Boat House in Laugharne, Wales, his home for the four and a half years before his death. Caitlin said of these trips that they were Thomas's excuse for "flattery, idleness and infidelity." The readings were supposed to provide quick money to pay off his debts accruing at home, yet he still managed to squander the money on spirits and women. He referred to his final weeks in New York on one tour as "one liquid, libidinous fortnight." He became ill after an evening at the White Horse Tavern in New York: he told his American mistress, Liz Reitell, "I've had eighteen straight whiskies. I think that's the record" — undoubtedly a gross exaggeration. A doctor was summoned three times during the night and gave Thomas an injection of morphine that skeptics believe was the real cause of his falling into a coma during the morning of 5 November 1953, from which he was not to awake. He died on 9 November, officially of pneumonia with "pial oedema," or water on the brain, as the "immediate cause" of the "insult to the brain." He left behind a mound of debts that private contributions helped to pay. He was buried in Laugharne.

Much of what made Thomas a major voice in twentieth-century poetry can be found in his early prose. Korg believes that "Thomas's early short stories often confirm the themes of his poems," themes steeped in mysticism. "Whatever the reason," Seib writes of the current lack of attention to Thomas's short fiction, "neglect is shameful, for Thomas' stories are artful contrivances, as complex as many of his better poems and worthy of careful consideration."

Letters:

Letters to Vernon Watkins, edited by Vernon Watkins (London: Dent & Faber, 1957; New York: New Directions, 1957);

"Love Letters from a Poet to His Wife," *McCall's,* 93 (February 1966): 78, 173;

Selected Letters of Dylan Thomas, edited by Constantine FitzGibbon (London: Dent, 1966; New York: New Directions, 1967);

Twelve More Letters (Stoke Ferry, U.K.: Turret, 1969);

The Collected Letters of Dylan Thomas, edited by Paul Ferris (London: Dent, 1985; New York: Macmillan, 1985).

Bibliographies:

J. Alexander Rolph, *Dylan Thomas: A Bibliography* (London: Dent, 1956; New York: New Directions, 1956);

Ralph Maud, *Dylan Thomas in Print: A Bibliographical History* (Pittsburgh: University of Pittsburgh Press, 1970);

Georg M. A. Gaston, *Dylan Thomas: A Reference Guide* (Boston: G. K. Hall, 1987).

Biographies:

John Malcolm Brinnin, *Dylan Thomas in America* (Boston: Atlantic/Little, Brown, 1955; London: Arlington, 1988);

Caitlin Thomas, *Leftover Life to Kill* (London: Putnam, 1957; Boston: Atlantic/Little, Brown, 1957);

Bill Read, *The Days of Dylan Thomas* (London: Weidenfeld & Nicolson, 1964; New York: McGraw-Hill, 1964);

Constantine FitzGibbon, *The Life of Dylan Thomas* (London: Dent, 1965; Boston: Atlantic/Little, Brown, 1965);

Andrew Sinclair, *Dylan Thomas: No Man More Magical* (New York: Holt, Rinehart & Winston, 1975);

Paul Ferris, *Dylan Thomas: A Biography* (London: Hodder & Stoughton, 1977; New York: Dial, 1977);

Daniel Jones, *My Friend Dylan Thomas* (London: Dent, 1977; New York: Scribners, 1977);

Gwen Watkins, *Portrait of a Friend* (Llandysul, Wales: Gomer Press, 1983);

Caitlin Thomas and George Tremlett, *Caitlin: A Warring Absence* (London: Secker & Warburg, 1986); republished as *Caitlin: Life with Dylan Thomas* (New York: St. Martin's Press, 1986);

Tremlett, *Dylan Thomas: In the Mercy of His Means* (London: Constable, 1992; New York: St. Martin's Press, 1992).

References:

John Ackerman, *A Dylan Thomas Companion* (London: Macmillan, 1991);

Ackerman, *Dylan Thomas: His Life and Work* (London: Oxford University Press, 1964);

Alan Bold, ed., *Dylan Thomas: Craft or Sullen Art* (London: Vision, 1990; New York: St. Martin's Press, 1990);

Gerald L. Bruns, "Daedalus, Orpheus, and Dylan Thomas's Portrait of the Artist," *Renascence,* 25 (Spring 1973): 147–156;

James A. Davies, "Dylan Thomas' 'One Warm Saturday' and Tennyson's *Maud,*" *Studies in Short Fiction,* 14 (Summer 1977): 284–286;

Richard A. Davies, "Dylan Thomas's Image of the 'Young Dog' in *Portrait,*" Anglo-Welsh Review, 26 (Spring 1977): 68–72;

Walford Davies, "Imitation and Invention: The Use of Borrowed Material in Dylan Thomas's Prose," *Essays in Criticism,* 18 (July 1968): 275–295;

Brian Finney, "Dylan Thomas's 'A Visit to Grandpa's,'" *London Review,* 8 (Winter 1971): 31–35;

Warren French, "Two Portraits of the Artist: James Joyce's *Young Man;* Dylan Thomas's *Young Dog,*" *University of Kansas City Review,* 33 (June 1967): 261–266;

Georg M. A. Gaston, *Critical Essays on Dylan Thomas* (Boston: G. K. Hall, 1989);

Burton S. Glick, "A Brief Analysis of a Short Story by Dylan Thomas," *American Imago,* 14 (Summer 1957): 149–154;

Allen Wallace Graves, "Difficult Contemporary Short Stories: William Faulkner, Katherine Anne Porter, Dylan Thomas, Eudora Welty, and Virginia Woolf," Ph.D. dissertation, University of Washington, 1954;

Richard Kelly, "The Lost Vision of Dylan Thomas' 'One Warm Saturday,'" *Studies in Short Fiction,* 6 (Winter 1969): 205–209;

Jacob Korg, *Dylan Thomas* (New York: Twayne, 1965; revised, 1992);

Harold F. Mosher, Jr., "The Structure of Dylan Thomas's 'The Peaches,'" *Studies in Short Fiction,* 6 (Fall 1969): 536–547;

William T. Moynihan, *The Craft and Art of Dylan Thomas* (Ithaca, N.Y.: Cornell University Press, 1966);

Linden Peach, *The Prose Writing of Dylan Thomas* (London: Macmillan, 1988);

Annis Pratt, *Dylan Thomas' Early Prose: A Study in Creative Mythology* (Pittsburgh: University of Pittsburgh Press, 1970);

Kenneth Seib, "*Portrait of an Artist as a Young Dog:* Dylan's *Dubliners,*" *Modern Fiction Studies,* 24 (Summer 1978): 239–246;

Derek Stanford, *Dylan Thomas: A Literary Study* (London: Spearman, 1954; New York: Citadel, 1954);

Henry Treece, *Dylan Thomas: "Dog among the Fairies"* (London: Drummond, 1949; revised edition, London: Benn, 1956).

Papers:

The majority of Dylan Thomas's papers and manuscripts are at the Harry Ransom Humanities Research Center, University of Texas at Austin. The four notebooks from his youth are at the Lockwood Memorial Library, State University of New York at Buffalo. Miscellaneous papers are at the Houghton Library, Harvard University; the New York Public Library; the Lilly Library, Indiana University; the National Library of Wales; the British Library; the BBC Written Archives Centre; the Swansea (Wales) Public Library; the Llanelli (Wales) Public Library; and at Swansea University College, Swansea, Wales.

William Trevor
(24 May 1928 –   )

Marjorie Podolsky
Pennsylvania State University – Erie

See also the Trevor entry in *DLB 14: British Novelists Since 1960: Part 2.*

BOOKS: *A Standard of Behaviour* (London: Hutchinson, 1958);

The Old Boys (London: Bodley Head, 1964; New York: Viking, 1964);

The Boarding House (London: Bodley Head, 1965; New York: Viking, 1965);

The Love Department (London: Bodley Head, 1966; New York: Viking, 1967);

The Day We Got Drunk on Cake and Other Stories (London: Bodley Head, 1967; New York: Viking, 1968);

The Girl (London: French, 1968);

Mrs. Eckdorf in O'Neill's Hotel (London: Bodley Head, 1969; New York: Viking, 1970);

The Old Boys [play] (London: Poynter, 1971);

Miss Gomez and the Brethren (London: Bodley Head, 1971);

A Night with Mrs. da Tonka (London: French, 1972);

The Ballroom of Romance and Other Stories (London: Bodley Head, 1972; New York: Viking, 1972);

Going Home (London: French, 1972);

Elizabeth Alone (London: Bodley Head, 1973; New York: Viking, 1974);

Marriages (London: French, 1974);

Angels at the Ritz and Other Stories (London: Bodley Head, 1975; New York: Viking, 1976);

The Children of Dynmouth (London: Bodley Head, 1976; New York: Viking, 1977);

Old School Ties (London: Lemon Tree, 1976);

Lovers of Their Time and Other Stories (London: Bodley Head, 1978; New York: Viking, 1978);

Other People's Worlds (London: Bodley Head, 1980; New York: Viking, 1981);

Beyond the Pale and Other Stories (London: Bodley Head, 1981; New York: Viking, 1982);

Fools of Fortune (London: Bodley Head, 1983; New York: Viking, 1983);

The Stories of William Trevor (Hammondsmith, Middlesex, U.K.: Penguin, 1983);

William Trevor

A Writer's Ireland: Landscape in Literature (New York: Viking, 1984; London: Thames & Hudson, 1984);

The News from Ireland and Other Stories (London: Bodley Head, 1986; New York: Viking, 1986);

Nights at the Alexandra (New York: Harper & Row, 1987);

The Silence in the Garden (London: Bodley Head, 1988; New York: Viking, 1988);

Family Sins and Other Stories (London: Bodley Head, 1990);

Two Lives: Reading Turgenev and My House in Umbria (New York: Viking, 1991);

Excursions in the Real World: Autobiographical Essays (New York: Knopf, 1994).

Collection: *The Collected Stories* (New York: Viking, 1992).

William Trevor is considered one of the masters of the contemporary short story. The author of eleven novels and seven collections of short fiction, he was recognized for his contributions to literature with the title of commander, Order of the British Empire in 1977. Trevor has also written three novellas, several plays, and radio and television adaptations of his short stories. However, he prefers writing short fiction, calling himself "a short story writer . . . who happens to write novels."

Trevor's short fiction has been praised for its delineation of character, especially its portrayal of ordinary people – the lonely, the alienated, the victims of society – as well as those who, at the extreme, are pathological evildoers. His stories have been called tragicomic or darkly comic; they create a wide range of effects from nostalgia for lost love to sardonically bitter commentary on evil. Trevor's artistic vision, however it may be interpreted, is rooted in his compassion for human suffering. Trevor's short fiction has been compared to that of James Joyce's *Dubliners* (1914). Like Joyce, Trevor often ends his stories with an epiphany, and both writers share the view that one can write well about Ireland only after leaving it. Trevor also has been compared to Elizabeth Bowen, both for their shared insights into the lives of the Anglo-Irish and their psychological exploration of character that takes precedence over plot.

Although Trevor's style and plot development are traditional rather than experimental, his fiction reveals him as a shrewd observer of events of his time, or, as he calls himself, an eavesdropper on conversations and situations. His early stories explore the worlds of the elderly, the eccentric, and society's misfits. The stories of his middle period reflect the social turmoil of Britain in the 1960s and 1970s. Forced out of their constricted environments, Trevor's characters must cope with such social phenomena as the effects of drugs and alcohol on themselves and others, the new sexual freedom and the changes it brings to marriage, the behavior of a generation of adolescents unleashed from adult supervision and loosed on society, and the disturbance of those who try in vain to re-create an idealized happiness of the past.

A theme that appears in Trevor's early work but is not fully developed until later is the suffering caused by the troubles between England and Ireland. With increasing depth and intensity his later fiction explores those crucial moments when the desires of the individual are constrained by the events of history. Trevor writes primarily about three groups: the provincial Irish, the English, and the Anglo-Irish Protestants. His home is a farm in Devon, but he spends some time in Italy every year, and this locale is the setting of some of his later stories.

Trevor's work, while capturing the cultural and historical nuances of the times of which he writes, concentrates on the behavior of those who must make moral choices. At such moments of decision he pins his characters to the mat and watches them squirm. Sometimes his protagonists achieve a revelation of truth; sometimes they further mire themselves in self-delusion. Often the truth they reveal results in betrayal by those whom they believed they could trust, or even in insanity as society defines it. In Trevor's canon these truth-tellers may accept their fate, seek meaning in the supernatural, or retreat into madness. Often they understand the tragedy of the joyless lives they must live, a viewpoint that has caused some of Trevor's critics to accuse him of a morose pessimism that exaggerates the plight of ordinary humanity.

Trevor commands his readers' attention and sustains interest with a strategy that Gregory A. Schirmer, in *William Trevor: A Study of His Fiction* (1990), calls "multiple centers of consciousness." That is, Trevor abruptly shifts the narrative point of view from one character to another and then stands back to view the action as the distant author. He often demands that the reader construct the meaning of the story by evaluating the credibility of these conflicting points of view, thus creating the irony in much of his fiction. In this way Trevor raises troubling moral issues without providing clear answers. The moral dimension of his fiction earns the highest praise from readers and critics.

William Trevor Cox was born on 24 May 1928 in Mitchelstown, County Cork, Ireland, to James William and Gertrude Davison Cox. His parents were Protestants, and his observation of provincial Irish society as an "outsider" informs much of his fiction. His father was a bank manager who frequently moved the family as he changed jobs; Trevor attended at least thirteen schools or was tutored by "mostly failed Christian brothers." He attended Saint Columba's College in Dublin and read history at Trinity College, where he earned a B.A. in 1950. He married Jane Ryan in 1952, and they are the parents of two sons.

For several years Trevor taught in Northern Ireland until the school went bankrupt. He moved to England when he could no longer support his family in Ireland and taught art for two years; he also achieved minor success as a church sculptor. For five years he worked – unhappily and unsuccessfully, he has said – as a copywriter for a London advertising agency. During this time he began publishing his short stories under the name of William Trevor. His first novel, *A Standard of Behaviour* (1958), which he does not regard highly, was written because he needed money. His first serious novel, *The Old Boys* (1964), is a satire about British schools. This book established his reputation and earned him the Hawthornden Prize. He has never had difficulty getting his short stories published, his earliest ones appearing in *Transatlantic Review* and the *London Magazine*. Since then his stories have been published in a wide variety of periodicals in Britain and the United States, including the *New Yorker, Atlantic, Antaeus, Encounter,* and the *Irish Press.*

Trevor followed his first success with *The Boarding House* (1965), a sprawling Dickensian novel about a group of eccentric people living together. In *The Love Department* (1966) he turns his attention to marriage and family life, subjects of continuing interest in succeeding works. His first collection of short fiction, *The Day We Got Drunk on Cake and Other Stories,* was published in 1967. This volume and the six collections that have followed have been highly praised by most critics, although not with uniform agreement as to the merit of certain stories. While Trevor's novels and short fiction share themes and subject matter, his short stories paint a darker picture of life.

The twelve stories in *The Day We Got Drunk on Cake* introduce character types and themes that Trevor has continued to explore. His style and technique are fully developed in these early stories, set in London, that reveal the lives of society's misfits. Several focus on the psychological relationship between victim and victimizer. As a character in "Miss Smith" says: "People who are weaker are always the ones who get hurt. . . . You've got to find the weak spot. Everyone has a weak spot."

"The Penthouse Apartment" portrays a trio of eccentric characters brought together by chance, one of Trevor's favorite strategies. The action begins, as Trevor's stories often do, with a cryptic slice of dialogue: " 'Flowers?' said Mr. Runca. . . . 'Shall we order flowers?' " A sophisticated couple are preparing their fashionable apartment for a magazine photograph. With typical spareness Trevor limns Mrs. Runca as she lights her first cigarette of the day: "She had a long, rather thin face and pale grey hair that had the glow of aluminum. Her hands were long also, hands that had grown elegant in childhood with fingernails that were of a fashion-

able length, metallically painted, a reflection of her hair."

The Runcas, however, are not the focus of the story. The center of consciousness shifts to Miss Winton, whose apartment is in dismal contrast to that of the elegant Runcas in the same building. Miss Winton, an elderly spinster, is pathologically shy and fearful of offending others. Accompanied by her cairn terrier she accepts the invitation of the Runcas' feckless maid, Bianca, to visit the penthouse for a cup of coffee in the owners' absence. Although Miss Winton is uneasy about the situation, she does not have the courage to extricate herself from it and becomes trapped in a swiftly developing comic disaster. The handyman Morgan, a boorish alcoholic, shows up and gets drunk on the Runcas' whiskey. Miss Winton, fearful of creating a scene, accepts several drinks offered by the maid and also becomes light-headed. The drunken Morgan smashes a vase of flowers that has been specially arranged for the photograph session and stains the carpet. He decides to blame the incident on Miss Winton's dog. The ill-assorted trio of Miss Winton, Morgan, and Bianca attempt to repair the damage, creating a series of wickedly comic scenes when they burn the carpet while trying to dry it with an electric heater. The Runcas are of course horrified by the wreckage when they return. Miss Winton tries to explain the situation but ends by defending Bianca and Morgan and taking the blame on herself.

The story illustrates some of Trevor's favorite fictional concerns. The arrogant handyman and the stupid maid exploit Miss Winton's misplaced sympathy and sense of guilt. The sophisticated Runcas are too self-concerned with their petty predicament to listen to the truth. Miss Winton, the only morally responsible person in the story, is one of Trevor's truth-tellers, but, like Cassandra, she is not believed. Ultimately she places the guilt for the misunderstanding on herself, saying: "I have failed to do something that might have been good in its small way." Her epiphany is a painful confrontation with reality: she has made a fool of herself and will live out her years in a constricted world that views her as an object of ridicule.

By giving the reader several points of view – those of Miss Winton, Mr. and Mrs. Runca, and the distant author – Trevor creates a disturbing effect. While the meticulously described scene is comic, Miss Winton's suffering is agonizingly real. Still, she has created her own disaster by allowing herself to be manipulated. The reader must decide where to place blame or sympathy, or may even wonder

Dust jacket for Trevor's first collection of short fiction, which focuses on the lives of misfits in London

whether the situation is too trivial to warrant serious consideration.

However, the truth-teller in Trevor's stories does not always invite sympathy. In "Raymond Bamber and Mrs. Fitch" Raymond is the weak one, a bachelor who lives "a tidy life" and looks forward to a yearly cocktail party given by friends. Mrs. Fitch, an unattractive woman who looks years older than her husband, attaches herself to Raymond and relates her tale of woe. Her husband, she says, plans to get rid of her and seduce the woman to whom he is talking. Quickly drinking herself into a rage, she tells Raymond the "truth" – that he is a "grinding bore" invited to the party only because of longstanding family obligations. Raymond's sympathy (and that of the reader) is with the unfortunate Mr. Fitch, who must take his disgusting wife home in embarrassment.

Mr. Fitch returns and does make sexual overtures to the woman at the party. Having to deal with Mrs. Fitch's revelations – both about her husband's behavior and her analysis of himself – Raymond maintains his precarious self-esteem by

deciding that Mrs. Fitch is unstable as, indeed, are the rest of the partygoers – an offense against the orderliness of society. By manipulating the narrative voices Trevor leads the reader to reject Raymond's "epiphany" and accept the version of reality uttered by Mrs. Fitch.

In "The Penthouse Apartment" and "Raymond Bamber and Mrs. Fitch" self-delusion and weakness have embarrassing but minor consequences; the protagonists are ordinary people with recognizable character flaws and whose actions are understandable. In other stories in the collection, however, the mischief approaches pure evil. Trevor's interest in the perversions of life in British schools (a theme developed in *The Old Boys*) is expressed in "A School Story." Williams, a malicious boy whose motivation is never clearly revealed, drives young Markham, supposedly his friend, into the insane belief that he has been responsible for the death of his parents. The young narrator, a friend of both boys, attempts to report the truth of this manipulative relationship to the headmaster – a pompous dolt, like many of his counterparts in Trevor's fiction – who interprets this awkward revelation as an "illicit relationship" among the boys, and once again the truth-teller is ignored. Markham, unbalanced by his delusion of guilt, is sent away to a "place they had found for him in Derbyshire."

In the most sinister story, "Miss Smith," evil is embodied in the schoolboy James. A pathologically sensitive child belittled by his teacher, Miss Smith, James bides his time to take his revenge. Miss Smith marries and bears a child. The neutral voice of a distant narrator relates a series of mysterious mishaps endangering the child. At the conclusion Miss Smith, whose child has disappeared, follows James to the place where he has promised she will find her missing child: "She heard him [James] laughing; she looked at him and saw his small weasel face twisted into a merriment that frightened her." Stories such as "Miss Smith," in which Trevor introduces near-demonic characters, are generally less satisfactory or credible than those in which he allows evil to result from understandable human error.

The theme of love and its delusions that Trevor explores more fully in later stories is suggested in the title story, a tale of a young man's betrayal by the woman he loves. His epiphany is a bleak revelation: "As for me, time would heal and time would cure. I knew it, and it was the worst thing of all. I didn't want to be cured." Schirmer, in praising Trevor's achievement in this story, compares it to T. S. Eliot's *The Wasteland* (1922) because its "fragmented relationships function as barometers of society's moral and spiritual impoverishment."

With the publication of *The Day We Got Drunk on Cake* Trevor was acknowledged as an accomplished storyteller and was praised for his mastery of plot, precisely detailed descriptions, character development, and ironic comic effects. However, Robert Hogan, in *The Irish Short Story: A Critical History* (1984), finds the pessimism of these and other stories disturbing: "In his low-keyed, businesslike fashion, he quietly proceeds, story by story, to transform the entirety of modern life into a gray, dank, commonplace asylum." This controversy continues to surface whenever Trevor publishes a new book. Most critics praise his mastery of form in both novels and short stories, but many of those who admire his artistry object to his dark view of human nature.

Trevor's next three novels, *Mrs. Eckdorf in O'Neill's Hotel* (1969), *Miss Gomez and the Brethren* (1971), and *Elizabeth Alone* (1973), reflect Trevor's fascination with the lives of women. He has said that he finds himself uninteresting, but he is intensely curious about the lives of people whose experiences he has not shared; he creates his characters so that he can learn from them. Apparently he succeeds, for his sympathetic portrayals of female characters in both his novels and stories are often praised by critics.

In his second collection of short fiction, *The Ballroom of Romance and Other Stories* (1972), Trevor continues to write about lonely and isolated people, but he begins to explore marriage and family life more extensively. In a 1986 interview with Nicholas Shakespeare he states that, as the child of an unhappy couple, he is fascinated by marriage as "It is the closest of all relationships because people choose. They dig their own graves." As one might expect from this comment, Trevor often paints a dark picture of marriage. The obvious resemblance of several married couples in his novels and short stories is intentional. When Trevor believes that a character is not developed as truthfully as possible, he repeats his experiment in another work until he is satisfied. In addition to portraying marriage as a social convention, his second collection probes the complexity of sexual relationships in ways only suggested in his earlier stories. His first stories of rural Ireland also appear in this volume, extending his concern not only for people as victims of each other but for "the sadness of fate, the things that just happen to people," as he observes in a 1983 interview with Amanda Smith.

In the title story a sad fate is borne by a woman in rural Ireland. Bridie – a plain, thirty-six-year-old spinster burdened with the care of her crippled father and the running of a farm – finds her only outlet in Saturday nights at the dance hall, a shabby setting that contrasts ironically with the romantic Cole Porter songs played by the local band. Years ago Bridie had lost her chance at marriage with Patrick Grady when he was stolen from her by another woman. The marriageable men, those with ability and ambition, have moved to the city or left Ireland. The available bachelors are three unattractive, middle-aged men as lethargic as their farm animals. These three are "wedded already, to stout and whiskey and laziness, to three old mothers somewhere up in the hills."

Dano Ryan, a musician with more sensitivity than the local farmers, is a possible husband, but Bridie sees that another woman intends to claim him. Refusing to indulge in self-pity, and understanding that she is becoming a foolish figure at the dance hall, Bridie decides to give up her Saturday nights. She allows herself to be taken home by the loutish Bowser Egan, who, during painfully fumbling attempts at lovemaking in a farmer's field, of-fers his half-drunken proposal. When his mother dies, he will sell his farm and use the money to im-prove someone else's property. After he has spent the money, Bridie believes, "he would think of get-ting married because he'd have nowhere to go, be-cause he'd want a fire to sit at and a woman to cook food for him." Bridie ends the story with her proph-ecy: "She would marry Bowser Egan because it would be lonesome being by herself in the farm-house." Bridie's small tragedy, her painful accep-tance of reality, is a metaphor for the economic real-ities of rural Ireland. As always in a Trevor story, however, the emphasis is less on the meaning of po-litical or historical events than on the compassion-ate portrayal of an ordinary person without heroic qualities who must settle for what little life has to offer.

In "Access to the Children" Malcolmson, a London father who has divorced his wife to take up with a younger woman, spends the day with his two daughters. The children, innocent truth-tellers who observe events beyond their understanding, report that their mother has a new friend (an Irishman, ironically). Malcolmson, whose lover has proved fickle and abandoned him, drinks his way through the day and is inebriated when he returns the chil-dren to his former wife. He begs her to resume their marriage, saying that he has made a mistake. The reader understands that Malcolmson's hope for achieving his past happiness is a delusion: his for-mer wife feels nothing for him but pity; she will in-deed marry her new lover, whom the daughters have already accepted as a father. His "mistake," like that of Miss Winton, is irredeemable. Malcolm-son may also be paying the price for the new free-dom of the 1960s that raised expectations for sexual adventure outside of marriage.

In another view of marriage, "The Grass Wid-ows," an older woman married to a boorish, selfish man sees an early version of her own unhappiness in a honeymooning couple. She tries to warn the young bride of the life that awaits her. In an espe-cially vivid scene the older woman overhears from an adjoining bedroom the shockingly insensitive be-havior of the young husband as he asserts his mari-tal rights. The truth-teller's message falls on deaf ears, of course; the bride naively believes that she and her husband will be happy together. Three other stories in the collection, "An Evening with John Joe Dempsey," "A Nice Day at School," and "A Choice of Butchers," have as their subject the initiation of children and adolescents into the dark side of sexuality. "O Fat White Woman" is another school story, this time concerning the death of a stu-dent caused by a sadistic master.

Auberon Waugh, in the *Spectator* (13 May 1972), while noting the bleakness of Trevor's imag-ined world, calls several of the stories in *The Ball-room of Romance* "as excellent as it is possible for a short story to be — as well-written, meticulously ob-served, ingeniously constructed, generously con-ceived — deserving to be treated as classics of the form." Schirmer praises Trevor's increasing skill in balancing multiple points of view to create an ironic distance between reality and the self-perceived world of his characters, with sympathy for their plights.

Trevor's next collection, *Angels at the Ritz and Other Stories,* was published in 1975. The title story describes the new sexual freedom of the time, with two London suburban couples engaging in the fash-ionable practice of wife swapping. The final disillu-sionment belongs to one of the wives who, comply-ing with her husband's need for new sexual ex-ploits, understands that they have lost their inno-cence and have "fallen" into the complacency of middle age. Trevor's title also suggests that they have fallen from a former state of grace.

"The Distant Past" is a much-praised story about a brother and sister, both elderly Irish Protes-tants. Economic hard times follow the renewal of "the troubles" in a small town dependent on tour-ism. As the woman understands at the end of the story, the good years of their friendly relations with the townspeople are over: "Because of the distant past they would be friendless. It was worse than being murdered in their beds." In "Angels of the Ritz" and "The Distant Past," as well as other sto-ries in the collection, Trevor portrays the small tragedies caused by the complex interweaving of individuals' actions and historical events.

"Teresa's Wedding" is a brutally painful ob-servation of an Irish Catholic marriage. The bride is pregnant, and while she and her fiancé do not care for each other, religion and social convention re-quire the ceremony. The wedding reception pro-ceeds with the ironic collusion of the relatives, the priest, and the other guests in the pretense that this is a happy occasion. In answer to her new hus-band's question Teresa admits that she did in fact have a brief affair with his best friend. But, as she observes, at least there can be absolute truth be-tween them because they have no illusions.

In two stories Trevor touches on racial issues which are a frequent subtext in his pieces. In "After-noon Dancing" a middle-aged London woman con-ducts a harmless flirtation with a Jamaican, but she

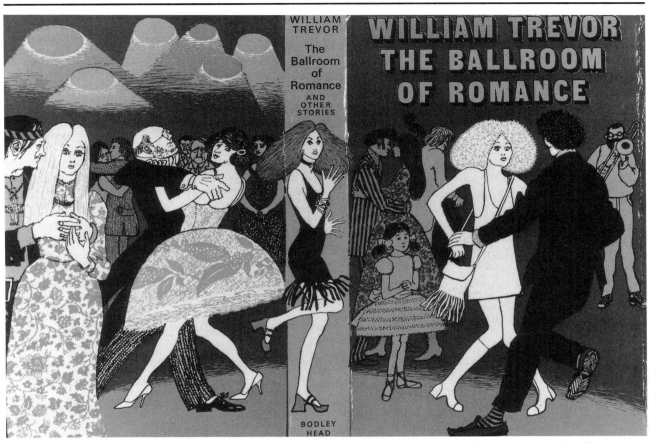

Dust jacket for Trevor's second collection of short fiction, which explores marriage, family life, and sexual realtionships

is unable to accept his friendship because of their racial difference. In "A Complicated Nature" an eccentric man is repelled by the exotic strangeness of a Jewish woman who enlists his help in concealing her love affair. The situation is comically bizarre: the woman's married lover has died in her bed, she thinks, and she must dispose of the body to avoid scandal. Ultimately the "dead" lover recovers and walks away.

In a more realistic story, "Mrs. Silly," Trevor dissects the painful experience of a British schoolboy who, in order to conform to his classmates' rigid adolescent code of behavior, must publicly reject his beloved mother for her lack of social class. As several reviewers have noted, Trevor seldom writes graphically about sex and violence; nevertheless, the reader is always aware of their presence in his stories. Paul Theroux observes that in *Angels at the Ritz* Trevor creates "the clearest and most original prose in this generation and a compassionate balance of fascination and sympathy, real people of flesh and blood out of characters another writer would dismiss as goons or drudges."

Trevor's next novel, *The Children of Dynmouth* (1976), describes the havoc wreaked by a malicious adolescent in an English resort town. Trevor's fourth collection of short fiction, *Lovers of Their Time and Other Stories* (1978), continues to describe the unhappiness of those damaged by life: an old woman victimized by lower-class teenagers, a vengeful homosexual who destroys several families by revealing former schoolboy indiscretions, and a neglected child who in his loneliness resurrects a ghost as a companion. Trevor also extends his range and his exploration of women's lives with a story about a lesbian relationship. He intensifies several of his themes, notably the suffering caused by the Anglo-Irish conflict and the futile attempt to recapture the past.

The title story, unusual for Trevor in its sympathetic portrayal of romantic love (the background music is the Beatles' "Eleanor Rigby"), celebrates an adulterous relationship consummated over a period of years in the public bathroom of an elegant hotel because of the couple's lack of money for a suitable meeting place. Three stories, sometimes called a novella within the collection, relate the life of Matilda, who, nostalgic for the bygone era of the pleasant English manor life, makes an impossible attempt to re-create the past and ends by destroying her marriage and descending into madness.

"Death in Jerusalem" is one of Trevor's most convincing stories of Irish Catholics. Two brothers – Father Paul, a priest, and Francis, a bachelor shopkeeper who remains at home to care for his aging mother – take a trip to Jerusalem. Father Paul, a generous man with strong physical appetites, wants to give his ascetic brother Francis a memorable experience to enliven his carefully regulated life. The actual death in the story is that of the old mother in Ireland during the brothers' trip. The Jerusalem "death" is caused by Father Paul, who, not wishing to deprive his brother of his travel experience and knowing that it will make no difference to the dead mother, delays telling him the news. Francis, consumed by guilt, insists on returning immediately. Father Paul consoles himself with drink, knowing that Francis "would sit alone in the lace-curtained sitting room, lonely for the woman who had made him what he was, married forever to her memory." Father Paul understands the death of the relationship with his brother and that he himself will never again return home.

The Anglo-Irish story "Another Christmas" describes the end of a friendship between the Protestant Mr. Joyce and a working-class Catholic couple over an incident of violence in Northern Ireland. The most highly praised story in the collection is "Attracta," whose heroine is a Protestant teacher in Northern Ireland. She attempts to deal with her past and the frightening emotions it evokes (her parents were mistakenly killed in a rebel attack) and to educate her young pupils to the horrors of the conflict. She tells them in graphic detail about two recent political murders. The penalty for her truth-telling, once the children report her behavior, is forced retirement.

In the *New York Review of Books* (19 April 1979) V. S. Pritchett praises the moral insights of "Attracta" and other stories by Trevor, seeing as a common theme the motif of the "explosion of conscience," or moment of rare courage when ordinary people revolt against events that others accept as reality. The characters, Pritchett remarks, are "crucified by the continuity of evil and cruelty in human history," and Trevor gives them "an obscure dignity and pride which they are either too shy or too unskilled to reveal at once." Benjamin DeMott (*Atlantic*, May 1978) calls the stories in *Lovers of Their*

Time "bold, original, energetically ambitious work, marvelously assured and . . . British to the core."

Trevor's next novel, *Other People's Worlds* (1980), is the story of a psychotic con man. Schirmer notes that this work demonstrates that Trevor is "necessarily and morally engaged with the society in which he lives." The title story of Trevor's fifth collection, *Beyond the Pale and Other Stories* (1981), attracted the usual divided critical commentary on both sides of the Atlantic. While some reviewers praised "Beyond the Pale" as one of his finest stories, others found the writing excessively emotional and the character motivation insufficiently developed. A story within a story, the framing narrative set in the 1960s introduces four English people who are vacationing, as they have done for several years, at Glencorn Lodge, a hotel in County Antrim owned by an English couple. The vacationers, all in their midfifties, are the narrator, Dorothy Milson, or Milly; Dekko, who "though he takes out girls who are half his age has never managed to get around to marriage"; and Major and Cynthia Strafe. They play bridge and roam the countryside, having "fallen hopelessly in love with every variation of this remarkable landscape."

Milly reports that the "unpleasantness" was not apparent at all, that "nothing could be further away from all the violence than Glencorn Lodge." Milly reveals that she and Major Strafe are lovers. Confident of her own sexual attraction, she pities "poor old Cynth," her lover's wife. The insensitivity of Major Strafe and Dekko is revealed in their malicious delight in practical jokes (they once sent a false telegram to a male friend from a housemaid, announcing her pregnancy).

The narrator and the Major return from a side trip to find Cynthia in a state of hysteria. An Irishman, after unburdening himself to her, has committed suicide by walking into the sea. Milly, Dekko, and the Major agree that the unfortunate event is not good for the hotel's business and should be hushed up. The distraught Cynthia, however, is compelled to tell the man's tale, which becomes the story within the framing narrative. The childhood sweetheart of the dead man had become a terrorist and was killed in London while assembling a bomb. Cynthia, the only one of the four who has troubled herself to learn something of Irish history, is an imaginative woman who re-creates these events in her mind. Her three listeners, as well as the owners of the hotel, believe she is inventing a fantasy and that the man's death was an accident. The Major and the hotel owners sternly advise Cynthia to pull herself together. Instead, she becomes even louder, crying out against the violence in Ireland, saying that the English "as civilized people create a garden" in Ireland, ignoring real life "beyond the Pale." Cynthia ends her outburst by announcing that she knows of the affair between the narrator and her husband.

As with many of Trevor's truth-tellers, Cynthia's moral sensitivity and loss of emotional control when she is not believed are interpreted by the others as madness. Milly selfishly regrets that her comfortable deception has been uncovered and that her pleasant vacation has been destroyed by Cynthia's incoherent revelations. The narrator completes her self-portrait (and ultimately discredits her own account) by saying it was unfortunate that Cynthia, rather than the Irishman, had not walked into the sea.

Trevor's connection of the English insensitivity to (and complicity in) the troubled history of Ireland is one of his recurring themes although not usually stated so unequivocally as in this story. Schirmer calls "Beyond the Pale" one of Trevor's most vital revelations of "a humanistic vision of moral responsibility." In a *New York Times* review (3 February 1982) Anatole Broyard, however, finds the character motivation weak, saying that in this instance Trevor is not a "master of understatement" but is seemingly "wary of inviting full-blooded people into his stories, as if they might break up the delicate furniture of his art."

Other stories in *Beyond the Pale* include "The Bedroom Eyes of Mrs. Vansittart," an observation of American tourists in Italy. Reflecting the concerns of his time, Trevor also writes of the anguish of a middle-aged London couple whose son is a drug addict in "Sunday Drinks." In "Autumn Sunshine" Trevor returns to his Anglo-Irish theme by portraying a widowed Irish Protestant clergyman who helplessly watches the development of a disastrous affair between his daughter and an irresponsible young Englishman who has a pseudo-interest in the history of the troubles as played out in the 1798 massacre of twelve Irish men and women in a local barn. "Mulvihill's Memorial," a wickedly humorous tale of the seedy side of London life, involves a commercial artist with a side interest in pornographic movies. He dies unexpectedly, leaving behind a voyeur's home movie of two fellow employees having sex. Three other stories in the collection concern Irish Catholics. Ted Solotaroff, evaluating Trevor's fiction and *Beyond the Pale* in particular (*New York Times Book Review*, 21 February 1982), says that "It strengthens the human bond in an age desperately in need of that, a task that most great fiction writers of previous centuries have taken for granted."

Trevor's tenth novel, *Fools of Fortune*, was published in 1983, along with the Penguin paperback *The Stories of William Trevor*, which includes the stories from his first five collections. *Fools of Fortune*, called variously a romance or a tragedy, is his first full-length treatment of the Anglo-Irish conflict. The novel is set in the twentieth century, but it calls up events from the famine years of the mid 1800s and relates the parallel stories of the doomed love of an Irishman and an Englishwoman. Schirmer calls this novel Trevor's best for its portrayal of character, thematic development, and use of multiple points of view, as well as "the sheer quality of its prose," which establishes Trevor as "a master of prose fiction." Although some reviewers have found the plot and character development melodramatic, Irish-American novelist Mary Gordon, in the *New York Review of Books* (22 December 1983), rejects this interpretation, calling the novel a highly moral and compassionate creation of characters "who are doomed not by their natures, but by the nature of Irish history."

In Trevor's seventh collection of short fiction, *The News from Ireland and Other Stories* (1986), six of the stories have an Irish setting, and four are set in Italy. The title story, echoing the theme and subject of *Fools of Fortune*, departs from convention both in its length (thirty-seven pages) and its historical setting during the famine years of 1837 to 1839. The Fogartys, an Irish Protestant brother and sister, are butler and cook for the Anglo-Irish Pulvertaft family. Again using multiple viewpoints Trevor alternates the perspectives of Mr. Fogarty; Mrs. Pulvertaft; the daughters of the house, who are contemplating marriage; and the diary entries of Anna Maria Heddoe, the homesick English governess. Mr. Fogarty, who wishes that the Pulvertaft family would die off so the estate can be "driven back into the clay it came from," further complicates the narrative viewpoint by reading and reacting to the governess's diary. The Pulvertafts, far from being stereotypically cruel English landlords, attempt to relieve the suffering of the Irish by providing a soup kitchen and employing the men to build an unnecessary road on the estate.

A local child is born with the stigmata of Christ, lives briefly, then dies. The Irish Catholics interpret the event as a miracle, but the Protestant English view this belief as characteristic Irish irrationality. Miss Heddoe, however, is deeply disturbed by the event and the suffering of the Irish, and she questions the meaning of her life. In the midst of the famine the daughters of the house are married and will presumably produce heirs to the family line. Eventually Miss Heddoe accepts the proposal of Erskine, the estate manager, in what promises to be one of the loveless, but practical, marriages so frequently described by Trevor. Miss Heddoe is described by Mr. Fogarty in the story's conclusion: "Stranger and visitor, she has learnt to live with things." Schirmer has judged the story's strength to be the contrasting viewpoints represented by Fogarty, the bitter man from the old tradition, and Miss Heddoe, the young innocent forced (to Fogarty's considerable satisfaction) to shape herself to reality.

"The Property of Colette Nervi," Trevor's homage to Guy de Maupassant, traces the confluence of history, the poverty of rural Irish life, and individual desires. Dolores Mullally, a twenty-six-year-old woman with an attractive face but a leg twisted by polio, is considered unmarriageable. She escapes by reading American Wild West novels and watching romantic films. The Irish crossroads town in which her mother keeps a shop has become a tourist attraction because of its ancient stones. Four years previously a Frenchwoman, Colette Nervi, accompanied by her lover, left her handbag on the roof of a rented car on her way to visit the stones.

Eventually Henry Garvey, "a large, slow man at forty, known in the neighborhood for his laziness and his easy-going nature," proposes to Dolores, an act the townspeople view as a stroke of fortune for the crippled woman. Garvey, lonely after the death of his father, intends to take over the shop when Dolores's mother dies. A miserly man, he gives his bride a gift that he claims belonged to his mother, a necklace with twenty-two blue jewels. Dolores, however, knows its origin. On her wedding day, suspecting that her husband will someday abandon her when he tires of her deformity, she acquiesces in the deception. Wearing the necklace of Colette Nervi concealed under her wedding dress, Dolores believes she can absorb the romance of its magic, imagining the sophisticated Frenchwoman in her lover's embrace: "The two faces were pressed into each other like the faces of the man and the woman in *From Here to Eternity*."

"Bodily Secrets," another Irish story, is an unsparing view of the compromises of marriage. The wealthy widow Mrs. O'Neill, fifty-nine and depressed by the deterioration of her once beautiful body, marries Mr. Agnew. She learns that he too has "bodily secrets," as he is a homosexual who spends weekends in Dublin with his lovers. In "Virgins," a story set in Ireland and Italy, two middle-

aged Irishwomen (one Catholic, one Protestant) recall their childhood friendship during World War II, one that was broken by the fatally ill Ralph de Courcy, who cultivated their adolescent romantic fantasies. This story is considered one of Trevor's best for its portrayal of the nostalgic longing for a past that cannot be recovered.

The News from Ireland was favorably reviewed, but with the usual reservations about the pessimism of Trevor's artistic vision. Elizabeth Spencer, in the *New York Times Book Review* (8 June 1986), finds the English stories less than convincing but praises the Irish ones for their "flow and power." She notes that the title story, "for its grasp of a historical moment, penetration of character, and dramatic force . . . comes close to creating the resonant effect of a full novel." Trevor's next novel, *The Silence in the Garden* (1988), like *Fools of Fortune,* is set in Ireland. Both deal with the declining fortunes of Anglo-Irish families in the wake of political upheavals.

While Trevor's collections of short fiction usually take their titles from one of the stories, his seventh volume, *Family Sins and Other Stories* (1990), reveals its theme in the title. Trevor's increasing concern with Ireland is evident; eight of the twelve stories are set in that country. Where *The Silence in the Garden* pits the desires of the individual against the events of history, *Family Sins* examines the relationships between individual sinners and their victims. In two stories the sinner is motivated by pure malice. More often, however, Trevor exposes the complexity of human relationships, with sin requiring both the vulnerability of the victim and the understandable – but unforgivable – needs of the exploiter.

In "Events at Drimaghleen," set in contemporary rural Ireland, the deaths of three people are solved to the satisfaction of the provincial religious community, which interprets the tragedy as a case of thwarted romantic love. An Irish mother, "strange in the head" and determined to keep her son to herself, has apparently killed the woman he loves rather than lose him. The young woman, Maureen, is seen as a martyr to love. However, cynical media people from Dublin, catering to their audience's appetite for scandal, arrive on the scene to ferret out a less comforting but more probable answer: the "saintly" Maureen was herself the killer. The question is not simply one of justice (the three principals are, after all, dead and beyond punishment), but the right of individual privacy versus public titillation. The story raises the question as to whether revelation of the truth justifies the anguish of the bereaved family and the retreat of Maureen's mother into insanity.

In "A Husband's Return" a rural Catholic family refuses to acknowledge the implications of the death of one daughter as the result of an abortion, illegal in Ireland and a sin in the eyes of the church. The dead daughter was the lover of her sister's husband, with whom she had run off. Family blame is placed on the wife for having chosen a "scoundrel" for her husband rather than on the behavior of the man, who clearly is the true sinner. In both "Events at Drimaghleen" and "A Husband's Return" Trevor pits the suffering of the individual against the community's need to maintain its conventional moral equilibrium. These stories suggest that it is not only the individual but the entire community that must create a mythology in order to accommodate the horror of reality. While his critics disagree, Trevor considers himself a religious writer, and these stories support his self-assessment.

In "Kathleen's Field" a poverty-stricken farmer needs a loan from a well-to-do tavern owner to purchase the field that will keep the family solvent. As a condition of the loan he agrees to exchange the services of his daughter Kathleen as a maid in the tavern owner's household. The true bargain, as Kathleen soon learns, is that she must serve the sexual needs of the man of the house, who well understands that she will not report him. The story is a grotesque inversion of the martyrdom of Maria Goretti, a figure from Roman Catholic hagiography. Goretti, an Italian peasant girl whose chastity is revered by Irish Catholics, chose to die a virgin rather than succumb to the advances of her seducer. Kathleen, damned by her sexual "sin" in both death and life, will assure the economic survival of her family.

"In Love with Ariadne" and "The Printmaker" explore, in a gentler tone, the theme of failed love haunted by events of the past. Ariadne, having internalized the shame of her father's death (he was a pedophile who committed suicide when discovered), is unable to find the thread that will rescue her from her prison and so retreats to a convent. As a teenager Charlotte, whose consciousness dominates "The Printmaker," formed a passionate attachment to a married man and is unable to find love again. She wonders: "Does it happen . . . in other people's lives that a single event influences all subsequent time?" The stories in *Family Sins* suggest Trevor's affirmative answer to this question, a prominent

theme in his fiction. While most reviewers saw this collection as confirming Trevor's mastery of the short story, several faulted him for plowing familiar ground. If, however, the characters and settings are familiar, Trevor has reinvented them to explore such contemporary issues as the abortion question and the increasing encroachment of the media into the lives of individuals – evidence that he continues to see moral questions as central to his artistic vision. *Two Lives: Reading Turgenev and My House in Umbria* (1991) includes two novellas that have elicited the usual conflicting judgments from critics.

Although Trevor abandoned his work as a sculptor early in his career, he believes that this artistic form has strongly influenced his fiction. When he writes, he said in a 1983 interview with Smith, he is "obsessed by form and pattern – the actual shape of things, the shape of a novel or the shape of a short story." Continuing his comparison of the visual arts to writing, Trevor sees the novel as a Renaissance painting, but the short story as an impressionist work. In a 1989 interview with Mira Stout he further defines the short story as "the art of the glimpse . . . an explosion of truth," whose "strength lies in what it leaves out . . . a total exclusion of meaninglessness." Although he is usually identified as a British author, Trevor calls himself an Irish writer. James F. Kilroy, describing the qualities that distinguish the Irish short story from American and British fiction, says that Irish writers excel in achieving irony through the authority of the narrator, who has the power to reveal or withhold information. Trevor is unquestionably a master of this narrative technique.

Trevor's best work reflects his obsession with the conflict between the individual's moral strivings and the demands of historical events beyond his or her control. Consistent with his belief that the experiences of childhood indelibly mark one's character, Trevor most often (and most believably) has chosen rural Ireland as the territory where this battle – both tragic and comic – is joined. Unlike some of his critics Trevor does not see in his fiction an absence of hope, but rather a vision of the truth. In his interview with Stout he states: "Truth is the most important thing there is, and if you lose sight of it, your writing will be destroyed in the end." The vigor of his fiction, particularly his short stories, is rooted in his belief in the significance of those anguished moments in the lives of ordinary people when they must struggle to make sense of their own limited choices in the time and place to which fate has assigned them.

Interviews:

"William Trevor," in *The Writer's Place: Interview on the Literary Situation in Contemporary Britain,* edited by Peter Firchow (Minneapolis: University of Minnesota Press, 1974), pp. 304–312;

Mark Ralph-Bowman, "William Trevor," *Transatlantic Review,* 53/54 (1976): 5–12;

Amanda Smith, "William Trevor," *Publishers Weekly,* 224 (28 October 1983): 80–81;

Nicholas Shakespeare, "Distiller of the Extraordinary: William Trevor," *Times* (London), 15 March 1986, p. 23;

Mira Stout, "The Art of Fiction CVIII: Interview with William Trevor," *Paris Review,* 31 (Spring 1989): 119–151.

References:

Julian Gitzen, "The Truth-Tellers of William Trevor," *Critique: Studies in Modern Fiction,* 21, no. 1 (1979): 59–72;

Robert Hogan, "Old Bucks, Young Bucks, and New Women: The Contemporary Irish Short Story," in *The Irish Short Story: A Critical History,* edited by James F. Kilroy (Boston: Twayne, 1984), pp. 169–215;

James F. Kilroy, Introduction to *The Irish Short Story: A Critical History,* pp. 1–19;

Robert E. Rhodes, "William Trevor's Stories of the Troubles," in *Contemporary Irish Writing,* edited by James D. Brophy and Raymond J. Porter (Boston: Twayne, 1983), pp. 95–114;

Gregory A. Schirmer, *William Trevor: A Study of His Fiction* (London & New York: Routledge, 1990);

John J. Stinson, "Replicas, Foils, and Revelation in Some Irish Short Stories of William Trevor," *Canadian Journal of Irish Studies,* 11 (December 1985): 17–26;

Paul Theroux, "Miseries and Splendors of the Short Story," *Encounter,* 39 (September 1972): 69–75.

Frank Tuohy

(2 May 1925 -)

Alan Price
Pennsylvania State University — Hazleton

See also the Tuohy entry in *DLB 14: British Novelists Since 1960: Part 2.*

BOOKS: *The Animal Game* (London: Macmillan, 1957; New York: Scribners, 1957);

The Warm Nights of January (London: Macmillan, 1960);

The Admiral and the Nuns, with Other Stories (London: Macmillan, 1962; New York: Scribners, 1963);

The Ice Saints (London: Macmillan, 1964; New York: Scribners, 1964);

Portugal (London: Thames & Hudson, 1968; New York: Viking, 1970);

Fingers in the Door, and Other Stories (London: Macmillan, 1970; New York: Scribners, 1970);

Yeats (London & New York: Macmillan, 1976);

Live Bait and Other Stories (London: Macmillan, 1978; New York: Holt, Rinehart & Winston, 1978);

The Collected Stories (London: Macmillan, 1984; New York: Holt, Rinehart & Winston, 1984; Harmondsworth, U.K.: Penguin, 1986).

OTHER: "Dreams of Unfair Women," in *Winter's Tales,* new series 1 (London: Constable, 1985), pp. 181–189.

Frank Tuohy is an accomplished prose stylist whose three collections of short stories and three novels have received critical praise in England and the United States. Having lived and taught for much of his adult life in foreign locales, Tuohy frequently chooses the lives of exiles as his subjects, setting his stories and novels in Brazil, Poland, and Japan, as well as in his native England. His fiction offers penetrating psychological insights, vivid settings, and exact — if often painful — renderings of social scenes. Reviewers have compared his traditional fictional forms and realistic technique with those of Anton Chekhov, V. S. Pritchett, William Trevor, and Elizabeth Bowen. Tuohy's stories have appeared in the *Transatlantic Review,* the *New Yorker, Cornhill Magazine, Encounter, Nova,* the *Listener,* the *Times* (London), *Harper's-Queen, Voices,* and *London Magazine;* and they have won many distinguished prizes and awards.

John Francis Tuohy was born on 2 May 1925 in Uckfield, Sussex, England, to Patrick Gerald and Dorothy Annandale Tuohy. His father's family was originally from county Cork, Ireland, and was distantly related through marriage to James Joyce. The Tuohy family immigrated to England in the late nineteenth century and joined the professional classes. Tuohy's father was a doctor. His mother's heritage was Scottish. His parents blended puritanical elements from their Catholic and Presbyterian backgrounds so that Tuohy, born when they were both nearly forty, remembers being brought up with a sense that "they had already retired, and . . . that nothing was as good as it had been." In addition to the psychological weight of his dour parents, Tuohy was born with a congenital heart defect that restricted his physical activities and undoubtedly affected his early view of the world. By the time the hole in his heart was surgically repaired in 1960, any romantic or idealistic vision of life appears to have escaped him completely.

As a young boy Tuohy was first sent to a rigorous preparatory school with a naval emphasis; there, he says, he "learned a fairly lasting sense of inadequacy." His situation was somewhat better at the Stowe School in Buckinghamshire, where he spent the early years of World War II. The consequence of his always "feeling rather ill" and necessarily being excluded from the rough-and-tumble of preparatory-school life seems to have confirmed him, as it did George Orwell, in the role of the critical observer.

Tuohy left the Stowe School in 1943 and was rejected by the army because of his heart condition. He entered King's College, Cambridge University, where he studied philosophy and English literature and was graduated with first class honors in 1946.

Frank Tuohy (courtesy of Texas A&M University)

That was the Cambridge of F. R. Leavis and his disciples, who, Tuohy remembered, "had a preemptive sneer for every living poet and novelist without exception." Tuohy, however, already knew that he wanted to write. He had composed some short stories, almost all of which were lost "by a well-known London literary figure" — a loss he recalled with bitterness more than twenty years later.

After World War II, as millions of demobilized men were being thrown into the labor pool, England was not a place ripe with prospects for a fresh university graduate. Therefore Tuohy sought teaching jobs at foreign universities. His first assignment was as a lecturer in English at the University of Turku in Finland. In 1950 he moved to Brazil, where he divided his time for the next six years between his writing and his teaching duties as a professor of English at the University of São Paulo.

Brazil provided the setting for his first two novels, *The Animal Game* (1957) and *The Warm Nights of January* (1960), as well as for the most fully developed stories in his first collection, *The Admiral and the Nuns, with Other Stories* (1962). *The Animal Game*

adumbrates several themes and techniques that follow in his stories and other novels. Set "far away, on the precarious underside of the world," in "the giant bone-white construction" of São Paulo, the novel examines an English expatriate ill-equipped to deal with the tangle of selfish and self-destructive lives he encounters in this exotic but potentially sinister location. The novel's dispassionate narrator, in the mode of those in works by Graham Greene and Joseph Conrad, records the downward spiral of the beautiful Celina Fonseca while the English exile, Robin Morris, finds himself "set apart, without even an attitude to fall back on."

In *The Animal Game* the grisly opening image of pigs beginning to devour one another after being locked in an unattended truck for three days becomes a central metaphor for the book. Soon the human characters in the international cast begin to take on animal traits. At a party, for example, a Polish film director's "vulture's eyes had unhooded and were glaring away" at his companion, a full-blooded Karaja Indian who "preened himself a little, like a wild bird." Tuohy's use of animal imagery to describe human behavior in this novel and his short stories reinforces an interpretation of life as a social jungle.

Tuohy's second novel, *The Warm Nights of January,* was written in Paris while he was thinking, he says, in Portuguese and French. Macmillan published the novel in England in 1960, but the principal story of an interracial love affair between a white woman and a black man led his American publisher, Scribners, to decline it. Tuohy acknowledges that it "is too special in background, I think, to be readily comprehensible."

The novel centers on the life of the divorced French expatriate artist Bella Magnard during the tumultuous days surrounding Christmas and Carnival in Rio de Janeiro. Again the cast is a deftly observed collection of international flotsam and jetsam. Bella maintains complex relationships with Hadriano, her black Brazilian lover; Alix, an aggressive Russian lesbian; Lucille, her philandering French sister-in-law; Mario, a deceitful young man who enters her life and causes chaos; and Eduardo, a puritanical Frenchman who tries to save her from the others. "Like all exiles," the narrator reminds the reader, "she experienced sudden yawning voids, where in her own country some habit of life or small social obligation would have offered fulfillment." Thus, the exile in Tuohy's fiction cannot depend on habit or custom to see him- or herself through an unknown situation but must constantly be inventing a reaction to the situation.

After publication of his novels Tuohy began to collect his short stories. In "Some Notes on Writing Stories" (*London Magazine,* March 1970) he offers a clear description of his approach to the short-story genre and his preferred subject: "Whenever I start writing a short story, I see the place first and then the people in it. . . . I write a lot about exiles who have gone too far to remain in any genuine contact with any social background." Each of Tuohy's three collections of short fiction, published at eight-year intervals, contains twelve stories. The progression of the geographical settings in the stories roughly parallels Tuohy's foreign university assignments. The first collection includes pieces set in South America, Poland, and England. Following the purchase of a house near Bath in 1967 and a prolonged residence in England, he placed the majority of the stories in the second collection in England. His third collection features a new fascination with Japan, along with continued attention to England and brief nods in the direction of the United States and France.

While the locations of his stories change, Tuohy maintains a constant theme: the alienation of the individual from a foreign culture or his own culture through the effects of class, age, or sexual orientation. What does change during the twenty-five years of his story writing is his attitude toward his subject, or his tone. His characters of the 1960s are the nihilistic and anomic heirs of the existential world of Jean-Paul Sartre and Albert Camus. For instance, when Celina in *The Animal Game* comes across a group of Japanese children on a Brazilian beach, she experiences "a feeling of complete alienation, of belonging to a world so broken up that no relationships exist at all, each person wading ahead alone through the mess until death." Tuohy's English characters of the 1960s have the scorched smell of the angry-young-man generation about them. During the 1970s his fictional world began to soften. While he still treated his characters with critical irony, satire and parody began to appear. In his most recent stories he has explored the genres of the ghost story and the political satire.

In *The Admiral and the Nuns* two of the most fully developed tales take place in South America. The title story concerns the hapless English wife of a Polish émigré who protects herself from the reality of her unhappy position in an industrial town in the interior of Brazil and evades responsibility for her squalid marriage by clutching her upper-class pedigree. Barbara Woroszylski relies on her heritage as the daughter of a British admiral, along with her Anglo-Catholic upbringing at the Holy Child convent school, to give her some standing in her alien community and marriage.

The detached first-person narrator comes to the settlement on a public-relations assignment and meets Stefan Woroszylski and his wife. He soon realizes his role in their personal drama: "They had used the truce provided by a stranger's presence for shock tactics, for outrageous raids into the other's emotional territory." Although Barbara counts on the background to make an ally of the narrator, his sympathies soon shift to Stefan, whose primitive pleasures of shooting wild dogs and drinking and whoring in the capital city have an understandable source in his peasant origins. As it frequently does in Tuohy's fiction, the landscape itself becomes an antagonist. After a riotous night in the city Stefan hitches a ride on a truck headed for the interior, "moving off into the dusty jail of this continent."

Tuohy's narrator is alert to the social and linguistic niceties of the local language: "In this country you asked about a child 'Is it a man or a woman?' " Tuohy's exiles depend on language and naming to allow them to know the limits and shapes of their foreign worlds. In a later story an Englishman visiting the "battered Eden" of Connecticut "wanted names to be given, not only to people but to things." (Also in later stories, Tuohy's adolescent characters self-consciously consider what to call their fathers: "Pa," "Daddy," "Father.") Tuohy captures the Germanic word placement of Stefan's explanation of his wife's isolation: " 'My friends are always speaking with me Polish. She [Barbara] have not friends among the womans in the settlement.' " As the faces and gestures of characters in *The Animal Game* are presented with bird imagery, Tuohy's characters here are frequently described in animal terms: Stefan "was short, with colorless hair and a snouty face. He reminded you of an otter or a pine marten – a benevolent, comic, European animal." When Stefan and the narrator have dinner in a German restaurant, the other diners are "Central European businessmen, of a tusked, wild-boar appearance."

The story's climax comes on the night of the Coronation Ball. When a florid Barbara tells the narrator that they "have a surprise for him," he thinks, with a deflationary irony, "Ever since I can remember, these words have possessed a more violent and sudden power to depress than almost any others." The British Club – decorated in red, white, and blue and hung with pictures of the queen and the duke of Edinburgh – is "like being inside a stamp album." When the drunken Stefan makes a pass at a young English girl, all the unpleasantness of his marriage comes out. In the end the narrator condemns Barbara for the failure of her marriage because she has used the easy "retreats into the cosiness of class and religion." "The Admiral and the Nuns" won the Katherine Mansfield Prize for 1960.

"Two Private Lives," another tale of alienation in an exotic location, takes place in the Spanish-speaking city of San Jaime in an unnamed South American country. The private lives of the title are those of the newly arrived English consul and Andrew Tripp, the British press officer in San Jaime since World War II. The story focuses on Tripp, who is lazy, lecherous, and, though his Spanish is excellent, "only reasonably conscientious at his job." Tripp and the consul maintain a public appearance of propriety and British reserve while privately letting their sexual lives run riot. The reader learns of the consul's perverted (though unnamed) pleasures with his camera during their afternoon and evening outings. Tuohy's irony can be corrosive: "In the Consul's defense, it must be said that his experience of nonprofessional love was limited."

And there is assurance in his laconic style: "He assumed that the Press Officer had slept with Candida and was prepared to run risks in order to do so again. He was wrong."

When the two go to an Italian restaurant before a prearranged debauchery, they split the bill exactly in half at the consul's insistence. The punctiliousness of the consul creates a smug, smarmy atmosphere reinforced later by the appearance of a brothel: "Downstairs the place had been clean-looking, almost smart, but here the walls were leprous, the floor covered with unanalyzable filth." Like Kurtz in Conrad's *Heart of Darkness* (1902), these colonial officers have become detached from their ethical moorings and are adrift. At the end of the story the press officer, remembering conventional British moral clichés about "not letting the side down" and team spirit, saves the consul from recognition and embarrassment at a police station. The consul, however, demands that they split the bribe exactly in half (though it was his camera crashing to the pavement that alerted the police and caused the arrest) because, as he lamely asserts, "After all, you were in this too." "Two Private Lives" was chosen for inclusion in the first number (1955) of *Winter's Tales,* an annual anthology published by Macmillan drawing the best from the year's crop of British and Irish short stories.

Three other stories in this first collection are also set in South America. "Showing the Flag" captures the jingoistic bravado of Englishmen at the British Club who argue that the accidental shooting of a drunken English sailor is reason enough to show the gunboats to the natives. The patina of democracy at the club shows thin when one of the English businessmen declares, "I've been out here thirty years and I'm proud to say that I've never had a conversation with one of 'em, – apart from line of business, mind." When someone suggests that they all attend the funeral as a gesture of solidarity and patriotism, however, each begs off with an excuse of a rugby match or an appointment; their braggadocio is exposed as hypocritical posturing. In "Luck" an unemployed native waiter cannot believe his good fortune when he is propositioned by a fat North American woman on the beach.

"A Survivor in Salvador" – later included in *Publisher's Choice: Ten Short Story Discoveries* (a 1967 anthology of British and American short stories compiled by the editors at Scribners) and also selected for the sixth number of *Winter's Tales* – begins in Brazil. The exiled fifty-three-year-old Polish prince Krzystof Wahorski agrees to be a courier for a package of cocaine. Just as he reaches Salvador, his contact there is picked up by the police. Without money, friends, or even a rudimentary understanding of the local language, he tries unsuccessfully to sell the drug himself. After days of wandering around the scorching city, he is saved by a young prostitute.

"A Survivor in Salvador" offers an example of Tuohy's dexterity with narrative technique. The story is told from a conventional third-person point of view, with occasional shifts to the second person: "Christophe was not angry at this. Instead he felt the masochistic pleasure you get when people revert to type and behave exactly as you expect them to." Tuohy's narrative strategy of allowing a third-person narrator to slip into the second person to generalize about human behavior or to comment on the human condition occurs again when Christophe's money runs out and he is forced to sell his watch to a jeweler for an absurdly small sum: "You got money out of the poor by surliness and anger, when they were too far gone to resist." The second-person voice draws the reader in, as if to validate the generalization.

From 1958 to 1960 Tuohy was a contract professor at Jagiellonian University in Kraków, Poland; four of the stories in *The Admiral and the Nuns* take place in Poland. The drab landscape of postwar Poland is matched by the flat affect (the psychological phenomenon of an emotionless appearance) and justifiable paranoia of the people. Two stories deal with the politics of Polish university life. The least successful stories in the collection are those set in England. Two deal with teenage girls who are exploited by recently demobilized men. A third, "At Home with the Colonel," involves an old man whose daughter and her lesbian lover mock his attempt to introduce a young man into the house.

The Admiral and the Nuns received positive critical notices. In the *Saturday Review* (23 March 1963) Hoke Norris commented on the stories' Chekhovian manner – "quiet, deceptively matter-of-fact, without compromise or illusion or any desire to prettify the ugly" – and called the collection "a splendid achievement." Michele Murray (*Commonweal,* 8 March 1963) repeated the comparison to Chekhov but objected to what she thought was Tuohy's attitude of an "emotional tourist." The tone in Tuohy's early stories is certainly somber and sometimes malevolent. Some reviewers criticized his unrelieved pessimism, commenting on his "morbid outlook on life" and his "lugubriousness." His characters are trapped in a quirky universe where life is frequently cruel and occasionally hopeless.

Dust jacket for Tuohy's first collection of short fiction, which includes five stories set in South America

Responding to charges against his dark philosophical view, Tuohy has said that "the sense of displacement, loss, anxiety which happens to people derives from the world outside them. If I thought of it as starting inside, as being part of the Self, I probably would not write at all." The best for which Tuohy's exiles can hope is to make a private accommodation with life that allows them some private sense of dignity.

Tuohy's third novel, *The Ice Saints* (1964), takes place during the raw, wet months of April and May – the time of Saint Pancras, Saint Servace, and Saint Boniface, the Ice Saints – in Poland. The opening contrast between the cozy cheerfulness of the British Embassy in Warsaw and the barbed wire and bullet-pocked walls of the buildings just beyond sets up the tension between Rose Nicholson and her brother-in-law Witold Rudowski. Rose has given up her job in London to come to Poland to persuade her sister and brother-in-law to allow her to take her nephew back to England, where he has been left a small inheritance. During her weeks in Poland Rose has an affair with a secret-police agent assigned to keep an eye on her and thus inadvertently scuttles all her planning. The only relief to the ruin brought about by Rose's patronizing plan is the energy exhibited by her determined brother-in-law, who maintains his ambition in spite of his difficult situation.

For his second collection, *Fingers in the Door, and Other Stories* (1970), Tuohy returns to England for his setting and frequently to the period of his own youth for his subject. All twelve stories take place in England during or just after World War II. "The Palladian Bridge" is a gentle reminiscence of a boy's first brush with sexuality, carried out against the drone of bombers flying overhead on their way to daylight raids in Germany. The mature narrator looks back at the incident through the rich mixture of nascent sexuality and nostalgia associated with "that winged freedom of girls on bicycles during the war years (they were everywhere, spokes flashing, skirts flying, bare legs pistoning, as they swept past whistling ambushes of soldiers, past elderly gossips in Victory Gardens, on their way to work in factories, to buy rations, to give love)." A serious boy, Page-Barlow passes the time trying to memorize some lines from an anthology of contemporary poetry. When a serving girl from the preparatory school's dining hall asks him why he has two names, he knows vaguely that it has to do with his family's wealth, but his mother's cautionary voice is immediately in his ear, telling him not to discuss money with servants. Later he hears his father's inflection: "Then his father's voice took over from his mother's: 'So you had to get mixed up with a thief and a whore.' No, 'tart' was the correct word: it had the sticky sourness of old men's desires. 'A thief and a tart.' "

A second wartime story, "A War of Liberation," originally published in *Encounter,* is again told by a mature narrator, who recalls the "enclosed aquarium of childhood, where the thick air is like clear water holding everything in its place." Miss Featherstone, a retired headmistress of a girls' school, has adopted the twin sisters Heather and Olive Willock. Their liberation from an isolated country village and Miss Featherstone's scheme of indenturing them to teaching school is the subject of the story: "Sons could manage to get away, but daughters at this date found escape much harder. Pretty girls especially, growing up, felt increasingly trapped." The coming of the troops from Canada and the United States created the possibility of escaping as war brides.

The young narrator, like Tuohy the son of a physician, overhears the sobs of outwardly contented wives who visit his mother during the afternoon. The climax of the story turns on an ill-timed visit by Miss Featherstone. His mother is out, and the narrator, armed only with the evasions in which his parents have instructed him, turns the old woman away. Later he wonders whether he is partially responsible for her suicide. He concludes, rather hopelessly, "If I had been able to speak to her she would not have died. But like everyone else, I too was a symptom, a part of the evidence: we classify in order to deal with one another, and then we die."

Tuohy's presentation of wartime and the immediate postwar period frequently dwells on characters with less-than-patriotic motives. In "A Life Membership" two young demobilized, unemployed middle-class men exploit a drunken laborer who is squandering his disability allowance. Other characters in Tuohy's stories are marginalized by the British class system, their sexual preferences, or sometimes both. In "A Reprieve" and "A Special Relationship" two men confined to hospitals on the National Health Service plan are made to feel that their care is a charity and a drain. In addition, both men feel distanced from family and fellow patients because of their homosexuality. In "Discontinued Lines" a middle-aged matron is embarrassed by the open relationship between her television-pundit son and his Greek driver-companion.

Another theme in the English stories is the loss of rituals that traditionally brought solace during times of pain and death. With an anthropological detachment Tuohy looks at the customs of the suburban upper-middle class and finds that they have lost their instinct for compassion. In "Fingers in the Door" a real-estate agent from Surrey is taking his spoiled daughter and insecure, snobbish wife to London on a birthday outing when his fingers are accidentally smashed in the door of a railway compartment. Rather than sympathize, the daughter and wife scold the man for ruining their day, while he tries to placate them by observing through his pain, "Look, love, there's an interesting yellow tint coming up." When Graham Corbett in "A Floral Tribute" realizes that sleeping drugs and the efficiency of the nursing home and undertaker have conspired to take any sting out of his father's death, he can think only of alternative rituals that are outrageously melodramatic: "We ought to have six horses and plumes, hired carriages and mourners, paid masses for the dead, and Ma and Priscilla along, half fainting, drenched in a cloudburst of black veiling. We ought to be declaring that my father actually existed, instead of hustling him out of mind with an unpretentiousness that is conveniently inexpensive." Even the elaborate wreath sent by their well-meaning Italian au pair and the children is quickly dismantled to become a table centerpiece.

Tuohy is a master of the socially grating tone. He grinds incidents of embarrassment and social uneasiness finer and finer until the reader's flayed sensibilities look for escape. In "The Trap," first published in *Encounter,* Professor Haworth, recently returned from a teaching assignment in Poland, receives a telephone call from his former student Marysia Rodzinska. She has followed him to London at her first opportunity. Tuohy is frank about the sometimes ungrateful and unhappy nature of refugees: "Miss Rodzinska was still in the first stage of refugeedom: she thought herself powerful and important through having come from where she did, for having lived the way she did, through those long, hungry winters in which it always seemed to be six o'clock on a freezing morning. She believed the unfortunate could make bullying demands on the fortunate, whoever they were, and was ready to try this out on him."

In the desperation of her position she tells him that she has come to England especially to be with him. He pulls back from this kind of obligation, this entrapment, and finally he pushes her into a subway car. The reader's final vision of Rodzinska is of her "making small half-blind movements, like an animal searching incredulously around the walls of its trap." But both Haworth and Rodzinska are trapped within political and social boxes. Tuohy suggests that the arrogance of the refugee from Eastern Europe is similar in its rigidity to English exiles' dependence on the British Club. In both cases there are the instant comparisons with home and the sudden emphasis on customs that elevate the authenticity of life there over life in the new country.

Tuohy is able to capture the spirit of an age with a few selective details. His description of the way Rodzinska is dressed, for example, captures the poverty of style in postwar Poland: "She was wearing a salmon pink coat with a single button, with sandals of a different gray; her handbag was gray plastic. She belonged in fact to the Plastic Age of communism, where people no longer look proletarian but lower middle class." Frequently his prose style takes on an epigrammatic terseness, as when the boy in "The Palladian Bridge" fails "to learn the pimp's arrogance, and without it he is only a mess." Tuohy's comparisons are brief and edged. Another

adolescent boy beginning a school holiday "still reeked of boarding school, as men do of prison."

Unobserved by all reviewers of the second collection is Tuohy's introduction of parody into several of the stories. In "Fingers in the Door" the sixteen-year-old daughter, for example, reads a trashy romantic horror novel, and with obvious relish Tuohy provides sample passages in the overblown style of the genre. In "A Special Relationship" he spoofs the theatrical genre of the sexual farce. He opens the slight tale "Thunderbolt" with a parody of the restaurant guidebook: "Colonel and Mrs. Stopham aim at providing 'traditional fare with variations of our own, as the whim takes us.' Booking advisable."

The most satiric of the stories is "Ructions, or A Historical Footnote to the Cold War," which casts the narrator as a fumbling historian looking into yet another British spy case. The humor derives partly from the juxtaposition of one of England's most conservative traditions — the nanny to wellborn children — with one of the most countercultural roles, the spy or secret agent. There are silly puns, as when Nanny filches detailed defense photographs from her employer's — Minister Grist-Miller's — briefcase. But Tuohy's richest comic moment comes when the narrator sifts his meager evidence to speculate on the moment of Nanny's recruitment and arrives at a hilarious Marxist literary interpretation of *Winnie-the-Pooh* (1926).

Three of the stories from *Fingers in the Door* were included in annual numbers of *Winter's Tales,* and the collection won Tuohy the E. M. Forster Memorial Award for 1971. In a review of the collection for the *New Leader* (5 October 1970) Kingsley Shorter acknowledged that "these stories are the work of a master craftsman," but he was repelled by the unrelieved gloom and "the pornography of social unease." Shorter also raised the question of whether Tuohy has a strain of misogyny because of the number of aggressive women in his stories. It is true that Tuohy's lesbian characters are unattractively presented; moreover, his homosexual men are frequently insecure and demanding. The charge of bias, however, is limited when one realizes that his heterosexual characters often exploit their partners. Other reviewers tempered their praise for Tuohy's technique with misgivings about his themes. For instance, while calling his style "sure-footed and supple" and complimenting his "ability to interlace his stories with well-observed details," Robert Moss, in the *Saturday Review* (7 November 1970) concluded that Tuohy's acknowledged skills as a social observer are "inadequate to his gloomy vision of life."

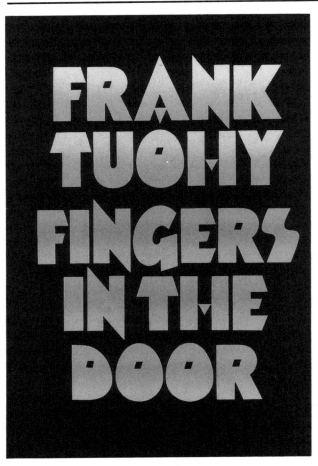

Dust jacket for Tuohy's 1970 collection of short stories, all of which are set in England during or just after World War II

Having done fiction – both long and short – and travel writing for a book of photographs of Portugal, Tuohy turned in the 1970s to biography. His life of W. B. Yeats was done at the suggestion of his publisher, Macmillan, which owned the American and British rights to the poet's papers. Tuohy had a longstanding interest in Yeats, aside from their shared Irish heritage, dating back to his undergraduate thesis on "Leda and the Swan." He frequently quotes Yeats in his stories. *Yeats* (1976) was greeted with warm praise from both the popular and scholarly press.

In Tuohy's third collection, *Live Bait and Other Stories* (1978), the stories continue to move toward satire and away from the detached, acerbic analyses of his first collection. They also reflect a geographical shift from South America and Poland to an interest in Japan and Japanese customs. From 1964 to 1967 Tuohy was a visiting professor at Waseda University in Tokyo, and he returned to Japan in the mid 1980s. Tuohy has commented on the uniqueness of Japan: "From having lived in other countries one can comprehend elements in Japanese life. But the contrary is not the case . . . Japan isn't like anywhere else."

The reader is eased into an introduction to Japan with "A Summer Pilgrim," set in the Sussex countryside. The story opens comically with a Japanese pilgrim, Professor Ukai, trying to negotiate the mysteries of the English coin telephone. Ukai arranges a visit with his friend Dunstan Roper, a poet who had lived in Japan for eight years and has written a book of verse about his impressions. The professor – accompanied by Miss Hitomi, Roper's former student and now a junior faculty member at Ukai's university in Kyoto – first makes a duty visit to Stratford-upon-Avon, where he sleeps through a Shakespeare play but insists on having his picture taken in front of the playwright's birthplace and Anne Hathaway's cottage.

While in Japan Roper, like other Westerners, clung to a belief in his personal distinctiveness:

> They had indeed accepted him, Miss Hitomi remembered, but as a typical English gentleman. Belonging to a nation of unwitting Platonists, they generalized from this single example to the ideal. When he tried not to be a bore, he bored them beautifully; followers of the Noh theater and the Tea Ceremony, they were connoisseurs of tedium. Dunstan Roper was sufficiently old (it is nearly impossible to guess the age of a Westerner), he was a poet, he was boring. They delighted in him.

Hearing that Roper has married for a second time, Ukai imagines the poet in his garden listening to the song of crickets (on announcing his return to England, Roper said that he missed the game of cricket) and attended by a respectful, subservient woman. When the day of the visit arrives, however, the professor begs off at the last minute on illness. (He spends the afternoon in a strip club in Soho.) So Miss Hitomi makes the visit alone, negotiating the second Mrs. Roper, who is large and garrulous, and laying her gifts before the poet. Complicating the national stereotype, the Japanese woman "despised the cultural training which made her look down at the carpet instead of directly into his blue eyes." She accepts lamb at lunch even though on a previous occasion the dish has made her sick.

When his wife leaves the room, the old poet fondles his shocked guest under the table. Later, after she has been ill but cannot bring herself to blame the lamb ("There can be no sense of proportion in such things. A story was told of a Japanese bride who, after breaking wind at her wedding ceremony, killed herself "), the old poet returns to his groping ways. The last obligation of the visit is for Miss Hitomi to take the ritual photograph of the poet in front of his house. She captures him "blinking a little but calm, like a rare animal that has grown used to its cage."

With "Nocturne with Neon Lights" Tuohy moves to Tokyo, and again the story turns on a confusing collision of customs. Despite courses in flower arranging, doll making, and brush drawing, Gillian Prescott cannot make herself content in Japan and after six months returns to England. Her businessman husband sees her off at Tokyo International Airport and then sets off almost immediately for an address sketched by the household maid, with whom he has begun an affair. The pictograph he hands the cabdriver is the only link he has to the girl, and "since Tokyo streets have no names, this was a vitally important document."

The cabdriver makes several inquiries, but his attempts to locate the address end in confusion. Finally he turns the exasperated Prescott over to three Japanese policemen, one of whom speaks English. The policeman explains that the Chinese character representing the address can be read in at least three ways. But the sexually consumed and intellectually exhausted Westerner cannot enjoy the ambiguity of his situation: "Prescott could only shout, and so nobody could hear what he said. He waved his arms, and so nobody could see him. By losing his temper, he entered the solipsist's nightmare in which everything exists except yourself." Reading his desperation the police direct him to a brothel, thinking sex is what Westerners are after anyway. Ironically in this case they are right.

"The Broken Bridge" is the third of the Japanese stories. The title is a parody of the bridge of cooperation between East and West and also an allusion to Arthur Miller's play The Bridge. The first-person narrator, a British professor of literature and composition at a university in Tokyo, meets Larry Breitmeyer, a young American theater director who is preparing a determinedly homosexual production of Miller's play. The leading actor, a student in the narrator's composition class, confides in an essay that he is disturbed by the director's concept of his role, especially the part where his character kisses another man: "It is very difficult for me to make this scene."

The narrator withholds judgment because he has seen Breitmeyer have success in action exercises pitting Japanese girls against boys and calling forth "that intense fury of the will which hides behind all the decorum and docility." The young student, however, does not claim his composition, and,

every time the narrator calls his name, the class hushes with "a sound of breath drawn in between closed teeth, followed by a small hard silence." Finally a delegation of students tells him that the student actor has committed suicide.

The description of Breitmeyer's departure written by the resident American gossip columnist allows Tuohy to indulge in his obvious enjoyment of parodying popular literary forms: "ABM's Tex Kirshenbaum and gorgeous Gaye (she of the thousand bangles!!) hosted a stand-up send-off last eve for Larry Breitmeyer. Larry, swinging theater buff, Noh-man and Kabuki expert, hies him westward this day on a wing-ding tour of Europe's capitals. Bon voyage, Larry, and Sayonara."

Two of the stories deal with the supernatural and delusional states of mind. "In the Hotel" is a report by an emotionally disturbed narrator spending the night with his brother in a country hotel on the edge of Wales. The narrator claims his "beast was in attendance," though the reader never learns what the "beast" is. "The Ghost Garden" features a much happier haunting. The spinster Susan Vincent restores Midsomer Cottage in Wiltshire so that her companion, the misanthropic biographer Bamford Chetwynd, may have a quiet place to write his lives of "redoubtable French ladies." Her consolation is to lay out a garden modeled on that of Victoria Sackville-West at Sissinghurst, with "visions of opening the garden to the public, in a year or two's time, in aid of the District Nurses."

In fitting up the house she employs two local carpenters and unexpectedly finds herself attracted to Sydney Woods, a forty-year-old craftsman. A problem arises when Sydney, a great gardener himself, looks at her imported hybrid plants and tells her they will not grow. He recommends that she switch to common varieties of flowers – delphiniums, goldenrod, and dahlias – and garden-variety vegetables, such as cabbages and scarlet runners. Sydney is killed one night in a motorbike accident, but he is not entirely gone. When spring arrives, Susan's garden looks "like something off a cheap calendar, or a picture to be cross-stitched on a tea cozy. No sooner had puce aubretia and yellow alyssum done their worst than pillar-box red poppies hurt the eyes, clashing with the hard orange of marigolds."

As if these common varieties of flowers were not reminder enough, she soon discovers a complete run of undistinguished vegetables: "Sydney Woods had won her heart and was proclaiming his triumph everywhere; everything was just as he would have wanted it." She smells the smoke of his bonfires and the aroma of his Player's Weights. In the final scene, having delivered a sullen Bamford Chetwynd to the airport to take off for a long research stay in Paris, she drives home in an ecstatic rush to be alone with her phantom lover. When she opens the door, she hears footsteps and whispers his name.

Some of the stories in the third collection deal satirically with class distinctions and patronizing exchanges between people of different backgrounds. In "The White Stick" the self-satisfied thirty-year-old writer Nigel Griffin is deputized to accompany a blind man on a subway trip across London. Griffin's moral superiority dissolves into shame when he discovers the man has lost a valuable briefcase. Griffin's wide mood swings show that his earlier condescending attitude toward the handicapped man actually masks a fragile sense of self-esteem. In his stories of the 1970s and 1980s Tuohy turns his satiric gaze on reflections of the moral smugness of young educated liberals.

Other stories in *Live Bait* return to his earlier subject of differences in language and national custom. Perhaps drawing on his experiences as a writer in residence at Purdue University, Tuohy sets "Evening in Connecticut" at an academic party. A British professor being interviewed for a job spends the evening in an alcoholic haze, trying to read the Americans' verbal cues. He carefully corrects himself in small matters ("I look forward to meeting him in the autumn – fall, I mean") but disastrously misinterprets a reference to "my boy" to mean a homosexual relationship when the speaker is in fact referring to his son. The rattled character explains, "Cultural differences. One doesn't always interpret the signals correctly."

In "Live Bait," the volume's final and most thoroughly developed story, Tuohy sides openly with the social underdog and against the abuse of power and privilege. Even physically the classes are divided: "Andrew, small for his age, which was thirteen, was snub-nosed, crooked, and guilty. Jeremy, his companion, was altogether easier to commend, a handsome boy with blond hair and a milky complexion." Andrew is well aware that he is not the right sort: "He already knew that he was physically unattractive, because people didn't much like him leaning on them at school."

Through Jeremy's family's connections the two have been allowed to fish in the lake at Braxby Hall – one of the few estates in the south of England not yet broken up into council-house developments or taken over as private hospitals or research institutes. A man who works on the estate tells the

boys that there is a twenty-pound pike in the lake, and Andrew takes the information as part of a religious quest: "The big pike was waiting like something in time rather than place." Andrew knows that to catch such a fish he will need heavier tackle with wire leader and a boat to get to the middle of the lake. To escape the hypocritical and exploitative world of adults, however, Andrew needs even greater skills. His absent military father prefers to spend his vacations on Cyprus with a woman other than Andrew's mother. His mother has taken solace with Group-Captain Godfrey Weare, whom Andrew is uncertain how to address. At Braxby Hall Andrew is dismissed by the ancient Mrs. Peverill, while her son tries to abuse him sexually.

Life is a continuous struggle for Andrew. He concentrates on the pike, for he knows that when the end of vacation comes "there was next term to think about, when he would sit the entrance scholarship to his Public School. It had been implied that, if he failed, he would be cast into some sort of outer darkness and his mother would be disappointed and weep. Nobody had ever explained why this had to happen; why it was that Jeremy, for instance, should proceed to Harrow without trouble, having been put down for the school at his birth." Tuohy uses Andrew as a center of consciousness to examine the world of English hereditary privilege, from which the boy learns to defend himself through silence and cunning.

Live Bait received a great deal of critical attention in the United States. Anatole Broyard, in the *New York Times* (6 January 1979), admired the fine sentences in the "rueful, rich, and surprising" stories. Julia O'Faolain, in the *New York Times Book Review* (25 February 1979), noted Tuohy's "cruelly compassionate eye for social flounderings."

During the late 1970s and early 1980s Tuohy reviewed books for *London Magazine* and the *Times Literary Supplement*. During late 1982 and early 1983 he reviewed fiction for the *Times Literary Supplement* almost weekly. Also in the 1980s Tuohy returned to Japan and to the United States as a writer in residence at Texas A&M University. In 1984 his three collections of short stories were brought together in a single volume, *The Collected Stories*. Peter S. Prescott began his full-page review in *Newsweek* (4 February 1985) by wondering "why Frank Tuohy's work isn't better known in this country I can't guess."

One measure of the esteem in which Tuohy was held as a short-story writer during the 1960s and 1970s was the inclusion of eleven of his stories in the first twenty numbers of *Winter's Tales*. His fellow contributors to *Winter's Tales* include Kingsley

Amis, Margaret Drabble, L. P. Hartley, Frank O'Connor, Anthony Powell, V. S. Pritchett, and Alan Sillitoe. An uncollected story by Tuohy, "Dreams of Unfair Women," was published in the first number of the new series of *Winter's Tales* (1985). Set in an English seaside town, the tale records the disturbing dreams of a 1960s political radical whose fantasies in middle age have turned embarrassingly conservative. In one dream he is dressed like a Tory, agreeing that people with social problems simply need discipline. In another dream the wife of a Tory M.P. mocks his shabby, radical existence, which in its studied unconventionality is all the more conventional. In a final dream he and his family have moved to London and are restoring a house in Fulham ("but very nearly in Chelsea"). The children are in boarding schools, and he is working in public relations. This satire of a political radical grown conservative with age and troubled by a growing taste for physical comfort is gently done. While not Tuohy's best short story, it shows

a satiric, humorous side, suggesting that perhaps Tuohy's own pessimistic edge has softened.

Tuohy writes most effectively when he presents exiles struggling with questions of personal identity in foreign settings. He treats differences in national customs with sensitivity and economy, and he has a projective sympathy that allows him to see Westerners from the point of view of the Japanese — or the English from the perspective of the Poles — thus complicating and enriching the reader's understanding of national stereotypes. His vision has always been detached and ironic, but his tone — originally nihilistic — has moved toward the satiric. A product of World War II England, Tuohy has remained a critic of class privilege, sexual exploitation, and inauthenticity.

Reference:

John Mellors, "Foreign Bodies: The Fiction of Frank Tuohy," *London Magazine*, new series 18 (February 1979): 59–63.

Fred Urquhart

(12 July 1912 –)

Colin Affleck

BOOKS: *Time Will Knit* (London: Duckworth, 1938);

I Fell for a Sailor (London: Duckworth, 1940);

The Clouds Are Big with Mercy (Glasgow: Maclellan, 1946);

Selected Stories (London & Dublin: Fridberg, 1946);

The Last G.I. Bride Wore Tartan (Edinburgh: Serif, 1948);

The Ferret Was Abraham's Daughter (London: Methuen, 1949);

The Year of the Short Corn (London: Methuen, 1949);

The Last Sister (London: Methuen, 1950);

Jezebel's Dust (London: Methuen, 1951);

The Laundry Girl and the Pole (London: Arco, 1955);

Scotland in Colour, text by Urquhart, photographs by Kenneth Scowen (London: Batsford, 1961; New York: Viking, 1961);

Camp-Follower (Edinburgh: Blackwood, 1977);

Palace of Green Days (London & New York: Quartet, 1979);

Proud Lady in a Cage (Edinburgh: Harris, 1980);

A Diver in China Seas (London & New York: Quartet, 1980);

Seven Ghosts in Search (London: Kimber, 1983).

Editions and Collections: *The Collected Stories, Volume One: The Dying Stallion* (London: Hart-Davis, 1967);

The Collected Stories, Volume Two: The Ploughing Match (London: Hart-Davis, 1968);

Full Score, edited, with an introduction, by Graeme Roberts (Aberdeen, Scotland: Aberdeen University Press, 1989).

OTHER: *No Scottish Twilight*, edited by Urquhart and Maurice Lindsay (Glasgow: Maclellan, 1947);

W.S.C.: A Cartoon Biography, compiled by Urquhart (London: Cassell, 1955);

Great True War Adventures, edited by Urquhart (London: Arco, 1956; New York: Arco, 1957);

Men at War, edited by Urquhart (London: Arco, 1957);

Scottish Short Stories, edited by Urquhart (London: Faber & Faber, 1957);

Great True Escape Stories, edited by Urquhart (London: Arco, 1958);

The Cassell Miscellany, 1848–1958, edited by Urquhart (London: Cassell, 1958);

"The Gay Gush Girls," in *Thy Neighbour's Wife*, edited by James Turner (London: Cassell, 1964; New York: Stein & Day, 1968), pp. 165–179;

"Scotland," in *A Traveller's Guide to Literary Europe*, volume 2, edited by Margaret Crosland (London: Evelyn, 1966), pp. 97–117;

Everyman's Dictionary of Fictional Characters, compiled by William Freeman, revised by Urquhart (London: Dent, 1973; New York: Dutton, 1973);

Modern Scottish Short Stories, edited by Urquhart and Giles Gordon (London: Hamish Hamilton, 1978);

"My Many Splendoured Pavilion," in *As I Remember*, edited by Lindsay (London: Hale, 1979), pp. 157–174;

The Book of Horses, edited by Urquhart (London: Secker & Warburg, 1981; New York: Morrow, 1981);

"Alice, the Baby and Bonnie Dundee," in *Stories of Haunted Inns*, edited by Denys Val Baker (London: Kimber, 1983), pp. 108–119;

"Dust Fills Helen's Eyes," in *Phantom Lovers*, edited by Baker (London: Kimber, 1984), pp. 29–40;

"The Straitened Cry," in *After Midnight Stories*, edited by Amy Myers (London: Kimber, 1985), pp. 39–55;

"Robert/Hilda," in *New Writing Scotland 5*, edited by Carl MacDougall and Edwin Morgan (Aberdeen: Association for Scottish Literary Studies, 1987), pp. 1–21;

Louise Callender, Fred Urquhart, and Rhys Davies in 1946

"Swing High, Willie Brodie," in *The Third Book of After Midnight Stories,* edited by Myers (London: Kimber, 1987), pp. 182–197;

"The Dead Blackbird," in *New Writing Scotland 6,* edited by MacDougall and Morgan (Aberdeen: Association for Scottish Literary Studies, 1988), pp. 40–58;

"Lillie Langtry's Silver Cup," in *The Fourth Book of After Midnight Stories,* edited by Myers (London: Kimber, 1988), pp. 119–134.

In the essay "Modern Scottish Novels" (*Time and Tide,* 19 April 1952) Fred Urquhart praises George Douglas Brown's savage work *The House with the Green Shutters* (1901) for giving "a picture of Scotland as it too often was – and still is," adding that realism in Scottish writing had gone even further since this violation of the falsely glowing picture painted by the Kailyard School (a group of Scottish writers who exploited a sentimental, romantic image of small-town life). Much of that advance is due to Urquhart's work, which for more than five decades has truthfully and revealingly illustrated the lives of the working people of Scotland, both rural and urban. His greatest achievement has been his brilliant use of dialogue to create a host of living characters: frequently women, old people, children, and other victims of social oppression.

He employs a detailed, realistic style to illustrate their lives in a way that is sometimes moving and often humorous, but never sentimental. The clarity, fluidity, and economy of his writing prevent any impediment to his irresistible narrative drive; his urge is always to tell the story, not to draw attention to the writing. He has created a record of the social context of Scottish life in the twentieth century and has vividly explored Scotland's past in historical stories. Other stories have examined the supernatural and have gone outside Scotland. The playwright Alexander Reid wrote in 1958 that Urquhart had a "strong claim" to be considered "Scotland's leading short story writer of the century"; in the outstanding quality, quantity, and range of his stories, Urquhart has amply substantiated that claim.

Frederick Burrows Urquhart was born on 12 July 1912 in Edinburgh, Scotland, the first of three brothers. He was named after his father, a chauffeur; his mother was Agnes (Nan) Harrower Urquhart. The family moved to Duns in the south of Scotland, then in 1914 to Fife, where Urquhart went to a village school at age five. He had already learned to read. Toward the end of World War I his father became chauffeur to the marquis of Breadalbane at Taymouth Castle in Perthshire. Beginning in 1919 Urquhart spent two years with his maternal grandparents back in Edinburgh and then lived in Kirkcolm, Wigtownshire, for four years.

Urquhart displayed an early interest in the arts, informing the marchioness of Breadalbane that he would be a great artist one day. When he was twelve, he had a fairy story published in the *Scotsman,* which also printed some of his drawings. He was encouraged by teachers at Stranraer High School, but in 1925 his family settled permanently in Edinburgh and he was sent to Broughton Secondary School, which he hated. He left at age fifteen to work in a secondhand bookshop. In Edinburgh he went regularly to the cinema and the theater. The importance of the movie house in popular culture is a recurring theme in his fiction, and many of his characters have theatrical connections. He aspired to be an actor, but after a less-than-inspiring experience as a spear carrier in Bernard Shaw's *Back to Methuselah* (1921) he began to concentrate on writing.

The job in the bookshop lasted seven and a half years. He read widely and wrote stories, poems, plays, and three novels, which were returned by publishers. Two authors had a great influence on his writing: Ernest Hemingway, whose staccato style and spare dialogue Urquhart admired, and H. E. Bates, whose slice-of-life stories about ordinary people set a model for Urquhart's early fiction. In "The Work of H. E. Bates" (*Life and Letters To-Day,* December 1939) Urquhart commends his "clear-cut and vigorous" writing and the fact that the "ordinary working man or woman would understand and appreciate" his characters, qualities that apply to Urquhart's work.

After leaving the bookshop in 1935, Urquhart experienced periods of unemployment between temporary jobs, but the following year he began to have stories accepted for publication in leading English literary magazines. First to appear in print was "The Daft Woman in Number Seven" (*Adelphi,* September 1936; *I Fell for a Sailor,* 1940), about a working-class couple who aspire to self-improvement but who are persecuted and dragged down by the lumpen proletarians among whom they live. Some characteristic features of Urquhart's stories are already apparent here: the depiction of "dreams . . . defeated by hostile circumstances," as Alan Bold put it in *Modern Scottish Literature* (1983); the stress on female characters;

and the clever use of dialogue. Urquhart follows the tradition, established by Sir Walter Scott, of setting Scots dialogue in a narrative that is basically in Standard English. Urquhart's left-wing leanings of the time are apparent from the first line – "Environment breeds character" – but he refuses to idealize or romanticize the working class.

"I Fell for a Sailor" (*London Mercury,* January 1937; *I Fell for a Sailor*) is a first-person narrative in which a naive American girl describes her relationship with a sailor who was clearly using her, although she does not realize it. The short, simple sentences reflect the influence of Hemingway, while the hard-boiled, demotic American language may partly derive from American pulp magazines that Urquhart read in the bookshop. "The Heretic" (*New Writing,* Spring 1937; *I Fell for a Sailor*), set among Irish Catholics in Edinburgh, deals with Timothy's rejection of his religion, his consequent ostracism and unemployment, and the ironic way in which his apparent sexual freedom leads to his forcible return to the church. Urquhart's dislike of organized religion and its repressive effects is clear, and Timothy's feelings when unemployed – "He felt beaten and useless and empty" – reflect the author's position.

"Those Things Pass" (*Left Review,* March 1937; *I Fell for a Sailor*) expresses a soldier's disillusionment with army life, which Urquhart observed at close quarters during a brief job in the armed-forces catering organization. Social inequality and the dehumanizing effect of the military machine are criticized. The piece is too much of a political statement and is insufficiently dramatized, but it was admired by J. R. Ackerley, literary editor of the *Listener* and one of the London literary figures from whom Urquhart sought advice. Ackerley told Urquhart that his stories needed more tightness and economy, advice that he took to heart.

Those qualities are certainly displayed in "Sweat" (*Fact,* July 1937; *I Fell for a Sailor*), as is Urquhart's concern with the appalling social conditions of the poor. Jeanie sews in a workroom appropriately described as a "sweat shop," since the air is filled with the stench of perspiration. She constantly worries that she smells, so she spends the pittance she receives for overtime on perfume, hoping to encourage her boyfriend to make advances that will lead to marriage and escape. In an ironic twist he objects to the smell of "cheap scent." The rather daring realism with which Urquhart describes intimate details of working-class life is typical, as is the simple narrative style that does not detract attention from these details.

Urquhart's stories were beginning to attract attention; the *Weekly Scotsman* (7 August 1937) described "They Foreigners!" (*London Mercury*, August 1937; *I Fell for a Sailor*) as "an extraordinary exposition of insularity." In this story three Scottish sailors in a French port are mainly concerned with discovering Scottish football results. They are taking supplies to the Republicans in Spain, but they have no interest in the Spanish civil war, suggesting the political backwardness of the Scottish working class. Urquhart includes lines from popular songs, a technique he often uses to provide a social context for his characters and to suggest the hackneyed sources of their means of emotional expression.

"The Christ Child" (*Penguin Parade 2*, 1938; *I Fell for a Sailor*) has a rather Jamesian theme concerning an artist whose knowledge of a beautiful child's spiritual depravity prevents him from painting his physical beauty unambivalently. The pace is more leisurely than usual in Urquhart's early work, and the descriptions of landscape are also unusually detailed. The sexual impulse underlying the artist's attraction to the boy is implied, and the sexual and artistic tensions eventually find a physical outlet when the artist beats him.

Urquhart's name as a writer was made with the publication of his novel *Time Will Knit* in May 1938. This amusing, tragic, and, above all, living picture of a working-class family in Edinburgh (with, like much of Urquhart's work, a strong autobiographical element) is ingeniously constructed. Alternate chapters are titled "Plain" and "Purl"; the former are narrated by Spike, an agreeable young American relation who comes for a visit, and the latter by members of the family. This structure reflects the influence of Virginia Woolf; Urquhart stated that at the time his "one desire was to write 'inner monologues' in Scots." As in the short stories the characters are revealed by the vivid vernacular of the dialogue. Both they and the social conditions in which they live are depicted with unsparing realism but also with humor often described as Rabelaisian.

The success of *Time Will Knit* meant a great deal to Urquhart. Now that he was an established writer, producing journalistic articles as well as fiction, he began to move in Scottish literary circles. He became friendly with broadcaster and author John R. Allan and his wife, Jean. She founded the Theatre Society of Scotland to campaign for a Scottish national theater, and Urquhart was active as its Edinburgh secretary. Urquhart joined many Scottish writers in signing a letter to the press in July 1938, calling for help for the Basques and Catalans in Spain.

In "It Always Rains in Glasgow" (*Sunday Post*, 3 July 1938; *I Fell for a Sailor*) a family visits the Empire Exhibition in that city. Mrs. Dunn is an archetypal Scottish figure, the eternal pessimist. She insists that it will rain and is triumphant when it does. She worries so much that she cannot enjoy herself, and she resents the enjoyment of others. And yet, because the reader is shown events from her point of view, one is aware of the pressures governing her behavior. The precisely observed social details and dialogue, including popular catchphrases, are completely convincing.

"Tomorrow Will Be Beautiful" (*New Writing*, Autumn 1938; *I Fell for a Sailor*) deals with an outing to a barracks open day. Eve goes reluctantly, having a cynical view of the military: "Give your heart to a man who was little better than a machine, a man who'd have to go at once if there was a war, and spend months, perhaps years of anxious worrying over him – No, sir!" The heat of the day is stressed, there is a sensuous description of horses ("sleek necks slippery as snake's skin and polished rumps gleamed like jewels"), and then the good looks of Scotty, a soldier, are detailed as they strike Eve. The erotic charge built up is such that the sudden love between Eve and Scotty is completely credible. Their idyll is abruptly interrupted by the sound of machine guns, at which Eve "felt terrified suddenly of what all this meant." The "all" is deliberately ambiguous, referring both to the start of an adult relationship and to the military machine (which, it was already clear, would soon enter a war). Her original view of soldiers is recalled. The behavior of all the characters is beautifully detailed, tying what could be a sentimental romance firmly to reality.

Another remarkable depiction of a young woman's emotions is "We Never Died in Winter" (*Penguin Parade 4*, 1938; *I Fell for a Sailor*), in which Mary describes how her friends and then her boyfriend stopped coming to see her after she went to a tuberculosis hospital. Her mother has taken her home because the hospital can do no more for her; her approaching death has been presaged by that of another patient who died at home. Mary engages the reader's sympathy because she lacks self-pity and is extremely objective about everyone, including herself. At one point she starts to cry, "but I stopped when I remembered that I hadn't any powder with me." The reader is even led to feel sympathy for the boyfriend. The language is that of lower-middle-class Edinburgh – English with a touch of Scots – and the slangy tone seems to place Mary exactly.

After war was declared in September 1939, Urquhart went to live with Mary Litchfield, a retired schoolteacher and admirer of his work, in Cupar, near Saint Andrews. He was fascinated by her reminiscences of theatrical circles in London. Through her he met others connected with literature and the theater, including Edwin and Willa Muir, whom they regularly visited. Edwin Muir encouraged Urquhart to use simple terms, avoiding pretension. Odd-looking visitors to Litchfield's house, including students, led to a police raid after the retreat from Dunkirk in June 1940, a neighbor having reported the presence of fifth columnists.

Urquhart's first collection of short fiction, *I Fell for a Sailor,* includes all his stories published to the end of 1939 and three broadcast by the British Broadcasting Corporation (BBC). Many of Urquhart's stories have been read on the radio over the years; their clarity of structure and vivid dialogue make them ideal for the medium. One of these, "The Bike" (*Full Score,* 1989), another example of the destruction of a working-class girl's dreams, is widely regarded as one of Urquhart's greatest stories.

In "The Bike" Annie has an almost spiritual longing to own a bicycle, on which she could assert her individuality by escaping from "the crowded pavements." After three years of sacrifices she buys one, which brings her close to the loutish Charlie because he criticizes her paying "some capitalist." The ambivalence of Urquhart's attitude toward socialism as an anti-individualistic force is demonstrated by his choosing such an unworthy representative as Charlie. Annie and Charlie go out, but her feelings for him are shattered, along with her bike, when he drunkenly drives over it and, displaying a shocking indifference to her, dismisses it as "just that lassie's bike." Annie knows that "nothing would ever be the same again": her youthful innocence has ended with the revelation of the unkindness of which men are capable. A level of moral ambiguity is built in, since Annie allows Charlie's good looks to blind her to his obviously evil nature, but the reader is still led to sympathize with her.

Two stories in *I Fell for a Sailor* had not appeared in magazines because of their homosexual themes. One, "The Lodger," is set among the Edinburgh working class. Two neighbors, Mrs. Currie and Mrs. Spence, gossip on a tenement landing, speaking in urban Scots so forceful that it seems to leap off the page. As they reveal their own characters, it becomes amusingly evident that Mrs. Currie's lodger, Victor, and her son, Jim, are enjoy-

ing a sexual relationship. The amusement derives from the two women's ignorance of this, with further humor from their bitchy remarks. Disaster strikes with the revelation that Victor and Jim have been arrested, but even this occurrence is treated humorously, with Mrs. Currie at first relieved that Victor is only in jail ("I thocht he'd got run ower or somethin' serious") and then requiring an explanation of what his crime means. The final comic touch comes when a young girl, having evidently misheard a reference to sodomy, tells her playmates, "Oor Jim an' the lodger are in the nick for stealin' soda!" In Urquhart's work unorthodox sexual behavior often underlies the action, sometimes coming devastatingly to the surface.

"Cleopatra Had Nothing On" (*I Fell for a Sailor*) is an amusing mixture of bawdy humor and satire in Urquhart's American vein, with famous residents of hell wisecracking wildly while trying to get into a film. The American stories did not receive the widespread admiration from contemporary critics that the Scottish stories did. In a review of *I Fell for a Sailor* in *John o' London's Weekly* (25 May 1940) Bates wrote, "So long as he elects to sketch the tenements of Edinburgh and the lives of Scottish provincials, Mr. Urquhart will be a regional writer well on the way to first rank." In the *Tribune* (26 April 1940) George Orwell picked out some stories from the book as "little masterpieces," while Stevie Smith, in *Life and Letters To-Day* (July 1940), praised Urquhart's "diamond style."

In July 1940 Urquhart appeared before a Conscientious Objectors' Tribunal in Edinburgh, stating that "I thought war the greatest of all evils. . . . I said that I'd always been a pacifist and that I'd tried to define my hatred of war in both of my published books." He was refused exemption from military service, but later that year the Appellate Tribunal ordered him to do agricultural work for the duration of the war. He went to Bent Farm near Laurencekirk in northeastern Scotland. There, in the fertile agricultural area known as the Howe o' the Mearns, which is the setting for the works of Lewis Grassic Gibbon (James Lewis Mitchell), Urquhart worked as a farm laborer and then as farm secretary. His experience of rural life and his close attention to the Scots spoken in the northeast had a considerable effect on his writing, which had previously concentrated on urban Scotland.

Most copies of *I Fell for a Sailor* were destroyed on 29 December 1940 when a book warehouse in London was bombed, but the publication of *Time Will Knit* in a 1943 Penguin paperback edition brought Urquhart wider fame. The increased demand for short fiction during World War II allowed him to publish stories in a wide range of magazines, from the intellectual *Horizon* to the more popular *Penguin Parade*, but the paper shortage and other difficulties prevented publication of further collections until 1946, when two volumes of his wartime stories appeared.

Most of the stories in *The Clouds Are Big with Mercy* (1946) have Scottish urban settings, and the main characters tend to be women or children in difficult situations. "The Loony" (*Spectator*, 22 March 1940; *The Clouds Are Big with Mercy*) shows the degeneration of the character of Miss Mayfield, companion to the rich, mentally deficient Miss Rhona. Miss Mayfield sees her charge as symbolic of the upper classes, who do nothing and get everything; this symbolism is more convincing because it is filtered through the character's consciousness. In the original magazine version Miss Mayfield pushes Miss Rhona down the stairs, but in the book she "would never have the courage to take the decisive step." The revision from a melodramatic ending to a more psychologically convincing one also increases the horror of the situation, since Miss Mayfield can never escape.

"Namietnosc – or The Laundry Girl and the Pole" (*The Clouds Are Big with Mercy*) is a novella written in 1940 in Cupar, where the arrival of a Polish regiment aroused the young women (*namietnosc* is Polish for "passion"). Familiar elements of Urquhart's fiction are present, including the erotic perceptions of a young woman intercut with a lively, antiromantic humor (when the soldier Jan abruptly makes love to the laundry girl Nettie, she experiences "waves and waves of ecstasy" but still manages to call out, "Mind ma stockin's!"). Urquhart creates convincing characters, largely through vivid, rough Scots dialogue; closely observes social details, including lines from popular songs, carefully chosen to counterpoint the characters' feelings and actions; and criticizes social and political conditions while still displaying the faults of his working-class characters.

In "Man about the House" (*Horizon*, November 1940; *The Clouds Are Big with Mercy*) a sinister atmosphere is built up touch by touch, as a charwoman's humorous attitude toward a strange young man gradually turns to panic. "Not So Pretty Polly" (*Writing Today*, October 1943; *The Clouds Are Big with Mercy*) conveys all the squalor of Edinburgh's Old Town slums. Old Polly is decrepit, but the vigor of her language demonstrates her unabated zest for life. As in many of Urquhart's stories, the main character's thoughts spill out into the

narrative passages, increasing one's sense of seeing life through her eyes. The protagonist of "Dirty Minnie" (*Life and Letters To-Day*, August 1942; *The Clouds Are Big with Mercy*) is slatternly but sympathetic. She banters with women in an air-raid shelter before going home to her lodgers, three realistically depicted sailors. They are established as separate individuals by differentiation in dialogue. Minnie's philosophy is "There's time enough to worry aboot snaw when it comes on," which the story suggests is the best way to live in wartime.

Selected Stories (1946) consists mainly of stories inspired by Urquhart's time in the Mearns; these are set in and around the fictional town of Auchencairn. Several feature a classic simplicity and resonant archetypes that have led some critics to regard them (and later stories in the same vein) as his best works. An outstanding example is "The Dying Stallion" (*Life and Letters To-Day*, September 1944; *Selected Stories*), in which a stallion is badly injured while leaping a gate to get at some mares. An old farmer, William Petrie, feels for the horse, a symbol of the old order. His sons-in-law lack sympathy, being part of the new world where tractors have replaced horses. The stallion is also a symbol of true virility. Young Dick's apparent manliness is false, and his resentment is seen in his striking the horse's genitals and finally saying, "Ye'd better cut him and yoke him to a cart." The clash between youth and age, old and new, is summed up as the horse is dying: "The old man wanted to stretch out his hands and touch it, willing to give all his own dying vigour to revive it, but he was afraid of the ridicule of the young men."

Other pieces in *Selected Stories* faithfully depict agricultural work. "The Tattie Dressers" (*Fantasy No. 27*, 1943) contains a comprehensive description of potato dressing (sorting out seed potatoes), and the portrayal of the characters establishes the natural rhythm of their lives. The ribald gossip and jokes convey the impression of a happy community carrying out work more significant than world events. "We maun get that Seed dressed, war or nae war," old Alec remarks when a German airplane is shot down, and he expresses the reality of war in human terms on hearing that a young German pilot was killed: "He was somebody's bairn."

Two stories set in northeastern Scotland are concerned with Italian prisoners of war used as agricultural laborers. "The Prisoner's Bike" (first published in the American magazine *Story*, November–December 1943; collected in *Selected Stories*) focuses on the attitude of Mrs. McBride, a farmer's wife, toward one of these men. She fears him and lacks gratitude when he helps her, but she sides with him when the authorities want to take his beloved bicycle away from him. Other local people become friendly with Giuseppe sooner: "They saw that the Italian was a decent man like themselves. . . . They saw that he was glad to be out of the war, and that he had not wanted to be a soldier any more than they wanted to be soldiers themselves." This antiwar message is strengthened by Mrs. McBride's conversion; at that moment she holds her tray "like a shield in front of her," a sign of determination against the military machine. "English in Three Months" (*Life and Letters To-Day,* December 1943; *Selected Stories*) is a deeply moving study of a relationship destroyed by the conditions of war. The prisoner Domenico and the farmer Alex try to learn each other's language and share a friendship that defies conventions. Despite Alex's attempt to keep Domenico on his farm, he is taken away suddenly. The abruptness of this denouement shocks the reader, making it easy to identify with the heartbroken Domenico.

Both *The Clouds Are Big with Mercy* and *Selected Stories* were, on the whole, well received by contemporary critics. Orwell, in the *Manchester Evening News* (28 March 1946), wrote that the stories lacked plot but that "few people now writing are able to handle dialogue more skilfully." The *North East Review* (May 1946) saw Urquhart's objective representation of the working class as "a welcome antidote to the Marxist glorification of the proletariat." Although Urquhart was often described as a proletarian writer, Michael Williams has pointed out that Urquhart and Christopher Isherwood differed from the proletarian school because they were "not out to bludgeon their readers into acquiescence, but to reveal and distil," presenting the truth as they observed it and not as propagandistic distortions.

Many critics have seen Urquhart's rural stories as influenced by Gibbon, but Urquhart resents this. He used the Kincardineshire dialect in many stories, but mainly in the dialogue, whereas Gibbon tried to reconstruct the "speak" throughout the narrative. (Urquhart has always been concerned that his writings should be comprehensible to non-Scots.) Sydney Goodsir Smith pointed out this difference in the *Edinburgh Evening Dispatch* (30 May 1947), remarking that he did not like the "rhapsodisings" of Gibbon. Furthermore, Urquhart's stories are free from the ideological "preaching" of Gibbon, as Denys Val Baker put it in *Edinburgh Today* (November 1954).

By the time these books were published, Urquhart was living in England, having moved

there in June 1944 to become farm secretary on the Woburn estate of the duke of Bedford. On weekends Urquhart visited the artists Robert Colquhoun and Robert MacBryde in London, meeting other literary and artistic figures. In late 1946, after taking a room in London, he became temporary literary editor of the *Tribune,* the Labourite weekly, to which he had already contributed stories and reviews. The publishers refused to pay his National Insurance contributions, causing him financial difficulties, and his observation of the hypocrisy of leading "socialists" further reduced his enthusiasm for the Left. In the pubs and clubs of Fitzrovia and Soho, London's bohemia, he mixed with more writers and artists, including Julian Maclaren-Ross, Dylan Thomas, William Sansom, John Minton, and Francis Bacon. Quentin Crisp was a friend, as were the writers Norah Hoult and Rhys Davies and the artist Nina Hamnett. On 25 May 1947 Hamnett introduced Urquhart to Peter Wyndham Allen, a former dancer, with whom he lived until Allen's death forty-three years later.

Toward the end of 1946 James Wedgwood Drawbell, editor of *Woman's Own,* invited Urquhart to write romantic stories for the magazine. Despite the harsh realism of his work, he had displayed a deep understanding of women's emotions. *Woman's Own* published works by such reputable writers as A. J. Cronin and Eric Linklater, and it paid well. Urquhart accepted for financial reasons. He now dismisses most of the stories he wrote for Drawbell as "rubbish," but some are of high literary quality. "Hunt the Slipper" (March 1947) tells of an Aberdeenshire farmer's wife who is irritated by a pretentious London shop assistant's flirting with her male friend. The wife is so irked that she rejects the shoes she really wanted, describing them as "far too fancy for a simple country cousin like me." Part of the point is that she is actually a sophisticated middle-class woman, but her Scottish accent makes her seem provincial to the English shop assistant. This story was collected in *The Last G.I. Bride Wore Tartan* (1948).

The title story in that collection is a sparkling novella about the cinema-obsessed Jessie McIntyre, in London to find a GI before they all return to the United States. She avidly reads *Gentlemen Prefer Blondes* (1925), and Urquhart's story can be seen as a Scottish version of Anita Loos's book. As the spirited Jessie, having married her GI, sails to America, it becomes clear that, despite her hard-boiled style, she is not as hard as she pretends. The first-person narrative makes this a process of self-revelation, more amusing and touching because it is inadvertent. After she humorously describes a voyage on a ship full of GI brides, Jessie realizes that she actually loves her husband. Their idyll is threatened, however, by another bride, who tells Lew that Jessie only married him to become a Hollywood star. All comes right, and Jessie seems to prefer love to stardom, but in the last line she still dreams about making films.

Even though the stories in this collection are lighter in tone than many of Urquhart's previous works, there is still no place for an unambiguously happy ending. In "Call Me Blondie" (*Tribune*, 16 May 1947) – which sets up an amusing but rather sinister contrast between its style (like that of a hard-boiled American detective story) and its subject (the attempted seduction of a Scottish workman by an eccentric married woman) – Mac escapes from Mrs. Ames's predatory clutches but still loses his job.

In a review of *The Last G.I. Bride Wore Tartan* for *Scotland* (August 1948) Edward Scouller wrote, "Probably the only thing that saves Mr. Fred Urquhart from being stabbed to death by indignant young women is that the type he vivisects does not read anything but film weeklies and untrue confessions," but he added that Urquhart was motivated by truthfulness, not malice. Like many reviewers he disliked Urquhart's American excursions – in which the influence of William Saroyan's lack of formality was often detected – but to the more modern reader they have an engaging individuality.

During the late 1940s and into the 1950s Urquhart became a prolific reviewer of fiction for such magazines as *Life and Letters To-Day* and *Time and Tide* (where he was hired by John Betjeman, an admirer of his work). In 1948 he obtained a part-time job with the Richmond Towers Literary Agency, living above the premises on Bloomsbury Street. There he wrote his second published novel, *The Ferret Was Abraham's Daughter* (1949), and its sequel, *Jezebel's Dust* (1951). These novels concern the life of Bessie Hipkiss from her girlhood in an Edinburgh slum through her attempt to better herself by working in a boardinghouse – along with her racy misadventures with the loose Lily McGillivray – to her eventual happiness as an American wife. Bessie has been deeply affected by romantic films and periodically escapes from harsh reality into fantasies of aristocratic life. Some critics disliked the loose structure of the books, but the authentic dialogue and details of working-class life attracted praise.

During the 1940s several of Urquhart's stories appeared in the prestigious American periodical *Story*, whose editor, Whit Burnett, had a high opinion of them: "They are human, warm and funny, with a deep sense of the oddities and frailties of humankind." He included one story in the 1949 anthology *Story: The Fiction of the Forties*, listing Urquhart with Tennessee Williams, Truman Capote, Norman Mailer, and J. D. Salinger as those who would be "the 'known' authors . . . of the fifties." Also in 1949, Urquhart's collection *The Year of the Short Corn* appeared. Many of its themes and settings are familiar from earlier books.

Of the three Auchencairn stories in *The Year of the Short Corn*, the most striking is "The Prisoners," the third of Urquhart's studies of Italian prisoners of war and Scottish reactions to them. Mary is ashamed of her husband's arrogant treatment of the prisoners on his farm, and, in a wider sense, she resents his lack of sensitivity and imagination. She identifies with the prisoners, partly because she feels like a "prisoner bound by her love and fear of Will." Her bitterness toward Will is clear because the reader is privy to her thoughts, which are underlined by her obliquely critical remarks. These undermine her attempts to remind herself of Will's good points. The result is a psychologically acute picture of Mary's contradictory feelings. A friendly prisoner is tricked into believing he will not be sent away, so Mary hates Will. When, at the end, Will expresses sympathy for the Italian, it comes as a considerable surprise, because Will has only been seen from the point of view of his resentful wife. Urquhart implies that people may suppress their finer feelings in order to get things done, but they do not necessarily lack empathy.

"The Red Stot" (*The Year of the Short Corn*) is a detailed account of the workday of a young farm laborer, or "loon." He looks after cattle, but the story gains poetic intensity from the precise details (which encourage identification with the loon's feelings), the beautiful descriptions of natural conditions, and the imputed parallels between the behavior of cattle and people. The physical environment is of utmost importance to the loon, so it is visualized more exactly than usual in Urquhart's stories. The ending, with its reflection of the eternal struggle of life, seems to resonate beyond the story:

> The snow fell faster and faster, and the flakes grew bigger. Soon they could see only a few yards in front of them. The going got more and more difficult. But on they struggled into the whiteness leading to Dallow, following the dark shape of the lumbering red stot.

Many stories in *The Year of the Short Corn* deal with people who believe themselves outsiders. In "Allow the Lodger" Mr. Bertram, the lodger, is first shown from the point of view of Mrs. Wright, his landlady, so he seems an unpleasant character, creeping about and prying. After the arrival of Mrs. Wright's extroverted sons and their wives, Urquhart shows events from Bertram's perspective. He is frightened by the noise and vivacity of the young people but is too shy to blend in with the tightly knit family. These tensions are expressed in the contrast between the rowdy behavior when Bertram is away and the strained atmosphere when he is present.

Some of the stories in *The Year of the Short Corn* are set in England. "Everybody Has Somebody Else" (first published in slightly different form in the American *Harper's Bazaar,* November 1945) is an extremely perceptive, psychologically revealing study of a physically unattractive, sexually frustrated young woman. She vainly longs for a handsome man to sit beside her on the train and is jealous of young couples who have the relationships she lacks. On a bus she manages to sit beside a young man, but the seat was vacant because someone had vomited on it. This is blackly humorous, especially when she thinks she could have sat across the aisle from the man and talked: "They could have started a conversation about the sickness." Finally she trudges through the snow to the farm where she works, still hoping that an attractive man might give her a lift. "Two Ladies" (*Illustrated,* 24 August 1946) is a short, sharp look at British snobbery, while Urquhart's love of the music hall and its performers is reflected in "He Called Me Girlie." Here Urquhart gives an uncomplimentary, objective view of an old stager's performance in a factory concert, but, by cutting to the enthusiastic reaction of an old worker, Urquhart shows movingly what the old songs can mean to people.

In a review of *The Year of the Short Corn* the *Times Literary Supplement* (4 November 1949) claimed that Urquhart "sets out to be the conscientious social realist who presents the reader with a slice of life. . . . The mood is uniformly grey." This view was contradicted in the *Spectator* (18 November 1949) by L. A. G. Strong, who praised the collection's "vigour, colour, *brio* and enjoyment." Some critics, deciding that books about the working class must be dull, blinded themselves to Urquhart's wit and gusto, but most recognized it.

The Last Sister (1950) begins with "Once A Schoolmissy . . . ," one of Urquhart's novellas. The central relationship here is between two teachers. Miss Perrott is English, proper, house-proud, and class-conscious, while Miss Riddell is Scottish, addicted to betting, untidy, and in the habit of obtaining sexual release with her handyman. Miss Perrott visits her friend in a Scottish village, intending to persuade her to live with her on her retirement, but Miss Riddell plans to marry Mr. Munro, a whiskey-drinking small farmer. The prim Miss Perrott's ordered view of life suffers various shocks, particularly during a visit to the outrageous Poppy Chiltern, another former colleague; it becomes evident that Miss Perrott has repressed sexual feelings toward Miss Riddell. Urquhart uses the space provided by the longer form to build up complex characters. Miss Riddell, with her eccentric school curriculum, and Mrs. Chiltern, with her difficulty in distinguishing between fantasy and reality, can be seen as predecessors of Muriel Spark's Miss Jean Brodie (*The Prime of Miss Jean Brodie,* 1961). Even Miss Perrott is allowed her virtues, such as opposition to war. She is defeated, but, like many of Urquhart's characters, she admirably refuses to give up hope.

Three other stories in the collection are set in northeastern Scotland. The outstanding one is "The Ploughing Match" (*Life and Letters To-Day,* November 1947; *The Last Sister*), which won the Tom-Gallon Award for 1952–1953. Here Annie Dey has achieved her long-standing ambition of holding a plowing match on her farm, but only after she is confined speechless to her bed following a stroke and has to watch the proceedings through binoculars. Furthermore the competition involves tractors, not horses, unlike the match she remembers from her girlhood. Her husband is dead, and her despised daughter-in-law has taken her place as hostess. None of the eminent visitors pays respects to her.

This is another of Urquhart's studies of the process of change and the embittering effects of conflict between generations on old people. Annie's feelings are described so precisely (as when she "writhed as she thought of what the grieve and the ploughman childes must say out there in the tractor-shed: 'Only an act o' God would make the auld bitch hold her tongue!' ") that the reader feels sympathy for her. The fact that she is not sentimentalized makes the story genuinely moving. In the last paragraph Annie dozes and starts to dream: "Scenes passed before her eyes, scenes for which she needed no spy-glass to see more clearly." At last she experiences the plowing match as it should have been, and "her greatest ambition had come true." She is allowed a happy ending, although it is obviously only temporary.

Urquhart frequently displays an incisive, unsentimental insight into the minds of children, and he effectively uses a child's point of view in "Alicky's Watch" (*Listener*, 11 August 1949; *The Last Sister*). The mother of nine-year-old Alicky has died, but, by the time of the funeral three days later, her death already seems remote to him, and the real tragedy is that his watch stops. Descriptions of childish concerns are intercut with blackly comic passages about the adults' activities, which take place over the children's heads. The dead woman's mother has insisted that her daughter be buried, not cremated, for practical reasons: "But we have the ground, Sandy! . . . It would be a pity not to use it."

Alicky's father experiences the "new-found dignity of widowerhood," while his grandmothers compete for precedence at the funeral meal, during which the minister stops praying to save the cold meats from the cat. Auntie Liz complains that (as was customary in Scotland until after World War II) women do not go to funerals: "You men ha'e all the fun." Ironically when Alicky, his spirits restored by the restarting of his watch, asks whether he and his brother may go to the movies, his father says, "We're no' here for fun," but it is obvious that the adults are. The nicer granny lets the boys out, and they run to the cinema. Urquhart shows that life, literally and symbolically, carries on after death, and the natural way in which children accept this is contrasted with the hypocritical rituals adults use to disguise the process.

In "Win Was Wild" (*Our Time*, May 1949; *The Last Sister*) Urquhart demonstrates his grasp of Cockney dialect. The loud Rosie stirs up trouble in a pub (many stories are set in pubs, about which Urquhart once planned to write a book) by amusingly maligning the morose Win. This short tale is a brilliant example of Urquhart's ability to create characters largely by carefully individualized dialogue. While praising the dialogue in *The Last Sister*, some reviewers felt that the stories lacked plots, missing the point of Urquhart's subtle revelations of character through speech rather than action.

Urquhart came to dislike working at the literary agency, so he left in 1952. For several years he was a reader for M-G-M, writing reports on novelettes that were never filmed. He acquired a longer-lasting position as a reader and editor for the publisher Cassell, for whom he read up to nine manuscripts each week until 1974. On his recommendation they published the work of Thomas Kenneally, but they turned down Flannery O'Connor's. During these decades he also read for several other publishers. From 1952 to 1958 he lived in various parts of southeastern England, residing in flats and houses that always turned out to be unsuitable in some way, and made frequent visits to London's bohemia. One of the writers he met there was Derek Stanford, who, in *Inside the Forties* (1977), recalls, "Fred was a wonderful mimic, and after he had impersonated someone, he would roll his eyes up to the ceiling in a gesture that paid tribute to human stupidity and pretension."

The falloff in the market for short stories after World War II prompted Urquhart to spend even more time on his other pursuits in order to make a living, in turn reducing his production of stories. *The Laundry Girl and the Pole* (1955) consists of previously collected stories, along with five new ones. The most important is the poignant "Elephants, Bairns and Old Men" (*Colophon*, September 1950), which returns to William Petrie, the old farmer in "The Dying Stallion." The stress is again on the division between generations. The occasion is the Scottish festival of Hogmanay – the last day of the year – a time for remembering. The three elements of the title – elephants, children, and old men – allegedly share the quality of never forgetting. For the children in the story remembering is part of the onward process of living, while for Petrie memory has effectively replaced life. He remembers his dead son, Alec; he perhaps idealizes him, but he identifies him with his own attachment to old ways. As the new year approaches, Petrie slips away from his noisy, unsympathetic family to join his stallion, representative of the past. The sense of loss and loneliness is intensely communicated.

Urquhart's first venture into historical fiction is "Kind Oblivion's Shade" (*Everybody's*, 21 March 1953; *The Laundry Girl and the Pole*), a more romantic narrative than is usual for him. It reconstructs the tragic tale of Robert Burns and Highland Mary. By stressing the harsh conditions of Mary's life, the story remains emotional without becoming sentimental. In a review of *The Laundry Girl and the Pole* for the *Daily Telegraph* (19 August 1955) Betjeman wrote that Urquhart "is to Scotland rather what Rhys Davies is to Wales, a short story writer who describes the poorer people of his native land and who is particularly good at portraying women." Urquhart admired the work of his friend Davies, who probably influenced his writing. Three years later Alexander Reid, in an essay on Urquhart's work, justifiably commented:

No modern writer in English has depicted the conscious worlds of the lost and lonely among the lower tenths of our population better than Urquhart. No other writer, with less moralising and sentimentality, has brought out the pathos of the lives of those who (to borrow a fine phrase first used of the characters of Hemingway) "have things done to them" in a world which, so far as they are aware, is utterly meaningless.

During the late 1950s Urquhart edited a cartoon biography of Winston Churchill and various anthologies, and he continued to review widely. In April 1958 he and Allen moved to Spring Garden Cottage in the middle of the Ashdown Forest in Sussex. This house, which was their home for more than thirty years, was found by a friend, the writer John Pudney, who lived nearby. At first Urquhart traveled to London twice weekly to collect books and manuscripts – particularly necessary when he was the London scout for Walt Disney Productions in 1960 – but as the years passed his visits became less frequent. In 1963 Brian Aldiss, then the literary editor, invited Urquhart to review for the *Oxford Mail,* and he contributed a monthly piece for many years.

In 1967 and 1968 Urquhart's *Collected Stories* appeared in two volumes. Despite the title, these books contain only a selection of twenty-five stories, which, apart from five in the first volume, had all appeared in previous collections. "Provide for Your Poor Sisters" (*London Magazine,* December 1963) is one of Urquhart's most devastating stories, revealing the sexual maelstrom that exists beneath Edinburgh's apparently respectable middle-class facade. Here Miss Macmillan, a genteel spinster, drinks because she is lonely. One afternoon she finds herself by chance on Rose Street, a once-notorious lane at the back of the respectable Princess Street stores, and enters a public house called Corbie's Hole, its name having incongruously reminded her of a nursery rhyme.

She falls in with two prostitutes but in her innocence does not recognize them for what they are. After frequent visits to the pub, Agnes and Nellie, having learned that she is a virgin, introduce her to one of Agnes's clients. The scales fall from Miss Macmillan's eyes, but another man insists on going home with her, inviting her to indulge in unorthodox sexual activities. She throws him out, goes into a decline, and is found dead some months later with an empty gin bottle in her hand. The black humor of the piece is so robust that in the confrontation between innocent respectability and foulmouthed harlotry the latter seems more appealing. One cannot help feeling that Urquhart takes his revenge on the

straitlaced, puritanical Edinburgh from which he, as a young man, was glad to escape.

"Maggie Logie and the National Health" (*Envoy,* November–December 1959; *Collected Stories*) is described by Bold in *Modern Scottish Literature* as "possibly the funniest story ever written by a Scotsman." It is certainly amusing in its satiric depiction of a Scotswoman who, following the introduction of the National Health Service after World War II, "made up her mind that she must get her money's worth" from her National Insurance payments. She plagues the doctor for medicines, has all her teeth extracted unnecessarily so she can get free false teeth, gets spectacles that she does not need, cuts off her hair so she can obtain a wig, and finally, while traveling in a motorbike sidecar, has the brilliant idea of having a leg amputated in order to get an artificial one: "It would maybe save the wear and tear on stockings." In her excitement she causes a crash in which she is killed.

There is less dialogue than usual in the story, but the narrator sounds like someone who knew the characters and is chattily telling their story, supplying a wealth of detail about changes in their social conditions. As with all satire there is a serious purpose. As Maggie's boyfriend Tam puts it, "Time was when ye went to the doctor, there was nobody waitin' but folk that were really ill. But now every man, woman and bairn in Cairncolm's sittin' there waitin' for a free dose o' cough-mixture."

"Weep No More, My Lady" (*Queen,* 4 August 1966) is Urquhart's first venture into the genre of the comic ghost story. Using a plot about eighteenth-century ghosts who have to perform an annual reenactment of a murder, Urquhart works in satiric attacks on aspects of the 1960s that repelled him: lazy young workmen with no imagination, ugly council houses, traffic, noisy teenagers, overreaching trade unions, and the overindulgence of the welfare state. The ghosts are victims of modernity; even when they escape to the Scottish Highlands they cannot get away from unwelcome changes. Urquhart is particularly fond of this piece, which he chose to represent his work in a 1977 anthology of favorite stories. That it reflects his personal rejection of British Labourism and its notions of progress is clear from his introduction to *Scotland in Colour* (1961), where he attacks "hideous pylons and rows of tasteless, coffin-shaped council houses – symbols of the twentieth century" and "the remorseless regimentation of the Welfare State."

The publication of *The Collected Stories* prompted an outpouring of praise from reviewers.

At last, it seemed, most critics could understand what Urquhart had been trying to do throughout his career. In the *Queen* (December 1967) Frank McGuinness wrote that Urquhart "has blazed the trail for so many modern writers." In the *New Statesman* (24 February 1967) V. S. Pritchett wrote that Urquhart's "proletarian studies . . . opened the way for the playwrights of the last decade." In the *Listener* (14 December 1967) Arnold Goldman compared the stories dealing with entire lives to the work of Bernard Malamud. Neville Braybrooke, in the *Spectator* (15 December 1967), referred to "moments when it is as if a veil were lifted and underlying secrets suddenly made clear"; this sense of mysteries beneath the surface is often experienced in the stories. In the *Sunday Telegraph* (31 December 1967) Francis King wrote that Urquhart's "prose lacks any sensuousness; but in its lucidity and restraint it becomes the perfect instrument for the expression of a view of life at once comic and despairing."

In the *Spectator* (24 May 1968) Iain Crichton Smith observed, "He has the significant deviousness of the true short-story writer as distinct from the flashy freeway style of the typical *New Yorker* contributor. . . . Urquhart never intellectualises, always allows each character his own speech and his own meanderings." Alexander Scott, in the *Scots Independent* (20 July 1968), commented, "He writes of the realities, the tragedies and the triumphs of ordinary life in a local setting, and his sympathetic insight and his unobtrusive skill result in the best of the localised stories becoming works of universal significance." This is an important point, given the danger of Scottish literature being dismissed as provincial. Urquhart's characters are so real because they are particularized in a Scottish identity. Having become real, they can then take on a universal relevance.

Urquhart has always taken an interest in other Scottish writers. With Giles Gordon, his former agent, he edited *Modern Scottish Short Stories* (1978), his third such anthology. In all three he sought to promote "Scottish authors who do not wish to write slick, popular, emasculated stories," especially those authors he felt were underrated. He thought that Scottish short stories descended from the traditional ballads. In the *Scotsman* (19 July 1980) Bold remarked that this origin is true for Urquhart's stories, which, like the ballads, "tell a story by combining narrative objectivity with the dramatic use of dialogue."

Palace of Green Days (1979), Urquhart's fourth published novel, is strongly autobiographical, looking back to his early childhood at Taymouth Castle. A chauffeur, his wife, and their three children arrive at the marquis of Bencraigon's Finlochrig Castle in 1918. Members of the community, eccentric aristocrats, and Canadian soldiers are seen largely through the eyes of the children, with an appropriate clearness and vividness. Adult sexuality (often with an element of violence) frightens the children, who are not ready to deal with it, but the glowing humor of the book infiltrates even that theme, as when the aroused, birch-wielding marchioness chases an orphan in a kilt. The themes and the use of dialogue are reminiscent of those in the short stories, but the book has a strongly novelistic narrative thrust.

In 1980 two volumes of Urquhart's stories were published. *Proud Lady in a Cage* brings together five of the Scottish historical pieces that Urquhart wrote in the previous decade for the Edinburgh-based *Blackwood's Magazine* and short-story anthologies. In all but one story the central character is a woman. These people of the past are faced with horror and violence; this is certainly not a romantic view of Scottish history. Urquhart may have been influenced by Dorothy K. Haynes, whose work he admires. Two of the pieces involve the supernatural, another genre in which he had occasionally written.

The title story tells of Bella Logan, a young supermarket worker who is periodically carried back into the body of Isabella, Countess of Buchan, as she suffers torments in a cage hanging from the wall of Berwick Castle. (The countess actually was so imprisoned in 1306 on the orders of Edward I of England.) Urquhart's imaginative description of the woman's sufferings is genuinely horrifying. The cleverly selected details of banal modern life make the contrast between Bella's two existences all the more harrowing. The story is ingeniously constructed on a series of parallels: Bella works at an inquiry desk with bars, and Isabella is in a cage; a witch and her grandson exist in both times, and they burn to death in both; and so on, down to such small details as Bella's father being a Scottish Nationalist, paralleling Isabella's anti-English father, the earl of Fife. Irony is added by Urquhart's making Bella "totally lacking in imagination," one symptom of which is her failure to understand her boyfriend's sexual needs.

"Pretty Prickly English Rose" (*Proud Lady in a Cage*), set in fifteenth-century Scotland, is told by the crippled Lady Grizel, a maid-in-waiting to Queen Joan Beaufort. Urquhart shows the events leading up to the assassination of James I and the cruel treatment of the assassins through the eyes of this fictional character, who is well situated to see the viciousness of the period. Lady Kate Douglas, one of the heroines of popular Scottish history, is the villainess of the piece and is amusingly portrayed. The Scots language of the time would be incomprehensible to most readers, so Urquhart uses a convincing, slightly archaic, but easily understandable form of Scots.

He moves forward to the Jacobite Rebellion of 1745 for "Your Grave Is My Only Landmark" (*Blackwood's Magazine,* September 1974; *Proud Lady in a Cage*), about the daughter of a bigoted minister who elopes with a handsome Jacobite officer. She meets Bonnie Prince Charlie in Edinburgh but ends up being raped by a Hanoverian soldier, beaten and imprisoned by her father, and condemned to look out at her lover's grave. The inhumanity of men to women and the opposition of supposed Christians to love are typical concerns for Urquhart.

In Urquhart's second 1980 collection, *A Diver in China Seas,* he reaches new heights in characterization, humor, and the reconstruction of the past. He also displays an apparently effortless technical skill in narrative construction and the use of different levels of time. This skill is particularly evident in "Pilgrimages to the Old Manse," in which the narrator, Lady Dalziel, intercuts accounts of her two visits to the home of the late Agnes Inglis with the story of her own life and her love of Miss Inglis's novels. The reader is told that Agnes Inglis was a friend of Henry James and wrote in a similar style. It is therefore appropriate that Urquhart's story — about the influence of Agnes's servant, Teenie Peebles, on her life and works — has a distinctly Jamesian theme, although the style is much more direct.

This is one of Urquhart's most complex and ambiguous stories; despite scattered clues, it is never completely clear how much Teenie actually contributed to the novels. The narrator does not seem to be entirely reliable, obsessed as she is with matters of social class, and the titles of Miss Inglis's novels (such as *A Laird in Old Siena*) are so trite and the excerpt from one of her letters so bad that one wonders about Lady Dalziel's literary taste. Urquhart's use of Scots is subtle; Teenie Peebles speaks much more broadly when talking to the narrator (of working-class origin) by herself than when Lord Dalziel is present, and she disapproves of Lord Dalziel's patronizing use of Scots expressions (or so the narrator thinks). The whole story promotes the feeling that what seems to be true is not necessarily so, especially where literature is concerned.

Another narrator who may not be telling the whole truth is Carrie in the title story of the collection, "A Diver in China Seas" (*Scottish Review,* Spring 1976). The opening sentence — "Now that I feel death's cauld hand crawling over me every night I keep turning my mind to the corpses I've seen in my day" — adds a sharper tone to her vivid account of her friendship with two old sisters in Leith. After one of them, Jessie, literally dies laughing, Carrie describes rather disingenuously how she married an elderly former suitor of Jessie. The reader gathers that Nora, the other sister, had her eye on him. Within three years Carrie inherited the old man's money, but now she envies Nora for having lived to the age of ninety. The unspoken — perhaps unrealized — guilt underlying the story adds to its power.

"A Gone Woman" (*Scottish Review,* November 1977; *A Diver in China Seas*) is also about memory, more directly in this case since the narrator is recalling her childhood. She describes in a matter-of-fact tone the lack of civilized facilities in her grandparents' cottage in Granton (the autobiographical strain in this story is strong). The lodger had to go into the kitchen every night to get the key to the outside lavatory. This situation prompts the narrator to consider people who "suffered in those times from lack of privacy and the subsequent loss of dignity that are so essential to human happiness. Or did they suffer? And do some people still?" This remark is far more effective coming from the fictional narrator than it would have been as an authorial intervention.

Intergenerational conflict surfaces in "Like Arrows in the Hands of a Giant" (*A Diver in China Seas*), in which two elderly sisters take a girl of fourteen from an orphanage to be their maid. Jess makes up stories about her employers, alleging that they beat her, but in fact she ruthlessly establishes control over them. With brutal irony Urquhart has her finally beating the surviving sister, forcing her to live out the fantasies of maltreatment in the orphanage that Jess once invented about herself. One of the local women remarks that Jess "has no imagination"; in fact, she has too much imagination, but of the wrong sort. The narrative tone is conversational, with the narrator using northeastern Scots expressions, as do Jess and the women of Auchencairn.

"Dusty Springtime" (*A Diver in China Seas*) is a hilarious account by Nelly Linton — a Scottish show-business celebrity and former music-hall star — of a visit to Paris. She has been summoned by her prim granddaughter, Pat, to help search for

Nelly's daughter and Pat's mother, the alcoholic nymphomaniac Addie, although the story is told so discursively that it is some time before Nelly explains this. In fact, Nelly tells the story of her life and provides a funny excerpt from her radio program before the reader learns why she is in Paris. This delay not only maintains a certain tension but also helps to establish Nelly's gossipy, energetic character. The style is so conversational that it seems as if Nelly is actually talking to the reader. The title refers to the fact that the visit takes place in July, although Nelly has always wanted to see Paris in the spring. It also relates to Nelly's being in the spring of life mentally but not physically: "Even though my heart was young and gay, my feet wouldn't let me, as my granny (and *she* never entered for the glamour stakes) used to say." She is still, however, "Not so dusty," as she puts it, and ends up trying to pick up her daughter's boyfriend.

Humor also predominates in "Local Boy Makes Good" (*Saltire Review,* Summer 1960; *A Diver in China Seas*). Urquhart once told Maclaren-Ross, when the latter asked him whether he would ever write about the artists Colquhoun and MacBryde, "They may look easy but they're difficult to do." However, the vividly bohemian characters of Kenneth and Davina are based on them. The central joke is that Kenneth, a famous Scottish artist and a drunk, is invited back to his hometown to open a reservoir. As Davina remarks, he never "touches water outside or in."

A Diver in China Seas also contains two longer stories. "Camp Follower" (*Blackwood's Magazine,* August 1977) is a historical fiction about Kirsty Gloag, whose love for a soldier leads her from prostitution in the slums of Edinburgh to follow him to the Peninsular Wars. She is at the mercy of forces beyond her control; she never has much idea of how the war is going, and she endures various privations and sufferings before ending up as Goya's model and housekeeper. Once again Urquhart sees the historical past as a time when ordinary people, particularly women, had to face terrible problems. The narrative is full of Scots words, which is particularly apt because all the action is seen from Kirsty's point of view.

"Princess McDougall" is a novella concerning the life story of a woman who is born into the respectable working class in Edinburgh. She becomes a shop assistant, develops an affected accent of the kind known in Edinburgh as "Morningside" (reproduced by Urquhart), acquires an equally affected friend, and then marries a rich Canadian. She makes almost-annual visits back to Scotland until

the outbreak of World War II, after which she resumes her trips. Her husband dies, her money dwindles, and she dies in poverty in a bed-sitting room near her birthplace.

Within this structure Urquhart fits in a wealth of details that illustrate not only the main character's life but also her relationships with her relatives and the processes of social change in Scotland. A careful balance is maintained between exposing Princess's pretension and coldness and sympathizing with her desire to improve herself and her treatment by her uninterested relatives. By the end she seems a sad character, unable to settle in Scotland or Canada because she is attracted by both countries. The conclusion is moving; her restlessness, it is suggested, continues even after death, when a young steward thinks he has seen her on a transatlantic liner.

Allan Massie, in the *Scotsman* (27 September 1980), described "Camp Follower" and "Princess McDougall" as "masterpieces," pointing to their "poignancy that is totally unsentimental." He praised the "accurate observation, wit, narrative skill and invention" of "a writer whose range is unequalled by anyone working in Scotland today." In *Books in Scotland* (Autumn–Winter 1980) Douglas Gifford remarked on "that bitter-sweet vitality and nostalgia for lost virility which is Urquhart's hallmark. No-one else can bring dead dreams and old ways of living back to life like him."

In March 1981 the BBC broadcast "Alice Buchan, Babysitter," a dark but humorous view of life on a modern Scottish public-housing estate, and the story was published shortly afterward (*Scottish Review,* May 1981). Another eighteen stories about the elderly, working-class Alice followed, all but the last one being broadcast. Unfortunately only two of these have appeared in print. Also in 1981 *The Book of Horses,* edited by Urquhart, was published. To celebrate, he spent three days with Margaret and Giles Gordon, his only visit to London in ten years. His life in the country was quiet but far from dull; he had a wide range of friends in the surrounding area, including many literary and artistic people.

Nine stories with supernatural themes are brought together in *Seven Ghosts in Search* (1983). Among the five that were previously uncollected is the novella "What's a Few More Deaths Between Friends?," written in the same satiric vein as "Weep No More, My Lady" and with the same targets, plus such additional manifestations of debased culture as pop stars, brainless avant-garde theater events, and intellectuals who pander to trendy youths. In

"Seven Ghosts in Search" (*Blackwood's Magazine,* May 1980) the ghost of actress Ellen Terry appears in seven guises to visitors to her old house, now a museum. She also remembers moments from her life and career, so well selected that in fewer than ten pages the reader gets what feels like a complete autobiography.

"The Saracen's Stick" (*Seven Ghosts in Search*) is constructed (like "Proud Lady in a Cage") as a series of parallels between modern life and past events. In Lebanon a small boy, Cameron Locherbie, meets the ghost of Simon, a collateral ancestor who looks just like him. Simon had joined the thirteenth-century Children's Crusade, was captured, and became the slave of Emir Sulieman. The latter's reincarnation, Sulieman Hikmet, has the same sexual interest in Cameron that the emir consummated with Simon. Both boys are befriended by Africans, and eventually Simon brings to Sulieman the same form of death that he suffered. The characters (apart from a Scottish nanny who complains about the Lebanese heat: "All my undies are sticking to me") seem more symbolic than real, which is unusual for Urquhart, but the powerful sense of evil pervading the story makes it memorable.

Urquhart's most recent collection, *Full Score* (1989), includes twenty stories selected by Graeme Roberts and intended to represent the range of Urquhart's writing. Scottish reviewers heaped praise on the book, but it was scarcely noticed in England. In *Chapman* (Autumn 1990) Gillian Ferguson was particularly impressed by Urquhart's understanding of women, especially "that self-effacing, objectified love which seems the special preserve of women," and suggested that he had earned "an honorary 'womanhood.' " One of the most striking features of the book is the extremely high standard of the early stories, something that Urquhart maintained throughout his career. His later work is more structurally complex, but from the start Urquhart has been capable of reaching the highest levels of characterization.

On 9 November 1990 Allen died. Urquhart was faced with living alone in their remote cottage, so the following year he moved to Musselburgh, just outside Edinburgh, where he bought a flat next door to his brother. Despite his long residence in England, he once wrote that he found it "harder to understand" the English than to imagine the lives of Scottish people. He has said, "I think in Scots and every character I write about seems to be Scottish," and he has always retained his Scottish accent. Nevertheless, he had said that he had no desire to live in Scotland again, so his return was a big step for him.

Urquhart's critical reputation in England has suffered from a growing dichotomy between the literatures of that country and Scotland; the same is true of another great Scottish writer, Robin Jenkins. When Urquhart began writing, his fiction was published in a wide range of English magazines. By the 1970s, however, there was a reluctance on the part of such publications to take Scottish stories, so his fiction was published more in Scottish periodicals and abroad. Correspondingly English critics took less interest in him, with such exceptions as Martin Seymour-Smith, who wrote that only Urquhart and Pritchett survive "of that group of story-writers of the Thirties which comprises the golden age, in this century, of the short story in England." In Scotland Urquhart's preeminent position as a short-story writer is recognized by such authors as Edwin Morgan, Naomi Mitchison, Massie, and Bold, who notes in *Modern Scottish Literature* that "Urquhart's ear for dialogue, especially Scots dialect, is unsurpassed in modern Scottish writing and it is matched by a mastery of descriptive detail and a command of understatement."

Urquhart's stories continue to appear in anthologies and to be taught in Scottish schools (where Scottish literature is sadly underrepresented), but references to him in academic surveys of Scottish literature tend to be unjustifiably perfunctory, misjudged, or nonexistent. With the stress that many literary academics put on attention-seeking style and the widespread misconception that difficulty is the emblem of seriousness in modern writing, Urquhart's achievement in writing deeply truthful, easily read stories is widely undervalued. In the *Spectator* (18 August 1979) King commented that he "writes so simply and so effortlessly that it is easy to underrate him." Massie, in the *Scotsman* (27 September 1980), pointed to the versatility of his writing as another reason "why he has not enjoyed the acclaim he deserves . . . there is nothing a critic resents like variety," adding that Urquhart's work "shows a large capacity which was always, till recently, regarded as one of the attributes of genius."

Now an octogenarian, Urquhart is still writing stories, has partly written a sequel to *Palace of Green Days,* reviews books occasionally, and plans to write an autobiography. Despite his present lack of fame among the reading public, his reputation is high among those who know his books, and it is only a matter of time before he gains proper recognition as one of the greatest British masters of the short story.

Interviews:

Hugh Macpherson, "Scottish Writers: Fred Urquhart," *Scottish Book Collector,* 3 (February–March 1992): 27–30;

Margaret Vaughan, "Author Returns to the Glour of No Publicity," *Herald,* 13 July 1992, p. 3;

Alexandra Henderson, "Too Old to Rock and Roll, Too Young to Rest on His Laurels," *Scotland on Sunday* (23 August 1992): 38;

Henderson, "Fred Urquhart," *Pink Paper,* 251 (8 November 1992): 14–15.

References:

Denys Val Baker, "Fred Urquhart," *Edinburgh Today,* 3 (November 1954): 23–25;

Alan Bold, "Rainbow over Clapham Common," *Scotsman,* 11 August 1979;

Bold, "The Reflective Novel: Jenkins and Urquhart," in his *Modern Scottish Literature* (London: Longman, 1983), pp. 205–212;

Bold, "Song for an Unsung Exile," *Scotsman* (supplement), 19 July 1980, p. 1;

Isobel Murray, "The Long and Short of a Tall Storyteller," *Scotsman,* 11 July 1992, p. 9;

Alexander Reid, "The Voice of the Lonely," *Scotland's Magazine* (February 1958): 55–56;

Graeme Roberts, "Fred Urquhart: Lad for Lassies," *Scottish Review,* 26 (May 1982): 18–23;

Martin Seymour-Smith, *Macmillan Guide to Modern World Literature* (London: Macmillan, 1985; New York: Bedrick, 1985), p. 312;

Michael Williams, "Class-Conscious Culture," *Voices,* 4 (1945): 27–30.

Papers:

The largest collection of Urquhart's manuscripts and letters is at Edinburgh University Library. Another important holding is at the Harry Ransom Humanities Research Center, University of Texas at Austin. The National Library of Scotland, Edinburgh, also has some of Urquhart's manuscripts, including those for his first two unpublished novels.

John Wain

(14 March 1925 –   )

Dean Baldwin
Pennsylvania State University – Erie

See also the Wain entries in *DLB 15: British Novelists, 1930–1959: Part 2* and *DLB 27: Poets of Great Britain and Ireland, 1945–1960.*

BOOKS: *Mixed Feelings* (Reading, Berkshire, U.K.: Reading University School of Art, 1951);

Hurry on Down (London: Secker & Warburg, 1953); republished as *Born in Captivity* (New York: Knopf, 1954);

Living in the Present (London: Secker & Warburg, 1955; New York: Putnam, 1960);

A Word Carved on a Sill (London: Routledge, 1956; New York: St. Martin's Press, 1956);

Preliminary Essays (London: Macmillan, 1957; New York: St. Martin's Press, 1957);

The Contenders (London: Macmillan, 1958; New York: St. Martin's Press, 1958);

A Travelling Woman (London: Macmillan, 1959; New York: St. Martin's Press, 1959);

Gerard Manley Hopkins: An Idiom of Desperation (London: Oxford University Press, 1959; Folcroft, Pa.: Folcroft Editions, 1974);

Nuncle and Other Stories (London: Macmillan, 1960; New York: St. Martin's Press, 1961);

A Song about Major Eatherly (Iowa City: Quara Press, 1961);

Weep Before God: Poems (London: Macmillan, 1961; New York: St. Martin's Press, 1961);

Strike the Father Dead (London: Macmillan, 1962; New York: St. Martin's Press, 1962);

Sprightly Running: Part of an Autobiography (London: Macmillan, 1962; New York: St. Martin's Press, 1963);

Essays on Literature and Ideas (London: Macmillan, 1963; New York: St. Martin's Press, 1963);

The Living World of Shakespeare: A Playgoer's Guide (London: Macmillan, 1964; New York: St. Martin's Press, 1964);

Wildtrack: A Poem (London: Macmillan, 1965; New York: Viking, 1965);

The Young Visitors (London: Macmillan, 1965; New York: Viking, 1965);

John Wain

Death of the Hind Legs and Other Stories (London: Macmillan, 1966; New York: Viking, 1966);

The Smaller Sky (London: Macmillan, 1967);

Arnold Bennett (New York: Columbia University Press, 1967);

Letters to Five Artists (London: Macmillan, 1969; New York: Viking, 1970);

A Winter in the Hills (London: Macmillan, 1970; New York: Viking, 1970);

The Life Guard (London: Macmillan, 1971);

The Shape of Feng (London: Covent Garden Press, 1972);

A House for the Truth: Critical Essays (London: Macmillan, 1972; New York: Viking, 1973);

Samuel Johnson (London: Macmillan, 1974; New York: Viking, 1975);

Feng (New York: Viking, 1975; London: Macmillan, 1975);

Professing Poetry (London: Macmillan, 1977; abridged edition, New York: Viking, 1978);

The Pardoner's Tale (London: Macmillan, 1978; New York: Viking, 1979);

King Caliban and Other Stories (London: Macmillan, 1978);

Poems: 1949–1979 (London: Macmillan, 1982);

Young Shoulders (London: Macmillan, 1982);

Mid-week Period Return: Home Thoughts of a Native (Stratford-upon-Avon: Celandine Press, 1982);

Frank (Oxford: AmberLane Press, 1984);

Dear Shadows (London: Murray, 1986);

Open Country (London: Hutchinson, 1987);

Where the Rivers Meet (London: Hutchinson, 1988);

Comedies (London: Hutchinson, 1990).

Edition: *A John Wain Selection,* edited by Geoffrey Halson (London: Longman, 1977).

OTHER: *Contemporary Reviews of Romantic Poetry,* edited by Wain (London: Harrap, 1953; New York: Barnes & Noble, 1953);

Interpretations: Essays on Twelve English Poems, edited by Wain (London: Routledge, 1955; New York: Hillary House, 1957);

Lives of the English Poets: A Selection, edited by Wain (London: Dent, 1975; New York: Dutton, 1975);

An Edmund Wilson Celebration, edited by Wain (Oxford: Phaidon Press, 1978);

The Seafarer, translated from the Anglo-Saxon by Wain (Warwick, U.K.: Grenville Press, 1980);

Everyman's Book of English Verse, edited by Wain (London: Dent, 1981);

The Journals of James Boswell, 1762–1795, edited, with an introduction, by Wain (New Haven: Yale University Press, 1991).

John Wain has achieved fame as a novelist, poet, critic, biographer, and short-story writer — in short, as a modern man of letters. Like his contemporaries Kingsley Amis, Philip Larkin, and John Braine, Wain came of age just before World War II and published his first works in the years just following — a time when Britain was recovering from the war's devastation and when young writers were reacting against the orthodoxies of modernism. Wain, though sometimes regarded primarily as a social critic, might better be characterized as a liberal humanist. Over the years his novels have become less comically boisterous and more pessimistic, as his thematic concerns have shifted from the repressions of society to "the effects of loneliness and the remoteness of love," according to Dale Salwak in *John Wain* (1981). Wain's short stories show similar concerns, but, particularly in the more successful ones, he examines evil, self-destruction, and interior corrosiveness. He treats these issues philosophically, even religiously, not as case studies in social or psychological "causes" but as mysteries of human nature to be explored but never fully understood.

John Barrington Wain was born 14 March 1925 in Stoke-on-Trent, Staffordshire, to Arnold and Anne Turner Wain. John Wain's forebears were working-class laborers on his father's side and peasant and working-class laborers on his mother's. In *Dear Shadows* (1986), a collection of semi-autobiographical essays, Wain sketches an admiring portrait of his father, who scrambled up from grim poverty to become a dentist and an influential lay preacher. In 1928 the family moved to Penkhull, a step up the social ladder. Although spared the barbarities of English boarding school, Wain learned at infant school and again at Newcastle-under-Lyme High School that the world divides itself roughly into two camps: the bullies and the bullied. He traces his hatred of totalitarianism to the routine violence of school life. Humor was young Wain's means of survival. Among his earliest memories are the feelings aroused by the beauty of nature, encouraged throughout his youth by his father, an avid walker in the Staffordshire countryside. Wain could in no sense be called a nature writer, but his fictional characters often find solace and direction in nature's calming influence.

Wain did not excel in school or at athletics. Scornful of discipline and somewhat of a prig, he could learn only from teachers he admired. Nevertheless, he read voraciously, began writing fiction at nine, and became a lifelong lover of jazz in his teens. At sixteen he joined the Officers' Training Corps as a curious act of defiance, but he was spared military service because of a detached retina. By his own admission, adopting his parents' pacifism made him self-righteous and enduring wartime privations made him pessimistic; but the war enabled him, in spite of poor preparation, to attend Oxford. Still nursing a defensive siege mentality and an un-

*Dust jacket for Wain's first collection of short fiction, which is
built around the novella-length title story*

earned youthful pessimism, Wain fell in love with
Oxford, poetry, and scholarship. While there he
was influenced by C. S. Lewis, Neville Coghill, and
the eccentric E. H. W. Meyerstein. Wain acted in
Coghill's production of Shakespeare's *Measure for
Measure* alongside Richard Burton. Wain also
founded a literary magazine, *Mandrake,* and upon
graduation in 1946 was appointed Fereday Fellow
at Saint John's College, eventually earning an M.A.

Wain describes himself in this period as wanting only to bury himself in the past and let the
world rush over him. This attitude, and a lectureship at the University of Reading, led him to marry
Marianne Urmstrom. In 1947 he had begun what
he assumed would be a settled academic career, a
view he maintained even after publishing a slim volume of poems, *Mixed Feelings* (1951). He was moving toward a literary career, however, beginning a
novel in 1949 and finishing it in 1952 amid the turmoil of a disintegrating marriage – which ended in

1956 – and resulting ill health. That novel, *Hurry on
Down* (1953), thrust Wain into the public eye as a
member of the so-called Angry Young Men, a label
that he, like the others, rejects. In 1955 he resigned
his post at the university in order to write, but
Wain has never been able to escape the lure of academia, either as a writer or teacher. He has since
taught in France, Canada, and the United States as
well as in England.

Wain was extremely productive in the 1950s,
his efforts resulting in the novels *Living in the Present*
(1955), *The Contenders* (1958), and *A Travelling Woman* (1959); two volumes of essays; a second collection of poetry, *A Word Carved on a Sill* (1956); and a
study of Gerard Manley Hopkins. In addition, he
published short stories in *Harper's Bazaar, Everywo-
man, Lilliput, London Magazine,* and *Suspense,* but the
postwar collapse of the magazine market for short
fiction was already evident. Five stories in his first
collection, *Nuncle and Other Stories* (1960), appeared
there for the first time. In a 1974 interview with
Peter Firchow, Wain recalls, "One of my least unsatisfactory stories ["Nuncle"] is about 20,000
words, but in order to get it into print at all, I had to
write a lot of other short stories to go with it."
Wain's first volume of short fiction reflects his
"angry" mood of these years but also shows concern for a wide range of topics and issues. Indeed,
one purpose of the collection may have been to
demonstrate Wain's distance from any particular
school of fiction, as emphasized by a brief preface:

> This is John Wain's first volume of short stories, and he
> has taken the opportunity offered by this form to de-
> velop his work in several directions. While some of the
> stories take us into the world of his novels, others move
> completely outside that world . . . and, while the earlier
> gift for comedy is present here as freshly as ever, the
> book as a whole represents a remarkable broadening of
> the writer's range.

Critical reception of the stories was predictably mixed. Gene Baro (*Books,* 10 September 1961)
complained that "this short fiction, for the most
part, lacks the insight of the poetry, the down-to-
earth vigor of the essays, or the satirical point of the
novels." Hallie Burnett (*Saturday Review,* 16 September 1961), however, was both more generous and
more perceptive in noting the variety of stories in
the collection and that "it is character with its incon-
sistencies – even its hallucinations – which holds
the reader's attention."

Two stories resemble Wain's novels in emphasizing the individual in society: "The Two Worlds
of Ernst" and "Christmas at Rillingham's." The

first grew out of Wain's 1953 experiences in Switzerland, where he went to recuperate from the emotional and physical ailments then afflicting him. "The Two Worlds of Ernst" is an accomplished but remote character sketch and hence not particularly successful.

"Christmas at Rillingham's" cuts deeper. Its main character and narrator, Sidney, resembles Charles Lumley in *Hurry on Down:* alienated, sexually frustrated, and sarcastic toward those around him. The objects of Sidney's sarcasm are his boss at Rillingham's appliance and record store, where Sidney works as a repairman, and Patty, the curvaceous young clerk whose bubbly personality attracts buyers of rock-and-roll records. Sidney drops the sarcasm when his repair rounds introduce him to a pretty Swiss au pair whom he tries to impress with his knowledge of electronics and the store's new answering machine. She is more interested in watching television, however, and in the end Sidney is defeated by the technology he thinks will assure his future. He resigns his position, consoling himself with the thought that he must soon do his national service anyway.

"Christmas at Rillingham's," unlike "The Two Worlds of Ernst," has a genuinely individual voice and the pressure of a felt society. Wain's Switzerland is dreamy and ethereal, but his England is palpable, rife with economic and class distinctions and peopled by talkative bores. Sidney's voice carries the alienation and enthusiasm of youth, alternately depressed and buoyed by sexual promise and irrationally self-destructive.

"Rafferty" and "The Quickest Way out of Manchester" are enlivened by details of lower-middle-class life, but the conflicts are interpersonal rather than social. In the former Walter is hopelessly in love with Isobel, but she continually puts him off, insisting he be patient and give her time. Finally he decides it is time to move on, just as she decides it is time to get serious.

In "The Quickest Way out of Manchester" Wain explores the contradictions of fatherhood and manhood through Mr. White, who has invited his workmate, Mr. Green, to his home for dinner. White envies Green because he is unmarried, and in hints and leering suggestions White tries to get Green to reveal his escapades in "gay Paree." Green is embarrassed and perplexed by White's behavior until he meets White's young daughter, Erica, and concludes that he has been invited to be considered as a potential husband for her. He is badly mistaken: White's paternal concerns are that Erica remain chaste and at home until he can find her a suit-

able young man, not a waster like (he implies) Green.

Wain has written that he has no patience with adults who forget what childhood is like. This conviction lies behind two of the collection's most telling stories, which are presented through the eyes of children. In the strikingly original "Master Richard" the voice belongs to a thirty-five-year-old consciousness trapped in a five-year-old's body — Wain's way of indicating that a child's mind is not free of adult anxieties. Caught between two worlds Richard first finds release by writing of his anger and frustration. When a brother is born, he finds a new outlet: a diabolical plan to use his brother to destroy his parents and avenge himself on God. That plan, however, is foiled by the brother's unconditional love for him, leaving the narrator resolved on suicide.

Much of the story's fascination comes from Richard's wholly convincing position as man/child. He sees through adults and children, yet his body and immature emotions betray him at every turn. His rage is both frightening and understandable; life has played him a dirty trick. The suggestion of religious allegory in the end is convincing, leaving readers in a perplexing, Manichaean universe of evil and love.

"A Message from the Pig-Man" is gentler in tone and more realistic in method. Six-year-old Eric is confused by adults and frightened by the Pig-Man, who in the boy's imagination is some monstrous combination of human and pig. But he is merely a farmer who collects table scraps from housewives to feed his pigs, as Eric discovers when he bravely faces up to his fear and confronts him. Applying this lesson to more complicated situations, however, leaves Eric as confused as ever, for neither his mother nor her live-in lover can explain why Daddy can no longer stay with them. Grownups, he concludes, are "mad and silly, and he hated them all, all, *all.*"

"A Few Drinks with Alcock and Brown" is in many ways the most pithy story in the collection. Events are seen through Eric Benlowes, an Oxford undergraduate who has written his fiancée, Ellen, to end their engagement. When he receives her letter in response, he takes it to a pub where, in the company of others, he can read it nonchalantly. As he listens with one ear to the story Digby is relating to Alcock and Brown, and with the other to the conversation of a young couple, tension in him rises, and his previous confidence erodes. He recalls the thrush that had witnessed his first kiss with Ellen as "the only real thing in his life." As he hurries off on an absurd errand with his fellow undergraduates, he still has not opened the letter, but the reader knows, as does Eric, that he has blundered in ending the engagement and that no amount of superficial posing will be able to compensate for the mistake.

Interior tension and the suspicion of an irretrievable error also surface in "A Stranger at the Party," in which the narrator is a recent refugee from an unnamed Eastern European Communist state. The events of the evening and the flow of his thoughts convince him that much of his former life was a lie and that, in spite of having to learn a new language, he can succeed as a poet; the circumstances of life matter less than the genuineness of his poetic vision. This story may well be the result of Wain's trip to the Soviet Union in 1960 and his resulting disapproval of the Soviet regime, particularly its systematic lying to itself.

The novella-length "Nuncle" provides an interesting example of the strengths and weaknesses of the volume as a whole. Its narrator is Tom Rogers, a fifty-year-old writer whose place in literary history is assured by his first two novels. Since writing them he has produced nothing. More to the point he must quit drinking. Rogers's solution is to find a wife, and he proposes to Daphne, an otherwise sensible and successful woman of twenty-five, who agrees to marry him, apparently to help him reform. They move into the country cottage already occupied by Daphne's retired father, Alex, but still Rogers cannot write. Ironically Alex can; in fact he is a genuine literary artist. However, he hates the publicity that writers attract, so he and Rogers strike a bargain: Alex will write, and Rogers will publish the stories under his name. Daphne acquiesces to this scheme, but before long she transfers her loyalties from Rogers to her father because those two, in effect, have exchanged roles. Rogers winds up leaving the cottage and returning to his former ways.

"Nuncle" illustrates many of Wain's finest qualities: his fertile invention, skill at characterization, unerring ear for dialogue, and ability to create an entirely convincing and individual voice for each story. The voice of Tom Rogers strikes just the right note of canny insight, humor, and self-deprecation. However, the plot twist that gives the story its individuality and unpredictable lifelike quality is hampered by the point of view, for the interesting change occurs in Daphne, and this the narrator can view only from the outside. In "Christmas at Rillingham's" and "Master Richard" the plot twists and character changes occur within the narrators. In "A

Few Drinks with Alcock and Brown" and "The Quickest Way out of Manchester" the omniscient narrators can peer into the protagonists' thoughts. In "Nuncle" the inside view of change is lost.

Nuncle and Other Stories shows Wain's versatility and talents as a short-story writer. His techniques are traditional: a plain, economical style; clear narrative line; and sharply etched characters. In the best stories there is also something of an edge, a grit in the psychological machinery that reveals the unpredictability, even cussedness, of the human psyche – the suggestion of inherent irrationality and mystery. Wain has described his approach to short fiction:

> The kind of short, compressed poem that I write . . . is meant to present its subject-matter with the immediacy of the sudden shocks you get in life. The short story, too, can work in something like the same way by picking the moment when a thing comes to the boil and relying on suggestion to convey what comes before and after.

In January 1960 Wain married Eirian James, and they had three sons. In 1960 Wain also was elected a fellow by the Royal Society of Literature, but he resigned in 1961. He continued to produce poetry, criticism, and short stories. In *Death of the Hind Legs and Other Stories* (1966) the fertility and inventiveness of *Nuncle and Other Stories* are still evident, but the tone is more mellow – the narrative voices have lost some of their edge. Reviewers, again, were divided. One particularly hostile critic, T. O'Hara (*Commonweal*, 10 February 1967), called Wain a "literary prankster" and dismissed most of the stories as failing in their objectives. Joseph Epstein (*Book Week*, 27 November 1966), however, claimed that the stories "constitute a delicate and remarkable probe of the modern heart of darkness."

"King Caliban" is the most successful of the collection, in part because of its narrator, Bert, who sounds like a moral adolescent attempting to explain why his "daft" brother, Fred, attacked a heckler at a wrestling match. By "daft" Bert means intellectually slow, emotionally childlike, and physically strong but gentle. Although younger, Bert has always been Fred's mentor, guide, and spokesman – a fast talker with a cocky attitude and an eye on material success. When Fred's wife, Doreen, asks Bert to help Fred make more money, Bert suggests professional wrestling. However, the gentle Fred dislikes the pseudoviolence of the sport and the evil persona, King Caliban, he must adopt. At his first bout he accidentally injures his opponent and cracks under the pressure of heckling. Hurdling from the ring he attacks the offending fan and must be subdued by police.

The story is a perfect vehicle for Wain's disgust at sham publicity and phoniness in art, as well as the love of violence and material possessions. Fred is almost a literary cliché – a gentle giant content with work and family. But Doreen wants all the modern appliances and conveniences, and Bert sees wrestling as a way to promote his own ambitions. Just before the first bout Doreen complains that she hardly knows Fred anymore. Bert replies, "When he's earning you eighty quid a week, you won't care whether you know him or not." Neither can understand Fred's simple moral outrage at the gratuitous violence and bloodthirsty taunting of the crowd. Bert walks away from the situation unscathed and uncomprehending, leaving his bewildered brother to face the consequences. Wain observes that his novel *The Contenders* "tries to tackle the problem of (a) material ambition as a corrupting power, (b) rivalry as ditto, (c) whether personal relationships or 'work' in the Carlylean sense is the better foundation for a life, (d) the metropolitan versus the provincial virtues, i.e. 'being in touch' versus 'sturdy independence.' " This is a perfect description of "King Caliban" as well.

Adultery is the subject of two fine stories, "Come in Captain Grindle" and "Further Education." The latter derives at some level from Wain's years at Oxford. The narrator, James Richards, is not a likable protagonist; he is philistine, self-centered, and smugly confident. When asked by a former Oxford acquaintance to donate money to an educational scheme in Africa, Richards is drawn not to the idea but to Laura, his friend's wife and a former love interest. From the well-rendered dialogue, the carefully observed social detail, and the shrewd psychology of the narrative emerges a picture of casual decay: Richards's seduction of Laura twenty years beforehand, her intervening infidelities, and his reseduction of her via his large donation to the African venture. Wain captures the casual, amoral sordidness of contemporary mores, but the issue is not simply sexual. At the core is the willingness to use and manipulate people for personal ends.

Yet a third view of these issues is afforded by "Giles and Penelope," in which a young woman comes to realize that her lover uses and manipulates her. In the end she demands to be treated as what she in fact is – a kept woman. At first appalled, Giles finally accepts, excited by the prospect of using, then discarding, Penelope when it suits him.

"Down Our Way" is the shortest and, perhaps for that reason, one of the most effective stories in the collection. The Robinson family, which rents its spare rooms to lodgers, has learned that a newspaper reporter has blackened his face and set out to test the racial climate by attempting to rent accommodations. The outraged Mrs. Robinson is prepared to defeat him by cheerfully renting him her room. When an authentic West Indian inquires about her vacancy, she agrees to accommodate him. Her family is horrified, but, even after discovering her error, she is not worried. She will find an excuse to get rid of him. At this moment Mr. Robinson sees his wife as if for the first time. The ending is perhaps a bit forced, and the story takes too-easy swipes at Christianity, but its humor is refreshing. The characterizations, especially of the smart-aleck Robinson children, are zesty, and the dialogue is masterful.

"Darkness" mixes comedy, pain, and panic in depicting an English tourist trying to find his way back to his hotel in a Spanish village where the electricity is turned off at night to save power. Wain's depiction of the tourist's struggle is fully and imaginatively realized, with a concentration of detail and suspense reminiscent of William Sansom at his best. The remaining five stories in the collection have individual merits but do not rise to the level of Wain's best. "A Vist at Tea-Time," for instance, presents a Mr. Williams who is nostalgically longing to tour his boyhood home. The visit is predictably disappointing but not because the house has changed; rather it is now inhabited by philistines. The couple's coldness, reflected in the sterile modern furniture, is effectively conveyed, but the ultimate effectiveness of the story depends on whether the reader can accept the ending, in which Williams enters into an elaborate fantasy with the couple's son.

"Manhood" is another of Wain's critical looks at adults but is far too obvious and predictable. Equally obvious is "Steam," which sentimentalizes its elderly protagonist. "Death of the Hind Legs" is sentimental in its depiction of aging theater people, their condemned playhouse, and the familiar "the show must go on" theme.

Generational conflict lies at the heart of "The Valentine Generation," in which a postal worker confronts a distraught young woman who wants him to return a letter she has written in anger to her boyfriend. Her request is contrary to regulations, but beyond this is his suspicion that she (and her generation) regard love as nothing but "Sex, sex, sex from morning to night and never a bit of sentiment." To her, he is part of the valentine generation, with chocolate-box ideas of love. In the end his

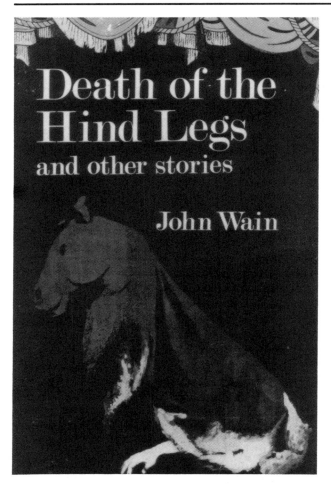

Dust jacket for Wain's 1966 collection of short fiction, which concerns such topics as adultery and racial tension

garded as merely reactionary, but that is a misrepresentation and oversimplification. According to Salwak (in *John Wain*) the author continues to observe worrisome cultural trends: "Art and imagination have been replaced by journalism, people by the machine, love by sex, folklore by popular movies, work by productivity, and villages by suburbs." Wain sees these forces partly as the result of choices made by individuals.

"The Life Guard" is a particularly disturbing study of a young man's attempt to make himself look good and please his boss. Jimmy is disaffected, uncertain of his future, and uninterested in school or anything except swimming. Luckily he has been hired as a lifeguard and swimming instructor at Red Rocks Beach as part of a promotional campaign by Mr. Prendergast to reinvigorate the local economy. But Prendergast's idea has not worked well. Business is not better than usual, and Jimmy fears he will lose his job, so he bribes his friend Hopper to fake drowning. Everything goes wrong, however, and even though Jimmy performs admirably, Hopper dies. No one suspects Jimmy, but Hopper's younger sister, Agnes, has overheard their plans. Jimmy's reaction to her threat to tell what she knows is swift and violent: " 'Listen,' Jimmy breathed. 'If you tell anybody what you heard, I'll kill you. I'll get at you and I'll kill you. You say I killed Hopper, well, if I can be a murderer once I can be one twice.' "

"While the Sun Shines" presents an interior view of moral choice as faced by a young tractor driver working for a vindictively jealous boss, Robert, who thinks his wife Yvonne has designs on the tractor driver. Hoping to force him to quit, Robert orders the driver to mow the hay on a steep slope that has already caused one driver severe injury. Tension between the driver and his boss builds, complicated by Yvonne's presence and "lecherous eye," until Robert relents and lets the driver decide whether or not to mow the dangerous hillside. Surprisingly he takes up the challenge, and Wain vividly dramatizes how the driver attacks the hill and controls his fear while maneuvering the tractor through this harrowing experience. When he has beaten the hill, the driver is exultant, singing "I am the king" and looking forward to future encounters with it. And, in a surprise twist, he accepts Yvonne's invitation for a drink: "Another time, I'd have gone straight back to Mary and the kids. But today I was the king, I'd won and it was a case of winner take all."

A similarly rich ambiguity emerges from "The Innocent," which at first reading may seem merely

sentimentality convinces him to return her letter, but, before their quarrel has ended, each has enlightened, if not convinced, the other. "I wonder" are the last words of the story, and they leave just the right note of doubt and inconclusiveness. If the situation seems contrived and the dialogue a bit too articulate to be believable, there is at least a satisfying complexity to the arguments presented.

The five years between *Death of the Hind Legs* and Wain's next collection, *The Life Guard* (1971), were apparently tranquil ones personally, devoted to teaching (Centre Universitaire Experimental, Vincennes and Oxford), criticism, and the novel *A Winter in the Hills* (1970), whose setting reflects Wain's summer holidays on his wife's ancestral farm in northern Wales. His third collection contains only six stories, but four are vintage Wain. His tone has lost the harsh edge and comic bite of the first collection, but the overall view has darkened, which is also true of his later novels. Among some reviewers this shift has been re-an inconclusive anecdote. After an unsatisfactory day in the country Heseltine is anxious, edgy, and eager to go home. A nameless fear causes him to drive cautiously, but he still runs over an animal. Forgetting his desire to be home Heseltine finds a dead badger and, digging the soft earth with his hands, buries it. This act relieves his causeless worries; he looks forward confidently to the rest of the drive home and a night's rest in his clean bed. Somehow immediate contact with elemental nature – the animal's blood, the soft earth – has allayed his fears. The mechanism remains a mystery – like nature itself – but the effect is real.

Fallen innocence and discovery of the evil within are the subjects of "I Love You, Ricky." Hilda has betrayed her friend by pretending to lose the cuff link Elizabeth tore from the shirt of Ricky, a pop star. Her brother's accidental discovery of the cuff link and deliberate disclosure of Hilda's lie mean the end of the girls' friendship and Hilda's love for Ricky: "To cheat and steal for Ricky was fine. But to cheat and steal and be found out – that was failure. And there was no place for failure in his young and shining face."

The incidents in "I Love You, Ricky" seem trivial but are layered with significance. Rivalry, revenge, hatred, and the joys of self-delusion and self-righteousness are all part of this simple story. Deeper than the rivalry between Hilda and Elizabeth is the conflict between Hilda and her brother, Rodney, who lives to inflict pain on his sister. Hilda hopes that "one day, one day, she would find some way of hurting him as much." This is a story of original sin, as elemental in its motives as the stories from Genesis and as refreshingly clear of irrelevant psychologizing. Wain is not afraid to confront evil as a simple fact of human nature, needing nothing more than its own delights as its reason for being.

Wain's place in literary history may in the end rest on his novels, though he prefers his poetry. In *Sprightly Running: Part of an Autobiography* (1962), he writes: "The chief snag I found then [at age nine] about novel-writing was the same one that I find today, the sheer difficulty of keeping the thing going on a level plane; I lack the power of sustaining large structures, and would be a short-story writer if it weren't so impossible to make a living by it." He also stated that "the artist's function is always to *humanize* the society he is living in, to assert the importance of humanity in the teeth of whatever is currently trying to annihilate that importance." In this respect Wain's stories succeed in their intention through their uncanny ability to reveal much about contemporary (and perennial) moral issues in a short space. Their artistry is traditional but unmistakable, and because of it Wain deserves serious consideration as an artist of uncommon insight and accomplishment.

Interviews:

"International Symposium on the Short Story, Part II," *Kenyon Review,* 31, no. 1 (1969): 58–94;

Peter Firchow, "John Wain," in his *The Writer's Place: Interviews on the Literary Situation in Contemporary Britain* (Minneapolis: University of Minnesota Press, 1974), pp. 313–330;

David Girard, *My Work as a Novelist: John Wain* (Cardiff: Drake Educational Associates, 1978).

Bibliography:

Dale Salwak, *John Braine and John Wain: A Reference Guide* (Boston, Twayne, 1980).

References:

James J. Gindin, *Postwar British Fiction: New Accents and Attitudes* (Berkeley & Los Angeles: University of California Press, 1962);

Jean Pickering, "The English Short Story in the Sixties," in *The English Short Story, 1945–1960,* edited by Dennis Vannatta (Boston: Twayne, 1985), pp. 75–119;

Dale Salwak, *John Wain* (Boston: Twayne, 1981).

Sylvia Townsend Warner

(6 December 1893 – 1 May 1978)

Barbara Brothers
Youngstown State University

See also the Warner entry in *DLB 34: British Novelists, 1890–1929: Traditionalists.*

BOOKS: *The Espalier* (London: Chatto & Windus, 1925; New York: Dial, 1925);

Lolly Willowes; or, The Loving Huntsman (London: Chatto & Windus, 1926; New York: Viking, 1926);

Mr. Fortune's Maggot (London: Chatto & Windus, 1927; New York: Viking, 1927);

The Maze: A Story to Be Read Aloud (London: Fleuron, 1928);

Time Importuned (London: Chatto & Windus, 1928; New York: Viking, 1928);

Some World Far from Ours; and "Stay, Corydon, Thou Swain" (London: Mathews & Marrot, 1929);

The True Heart (London: Chatto & Windus, 1929; New York: Viking, 1929);

Elinor Barley (London: Cresset, 1930);

This Our Brother (London: Cambridge, 1930);

Opus 7 (London: Chatto & Windus, 1931; New York: Viking, 1931);

A Moral Ending and Other Stories (London: Jackson, 1931); enlarged as *The Salutation* (London: Chatto & Windus, 1932; New York: Viking, 1932);

Rainbow (New York: Knopf, 1932);

Whether a Dove, or Seagull, by Warner and Valentine Ackland (New York: Viking, 1933; London: Chatto & Windus, 1934);

More Joy in Heaven, and Other Stories (London: Cresset, 1935);

Summer Will Show (London: Chatto & Windus, 1936; New York: Viking, 1936);

After the Death of Don Juan (London: Chatto & Windus, 1938; New York: Viking, 1939);

24 Short Stories, by Warner, Graham Greene, and James Laver (London: Cresset, 1939);

The Cat's Cradle-Book (New York: Viking, 1940; London: Chatto & Windus, 1960);

The People Have No Generals (London: Newport, 1941);

Sylvia Townsend Warner, 1954 (photograph by F. Carlos Pickering)

A Garland of Straw and Other Stories (London: Chatto & Windus, 1943); republished as *A Garland of Straw: Twenty-Eight Stories* (New York: Viking, 1943);

Two Poems (Derby, U.K.: Hopkins, 1945);

The Museum of Cheats (London: Chatto & Windus, 1947; New York: Viking, 1947);

The Corner That Held Them (London: Chatto & Windus, 1948; New York: Viking, 1948);

Somerset (London: Elek, 1949);

Jane Austen, 1775–1817 (London & New York: Published for the British Council and the National Book League by Longmans, Green, 1951; revised, London & New York: Longmans, Green, 1957);

The Flint Anchor (London: Chatto & Windus, 1954; New York: Viking, 1954); republished as *The Barnards of Loseby* (New York: Popular Library, 1974);

Winter in the Air, and Other Stories (London: Chatto & Windus, 1955; New York: Viking, 1956);

Boxwood (London: Privately printed, 1957; enlarged, London: Chatto & Windus, 1960);

A Spirit Rises (London: Chatto & Windus, 1962; New York: Viking, 1962);

Sketches from Nature (Wells, U.K. & London: Clare, 1963);

A Stranger with a Bag, and Other Stories (London: Chatto & Windus, 1966); republished as *Swans on an Autumn River* (New York: Viking, 1966);

T. H. White: A Biography (London: Cape/Chatto & Windus, 1967; New York: Viking, 1968);

King Duffus and Other Poems (Wells, U.K.: Clare, 1968);

The Innocent and the Guilty: Stories (London: Chatto & Windus, 1971; New York: Viking, 1971);

The Kingdoms of Elfin (London: Chatto & Windus, 1977; New York: Viking, 1977);

Azrael and Other Poems (Newbury: Libanus, 1978); republished as *Twelve Poems* (London: Chatto & Windus, 1980);

Scenes of Childhood (London: Chatto & Windus, 1981; New York: Viking, 1982);

Collected Poems, edited by Claire Harman (Manchester, U.K.: Carcanet, 1983; New York: Viking, 1983);

One Thing Leading to Another: And Other Stories, edited by Susanna Pinney (London: Chatto & Windus, 1984; New York: Viking, 1984);

Selected Poems, edited by Harman (Manchester: Carcanet, 1985);

Selected Stories (London: Chatto & Windus, 1988; New York: Viking, 1988).

OTHER: *Alleluia, Anthem for Five Voices*, score by Warner (London: Oxford University Press, 1925);

"Notation: The Growth of a System," in *The Oxford History of Music*, volume 1 (London: Oxford University Press, 1929), pp. 66–84;

The Week-End Dickens, edited by Warner (London: Maclehose, 1932; New York: Lorring & Mussey, 1932?);

"Man's Moral Law," in *Man, Proud Man*, edited by Mabel Ulrich (London: Hamish Hamilton, 1932), pp. 221–245;

Ilya Ehrenburg, *The Fall of France Seen through Soviet Eyes*, foreword by Warner (London: Modern Books, 1941);

Gilbert White, *The Portrait of a Tortoise: Extracted from the Journals of Gilbert White*, edited by Warner (London: Chatto & Windus, 1946; Toronto: Oxford University Press, 1946);

T. H. White, *The Book of Merlyn*, prologue by Warner (Austin: University of Texas Press, 1977);

"Theodore Powys at East Chaldon," in *Recollections of the Powys Brothers: Llewelyn, Theodore and John Cowper*, edited by Belinda Humfrey (London: Owen, 1980), pp. 127–136.

TRANSLATIONS: Marcel Proust, *(Contre Sainte-Beuve) By Way of Saint-Beuve* (London: Chatto & Windus, 1958); republished as *On Art and Literature* (New York: Meridien, 1958);

Jean René Huguenin, *A Place of Shipwreck* (London: Chatto & Windus, 1963).

SELECTED PERIODICAL PUBLICATIONS – UNCOLLECTED:

FICTION

"Haig," *Time and Tide*, 14 November 1931, pp. 1305–1307;

"The Doll's House," *Time and Tide*, 13 January 1934, pp. 35–36;

"Story with an Hypothesis," *London Mercury*, 31 (February 1935): 341–345;

"An English Fable," *Left Review*, 3 (August 1937): 406;

"Bathrooms Remembered," *New Yorker*, 39 (11 January 1964): 33–36.

POETRY

"In This Midwinter," *Left Review*, 1 (January 1935): 101;

"Red Front!," *Left Review*, 1 (April 1935): 255–257.

NONFICTION

"Behind the Firing Line: Some Experiences in a Munition Factory. By a Lady Worker," anonymous, *Blackwood's*, 199 (February 1916): 191–207;

"Modern Witches," *Eve* (18 August 1926): 331, 336;

"Recommendations to Starvation," *Countryman*, 12 (January 1936): 563–567;

"Barcelona," *Left Review*, 2 (December 1936): 812–816;

"The Drought Breaks," *Life and Letters Today*, 16 (Summer 1937): 68–71;

"Harvest in 1937," *New Statesman and Nation* (31 July 1937): 184;

"What the Soldier Said," *Time and Tide*, 14 August 1937, p. 1091;

"The Way by Which I Have Come," *Countryman*, 19 (July 1939): 472–486;

"Fifty Girls Who Shouldn't," *Our Time*, 1 (December 1941): 11–17;

"Here in This Narrow Room," *Our Time*, 2 (April 1942): 1–2;

"Elizabeth Gaskell," *Our Time*, 4 (February 1945): 8–9;

"Love of France," *Our Time*, 5 (August 1945): 5–6;

"The Jungle Blossom," *Our Time*, 7 (August 1948): 287–292.

Sylvia Townsend Warner's short stories are remarkable both for the diversity of their subject matter and for their number. Most frequently Warner's narratives are a blend of realism and the fantastic. Before the works of such writers as Gabriel García Marquez and Salman Rushdie lent fashionability to the term *magic realism,* Warner was creating her fictional worlds by combining what the eye of fancy fathoms with what the eye of nature observes. In some cases the place and its inhabitants are imaginary, as are the kingdoms of Zuy, Elfhame, Wirre Gedanken, Bourrasque, Castle Ash Grove, Brocéliande, and the dozen other elfin courts that Warner depicts as scattered throughout Europe. In other cases the settings and characters are scrupulously true to life. As in Marquez's and Rushdie's fiction, real people, places, and events from the past come to life in the present.

Warner was born on 6 December 1893 to the Harrow schoolmaster George Townsend Warner and his independent-minded wife, Nora Hudleston Warner. While much can be learned about Warner's life from her published letters (1983), the best picture of her early years is found in her collection of semi-autobiographical stories, *Scenes of Childhood* (1981). She recounts vacations in "Wild Wales," at a cousin's home that was "reputed to be one of the best-haunted houses in Ireland," in Cologne, and at the family holiday cottage in Devonshire. The cottage was built as her mother had directed: "My father was a schoolmaster – a rather naysaying profession. In private life, he redressed the balance by falling in with my mother's wishes whenever this did not lead directly to crime or public riot." Warner also remarks: "My mother was infallible. My father made no such claim." Warner clearly found her father's company more pleasant than her mother's. She was, however, entranced by her mother's tales of her girlhood in India, "this astonishing storehouse, full of scents and terrors, flowers, tempests, monkeys, beggars winding worms out of their feet." While Warner's fiction exhibits the influence of her historian father, it bears the imprint of her mother in the way Warner makes the exotic part of the everyday.

Like most middle-class women of her generation who were the daughters of educated men, Warner received her schooling at home. Her father did not encourage her to learn to read, believing that the mind develops better through observation, memory, and "thinking for itself" than through books. Perhaps her powers of perception and her mother's use of the Bible as her reading book may have contributed to the originality of Warner's tales.

In 1913 Warner began an affair with her music teacher, Sir Percy Buck, who was twenty-two years older than she and married. The outbreak of World War I ended her plans to go to Europe to study with the composer Arnold Schoenberg; instead, she helped to raise money for the Red Cross and to settle Belgian refugees in Harrow. In 1915 she went to work in a munitions factory. Warner's father died in 1917; shortly thereafter she moved to London, where she worked as a musicologist, serving on the editorial committee for *Tudor Church Music* (1923–1929), and composed music. Chatto and Windus published her first volume of poetry, *The Espalier* (1925), and her novels *Lolly Willowes; or, The Loving Huntsman* (1926) and *Mr. Fortune's Maggot* (1927); both novels were best-sellers. From 1927 on she supported herself by her writing, though she continued to work on the *Tudor Church Music* project until 1929. Her first short story, "The Maze," appeared in 1928. The next year two more stories were published in the same volume with her third novel, *The True Heart*.

From the first, Warner's books were even more popular in America than in England. The *New York Herald Tribune* contracted with her for four articles, and she was treated as a celebrity during a visit to New York in 1929. There she formed lifetime friendships with prominent women in American literary circles, including Dorothy Parker, Elinor Wylie, Anne Parrish, and Jean Untermeyer. Warner was the toast of prominent reviewers as well.

In 1930 Buck ended their long relationship. That summer Warner bought a country house, Chaldon; in the fall she and Valentine Ackland began their life together there. The relationship lasted until Ackland's death in 1969.

"Some World Far from Ours," which opens Warner's collection *The Salutation* (1932), is typical of her stories. Minnie is a maid in a house of prostitution that masquerades as a restaurant. Between stripping the beds, she reads novels: "The novels were all about love, passionate love. Strong millionaires won the hearts of slender girls who had scorned their millions through a misunderstanding; airmen came back from Biskra just in time, nosediving into the yew walk; a red-haired typist became the world's darling, but even on the Lido was true to a memory, and the prattle of a child wiped out years of estrangement between a taciturn husband and a fashionable wife." The novels present a world far from the one that Minnie inhabits with the husband and three children she supports in a basement room. Not even a visit to the ocean, from which her grandfather earned his living as a seaman, is possible for such a woman.

Like Anton Chekhov's stories, Warner's are plotless evocations of character and place. And, like Chekhov's, Warner's characters are usually failures – or, if not failures, they are unhappy and haunted. While Chekhov's characters are from the upper classes, however, Warner most often depicts proletarian characters such as Minnie. Warner seems to identify with them; never does the reader get the sense that she either pities or idealizes them. Perhaps she has this attitude because, as she remarks in her 1959 article "Women as Writers" (reprinted in her *Collected Poems,* 1983), a woman looks on life through the "pantry window," writes on the pantry table, and is "at ease in low company."

Warner writes with compassion and acceptance of human flaws and avoids sentimentality. In "The Salutation" the narrator comments, "If from the first we could look into the hearts of those we meet, we should look on all men mildly. It is not our enemies that we seek to destroy, but our own illusions which mistook them for friends."

The stories in her collection *More Joy in Heaven, and Other Stories* (1935) are similar to those in her first volume. "The Democrat's Daughter," like "Emily" in *The Salutation,* is fictionalized history; it is also a satiric look at class. Class and age are the subjects of "Nosegay." There are stories of the unnoticed, such as Amy Cruttwell in "The Property of a Lady," who flagrantly shoplifts to gain attention by being arrested, and of the greedy, such as the family who waits for an aunt to die in "Try There." Two of the stories, "A Village Death" and "More Joy in Heaven," attack organized religion. Pinkie Lucas, the protagonist of "More Joy in Heaven," is a seventeen-year-old streetwalker. Warner opens the story with a description of the cats in the warehouse district along the Thames: "But for each of these there are a thousand lesser cats, depending solely upon their wits, never rising above the poverty-line, short-lived for all their sharpened cunning, dying of famine, mange or poison, worried by dogs, crushed under lorries, or tossed into a lock to drown and give some angry idler a moment's spectacle." By first describing the cats and then allowing the reader to see the similarities of their lives to Pinkie's, Warner makes her social comment with-

Dust jacket for Warner's 1943 collection of short stories, three of which concern the Spanish Civil War

out being maudlin. In the story she attacks the self-righteous teachings of the Church that deprive Pinkie of the one person who provided her with human contact.

In the mid 1930s Warner and Ackland joined the Communist party and began to write for the *Left Review*. Supporting the Republican side in the Spanish civil war, Warner led appeals for the Committee for Spanish Medical Aid, visited Spain for the committee, and participated in rallies and demonstrations. As she comments in her article "The Way by Which I Have Come" (1939), even better than the discovery that a woman could earn her living by writing was "the discovery that the pen could be used as a sword." She became friends with other leftist writers and editors, including Edgell Rickwood, Julius Lipton, Montagu Slater, Tom Wintringham, Amabel Williams-Ellis, and Nancy Cunard. She attended the International Writers' Congress in Spain with Stephen Spender, but they developed a mutual distrust. She later attended the Writers' Congress in New York. She was active in P.E.N. and was a member of the executive committee of Writers for Intellectual Liberty.

The Cat's Cradle-Book was published in the United States in 1940 but did not appear in England until twenty years later. In this collection Warner introduces the unnamed female narrator, who can understand a bit of the language of cats, and the handsome young William Farthing, who is fluent in it. He has discovered that mother cats tell fables to their kittens and that these stories are the same all over the world:

> "For ages the languages of men have kept them apart. For ages the cat language has been catholic, explicit, unvarying. I understand it, you understand it, every child picks up an inkling of it. When cats creep into children's cradles, and the old women say they are sucking the child's breath, what do you suppose they are doing? Keeping them quiet with a story — and better than their mothers can!
> . . . .
> "You may object that these stories do not deal exclusively with cats, that they are stories of mankind as much (or more) as stories of catkind. But why not? Cats have chosen to live among us, they have to reckon with us, analyse our motives, trace our weaknesses and peculiarities. The proper study of catkind is man. The results of this study they have embodied in narratives, which they tell to their children, and by superflux to our children. No highly cultured race keeps its culture to itself."

Thus, folktales originate with cats, among whom "we find the stories most constant, most uncontaminated. . . . It is among the misunderstanding forgetful humans that they become corrupt and prejudiced." Farthing has collected these stories, and the rest of the book is a selection of them compiled by the narrator after his death.

The tales wittily undermine notions of hierarchy and patriotism and traditional concepts of virtue. Although the endings of the stories are frequently ambiguous, there is no question whose side Warner is on in the debate between a ewe and a wild cat in "The Two Mothers":

> "The polecat kills my young ones," said the wild cat. "And the eagle and the butcher kill yours. I see no difference."
> The ewe drew herself up.
> "Your children are killed by a common low polecat. Mine are taken by the eagle, who is the King of Birds, or the butcher, who is a man and Lord of Creation. Such deaths are splendid and honourable. *Dulce et decorum est.*"

In her novel *Lolly Willowes* Warner had made the point that women become the storytellers of society precisely because they are ignored by society: forced into the role of observers, women tell stories to relieve the boredom of their lives and to pass on their history and their learning to their children. The cats' tales are not only told by females to the kittens they nurse, but they also are given to the world by a woman – the unnamed female editor of Farthing's transcripts.

Warner's political sympathies and commitment are evident in *A Garland of Straw and Other Stories* (1943). She shows the hideousness of war, the smugness of the bourgeois and the chauvinist, the innocence of the young and uninformed, and the anti-Semitism of the Fascists. She protests England's noninterventionist policy in the Spanish civil war and its failure to respond to the threat of Nazism. The stories are set in England, Spain, Poland, Germany, Mexico, New York, and North Carolina. In "Apprentice" a Polish woman is hired to clean the home of the ten-year-old Lili, who is fancied by the German major. The woman faints from hunger, but she is nothing more than a curiosity to Lili, who has made a game of dangling food just out of the reach of starving Polish children.

"Emil" is one of several stories that look at how prewar life in England was affected by the events on the Continent. Emil is a twenty-one-year-old refugee from Austria; his parents are both dead, and his brother is a Nazi. In the village where he has come to live he is feared, pitied, and treated as an object. Suspected of being a spy by one family and defended as a Jew by another, he is neither. The story shows England preparing for war in the summer of 1938 as well as the mixed feelings produced by the Munich agreement. Warner does not provide a commentary on her characters; readers, like the audience at a play, are left to draw their own conclusions. For example, neither Emil nor the narrator says how Emil feels about the Hathaways, the family with whom he lives, or the other villagers of France Green; the narrator says only that Emil prefers to spend long solitary hours at the piano. When Emil asks Mrs. Hathaway to join him at the piano to play a duet for the first time since arriving at their home, the reader is not told the reason for the change, though it appears to be that Emil shares a distaste with other members of the household for Prime Minister Neville Chamberlain's concessions to Hitler.

Three of the stories in *A Garland of Straw and Other Stories* focus on the Spanish civil war. "With the Nationalists" is a satire on the British government, the English and Spanish churches, and the capitalists, whose only allegiance is to money. In "The Language of Flowers" a principal's efforts to send teaching materials to Spain results in her being labeled a Bolshevist; instead of supplies for needy Spanish civilians, flowers are sent to Germany as a gesture of friendship. "The Red Carnation" depicts a young German soldier who has been duped by his government: in Spain he finds neither Communists nor romance, only poverty and dirt.

More than a third of the stories in *The Museum of Cheats* (1947) were first published in the *New Yorker*. Some of the anger so apparent in *A Garland of Straw and Other Stories* is still close to the surface, but here Warner uses her pen as a foil rather than as a bludgeon. Mary of "Poor Mary" has seemingly gone off to war while her conscientious-objector husband has remained at home: "She smells of metal, he thought, as I smell of dung." But she has not gone off to war; she has joined the Adventures Through Service (A.T.S.), a program in which women received nondangerous wartime assignments: "If they'd let me fight, as I wanted to, I might be killed by now. If we'd stayed in London and I'd driven an ambulance or a pump I might be killed by now. As it is, I've never been so healthy in all my life." Mary's husband thinks that she must be pregnant because she has gained weight; actually, she has gained weight because of too much starchy food. Her life has not been much better than that of the pigs he raises; she has been penned in an overcrowded building with floors of concrete slabs. Thus, it is only in his eyes that she is the stronger of the two. The story asks the reader to examine gender stereotypes and assumptions about strength, weakness, honor, and purity.

In "Time's Silvering Hand" old Miss Albury listens to her grandnephew's stories of air raids, grunting with so much pleasure at the grisly details that he feels called upon to embroider them. The women in "English Climate" are, like Miss Albury, overly patriotic, almost ghoulish in their delight at the sacrifice war demands; they feel cheated that they cannot fight or that a bomb has not been dropped on their town. Details of everyday life during the war in *The Museum of Cheats* include food, fuel, and housing shortages; constant fear of bombing; and returning soldiers suffering from shell shock. But not all of the effects of war that Warner depicts are negative. In "Sweethearts and Wives" the war teaches women to draw their strength from one another rather than from a man. The effects of war on the people of England are, however, not the only subjects Warner treats in *The Museum of Cheats.*

Several stories depict the betrayals to which women are particularly vulnerable. In "A Pigeon" Teresa tries not to be "narrow-minded" about her husband's infidelity; her self-betrayal is as damaging to her as her betrayal by her husband, for she dams up not only her anger but also all her emotions. The women Warner portrays live in fear of their husbands and of unwanted pregnancies, whether their own or those of their daughters.

Warner remained a Communist in the 1950s, but she was no longer an activist. Her stories continue to attack the rich, the self-righteous, and self-styled important people, but her tone loses some of its caustic edge. She seems to be more accepting of the human weaknesses she depicts.

The stories in *Winter in the Air, and Other Stories* (1955) are character studies. In "A Second Visit" a former soldier returns to a house on the southeast coast of England that he had requisitioned during the war for military use; for him, the house represents family and belonging. In "The Children's Grandmother" a woman brings her four children, left fatherless by the war, to live with their paternal grandmother. Warner does not give the narrator a name, identifying her as the "daughter-in-law . . . now a daughter of the house, the faithful, negligible daughter who has never left home" and suggests that there are other ways than death in which to lose one's children. But more than the change in subject matter from the previous collection of stories, the reader notes the change in tone. Compassion has replaced the satire that characterized the two previous volumes of stories; as Dean Baldwin remarks in "The Stories of Sylvia Townsend Warner," these are stories of "quiet resignation."

In the title story a woman whose husband is divorcing her to marry another woman moves to London because it offers her an anonymous existence. She prefers to bear her pain and loss alone, to "regroup" and "lick one's wounds and wring the sea-water of shipwreck out of [her] hair" without prying eyes. "Hee-Haw!" is also a story of lost love. A woman returns thirty years later to the village where she lived with her first husband, but in this case he had loved her: it was she who had been unable to bear the "agony" of such intense passion, throwing it away for a safe and sedate life. "At the Trafalgar Bakery" tells of a woman whose life with her domineering mother has become so unbearable that she runs off to Paris with a man who cannot marry her because his wife is "too religious ever to divorce him." "A Kitchen Knife" depicts a young woman who awakens to the knowledge that marriage and rearing children are not romantic. In

Dust jacket for Warner's 1971 collection of short stories, all of which were written while she was in her seventies

"Absalom, My Son" an old writer recognizes his lack of success and attempts to commit suicide. In "Idenborough" a middle-aged woman feels guilty when her stepson from her first marriage gives her and her new husband her first husband's car as a wedding gift: "It seemed to her like robbing a blind beggar to accept so much kind approval from her stepson when for the second time in her life she was violently in love, and on this occasion, too, not with his father." "Uncle Blair" is one of the few comic stories in the volume, including such sentences as: "The Committee accordingly decided that the memorial should be a Tittingham Folk Museum, which would house Miss Foale's collection of eighteenth and early nineteenth century boots, and shelter the Mopselling Maiden's dances when Mopsell Day happened to be a wet one."

While the reviewers praised *Winter in the Air, and Other Stories* for its craftsmanship and sensitivity, they decried the author's lack of concern for moral issues. Warner never punishes her "villains," nor does she condemn characters who sin in the eyes of the church or society. Rather than being concerned about such moral issues as adultery or prostitution, Warner focuses on social issues: how a young girl with no education can support herself, or how the human spirit survives in the poor, the old, and the outcasts of society.

The reviewers also praised *A Spirit Rises* (1962). In "The Locum Tenens" Adam Hutton, a middle-aged, successful doctor who had escaped through education from the poverty of his Yorkshire upbringing – "he had finally learned himself out of his station and away from his birthplace" – returns home to take over a vacationing doctor's practice for two weeks, giving up his own planned vacation in Rome. Just when Adam seems to be falling in love with Dr. Walker's daughter and to have discovered how good it is to return to one's roots, Dr. Walker comes home and announces that he has taken a partner: a married man he met on his vacation. This act seals the fate of Walker's daughter, who will continue to live with her parents and work for her father. The unsatisfying ending that leaves the characters no better off than at the beginning of the story characterizes Warner's fiction for many readers.

A Stranger with a Bag, and Other Stories (1966), republished as *Swans on an Autumn River* (1966), includes "A Love Match," about the incestuous love of a brother and a sister. That the story is beautiful and not offensive is a testament to Warner's skill as a writer. "Quiet Lives" is full of the details of everyday life, from the sound of a cuckoo's call to the price of duck. The characters are an elderly woman; her middle-aged son and daughter, Donald and Audrey; and a houseguest, Betty Sullivan, a childhood friend of the mother's whose husband has died. Long-suffering Audrey, from whose point of view the story is told, is to be given the spare room since it would be too small for Betty. Betty's visit turns out to be something of a blessing: their mother is more interested in talking over old times with her friend than in tormenting her children with her demands and admonitions. Nevertheless, it seems as if Betty has come to stay, making one more person for Audrey to care for. Her perfume is so offensive that Donald sprays every room with aerosols and irritates his nose by constantly applying a handkerchief soaked in citronella. He then has to use "carbolic soap and a nailbrush" to remove the odor of a perfumed lotion Betty applies to his nose to take away the redness. When Hannah, Betty's cook and housekeeper, is added to the household during Audrey's emergency appendectomy, it appears that the middle-aged children's lives will go from bad to worse. Yet the ending – untypically for Warner – is happy and conclusive: Audrey goes off to Africa; the mother dies; and Donald and his bride take over the house.

That Warner's creative talents did not fall off as she approached eighty is evident from stories such as "But at the Stroke of Midnight" in her collection *The Innocent and the Guilty: Stories* (1971). Lucy Ridpath leaves her husband, a "born bachelor" who registers her absence only by the fact that no food awaits him. He assumes that she has gone off on one of her visits to her cousin Aurelia Lefanu. But the cousin is a creation of Lucy's, who periodically leaves her life as Mrs. Ridpath to become Aurelia. Lucy is eventually forced back to her old identity, but only long enough for her and her husband to be carried off in a flood.

In *The Kingdoms of Elfin* (1977) Warner creates a fairy world to comment on the real one. The societies of elfindom are hierarchical, but the rulers are women. Flying is considered plebeian; thus, only the servant class can indulge in an activity that is both convenient and fun:

> There was a regular programme of racing events – the Scullery Cup, the Laundry Half-Mile, the Staff Handicap. Lineaged fairies, who would rather be seen dead than seen flying, felt a practical admiration for the speed of those who flew on errands or obeyed the summons of a silver whistle. Servants who excelled in pace or endurance were transferred to the specialized seclusion of race horses and exercised morning and evening; a famous valet who had the misfortune to break a wing was kept at stud and sired several winners.

Like humans, the elfins show great disdain for the old: they discard their kidnapped human pets when the latter lose their youth. The kingdoms suffer from great rivalries, and the inhabitants, in spite of leading lives of ease and pleasure, nurse petty grievances: "The Elfhame Dissidents had sickened of the frivolity of court life: pleasure was a burden to them; so was politeness. Beset with banquetings, love affairs, sonnets, whist drives, masquerades, and lotteries, they had no time to take themselves seriously." But they soon tire of the "noise, disorder, and dirt of the manse" in which they have taken refuge. The elfins seem as contrary as human beings: "Being young and perfectly happy and pledged to love each other till the remote end of their days, they naturally talked of death."

Warner comments ironically on religion, government, pride, and foolishness, but some of her tales are more compassionate. "Winged Creature," for example, is the story of an unlikely friendship between a young elfin, Grive, and an old changeling, Gobelet. When the elfin is dashed into the sea, Gobelet is inconsolable in his loss. The mixtures of tenderness, understanding, and compassion with playfulness, wit, satire, and fantasy that characterize the stories in *The Kingdoms of Elfin* are to be found in all of Warner's fiction. She always mixes comedy and tragedy, the imaginary and the real.

In June 1977 the Aldeburgh Festival put on a Sylvia Townsend Warner day, which included a reading of her poetry and a short story, "The Cold"; some of her poems were set to music by Alan Bush and John Ireland. She died on 1 May of the following year. Her remaining works were published by her literary executors, William Maxwell and Susanna Pinney, and her biographer Claire Harmon.

Reviewers generally praised Warner's work, but some criticized her for being "too neat and abstract" in her treatment of characters and too abrupt and enigmatic in her endings. Feminist critics have been almost the only ones to appreciate the satirical and political content of her work. Although fellow artists such as John Updike and H. E. Bates expressed their appreciation of Warner's fiction, scholarly books by academics on the history of the short story did not even mention her before the 1980s. Perhaps the only close critical examination of Warner's short stories is Robert Crossley's "A Long Day's Dying: The Elves of J. R. R. Tolkien and Sylvia Townsend Warner" (1985).

Letters:

Letters, edited by William Maxwell (London: Chatto & Windus, 1982; New York: Viking, 1983).

Interview:

Louise Morgan, *Writers at Work* (London: Chatto & Windus, 1931), pp. 27–35.

Biographies:

Valentine Ackland, *For Sylvia: An Honest Account* (New York & London: Norton, 1985);

Wendy Mulford, *This Narrow Place: Sylvia Townsend Warner and Valentine Ackland. Life, Letters and Politics, 1930–1951* (London: Pandora, 1988);

Claire Harmon, *Sylvia Townsend Warner: A Biography* (London: Chatto & Windus, 1989; New York: Viking, 1989).

References:

Walter Allen, *The Short Story in English* (Oxford: Clarendon / New York: Oxford University Press, 1981), pp. 251–256;

Dean Baldwin, "The English Short Story in the Fifties," in *The English Short Story, 1945–1980,* edited by Dennis Vannatta (Boston: Twayne, 1985), pp. 34–74;

Baldwin, "The Stories of Sylvia Townsend Warner," *Crazyhorse,* 31 (Fall 1986): 71–80;

Barbara Brothers, "Flying the Nets at Forty: *Lolly Willowes* as Female Bildungsroman," in *Old Maids to Radical Spinsters: Unmarried Women in the Twentieth-Century Novel,* edited by Laura L. Doan (Champaign: University of Illinois Press, 1991), pp. 195–212;

Brothers, " 'Through the 'Pantry Window,' " in *Rewriting the Good Fight: Critical Essays on the Literature of the Spanish Civil War,* edited by Frieda S. Brown, Malcolm Alan Compitello, Victor M. Howard, and Robert A. Martin (East Lansing: Michigan State University Press, 1989), pp. 161–174;

Brothers, "Writing against the Grain: Sylvia Townsend Warner and the Spanish Civil War," in *Women's Writing in Exile,* edited by Mary Lynn Broe and Angela Ingram (Chapel Hill: University of North Carolina Press, 1989), pp. 349–368;

Terry Castle, "Sylvia Townsend Warner and the Counterplot of Lesbian Fiction," *Textual Practice,* 4 (Summer 1990): 213–235;

Robert Crossley, "A Long Day's Dying: The Elves of J. R. R. Tolkien and Sylvia Townsend Warner," in *Death and the Serpent: Immortality in Science Fiction and Fantasy,* edited by Carl B. Yoke and Donald M. Hassler (Westport, Conn.: Greenwood Press, 1985), pp. 57–70;

Joseph M. Flora, ed., *The English Short Story 1880–1945: A Critical History* (Boston: Twayne, 1985);

Claire Harmon, ed., "Sylvia Townsend Warner 1893–1978: A Celebration," *PN Review 23,* 8 (1981–1982): 30–61;

Jane Marcus, "Sylvia Townsend Warner," in *The Gender of Modernism,* edited by Bonnie Kime Scott (Bloomington: Indiana University Press, 1990), pp. 531–559;

Marcus, "A Wilderness of One's Own: Feminist Fantasy Novels of the Twenties, Rebecca West and Sylvia Townsend Warner," in *Women Writers and the City,* edited by Susan Merrill Squier (Knoxville: University of Tennessee Press, 1984), pp. 134–160;

John J. Stinson, "The English Short Story, 1945–50," in *The English Short Story, 1945–1980,* pp. 1–33;

John Updike, "The Mastery of Miss Warner," *New Republic,* 154 (5 March 1966): 23–25.

Papers:

The Sylvia Townsend Warner and Valentine Ackland collection in the Dorset County Museum, Dorchester, includes diaries of Warner from 1927 and 1928. Letters from Warner to George Plank are in the Beinecke Rare Book and Manuscript Library, Yale University. Letters from Warner to Nancy Cunard and Alyse Gregory are in the collection of the Harry Ransom Humanities Research Center, University of Texas at Austin.

Angus Wilson

(11 August 1913 – 31 May 1991)

Fiona R. Barnes
University of Wisconsin – Madison

See also the Wilson entry in *DLB 15: British Novelists, 1930–1959: Part 2.*

SELECTED BOOKS: *The Wrong Set and Other Stories* (London: Secker & Warburg, 1949; New York: Morrow, 1950);

Such Darling Dodos and Other Stories (London: Secker & Warburg, 1950; New York: Morrow, 1951);

Emile Zola (London: Secker & Warburg, 1952; New York: Morrow, 1952; revised edition, London: Secker & Warburg, 1964);

Hemlock and After (London: Secker & Warburg, 1952; New York: Viking, 1952);

For Whom the Cloche Tolls: A Scrap-Book of the Twenties (London: Methuen, 1953; New York: Curtis, 1953; revised edition, Harmondsworth, U.K.: Penguin, 1976);

The Mulberry Bush (London: Secker & Warburg, 1956);

Anglo-Saxon Attitudes (London: Secker & Warburg, 1956; New York: Viking, 1956);

A Bit off the Map (London: Secker & Warburg, 1957; New York: Viking, 1957);

The Middle Age of Mrs. Eliot (London: Secker & Warburg, 1958; New York: Viking, 1959);

The Old Men at the Zoo (London: Secker & Warburg, 1961; New York: Viking, 1961);

The Wild Garden; or, Speaking of Writing (Berkeley: University of California Press, 1963; London: Secker & Warburg, 1963);

Tempo: The Impact of Television on the Arts (London: Studio Vista, 1964; Chester Springs, Pa.: Dufour, 1966);

Late Call (London: Secker & Warburg, 1964; New York: Viking, 1965);

No Laughing Matter (London: Secker & Warburg, 1967; New York: Viking, 1970);

Death Dance: Twenty-Five Stories by Angus Wilson (New York: Viking, 1969);

The World of Charles Dickens (London: Secker & Warburg, 1970; New York: Viking, 1970);

Angus Wilson (photograph by Tony Garrett)

As If by Magic (London: Secker & Warburg, 1973; New York: Viking, 1973);

The Strange Ride of Rudyard Kipling (London: Secker & Warburg, 1977; New York: Viking, 1978);

Setting the World on Fire (London: Secker & Warburg, 1980; New York: Viking, 1980).

Editions and Collections: *Diversity and Depth in Fiction: Selected Critical Writings of Angus Wilson,* edited by Kerry McSweeney (London: Secker & Warburg, 1983; New York: Viking, 1984);

The Collected Stories of Angus Wilson (London: Secker & Warburg, 1987).

OTHER: "Who for Such Dainties?," in *The Pick of Today's Short Stories,* third series, selected by

311

John Pudney (London: Oldhams, 1952), pp. 232–236;

"Animals or Human Beings," in *The Third Ghost Book,* edited by Cynthia, Lady Asquith (London: Barrie, 1955), pp. 265–270;

"Her Ship Came Home," in *Did It Happen? Stories* (London: Oldbourne, 1956), pp. 211–216;

Somerset Maugham, *A Maugham Twelve,* edited by Wilson (London: Heinemann, 1966);

Maugham, *Cakes and Ale, and Twelve Short Stories,* edited by Wilson (Garden City, N.Y.: Doubleday, 1967);

Writers of East Anglia, edited by Wilson (London: Secker & Warburg, 1977);

The Portable Dickens, edited, with an introduction, by Wilson (New York: Viking, 1983).

SELECTED PERIODICAL PUBLICATIONS – UNCOLLECTED:

FICTION

"Aunt Cora," *Contact,* 1 (May–June 1950): 31;

"An Elephant Never Forgets," *Panorama and Harlequin,* 5 (1951): 30–35;

"Aunt Mathilde's Drawings," *Evening Standard* (London), 11 September 1952, p. 8;

"Silent Pianist," *Evening Standard* (London), 11 September 1952, p. 8;

"The Men with Bowler Hats," *Evening News* (London), 5 May 1953, p. 9; reprinted as "Men with Bowler Hats," *Argosy* (November 1957): 105–109;

"Unwanted Heroine," *Homes and Gardens* (March 1954): 38–40, 124, 127, 129;

"Mrs. Peckover's Sky . . . ," *Evening Standard* (London), 13 December 1955, p. 19;

"My Husband Is Right," *Texas Quarterly,* 4, no. 3 (1961): 139–145.

NONFICTION

"A Conversation with E. M. Forster," *Encounter,* 9 (November 1957): 52–57;

"Bexhill and After," *Spectator,* 200 (9 May 1958): 583–584;

"Diversity and Depth," *Times Literary Supplement,* 15 August 1958, p. 8;

"Charles Dickens: A Haunting," *Critical Quarterly,* 2 (Summer 1960): 101–108;

"The Whites in South Africa," *Partisan Review,* 28 (Autumn 1961): 612–632;

"Skeletons and Assegais: Family Reminiscences," *Transatlantic Review,* 9 (Spring 1962): 19–43;

"Evil in the English Novel," *Kenyon Review,* 29 (March 1967): 167–194;

"The Politics of the Family," *Listener,* 91 (10 January 1974): 40–43;

"Art and the Establishment," *Listener,* 91 (17 January 1974): 78–80.

Angus Wilson was the first prominent new English writer to emerge in the post–World War II era. In *Critical Essays on Angus Wilson* (1985) Malcolm Bradbury calls him "one of four or five great English post-war writers," placing him in the company of William Golding, Graham Greene, Doris Lessing, and Iris Murdoch. Wilson is best known as a chronicler of the postwar social revolution in England and for his construction of a narrative mode that encompasses both the more successful experimentations of modernism and the strengths of the traditional novel of social realism. In his short fiction he portrays a world in flux – that of the 1930s to the 1950s, frequently looking back on these times with an ambivalent mixture of satire and pathos.

Angus Frank Johnstone Wilson was born in Dumfriesshire, England, on 11 August 1913 to William Johnstone-Wilson, who was of Scottish origin, and Maude Caney Johnstone-Wilson, who was from South Africa. Wilson was the youngest of five sons, thirteen years younger than the fourth child. Consequently, Wilson spent a somewhat lonely childhood with adults as companions, and this isolation from other children was further compounded by his parents' frequent moving about as a result of their deteriorating fortunes. He took refuge in his imagination, in role-playing and mimicry, an early talent the effects of which he explores in the child characters in such stories as "Raspberry Jam" (*The Wrong Set and Other Stories,* 1949) and "Necessity's Child" (*Such Darling Dodos and Other Stories,* 1950).

Wilson spent a year in Durban, South Africa, with his mother's relatives during his early childhood, and that visit inspired the story "Union Reunion" (*The Wrong Set*). This cross-cultural experience at such an early age no doubt contributed to his sense of displacement as a young child, for the condition of exile is frequently explored in his short fiction. Both of his parents had small private incomes that became increasingly inadequate as he grew up, so the family lived in genteel poverty in various hotels in the south of England. Wilson attended a series of kindergartens, then a prep school managed by one of his brothers, and went on to attend Westminster School in 1927. When he was fifteen his mother died, which affected him profoundly. Childhood, family dynamics, and the effects of the loss of a close relative are recurring subjects in Wilson's short fiction.

In 1932 Wilson went to Merton College, Oxford, to study medieval history. In the 1930s Freudian theory and Marxism were the most influential ideas at Oxford, and they are clearly detectable in Wilson's short fiction. While at the university, he made many good friends from various backgrounds, which helped to widen his experience and social range, although he is best known for his depiction of the middle class. During the Depression Wilson took a variety of jobs, including tutoring and secretarial work, until 1936, when he found a position in the Department of Printed Books at the British Museum, where he worked for almost twenty years. From 1947 to 1955 Wilson was deputy superintendent of the Reading Room, where he was in charge of replacing three hundred thousand volumes lost in the bombings of World War II. His work in the museum and the Foreign Office provided him with important insights into the world of the cultural establishment and into the workings of bureaucratic administration, both of which he frequently criticizes in his stories.

In the years before the war he became involved in working for liberal intellectual groups that were endeavoring to avert war. From 1939 to 1945 he worked in the Foreign Office and was billeted with a widow and her daughter. His sense of loneliness and alienation at work and at his lodgings, together with an unsuccessful love affair, brought him to the point of a nervous breakdown, for which he underwent psychotherapy.

In 1946, at the age of thirty-three, he began to write short stories on his weekends in the country as a form of therapy for his depression. Wilson explains his venture into writing in a 1957 interview with Michael Millgate: "Writing seemed a good way of diversifying my time. I was living in the country and commuting to London then and I could only do it at weekends. That's why I started with short stories: this was something I could finish, realize completely in a weekend." He wrote his first story, "Raspberry Jam," in one Sunday. Three of these early stories were published in literary magazines, two of them, "Mother's Sense of Fun" and "Crazy Crowd," in *Horizon* and the third, "Realpolitik," in the *Listener*. Impressed by the quality of these stories and their popularity, Secker and Warburg published twelve of them in *The Wrong Set*.

The collection had favorable reviews, and the first impression sold out in two weeks. Its rapid success was surprising because of the limited market for short stories, but its eager reception owed partially to the fact that so few new voices had emerged after the war. The English literary scene was still dominated by older writers such as Anthony Powell, Evelyn Waugh, and Aldous Huxley. Edmund

Wilson's review of *The Wrong Set* in the *New Yorker* welcomed him as a writer who signaled a new literary direction from the conventional "well-bred and well-turned entertainment that we have lately been getting from England." However, the reviewer reacted strongly against what he termed the "horror" and "cruelty" of the stories, yet he also acknowledged that Wilson accurately reflected the sickness of the postwar period.

Wilson's stories fictionalize much of his childhood and experiences during the war. In a 1972 interview with Frederick P. W. McDowell he describes his stories as being "little bits of my life which I had transformed into stories." Consequently, aside from its literary merit, his work has value as a detailed social history of the times. In *Angus Wilson* (1969) K. W. Gransden writes:

> Wilson's work is valuable as social documentary. He records with great accuracy the changing idiom, habits and fashions of English society in his lifetime.... But the primary aim of his early stories is satirical, not sociological. In story after story he ruthlessly exposes the naked truth, the secret motives and humiliations, behind the public mask of pomposity and self-deception.

Wilson describes and criticizes simultaneously, with a volatile mixture of nostalgia and mordant wit. His prime targets are anachronistic middle-class aspirations and traditional liberal values.

Most of the stories in *The Wrong Set* are set in the 1930s, and Wilson uses jargon and fashions to place the characters and their backgrounds. Many of the stories focus on the uncertainties and clashes caused by the postwar unsettling of class barriers. "Saturnalia," set on New Year's Eve, 1931, dramatizes a doomed attempt in a seedy private hotel to create a momentary harmony among the disparate elements of the establishment's guests and workers. It is clear that the class barriers are dissolving uncomfortably and reluctantly, so that the unsuccessful sexual encounters between the servants and the guests are the only form of interaction that night. Yet all the relationships – filial, marital, and professional – are diseased or misdirected. Wilson satirizes the failure of this traditional party to celebrate a new start.

"The Wrong Set" explores the diametrically opposed political and social values that split a family. Wilson's pointed titles are frequently clichés taken from conversations in the stories, as he explains in the interview with Millgate: "I take a platitude – 'the wrong set,' for example: the point is that no one knows what the wrong set is, and one person's wrong set is another's right set. And you get the pay-off, which is something I like." The protagonist, a nightclub piano player called Vi, is unaware that her alienation from her family is caused by her absurd pretense at gentility despite the shabbiness of her existence and the parasitic quality of her relationship with the unemployed Trevor. She, in turn, is disturbed by her nephew's political affiliations with "Reds" and "Conchies" and ironically sends a telegram to her sister warning her that her son is in with "the wrong set." Vi's complete lack of self-knowledge protects her from painful enlightenment, while her family's snobbishness makes a mockery of their enlightened political beliefs. Neither "set" is "right" in Wilson's scheme of things.

"Realpolitik" also dramatizes the total incomprehension of two worlds for each other. John Hobday is a callow representative of the new-world business order who sees the old liberal and scholarly ideals as obstacles to the financial success of the gallery that he now manages. The art experts who loyally staffed the gallery under the former owner, Sir Harold, are incapable of absorbing the new realities of a "progressive" society into their scholarly ideals, and they find Hobday's business skills antithetical to the gallery's ethos. The struggle for power is unequal, and Wilson's experiences at the British Museum and at Oxford obviously shape the tensions and drama of this story, which is played out almost entirely in dialogue.

In contrast to the social realism of "Realpolitik," "Totentanz" is a gothic story that relates the trials of a social climber, Isobel Capper. After her first successful social gathering, a bizarre set of circumstances – death, suicide, and murder – keep her from achieving her dream of becoming a salon leader in London. This tale of social pretension is framed by the snobbishness and ugliness of the academic world that her husband inhabits, one from which Isobel desperately wants to escape. The humor is mordant and macabre, and Wilson shows no compassion for any of the characters. In *Angus Wilson* (1985) Averil Gardner claims that this story is "unique" in its "heartless yet zestful extravagance."

The limitations of the academic life are also explored in the first story in the collection, "Fresh Air Fiend," which begins with Wilson's characteristic urbanity but ends fatally. A brisk young graduate student, Elspeth Eccles, becomes determined to save her mentor and hero, Professor Searle, from the burden of his overbearing, alcoholic wife. However, she is supremely unaware of his underlying weaknesses and ironically destroys his security while attempting to save him. Her target, the alco-

holic wife, simply takes refuge from Elspeth's accusations in drink, but the academic has no such protection. Wilson deliberately focuses on the conflict between the two women, so that the news of the professor's collapse is as much a shock for the reader as it is for Elspeth. The *fiend* of the title takes on its original demonic meaning as the insensitive young meddler destroys the fragile equilibrium of the Searle household. Wilson dramatizes the dangers of the smug self-righteousness of a new generation that intends to sweep clean without fully understanding the history of the old world.

"Et Dona Ferentes" – the title comes from a quotation from Virgil's *Aeneid:* "Timeo Danaos et dona ferentes" (I fear the Greeks, particularly when bearing gifts) – also presents the damaging effects of an outsider's visit, in this case a handsome Swedish student, Sven, on an unstable family situation. The repressed homosexuality of the father, Edwin Newman, produces the unspoken fear and guilt that propel the action of the story. Wilson acknowledges in *The Wild Garden; or, Speaking of Writing* (1963) that "the homosexual emotions in this story of a man taken for a ride by a calculating flirtatious Swedish boy are in some part my own at the adolescent period of my life." Wilson subtly portrays the brittle sociability of the family group at a picnic and gradually builds the dramatic tension by alternating the conflicting interior monologues of the characters, until the storm literally and figuratively explodes around them.

This tendency of Wilson's stories to begin quietly lulls the reader into security and complacency; then one is shocked by an explosion into a verbally or emotionally violent denouement, or the collapse into farce. At the center of most of the stories is a confrontation with the naked truth – a moment of disillusionment with others or a shocking self-realization. As Bradbury explains in "The Short Stories of Angus Wilson" (1966), many of Wilson's stories "turn on a moment of moral realism, a moment of truth – a moment when, often, he reveals the grotesque as the grotesque."

These moments of truth are often precipitated by family gatherings, for Wilson is fascinated with the dialectic between isolation and imprisonment in the family structure. Hence the wider social emphasis of his stories is complemented by the powerful psychological analyses of individuals in relation to each other. Wilson's stories nearly always focus on the dramatic conflicts between inimical people trapped in each other's company: family members, employees, colleagues, and spouses. As Kingsley Amis notes in a 1957 review of *A Bit off the Map*

(1957): "His subject is most often the explosions and embarrassments touched off when people of different class, training, or culture are made to confront one another." These stories frequently chronicle failure; they are dramas that end in miscommunication and misunderstanding.

"Union Reunion" is a typical Wilson story of family confrontation – except that it is the only one of his stories set in South Africa – in which the English visitors set off a chain of events that exposes the dissensions within the South African family nexus. As with the other pieces in *The Wrong Set,* the initial paragraphs are designed to set the scene and tone of the story and to build expectations. The stunned reaction of the English visitors to the harsh brilliancy of the African landscape and the violent contrast of the white colonial house with the bright red flowers stress the menace underlying the carefully "civilized" facade of white colonial society in South Africa:

> They could hardly keep their gaze on the low, one-storeyed house as they came up the long, straight drive, so did the sunlight reflected from the glaring white walls hurt and crack their eyeballs. Down the staring white facade ran the creepers in streams of blood – splashes of purple and crimson bouganvillea pouring into vermillion pools of cannas in the flower beds below, the whole massed red merging into the tiny scarlet drops of Barbton daisies and salvia that bordered the garden in trim ranks.

The savagery held barely in check in the garden symbolizes the evil of colonialism and the desensitization of the white colonials who support the system. While the South African relatives in the story are made to look crude and brutal, their English sister and her husband are just as offensive in their snobbery and selfishness. An underlying secret emerges near the end of the visit to destroy the tenuous camaraderie of the family reunion. Wilson supported the antiapartheid cause and wrote a perceptive article on the future of the whites and apartheid in South Africa, "The Whites in South Africa" (1961).

In "A Story of Historical Interest" Wilson explores the disillusionment and self-realization of a daughter who has nursed her ailing, elderly father to the detriment of her own life. Wilson admits in *The Wild Garden* that this story is autobiographical, "an almost direct relation of my father's death in which I have cast myself in the role of a daughter," and he portrays both the pathos and the ironies of her situation with great understanding. The flashbacks that reveal Lois's past sacrifices for her fa-

ther's welfare also show her selfish dependence on her roles as savior and favorite daughter. The conclusion is unusual for Wilson's short stories but prefigures his novels, in that it shows a positive development in Lois's life despite her deep hurt and disillusionment. She determinedly shuts her mind to the inevitable death of her ungrateful father and turns to her new life as a single woman without dependents. However, Lois's final determination to start a new life of gaiety is ironic in the light of future political events: the slow death of Lois's father runs parallel to Neville Chamberlain's weak attempts to delay the inevitable war with Germany. The title therefore epitomizes the dual emphasis often displayed in Wilson's stories. Lois's response to her own life is complicated by developments on a much broader horizon.

The mixture of irony and pathos with which so many of Wilson's stories are told makes the moral judgments of the reader difficult to crystallize. In *The Wild Garden* Wilson acknowledges this complexity of perspective as "the ambiguous tone, somewhere between satirical and admiring, with which I describe the resistance of many of my middle-class characters, particularly women, to economic and social decline and the empty disappointment of a life that is going downhill. I suppose that this portrayal is deeply embedded in my attitude to my mother, whose life, to say the least, was hard and heartbreaking." "Mother's Sense of Fun" reverses the roles of "A Story of Historical Interest" and analyzes the difficulties of a son who has to live with a woman such as Wilson describes.

The story recounts the mutual dependence and disappointments of an overprotective, overbearing mother and her resentful but weak son. Donald's interior monologues, presented in the third person, reveal his distaste for her superficial social graces and the hackneyed language that underscores her borrowed values:

> He had often thought that to find his mother's phrases one would have to go to English translations of opera or the French and German prose books that he had used at school. It always "rained cats and dogs," that is if the rain did not "look like holding off;" Alice Stockfield was "a bit down in the mouth" but then she "let things get on top of her;" Roger Grant was "certainly no Adonis" but she had "an awfully soft spot in her heart for him."

The son's life appears to be simplified when his mother dies, but ironically it is then that he discovers his deep need for her and loneliness without her.

In Wilson's fiction language is the most important indicator of a character's sincerity and self-awareness, or lack thereof. He is justly acclaimed for his dialogue presentation, which stems from a tremendous talent for mimicry. The energetic exchanges between characters of different age, gender, and class give Wilson's short fiction a dramatic quality. His representations of dialogue, dialect, jargon, and clichés also serve to capture vividly the times and places of his highly specific worlds.

In "A Visit in Bad Taste," which reads like a one-act play, the husband and wife, Margaret and Malcolm Tarrant, reveal their dishonesties and hypocrisies in their use of language. Words and deeds contradict one another as the elegantly dressed couple discuss how to divest themselves of their embarrassing houseguest. The protagonists' evasive language exposes all the hollowness of their liberal pretensions when confronted by real human error and need. The "bad taste" of which they accuse Margaret's deviant brother, Arthur, is clearly unimportant on Wilson's scale of ethics, while their purely theoretical humanism and ruthless egotism condemn them utterly.

In "Crazy Crowd" the visitor does not cause a rift within the family but exposes for himself and the reader the deluded, incestuous makeup of the Cockshutt family. Blinded by the virtues of his fiancée, Jennie, Peter is initially overawed by the family myths with which he has been regaled. However, once he recognizes that their regressive family language and antics are designed merely to disguise their egotism, he is alienated and disgusted by their eccentricities. The entire family becomes the butt of Wilson's satire on adults who have never grown up, and in whose lives imagination has been degraded to a tool for continuous escape from reality. As a young man whose childish innocence makes him the easy victim of other people's manipulations, Peter does not escape censure. Wilson condones neither immature nor willful ignorance; self-awareness is the quality most lacking in his characters.

The education of yet another callow young man, Jeremy, is featured in "Significant Experience." The title is typically ironic, for Wilson parodies the conventions of romantic love in this tale of a young student's summer affair with an older woman. The story is framed by the immature pontifications of Jeremy's fellow students, whose remarks emphasize the gap between the ideal and the reality of his sexual adventure with Prue, his temperamental mistress.

The evils of excessive imagination in the adult world are grotesquely dramatized in what is probably Wilson's most notorious story, "Raspberry Jam," which focuses on a child's first confrontation with the irrational cruelty and untrustworthiness of adults. Wilson uses the familiar tradition of the eccentric English lady to lull the reader, together with the unsuspecting boy, into complacency, so that the vicious ending, where two sisters torture a bird in front of Johnnie, is as shocking for the reader as it is for him. Despite Wilson's sympathy both for eccentric old ladies and lonely young children, his characterizations are never sentimental, nor does he glorify the role of imagination in daily life.

Many critics have attacked Wilson for the thread of violence that runs throughout his work, but he speaks with characteristic honesty of his own thoughts on the subject in the lecture "The Novelist and the Narrator" (*Diversity and Depth in Fiction: Selected Critical Writings of Angus Wilson,* 1983), particularly on its effects in "Raspberry Jam":

> The theme – a recurring one in my work: the co-existence of a fierce sadism and a compensating gentleness – comes from deep within me. It lies perhaps at the root of what has puzzled many readers about my characters: I have towards people sometimes at the same moment intense interest and stifling boredom, love and strong hate. That this theme, of which I was unconscious at the time, should have found shape in my first story is not perhaps surprising, but as a result of its intensity and the depth from which it came, the narrator in me was never able to control it, and the story is, as a result, very badly told.

Not everyone would agree with Wilson about the failure of his narrative method in "Raspberry Jam," but most critics agree that the story is powerful in its indictment of the self-protective fantasies of adults. The two old ladies escape from the harshness of the outside world in anachronistic role-playing. The other adults in the story know about the excesses of the two old ladies but nonetheless continue to delude themselves that they are fit companions for an impressionable young boy. These delusions are portrayed as a debasement of the imaginative play of the child protagonist, Johnnie.

"Totentanz" and "Raspberry Jam" feature elements of the supernatural, the grotesque, and the macabre. However, even those stories in *The Wrong Set* that seem most realistic and ordinary usually confront the reader with an unexpected glimpse of the void or abyss that lies below the surface of commonplace reality. Wilson excels at portraying the way in which violence can erupt into ordinary existence, and the ever-present possibility of evil remains a preoccupation in his later short fiction and novels. Many of his stories seemed depressing, for Wilson depicts personal happiness as precarious and the unity of family groups as an illusion. Yet, if his characters can face this darkness and move on, they achieve a type of heroism. As Wilson remarks in the interview with Millgate: "The opportunities for heroism are limited in this kind of world: the most people can do is sometimes not to be as weak as they've been at other times."

Wilson's second collection of short fiction, *Such Darling Dodos and Other Stories,* was published in 1950. Many of the preoccupations, themes, narrative methods, and character types that he explores in his first collection appear in the second. Many critics have commented on Wilson's use of certain stock-character types in his early work, particularly in his short fiction, where character development is necessarily limited. Wilson calls his early characters "raffish flotsam" who are modeled on the inhabitants of the hotels in which he spent his childhood. In *Angus Wilson* (1964) Jay Halio lists four character types that recur, with variations, in Wilson's early short fiction: "the Raffish Old Sport," "the Intense Young Woman," "the Young Intellectual," and "the Widow who Copes." Wilson is unsparing in his presentation of their moral failures and self-delusions, yet he manages to create brief moments of pathos and compassion along with the ironies.

Many of the stories in the second collection resemble those in *The Wrong Set* in dealing with dysfunctional family relationships. The first story, "Rex Imperator," dramatizes an entire family that feeds parasitically yet resentfully on one member: "They were like parasites washed up by the tide, hanging like limpets to the rock, hating and loathing it, yet waxing fat upon it, devitalizing the air they breathed." The despicable behavior of these egotistical hangers-on completely alienates the reader, particularly as they vent their displeasure on Rex's wife, Brenda, who seems innocuous and long suffering.

Wilson, however, allows no easy moral judgments, for he deliberately withholds acquaintance with the family provider until the conclusion is near. The sympathy the reader feels for the unknown brother is soon alloyed by his egotistical behavior, as he complicates the balance of power by playing what Wilson calls the "Tyrant-Victim" role. The story ends with a melodramatic, hysterical outburst from Rex, whose hatred of the family leeches is counteracted by his desire to remain the omnipotent patriarch who dispenses riches to poor relations. His harangue is made anticlimactic, however, by Brenda's housewifely doling out of chores to keep these immature "children" out of trouble.

"Heart of Elm" parodies the responses and attitudes displayed by the families of the faithful old retainer, Ellen, and by her employer, Constance, at Ellen's deathbed. The sentimentality of the mourners is undercut by the relief of Constance, the mother, who longs to break away from her old pattern of life, in which Ellen's old-fashioned ideas have played such a large role in prolonging Constance's children's immaturity. Ellen's death signals the end of Constance's servitude as well, which makes Ellen's last gestures of love seem ironic. While Constance's two children struggle over possession of Ellen's love, Ellen's relatives vie for her possessions.

In "Sister Superior" Claire, the older sister, is not content with the easy extraction of money from her naive, generous younger sister, Mary. Envious of her sister's financial security and close family life, Claire proceeds, with insidious ease and Machiavellian cunning, to manipulate her sister's children in order to ruin the family's harmony. Ultimately, however, the reader is alienated from the hapless Mary and her two unimaginative children, as Wilson gradually exposes the danger of their stupidity and their state of "preserved innocence." Such innocence is too akin to ignorance and all too frequently involves a blindness to the realities of adult life and society.

Three other stories of family affairs and childhood needs are further ventures into the realms of the grotesque and surrealistic. "A Little Companion" begins conventionally enough, with references to Jane Austen spinsters in the reassuringly sensible description of Miss Arkwright. Yet Wilson proceeds to undercut the literary convention by using it only to demonstrate how different and unwelcoming the world has become since Austen wrote. The hallucinations that follow Miss Arkwright's forty-seventh birthday make her an eccentric whose condition is airily explained away by a vicar as being "just another war casualty." Yet "A Little Companion" is a sad tale about a woman who has filled her life with social work and other compensations, but whose longings for companionship and motherhood can not be suppressed. Wilson's ability to portray female characters with depth and compassion is well recognized, and he attributes this talent to his homosexuality, which he describes as giving him a "greater power of identifying truly sympathetically with my women characters."

"Necessity's Child" explores the loneliness of a child, making it reminiscent of "Raspberry Jam." The alienation of an overimaginative child from adult society is compounded by the neglect and disappointment of his parents. Rodney takes refuge from his loveless life in his imagination and in

Dust jacket for Wilson's last collection of short stories, most of which depict generational and class conflicts

books, but his protective fantasies generally lead to lies and punishment. His final flight of imagination is a revenge fantasy that pits him against the sea as a survivor of the *Titanic,* a disaster during which both his parents drown. Wilson admits in *The Wild Garden* that this story "is a near-autobiography (somewhat self-pityingly set out) of my last childhood seaside years."

In "Mummy to the Rescue" Wilson once again tricks the reader into accepting the normality of a situation that turns out to be grotesque. This story clearly demonstrates that Wilson was well aware of the deceptive arts of the storyteller. He remarks in the interview with Millgate that "all fiction for me is a kind of magic and trickery – a confidence trick, trying to make people believe something is true that isn't." The dreary complaints of Nurse Ramsay that open the story are the prelude to a strange tale of neglect, suffering, and death. Celia, Nurse Ramsay's charge, is a "poor lunatic" who strangles herself with the beloved cardigan that is her final link to her lost mother. Wilson himself refers to this story as "macabre."

The other four stories in the collection deal with clashes between various class, work, and generational groups. They are more satiric than shocking and reveal the opposed values of a society that was once constructed along clearly demarcated lines of class, wealth, and politics but that is now devoid of such certainties and uncertain how to reconfigure itself. Most of these stories end in mutual misunderstandings and hurtful humiliations, and there is little promise of reconciliation or constructive exchange.

"Learning's Little Tribute" satirizes the clash between a snobbish group of encyclopedists and the realistic lower-middle-class widow who confronts them. Their egotism and condescension are confronted by her honesty and commonsense refusal of their self-serving charity after her husband's death. As mediocre academics wrapped up in scholarly ideals that are their replacements for ethical standards, they remain unaware of their own alienation from contemporary society. Mrs. Craddock is courageously determined to make her own way and to preserve the independence and potential of her children, despite her own lack of education. The story ends with the total incomprehension by each party of the other's standards. Mrs. Craddock's honesty contrasts with the high-flown, specious rhetoric of the scholars.

"Such Darling Dodos" has been acclaimed as the best story of the collection for its integration of psychological and historical details. Robin Harker's terminal illness symbolizes the death of the 1930s left-wing ideals that are the focus of the Harker couple's lives. Priscilla is dominated by feelings of pathos for others, fixing "her emotionally as a child playing dolls' hospitals," while her husband is determinedly materialistic in his social work. Neither is capable of confronting the meaning of Robin's death, for both have sought refuge in progressive "good works" rather in their own emotional or spiritual development. The criticism of this lifestyle by their conservative, yet pragmatic, homosexual cousin Tony unveils the anachronistic nature of their lives and ideals, as well as the limitations of liberalism in a postwar world. The Harkers are unable to integrate into contemporary society and are therefore unable to answer its needs. However, the new alternative in society, typified by a visiting young couple, appears to be a reactionary smugness that does not improve on the Harkers' ineffectual humanism.

"Christmas Day in the Workhouse" is a Dickensian title that encapsulates both the Victorianism of the protagonist's values and the joyless-ness of a traditionally joyful season. This Christmas is being celebrated during wartime in a gray, bureaucratic department, and the breakdown of class barriers – supposedly a by-product of the war – is portrayed as superficial. The possible warmth of Christmas dinner is ruined for Thea, the protagonist, by what she sees as her betrayal by an upper-class workmate, Stephanie, whose aloofness and snobbery have ironically won Thea's admiration. In turn Thea treats the overtures of an unattractive subordinate, Joan, with condescension and snobbery, learning little from her own suffering. Like "Learning's Little Tribute" the story ends in misunderstanding and humiliation, for none of the protagonists is capable of self-awareness or moral development.

The last story in the collection, "What Do Hippos Eat?," exposes the symbiotic relationship between Maurice, a gentleman now down on his luck, and Greta, a savvy working-class woman, who reluctantly depend on each other to survive. Their gay time at the zoo is interspersed with their realistic perceptions about the ulterior motives of the other, yet neither is capable of self-criticism. The darkness that underlies their relationship is dramatized in a vision of the hippos as threatening denizens of the muddy deep:

> The hot steam from the muddy water smelt abominably and the sides of the pool were slippery with slime. Every now and again the huge black forms would roll over, displacing ripples of brown foam-flecked water, and malevolent eyes on the end of stalks would appear above the surface for the moment.

The hippos are metaphors for the human evil that lurks in the protagonists' sordid lives. The zoo is an appropriate setting for their animal cunning and baser emotions, and Wilson uses this locale effectively in the surrealistic novel *The Old Men at the Zoo* (1961).

One of the strengths of Wilson's fiction is its avoidance of didacticism; he never preaches or moralizes but allows the characters to reveal and condemn themselves. Few of the characters in his short fiction are admirable or strong, so the reader knows only by implication that Wilson admires those who are self-aware and morally courageous. His stories and characterizations have an innate moral structure, what Wilson calls "a kind of immediate ethical text," and he expects the reader to be equal to making his or her own moral judgments. He facilitates this active role of the reader by interspersing interior monologues with the third-person narration in order to reveal the characters in dramatic conflict.

These alternating perspectives give a jigsaw-puzzle effect to the stories that compels the reader to interact in order to create a coherent viewpoint.

The interplay between interior monologues and omniscient narration also creates ambiguity and tension that remain unresolved. The many powerful emotions that readers experience as they enter the minds of the characters are rendered merely pathetic when the narrator intervenes and provides a detached perspective. These two narrative modes dramatize the tensions between traditionalism and modernism in Wilson's work. His affinity for social realism finds expression in the controlling voice of the third-person narrator, while his interest in modernist experimentations in subjectivity finds expression in his characters' pastiche of voices and thoughts.

In 1952 Secker and Warburg published Wilson's critical study of Emile Zola, which he had been commissioned to write for a writers' series that failed. Wilson was obviously influenced by Zola's composition method in the preparation of his own novels, and the study displays Wilson's Freudian critical methods. After completing *Emile Zola* Wilson wrote his first novel, *Hemlock and After* (1952), in four weeks. He successfully repeated its retrospective mode in some of his subsequent novels. Many of its themes are immediately recognizable to the reader of his short stories: the necessary confrontation of the protagonist with his own capacity for evil; the clash between freedom and responsibility, imagination and authoritarianism; and the powerful influence of the family on the individual. *For Whom the Cloche Tolls* (1953), aptly subtitled *A Scrap-Book of the Twenties,* is a retrospective of the 1920s written in epistolary and diary form, with pen-and-ink drawings by Wilson's friend Philippe Jullian. This innovative fictional treatment of a memoir gives some hint of Wilson's future experimentations with narrative technique in his novels.

While still working in the Reading Room at the British Museum, Wilson wrote his only play, *The Mulberry Bush* (1956). This drama explores the fortunes of a middle-class family and treats such familiar Wilson themes as the willful ignorance of liberalism and the corrupting effects of power. The play was a great success in Bristol but failed in London. Soon afterward the dramas of the angry young men took over the West End, and, aside from one radio script ("Skeletons and Assegais," 1962) and a few teleplays, Wilson made no further attempts at drama.

In 1955 Wilson resigned from the British Museum to become a full-time writer, a courageous move for a middle-aged author with only three hundred pounds in the bank and no pension. As a result of this decision Wilson turned from short fiction to longer narrative forms, and *A Bit off the Map* was to be his last collection of short stories. *Anglo-Saxon Attitudes* (1956) remains one of his most popular novels, even though Wilson describes it in *The Wild Garden* as "the most 'thought' of my novels, the least 'felt.' "

During the years in which Wilson was writing his early novels and reviews, he was also composing short stories, most of which are collected in *A Bit off the Map*. Two of the volume's stories, "More Friend than Lodger" and "Once a Lady," were initially published in the *New Yorker* (August 1957) rather than his customary British journals. In the 1957 interview Wilson said the stories in *A Bit off the Map* are exemplary of the "false answers people provide today to get back some sense of position in society. These new stories are all satirical of the old philosophies that have now become fashionable again – neo-Toryism, Colin Wilson's Nietzscheanism, and so on – of people seeking after values which now no longer apply."

This assessment sums up the difference between most of Wilson's short stories and his novels. In his novels Wilson generally portrays the protagonists as breaking through to an understanding of their own self-deceptions. Thus the final effect of the novels is positive, for most of his protagonists ultimately adopt new ways of life based on self-awareness and individual happiness. In contrast his short fiction, because of its more limited scope, focuses on the shortcomings of his characters and the corresponding collapse of society, therefore appearing much more negative than his longer fiction.

Most of the pieces in the last collection are much longer stories that display the influence of his novel writing through more-developed plot lines and more-rounded characterizations. In these stories he also experiments with narrative technique and character development in preparation for other novels. Even in the two shortest stories, "Higher Standards" and "A Flat Country Christmas," Wilson's development as a writer is clear. Both are less one-dimensional than some of his earlier and shorter stories. Neither story is a simple character sketch, and both sensitively interweave the effects of a shifting class structure with individual hopes. Wilson portrays how "getting ahead" means that sacrifices and compromises must be made; social and material "success" are bought dearly, at the price of displacement and loneliness. The tone of both stories is somber and disillusioned.

"A Flat Country Christmas" explores the social problems of the suburbs, for the flatness of the landscape is reflected in the dullness of the human life it supports. The new housing estates flatten out class differences and facilitate the gathering of an amorphous collection of people without common values. The two couples celebrating the season are connected only by the men's work, and they adopt party personas in order to get through the evening without dissension and boredom. However, their masks are shattered by a seemingly harmless party game. One of the men confronts his own nothingness in the mirror, yet this vital self-revelation is typically brushed under the rug in order to maintain appearances.

In "Higher Standards" Wilson sensitively depicts both the tensions between mother and daughter and the split between the daughter's longing for a better life and her loneliness as an educated outsider in her village. Wilson evocatively sets the scene, and the details of time and place are woven seamlessly into the action. Elsie Corfe is trapped between two social classes, a situation that mocks the liberal idea of education as bringing freedom and progress. Her success in bettering herself has only served to alienate her from her home life and erstwhile friends while not providing her with opportunities to move on to better things.

"Once a Lady" and "A Sad Fall" portray the struggling female characters whom Wilson both admires and satirizes. The protagonist of "Once a Lady," Esther Barrington, is also a victim of class barriers. Her marriage to a man far beneath her socially was a courageous act of love that has been rewarded by a lonely, arduous life alienated from her peers. Her sacrifice has meant that she is no longer at home in either her old world or the new, and her heroic attempts to retain her dignity are assailed by Eileen Carter, her only friend, whose love for Esther makes her jealous and possessive.

Like "Such Darling Dodos," "A Sad Fall" chronicles the passing of an era, this time in the ineffectual platitudes of old Mrs. Tanner. Yet while her clichés and martyred role-playing as the useless old mother are obviously outdated, the moral atrophy of John Appleby, her son's friend, is equally horrible. When the young boy in Mrs. Tanner's charge falls off the roof, John sees him as merely a statistic in contrast to her sentimental hysteria. Wilson makes it clear that Mrs. Tanner's values are anachronistic, but the scientific ideas espoused by John have no moral value at all and are therefore no replacement for the old ways.

The amorality of the new generation is wittily and dispassionately on display in "More Friend than Lodger." This story is in the mold of "Superior Sister" in its protagonist's candidly calculating tone and evil intent. The predatory June Raven coyly addresses the reader, and the continuous first-person narrative is striking. (Wilson uses the extended interior monologue in his next novel, *The Middle Age of Mrs. Eliot,* published in 1958.) Despite June's skillful dissection of her own motives and those of others, there is no dawning of self-awareness in her musings. She is an incorrigible hedonist with no emotional depth who manipulates and controls both her husband and her lover in her determination to "have her cake and eat it."

"After the Show" and "A Bit off the Map" unveil the delusions and ambitions of two young men who find themselves living in a society that cannot provide them with the experiences and answers that they need. "After the Show," like "Significant Experience," portrays a young man's journey into (limited) experience through an acquaintance with an older woman. In this instance Maurice desperately wants to escape from the "fraudulent flatness of his own life" and the controlling influence of his family into a world in which he can serve a cause of some kind. The ironic parallels in the story with Henrik Ibsen's *The Wild Duck* (1884) — the "show" that Maurice attends with his grandmother at the beginning of the tale — only serve to highlight the impoverished world in which Maurice has to operate. He has entered life after the show has ended, but he still wants to assume a central role as romantic hero. His self-conscious theatricality exposes the self-deceptions and masquerades to which so many of Wilson's characters are prone.

"A Bit off the Map" is a rather uneven piece that moves from the perspective of a psychotic teddy boy, Kennie, to the affected Nietzscheanism of his adoptive group of intellectuals, "The Crowd." The story enacts an allegorical search for "Truth" by various groups in England, all of which are obviously misdirected and hence "off the map." Unfortunately the story is dull and turgid until the sudden violent ending, partly because the device of dramatizing the thoughts of someone who is mentally deficient proves unconvincing and limited.

The collection ends on an apocryphal note with the somber 1956 New Year's Eve celebrations of the Peacehaven family, whose tyrannical patriarch lies upstairs with his mind wandering. The title "Ten Minutes to Twelve" speaks of doom and apprehension. The year 1956 brought the Suez crisis, and the old forms of English imperialism were reawakening. The disturbing revival of authoritarianism is enacted in the enthusiasm and support of

the young grandson, Geoff, for his grandfather's dictatorial management, despite the old man's ignoble end. In "Ten Minutes to Twelve" Wilson brilliantly portrays what he sees as the predicament of his society: the old world and its ways are in decline, but there are no new alternatives to replace it.

Three other stories by Wilson, "Aunt Cora" (1950), "Her Ship Came Home" (*Evening Standard* [London], 9 May 1955; collected in *Did It Happen? Stories,* 1956) and "The Men with Bowler Hats" (1953), contrast the delusions, miscommunication, and role-playing of the adult world with the child's limited, innocent attempts to understand. Imagination, the child's important tool for interpreting and understanding the adult world, all too frequently becomes an escape mechanism for the warped adult to hide the harshness of reality and to prohibit self-awareness.

The willful self-deception of adults is portrayed in "Aunt Mathilde's Drawings" and "Silent Pianist" (both published in 1952). Both stories feature old-lady protagonists who live in the fantasy past in preference to the heartless present. They are "such darling dodos" who are impatiently treated as burdens by family and society. In these character sketches Wilson succeeds not only in dramatizing the delusions of these women but also in exposing the callousness of contemporary society.

"An Elephant Never Forgets" (1951) and "Who for Such Dainties?" (1952) lampoon the struggles of the middle class to remain respectable by keeping up appearances. None of the characters is spared Wilson's satiric touch, and the pretentious receive their comeuppance in the end. Yet neither of these stories achieves the depth of moral vision of similar stories in Wilson's collections. "Unwanted Heroine" (1954) is reminiscent of "A Story of Historical Interest," as the self-centered female protagonist moves reluctantly to an understanding of her own egotistical motives and tendency to self-dramatization. "Mrs. Peckover's Sky . . ." (1955) focuses on another self-centered female protagonist and her inevitable loss of domain and happiness during World War II.

In "Animals or Human Beings" (1955) Wilson returns successfully to the macabre and the gothic as they are revealed in the human psyche. The story satirizes British and German attitudes toward spinsterhood while creating a "horror" tale from what seem initially to be commonplace circumstances. Irony, humor, and pathos are mixed in the portrayal of Fraulein Partenkirchen's attempts to find a place in society: the violent death that precipitates her departure from England symbolically repeats the brutality that she suffered in Adolf Hitler's Germany. The title, deliberately not phrased as a question, raises the issue of the human brutality that underlies modern society.

After the 1950s Wilson published only two other stories, "My Husband Is Right" (1961) and "The Eyes of the Peacock" (*Sunday Times Magazine*, 14 December 1975; *The Collected Stories of Angus Wilson*, 1987). While these stories show thematic continuity with his previous short fiction, the style and tone of both are markedly different from his earlier short stories. Wilson wrote "My Husband Is Right" as a prologue to a novel, "Goats and Compasses," which he abandoned after one chapter. This story shows the benefits of Wilson's novel writing in its careful crafting and consistent tone, and it is far more compassionate and less satiric than his earlier short stories. The interplay between a husband suffering a nervous breakdown and a protective wife is convincing and tense. The therapeutic escape abroad that she has planned for her husband goes awry, and it is clear that nothing can save them from his mental collapse. The ending, with its bitterly humorous double entendre, emphasizes the miscommunication and alienation that haunt the couple wherever they go.

"The Eyes of the Peacock" is a satiric fairy tale for adults that once more features a lonely boy and his relationship with an eccentric old female relative. The story is told from a child's perspective, in simple, matter-of-fact style, and mixes realistic social details with supernatural and gothic elements. It successfully includes both Wilson's customary satire of the middle class and a parable about the ability of beauty and imagination to conquer fascism and conformity in their many shapes. The story is a prelude to Wilson's novel *Setting the World on Fire* (1980) in character, theme, atmosphere, and setting.

Alienation and dispossession are the common themes that haunt these stories, as in Wilson's three collections; it is also clear that much of the material is autobiographically based. Yet the last two stories display the maturity of style and vision that he developed as he exercised his writing talent more fully in the novels. Margaret Drabble – in a 1980 article, " 'No Idle Rentier': Angus Wilson and the Nourished Literary Imagination," collected in *Critical Essays on Angus Wilson* – comments on his progression as a writer:

> The success of his first collections of stories, *The Wrong Set* and *Such Darling Dodos* (1949 and 1950), brought him fame as a social satirist, earning him such epithets as "merciless" and "savage," but ... he soon found this

kind of recognition restricting and moved into larger fields, writing, with equal and increasing success, of wider themes, drawing together the random subjects of his stories into a more comprehensive portrait of British life.

From 1966 to 1978 Wilson was a professor in the School of English and American Studies at the University of East Anglia in Norwich, but he continued to travel and lectured extensively all over the world. In 1978, at age sixty-five, Wilson retired from his teaching post, but he continued to take guest professorships at various universities in the United States. He was knighted in 1980 both for his literary achievements and his contributions to the arts and service organizations. His last novel, *Setting the World on Fire*, explores the influence of place on human character and is largely constructed of dramatic dialogue. He served as president of the Royal Society of Literature from 1982 to 1988. Wilson died of a stroke on 31 May 1991 at a nursing home in Bury Saint Edmunds, where he had spent his last few years.

Wilson's influence extends beyond his fiction, for he was a respected critic, reviewer, and biographer. These writings, together with his work as a professor and international public lecturer, have had a profound effect on the shape of English literature from the 1940s onward. Wilson is regarded by many literary historians as a transitional figure from the modernist to the postmodernist era because of his unusual melding of traditional subjects with experimental methods. No other writer at the time so clearly dramatized the collapse of the upper middle class in England, and his social satire opened the way for the works of social protest by the angry young men in the 1950s.

Interviews:

Michael Millgate, "Angus Wilson," *Paris Review* (New York), 17 (Autumn–Winter 1957): 88–105; reprinted as "Angus Wilson: The Art of Fiction," in *Critical Essays on Angus Wilson*, edited by Jay L. Halio (Boston: G. K. Hall, 1985), pp. 39–48;

Jack I. Biles, "An Interview in London with Angus Wilson," *Studies in the Novel*, 2 (Spring 1970): 76–87; reprinted in *Critical Essays on Angus Wilson*, pp. 48–59;

Frederick P. W. McDowell, "An Interview with Angus Wilson," *Iowa Review*, 3 (Fall 1972): 77–105;

Jonathan Raban, "Profile of Angus Wilson," *New Review*, 1 (April 1974): 16–24;

Betsy Draine, "An Interview with Angus Wilson," *Contemporary Literature,* 21 (Winter 1980): 1–14; reprinted in *Interviews with Contemporary Writers,* edited by L. S. Dembo (Madison: University of Wisconsin Press, 1983), pp. 270–283;

Joseph Kissane, "Talking with Angus Wilson," *Twentieth Century Literature,* 29 (Summer 1983): 142–150;

Biles, "Some Words More, Some Years Later: A Talk with Angus Wilson," in *Critical Essays on Angus Wilson,* pp. 59–69.

Bibliographies:

Rubin Rabinovitz, *The Reaction Against Experiment in the English Novel, 1950–60* (New York & London: Columbia University Press, 1967), pp. 184–195;

Frederick P. W. McDowell and Sharon E. Graves, *The Angus Wilson Manuscripts in the University of Iowa Libraries* (Iowa City: Friends of the University of Iowa Libraries, 1969);

J. H. Stape and Anne N. Thomas, *Angus Wilson: A Bibliography, 1947–1987* (London: Mansell, 1988).

References:

Malcolm Bradbury, "The Fiction of Pastiche: The Comic Mode of Angus Wilson," in his *Possibilities: Essays on the State of the Novel* (London & New York: Oxford University Press, 1973), pp. 211–230;

Bradbury, "The Novel as Pastiche: Angus Wilson and Modern Fiction," in his *No, Not Bloomsbury* (London: Deutsch, 1987), pp. 219–243;

Bradbury, "The Short Stories of Angus Wilson," *Studies in Short Fiction,* 3 (Winter 1966): 117–125;

C. B. Cox, *The Free Spirit* (London: Oxford University Press, 1963);

Peter Faulkner, *Angus Wilson: Mimic and Moralist* (New York: Viking, 1980);

Averil Gardner, *Angus Wilson* (Boston: Twayne, 1985);

James Gindin, *Harvest of a Quiet Eye: The Novel of Compassion* (Bloomington: Indiana University Press, 1971);

K.W. Gransden, *Angus Wilson* (London: Longman, 1969);

Jay Halio, *Angus Wilson* (Edinburgh: Oliver & Boyd, 1964);

Halio, ed., *Critical Essays on Angus Wilson* (Boston: G. K. Hall, 1985);

Kerry McSweeney, *Four Contemporary Novelists* (Montreal: McGill-Queen's University Press, 1983).

Papers:

A collection of Wilson's manuscripts is housed at the University of Iowa Library, Iowa City.

Books for Further Reading

Allen, Walter. *The Short Story in English.* New York: Oxford University Press, 1981.

Aycock, Wendell M., ed. *The Teller and the Tale: Aspects of the Short Story.* Lubbock: Texas Tech Press, 1982.

Bates, H. E. *The Modern Short Story: A Critical Survey,* second edition. London: M. Joseph, 1972.

Bayley, John. *The Short Story: Henry James to Elizabeth Bowen.* New York: St. Martin's Press, 1988.

Beachcroft, T. O. *The Modest Art: A Survey of the Short Story in English.* London: Oxford University Press, 1968.

Bergonzi, Bernard. *The Situation of the Novel,* second edition. London: Macmillan, 1979.

Daiches, David. *The Present Age in British Literature.* Bloomington: Indiana University Press, 1958.

Flora, Joseph M., ed. *The English Short Story, 1880–1945: A Critical History.* Boston: Twayne, 1985.

Gelb, Norman. *The British: A Portrait of an Indominitable Island People.* New York: Everest House, 1982.

Gindin, James. *Postwar British Fiction: New Accents and Attitudes.* Berkeley & Los Angeles: University of California Press, 1962.

Hanson, Clare. *Short Stories and Short Fictions, 1880–1980.* London: Macmillan, 1984.

Hanson, ed. *Re-reading the Short Story.* New York: St. Martin's Press, 1989.

Lohafer, Susan. *Coming to Terms with the Short Story.* Baton Rouge: Louisiana State University Press, 1983.

Lohafer and Jo Ellyn Clarey, eds. *Short Story Theory at a Crossroads.* Baton Rouge: Louisiana State University Press, 1989.

Magill, Frank, ed. *Critical Survey of Short Fiction,* 7 volumes. Englewood Cliffs, N. J.: Salem Press, 1981.

Marwick, Arthur. *British Society Since 1945.* London: John Lane, 1982.

Maschler, Tom, ed. *Declaration: Colin Wilson and Others.* New York: Dutton, 1958.

May, Charles E., ed. *Short Story Theories.* Athens: Ohio University Press, 1976.

O'Connor, Frank. *The Lonely Voice: A Study of the Short Story.* Cleveland: World, 1963.

Reid, Ian. *The Short Story.* New York: Barnes & Noble, 1977.

Sutherland, J. A. *Fiction and the Fiction Industry.* London: Athlone, 1978.

Vannatta, Dennis, ed. *The English Short Story, 1945–1980: A Critical History.* Boston: Twayne, 1985.

Contributors

Colin Affleck ....*Edinburgh, Scotland*
Stevens Amidon ....*Goddard College*
Dean Baldwin..*Pennsylvania State University — Erie*
John S. Bak ....*Ball State University*
Fiona R. Barnes ....*University of Wisconsin — Madison*
Barbara Brothers ....*Youngstown State University*
D. A. Callard..*Cardiff, Wales*
Ann Gibaldi Campbell ....*University of North Carolina at Chapel Hill*
Joanne Mathias Emig.......................................*York College of Pennsylvania*
David W. Endicott..*Ball State University*
Mathew David Fisher ....*Ball State University*
Julia M. Gergits..*Youngstown State University*
John L. Grigsby ....*Lincoln Memorial University*
Edward T. Jones..*York College of Pennsylvania*
Michael Kleeberg..*Ball State University*
Vern Lindquist......................................*Sullivan Community College*
Marjorie Podolsky......................................*Pennsylvania State University — Erie*
Alan Price ....*Pennsylvania State University — Hazleton*
Esther P. Riley ....*East Tennessee State University*
David S. Robb..*University of Dundee*
James J. Schramer.......................................*Youngstown State University*
Jennifer Semple Siegel..*York College of Pennsylvania*
Bes Stark Spangler...*Peace College*
Marina Spunta..*Bologna, Italy*
K. M. Stemmler ....*Clarion University of Pennsylvania*
John J. Stinson..*SUNY College at Fredonia*
Alice L. Swensen...................................*University of Northern Iowa*
Val Warner ....*Kenton, Harrow, England*

Cumulative Index

Dictionary of Literary Biography, Volumes 1-139
Dictionary of Literary Biography Yearbook, 1980-1992
Dictionary of Literary Biography Documentary Series, Volumes 1-11

Cumulative Index

DLB before number: *Dictionary of Literary Biography*, Volumes 1-139
Y before number: *Dictionary of Literary Biography Yearbook*, 1980-1992
DS before number: *Dictionary of Literary Biography Documentary Series*, Volumes 1-11

A

Abbey Press DLB-49

The Abbey Theatre and Irish Drama,
1900-1945 ....DLB-10

Abbot, Willis J. 1863-1934 ....DLB-29

Abbott, Jacob 1803-1879 ....DLB-1

Abbott, Lee K. 1947- DLB-130

Abbott, Lyman 1835-1922 ....DLB-79

Abbott, Robert S. 1868-1940 ....DLB-29, 91

Abelard, Peter circa 1079-1142 .....DLB-115

Abelard-Schuman DLB-46

Abell, Arunah S. 1806-1888 ....DLB-43

Abercrombie, Lascelles 1881-1938 ...DLB-19

Aberdeen University Press
Limited DLB-106

Abish, Walter 1931- DLB-130

Abrahams, Peter 1919- DLB-117

Abrams, M. H. 1912- DLB-67

Abse, Dannie 1923- DLB-27

Academy Chicago Publishers DLB-46

Accrocca, Elio Filippo 1923- DLB-128

Ace Books DLB-46

Achebe, Chinua 1930- DLB-117

Achtenberg, Herbert 1938- DLB-124

Ackerman, Diane 1948- DLB-120

Acorn, Milton 1923-1986 ....DLB-53

Acosta, Oscar Zeta 1935?- DLB-82

Actors Theatre of Louisville DLB-7

Adair, James 1709?-1783? DLB-30

Adam, Graeme Mercer 1839-1912 ...DLB-99

Adame, Leonard 1947- DLB-82

Adamic, Louis 1898-1951 ....DLB-9

Adams, Alice 1926- Y-86

Adams, Brooks 1848-1927 ....DLB-47

Adams, Charles Francis, Jr.
1835-1915 ....DLB-47

Adams, Douglas 1952- Y-83

Adams, Franklin P. 1881-1960 ...... DLB-29

Adams, Henry 1838-1918 .... DLB-12, 47

Adams, Herbert Baxter 1850-1901 ... DLB-47

Adams, J. S. and C.
[publishing house] DLB-49

Adams, James Truslow 1878-1949 ... DLB-17

Adams, John 1735-1826 .... DLB-31

Adams, John Quincy 1767-1848 ..... DLB-37

Adams, Léonie 1899-1988 .... DLB-48

Adams, Levi 1802-1832 .... DLB-99

Adams, Samuel 1722-1803 ...... DLB-31, 43

Adams, William Taylor 1822-1897 .. DLB-42

Adamson, Sir John 1867-1950 ...... DLB-98

Adcock, Arthur St. John
1864-1930 .... DLB-135

Adcock, Betty 1938- DLB-105

Adcock, Betty, Certain Gifts DLB-105

Adcock, Fleur 1934- DLB-40

Addison, Joseph 1672-1719 .... DLB-101

Ade, George 1866-1944 .... DLB-11, 25

Adeler, Max (see Clark, Charles Heber)

Advance Publishing Company DLB-49

AE 1867-1935 .... DLB-19

Aesthetic Poetry (1873), by
Walter Pater DLB-35

After Dinner Opera Company Y-92

Afro-American Literary Critics:
An Introduction DLB-33

Agassiz, Jean Louis Rodolphe
1807-1873 .... DLB-1

Agee, James 1909-1955 .... DLB-2, 26

The Agee Legacy: A Conference at
the University of Tennessee
at Knoxville Y-89

Ai 1947- DLB-120

Aichinger, Ilse 1921- DLB-85

Aidoo, Ama Ata 1942- DLB-117

Aiken, Conrad 1889-1973 ....DLB-9, 45, 102

Ainsworth, William Harrison
1805-1882 ....DLB-21

Aitken, Robert [publishing house] ...DLB-49

Akenside, Mark 1721-1770 ....DLB-109

Akins, Zoë 1886-1958 ....DLB-26

Alabaster, William 1568-1640 ......DLB-132

Alain-Fournier 1886-1914 ....DLB-65

Alarcón, Francisco X. 1954- DLB-122

Alba, Nanina 1915-1968 ....DLB-41

Albee, Edward 1928- DLB-7

Albert the Great circa 1200-1280 ...DLB-115

Alberti, Rafael 1902- DLB-108

Alcott, Amos Bronson 1799-1888 .....DLB-1

Alcott, Louisa May
1832-1888 ....DLB-1, 42, 79

Alcott, William Andrus 1798-1859 ....DLB-1

Alden, Henry Mills 1836-1919 ......DLB-79

Alden, Isabella 1841-1930 ....DLB-42

Alden, John B. [publishing house] DLB-49

Alden, Beardsley and Company DLB-49

Aldington, Richard
1892-1962 .... DLB-20, 36, 100

Aldis, Dorothy 1896-1966 ....DLB-22

Aldiss, Brian W. 1925- DLB-14

Aldrich, Thomas Bailey
1836-1907 .... DLB-42, 71, 74, 79

Alegría, Ciro 1909-1967 ....DLB-113

Aleixandre, Vicente 1898-1984 .....DLB-108

Aleramo, Sibilla 1876-1960 ....DLB-114

Alexander, Charles 1868-1923 ......DLB-91

Alexander, Charles Wesley
[publishing house] DLB-49

Alexander, James 1691-1756 ....DLB-24

Alexander, Lloyd 1924- DLB-52

Alexander, Sir William, Earl of Stirling
1577?-1640 ....DLB-121

Alexis, Willibald 1798-1871 ....DLB-133

B

Cumulative Index

H

J

ISBN 0-8103-5398-9

(Continued from front endsheets)

116 *British Romantic Novelists, 1789-1832,* edited by Bradford K. Mudge (1992)

117 *Twentieth-Century Caribbean and Black African Writers,* First Series, edited by Bernth Lindfors and Reinhard Sander (1992)

118 *Twentieth-Century German Dramatists, 1889-1918,* edited by Wolfgang D. Elfe and James Hardin (1992)

119 *Nineteenth-Century French Fiction Writers: Romanticism and Realism, 1800-1860,* edited by Catharine Savage Brosman (1992)

120 *American Poets Since World War II,* Third Series, edited by R. S. Gwynn (1992)

121 *Seventeenth-Century British Nondramatic Poets,* First Series, edited by M. Thomas Hester (1992)

122 *Chicano Writers,* Second Series, edited by Francisco A. Lomelí and Carl R. Shirley (1992)

123 *Nineteenth-Century French Fiction Writers: Naturalism and Beyond, 1860-1900,* edited by Catharine Savage Brosman (1992)

124 *Twentieth-Century German Dramatists, 1919-1992,* edited by Wolfgang D. Elfe and James Hardin (1992)

125 *Twentieth-Century Caribbean and Black African Writers,* Second Series, edited by Bernth Lindfors and Reinhard Sander (1993)

126 *Seventeenth-Century British Nondramatic Poets,* Second Series, edited by M. Thomas Hester (1993)

127 *American Newspaper Publishers, 1950-1990,* edited by Perry J. Ashley (1993)

128 *Twentieth-Century Italian Poets,* Second Series, edited by Giovanna Wedel De Stasio, Glauco Cambon, and Antonio Illiano (1993)

129 *Nineteenth-Century German Writers, 1841-1900,* edited by James Hardin and Siegfried Mews (1993)

130 *American Short-Story Writers Since World War II,* edited by Patrick Meanor (1993)

131 *Seventeenth-Century British Nondramatic Poets,* Third Series, edited by M. Thomas Hester (1993)

132 *Sixteenth-Century British Nondramatic Writers,* First Series, edited by David A. Richardson (1993)

133 *Nineteenth-Century German Writers to 1840,* edited by James Hardin and Siegfried Mews (1993)

134 *Twentieth-Century Spanish Poets,* Second Series, edited by Jerry Phillips Winfield (1994)

135 *British Short-Fiction Writers, 1880-1914: The Realist Tradition,* edited by William B. Thesing (1994)

136 *Sixteenth-Century British Nondramatic Writers,* Second Series, edited by David A. Richardson (1994)

137 *American Magazine Journalists, 1900-1960,* Second Series, edited by Sam G. Riley (1994)

138 *German Writers and Works of the High Middle Ages: 1170-1280,* edited by James Hardin and Will Hasty (1994)

139 *British Short-Fiction Writers, 1945-1980,* edited by Dean Baldwin (1994)

Documentary Series

1 *Sherwood Anderson, Willa Cather, John Dos Passos, Theodore Dreiser, F. Scott Fitzgerald, Ernest Hemingway, Sinclair Lewis,* edited by Margaret A. Van Antwerp (1982)

2 *James Gould Cozzens, James T. Farrell, William Faulkner, John O'Hara, John Steinbeck, Thomas Wolfe, Richard Wright,* edited by Margaret A. Van Antwerp (1982)

3 *Saul Bellow, Jack Kerouac, Norman Mailer, Vladimir Nabokov, John Updike, Kurt Vonnegut,* edited by Mary Bruccoli (1983)

4 *Tennessee Williams,* edited by Margaret A. Van Antwerp and Sally Johns (1984)

5 *American Transcendentalists,* edited by Joel Myerson (1988)

6 *Hardboiled Mystery Writers: Raymond Chandler, Dashiell Hammett, Ross Macdonald,* edited by Matthew J. Bruccoli and Richard Layman (1989)

7 *Modern American Poets: James Dickey, Robert Frost, Marianne Moore,* edited by Karen L. Rood (1989)

8 *The Black Aesthetic Movement,* edited by Jeffrey Louis Decker (1991)

9 *American Writers of the Vietnam War: W. D. Ehrhart, Larry Heinemann, Tim O'Brien, Walter McDonald, John M. Del Vecchio,* edited by Ronald Baughman (1991)

10 *The Bloomsbury Group,* edited by Edward L. Bishop (1992)

11 *American Proletarian Culture: The Twenties and The Thirties,* edited by Jon Christian Suggs (1993)

Yearbooks

1980 edited by Karen L. Rood, Jean W. Ross, and Richard Ziegfeld (1981)

1981 edited by Karen L. Rood, Jean W. Ross, and Richard Ziegfeld (1982)

1982 edited by Richard Ziegfeld; associate editors: Jean W. Ross and Lynne C. Zeigler (1983)

1983 edited by Mary Bruccoli and Jean W. Ross; associate editor: Richard Ziegfeld (1984)

1984 edited by Jean W. Ross (1985)

1985 edited by Jean W. Ross (1986)

1986 edited by J. M. Brook (1987)

1987 edited by J. M. Brook (1988)

1988 edited by J. M. Brook (1989)

1989 edited by J. M. Brook (1990)

1990 edited by James W. Hipp (1991)

1991 edited by James W. Hipp (1992)

1992 edited by James W. Hipp (1993)